Worlds of History

A Comparative Reader

Worlds of History

A Comparative Reader

Volume One: To 1550

Sixth Edition

Kevin Reilly
Raritan Valley College

bedford/st.martin's
Macmillan Learning

Boston • New York

For Bedford/St. Martin's

Vice President, Editorial, Macmillan Learning Humanities: Edwin Hill
Publisher for History: Michael Rosenberg
Acquiring Editor for History: Laura Arcari
Director of Development for History: Jane Knetzger
Developmental Editor: Tess Fletcher
Production Editor: Matt Glazer
Production Supervisor: Lisa McDowell
History Marketing Manager: Melissa Famiglietti
Assistant Editor: Mary Posman
Copy Editor: Susan Moore
Photo Editor: Robin Fadool
Photo Researcher: Naomi Kornhauser
Permissions Editor: Jen Roach
Senior Art Director: Anna Palchik
Cover Design: William Boardman
Cover Art/Cover Photo: (Top) Ms 1186 f.1 Astrologer with an astrolabe, a Scribe
   and a Mathematician, from a Latin psalter from the Psalter of St. Louis and
   Blanche of Castile, 1225-1250 (vellum), French School, (13th century) /
   Bibliotheque de L'Arsenal, Paris, France / Flammarion / Bridgeman Images;
   (Bottom) The Astronomy Lesson (ink & gold on vellum), Ottoman School,
   (15th century) / Private Collection / © Leemage / Bridgeman Images
Composition: Cenveo Publisher Services
Printing and Binding: RR Donnelley and Sons

Manufactured in the United States of America.

1 0 9 8 7 6
f e d c b a

For information, write: Bedford/St. Martin's, 75 Arlington Street, Boston, MA 02116
(617-399-4000)

ISBN 978-1-319-03258-6

Acknowledgments

*Text acknowledgments and copyrights appear at the back of the book on pages ACK-1–
ACK-6, which constitute an extension of the copyright page. Art acknowledgments
and copyrights appear on the same page as the art selections they cover.*

Preface

The college-level world history course is undergoing another transformation: the third since I first wrote about the subject for the American Historical Association in 1984.[1] The first two were the almost contemporaneous conceptual jump from Western history to world history and the inclusion of a vast array of new subject areas, especially in social and cultural history. The third, occurring now, is a trend toward engaging students with sources rather than solely with writings about those sources, "flipping" the course from lecture to discussion, and teaching historical thinking skills rather than merely transferring information. The purpose of this book is to satisfy the needs expressed in these three revolutions. The switch to world history from courses in "Western Civilization" that rarely ventured over the Alps or the Pyrenees is an obvious need of students in the twenty-first century. So, too, is the addition of topics on gender, race, and class; migrations, trade, and encounters; religion, sexuality, and work; climate, ecology, and disease; and so many more fruits of contemporary scholarship, micro and global. Our title, *Worlds of History*, is a reflection of both these goals.

The need to teach students to think critically and independently, an often unspoken goal of history education over the past several decades, is now receiving explicit formulation and vigorous advocacy in the efforts of institutions like the American Historical Association and the College Board to answer public unease about the value of college degrees in history and the other humanities. What are the thinking skills or "habits of mind" that we teach or can teach when we teach history? This book suggests answers to that question and prepares teachers to demonstrate them.

To engage students who are not only new to the college experience but new to reading source material as well, I have continued my efforts to provide accessible readings that pique their interest. This new edition aims to maintain that high level of reader interest with new selections, like an explanation from the fourteenth-century College of Physicians in Paris for the causes of the Black Death and an image depicting Aztec education from the *Codex Mendoza*. As in previous editions, I have also included secondary as well as primary texts. In some chapters the secondary text introduces an issue that the primary sources then address, while at other times the secondary source offers a summary or suggestions for new directions. My aim in combining these two types of sources is for students to learn how texts, whether primary or secondary, talk to each other—and without having to buy separate books of each.

[1] Kevin Reilly, ed., *The Introductory History Course: Six Models* (American Historical Association), 1984.

As a framework, I've used a thematic and topical organization that also proceeds chronologically, with each chapter focusing on a captivating topic within a particular time period. I have long found a comparative approach to be a useful tool for approaching world history, and for this sixth edition, I have continued to use this tool, examining two or more cultures at a time. In some chapters students can trace parallel developments in separate regions, such as the development of society in ancient Greece and India in Chapter 3, or the advent of nationalism in Japan and India in Chapter 23. In other cases students can examine the enduring effects of contact and exchange between cultures, as in the chapter on Mongol and Viking raiding and settlements from the tenth to the fourteenth centuries, or Volume 2's chapter on the scientific revolution in Europe, the Ottoman Empire, China, Japan, and the Americas. Even the normally bipolar study of the Cold War can be expanded, as documents in Chapter 26 relating to the superpowers' fight to control the emerging "Third World" show.

I continue to include a wealth of pedagogical tools to help students unlock the readings and hone their critical thinking skills. Each chapter begins with a "Historical Context" introduction that sets the stage for directed comparisons among the chapter's readings. A "Thinking Historically" section follows, which introduces a particular critical thinking skill—such as asking about author, audience, and agenda or distinguishing causes of change—that is designed to mine the chapter's selections. Introductions preceding each selection provide additional context, while document-specific "Thinking Historically" content poses questions to encourage close analysis of the selections using the critical thinking skill introduced at the beginning of the chapter. Explanatory gloss notes and pronunciation guides throughout help ensure comprehension of the readings. A set of "Reflections" that both summarizes and extends the chapter's lessons concludes each chapter.

■ NEW TO THIS EDITION

While I am continually testing selections in my own classroom, I appreciate input from readers and adopters, and I want to thank them for their many suggestions for exciting new chapters and selections. Having incorporated some of this feedback, I think those who have used the reader previously will find the sixth edition even more geographically and topically comprehensive, interesting, and accessible to students. Close to a third of its selections are new, resulting in fresh material in almost every chapter. In addition, I have added two new chapters, an exploration of traditions of students and education across the world (Chapter 13) and a look at empire, religion, and war in Asian, Islamic, and Christian states (Chapter 17).

In my ongoing efforts to make the book more accessible, I have added new Thinking Historically skills to both new and existing chapters. Chapter 10 includes a new section on Understanding Causes; Chapter 13 asks students to think critically about Texts and Contexts; Chapter 17 deepens students' understanding of Author, Audience, and Agenda; and Chapter 25 has been reframed to encourage students to delve into World War II–era documents through the lens of Empathetic Understanding.

I am not a believer in change for its own sake; when I have discovered a successful way of teaching a subject, I am not disposed to jettison it for something new. Consequently, many of my most satisfying changes in this edition are incremental: a better translation of a document, the addition of a newly discovered source, or additional questions to further inspire critical thinking. In some cases I have been able to further edit a useful source, retaining its muscle while also providing space for a precious new find. I begin each round of revision with the conviction that the book is already as good as it can get. And, as history happens all around us in the years between editions, I end each round with a book that is not only updated but also better than it was.

What's more, *Worlds of History* is being offered in an electronic format this year for the first time. The new PDF e-book can be read on a variety of devices, including e-readers, laptops, and tablets. For more information, you or your students can visit macmillanhighered.com/ebookpartners.

■ ACKNOWLEDGMENTS

A book like this cannot be written without the help and advice of a vast army of colleagues and friends. I consider myself enormously fortunate to have met and known such a large group of gifted and generous scholars. Some were especially helpful in the preparation of this new edition. They include: Lawrence Backlund, Montgomery County Community College; Roger Deal, University of South Carolina–Aiken; Grant Hardy, University of North Carolina at Asheville; Obbe Haverkamp, Davidson Community College; Martin Kalb, Northern Arizona University; Dana Wessell Lightfoot, University of Northern British Columbia; Matthew Maher, Metropolitan State College of Denver; Kate McGrath, Central Connecticut State University; Kelli Nakamura, Kapiolani Community College; Raphael Njoku, Idaho State University; Janine Peterson, Marist College; Marynel Ryan Van Zee, University of Minnesota, Morris; and Peter Winn, Tufts University.

Over the years I have benefited from the suggestions of innumerable friends and fellow world historians. Among them: Michael Adas, Rutgers University; the late Jerry Bentley, University of Hawai'i; David

Berry, Essex County Community College; Edmund (Terry) Burke III, University of California–Santa Cruz; Catherine Clay, Shippensburg University; the late Philip Curtin, Johns Hopkins University; S. Ross Doughty, Ursinus College; Ross Dunn, San Diego State University; Marc Gilbert, Hawai'i Pacific University; Steve Gosch, University of Wisconsin–Eau Claire; Sue Gronewold, Kean University; Gregory Guzman, Bradley University; Brock Haussamen, Raritan Valley College; Allen Howard, Rutgers University; Sarah Hughes, Shippensburg University; Karen Jolly, University of Hawai'i; Stephen Kaufman, Raritan Valley College; Maghan Keita, Villanova University; Craig Lockard, University of Wisconsin–Green Bay; Pat Manning, University of Pittsburgh; Adam McKeown, Columbia University; John McNeill, Georgetown University; William H. McNeill, University of Chicago; Gyan Prakash, Princeton University; Lauren Ristvet, University of Pennsylvania; Robert Rosen, University of California–Los Angeles; Heidi Roupp, Aspen High School; John Russell-Wood, Johns Hopkins University; Lynda Shaffer, Tufts University; Ira Spar, Ramapo College; Robert Strayer, California State University–Monterey Bay; George Sussman, LaGuardia Community College; Robert Tignor, Princeton University; John Voll, Georgetown University; and Peter Winn, Tufts University.

I also want to thank the people at Bedford/St. Martin's: Michael Rosenberg, publisher for history; Jane Knetzger, director of development for history; Laura Arcari, acquiring editor for world history; Tess Fletcher, developmental editor for this edition; Mary Posman, editorial assistant; my copy editors, Susan Moore and Melissa Cook; the book's cover designer, William Boardman; and Matt Glazer, production editor. None of this would have been possible if I had not been blessed in my own introduction to history and critical thinking at Rutgers in the 1960s with teachers I still aspire to emulate. Eugene Meehan taught me how to think and showed me that I could. Traian Stoianovich introduced me to the world and an endless range of historical inquiry. Warren Susman lit up a room with more life than I ever knew existed. Donald Weinstein guided me as a young teaching assistant to listen to students and talk with them rather than at them. And Peter Stearns showed me how important and exciting it could be to understand history by making comparisons. I dedicate this book to them.

Finally, I want to thank my own institution, Raritan Valley College, for nurturing my career, allowing me to teach whatever I wanted, and entrusting me with some of the best students one could encounter anywhere. I could not ask for anything more. Except, of course, a loving wife like Pearl.

Kevin Reilly

Introduction for Students

When most people think of history books, they think of books that tell a story about the past. It may be a small part of the past, like a presidential election or the making of the atomic bomb, or a large chunk of the past like the history of China or the history of warfare. In either case, these are books that tell a continuous story from beginning to end. The story might evolve gradually or reveal a conclusion at the start. It might be dramatic or plodding. There may be quotations from various people scattered throughout or indented in long paragraphs, but the book is written by a single author (or sometimes a few who agree on what to say) and presented with a single voice. The voice of a single storyteller gives this kind of history book a strong sense of authority. The reader is not invited to question anything, much less disagree. Any doubts are met by an implicit: "Wait, let me finish," and the author's conclusions follow inevitably from the facts that he or she has determined best fit the story.

The book you are holding in your hands is a different kind of history book. It does not tell a single story, but many. And while these selections are gathered by a single editor (a not unimportant matter), they were originally crafted by hundreds of different people. These people came from various places throughout the world, lived at different times, and were addressing different subjects, often with no awareness of what any of the other authors in this book said—or even of their existence.

This book contains many different stories. But it contains much more. Most of the selections are not stories in the way that history books are. First of all, most were not written by historians. Some of the stories in this book are literary or imaginary, while others come from personal letters or diaries. And many are not even stories. There are selections from treaties, philosophy books, scientific treatises, holy books, telegrams, letters, and diaries. Further, some of the selections are not even writings. There are paintings, art works, photographs, pictures of things, and cartoons. There would be music too, if it could fit into a book.

The point is that this book contains what are called **historical sources** rather than histories. Historical sources are the raw materials that historians use to construct histories. Of course, when you think of all the possible sources available to historians, you realize that even a book of this size can contain only a miniscule number of sources. There are in fact whole libraries devoted to archiving historical sources—from presidential libraries that contain the papers of a president to the archives of government offices. In addition, museums, university libraries, film archives, and ever-expanding online collections include sources ranging from newspapers, magazines, and books to images, letters, e-mails, and more.

Historians use these collections in order to find the sources they need to tell a particular story. The sources are as varied as the questions historians ask. Say, for instance, you are studying the history of individuality and you want to see if the use of the pronoun *I* increased in the late Middle Ages. There happens to be an archive that includes every scrap of writing from a medieval Jewish community in Cairo that saved everything on the chance that a piece of paper might contain the word for God, and therefore, under Jewish tradition, could not be destroyed. With this archive, tedious work, and a good computer, you could chart the use of a single word like *I* over the hundreds of years in which these papers were gathered. It would be within one community, to be sure; but there are few, if any, comparable source collections for this period. Someday a historian may even try to figure out what college students were thinking in the last years of the Age of Reading by a study of your e-mail, essays, or other personal possessions.

This book, then, is one of the two types of books most often used in a history course. The first type is the survey textbook. This book is the second type. It is variously called a "reader," "source book," or an anthology, and it collects a variety of sources in one book. It is designed to introduce you to working with historical sources. The reason for using a reader in addition to, or instead of, a survey text is that it allows us to do those things that the text makes so difficult. It allows us to interpret sources on our own, ask questions, solve problems, and actively build our understanding. Sources can engage our minds in ways that narrative textbooks, with their sense of authority and finality, do not.

Many source books contain only what are called **primary sources**, pieces from the past that were created in the period we are studying. This book contains some **secondary sources** as well. Secondary sources are pieces *about* the period we are studying. They are usually written by scholars. Most of the secondary sources in this book were written fairly recently by modern historians. My reason for including secondary sources is to provide some context or perspective to consider the primary sources (which make up most of the selections in each chapter). Historians read and write secondary sources, continually checking and revising them to conform to primary sources—the actual evidence from the past.

Primary sources can be difficult to interpret because they were often written in a time that is not familiar to us, and the context specific to their creation may be unknown. They use funny words, address weird issues, say strange things, and are sometimes written in a language that we have to struggle to make sense of. I have tried to minimize some of these problems with footnotes, pronunciation help, and some modernization of the language.

I've also included headnotes before each source that give you some historical background about the author and the source. But I can't do too much of that because it is important for you to appreciate the unfamiliarity of these sources in order to do your own analysis. A wise novelist once said: "The past is a foreign country: They do things differently there."[1] These sources were created in a different time, which often makes them seem foreign and remote. So it is precisely this context of a different time that we have to immerse ourselves in to understand the source and the world from which it came. Primary sources require and enable a kind of time travel to knowledge in which we have to leave many of our assumptions behind as excess baggage.

Because the authors of primary sources were not writing for us, and indeed had no idea we'd ever exist, they can't lie to us (at least as they might have, had they been given the opportunity). They tell us so much more than they intended. Primary sources can also be full of deceit, based on illusion, and riddled with error. They can even seem bonkers—and by those very characteristics, tell us much. Working with primary sources is like being a fly on the wall or being able to see things while remaining invisible. It is like having a superpower—gained from the study of history.

Throughout both volumes of this reader you have chapters in world history, which deal with particular historical periods and topics. Some topics cover long periods, like the rise of civilization and patriarchy (Chapter 1) or migrations, travel, and trade from 3000 B.C.E to 1350 C.E. (Chapter 8). Some topics cover brief periods, like the First Crusade from 1095–1099 (Chapter 10) and the Black Death from 1346–1350 (Chapter 12). Most fall in between these extremes. There are, for example, chapters on the topics of women, marriage, and family in most of the large periods that divide the book, i.e., ancient, classical, medieval, and early modern. There are also chapters that compare different societies: classical India and Greece, the Roman and Chinese empires, and Mongols and Vikings. There are chapters on such conventionally defined topics as the Atlantic Slave Trade, the Scientific Revolution, the Enlightenment, the First and Second World Wars, and the Cold War. There are also chapters that pose new historical frameworks like secularization, democratization, and globalization.

As you learn about historical periods and topics, you will also be learning to explore history by analyzing primary and secondary sources systematically. The "Thinking Historically" exercises in each chapter encourage habits of mind that I associate with my own study of history. They are not necessarily intended to turn you into historians but, rather, to give you skills that will help you in all of your college courses. Indeed, these are skills for life: for jury duty and the voting booth; for writing letters or drafting memos on the job; for weighing options and making smart decisions. Hopefully these new habits of mind will also expand your interests and nourish your self-confidence.

---

[1] L. P. Hartley, *The Go-Between* (New York: NYRB Classics, 2002), 17. First published in London in 1953.

These skills are organized from the simple to the more complex. Since skill building is cumulative, your ability to understand, analyze, and use sources will become increasingly sophisticated as you read through this text. But you need not wait for the end of the course to begin your analysis of these sources. Rather, it would be useful to develop the habit of asking the basic questions that journalists are trained to ask whenever they are assigned a story: who, what, where, when, and why?

Whether the source is primary or secondary, a piece of writing or a work of art, a run-through of these basic "w" questions is a good place to start when analyzing sources:

- **Who** wrote or created the source? If the author is unknown or anonymous, what sort of person does the author appear to be? An observer, participant, or eyewitness? A later historian? This will establish whether it is a primary or secondary source. Are there any clues to the identity of the author in the source itself? Are there signs of the author's social class, political position, and attitudes toward the subject of the source?
- **What** is the source? Is it a history by a modern historian and, therefore, a secondary source? Or is it a primary source from the past? If so, what kind of primary source? Is it an engraved stone, a poem, a love letter, a diary entry, a chapter from an ancient book of philosophy, a prayer?
- **Where** does it come from? China? Ancient Mesopotamia? France? Paris? Has it traveled from one place to another, or has it always been in the same place?
- **When** was it created? If it is writing, was it revised? Was there an earlier written or oral version? Is it an example of an older style? How new is it?
- **Why** was it created? To entertain, exorcise, instruct, persuade? **What** was the purpose? **Who** was the audience?

Ultimately, our answers to these questions might help us answer the most important question of all: **What** does this source tell us about the world from which it came?

World history is nothing less than everything ever done or imagined, so we cannot possibly cover it all; we are forced to choose among different places and times in our study of the global past. Our choices do include some particular moments in time, like the one in 111 C.E. in the first half of this reader, when the Roman governor of Bithynia consulted Emperor Trajan about proper treatment of Christians. But our attention will be directed toward much longer periods as well. While we will visit particular places in time like Imperial Rome in the second century or Africa in the nineteenth century, typically we will study more than one place at a time by using a comparative approach.

Comparisons can be enormously useful in studying world history. When we compare the raiding and trading of Vikings and Mongols, the scientific revolution in Europe and Japan, and the Cold War in Cuba and Afghanistan, we learn about the general and the specific at the same time. My hope is that by comparing some of the various worlds of history, a deeper and more nuanced understanding of our global past will emerge. With that understanding, we are better equipped to make sense of the world today and to confront whatever the future holds.

Contents

> The agricultural revolution ten thousand years ago and the urban
> revolution five thousand years ago were probably the two most important
> events in human history. Did they "revolutionize" the power of women
> or begin the age of male domination? Thinking in "stages" can be more
> useful than thinking in years.

4. Empire and Government: China and Rome, 300 B.C.E.–300 C.E. 117

Roughly two thousand years ago the Chinese Empire and the Roman Empire spanned Eurasia. In comparing these ancient empires, we seek to understand how they were governed. Both required officials, armies, and governing ideologies, but these and other tools of rule were not the same in each. How was the government of the Chinese Empire different from that of the Roman Empire? What were the consequences of those differences?

5. Gender, Sex, and Love in Classical Societies: India, China, and the Mediterranean, 500 B.C.E.–550 C.E. 153

The identities and experiences of women and men of the classical era varied from East Asia to the Mediterranean. Nevertheless, the predominance of patriarchy in all of the societies of these regions limited possibilities for women and, in each case, shaped the way men and women related to each other. We can better understand the great works

6. From Tribal to Universal Religion: Hindu-Buddhist and Judeo-Christian Traditions, 1000 B.C.E.–100 C.E. 187

Two religious traditions transformed themselves into universal religions at about the same time in two different parts of Asia, as each became part of a more connected world. Their holy books reveal these changes as well as a desire to hold on to the tried and true.

7. The Spread of Universal Religions: Afro-Eurasia, 100–1000 C.E. 224

Christianity, Buddhism, and, later, Islam spread far across Eurasia, often along the same routes in the first thousand years of the Common Era. Perhaps Judaism did as well. What made these religions so expansive? How were they alike and different? Who converted whom? What did these religions change, and what did they leave the same?

10. Muslim, Christian, and Jewish Encounters: Afro-Eurasia, 1000–1300 349

Islam, Christianity, and Judaism came into frequent contact in the centuries after 1000. In this chapter, we examine these post-1000 encounters and recognize their diversity. Why did the German city of Speyer invite Jews in 1084 and then allow them to be killed by crusaders in 1095? How do we account for the cooperation between Muslim and Christian armies? When did Muslim hostility toward Christians harden? History is a process of continual change, and here we seek to understand causes.

11. Raiders of Steppe and Sea: Vikings and Mongols: Eurasia and the Atlantic, 900–1350 376

From the late ninth through the tenth century, waves of Viking ships attacked across Europe; a few centuries later, beginning in 1200, the

Mongols swept across Eurasia, conquering all in their path and creating the largest empire the world had ever seen. What was the impact of these raiding peoples on settled societies and vice versa? In considering this question and the violent and destructive nature of these "barbarian" raids, we will consider the relationship of morality to history.

12. The Black Death: Afro-Eurasia, 1346–1350 418

The pandemic plague ravaged the population of Afro-Eurasia, killing about one-third of the population of Europe and Egypt. In this chapter, we examine the impact of the plague in various locales while also contemplating its causes and the relationship between cause and effect.

13. Students and Education: The World, 800–1400 449

This chapter looks at students and education over the long course of human history, from Buddhist monks in Japan and societies in central Sudanic Africa in the ninth century to Aztec society in the fifteenth century. In addition to asking about the context in which a source was composed, we will ask about the context in which the source presented its subject.

14. Environment, Culture, and Technology: Europe, Asia, and Oceania, 500–1500 477

Since the Middle Ages, the most significant changes have occurred in the fields of ecology, technology, and science. In this chapter we read and assess three grand theories about the origins of our technological transformation and of our environmental problems, drawing on written and visual primary source evidence to develop our conclusions.

LIST OF MAPS

Geographic Contents

Middle East (West Asia)

Central Asia

South Asia

East Asia

Southeast Asia

Australasia and the Pacific

Europe and Russia

The Americas

Interregional Contacts

Worlds of History

A Comparative Reader

1

Prehistory and the Origins of Patriarchy

Gathering, Agricultural, and Urban Societies, 40,000–1000 B.C.E.

■ HISTORICAL CONTEXT

Men control more of the world's income, wealth, and resources; enjoy more opportunities, freedoms, and positions of power; and exercise greater control over the bodies, wishes, and lives of others than do women. In most of the world, men dominate, parents prefer sons to daughters, and most people—even women—associate maleness with strength, energy, reason, science, and the important public sphere. A system of male rule—"patriarchy"—seems as old as humanity itself. But is it? This chapter will ask if patriarchy is natural or historical. If patriarchy did not always exist, did it have a historical beginning, middle, and, therefore, potentially a historical end? If patriarchy had human causes, can humans also create a more equal world?

The selections in this chapter span the three types of societies known to human history: hunting and gathering (the earliest human lifestyle), agricultural and pastoral (beginning about ten thousand years ago), and urban (beginning about five thousand years ago). Thus, we can speak of the agricultural revolution (8000 B.C.E.) and the urban revolution (3000 B.C.E.) as two of the most important changes in human history. These events drastically transformed the way people earned a living and led to increased populations, greater productivity, and radically changed lifestyles.

As you read, consider how the lives of men and women changed with these revolutions. How did the relationships between men and women change? As people settled in agricultural villages, and later in cities, economic and social differences between groups became more marked. Did differences between the sexes increase as well? Did men and women have relatively equal power before the development of agriculture and the rise of cities? Did patriarchy originate as part of the transition from agricultural to urban society, or did men always have more power?

■ THINKING HISTORICALLY

Thinking about History in Stages

To answer these questions, one must think of early human history in broad periods or stages. However, history does not develop in neat compartments, one clearly distinguished from the other. Historians must organize and analyze disparate events and developments that occur over time to make sense of them. This chapter follows a widely accepted division of early history into the hunting-gathering, agricultural-pastoral, and urban stages. Reflect on how this system of structuring the past makes history more intelligible, and consider the shortcomings of such a system. What challenges to the idea of historical stages do the readings in the chapter pose? On balance, does organizing history into stages make it easier or more difficult to understand complex changes, such as evolving gender roles?

1

VIRGINIA HUGHES

Were the First Artists Mostly Women? 2013

Earliest human societies are called "hunting and gathering" because that is how the first humans got their food — they hunted animals and gathered plants. The hunters were more frequently men, and the gatherers were more often women. Perhaps because hunting seems more glamorous than gathering, people think of this early period as patriarchal — dominated by men. In fact, in many hunting-gathering societies, gathering provided more food than hunting. Women's work was every bit as important as men's.

Still, we might ask if people or places that relied heavily on hunting were patriarchal. The first places to look would be those where

---

Source: Virginia Hughes, "Were the First Artists Mostly Women?" *National Geographic*, October 9, 2013.

we find cave paintings of the animals that men hunted. The caves in Europe, which have received considerable attention, often also reveal images of human hands — a frequent image of hunting-gathering or Paleolithic art throughout the world. The hand images are either printed on cave walls by hands doused in a kind of paint or stenciled by someone who placed a hand on the wall and then sprayed paint around it. The latter method, which was more common in the European caves, was a complex process of blowing paint through a bone straw.

This article relates the argument that these early paintings of hands — and therefore maybe animals as well — were the work of women. What is the evidence? What do you think? How might this affect your ideas about early men and women?

THINKING HISTORICALLY

People used to call early humans "Cave Men" and imagined fur-clad men and women living in cold caves. One reason for that idea was the discovery of the paintings of animals in caves in Spain in 1870, in France in 1940, and since then in numerous places in Europe and Asia as far as the Indonesian Island of Sulawesi in 2014. These caves were painted over a period of tens of thousands of years, the earliest (at Sulawesi) dating to 40,000 years ago. In popular imagination, they all came from the same era: the period of the Cave Men. This was a simple idea of a stage of history: First there were the cave men, and then came us. Whether the intent was to emphasize the changes between the Cave Men era and the modern era, or the relative continuity since then, people found it helpful to think of human history in these two stages.

Modern anthropologists and historians divide time into more sophisticated stage theories for the same reason — to help us think of human history. More precisely, stages (or periods, eras, even "times") are tools for ordering the vast abundance of data we have about the past. Today, we dismiss the term *Cave Man* because we recognize that many, if not most, early humans did not live in caves. What they did share, however, was a dependence on hunting and gathering food for survival — at least until they discovered how to plant food and domesticate animals 10,000–12,000 years ago.

The value of thinking in stages is that it allows us to generalize beyond the clutter. The danger is in generalizing too far. How does the author of this selection generalize from hands to animals, and from hunters in caves to hunting and gathering societies?

Women made most of the oldest-known cave art paintings, suggests a new analysis of ancient handprints. Most scholars had assumed these

ancient artists were predominantly men, so the finding overturns decades of archaeological dogma.

Archaeologist Dean Snow of Pennsylvania State University analyzed
hand stencils found in eight cave sites in France and Spain. By comparing the relative lengths of certain fingers, Snow determined that three-
quarters of the handprints were female.

"There has been a male bias in the literature for a long time," said
Snow, whose research was supported by the National Geographic
Society's Committee for Research and Exploration. "People have
made a lot of unwarranted assumptions about who made these things,
and why."

Archaeologists have found hundreds of hand stencils on cave
walls across the world. Because many of these early paintings also
showcase game animals — bison, reindeer, horses, woolly mam-
moths — many researchers have proposed that they were made by
male hunters, perhaps to chronicle their kills or as some kind of
"hunting magic" to improve success of an upcoming hunt. The new
study suggests otherwise.

"In most hunter-gatherer societies, it's men that do the killing.
But it's often the women who haul the meat back to camp, and women
are as concerned with the productivity of the hunt as the men are,"
Snow said. "It wasn't just a bunch of guys out there chasing bison
around."

Experts expressed a wide range of opinions about how to interpret
Snow's new data, attesting to the many mysteries still surrounding this
early art.

"Hand stencils are a truly ironic category of cave art because they
appear to be such a clear and obvious connection between us and the
people of the Paleolithic," said archaeologist Paul Pettitt of Durham University in England. "We think we understand them, yet the more you dig
into them you realize how superficial our understanding is."

Sex Differences

Snow's study began more than a decade ago when he came across the
work of John Manning, a British biologist who had found that men and
women differ in the relative lengths of their fingers: Women tend to have
ring and index fingers of about the same length, whereas men's ring fingers tend to be longer than their index fingers.

One day after reading about Manning's studies, Snow pulled a
40-year-old book about cave paintings off his bookshelf. The inside
front cover of the book showed a colorful hand stencil from the famous
Pech Merle cave in southern France. "I looked at that thing and I thought,

man, if Manning knows what he's talking about, then this is almost certainly a female hand," Snow recalled.

Hand stencils and handprints have been found in caves in Argentina, Africa, Borneo, and Australia. But the most famous examples are from the 12,000- to 40,000-year-old cave paintings in southern France and northern Spain.

For the new study, out this week in the journal *American Antiquity*, Snow examined hundreds of stencils in European caves, but most were too faint or smudged to use in the analysis. The study includes measurements from 32 stencils, including 16 from the cave of El Castillo in Spain, 6 from the caves of Gargas in France, and 5 from Pech Merle.

Snow ran the numbers through an algorithm that he had created based on a reference set of hands from people of European descent who lived near his university. Using several measurements—such as the length of the fingers, the length of the hand, the ratio of ring to index finger, and the ratio of index finger to little finger—the algorithm could predict whether a given handprint was male or female. Because there is a lot of overlap between men and women, however, the algorithm wasn't especially precise: It predicted the sex of Snow's modern sample with about 60 percent accuracy.

Luckily for Snow, that wasn't a problem for the analysis of the prehistoric handprints. As it turned out—much to his surprise—the hands in the caves were much more sexually dimorphic than modern hands, meaning that there was little overlap in the various hand measurements.

"They fall at the extreme ends, and even beyond the extreme ends," Snow said. "Twenty thousand years ago, men were men and women were women."

Woman, Boy, Shaman?

Snow's analysis determined that 24 of the 32 hands—75 percent—were female.

Some experts are skeptical. Several years ago, evolutionary biologist R. Dale Guthrie performed a similar analysis of Paleolithic handprints. His work—based mostly on differences in the width of the palm and the thumb—found that the vast majority of handprints came from adolescent boys.

For adults, caves would have been dangerous and uninteresting, but young boys would have explored them for adventure, said Guthrie, an emeritus professor at the University of Alaska, Fairbanks. "They drew what was on their mind, which is mainly two things: naked women and large, frightening mammals."

Other researchers are more convinced by the new data.

"I think the article is a landmark contribution," said archaeologist Dave Whitley of ASM Affiliates, an archaeological consulting firm in Tehachapi, California. Despite these handprints being discussed for half a decade, "this is the first time anyone's synthesized a good body of evidence."

Whitley rejects Guthrie's idea that this art was made for purely practical reasons related to hunting. His view is that most of the art was made by shamans who went into trances to try to connect with the spirit world. "If you go into one of these caves alone, you start to suffer from sensory deprivation very, very quickly, in 5 to 10 minutes," Whitley said. "It can spin you into an altered state of consciousness."

The new study doesn't discount the shaman theory, Whitley added, because in some hunter-gatherer societies shamans are female or even transgendered.

The new work raises many more questions than it answers. Why would women be the primary artists? Were they creating only the handprints, or the rest of the art as well? Would the hand analysis hold up if the artists weren't human, but Neanderthal?

The question Snow gets most often, though, is why these ancient artists, whoever they were, left handprints at all.

"I have no idea, but a pretty good hypothesis is that this is somebody saying, 'This is mine, I did this,'" he said.

2

OLGA SOFFER, JAMES M. ADOVASIO,
AND DAVID C. HYLAND

The "Venus" Figurines: Textiles, Basketry, Gender, and Status in the Upper Paleolithic, 2000

In addition to paintings of hands and animals on cave walls, the Paleolithic (or Old Stone Age) peoples of Europe and Asia have left us many small statues of women. These sculptures are naked or partially clothed and often emphasize women's sexual features, sometimes suggesting pregnancy. Because of this, the classically educated archaeologists who

---

Source: Olga Soffer, James M. Adovasio, and David C. Hyland, "The 'Venus' Figurines: Textiles, Basketry, Gender, and Status in the Upper Paleolithic, 2000," *Current Anthropology*, August/October 2000, Vol. 41, Issue 4, pp. 511–537. Published by The University of Chicago Press.

discovered them beginning in the nineteenth century labeled them "Venus figurines," after the Roman goddess of love, sex, and fertility.

As the authors of this article point out, much has been written about these Venus figurines, but they believe they have discovered something others have missed. What is that something? Why do they think it is important? What do you think?

THINKING HISTORICALLY

Stages can be very different from chronological periods. The time from 40,000 years ago to 12,000 years ago constitutes a chronological period in which all humans were hunters and gatherers. But the hunting–and-gathering style of life did not disappear from the world when agriculture first appeared. Indeed, it continues today in some of the more remote parts of the world. So, the hunting-and-gathering stage includes some people living today. It is useful to include them with our early ancestors because of the similarities in the hunting-and-gathering life. For one thing, their technology is the same: They all use hacked stone for tools and weapons. Thus, we can use the term *Old Stone Age* (or *Paleolithic*) to describe them. The Old Stone Age is not a period. Some human beings alive today still live as people did in the Stone Age.

Buried things that we dig up provide one route to the past. But it is a silent one. Our knowledge of the Old Stone Age is based on a combination of the excavated artifacts that archaeologists uncover and what we can learn from modern-day hunter-gatherers. Ethnographers who live with hunting-gathering people today can give voice to the silent artifacts. Toward the end of this article, the authors refer to the "ethnographic record" as support for their interpretation of the "iconography" (or the silent "Venus" figurines). What do they mean by that? What might be the drawback of using twenty-first-century hunter-gatherers to understand those who lived tens of thousands of years ago?

Our images of Upper Paleolithic Europe are a curious lot, abounding with depictions of brave Ice-Age hunters preparing for the hunt, stalking and killing megafauna, or celebrating the kill. This is true for written and visual representations alike, which, by omitting from consideration the activities of not only older individuals but also women and children, present extremely limited and biased reconstructions of the past. These reconstructions of the imagined stereotypical activities of prime-age males leave us in the proverbial outer darkness as to what the Paleolithic "silent majority"—the mates, children, and parents of such brave prehistoric men—may have been doing with their lives in addition to admiring and assisting them. . . .

No item of Upper Paleolithic material culture has received as much attention, from amateurs and professionals alike, as depictions of humans. Particular attention has been paid to Paleolithic depictions of women, commonly termed "Venuses" in the literature. This attention has, by and large, been directed to certain features common to many of them, namely, the emotionally charged primary and secondary sexual characteristics—vulvae, breasts, stomachs, and buttocks. This selective focus on just a few features, presumed but never demonstrated to be the critical ones, has led to the well-known myriad of conflicting unitary explanations for the Venus figurines. These explanations are as numerous as commentators venturing an opinion and range from seeing the depictions as "fertility" symbols or "mother goddesses," paleoerotica, gynecological primers, and self-portraiture to suggestions that they were signifiers of widespread social ties. Other scholars have raised serious objections to such explanations, pointing to their selectivity, lack of attention to context, uncontrolled chronologies, and unjustified assumptions. . . .

Upper Paleolithic female figurines, naked as well as partially clad, occur across Eurasia from the Atlantic Ocean to Lake Baikal.[1] Their distribution contrasts sharply with the scarcity of unambiguous depictions of Paleolithic males and humans of unknown sex who are depicted either naked (in the case of unambiguous males) or lacking any marking.

Abramova (1960) and Gvozdover (1989) were the first scholars to study the patterning of the decorations on the Venus bodies and to suggest that some of them might represent clothing. Our study continues this research, focusing on the close reading of these decorations and demonstrating that they do indeed depict clothing. . . .

While the few scholars who have commented on likely Paleolithic clothing have argued that it was surely made of such animal by-products as furs and hides, we argue here that the garments depicted on the European Venus figurines clearly and unambiguously reflect plant-based textiles and basketry. . . .

The head of the [Venus of] Willendorf figurine [Figure 1.1] offers the clearest evidence that what we see here is a depiction of headgear—a fiber-based woven cap or hat—rather than a hairdo, or a cap made of shells. Our close examination of this specimen shows a spirally or radially hand-woven item which may be initiated by a knotted center in the manner of some kinds of coiled baskets. The technique represented is a two-element structure in which an apparently flexible, horizontal foundation element or warp is vertically wrapped with stem stitches. The foundation element is clearly visible between the stitches, some of which

---

[1] In central Russia. [Ed.]

Figure 1.1   The Venus of Willendorf.
Source: © The Art Gallery Collection/Alamy Stock Photo.

are plain while others are countered. Work direction is right to left, and at least seven circuits encircle the head, with two extra half-circuits over the nape of the neck. . . . Several areas on the body of the cap appear to illustrate splices, where new material has been added. Suffice it to say that this complex construction cannot be produced with growing (that is, attached) human hair. . . .

Our examination of the original [Venus of] Lespugue piece [Figure 1.2] via unaided eye and low-power magnification reveals remarkable attention to detail. The Lespugue skirt is composed of 11 cords plied around a base cord which serves as the belt. . . . The overall configuration of the skirt is tapered not unlike a tail by employing a long central cord and immediately contiguous segments with progressively shorter cords toward the lateral margins of the skirt. Although no details of cord splicing are evident, our

Figure 1.2　The Venus of Lespugue.

Source: © Roger-Viollet / The Image Works.

examination confirms Barber's (1991, 1994) observation that the garment depicted was clearly made of plant fiber. . . .

As we have noted above, the unambiguous assignment of particular technologies to any particular social grouping of individuals is a difficult endeavor in archaeology. This is especially so as one moves farther back in time and can no longer convincingly use arguments of historical continuity. Separated as we are by some 27 millennia from the first documentation about who wove and made baskets in prehistoric Europe, the gendering of textile technologies must rely on parsimony, at best. Nonetheless, iconography and analogy with the ethnographic record clearly indicate that it was Paleolithic women who were most likely the weavers and basket makers in Gravettian times.[2]

We have already presented iconographic evidence for this. Here we briefly refer to the ethnographic record, which documents the close association of women not only with plant harvesting and processing but also with the transformation of plant products into more complex structures through weaving and the processing of woody materials into basketry. This association is valid for all simpler societies where textiles and basketry are produced for domestic and communal needs and breaks

---

[2] About 29,000–22,000 B.C.E. [Ed.]

down only when such perishable products enter the sphere of market exchange.

Our documentation of extensive textile production in prehistoric Europe and of the gendering of these technologies sheds new light not only on the labor of a heretofore unrecognized segment of Upper Paleolithic people, women, but also on the high value of this labor. The exquisite and labor-intensive detailing employed in the depiction of the woven garments worn by one group of Venuses clearly shows that weaving and basket-making skills and their products were valued enough to be transformed into transcendent cultural facts carved into stone, ivory, and bone. Simply put, we suggest that being depicted wearing such garments associated the wearer and, by extension, the maker of them with a marked position of prestige.

3

Paleolithic and Neolithic Art from Europe, Africa, Asia, and the Middle East, c. 15,000–2000 B.C.E.

Paleolithic (Old Stone Age) art made by hunters and gatherers was common everywhere before the agricultural revolution. Here we see two examples, from Europe and North Africa. The hunter and bison shown in Figure 1.3 were carved onto the wall of a cave in Lascaux, France, around 15,000 B.C.E. Figure 1.4 comes from a large collection of rock art dating from 10,000 B.C.E. in Algeria. The origins of agriculture led to the creation of a greater range of art forms and images in what we call the Neolithic or New Stone Age. We see here examples from Jordan and northern China. Among the earliest representations of humans are the half-sized human figures from c. 7000 B.C.E. found near Ain Ghazal in Jordan (Figure 1.5). Figure 1.6 is a Neolithic ceramic vase from Gansu province in China. What do these images suggest about the interests of hunters and gatherers? How was Neolithic art different from Paleolithic art?

Figure 1.3   Cave drawing from Lascaux, France, c. 15,000 B.C.E.
Source: © AAAC / TopFoto / The Image Works.

Figure 1.4   Rock carving from Tassili n'Ajjer, Algeria, c. 10,000 B.C.E.
Source: imageBROKER / SuperStock.

Figure 1.5 Plaster head from Ain Ghazal, Jordan, c. 7000 B.C.E.

Source: © Louvre Museum, Paris / Werner Forman Archive / The Image Works.

THINKING HISTORICALLY

Dating a work of art or any artifact from the past is a complex process that involves carbon dating (measuring the lost carbon-14 isotopes) of nearby organic remains and other scientific methods. But, as complex as it may be, all historical understanding begins with reliable dates. The date of an object allows us to place it on a real or imagined timeline that reveals the relationship of the object to everything else.

Create a timeline from 40,000 years ago until 2,000 years ago, and place each of these works in its proper place. What, if anything, does this visual representation of actual dates suggest to you? Then on the same timeline mark the beginning of the Neolithic Age and the beginning of the Urban or Bronze Age. This is the difference between raw dating and organizing the past into technological stages. What advantages do you see in organizing the past in stages? What might be the disadvantages?

Figure 1.6 Neolithic vase from Gansu province in China, c. 2000 B.C.E.

Source: DeAgostini / SuperStock.

4

MARGARET EHRENBERG

Women in Prehistory, 1989

British anthropologist Margaret Ehrenberg argues here that women were likely the first farmers as well as the originators of many of the innovations of the agricultural revolution. What evidence does she offer? What was the importance of the agricultural revolution? When and how, according to Ehrenberg, did men take over?

THINKING HISTORICALLY

In this selection much of the author's evidence is anthropological or ethnographic (rather than archaeological). That is, it comes from our contemporary world, not from digging up the past. How does the use of this kind of evidence depend on the idea of historical stages? From

Source: Margaret Ehrenberg, *Women in Prehistory* (Norman: University of Oklahoma Press, 1989), 77–81, 99–100, 103–7.

the standpoint of women, was the agricultural revolution a single stage of history, or should we think of it as two stages? If so, what were those stages?

From the point of view of the lives of women, the Neolithic period is perhaps the most important phase of prehistory. . . . It is likely that at the end of the Palaeolithic and Mesolithic, women enjoyed equality with men. They probably collected as much, if not more, of the food eaten by the community and derived equal status from their contribution. But by about four thousand years ago, in the Bronze Age, many of the gender roles and behaviour typical of the world today had probably been established. The implication is that the crucial changes must have taken place during the Neolithic period. . . .

The discovery of farming techniques has usually been assumed to have been made by men, but it is in fact very much more likely to have been made by women. On the basis of anthropological evidence for societies still living traditional foraging lifestyles and those living by simple, non-mechanised farming, taken in conjunction with direct archaeological evidence, it seems probable that it was women who made the first observations of plant behaviour, and worked out, presumably by long trial and error, how to grow and tend crops.

This transition from foraging to farming, which marks the change from the Palaeolithic and Mesolithic or Old and Middle Stone Ages to the period known to archaeologists as the Neolithic or New Stone Age, seems to have taken place initially in south-west Asia some time after 10,000 BC. By 6000 BC farming was well established throughout that part of the world. . . .

How and why did this change to agriculture take place, and, more particularly, what can we say about the role of women in this process? . . . Foraging societies still living in the world today . . . gather and hunt food in a way similar to Palaeolithic societies before the invention of agriculture; among these people there is a regularly recurring pattern of food procurement. . . . Women are mainly concerned with gathering plant food, which provides the bulk of the diet of nearly all foragers, while men spend much time hunting animals. Although animal products form an important source of proteins in the diet, meat actually makes up a relatively small proportion of the food intake of these societies. We can also study other groups of people in places such as New Guinea and parts of Africa who still grow crops and keep animals with the aid of only the very simplest technology, in much the same way as we may imagine Neolithic societies would have done. These societies do not use ploughs or artificial irrigation, and they keep few, if any, animals. To distinguish them from people using more mechanised agricultural technologies, anthropologists usually call this type of farming horticulture, and the people using it horticultural societies. . . .

Although present-day horticulturalists live in a wide variety of places around the world, many remarkably regular patterns of behaviour can be observed, and this gives us some degree of confidence in using their lifestyles as a model for the Neolithic, particularly if some of the behaviour patterns can be seen to be reflected in evidence from archaeological sites.

Studies of the roles of women in different types of agricultural communities show a remarkably consistent pattern. In societies where plough agriculture is practised and animals are kept on a significant scale, most of the agricultural work is done by men, with women playing no direct part, or only a very subsidiary role. On the other hand, in horticultural societies, in which hoes or digging sticks are used for making holes or drills in which to plant roots or seeds, women are usually almost wholly responsible for agricultural production. A study of 104 horticultural societies existing today showed that in 50 per cent of them women were exclusively responsible for agriculture, in 33 per cent women and men shared various tasks, and in only 17 per cent were men wholly responsible for farming, and this is after decades or even centuries of contact with societies whose ideology would encourage men to take on greater roles in production. Horticultural societies are still widespread, mainly within the Tropics, in many parts of Africa, central America and Asia. The typical pattern in these areas is one of shifting cultivation, where patches of land are worked for a few years, and then when soil fertility declines another plot is cleared and cultivated. Although men often help to clear the plots of trees and undergrowth, women usually hoe, sow, tend and harvest the crops. Studies carried out early this century suggest that this pattern of cultivation was more common then than it is today. It also seems very likely that it was even more typical before most parts of the world had contact with European traders and missionaries, with their preconceived ideas about what it was right and proper for women and men to do. . . .

The Secondary Products Revolution, or the Great Male Takeover Bid

In an earlier section it was argued that women almost certainly "invented" or worked out the principles of farming as well as many of the concomitant skills and tools which go to make crop agriculture possible and profitable. As principal food providers they were probably respected and had equal status with men. But between then and now, in all but the most traditional hunter-gatherer and horticultural societies, the status of women has been drastically reduced, and in many areas farming has become a predominantly male preserve. Why the change, and when did it happen? Two facts are certain: Firstly, by the time of the earliest written records, everywhere in Europe farming was primarily a male occupation, and men owned the farmland and the tools. Secondly, in those areas of the world where women are still the main agricultural producers, most of the farming is concerned with crop production, and if animals are kept at all, it is usually on a small farmyard scale, rather than as large herds or flocks. The change to male dominance in agriculture, therefore, took place at some time between the first stages of the Neolithic period and the advent of written records, and may be related to the changing role of animals within the farming economies of prehistoric Europe. It also seems likely that such a drastic shift in lifestyle, whether it took place gradually over millennia or as a sudden "revolution," would have been associated with other changes within society. Anthropologists have shown that in present-day societies a significant (though not 100 per cent) correlation exists between plough agriculture and patrilineal descent and land ownership in the same way as there is a correlation between non-plough agriculture and the heavy involvement, and consequent enhanced status, of women. We can look for evidence of this shift in the archaeological record: for example, changes in family structure, wealth or ownership patterns may show up in settlement sites or in burials. . . .

The crucial changes in farming practice are thought to have taken place around 3000 BC, in the later Neolithic period. This would have been some five millennia after the introduction of farming in the Near East, and similar economic shifts can be detected in many areas of Europe at about the same time. Andrew Sherratt has suggested that although domesticated animals were kept during the early Neolithic, they were used only as a source of meat; the consumption of milk or milk products was probably not significant, nor were the animals used for pulling ploughs or carts. All these innovations came later and not only revolutionised agricultural productivity, but also reduced the amount of labour involved in farming. Moreover, the greater importance of domesticated animals and their products would have reduced the necessity for hunting wild animals. As the balance of work changed from part hunting, part crop cultivation and tending a small number of animals to an economy dependent on mixed farming, so the roles and duties of women and men may have shifted. Let us examine the evidence and arguments. . . .

Both carts and ploughs first appear in depictions on clay tablets and cylinder seals in Mesopotamia, around the beginning of the fourth millennium BC, and both seem to have spread to Europe fairly rapidly over 500 years or so. One of the earliest depictions of ploughing [Figure 1.7] shows an ox drawing a two-handled plough with a sowing funnel, a device used for sowing seed deeply in the soil and often associated with areas where irrigation is needed. Most significantly the

Figure 1.7   Men leading and guiding a two-handled plough, depicted on a cylinder seal from Mesopotamia, late third millennium B.C.

Source: Ashmolean Museum, University of Oxford, UK / Bridgeman Images.

two individuals involved, one guiding the animal from the front, the other guiding the plough, both appear to be men with beards. Early depictions of ploughs in Egypt, from Old Kingdom tombs, also show them being used by men. . . .

In areas of the world where plough agriculture and the herding of animals are the predominant form of farming, men universally play the major role in agricultural tasks. Women either take no part in farming or only a small one. They may sometimes contribute to harvesting, or to the care of domestic animals, if these are kept only in small numbers. An important distinction exists today between Africa, where horticulture predominates, and Asia, where plough agriculture is far more common and where domesticated animals are kept. Even in those areas of Asia, for example, where women are involved to some extent in aspects of plough agriculture, they work fewer hours than men; whereas in Africa, where farming is predominantly carried out without the use of the plough, and primarily by women, they do far more work than men. The other main difference between these two farming regimes is that social and economic stratification is a far more significant factor, with greater extremes of poverty and wealth and of land ownership amongst the Asian plough agriculturalists than amongst the African hoe agriculturalists or horticulturalists. . . .

Patterns of social organisation in horticultural societies today are quite different from those of intensive agriculturalists: these seem to be linked to the balance of agricultural tasks and to their allocation to each sex. One of the greatest differences is in the position of women. This reinforces the theory that it was in the later Neolithic, when men began to take over most agricultural work, that the social status of women declined.

... It is likely that most of the tending of animals was done by men. Large-scale herding often takes place some way from the farm or settlement, as fresh grazing land is continually sought. Raiding by neighbouring tribes seems to be an endemic part of most cattle herding—almost a variation on hunting! This has been seen as the origin of warfare, when for the first time people owned a resource which it was both worthwhile and fairly easy to steal.

Secondly, the invention of plough agriculture, too, would probably have resulted in farming becoming predominantly a male activity, while on the basis of ethnographic analogy, at least, women would probably have spent more time in food preparation, child-rearing and textile and perhaps other craft production.

Thirdly, although less land is needed for the same amount of production, plough agriculture is far more labour-intensive than hoe agriculture: where land is poor, ploughing makes agriculture possible. In some areas of prehistoric Europe it had the effect of making large tracts of lighter, sandy soil available, but in other areas it may have allowed an increase in population where there was a real or perceived shortage of land. In the earliest phases of the Neolithic, land shortages would certainly not have been a problem, as witnessed by the rapid population spread discussed in an earlier section. However, in the later Neolithic there may have been a shortage of land perceived to be suitable for agriculture. Women would therefore have been expected to produce more children and thus more labourers. This would have been seen as their major role. Moreover, male children might have been valued most highly, as future farm workers. Women, meanwhile, would have become less valued by men in their own right: as more time was spent in pregnancy and the care of very young infants, so less time could be spent on farming activities. As men took over many of their tasks, they no longer contributed so much to the daily production of food, which had been a crucial factor in maintaining the equal status they had previously enjoyed.

Fourthly, another social change which might have been an indirect result of the secondary products revolution was the switch from matrilocal residence and matrilineal descent to patrilocal residence and patrilineal descent. There is a very strong ethnographic correlation between male-dominated farming and patrilineal descent and patrilocal residence. A male farmer will teach his sons the necessary skills and expect them to tend his land and animals. In a matrilineal system his sister's sons, rather than his own sons, inherit these herds, land and equipment on his death. This is not in the male interest if men are the main agriculturalists. When women were involved in the land-based tasks, they would have learnt the basic skills from their mothers, so it would have been more obvious for them also to inherit their land and equipment. However, it also seems that individual land ownership is less common amongst hoe agriculturalists, and, by definition, less equipment is used. Therefore, at least in terms of material goods, far less is typically at stake in matrilineal than in patrilineal systems.

Finally, the development of agriculture brought with it a large increase, not only in the number of related tasks, including several which are very time-consuming, but also in the range of material possessions such as farming and food-preparation tools and storage vessels. Two consequences would have resulted. On the one hand, this may be seen as the spur to the development of craft specialisation, as some individuals concentrated on the production of one particular item, which they would exchange for other products or services. At first this could have been in addition to normal farming tasks, but increasingly some people might have found that they could acquire enough food and other necessities by producing only their specialised article. In this way exchange must have become more common, and more sophisticated. On the other hand these material possessions, as well as the domesticated animals themselves, would have constituted considerable wealth, which could be accumulated and handed on from one generation to the next. . . .

The wealthy can become powerful by lending to poorer families in return for services, such as farm labour, or support in combat against other groups. By this means the rich are able to become more wealthy, while the poorer become indebted to other families, and have to produce more and more, or spend time on tasks other than directly for their own subsistence. So the vicious circle develops, and it is easy to see how from this point permanent hierarchies not only of wealth, but of power and status come about, in a way which is impossible in forager societies. This is also the context in which a society can begin to think of people, as well as material possessions and land, as objects of value and exchange. A child could be given as labour to a family to whom the child's parents were indebted, or a woman given to work or to produce extra children.

How such fundamental changes actually took place is not clear, even if we assume they were a gradual process in each community. The full consequences which have just been discussed would have developed very slowly, even over millennia, and are difficult to pinpoint chronologically. In any case, as women were increasingly relegated to secondary tasks, by the end of the Neolithic period they had fewer personal resources with which to assert their status. Presumably, as with so many innovations even in the modern world, the social and economic consequences of seemingly minor innovations would not have been apparent until it was too late to return to former *mores*. The discovery of agriculture, which at the beginning of the Neolithic had been such a positive step by women, was by the end of the period to have had unforeseen, and unfortunate, consequences for them.

5

CATHERINE CLAY, CHANDRIKA PAUL, AND CHRISTINE SENECAL

Women in the First Urban Communities, 2009

This selection comes from a text on women in world history. Since world history is full of patriarchal, or male-dominated, societies, one of the thorniest problems is to determine just how widespread patriarchy was. Against the commonly held assumption that patriarchy has always existed, that it is universal or natural, we have seen that male domination was not common in most hunting-gathering and early agricultural societies—that is, throughout most of human history. When and how did it come about? What is the answer given in this selection? What kind of evidence best supports the author's conclusion?

THINKING HISTORICALLY

As already mentioned, one of the earliest, and still widely accepted, stage theories of human history posits three important stages: hunter-gatherer, agricultural-pastoral, and city-based or urban. Archaeologists use the corresponding terms of Paleolithic (Old Stone Age), Neolithic (New Stone Age), and Bronze Age. This reading suggests other developments of the urban or Bronze Age that might be better descriptions of the "third" stage than cities or bronze: states, plow agriculture, stratified societies, slave-owning societies, and literate and writing-based societies. How does each of these new developments affect the lives of women? If you were to divide only women's history into two, three, or four stages, what would they be?

The world's first cities emerged in Eurasia around 3500 BCE. Fostered by the spread of villages, the urban centers of this continent grew up along major river systems—an environment conducive to planting and harvesting crops with relatively predictable patterns. There were four major regions where urban civilizations developed: in the Fertile Crescent along the Tigris and Euphrates* Rivers (also known as Mesopotamia, "the land between the two rivers"), along the Nile in Egypt, along the Indus River in modern Pakistan, and along the Yellow and Yangtze† Rivers in China.

---

* TY gruhs and yu FRAY teez
† yang zuh
Note: Pronunciations of difficult-to-pronounce terms will be given throughout the book. The emphasis goes on the syllables appearing in all capitals. [Ed.]

Source: Catherine Clay, Chandrika Paul, and Christine Senecal, *Envisioning Women in World History* (New York: McGraw-Hill, 2009), 20–23.

Eurasia's urban centers brought rapid changes in the organization of populations. Institutional patriarchy probably developed alongside the state, tribute extraction, social stratification, and slavery. The state, especially, was a political institution that organized, disciplined, and enslaved numerous inhabitants in order to provide security and order for itself. Law codes to promote universal standards of behavior, irrigation projects to ensure food supply, and extensive military defense were now possible and deemed necessary. Of course, in order to manage this type of society, institutional governments were needed, and the leaders who ran these growing states exercised a disproportionate share of power. State power transformed everything.

At the same time the world's first urban political institutions were taking shape, a disparity of wealth also grew in urban centers. Gaps between the haves and the have-nots of society appeared in heretofore unseen proportions. Slavery and the slave trade, essential to ancient Eurasian civilizations, are first in evidence. Some have argued that men's control and exchange of women's sexuality and reproductive capacity generally became the basis of private property in Mesopotamia between 3100 and 600 BCE. This affected not only female slaves and concubines but also the daughters of elite and free men. A bride's father, representing his family, exchanged her reproductive capacity for wealth and household goods and sometimes less tangible objects, such as status and/or influence. Sometimes payments were made in installments, and after a marriage, when her first child was born, the balance of bridewealth or dowry payments became due. This overall disparity in status, wealth, and power spelled a worsening of women's position.

Another explanation for the worsening of women's position and the emergence of patriarchy focuses on demography and technology, beginning with burgeoning populations of village communities, which, as discussed above, encouraged women's fertility to supply the needed workforce. Populous urban centers could no longer practice *hoe* agriculture, but often needed intensive *plow* agriculture to feed everyone. With more children, urban women had less time for heavier agricultural work and the long, intensive hours needed for cultivation. Women of plow-using cultures may have preferred and chosen to work around the house and to perform lighter agricultural work. This scenario resulted in a gradual loss of women's social power and prestige—sometimes through their own choices that made sense to them at the time, but that accelerated men's control over economic activity and social resources. Ultimately, then, when the communities began using plows and more laborious, intensive methods of cultivation (and the groups prospered materially), women's status changed.

Women's experience in the first urban centers was marked by a general devaluation of their social freedoms, a denial of their claims to the results of their labor, and sometimes even a reshaping of their religious expression. This decline did not affect all women's communities in the same way or at the same time. We notice this in the great variety of women's experiences across Eurasia in all four of the earliest urban areas.

Women and Society in the Earliest Civilizations

Although some villages had begun to experience greater social stratification by 3500 BCE, the difference between the powerful and the powerless was not nearly as marked as it was in the earliest cities. The increased wealth possessed by a small proportion of the urban population led to a growing interest in keeping wealth and power within familial units. And it led in many ways to the constriction of women's lives, whether slave, concubine, free, or elite.

The social experience of many women was shaped by the flourishing Eurasian slave trade. In Mesopotamia as early as 2300 BCE, inscriptions for "slave girl" appear earlier than those translating as "slave male." Female slaves in Mesopotamia often originated as captives of raids and were more plentiful than male slaves. They also seem to have been valued more than male slaves. In Syria, the reward for the return of fleeing females was double that for male fugitive slaves. Enslaved women lived under a wide range of conditions, from the relative comfort of high-level slaves important in the domestic realm, such as concubines (unfree females purchased for reproduction) to female slaves used for their brute physical labor. Thus, although many enslaved women held very low positions in society, the status of some was not as low as slaves in other time periods. For instance, a second-generation slave was often valued more than one that had been recently captured. Furthermore, female slaves could upon occasion be freed from their servitude. In Babylon around 1750 BCE, slave concubines were frequently freed after the demise of their masters. Additionally, the children of freewomen and male slaves were considered to be of free status there. High slave mortality and these legal paths to slave freedom made slave raiding for new supplies a constant imperative.

The situation of free and elite women was shaped by family control. Ensuring the lineage of a family meant keeping ever-closer tabs on women's morality, which could include preserving a woman's virginity until marriage and ensuring that she had only her husband for a sexual partner. This would guarantee that the paternity of family members would be unquestioned. Even a woman's reputation could be of critical interest to her family. We see this in practices such as veiling and seclusion, which marked women's high familial social standing and reputation for chastity (meaning virginity when single and fidelity in marriage), and actually prevented her from any sexual contact with males other than her husband.

As mentioned above, the decrease in women's social influence did not strike equally in all places. For instance, little evidence points to women's morality being constrained in the cities of Harappa and Mohenjo Daro in the Indus River Valley around 2500 BCE. The thousands of written sources from this civilization have yet to be deciphered, and thus it would be hazardous to assume that women's social position never declined there, and yet archaeological evidence suggests that the gap between the haves and the have-nots might not have been terribly significant to the urban population. The façades of the residential buildings in those cities were relatively similar, even though some families possessed much larger storerooms than others. This evidence therefore suggests that maintaining a family's wealth and power, and the corresponding demotion that meant for women, was not as marked there. . . . Similarly, in the less urbanized Egyptian civilization, evidence suggests that women held positions of relative social equality and enjoyed freedom of movement unlike in other ancient societies. Given geographic barriers protecting them from warlike neighbors, Nile and Indus River civilizations were more militarily secure generally than civilizations in Mesopotamia and East Asia, and this may have resulted in fewer constraints on women.

Insight from Law Codes

We can see the inferior social position of urban women in law codes. Although legal texts from Mesopotamia often reflected social guidelines rather than actual practice, they nevertheless give critical insight to the way a society's most powerful people intended to govern. For example, in one Mesopotamian city in 2000 BCE, the murder of a woman was a capital offense. But by the time of Hammurabi‡ (d. 1750 BCE), a Babylonian ruler and famous lawmaker in Mesopotamia, killing a common woman only resulted in a fine according to the law code. (There was a stronger punishment if an elite woman were the victim.)

We can also see the uneven treatment of urban women in the law and practices surrounding marriage and divorce. For instance, wives' positions in Mesopotamia differed from city to city even within the same time frame. Whereas one law code from the urban civilization of Sumer made it legal for a new bride to refuse intercourse without punishment, later, a woman could be drowned if she refused to consummate her marriage. By 2500 BCE a law allowed a man to break his wife's teeth with a burnt brick if she disagreed with him. Divorce laws from

‡ ha muh RAH bee

Mesopotamian civilizations show that, although women experienced new inequities and constraints, they continued to enjoy some protections also. The cases compiled by the Babylonian ruler Hammurabi about 1700 BCE forbade women from divorcing, yet allowed men to terminate their marriages. Nevertheless, even Hammurabi's law code required divorced men to support their former spouses and any children they had together.

■ REFLECTIONS

A historical stage is a specific example of a larger process that historians call *periodization*. Dividing history into periods is one way historians make the past comprehensible. Without periodization, history would be a vast, unwieldy continuum, lacking points of reference and intelligibility.

One of the earliest forms of historical periodization—years of reign—was a natural system of record keeping in the ancient cities dominated by kings. Each kingdom had its own list of kings, and each marked the current date by numbering the years of the king's reign. Some ancient societies periodized their history according to the years of rule of local officials or priesthoods. In the ancient Roman Republic, time was figured according to the terms of the elected consuls. The ancient Greeks used four-year periods called Olympiads, beginning with the first Olympic games in 776 B.C.E.

The ancient Greeks did not use "B.C." or "B.C.E.," of course. The periodization of world history into B.C. ("before Christ") and A.D. (*anno Domini*, "the Year of Our Lord" or "after Christ") did not come until the sixth century A.D., when a Christian monk hit upon a way to center Christ as the major turning point in history. We use a variant of this system in this text, when designating events "B.C.E." for "before the common era" or "C.E." for "of the common era." This translation of "B.C." and "A.D." avoids the Christian bias of the older system but preserves the simplicity of this common dating system, one used worldwide by most people today—even many non-Christians—because of its convenience.

All systems of periodization implicitly claim to designate important transitions in the past. The B.C. periodization inscribed the Christian belief that Christ's life, death, and resurrection fundamentally changed world history. Muslims count the years from a year one A.H. (*anno Hegire*, designating the year of the Prophet Muhammad's escape from Mecca to Medina) in 622 A.D. of the Christian calendar, and Jews date the years from a biblical year one.

Millennia, centuries, and decades are useful periods for societies that count by tens. Although such multiples are only mathematical, some historians use them for rough periodization, to distinguish between the 1950s and the 1960s or between the eighteenth and nineteenth centuries, for example, as if there were a genuine and important transition between one period and the other. Sometimes historians "stretch" the boundaries of centuries or decades to account for earlier or later changes. For example, some historians speak of "the long nineteenth century," embracing the period from the French Revolution in 1789 to the First World War in 1914, on the grounds that peoples' lives were transformed in 1789 rather than in 1800 and in 1914 rather than in 1900. Similarly, the "sixties," as a term for American society and culture during the Vietnam War era, often means the period from about 1963 to about 1975, since civil rights and antiwar activity became significant a few years after the beginning of the decade and the war continued until 1975.

Characterizing and defining a decade or century in chronological terms is only one method of periodization, however. Processes can also be periodized, as we saw in this chapter. All of world history can be divided into three periods: hunting-gathering, agricultural-pastoral, and urban. These are overlapping and continuing periods, and we can date only the beginning of the agricultural-pastoral and the urban periods, at about ten thousand and five thousand years ago, respectively. Further, we found it useful to divide the agricultural-pastoral period into two parts: early hoe agriculture or horticulture, when women still played a primary role, and later plow agriculture and the pastoral "secondary products revolution," when men's work predominated. Thus, our effort to understand the origins of patriarchy benefited from a four-stage periodization in which patriarchy began in an advanced agricultural-pastoral society and subsequent urban societies. These periods began at different times in different places: generally earliest in the Middle East and later in the Americas. To note how processes like plow agriculture or cities change people's lives (so much that we see a new stage of history) is not to say that all societies must take the same route. There may be different historical processes that lead to the same stage, as either plows or irrigation may produce enough food for cities (and lead to patriarchies). All societies do not go through all the same stages. Some today remain at a nonurban stage (making it possible to extrapolate about the past using recent information from anthropologists). Still, some historical processes—the adoption of new technologies or ways of life—can be so powerful that they effect changes almost everywhere. Can you think of other examples of such stage-making processes besides those mentioned in this chapter?

You might also get a sense of how the historian goes about periodizing and a feeling for its value if you periodize something you know a lot about—your own life, for instance. Think of the most important change or changes in your life. How have these changes divided your life into certain periods? Outline your autobiography by marking these periods as parts or chapters of the story of your life so far. To gain a sense of how periodization is imposed on reality and how arbitrary this structuring of the past can be, imagine how a parent or good friend would periodize your life. Would it be different from the way you did it? How and why? How might you periodize your life ten or twenty years from now? How would you have done it five years ago?

2.

The Urban Revolution and "Civilization"

Ancient City Societies in Mesopotamia, Egypt, and Peru, 3500–1000 B.C.E.

■ HISTORICAL CONTEXT

The urban revolution that began approximately five thousand years ago produced a vast complex of new inventions, institutions, and ideas in the cities that dominated surrounding farms and pastures. The first selection in this chapter surveys the wide range of innovations in these earliest civilizations.

The term *civilization* has to be used cautiously. Especially when the idea of civilization is used as part of a stage theory of human history, we tend to assume that technological advancement means moral advancement. For instance, one hundred years ago scholars described ancient history as the progression from "savagery" to "barbarism" to "civilization."

It would be a shame to throw out the word *civilization* because it has been written more often with an axe than with a pen. The fact remains that the ancient cities created new ways of life for better or worse that were radically different from the world of agricultural villages. If we discard the word *civilization* as too overburdened with prejudice, we will have to find another one to describe that complex of changes. The term *civilization* comes from the Latin root word for city, *civitas*, from which we also get *civic*, *civilian*, and *citizen*. But, as the first reading argues, cities also created social classes, institutionalized inequalities, and calls to arms; most civilizations created soldiers as well as civilians.

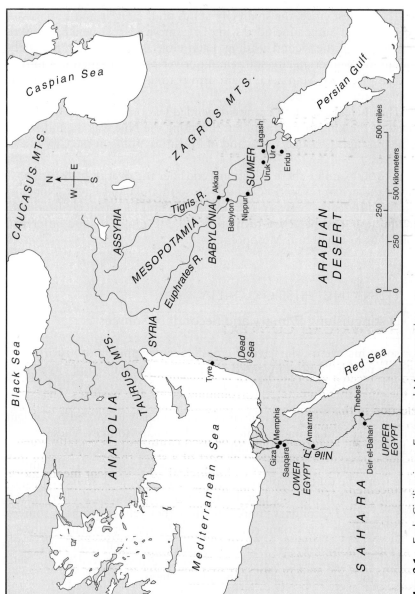

Map 2.1 Early Civilizations: Egypt and Mesopotamia.

The earliest cities, the small city-states on the Tigris and Euphrates* in ancient Sumer, included King Gilgamesh's Uruk, which is recounted in the second reading. Later cities, like Hammurabi's† Babylon, united Sumerian city-states and upriver pastoral kingdoms into giant empires (see Map 2.1). The fourth reading presents excerpts from Hammurabi's law code.

The ancient Egyptian empire depended less on cities than on the power of the king or pharaoh, but life along the Nile was magnified in the pharaoh's residence city and in his future home in the City of the Dead.

As you examine these selections, consider the overall transformation of the urban revolution in both Mesopotamia and Egypt. Note also the differences between Mesopotamian and Egyptian civilizations. Finally, how was the urban revolution in Peru similar to, and different from, that in Egypt and Mesopotamia?

■ THINKING HISTORICALLY

Distinguishing Primary and Secondary Sources

For some historians, the "age of cities" is the beginning of history because people in cities invented writing. The period before city building and the creation of writing systems thus is often called "prehistory."

Our knowledge of ancient cities is enormously enhanced by ancient writings, art, and artifacts, which we call primary sources. These include literature, law codes, and inscriptions but also sculpture, murals, building remains, tools, and weapons—indeed, virtually anything from the time and place being studied. Secondary sources differ: They are written after the fact. History books or historical interpretations are called secondary sources because they rely on primary sources for information. Historians read, study, and interpret primary sources to compose secondary sources. In this chapter, you will read both primary and secondary sources to help you learn ways to discern sources and extrapolate information from them.

---

* TY gruhs and yu FRAY teez

KEVIN REILLY

Cities and Civilization, 1989

This selection from a college textbook is an obvious secondary source. You know it is a secondary source because it was written long after the events described by a modern historian — me.

This selection does two things. First, it explores the wide range of changes brought about by the urban revolution, from particulars like writing and money and metallurgy to abstractions like social class, visual acuity, and anonymity. After you read the selection, you might make a list of all the inventions and new phenomena of cities. You will likely be surprised by the great number of ideas, institutions, and activities that originated in the first cities. You might also find it interesting to place pluses and minuses next to the items on your list to help you determine whether "civilization" (city life) was, on balance, beneficial or harmful.

Second, the selection compares the "civilizations" of Mesopotamia and Egypt. According to the selection, what are the chief differences between Mesopotamian and Egyptian civilization? What accounts for these differences?

THINKING HISTORICALLY

To get a feel for the differences between a primary source and a secondary source, try to determine what primary sources might lead to some of these interpretations. Choose a sentence or two that appear specific enough to be based on a primary source. What kind of source could lead to such an interpretation? Conversely, find interpretations in this selection that *could not possibly* derive from a primary source and ask yourself, why not? Finally, consider what kind of nonwritten sources and evidence inform this account.

The Urban Revolution: Civilization and Class

The full-scale urban revolution occurred not in the rain-watered lands that first turned some villages into cities, but in the potentially more productive river valleys of Mesopotamia around 3500 B.C.E. Situated along the Tigris and Euphrates rivers, large villages like Eridu, Erech, Lagash, Kish, and later Ur and Babylon built irrigation systems that increased farm production enormously. Settlements like these were able

---

Source: Kevin Reilly, *The West and the World: A History of Civilization*, 2nd ed. (New York: Harper & Row, 1989), 48–54, 56, 58, 60.

to support five thousand, even ten thousand people, and still allow something like 10 percent of the inhabitants to work full-time at nonfarming occupations.

A change of this scale was a revolution, certainly the most important revolution in human living since the invention of agriculture five thousand years earlier. The urban revolution was prepared by a whole series of technological inventions in agricultural society. Between 6000 and 3000 B.C.E. people not only learned how to harness the power of oxen and the wind with the plow, the wheeled cart, and the sailboat; they also discovered the physical properties of metals, learned how to smelt copper and bronze, and began to work out a calendar based on the movements of the sun. River valleys like those of the Tigris and Euphrates were muddy swamps that had to be drained and irrigated to take advantage of the rich soil deposits. The dry land had literally to be built by teams of organized workers.

Therefore, cities required an organizational revolution that was every bit as important as the technological one. This was accomplished under the direction of the new class of rulers and managers—probably from the grasslands—who often treated the emerging cities as a conquered province. The work of irrigation itself allowed the rulers ample opportunity to coerce the inhabitants of these new cities. Rain knows no social distinctions. Irrigated water must be controlled and channeled.

It is no wonder then that the first cities gave us our first kings and our first class societies. In Mesopotamia, along the Nile of Egypt, in China, and later in Middle America the king is usually described as the founder of cities. These kings were able to endow their control with religious sanction. In Egypt and America the king was god. In Mesopotamia a new class of priests carried out the needs of the king's religion of control.

In some cities the new priesthood would appoint the king. In others, the priests were merely his lieutenants. When they were most loyal, their religion served to deify the king. The teachings of the new class of Mesopotamian priests, for instance, were that their god had created the people solely to work for the king and make his life easier. But even when the priesthood attempted to wrest some of the king's power from him, the priests taught the people to accept the divided society, which benefited king and priesthood as providers of a natural god-given order. The priesthood, after all, was responsible for measuring time, bounding space, and predicting seasonal events. The mastery of people was easy for those who controlled time and space.

The priesthood was only one of the new classes that insured the respectability of the warrior-chieftain turned king. Other palace intellectuals—scribes (or writers), doctors, magicians, and diviners—also struggled to maintain the king's prestige and manage his kingdom. This new class was rewarded, as were the priests, with leisure, status, and magnificent buildings, all of which further exalted the majesty of the king and his city.

Beneath the king, the priesthood, and the new class of intellectuals-managers was another new class charged with maintaining the king's law and order. Soldiers and police were also inventions of the first cities. Like the surrounding city wall, the king's military guard served a double function: It provided defense from outside attack and an obstacle to internal rebellion.

That these were the most important classes of city society can be seen from the physical remains of the first cities. The archeologist's spade has uncovered the monumental buildings of these classes in virtually all of the first cities. The palace, the temple, and the citadel (or fort) are, indeed, the monuments that distinguish cities from villages. Further, the size of these buildings and the permanency of their construction (compared with the small, cheaply built homes of the farmers) attest to the fundamental class divisions of city society.

Civilization: Security and Variety

The most obvious achievements of the first civilizations are the monuments—the pyramids, temples, palaces, statues, and treasures—that were created for the new ruling class of kings, nobles, priests, and their officials. But civilized life is much more than the capacity to create monuments.

Civilized life is secure life. At the most basic level this means security from the sudden destruction that village communities might suffer. Civilized life gives the feeling of permanence. It offers regularity, stability, order, even routine. Plans can be made. Expectations can be realized. People can be expected to act predictably, according to the rules.

The first cities were able to attain stability with walls that shielded the inhabitants from nomads and armies, with the first codes of law that defined human relationships, with police and officials who enforced the laws, and with institutions that functioned beyond the lives of their particular members. City life offered considerably more permanence and security than village life.

Civilization involves more than security, however. A city that provided only order would be more like a prison than a civilization. The first cities provided something that the best-ordered villages lacked. They provided far greater variety: More races and ethnic groups were speaking more languages, engaged in more occupations, and living a greater variety of lifestyles. The abundance of choice, the opportunities for new sensations, new experiences, knowledge—these have always been the appeals of city life. The opportunities for growth and enrichment were far greater than the possibilities of plow and pasture life.

Security plus variety equals creativity. At least the possibility of a more creative, expressive life was available in the protected, semipermanent city enclosures that drew, like magnets, foreign traders and diplomats, new ideas about gods and nature, strange foods and customs, and the magicians, ministers, and mercenaries of the king's court. Civilization is the enriched life that this dynamic urban setting permitted and the human creativity and opportunity that it encouraged. At the very least, cities made even the most common slave think and feel a greater range of things than the tightly knit, clannish agricultural village allowed. That was (and still is) the root of innovation and creativity—of civilization itself.

The variety of people and the complexity of city life required new and more general means of communication. The villager knew everyone personally. Cities brought together people who often did not even speak the same language. Not only law codes but written language itself became a way to bridge the many gaps of human variety. Cities invented writing so that strangers could communicate, and so that those communications could become permanent—remembered publicly, officially recorded. [Writer and philosopher Ralph Waldo] Emerson was right when he said that the city lives by memory, but it was the official memory that enabled the city to carry on its business or religion beyond the lifetime of the village elders. Written symbols that everyone could recognize became the basis of laws, invention, education, taxes, accounting, contracts, and obligations. In short, writing and records made it possible for each generation to begin on the shoulders of its ancestors. Village life and knowledge often seemed to start from scratch. Thus, cities cultivated not only memory and the past, but hope and the future as well. City civilizations invented not only history and record keeping but also prophecy and social planning.

Writing was one city invention that made more general communication possible. Money was another. Money made it possible to deal with anyone just as an agreed-upon public language did. Unnecessary in the village climate of mutual obligations, money was essential in the city society of strangers. Such general media of communication as writing and money vastly increased the number of things that could be said and thought, bought and sold. As a consequence, city life was more impersonal than village life, but also more dynamic and more exciting.

The "Eye" and "I"

[Communication theorist] Marshall McLuhan has written that "civilization gave the barbarian an eye for an ear." We might add that civilization also gave an "I" for an "us." City life made the "eye" and the "I" more important than they had been in the village. The invention of writing made knowledge more visual. The eye had to be trained to recognize the minute differences in letters and words. Eyes took in a greater abundance of detail: laws, prices, the strange cloak of the foreigner, the odd type of shoes made by the new craftsworker from who-knows-where, the colors of the fruit and vegetable market, and elaborate painting in the temple, as well as the written word. In the village one learned by listening. In the city seeing was believing. In the new city courts of law an "eyewitness account" was believed to be more reliable than "hearsay evidence." In some villages even today, the heard and the spoken are thought more reliable than the written and the seen. In the city, even spoken language took on the uniformity and absence of emotion that is unavoidable in the written word. Perhaps emotions themselves became less violent. "Civilized" is always used to mean emotional restraint, control of the more violent passions, and a greater understanding, even tolerance, of the different and foreign.

Perhaps empathy (the capacity to put yourself in someone else's shoes) increased in cities—so full of so many different others that had to be understood. When a Turkish villager was recently asked, "What would you do if you were president of your country?" he stammered: "My God! How can you ask such a thing? How can I . . . I cannot . . . president of Turkey . . . master of the whole world?" He was completely unable to imagine himself as president. It was as removed from his experience as if he were master of the world. Similarly, a Lebanese villager who was asked what he would do if he were editor of a newspaper accused the interviewer of ridiculing him, and frantically waved the interviewer on to another question. Such a life was beyond his comprehension. It was too foreign to imagine. The very variety of city life must have increased the capacity of the lowest commoner to imagine, empathize, sympathize, and criticize.

The oral culture of the village reinforced the accepted by saying and singing it almost monotonously. The elders, the storytellers, and the minstrels must have had prodigious memories. But their stories changed only gradually and slightly. The spoken word was sacred. To say it differently was to change the truth. The written culture of cities taught "point of *view*." An urban individual did not have to remember everything. That was done permanently on paper. Knowledge became a recognition of different interpretations and the capacity to look up things. The awareness of variety meant the possibility of criticism, analysis, and an ever-newer synthesis. It is no wonder that the technical and scientific knowledge of cities increased at a geometric rate compared with the knowledge of villages. The multiplication of knowledge was implicit in the city's demand to recognize difference and variety. Civilization has come to mean that ever-expanding body of knowledge and skill. Its finest achievements have been that knowledge, its writing, and its visual art. The city and civilization (like the child) are to be seen and not heard.

It may seem strange to say that the impersonal life of cities contributed greatly to the development of personality—the "I" as well as the "eye." Village life was in a sense much more personal. Everything was taken personally. Villagers deal with each other not as "the blacksmith," "the baker," "that guy who owes me a goat," or "that no-good bum." They do not even "deal" with each other. They know each other by name and family. They love, hate, support, and murder each other because of who they are, because of personal feelings, because of personal and family responsibility. They have full, varied relationships with each member of the village. They do not merely buy salt from this person, talk about the weather with this other person, and discuss personal matters with only this other person. They share too much with each other to divide up their relationships in that way.

City life is a life of separated, partial relationships. In a city you do not know about the butcher's life, wife, kids, and problems. You do not care. You are in a hurry. You have too many other things to do. You might discuss the weather—but while he's cutting. You came to buy meat. Many urban relationships are like that. There are many business, trading, or "dealing" relationships because there are simply too many people to know them all as relatives.

The impersonality of city life is a shame in a way. (It makes it easier to get mugged by someone who does not even hate you.) But the luxurious variety of impersonal relationships (at least some of the time) provides the freedom for the individual personality to emerge. Maybe that is why people have often dreamed of leaving family and friends (usually for a city) in the hope of "finding themselves." Certainly, the camaraderie and community of village life had a darker side of surveillance and conformity. When everything was known about everyone, it was difficult for the individual to find his or her individuality. Family ties and village custom were often obstacles to asserting self-identity. The city offered its inhabitants a huge variety of possible relationships and personal identities. The urban inhabitant was freer than his village cousin to choose friends, lovers, associates, occupation, housing, and lifestyle. The city was full of choices that the village could not afford or condone. The village probably provided more security in being like everyone else and doing what was expected. But the city provided the variety of possibilities that could allow the individual to follow the "inner self" and cultivate inner gardens.

The class divisions of city society made it difficult for commoners to achieve an effective or creative individuality. But the wealthy and powerful—especially the king—were able to develop models of individuality and personality that were revolutionary. No one before had ever achieved such a sense of the self, and the model of the king's power and freedom became a goal for the rest of the society. The luxury, leisure, and opportunity of the king was a revolutionary force. In contrast to a village elder, the king could do whatever he wanted. Recognizing that, more and more city inhabitants asked, "Why can't we?" City revolutions have continually extended class privilege and opportunities ever since.

Once a society has achieved a level of abundance, once it can offer the technological means, the educational opportunities, the creative outlets necessary for everyone to lead meaningful, happy, healthy lives, then classes may be a hindrance. Class divisions were, however, a definite stimulus to productivity and creativity in the early city civilizations. The democratic villagers preferred stability to improvement. As a result, their horizons were severely limited. They died early, lived precipitously, and suffered without much hope. The rulers of the first cities discovered the possibilities of leisure, creation, and the good life. They invented heaven and utopia—first for themselves. Only very gradually has the invention of civilization, of human potential, sifted down to those beneath the ruling class. In many cases, luxury, leisure, freedom, and opportunity are still the monopolies of the elite. But once the powerful have exploited the poor enough to establish their own paradise on earth and their own immortality after death, the poor also have broader horizons and plans.

Mesopotamian and Egyptian Civilizations: A Tale of Two Rivers

Experts disagree as to whether Mesopotamian or Egyptian civilization is older. Mesopotamian influence in Egypt was considerable enough to suggest slightly earlier origins, but both had evolved distinct civilizations by 3000 B.C.E. Indeed, the difference between the two civilizations attests to the existence of multiple routes to civilized life. In both cases, river valleys provided the necessary water and silt for an agricultural surplus large enough to support classes of specialists who did not have to farm. But the differing nature of the rivers had much to do with the different types of civilization that evolved.

The Egyptians were blessed with the easier and more reliable of the two rivers. The Nile overflowed its banks predictably every year on the parched ground in the summer after August 15, well after the harvest had been gathered, depositing its rich sediment, and withdrawing by early October, leaving little salt or marsh, in time for the sowing of winter crops. Later sowings for summer crops required only simple canals that tapped the river upstream and the natural drainage of the Nile Valley. Further, transportation on the Nile was simplified by the fact that the prevailing winds blew from the north, while the river flowed from the south, making navigation a matter of using sails upstream and dispensing with them coming downstream.

The Euphrates offered none of these advantages as it cut its way through Mesopotamia. The Euphrates flowed high above the flood plain (unlike the neighboring Tigris) so that its waters could be used, but it flooded suddenly and without warning in the late spring, after the summer crops had been sown and before the winter crops could be harvested. Thus, the flooding of the Euphrates offered no natural irrigation. Its waters were needed at other times, and its flooding was destructive. Canals were necessary to drain off water for irrigation when the river was low, and these canals had to be adequately blocked, and the banks reinforced, when the river flooded. Further, since the Euphrates was not as easily navigable as the Nile, the main canals had to serve as major transportation arteries as well.

In Mesopotamia the flood was the enemy. The Mesopotamian deities who ruled the waters, Nin-Girsu and Tiamat, were feared. The forces of nature were often evil. Life was a struggle. In Egypt, on the other hand, life was viewed as a cooperation with nature. Even the Egyptian god of the flood, Hapi, was a helpful deity, who provided the people's daily bread. Egyptian priests and philosophers were much more at ease with their world than were their Mesopotamian counterparts. And, partly because of their different experiences with their rivers, the Mesopotamians developed a civilization based on cities, while the Egyptians did not. From the first Sumerian city-states on the lower Euphrates to the later northern Mesopotamian capital of Babylon, civilization was the product and expression of city life. Egyptian civilization, in contrast, was the creation of the pharaoh's court rather than of cities. Beyond the court, which was moved from one location to another, Egypt remained a country of peasant villages.

A prime reason for Egypt's lack of urbanization was the ease of farming on the banks of the Nile. Canal irrigation was a relatively simple process that did not demand much organization. Small market towns were sufficient for the needs of the countryside. They housed artisans, shopkeepers, the priests of the local temple, and the agents of the pharaoh, but they never swelled with a large middle class and never developed large-scale industry or commerce.

In Sumer, and later in Mesopotamia, the enormous task of fighting the Euphrates required a complex social organization with immediate local needs. Only communal labor could build and maintain the network of subsidiary canals for irrigation and drainage. Constant supervision was necessary to keep the canals free of silt, to remove salt deposits, to maintain the riverbanks at flood-time, and to prevent any farmer from monopolizing the water in periods of drought. Life on the Euphrates required cooperative work and responsibility that never ceased. It encouraged absolute, administrative control over an area larger than the village, and it fostered participation and loyalty to an irrigated area smaller than the imperial state. The city-state was the political answer to the economic problems of Sumer and Mesopotamia.

The religious practices in the Euphrates Valley reflected and supported city organization. Residents of each local area worshiped the local god while recognizing the existence of other local gods in a larger Sumerian, and eventually Mesopotamian, pantheon of gods. The priests of the local temple supervised canal work, the collection of taxes, and the storage of written records, as well as the proper maintenance of religious rituals. Thus, religious loyalty reinforced civic loyalty. Peasant and middle-class Sumerians thought of themselves as citizens of their particular city, worshipers of their particular city god, subjects of their particular god's earthly representative, but not as Sumerian nationals. By contrast, the Egyptian peasant was always an Egyptian, a subject of the pharaoh, but never a citizen.

The local, civic orientation of Mesopotamian cities can be seen in the physical structure of the capital city of Sumer, the city of Ur. Like other cities on the Euphrates, Ur was surrounded by a wall. It was dominated by the temple of Nannar, the moon-god who owned the city, and the palace complex beneath the temple. The residential areas were situated outside of the sacred Temenos, or temple compound, but within the walls, between the river and the main canal. The well-excavated remains of Ur of the seventeenth century B.C.E. show a residential street plan that looks like many Middle Eastern cities of today. A highly congested area of winding alleys and broad streets sheltered one- and two-story houses of merchants, shopkeepers, tradespeople, and occasional priests and scribes that suggest a large, relatively prosperous middle class. Most houses were built around a central courtyard that offered shade throughout the day, with mud-brick, often even plastered, outside walls that protected a number of interior rooms from the sun and the eyes of the tax inspector. The remains of seventeenth-century Ur show both the variety and the density of modern city life. There are specialized districts throughout the city. Certain trades have their special quarters: a bakers' square, probably special areas for the dyers, tanners, potters, and metalworkers. But life is mixed together as well. Subsidiary gods have temples outside the Temenos. Small and large houses are jumbled next to each other. There seems to be a slum area near the Temenos, but there are small houses for workers, tenant farmers, and the poor throughout the city. And no shop or urban professional is more than a short walking distance away. The entire size of the walled city was an oval that extended three-quarters of a mile long and a half a mile wide.

A well-excavated Egyptian city from roughly the same period (the fourteenth century B.C.E.) offers some striking contrasts. Akhetaton, or Tell el Amarna, Pharaoh Akhenaton's capital on the Nile, was not enclosed by walls or canals. It merely straggled down the eastern bank of the Nile for five miles and faded into the desert. Without the need for extensive irrigation or protection, Tell el Amarna shows little of the crowded, vital density of Ur. Its layout lacks any sense of urgency. The North Palace of the pharaoh is a mile and a half north of the temple complex and offices, which are three and a half miles from the official pleasure garden. The palaces of the court nobility and the large residences of the court's officials front one of the two main roads that parallel the river, or they are situated at random. There is plenty of physical space (and social space) between these and the bunched villages of workers' houses. The remains suggest very little in the way of a middle class or a merchant or professional class beyond the pharaoh's specialists and retainers. Life for the wealthy was, judging from the housing, more luxurious than at Ur, but for the majority of the population, city life was less rich. In many ways, the pharaoh's court at Tell el Amarna was not a city at all.

2

The Epic of Gilgamesh, c. 2700 B.C.E.

The Epic of Gilgamesh is the earliest story written in any language. It also serves as a primary source for the study of ancient Mesopotamia—the land between the two great rivers, the Tigris and Euphrates.

Gilgamesh was an ancient king of Sumer who lived about 2700 B.C.E. Since *The Epic* comes from a thousand years later, we can assume Sumerians kept telling this tale about King Gilgamesh for some time before it was written down. In Sumer, writing was initially used by temple priests to keep track of property and taxes. Soon, however, writing was used to preserve stories and to celebrate kings.

The more you know about the Sumerian people, the more information you will be able to mine from your source. In the previous secondary selection, you read some historical background that will help you make sense of this story. Look in *The Epic* for evidence of the urban revolution discussed in the previous selection. What is the meaning of the story of the taming of Enkidu by the harlot? Does Enkidu also tame Gilgamesh? What two worlds do Enkidu and Gilgamesh represent?

Do the authors or listeners of *The Epic* think city life is better than life in the country? According to *The Epic*, what are the advantages of the city? What problems does it have?

What does the story of the flood tell you about life in ancient Mesopotamia? Would you expect the ancient Egyptians to tell a similar story?

THINKING HISTORICALLY

Reading a primary source differs markedly from reading a secondary source. Primary sources were not written with you or me in mind. It is safe to say that the author of *The Epic of Gilgamesh* never even imagined our existence. For this reason, primary sources are a bit difficult to access. Reading a primary source usually requires some intensive work. You have to keep asking yourself, why was this story told? How would a story like this help or teach people at that time? That is, you must put yourself in the shoes of the original teller and listener.

Primary sources offer us a piece of the past. No historian is in your way explaining things. With your unique perspective, you have an advantage over the intended audience: You can ask questions about the source that the author and original audience never dared, needed, or thought to ask.

Ask questions that the source answers unintentionally; for example: Did the ancient Mesopotamians have copper?

Source: *The Epic of Gilgamesh*, trans. N. K. Sandars (London: Penguin Books, 1972), 61–69, 108–13.

Prologue: Gilgamesh King in Uruk

I will proclaim to the world the deeds of Gilgamesh. This was the man to whom all things were known; this was the king who knew the countries of the world. He was wise, he saw mysteries and knew secret things, he brought us a tale of the days before the flood. He went on a long journey, was weary, worn-out with labor; returning he rested, he engraved on a stone the whole story.

When the gods created Gilgamesh they gave him a perfect body. Shamash the glorious sun endowed him with beauty, Adad the god of the storm endowed him with courage, the great gods made his beauty perfect, surpassing all others, terrifying like a great wild bull. Two thirds they made him god and one third man.

In Uruk he built walls, a great rampart, and the temple of blessed Eanna for the god of the firmament Anu, and for Ishtar the goddess of love. Look at it still today: the outer wall where the cornice runs, it shines with the brilliance of copper; and the inner wall, it has no equal. Touch the threshold; it is ancient. Approach Eanna the dwelling of Ishtar, our lady of love and war, the like of which no latter-day king, no man alive can equal. Climb upon the wall of Uruk; walk along it, I say; regard the foundation terrace and examine the masonry; is it not burnt brick and good? The seven sages laid the foundations.

The Coming of Enkidu

Gilgamesh went abroad in the world, but he met with none who could withstand his arms till he came to Uruk. But the men of Uruk muttered in their houses, "Gilgamesh sounds the tocsin for his amusement, his arrogance has no bounds by day or night. No son is left with his father, for Gilgamesh takes from all, even the children; yet the king should be a shepherd to his people. His lust leaves no virgin to her lover, neither the warrior's daughter nor the wife of the noble; yet this is the shepherd of the city, wise, comely, and resolute."

The gods heard their lament, the gods of heaven cried to the Lord of Uruk, to Anu the god of Uruk: "A goddess made him, strong as a savage bull, none can withstand his arms. No son is left with his father, for Gilgamesh takes them all; and is this the king, the shepherd of his people? His lust leaves no virgin to her lover, neither the warrior's daughter nor the wife of the noble." When Anu had heard their lamentation the gods cried to Aruru, the goddess of creation, "You made him, O Aruru, now create his equal; let it be as like him as his own reflection, his second self, stormy head for stormy heart. Let them contend together and leave Uruk in quiet."

So the goddess conceived an image in her mind, and it was of the stuff of Anu of the firmament. She dipped her hands in water and pinched off clay, she let it fall in the wilderness, and noble Enkidu* was created. There was virtue in him of the god of war, of Ninurta himself. His body was rough; he had long hair like a woman's; it waved like the hair of Nisaba, the goddess of corn. His body was covered with matted hair like Samuqan's, the god of cattle. He was innocent of mankind; he knew nothing of cultivated land.

Enkidu ate grass in the hills with the gazelle and lurked with wild beasts at the water-holes; he had joy of the water with the herds of wild game. But there was a trapper who met him one day face to face at the drinking-hole, for the wild game had entered his territory. On three days he met him face to face, and the trapper was frozen with fear. He went back to his house with the game that he had caught, and he was dumb, benumbed with terror. His face was altered like that of one who has made a long journey. With awe in his heart he spoke to his father: "Father, there is a man, unlike any other, who comes down from the hills. He is the strongest in the world, he is like an immortal from heaven. He ranges over the hills with wild beasts and eats grass; he ranges through your land and comes down to the wells. I am afraid and dare not go near him. He fills in the pits which I dig and tears up my traps set for the game; he helps the beasts to escape and now they slip through my fingers."

His father opened his mouth and said to the trapper, "My son, in Uruk lives Gilgamesh; no one has ever prevailed against him, he is strong as a star from heaven. Go to Uruk, find Gilgamesh, extol the strength of this wild man. Ask him to give you a harlot, a wanton from the temple of love; return with her, and let her woman's power overpower this man. When next he comes down to drink at the wells she will be there, stripped naked; and when he sees her beckoning he will embrace her, and then the wild beasts will reject him."

So the trapper set out on his journey to Uruk and addressed himself to Gilgamesh saying, "A man unlike any other is roaming now in the pastures; he is as strong as a star from heaven and I am afraid to approach him. He helps the wild game to escape; he fills in my pits and pulls up my traps." Gilgamesh said, "Trapper, go back, take with you a harlot, a child of pleasure. At the drinking-hole she will strip, and when he sees her beckoning he will embrace her and the game of the wilderness will surely reject him."

Now the trapper returned, taking the harlot with him. After a three days' journey they came to the drinking-hole, and there they sat down; the harlot and the trapper sat facing one another and waited for the game to come. For the first day and for the second day the two sat

---

* EHN kee doo

waiting, but on the third day the herds came; they came down to drink and Enkidu was with them. The small wild creatures of the plains were glad of the water, and Enkidu with them, who ate grass with the gazelle and was born in the hills; and she saw him; the savage man, come from far-off in the hills. The trapper spoke to her: "There he is. Now, woman, make your breasts bare, have no shame, do not delay but welcome his love. Let him see you naked, let him possess your body. When he comes near uncover yourself and lie with him; teach him, the savage man, your woman's art, for when he murmurs love to you the wild beasts that shared his life in the hills will reject him."

She was not ashamed to take him, she made herself naked and welcomed his eagerness; as he lay on her murmuring love she taught him the woman's art. For six days and seven nights they lay together, for Enkidu had forgotten his home in the hills; but when he was satisfied he went back to the wild beasts. Then, when the gazelle saw him, they bolted away; when the wild creatures saw him they fled. Enkidu would have followed, but his body was bound as though with a cord, his knees gave way when he started to run, his swiftness was gone. And now the wild creatures had all fled away; Enkidu was grown weak, for wisdom was in him, and the thoughts of a man were in his heart. So he returned and sat down at the woman's feet, and listened intently to what she said. "You are wise, Enkidu, and now you have become like a god. Why do you want to run wild with the beasts in the hills? Come with me. I will take you to strong-walled Uruk, to the blessed temple of Ishtar and of Anu, of love and of heaven: there Gilgamesh lives, who is very strong, and like a wild bull he lords it over men."

When she had spoken Enkidu was pleased; he longed for a comrade, for one who would understand his heart. "Come, woman, and take me to that holy temple, to the house of Anu and of Ishtar, and to the place where Gilgamesh lords it over people. I will challenge him boldly, I will cry out aloud in Uruk, 'I am the strongest here, I have come to change the old order, I am he who was born in the hills, I am he who is strongest of all.'"

She said, "Let us go, and let him see your face. I know very well where Gilgamesh is in great Uruk. O Enkidu, there all the people are dressed in their gorgeous robes, every day is holiday, the young men and the girls are wonderful to see. How sweet they smell! All the great ones are roused from their beds. O Enkidu, you who love life, I will show you Gilgamesh, a man of many moods; you shall look at him well in his radiant manhood. His body is perfect in strength and maturity; he never rests by night or day. He is stronger than you, so leave your boasting. Shamash the glorious sun has given favors to Gilgamesh, and Anu of the heavens, and Enlil, and Ea the wise has given him deep understanding. I tell you, even before you have left the wilderness, Gilgamesh will know in his dreams that you are coming."

Now Gilgamesh got up to tell his dream to his mother, Ninsun, one of the wise gods. "Mother, last night I had a dream. I was full of joy, the young heroes were round me and I walked through the night under the stars of the firmament, and one, a meteor of the stuff of Anu, fell down from heaven. I tried to lift it but it proved too heavy. All the people of Uruk came round to see it, the common people jostled and the nobles thronged to kiss its feet; and to me its attraction was like the love of woman. They helped me, I braced my forehead and I raised it with thongs and brought it to you, and you yourself pronounced it my brother."

Then Ninsun, who is well-beloved and wise, said to Gilgamesh, "This star of heaven which descended like a meteor from the sky; which you tried to lift, but found too heavy, when you tried to move it it would not budge, and so you brought it to my feet; I made it for you, a goad and spur, and you were drawn as though to a woman. This is the strong comrade, the one who brings help to his friend in his need. He is the strongest of wild creatures, the stuff of Anu; born in the grasslands and the wild hills reared him; when you see him you will be glad; you will love him as a woman and he will never forsake you. This is the meaning of the dream."

Gilgamesh said, "Mother, I dreamed a second dream. In the streets of strong-walled Uruk there lay an axe; the shape of it was strange and the people thronged round. I saw it and was glad. I bent down, deeply drawn towards it; I loved it like a woman and wore it at my side." Ninsun answered, "That axe, which you saw, which drew you so powerfully like love of a woman, that is the comrade whom I give you, and he will come in his strength like one of the host of heaven. He is the brave companion who rescues his friend in necessity." Gilgamesh said to his mother, "A friend, a counsellor has come to me from Enlil, and now I shall befriend and counsel him." So Gilgamesh told his dreams; and the harlot retold them to Enkidu.

And now she said to Enkidu, "When I look at you you have become like a god. Why do you yearn to run wild again with the beasts in the hills? Get up from the ground, the bed of a shepherd." He listened to her words with care. It was good advice that she gave. She divided her clothing in two and with the one half she clothed him and with the other herself; and holding his hand she led him like a child to the sheepfolds, into the shepherds' tents. There all the shepherds crowded round to see him, they put down bread in front of him, but Enkidu could only suck the milk of wild animals. He fumbled and gaped, at a loss what to do or how he should eat the bread and drink the strong wine. Then the woman said, "Enkidu, eat bread, it is the staff of life; drink the wine, it is the custom of the land." So he ate till he was full and drank strong wine, seven goblets. He became merry, his heart exulted and his face shone. He rubbed down the matted hair of his body and anointed himself with oil. Enkidu had become a man; but when he had put on man's clothing he appeared like a bridegroom. He took arms to hunt the lion so that the shepherds could rest at night. He caught wolves and lions and the herdsmen lay down in peace; for Enkidu was their watchman, that strong man who had no rival.

He was merry living with the shepherds, till one day lifting his eyes he saw a man approaching. He said to the harlot, "Woman, fetch that man here. Why has he come? I wish to know his name." She went and called the man saying, "Sir, where are you going on this weary journey?" The man answered, saying to Enkidu, "Gilgamesh has gone into the marriage-house and shut out the people. He does strange things in Uruk, the city of great streets. At the roll of the drum work begins for the men, and work for the women. Gilgamesh the king is about to celebrate marriage with the Queen of Love, and he still demands to be first with the bride, the king to be first and the husband to follow, for that was ordained by the gods from his birth, from the time the umbilical cord was cut. But now the drums roll for the choice of the bride and the city groans." At these words Enkidu turned white in the face. "I will go to the place where Gilgamesh lords it over the people, I will challenge him boldly, and I will cry aloud in Uruk, 'I have come to change the old order, for I am the strongest here.'"

Now Enkidu strode in front and the woman followed behind. He entered Uruk, that great market, and all the folk thronged round him where he stood in the street in strong-walled Uruk. The people jostled; speaking of him they said, "He is the spit of Gilgamesh." "He is shorter." "He is bigger of bone." "This is the one who was reared on the milk of wild beasts. His is the greatest strength." The men rejoiced: "Now Gilgamesh has met his match. This great one, this hero whose beauty is like a god, he is a match even for Gilgamesh."

In Uruk the bridal bed was made, fit for the goddess of love. The bride waited for the bridegroom, but in the night Gilgamesh got up and came to the house. Then Enkidu stepped out, he stood in the street and blocked the way. Mighty Gilgamesh came on and Enkidu met him at the gate. He put out his foot and prevented Gilgamesh from entering the house, so they grappled, holding each other like bulls. They broke the doorposts and the walls shook, they snorted like bulls locked together. They shattered the doorposts and the walls shook. Gilgamesh bent his knee with his foot planted on the ground and with a turn Enkidu was thrown. Then immediately his fury died. When Enkidu was thrown he said to Gilgamesh, "There is not another like you in the world. Ninsun, who is as strong as a wild ox in the byre, she was the mother who bore you, and now you are raised above all men, and Enlil has given you the kingship, for your strength surpasses the strength of men." So Enkidu and Gilgamesh embraced and their friendship was sealed.

The Story of the Flood

[Utnapishtim, the old man, tells the story to Gilgamesh.]

"You know the city Shurrupak, it stands on the banks of Euphrates? That city grew old and the gods that were in it were old. There was Anu, lord of the firmament, their father, and warrior Enlil their counsellor, Ninurta the helper, and Ennugi watcher over canals; and with them also was Ea. In those days the world teemed, the people multiplied, the world bellowed like a wild bull, and the great god was aroused by the clamour. Enlil heard the clamour and he said to the gods in council, 'The uproar of mankind is intolerable and sleep is no longer possible by reason of the babel.' So the gods agreed to exterminate mankind. Enlil did this, but Ea because of his oath warned me in a dream. He whispered their words to my house of reeds, 'Reed-house, reed-house! Wall, O wall, hearken reed-house, wall reflect; O man of Shurrupak, son of Ubara-Tutu; tear down your house and build a boat, abandon possessions and look for life, despise worldly goods and save your soul alive. Tear down your house, I say, and build a boat. These are the measurements of the barque as you shall build her: let her beam equal her length, let her deck be roofed like the vault that covers the abyss; then take up into the boat the seed of all living creatures.'

"When I had understood I said to my lord, 'Behold, what you have commanded I will honour and perform, but how shall I answer the people, the city, the elders?' Then Ea opened his mouth and said to me, his servant, 'Tell them this: I have learnt that Enlil is wrathful against me, I dare no longer walk in his land nor live in his city; I will go down to the Gulf to dwell with Ea my lord. But on you he will rain down abundance, rare fish and shy wild-fowl, a rich harvest-tide. In the evening the rider of the storm will bring you wheat in torrents.'

"In the first light of dawn all my household gathered round me, the children brought pitch and the men whatever was necessary. On the fifth day I laid the keel and the ribs, then I made fast the planking. The ground-space was one acre, each side of the deck measured one hundred and twenty cubits, making a square. I built six decks below, seven in all, I divided them into nine sections with bulkheads between. I drove in wedges where needed, I saw to the punt-poles, and laid in supplies. The carriers brought oil in baskets, I poured pitch into the furnace and asphalt and oil; more oil was consumed in caulking, and more again the master of the boat took into his stores. I slaughtered bullocks for the people and every day I killed sheep. I gave the shipwrights wine to drink as though it were river water, raw wine and red wine and oil and white wine. There was feasting then as there is at the time of the New Year's festival; I myself anointed my head. On the seventh day the boat was complete.

"Then was the launching full of difficulty; there was shifting of ballast above and below till two thirds was submerged. I loaded into her all that I had of gold and of living things, my family, my kin, the beast of the field both wild and tame, and all the craftsmen. I sent them on board, for the time that Shamash had ordained was already fulfilled when he said 'In the evening, when the rider of the storm sends down the destroying rain, enter the boat and batten her down.' The time was fulfilled, the evening came, the rider of the storm sent down the rain. I looked out at the weather and it was terrible, so I too boarded the boat and battened her down. All was now complete, the battening and the caulking; so I handed the tiller to Puzur-Amurri the steersman, with the navigation and the care of the whole boat.

"With the first light of dawn a black cloud came from the horizon; it thundered within where Adad, lord of the storm, was riding. In front over hill and plain Shullat and Hanish, heralds of the storm, led on. Then the gods of the abyss rose up; Nergal pulled out the dams of the nether waters, Ninurta the war-lord threw down the dykes, and the seven judges of hell, the Annunaki, raised their torches, lighting the land with their livid flame. A stupor of despair went up to heaven when the god of the storm turned daylight to darkness, when he smashed the land like a cup. One whole day the tempest raged, gathering fury as it went, it poured over the people like the tides of battle; a man could not see his brother nor the people be seen from heaven. Even the gods were terrified at the flood, they fled to the highest heaven, the firmament of Anu; they crouched against the walls, cowering like curs. . . .

"For six days and six nights the winds blew, torrent and tempest and flood overwhelmed the world, tempest and flood raged together like warring hosts. When the seventh day dawned the storm from the south subsided, the sea grew calm, the flood was stilled; I looked at the face of the world and there was silence, all mankind was turned to clay. The surface of the sea stretched as flat as a roof-top; I opened a hatch and the light fell on my face. Then I bowed low, I sat down and I wept, the tears streamed down my face, for on every side was the waste of water. I looked for land in vain, but fourteen leagues distant there appeared a mountain, and there the boat grounded; on the mountain of Nisir the boat held fast, she held fast and did not budge. One day she held, and a second day on the mountain of Nisir she held fast and did not budge. A third day, and a fourth day she held fast on the mountain and did not budge; a fifth day and a sixth day she held fast on the mountain. When the seventh day dawned I loosed a dove and let her go. She flew away, but finding no resting-place she returned. Then I loosed a swallow, and she flew away but finding no resting-place she returned. I loosed a raven, she saw that the waters had retreated, she ate, she flew around, she cawed, and she did not come back. Then I threw everything open to the four winds, I made a sacrifice and poured out a libation on the mountain top. Seven and again seven cauldrons I set up on their stands, I heaped up wood and cane and cedar and myrtle. When the gods smelled the sweet savour, they gathered like flies over the sacrifice. Then, at last, Ishtar also came, she lifted her necklace with the jewels of heaven that once Anu had made to please her. 'O you gods here present, by the lapis lazuli round my neck I shall remember these days as I remember the jewels of my throat; these last days I shall not forget. Let all the gods gather round the sacrifice, except Enlil. He shall not approach this offering, for without reflection he brought the flood; he consigned my people to destruction.'

"When Enlil had come, when he saw the boat, he was wrath and swelled with anger at the gods, the host of heaven, 'Has any of these mortals escaped? Not one was to have survived the destruction.' Then the god of the wells and canals Ninurta opened his mouth and said to the warrior Enlil, 'Who is there of the gods that devise without Ea? It is Ea alone who knows all things.' Then Ea opened his mouth and spoke to warrior Enlil, 'Wisest of gods, hero Enlil, how could you so senselessly bring down the flood?

> Lay upon the sinner his sin,
> Lay upon the transgressor his transgression,
> Punish him a little when he breaks loose,
> Do not drive him too hard or he perishes;
> Would that a lion had ravaged mankind
> Rather than the flood,
> Would that a wolf had ravaged mankind
> Rather than the flood,
> Would that famine had wasted the world
> Rather than the flood,
> Would that pestilence had wasted mankind
> Rather than the flood.

It was not I that revealed the secret of the gods; the wise man learned it in a dream. Now take your counsel what shall be done with him.'

"Then Enlil went up into the boat, he took me by the hand and my wife and made us enter the boat and kneel down on either side, he standing between us. He touched our foreheads to bless us saying, 'In time past Utnapishtim was a mortal man; henceforth he and his wife shall live in the distance at the mouth of the rivers.' Thus it was that the gods took me and placed me here to live in the distance, at the mouth of the rivers."

3

ENHEDUANNA

The Exaltation of Inana, c. 2250 B.C.E.

If the *Epic of Gilgamesh* is the oldest story we have, Enheduanna may be the first author we know by name. We know her from the many poems and prayers she wrote to the gods and goddesses, especially

Source: Jeremy Allen Black, Graham Cunningham, J. Ebeling, Esther Fluckiger-Hawker, Eleanor Robson, Jonathan Taylor, and Gabor Zolyomi, *The Electronic Text Corpus of Sumerian Literature,* Oxford, 1998–2006.

the goddess Inana. Enheduanna was the daughter of King Sargon of Akkad who created the first Mesopotamian Empire by conquering the Sumerian cities of Ur and Uruk and southern Mesopotamia. Sargon appointed his daughter High Priestess to the goddess Inana, the most important deity of the city of Ur. Politically, her work helped to consolidate Sargon's rule over southern Mesopotamia by melding northern Akkadian religion with that of the Sumerians of the south. The *Exaltation of Inana* is said to be one of Enheduanna's more personal prayers, as it includes a reference to her own expulsion from Ur. (She was expelled in a temporarily successful revolt against Sargon by the deposed Sumerian king Lugal-ane.) What does Enheduanna want from Inana? How does she attempt to get it?

THINKING HISTORICALLY

An epic, like Gilgamesh, is filtered through many voices so that the version we read may distill the essence of a culture, but not a single voice. The prayer of Enheduanna, on the other hand, is a very personal document, an expression of one woman's plea. And yet, as a prayer, it follows a pattern honed by a culture over time. It shows us what a prayer can be, what one can request, what a god can grant, and even what they may want to hear. How does Enheduanna's exaltation to Inana answer some of these questions? What does it tell you about Mesopotamian religion?

Lady of all the divine powers, resplendent light, righteous woman clothed in radiance, beloved of An and Uraš! Mistress of heaven, with the great diadem, who loves the good headdress befitting the office of en priestess, who has seized all seven of its divine powers! My lady, you are the guardian of the great divine powers! You have taken up the divine powers, you have hung the divine powers from your hand. You have gathered up the divine powers, you have clasped the divine powers to your breast. Like a dragon you have deposited venom on the foreign lands. When like Iškur you roar at the earth, no vegetation can stand up to you. As a flood descending upon those foreign lands, powerful one of heaven and earth, you are their Inana . . .

At your battle-cry, my lady, the foreign lands bow low. When humanity comes before you in awed silence at the terrifying radiance and tempest, you grasp the most terrible of all the divine powers. Because of you, the threshold of tears is opened, and people walk along the path of the house of great lamentations. In the van of battle, all is struck down before you. With your strength, my lady, teeth can crush flint. You charge forward like a charging storm. You roar with the roaring storm, you continually thunder with Iškur. You spread exhaustion with the stormwinds, while your own feet remain tireless. With the lamenting balaĝ drum a lament is struck up. . . .

Lady supreme over the foreign lands, who can take anything from your province? If you frown at the mountains, vegetation there is ruined. Their great gateways are set afire. Blood is poured into their rivers because of you, and their people could not drink. They must lead their troops captive before you, all together. They must scatter their élite regiments for you, all together. They must stand their able-bodied young men at your service, all together. Tempests have filled the dancing-places of their cities. They drive their young men before you as prisoners. Your holy command has been spoken over the city which has not declared "The foreign lands are yours!", wherever they have not declared "It is your own father's!;" and it is brought back under your feet. Responsible care is removed from its sheepfolds. Its woman no longer speaks affectionately with her husband; at dead of night she no longer takes counsel with him, and she no longer reveals to him the pure thoughts of her heart. Impetuous wild cow, great daughter of Suen, lady greater than An, who can take anything from your province?

Great queen of queens, issue of a holy womb for righteous divine powers, greater than your own mother, wise and sage, lady of all the foreign lands, life-force of the teeming people: I will recite your holy song! True goddess fit for divine powers, your splendid utterances are magnificent. Deep-hearted, good woman with a radiant heart, I will enumerate good divine powers for you!

I, En-hedu-ana the en priestess, entered my holy ĝipar[1] in your service. I carried the ritual basket, and intoned the song of joy. But funeral offerings were brought, as if I had never lived there. I approached the light, but the light was scorching hot to me. I approached that shade, but I was covered with a storm. My honeyed mouth became scum. My ability to soothe moods vanished.

Suen, tell An about Lugal-Ane and my fate! May An undo it for me! As soon as you tell An about it, An will release me. The woman will take the destiny away from Lugal-Ane; foreign lands and flood lie at her feet. The woman too is exalted, and can make cities tremble. Step forward, so that she will cool her heart for me. . . .

In connection with the purification rites of holy An, Lugal-Ane has altered everything of his, and has stripped An of the E-ana. He has not stood in awe of the greatest deity. He has turned that temple, whose attractions were inexhaustible, whose beauty was endless, into a destroyed temple. While he entered before me as if he was a partner, really he approached out of envy.

My good divine wild cow, drive out the man, capture the man! In the place of divine encouragement, what is my standing now? May An extradite the land which is a malevolent rebel against your Nanna! May An smash that city! May Enlil curse it! May its plaintive child not be placated by his mother! Lady, with the laments begun, may your ship of lamentation be

---

[1] Temple. [Ed.]

abandoned in hostile territory. Must I die because of my holy songs? My Nanna has paid no heed to me. He has destroyed me utterly in renegade territory. Ašimbabbar has certainly not pronounced a verdict on me. What is it to me if he has pronounced it? What is it to me if he has not pronounced it? He stood there in triumph and drove me out of the temple. He made me fly like a swallow from the window; I have exhausted my life-strength. He made me walk through the thorn bushes of the mountains. He stripped me of the rightful crown of the en priestess. He gave me a knife and dagger, saying to me "These are appropriate ornaments for you."

Most precious lady, beloved by An, your holy heart is great; may it be assuaged on my behalf! Beloved spouse of Ušumgal-ana, you are the great lady of the horizon and zenith of the heavens. The Anuna have submitted to you. From birth you were the junior queen: how supreme you are now over the Anuna, the great gods! The Anuna kiss the ground with their lips before you. But my own trial is not yet concluded, although a hostile verdict encloses me as if it were my own verdict. I did not reach out my hands to the flowered bed. I did not reveal the pronouncements of Ningal to anybody. My lady beloved of An, may your heart be calmed towards me, the brilliant en priestess of Nanna!

It must be known! It must be known! Nanna has not yet spoken out! He has said, "He is yours!" Be it known that you are lofty as the heavens! Be it known that you are broad as the earth! Be it known that you destroy the rebel lands! Be it known that you roar at the foreign lands! Be it known that you crush heads! Be it known that you devour corpses like a dog! Be it known that your gaze is terrible! Be it known that you lift your terrible gaze! Be it known that you have flashing eyes! Be it known that you are unshakeable and unyielding! Be it known that you always stand triumphant! That Nanna has not yet spoken out, and that he has said "He is yours, has made you greater, my lady; you have become the greatest! My lady beloved by An, I shall tell of all your rages! I have heaped up the coals in the censer, and prepared the purification rites. Might your heart not be appeased towards me?" . . .

Hammurabi's Code, c. 1800 B.C.E.

King Hammurabi of Babylon conquered the entire area of Mesopotamia (including Sumer) between 1793 and 1750 B.C.E. His law code provides us with a rare insight into the daily life of ancient urban society.

Source: Martha T. Roth, *Law Collections from Mesopotamia and Asia Minor*, 2nd ed. (Atlanta: Scholar's Press, 1997), 82–128 (selections as numbered).

Law codes give us an idea of a people's sense of justice and notions of proper punishment. This selection includes only parts of Hammurabi's Code, so we cannot conclude that if something is not mentioned here it was not a matter of legal concern. We can, however, deduce much about Babylonian society from the laws mentioned in this selection.

What do these laws tell us about class divisions or social distinctions in Babylonian society? What can we learn from these laws about the roles of women and men? Which laws or punishments seem unusual today? What does that difference suggest to you about ancient Babylon compared to modern society?

THINKING HISTORICALLY

As a primary source, law codes are extremely useful. They zero in on a society's main concerns, revealing minutiae of daily life in great detail. But, for a number of reasons, law codes cannot be viewed as a precise reflection of society.

We cannot assume, for instance, that all of Hammurabi's laws were strictly followed or enforced, anymore than we can assume that for our own society. If there was a law against something, we can safely assume that some people obeyed it and some people did not. (That is, if no one engaged in the behavior, there would be no need for the law.) Therefore, law codes suggest a broad range of behaviors in a society.

While laws tell us something about the concerns of the society that produces them, we cannot presume that all members of society share the same concerns. Recall that, especially in ancient society, laws were written by the literate, powerful few. What evidence do you see of the upper-class composition of Babylonian law in this code?

Finally, if an ancient law seems similar to our own, we cannot assume that the law reflects motives, intents, or goals similar to our own laws. Laws must be considered within the context of the society in which they were created. Notice, for instance, the laws in Hammurabi's Code that may seem, by our standards, intended to protect women. On closer examination, what appears to be their goal?

Property and Theft[1]

6. If a man steals valuables belonging to the god or to the palace, that man shall be killed, and also he who receives the stolen goods from him shall be killed.

---

[1] Topical headings added by the editor of this volume are in neither the original nor translated source. [Ed.]

8. If a man steals an ox, a sheep, a donkey, a pig, or a boat — if it belongs either to the god or to the palace, he shall give thirtyfold; if it belongs to a commoner, he shall replace it tenfold; if the thief does not have anything to give, he shall be killed.

14. If a man should kidnap the young child of another man, he shall be killed.

15. If a man should enable a palace slave, a palace slave woman, a commoner's slave, or a commoner's slave woman to leave through the main city-gate, he shall be killed.

17. If a man seizes a fugitive slave or a slave woman in the open country and leads him back to his owner, the slave owner shall give him 2 shekels of silver.

21. If a man breaks into a house, they shall kill him and hang him in front of that very breach.

22. If a man commits a robbery and is then seized, that man shall be killed.

24. If a life (is lost during the robbery), the city and the governor shall weigh and deliver to his kinsmen 60 shekels of silver.

Economics and Contracts

48. If a man has a debt lodged against him, and the storm god Adad devastates his field or a flood sweeps away his crops, or there is no grain grown in the field due to insufficient water — in that year he will not repay grain to his creditor; he shall suspend performance of his contract and he will not give interest payments for that year.

53. If a man neglects to reinforce the embankment of (the irrigation canal of) his field and does not reinforce its embankment and allows the water to carry away the common irrigated area, the man in whose embankment the breach opened shall replace the grain whose loss he caused.

59. If a man cuts down a tree in another man's date orchard without the permission of the owner of the orchard, he shall weigh and deliver 30 shekels of silver.

117. If an obligation is outstanding against a man and he sells or gives into debt service his wife, his son, or his daughter, they shall perform service in the house of their buyer of the one who holds them in debt service for three years; their release shall be secured in the fourth year.

Family and Marriage

128. If a man marries a wife but does not draw up a formal contract for her, that woman is not a wife.

129. If a man's wife should be seized lying with another male, they shall bind them and cast them into the water; if the wife's master allows his wife to live, then the king shall allow his subject (i.e., the other male) to live.

130. If a man pins down another man's virgin wife who is still residing in her father's house, and they seize him lying with her, that man shall be killed; that woman shall be released.

142. If a woman repudiates her husband, and declares, "You will not have marital relations with me"—her circumstances shall be investigated by the authorities of her city quarter, and if she is circumspect and without fault, but her husband is wayward and disparages her greatly, that woman will not be subject to any penalty; she shall take her dowry and she shall depart for her father's house.

143. If she is not circumspect but is wayward, squanders her household possessions, and disparages her husband, they shall cast that woman into the water.

155. If a man selects a bride for his son and his son carnally knows her, after which he himself then lies with her and they seize him in the act, they shall bind that man and cast him into the water.

156. If a man selects a bride for his son and his son does not yet carnally know her, he shall weigh and deliver to her 30 shekels of silver; moreover, he shall restore to her whatever she brought from her father's house, and a husband of her choice shall marry her.

Assault and Personal Injury

195. If a child should strike his father, they shall cut off his hand.

196. If an *awīlu* [highest class] should blind the eye of another *awīlu*, they shall blind his eye.

197. If he should break the bone of another *awīlu*, they shall break his bone.

198. If he should blind the eye of a commoner or break the bone of a commoner, he shall weigh and deliver 60 shekels of silver.

199. If he should blind the eye of an *awīlu*'s slave or break the bone of an *awīlu*'s slave, he shall weigh and deliver one half of his value (in silver).

200. If an *awīlu* should knock out the tooth of another *awīlu* of his own rank, they shall knock out his tooth.

201. If he should knock out the tooth of a commoner, he shall weigh and deliver 20 shekels of silver.

202. If an *awīlu* should strike the cheek of an *awīlu* who is of status higher than his own, he shall be flogged in the public assembly with 60 stripes of an ox whip.

Responsibility and Liability

229. If a builder constructs a house for a man but does not make his work sound, and the house that he constructs collapses and causes the death of the householder, that builder shall be killed.

230. If it should cause the death of a son of the householder, they shall kill a son of that builder.

231. If it should cause the death of a slave of the householder, he shall give to the householder a slave of comparable value for the slave.

232. If it should cause the loss of property, he shall replace anything that is lost; moreover, because he did not make sound the house which he constructed and it collapsed, he shall construct (anew) the house which collapsed at his own expense.

251. If a man's ox is a known gorer, and the authorities of his city quarter notify him that it is a known gorer, but he does not blunt its horns or control his ox, and that ox gores to death a member of the *awīlu* class, he (the owner) shall give 30 shekels of silver.

252. If it is a man's slave (who is fatally gored), he shall give 20 shekels of silver.

5

The Tale of the Eloquent Peasant, c. 1850 B.C.E.

Archaeologists have yet to discover an equivalent of Hammurabi's Code in the dry sands of Egypt. A few Egyptian Pharaohs were known as law givers, but Egyptian law seems to have emerged more from court cases, the decrees of the Pharaoh, and the decisions of his appointed judges than from law codes. Thanks to an Egyptian tradition that court cases should be written down (and those dry sands), we have a few vivid examples of the workings of Egyptian justice three thousand years ago. "The Tale of the Eloquent Peasant" comes down to us from such a court case, committed to papyrus leaves about 1850 B.C.E. What does this fragment tells us about the life of peasants in ancient Egypt? What makes this peasant different from most others? What do we learn about ancient Egyptian justice?

Source: "The Tale of the Eloquent Peasant," in The *Tale of Sinuhe and Other Ancient Egyptian Poems 1940–1640 B.C.*, trans. R.B. Parkinson (Oxford: Oxford University Press, 1997), 58–63, 65, 67–68, 73–75. © R.B. Parkinson.

THINKING HISTORICALLY

Primary sources are not always exactly what they seem. While this
source clearly originated in a legal dispute that was transcribed,
"The Tale of the Eloquent Peasant" spins a story that appears more
entertainment and moral lesson than verbatim court record. What
elements of the tale seem to be exaggerations or elaborations
intended for dramatic or moral purposes? If you discount these
elements as unlikely, what do you think really happened? We cannot
be sure, of course, but to read this source as literal truth would lead
us to inaccuracies about ancient Egypt. It would be a mistake, for
instance, to conclude that the king routinely heard peasant
complaints. What other inaccurate conclusions might be drawn
from a literal reading of the source? What accurate conclusions
about ancient Egypt can you draw from a less literal reading?

There was once a man
called Khunanup;
he was a peasant of the Wadi Natrun,
whose wife was called Meret.
And this peasant said to this wife of his,
'Look, I am going to Egypt
to buy provisions there for my children.
Go and measure for me
the grain which is left in the storehouse from [yesterday].'
And he measured out for her six gallons of grain.
And this peasant said to this wife of his,
'Look, twenty gallons of grain [are given] to you
and your children for provisions.
But you shall make these six gallons of grain
into bread and beer
for every day, for me to live on.'

This peasant then went down to Egypt,
having loaded his asses with reeds and fan palms,
natron[1] and salt,
sticks . . .
and staffs from Farafra,
leopard skins
and wolf hides,
[pebbles] and [serpentine],
wild mint-plants and *inbi*-fruits,

---

[1] natron: a mineral used for cleaning and mummification. [Ed.]

tebu- and *uben*-plants,
—with all the fair produce of Wadi Natrun.

This peasant then went
south to Heracleopolis.
He then arrived
in the area of Per-Fefi, north of Mednit.
There he met a man, called Nemtinakht,
standing on the riverbank.
He was the son of a gentleman called Isry;
they were liegemen of the High Steward
Meru's son Rensi.
And this Nemtinakht, when he saw this peasant's asses
which tempted his heart, said,
'If only I had some effective charm,
with which to steal this peasant's belongings!'
Now the house of this Nemtinakht was on the water edge,
    which was a path.
It was narrow; it was not broad,
but only as wide as a kilt.
One of its sides was under water,
and the other under grain.
And this Nemtinakht said to his follower,
'Go bring me a sheet from my house!'
It was brought immediately.
Then he spread the sheet on the water-edge pathway.
And its fringe rested on the water,
with its hem on the barley.
And this peasant came on the public path.
And this Nemtinakht said, 'Take care, peasant!
Will you tread on my clothes?'
And this peasant said, 'I'll do as you wish; my way is good.'
He then went upwards.
And this Nemtinakht said, 'Will my barley be your path?'
And this peasant said, 'My way is good,
for the bank is high and the way under barley,
and you block our path with clothes.
Won't you even let us go past the path?'

Then one of the asses took a mouthful
from a clump of barley.
And this Nemtinakht said, 'Look, peasant, I will take your
    ass,
for eating my barley,
and it will tread grain for its offence.'
And this peasant said, 'My way is good;

one clump is destroyed—
one destroying ten!
For ten units I bought my ass
and you seize it for a mouthful
of a clump of grain!
Now, I know the lord of this estate;
it belongs to the High Steward Meru's son Rensi.
Now, he punishes every robber in this entire land.
Am I robbed in his estate?'
And this Nemtinakht said, 'Isn't this
the proverb that people say—
"A wretch's name is uttered only because of his master"?
Even though it's the High Steward you recall,
I'm the one who speaks to you.'

Then he took a stick of fresh tamarisk to him.
Then he beat all his limbs with it,
and his asses were taken, and entered into his estate.
And this peasant now wept very much,
for the pain of what was being done to him.
And this Nemtinakht said, 'Don't raise your voice, peasant,
or, look, you're for the harbour of the Lord of Silence!'
And this peasant said, 'You beat me and steal my belongings?
And then you'll rob my mouth of complaint?
O Lord of Silence, may You give me back my belongings,
so I shan't cry out to Your fearsomeness!'
And this peasant spent a full week
petitioning this Nemtinakht, but he paid no attention.

This peasant then went
to Heracleopolis to petition
the High Steward Meru's son Rensi.
He met him coming out
of the door of his house,
about to board his official barge.
And this peasant said, 'Might I acquaint you with this complaint!
There is a reason to send one of your choice followers
to me, about which I shall send him back to you.'
And the High Steward Meru's son Rensi sent
a choice follower to him,
and this peasant sent him back
about this matter in every detail.
And the High Steward Meru's son Rensi
accused this Nemtinakht to the officials who were with him.

And they said to him, 'Surely it's only a peasant of his
who's run off to someone else.

Look, this is what people do to their peasants
who run off to others.
Is there cause to punish this Nemtinakht
for a little natron,
and a little salt?
Order him to repay it, and he'll repay it.'
The High Steward Meru's son Rensi
was then quiet.
He answered neither the officials,
nor the peasant.

And this peasant came to petition
the High Steward Meru's son Rensi,
and said, 'High Steward, toy lord!
Great of the great,
leader of all that is not and all that is!

If you go down to the Sea of Truth,
you will sail on it with true fair wind;
the bunt will not strip off your sails, not your boat delay;
nor will misfortune come upon your mast, nor your yards
        break;
you will not go headlong, and be grounded;
nor will the flood carry you off;
nor will you taste the river's evil, nor stare in the face of fear.
But to you the fish will come caught;
you will catch fatted fowl.

For you are a father to the orphan
and a husband to the widow,
a brother to the divorced,
an apron to the motherless.
Let me make your name in this land, with every good law:
Leader free from selfishness!
Great one free from baseness!
Destroyer of Falsehood! Creator of Truth!
Who comes at the voice of the caller!

I speak so that you will hear.
Do Truth, praised one whom the praised praise!
Drive off my need—look, I am weighed down!
Examine me—look, I am at a loss!'

Now this peasant made this speech
in the reign of the Majesty of the Dual King Nebkaure, the
        justified.
The High Steward Meru's son Rensi

then went before his Majesty
and said, 'My lord, I have found one of the peasants,
whose speech is truly perfect, and whose goods have been
    stolen.
And, look, he has come to me to appeal about it.'

And his Majesty said, 'As you wish to see me in health
you shall delay him here,
without answering anything he says!
For the sake of his speaking, be quiet
Then we shall be brought it in writing, and we shall hear it.
But provide sustenance for his wife and children!
Look, one of these peasants only comes
to Egypt when his house is all but empty.
Also, provide sustenance for this peasant himself!
You shall have the provisions given to him
without letting him know that you are giving him them!'

And he was given ten loaves of bread,
and two jars of beer daily.
The High Steward Meru's son
Rensi gave them —
gave them to his friend, and his friend gave them to him.
Then the High Steward Meru's son Rensi sent
to the mayor of the Wadi Natrun
about making provisions for this peasant's wife,
three gallons daily.

And this peasant came to appeal to him a second time,
and said, 'High Steward, my lord!
Greatest of the great!
Richest of the rich!
Whose great ones have one greater!
whose rich, one richer!
Helm of heaven!
Beam of earth!
Plumbline bearing the weight!
Helm, drift not!
Beam, tilt not!
Plumbline, go not wrong!
For a lord great through taking what is ownerless
is now robbing someone, while your share is in your
    house.
A jar of beer and three loaves of bread —
what else need you give out to satisfy your dependents?
A mortal must die with his underlings.

Will you then be a man of eternity?
Yet is it not wrong? — the scales tilting,
the weight wandering
the truly upright man turned aside?
Look, Truth flees from under you,
exiled from its place;
the officials are doing evil;
the standard of speech
is now partial,
and the judges snatch when it carries things off —
this means that he who twists speech from its rightness
makes himself go wrong thereby;
the breath-giver is now at a loss on the ground;
he who breathes calmly makes people pant;
the apportioner is greedy,
the dispeller of need is the commander of its making,
and the harbour is its own flood;
the punisher of wrong does evil.' . . .

And this peasant came to appeal to him a third time
and said, 'High Steward, my lord!
You are a Sungod, lord of heaven, with your entourage.
Everyone's portion is with you, like a flood.
You are a Nileflood who revives the water-meadows, and
      restores the ravaged mounds.
Punisher of the robber, protector of the poor —
become not a torrent against the appealer!

Take heed of eternity's approach! Wish to endure,
as is said, "Doing Truth is the breath of life."
Deal punishment to the punishable!
May your standard never be equalled!
Do the scales wander?
Is the balance partial?
And is Thoth lenient? If so, then you should do evil! . . .

And this peasant came to appeal to him a fourth time;
he met him coming out of the gate
of the temple of Herishef,
and said, 'O praised one, may Herishef
from whose temple you have come, praise you!

Destroyed is goodness, it has no unity,
and nothing can hurl Falsehood to the ground.
Has this ferry not gone down? So who can be taken across,
when crossing is made hateful?

Crossing the river on foot—
is that a good crossing? No!
So who now can sleep till dawn?
For destroyed is going by night
and travelling by day,
and making a man attend his good true right.
Look, it is no use to tell you this,
for mercy has passed you by: how miserable is the poor man
    you destroy!

Look, you are a hunter who slakes his desire,
who reaches out and does what he wants,
who harpoons hippopotami and shoots wild bulls,
catches fish and snares fowl.
Yet none hasty-mouthed is free from recklessness;
none light of heart is cautious of intent.
Your heart should be patient, so that you will know Truth!
Suppress your choice for the good of him who would depart
    quietly!
No rapid man cleaves to excellence; no hasty-hearted man
    will exist.

Stretch out to act, now your eyes are opened!
Inform the heart!
Be not harsh because you are powerful, so that evil may
    not reach you!
Pass over a misdeed, and it will be two.
Only the eater tastes;
so the accused replies.
Only the sleeper sees the dream;
so the punishable judge
is an archetype for the evildoer. . . .

If Falsehood sets out, it strays;
it cannot cross in a ferry, and has not altered its course.
He who is rich with it has no children,
and no heirs on earth.
And he who sails with it cannot touch land,
his boat cannot moor in its harbour.

Be heavy no more, you have not yet been light!
Delay no more, you have not yet been swift!
Be not partial! Do not listen to the heart!
Do not disregard one you know!
Do not blind yourself against one who looks to you! Do not
    fend off a supplicator!

You should abandon this negligence, so that your sentence
    will be renowned!
Act for him who acts for you
and listen to none against him,
so that a man will be summoned according to his true right!
There is no yesterday for the negligent,
no friend for him who is deaf to Truth,
no holiday for the selfish.
The accuser becomes wretched,
more wretched than when a pleader,
and the opponent becomes a murderer.
Look, I am pleading to you, and you do not hear—
I will go and plead about you to Anubis.'

And the High Steward Meru's son Rensi
sent two attendants to turn him back.
And this peasant was afraid, thinking this was done
to punish him for the speech he had made.
And this peasant said, 'The thirsty man
approaching water,
the nurseling reaching his mouth
for milk—they die,
while for him who longs to see it come,
death comes slowly.'
And the High Steward Meru's son Rensi said,
'Don't be afraid peasant!
Look, you will be dealing with me.'
And this peasant swore an oath,
'So, shall I live on your bread,
and drink your beer for ever?'
And the High Steward Meru's son Rensi said,
'Now wait here and hear your petitions!'
And he caused every petition to be read out
from a fresh roll according to [its] content.
And the High Steward Meru's son Rensi had them
    presented
before the Majesty of the Dual King Nebkaure, the
    justified.
And they seemed more perfect to his heart
than anything in this entire land.
And his Majesty said, 'Judge yourself, Meru's son!'

And the High Steward Meru's son Rensi
sent two attendants to [bring this Nemtinakht].

Then he was brought, and an inventory made [of his
   household].
Then he found six persons, as well as [his . . .],
his barley, his emmer,
his donkeys, his swine, and his flocks.
And this Nemtinakht [was given] to this peasant,
[with all his property, all his] ser[vants],
[and all the belongings] of this Nemtinakht.

So it ends, [from start to finish,
as found in writing].

6

Images from Hunefer's *Book of the Dead,*
c. 1275 B.C.E.

Thanks to the preservative dry climate and the ancient Egyptian interest in illustrating books of papyrus and painting the interiors of pyramids, temples, and tombs, we have excellent visual primary sources
on the daily life of ancient Egypt. These two images are from a papyrus called Hunefer's *Book of the Dead*. Hunefer was a royal official of
the thirteenth century B.C.E. Like other wealthy or powerful Egyptians,
Hunefer had a version of the *Book of the Dead*, with all its prayers and
incantations, prepared especially for him.

In Figure 2.1, Hunefer's mummy is prepared to enter the afterlife.
His wife and daughter dab their heads with dirt. Three priests administer the rituals. The priest on the far left, dressed in a leopard skin,
burns incense and readies the food offerings. Two others prepare the
important ceremony of opening the mummy's mouth so that it can
breathe and eat. Anubis, the jackal-headed god of death, holds the
mummy. Behind him we can read an enlarged version of Hunefer's
tombstone, which will be placed in front of his tomb, a miniature
image of which we see on the far right.

In Figure 2.2 we see Hunefer led by Anubis, about to be judged.
In the center of the frame Hunefer's heart is weighed against a
feather. If his heart is lighter than the feather, he will be admitted
to the presence of Osiris and enter the afterlife. If not, his heart
will be devoured by the demon Ammut, whose crocodile head is

Source: *Book of the Dead* of Hunefer, Thebes, Egypt, 19th Dynasty, around 1275 B.C.E.

Figure 2.1 Entering the Afterlife.
Source: © The Trustees of the British Museum / Art Resource, NY.

turned to the ibis-headed god Thoth, standing to the right of the scales and writing the verdict. In that case, his existence will end forever. Fortunately, Hunefer's artist assures him of a happy ending. Thoth conducts Hunefer to Osiris seated on a throne, behind his four sons standing on a lotus leaf and in front of his wife, the goddess Isis, and her sister. What do these images tell you about Egyptian society? How do they compare to your own ideas of death?

THINKING HISTORICALLY

Reading primary sources, whether they be words or images, is always tricky. Unlike secondary sources, they were not written, painted, or left for us. The assumptions and intentions of the writer or artist may be very different from our own, and so we may misunderstand the meaning or purpose of a work.

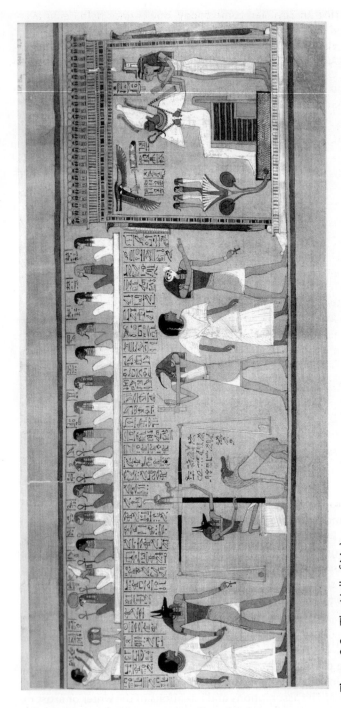

Figure 2.2 The Hall of Ma'at.

Entering an Egyptian tomb today, one cannot help being over-whelmed by the beauty of the paintings. Their vitality can be breathtaking. To the modern viewer, especially in museums where paintings and papyrus are torn from their original setting, they appear to us as beautiful works of art. And so they are. But for the ancient Egyptians, these images were more than representations, more than art. They were the things depicted. The food that was displayed was food for the deceased in the afterlife; the people painted on the walls were there to provide and serve. The pictures were intended to be more vital than we can imagine. Are visual images more or less reliable as primary sources than written words? What do visuals add to our understanding? How might they mislead us?

Images are different from written words in another way. You are able to make sense of these images from Hunefer's *Book of the Dead* because primary and secondary texts enable us to provide a summary of the story behind them. But the Egyptian artist and viewer knew that story, and hundreds of subplots, by heart. Imagine "reading" the images the way an ancient Egyptian viewer would have. Would the difference between your modern interpretation and the Egyptian viewer's interpretation be similar to the difference between seeing a movie and reading the book? And if "the book" was the wisdom of the ages as everyone knew it, and images could be real, what sort of movie would that be?

7

An Assyrian Law and a Palace Decree, c. 1100 B.C.E.

This selection consists of two official documents from a Mesopotamian city-based empire of about 1100 B.C.E., known today as the Middle Assyrian Empire because it followed the early Assyrian period (twentieth to fifteenth century B.C.E.) and preceded the Neo-Assyrian era (tenth to seventh century B.C.E.). Archaeologists working in Syria and Iraq continue to unearth many laws from all Assyrian eras.

The first document is only one of many laws, and sections are missing. Nevertheless, it provides a rare window onto one urban

Source: Martha T. Roth, *Law Collections from Mesopotamia and Asia Minor*, 2nd ed. (Atlanta: Scholar's Press, 1997), 167–68, 205–6.

society at the end of the second millennium B.C.E. What does it tell you about the role of women in this place at this time? What does it tell you about the attitudes of men toward women? What do you think was the purpose of passing this law?

The second document was a palace regulation meant to apply only to a select group of men and women, not the entire Assyrian society. What does this decree tell you about the lives of men and women in the palace? How were matters at the palace similar to, and different from, those of the larger society?

THINKING HISTORICALLY

Primary sources can be rich repositories of information. They can correct misconceptions and answer questions, even those we never thought to ask. These two Assyrian sources are particularly valuable in telling us about the intersection of gender and social class in 1100 B.C.E. Create two questions that one or both of these documents answer. Then compose two sentences that these documents show are clearly proved errors or misconceptions. For example, if someone believed the practice of veiling women had its origins in Muslim society, how would these documents show that this is a misconception?

Assyrian Law

Wives of a man, or [widows], or any [Assyrian] women who go out into the main thoroughfare [shall not have] their heads [bare]. Daughters of a man . . . [with] either a . . . -cloth or garments or . . . shall be veiled, . . . their heads. . . . When they go about . . . in the main thoroughfare during the daytime, they shall be veiled. A concubine who goes about in the main thoroughfare with her mistress is to be veiled. A married *qadiltu*-woman[1] is to be veiled (when she goes about) in the main thoroughfare, but an unmarried one is to leave her head bare in the main thoroughfare, she shall not veil herself. A prostitute shall not be veiled, her head shall be bare. Whoever sees a veiled prostitute shall seize her, secure witnesses, and bring her to the palace entrance. They shall not take away her jewelry, but he who has seized her takes her clothing; they shall strike her 50 blows with rods; they shall pour hot pitch over her head. And if a man should see a veiled prostitute and release her, and does not bring her to the palace

---

[1] A class of templewomen. [Ed.]

entrance, they shall strike the man 50 blows with rods; the one who informs against him shall take his clothing; they shall pierce his ears, thread them on a cord, tie it at his back; he shall perform the king's service for one full month. Slave women shall not be veiled, and he who should see a veiled slave woman shall seize her and bring her to the palace entrance; they shall cut off her ears; he who seizes her shall take her clothing.

Palace Decree of Tiglath-Pileser I
(r. 1114–1076 B.C.E.)

Tiglath-pileser, king of the universe, king of Assyria, son of Ashur-rēsa-ishi, himself also king of Assyria, issued a decree for the palace commander of the Inner City, the palace herald, the chief of the water sprinklers of the Processional Residence, the physician of the Inner Quarters, and the administrator of all the palaces of the entire extent of the country:

Royal court attendants or dedicatees of the palace personnel who have access to the palace shall not enter the palace without an inspection; if he is not (properly) castrated, they shall turn him into a (castrated) court attendant for a second time.

If either the palace commander of the Inner City, or the palace herald, or the chief of the water sprinklers of the Processional Residence, or the physician of the Inner Quarters, or the administrator of all the palaces of the entire expanse of the country allows an uncastrated court attendant to enter into the palace, and he is later discovered, they shall amputate one foot of each of these officials.

8

SMITHSONIAN MAGAZINE

First City in the New World? 2002

Historians used to think that the urban revolution occurred in the Western Hemisphere much later than in the Eastern. However, as earlier urban sites were uncovered, like Olmec cities in Mexico over 3,000 years old, the origins of civilization in the Americas has been pushed back earlier and earlier. Now archaeologists have dated a site

---

Source: *Smithsonian* Magazine, "First City in the New World?" 2002, http://www.smithsonianmag.com/history-archaeology/firstcity.html?c=y&page=1.

in Peru over a thousand years earlier than the Olmec. That would make the urban revolution in the Americas virtually contemporary with that of the Middle East. What is the evidence for this claim? In what ways was Peru's Caral similar to the cities of Mesopotamia or Egypt? In what ways was it different?

THINKING HISTORICALLY

The author of this secondary source says nothing about written re-cords from this site, but primary sources — pieces of the past — are not limited to writing. We have already seen how historians and archaeologists can interpret the past through the study of physical and organic remains, especially art and artifacts. In fact, one arti-fact in particular was very important in understanding Caral. What was this, and what was its importance? What other artifacts from the site proved to be useful primary sources for the under-standing of Caral?

Six earth-and-rock mounds rise out of the windswept desert of the Supe Valley near the coast of Peru. Dunelike and immense, they appear to be nature's handiwork, forlorn outposts in an arid region squeezed between the Pacific Ocean and the folds of the Andean Cordillera. But looks de-ceive. These are human-made pyramids, and compelling new evidence indicates they are the remains of a city that flourished nearly 5,000 years ago. If true, it would be the oldest urban center in the Americas and among the most ancient in all the world.

Research developed by Peruvian archaeologist Ruth Shady Solís of San Marcos University suggests that Caral, as the 150-acre complex of pyramids, plazas and residential buildings is known, was a thriving me-tropolis as Egypt's great pyramids were being built. The energetic ar-chaeologist believes that Caral may also answer nagging questions about the long-mysterious origins of the Inca, the civilization that once stretched from modern-day Ecuador to central Chile and gave rise to such cities as Cuzco and Machu Picchu. Caral may even hold a key to the origins of civilizations everywhere.

Though discovered in 1905, Caral first drew little attention, largely because archaeologists believed the complex structures were fairly re-cent. But the monumental scale of the pyramids had long tantalized Shady. "When I first arrived in the valley in 1994, I was overwhelmed," she says. "This place is somewhere between the seat of the gods and the home of man." She began excavations two years later, braving primitive conditions on a tight budget. Fourteen miles from the coast and 120 miles north of Peru's capital city of Lima, Caral lies in a desert region that lacks paved roads, electricity and public water. Shady, who enlisted

25 Peruvian soldiers to help with the excavations, often used her own money to advance the work.

For two months she and her crew searched for the broken remains of pots and containers, called potsherds, that most such sites contain. Not finding any only made her more excited; it meant Caral could be what archaeologists term pre-ceramic, or existing before the advent of pot-firing technology in the area. Shady eventually concluded that Caral predated Olmec settlements to the north by 1,000 years. But colleagues remained skeptical. She needed proof.

In 1996, Shady's team began the mammoth task of excavating Pirámide Mayor, the largest of the pyramids. After carefully clearing away several millennia's worth of rubble and sand, they unearthed staircases, circular walls covered with remnants of colored plaster, and squared brickwork. Finally, in the foundation, they found the preserved remains of reeds woven into bags, known as shicras. The original workers, she surmised, must have filled these bags with stones from a hillside quarry a mile away and laid them atop one another inside retaining walls, gradually giving rise to the city of Caral's immense structures.

Shady knew that the reeds were ideal subjects for radiocarbon dating and could make her case. In 1999, she sent samples of them to Jonathan Haas at Chicago's Field Museum and to Winifred Creamer at Northern Illinois University. In December 2000, Shady's suspicions were confirmed: the reeds were 4,600 years old. She took the news calmly, but Haas says he "was virtually in hysterics for three days afterward." In the April 27, 2001, issue of the journal *Science*, the three archaeologists reported that Caral and the other ruins of the Supe Valley are "the locus of some of the earliest population concentrations and corporate architecture in South America." The news stunned other scientists. "It was almost unbelievable," says Betty Meggers, an archaeologist at the Smithsonian Institution. "This data pushed back the oldest known dates for an urban center in the Americas by more than 1,000 years."

What amazed archaeologists was not just the age but the complexity and scope of Caral. Pirámide Mayor alone covers an area nearly the size of four football fields and is 60 feet tall. A 30-foot-wide staircase rises from a sunken circular plaza at the foot of the pyramid, passing over three terraced levels until it reaches the top of the platform, which contains the remains of an atrium and a large fireplace. Thousands of manual laborers would have been needed to build such a mammoth project, not even counting the many architects, craftsmen, supervisors and other managers. Inside a ring of platform pyramids lies a large sunken amphitheater, which could have held many hundreds of people during civic or religious events. Inside the amphitheater, Shady's team found 32 flutes made of pelican and condor bones. And, in April 2002, they uncovered

37 cornets[1] of deer and llama bones. "Clearly, music played an important role in their society," says Shady.

The perimeter of Caral holds a series of smaller mounds, various buildings and residential complexes. Shady discovered a hierarchy in living arrangements: large, well-kept rooms atop the pyramids for the elite, ground-level complexes for craftsmen, and shabbier outlying shanty-towns for workers.

But why had Caral been built in the first place? More important, why would people living comfortably in small communities perched on the Pacific Ocean with easy access to abundant marine food choose to move inland to an inhospitable desert? If she could answer this question, Shady believed she might begin to unravel one of the knottiest questions in the field of anthropology today: What causes civilizations to arise? And what was it about the desert landscape of Peru's Supe Valley that caused a complex, hierarchical society to flourish there?

Her excavations convinced Shady that Caral had served as a major trade center for the region, ranging from the rain forests of the Amazon to the high forests of the Andes. She found fragments of the fruit of the *achiote*, a plant still used today in the rain forest as an aphrodisiac. And she found necklaces of snails and the seeds of the coca plant, neither of which was native to Caral. This rich trading environment, Shady believes, gave rise to an elite group that did not take part in the production of food, allowing them to become priests and planners, builders and designers. Thus, the class distinctions elemental to an urban society emerged.

But what sustained such a trading center and drew travelers to it? Was it food? Shady and her team found the remains of sardines and anchovies, which must have come from the coast 14 miles to the west, in the excavations. But they also found evidence that the Caral people ate squash, sweet potatoes and beans. Shady theorized that Caral's early farmers diverted area rivers into trenches and canals, which still crisscross the Supe Valley today, to irrigate their fields. But because she found no traces of maize (corn) or other grains, which can be traded or stored and used to tide a population over in difficult times, she concluded that Caral's trade leverage was not based on stockpiling food supplies.

It was evidence of another crop in the excavations that gave Shady the best clue to the mystery of Caral's success. In nearly every excavated building, her team discovered great quantities of cotton seeds, fibers and textiles. Her theory fell into place when a large fishing net, unearthed at an unrelated dig on Peru's coast, turned out to be as old as Caral. "The farmers of Caral grew the cotton that the fishermen needed to make the nets," Shady speculates. "And the fishermen gave them shellfish and dried fish in exchange for these nets." In essence, the people of Caral

---

[1] Trumpet-like instrument. [Ed.]

enabled fishermen to work with larger and more effective nets, which made the resources of the sea more readily available. The Caral people probably used dried squash as flotation devices for nets and also as containers, thus obviating any need for ceramics.

Eventually Caral would spawn 17 other pyramid complexes scattered across the 35-square-mile area of the Supe Valley. Then, around 1600 B.C., for reasons that may never be answered, the Caral civilization toppled, though it didn't disappear overnight. "They had time to protect some of their architectural structures, burying them discreetly," says Shady. Other nearby areas, such as Chupacigarro, Lurihuasi and Miraya, became centers of power. But based on Caral's size and scope, Shady believes that it is indeed the mother city of the Incan civilization.

She plans to continue excavating Caral and says she would someday like to build a museum on the site. "So many questions still remain," she says. "Who were these people? How did they control the other populations? What was their main god?"

■ REFLECTIONS

To focus our subject in a brief chapter, we have concentrated on Mesopotamia and Egypt almost exclusively. This enabled us to observe the beginnings of the urban revolution in Mesopotamia and one of the most spectacular and best preserved of ancient civilizations in Egypt. The city-states of Mesopotamia and the territorial state of Egypt were the two extremes of ancient civilization. City-states packed most people tightly within their walls. Eighty percent of Mesopotamians lived within city walls by 2800 B.C.E. By contrast, less than 10 percent of Egyptians lived in cities—if we can call their unwalled settlements, palace compounds, and pyramid construction sites "cities" at all. The lesser role of cities in Egypt has led some historians to drop the term *urban revolution* for *the rise of civilization.* Other historians, objecting to the moralistic implications of the term *civilization,* prefer *the rise of complex societies. Complex* is not a very precise term, but it would refer to the appearance of social classes; the mixing of different populations; a multilayered governmental structure with rulers, officials, and ordinary people; and numerous specialists who are not full-time farmers or herders. More specifically, we might include kings, priests, writing, wheels, monumental building, markets, and money.

Our addition of early Peruvian civilization widens our lens. The unusually rich anchovy fisheries of Peru enabled the development of complex societies in the desert interior with limited agriculture through irrigation, but without some of the features of civilization in the Eastern Hemisphere. We read that Caral used gourds instead of ceramic containers, but later

Peruvians and other Americans fired clay and made ceramics. It used to be said that American Indians lacked writing (as Caral might have), but we can now translate the pictorial writing of Mexico and recognize Peruvian quipus of colored strings as a kind of writing. Wheeled vehicles were absent from the Americas (with the interesting exception of children's toys). Most Americans lacked beasts of burden (though Peruvians used llamas and alpacas). Peruvians and some Mexicans had bronze, but not all were literally "bronze age," and no American Indians had iron.

If we broaden our view to include the "complex societies" of South Asia and China as well as the Americas, similar types of cities pop up like mushrooms after a spring rain. Along the Indus River in Pakistan dozens of small and midsize cities formed independent clones of Harappa and Mohenjo-Daro (see Map 3.1 on p. 77). These numerous cities seem to have enjoyed the independence of city-states, linked more by culture and trade than by powerful kings or large armies. A vast web of such cities is still being excavated, stretching from Iran to India and from the coast of East Africa to southern Russia. In China, by contrast, vast territorial states integrated dozens of cities along river valleys and trade routes and throughout the interior, creating a cultural and political unity more like Egypt than Mesopotamia. Thus, a larger lens raises more questions than we have allowed in our brief examination of Mesopotamia and Egypt. How important were such "urban inventions" as kings, soldiers, warfare, wheels, and writing if they did not exist everywhere cities were created? Furthermore, how important were cities in the creation of the complex lives we have lived for the last five thousand years?

We might also ask the larger question: Has the urban revolution improved our lives? The belief that it has lies behind the use of the word *civilization*. Though the root of the word is the same as *city, civil,* and *civilian*, the word *civilization* came into the modern vocabulary of historians and social scientists in the nineteenth century. At this time anthropologists were working to distinguish stages of history and to illustrate the differences between what were then called "primitive" peoples and people of the modern world whom anthropologists considered "civilized." Thus, they contended there had been three stages of history that could be summarized, in chronological order, as savagery, barbarism, and civilization. By the early twentieth century, in the work of the great prehistorian V. Gordon Childe, these terms stood for hunting-gathering, agricultural, and urban societies.

The belief that the world of the anthropologists and the "moderns" of the nineteenth and twentieth centuries was more civilized than the preurban world that they studied was more than a bit presumptuous. But this presumption continues today, in the popular mythology of "country bumpkins" who lack the manners and savoir-faire of their city cousins. Interestingly, it was also the assumption of the earliest founders of cities. *The Epic of Gilgamesh* tells of the need of the city to tame the wild Enkidu so that he can take his place in

> ...ramparted Uruk,
> Where fellows are resplendent in holiday clothing,
> Where every day is set for celebration.

There are many reasons to be skeptical of the so-called achievements of city life: increased inequality, suppression of women, slavery, organized warfare, conscription, heavy taxation, and forced labor, to name some of the most obvious. But our museums are full of the art and artifacts that testify to what the ancients meant by "civilization." The pyramids of Egypt and of South America and the ziggurats of Mesopotamia are among the wonders of the world. Does it matter that the great pyramids of Egypt were built from the forced labor of thousands to provide a resting place for a single person and that people were entombed alive in order to serve him? We can view the pyramids today as a remarkable achievement of engineering and organization while still condemning the manner of their execution. We can admire the art in the tombs, thrill to the revealing detail of ancient Egyptian life, marvel at the persistence of vivid colors mixed almost five thousand years ago, and treasure the art for what it reveals of the world of its creators, while we still detest its purpose.

We can do this because these monuments have become something different for us than what they were for the ancients. They have become testaments to human achievement, regardless of the cost. These ancient city-based societies were the first in which humans produced abundant works of art and architecture, which still astound us in their range, scope, and design.

The significance of the urban revolution was that it produced things that lasted beyond their utility or meaning—thanks to new techniques in cutting and hauling stone; baking brick, tile, and glass; and smelting tin, copper, and bronze—as a legacy for future generations. Even three thousand years ago, Egyptian engineers studied the ancient pyramids to understand a very distant past, 1,500 years before, and to learn, adapt, revive, or revise ancient techniques. In short, the achievement of the urban revolution is that it made knowledge cumulative, so that each generation could stand on the shoulders of its predecessors.

3

Identity in Caste and Territorial Societies

Greece and India, 1000–300 B.C.E.

■ HISTORICAL CONTEXT

Both India and Greece developed ancient city-based civilizations within a thousand years of the urban revolution. In India that civilization was concentrated on the Indus River Valley in what is today Pakistan. (See Map 3.1.) In Greece the Minoan civilization on the island of Crete was followed by the Mycenaean civilization on the mainland. (See Map 3.2.) But both ancient Indian and ancient Greek civilizations were transformed by new peoples from the grasslands of Eurasia, who settled in both areas between 1500 and 1000 B.C.E. Called by later generations the Aryans in India and the Dorians in Greece, these pastoral peoples arrived with horses, different customs, and new technologies. The Aryans came with chariots (as had the early Mycenaeans), while the Dorians, somewhat later, brought iron tools and weapons.

Despite the similar origins of the newcomers and the similar urban experience of the lands in which they settled, Aryan India and Dorian Greece developed in significantly different ways. As William H. McNeill writes in the first selection, by the year 500 B.C.E. Indian and Greek civilizations had found entirely different ways of organizing and administering their societies. And these differences had profound effects on the subsequent history of Indian and European society.

■ THINKING HISTORICALLY

Interpreting Primary Sources in Light of a Secondary Source

In Chapter 2, we distinguished between primary and secondary sources. Similarly, we begin here with a secondary source, or an interpretation. We then turn, as we did in the last chapter, to a series of primary sources. But whereas the last chapter focused on recognizing and distinguishing primary from secondary sources, here we concentrate on the relationship of the primary sources to the secondary interpretation—how one affects our reading of the other.

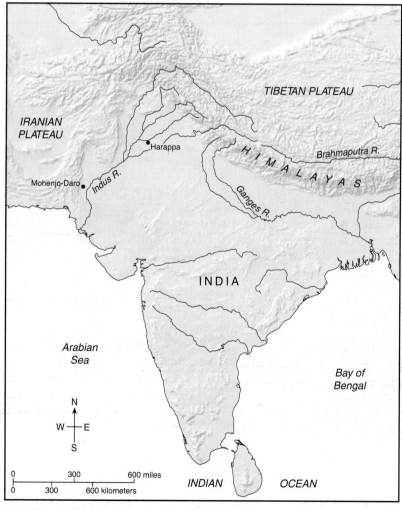

Map 3.1 India and the Indus River Valley, c. 500 B.C.E.

In this chapter, the primary sources were chosen to illustrate points
made in the introductory interpretation. This provides an opportunity
to understand the interpretation in some detail and with some degree
of subtlety. The primary sources do not give you enough material to
argue that McNeill is right or wrong, but you will be able to flesh out
some of the meaning of his interpretation. You might also reflect more
generally on the relationship of sources and interpretations. You will be
asked how particular sources support or even contradict the interpretation. You will consider the relevance of sources for other interpretations, and you will imagine what sort of sources you might seek for
evidence.

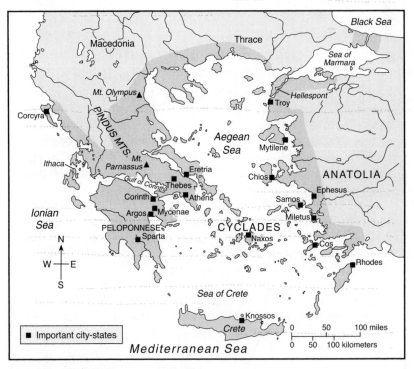

Map 3.2   Archaic Greece, c. 750–500 B.C.E.

WILLIAM H. McNEILL

Greek and Indian Civilization, 1971

William H. McNeill is one of the leading world historians in the
United States. In this selection from his college textbook *A World
History*, he compares the different ways in which Indian and Greek
civilizations of the classical age (by around 500 B.C.E.) organized
themselves. He distinguishes between Indian *caste* and Greek *territorial sovereignty*. These concepts are complex but useful in distinguishing between two of the basic ways societies organize and
identify themselves. As you read, try to define what each
term means. McNeill argues that caste and territorial sovereignty
had enormously different effects on the subsequent development
of Indian and European society. What were some of these
different effects?

THINKING HISTORICALLY

As you read this secondary source or historical interpretation, consider what sort of primary sources might have led McNeill to this view
or support his interpretation. Notice especially that in the first half of
the selection, McNeill mentions specific ancient Indian writings:
These are obvious primary sources for his interpretation. Not having
read McNeill's primary sources, can you imagine what in them would
lead to this interpretation?

Less of McNeill's interpretation of Greece is included in this selection; consequently, there is no mention of primary sources. In this
chapter, you will read a number of Greek primary sources, but at this
point can you speculate about what types of sources would demonstrate the Greek idea of territorial sovereignty?

Keep in mind that caste and territorial sovereignty are
modern terms not known or used by the ancients; therefore, you
will not find them in the primary sources that follow. What words
might the ancient Indians or Greeks have used to denote these
concepts?

Source: William H. McNeill, *A World History*, 2nd ed. (New York: Oxford University Press,
1971), 78–83, 88, 90, 95, 99–100.

Caste

A modern caste is a group of persons who will eat with one another and intermarry, while excluding others from these two intimacies. In addition, members of any particular caste must bear some distinguishing mark, so that everyone will know who belongs and who does not belong to it. Definite rules for how to behave in the presence of members of other castes also become necessary in situations where such contacts are frequent. When an entire society comes to be organized on these principles, any group of strangers or intruders automatically becomes another caste, for the exclusive habits of the rest of the population inevitably thrust the newcomers in upon themselves when it comes to eating and marrying. A large caste may easily break into smaller groupings as a result of some dispute, or through mere geographical separation over a period of time. New castes can form around new occupations. Wanderers and displaced individuals who find a new niche in society are automatically compelled to eat together and marry one another by the caste-bound habits of their neighbors.

How or when Indian society came to be organized along these lines remains unclear. Perhaps the Indus civilization itself was built upon something like the caste principle. Or perhaps the antipathy between Aryan invaders and the dark-skinned people whom they attacked lay at the root of the caste system of later India. But whatever the origins of caste, three features of Indian thought and feeling were mobilized to sustain the caste principle in later times. One of these was the idea of ceremonial purity. Fear of contaminating oneself by contact with a member of a lower, "unclean" caste gave Brahmans and others near the top of the pyramid strong reasons for limiting their association with low-caste persons.

From the other end of the scale, too, the poor and humble had strong reasons for clinging to caste. All but the most miserable and marginal could look down upon somebody, a not unimportant psychological feature of the system. In addition, the humbler castes were often groups that had only recently emerged from primitive forest life. They naturally sought to maintain their peculiar customs and habits, even in the context of urban or mixed village life, where men of different backgrounds and different castes lived side by side. Other civilized societies usually persuaded or compelled newcomers to surrender their peculiar ways, and assimilated them in the course of a few generations to the civilized population as a whole. In India, on the contrary, such groups were able to retain their separate identities indefinitely by preserving their own peculiar customs within the caste framework, generation after generation.

The third factor sustaining the caste principle was theoretical: the doctrine of reincarnation and of "varna." The latter declared that all men were naturally divided into four castes: the Brahmans who prayed, the Kshatriyas* who fought, the Vaisyas† who worked, and the Sudras who performed unclean tasks. Official doctrine classified the first three castes as Aryan, the last as non-Aryan, and put much stress on caste rank, from Brahmans at the top to Sudras at the bottom. Reality never corresponded even remotely to this theory. There were hundreds if not thousands of castes in India, rather than the four recognized in Brahmanical teaching. But apparent injustices and anomalies disappeared when the doctrine of reincarnation was combined with the doctrine of varna. The idea of reincarnation, indeed, gave logical explanation and justification to the system by explaining caste as a divinely established institution, hereditary from father to son, and designed to reward and punish souls for their actions in former lives. This undoubtedly helped to stabilize the confused reality. A man of unblemished life, born into the lowest caste, could hope for rebirth higher up the ladder. Conversely, a man of high caste who failed to conform to proper standards could expect rebirth in a lower caste. A man even risked reincarnation as a worm or beetle, if his misbehavior deserved such a punishment.

Clearly, the caste system as observed today did not exist in ancient India. Yet modern castes are the outgrowth of patterns of social organization that are as old as the oldest records. Early Buddhist stories, for instance, reveal many episodes turning upon caste distinctions, and passages in the *Rig Veda*‡ and other ancient writings imply caste-like practices and attitudes. By 500 B.C.E. we can at least be sure that the seeds from which the modern caste organization of society grew had already sprouted luxuriantly on Indian soil.

Caste lessened the significance of political, territorial administration. Everyone identified himself first and foremost with his caste. But a caste ordinarily lacked both definite internal administration and distinct territorial boundaries. Instead, members of a particular caste mingled with men of other castes, observing the necessary precautions to prevent contamination of one by the other. No king or ruler could command the undivided loyalty of people who felt themselves to belong to a caste rather than to a state. Indeed, to all ordinary caste members, rulers, officials, soldiers, and tax collectors were likely to seem mere troublesome outsiders, to be neglected whenever possible and obeyed only as far as

* KSHAH tree uh z
† VYS yuh z
‡ rihg VAY dah

necessary. The fragile character of most Indian states resulted in large part from this fact. A striking absence of information about war and government is characteristic of all early Indian history; and this, too, presumably reflects Indian peoples' characteristic emotional disengagement from the state and from politics. . . .

The Vedas and Brahmanas

Our knowledge of Aryan religion derives from the Vedas. The Vedas, used as handbooks of religious ritual, consist of songs that were recited aloud during sacrifices, together with other passages instructing the priests what to do during the ceremony. In course of time, the language of the Vedas became more or less unintelligible, even to priests. A great effort was thereupon made to preserve details of accent and pronunciation, by insisting on exact memorization of texts from master to pupil across the generations. Every jot and tittle of the inherited verses was felt to matter, since a misplaced line or mispronounced word could nullify a whole sacrifice and might even provoke divine displeasure.

Preoccupation with correctness of detail speedily shifted emphasis from the gods of the Aryan pantheon to the act of worship and invocation itself. Aryan priests may also have learned about magical powers claimed by priests of the Indus civilization. At any rate, some Brahmans began to argue that by performing rituals correctly they could actually compel the gods to grant what was asked of them. Indeed, proper sacrifice and invocation created the world of gods and men anew, and stabilized afresh the critical relation between natural and supernatural reality. In such a view, the importance and personalities of the separate gods shrank to triviality, while the power and skill of the priesthood was greatly magnified. These extravagant priestly claims were freely put forward in texts called Brahmanas. These were cast in the form of commentaries on the Vedas, purportedly explaining what the older texts really meant, but often changing meanings in the process.

The Upanishads and Mysticism

Priestly claims to exercise authority over gods and men were never widely accepted in ancient India. Chiefs and warriors might be a bit wary of priestly magic, but they were not eager to cede to the priests the primacy claimed by the Brahmanas. Humbler ranks of society also objected to priestly presumption. This is proved by the fact that a rival type of piety took hold in India and soon came to constitute the most distinctive element in the whole religious tradition of the land. Another body of oral literature, the Upanishads,* constitutes our evidence of this religious development. The Upanishads are not systematic treatises nor do they agree in all details. Yet they do express a general consensus on important points.

First of all, the Upanishads conceive the end of religious life in a radically new way. Instead of seeking riches, health, and long life, a wise and holy man strives merely to escape the endless round of rebirth. Success allows his soul to dissolve into the All from whence it had come, triumphantly transcending the suffering, pain, and imperfection of existence.

In the second place, holiness and release from the cycle of rebirths were attained not by obedience to priests nor by observance of ceremonies. The truly holy man had no need of intermediaries and, for that matter, no need of gods. Instead, by a process of self-discipline, meditation, asceticism, and withdrawal from the ordinary concerns of daily life, the successful religious athlete might attain a mystic vision of Truth—a vision which left the seer purged and happy. The nature and content of the mystic vision could never be expressed in words. It revealed Truth by achieving an identity between the individual soul and the Soul of the universe. Such an experience, surpassing human understanding and ordinary language, constituted a foretaste of the ultimate bliss of self-annihilation in the All, which was the final goal of wise and holy life. . . .

While India worked its way toward the definition of a new and distinctive civilization on one flank of the ancient Middle East, on its other flank another new civilization was also emerging: the Greek. The principal stages of early Greek history closely resemble what we know or can surmise about Indian development. But the end product differed fundamentally. The Greeks put political organization into territorial states above all other bases of human association, and attempted to explain the world and man not in terms of mystic illumination but through laws of nature. Thus despite a similar start, when fierce "tamers of horses"—like those of whom Homer[1] later sang—overran priest-led agricultural societies, the Indian and Greek styles of civilization diverged strikingly by 500 B.C.E. . . .

The self-governing city-states created by Greeks on the coast of Asia Minor had . . . great . . . importance in world history. For by inventing the city-state or *polis* (hence our word "politics"), the Greeks of Ionia established the prototype from which the whole Western world derived its penchant for political organization into territorially defined sovereign

---

* oo PAH nee shahdz
[1] Greek poet c. 800 B.C.E.; author of *The Iliad* and *The Odyssey*. [Ed.]

units, i.e., into states. The supremacy of territoriality over all other forms of human association is neither natural nor inevitable, as the Indian caste principle may remind us. . . .

Dominance of the Polis in Greek Culture

So powerful and compelling was the psychological pull of the polis that almost every aspect of Greek cultural activity was speedily caught up in and — as it were — digested by the new master institution of Greek civilization. Religion, art, literature, philosophy, took shape or acquired a new accent through their relationship with the all-engulfing object of the citizens' affection. . . .

Despite the general success of the polis ordering of things, a few individuals fretted over the logical inconsistencies of Greek religion and traditional world view. As trade developed, opportunities to learn about the wisdom of the East multiplied. Inquiring Greeks soon discovered that among the priestly experts of the Middle East there was no agreement about such fundamental questions as how the world was created or why the planets periodically checked their forward movement through the heavens and went backward for a while before resuming their former motion. It was in Ionia that men first confronted this sort of question systematically enough to bother recording their views. These, the first philosophers, sought to explain the phenomena of the world by imaginative exercise of their power of reason. Finding conflicting and unsupported stories about the gods to be unsatisfactory, they took the drastic step of omitting the gods entirely, and boldly substituted natural law instead as the ruling force of the universe. To be sure, the Ionian philosophers did not agree among themselves when they sought to describe how the laws of nature worked, and their naive efforts to explain an ever wider range of phenomena did not meet with much success.

Nevertheless, their attempts at using speculative reason to explain the nature of things marked a major turning point in human intellectual development. The Ionian concept of a universe ruled not by the whim of some divine personality but by an impersonal and unchangeable law has never since been forgotten. Throughout the subsequent history of European and Middle Eastern thought, this distinctively Greek view of the nature of things stood in persistent and fruitful tension with the older, Middle Eastern theistic explanation of the universe. Particular thinkers, reluctant to abandon either position entirely, have sought to reconcile the omnipotence of the divine will with the unchangeability of natural law by means of the most various arguments. Since, however, the two views are as logically incompatible with one another as were the myths from which the Ionian philosophers started, no formulation or reconciliation ever attained lasting and universal consent. Men always had to start over again to reshape for themselves a more satisfactory metaphysic and theology. Here, therefore, lay a growing point for all subsequent European thought which has not yet been exhausted.

Indeed, the recent successes of natural science seem to have vindicated the Ionian concept of natural law in ways and with a complexity that would have utterly amazed Thales* (d. c. 546 B.C.E.) or any of his successors, who merely voiced what turned out to be amazingly lucky guesses. How did they do it? It seems plausible to suggest that the Ionians hit upon the notion of natural law by simply projecting the tight little world of the polis upon the universe. For it was a fact that the polis was regulated by law, not by the personal will or whim of a ruler. If such invisible abstractions could govern human behavior and confine it to certain roughly predictable paths of action, why could not similar laws control the natural world? To such a question, it appears, the Ionians gave an affirmative answer, and in doing so gave a distinctive cast to all subsequent Greek and European thought.

Limitations of the Polis

It would be a mistake to leave the impression that all facets of Greek life fitted smoothly and easily into the polis frame. The busy public world left scant room for the inwardness of personal experience. Striving for purification, for salvation, for holiness, which found such ample expression in the Indian cultural setting, was almost excluded. Yet the Greeks were not immune from such impulses. Through the ancient mystery religions, as well as through such an association as the "Order" founded by Pythagoras,† the famous mathematician and mystic (d. c. 507 B.C.E.), they sought to meet these needs. But when such efforts took organized form, a fundamental incompatibility between the claims of the polis to the unqualified loyalty of every citizen and the pursuit of personal holiness quickly became apparent. This was illustrated by the stormy history of the Pythagorean Order. Either the organized seekers after holiness captured the polis, as happened for a while in the city of Croton in southern Italy, or the magistrates of the polis persecuted the Order, as happened in Pythagoras' old age. There seemed no workable ground of compromise in this, the earliest recorded instance of conflict between church and state in Western history.

* THAY leez
† py THAG uhr ahs

The fundamental difference between Greek and Indian institutions as shaped by about 500 B.C.E. was made apparent by this episode. The loose federation of cultures allowed by the caste principle in India experienced no difficulty at all in accommodating organized seekers after holiness such as the communities of Buddhist monks. By contrast, the exclusive claim upon the citizens' time, effort, and affection which had been staked out by the Greek polis allowed no sort of corporate rival.

Enormous energies were tapped by the polis. A wider segment of the total population was engaged in cultural and political action than had been possible in any earlier civilized society, and the brilliant flowering of classical Greek civilization was the consequence. Yet the very intensity of the political tie excluded ranges of activity and sensitivity that were not compatible with a territorial organization of human groupings, and sowed seeds of civil strife between the Greek cities which soon proved disastrous. But every achievement involves a surrender of alternatives: It is merely that the Greek achievement, by its very magnitude, casts an unusually clear light upon what it also excluded.

2

The Rig Veda: Sacrifice as Creation, c. 1500–500 B.C.E.

As McNeill discusses in the previous selection, the Vedas* are the writings of the ancient Brahman priests in India. They cover a wide variety of religious subjects and concerns: ritual, sacrifice, hymns, healing, incantations, allegories, philosophy, and the problems of everyday life. In general, the earliest Vedas (like the Rig Veda) focus more on the specifics of ritual and sacrifice, reflecting the needs and instructions of the priests more than the Upanishads. The last of the Vedas (like the Upanishads) are more philosophical and speculative.

This selection is from the Rig Veda. What happened when Purusha was sacrificed? What is the meaning of this first sacrifice? How does this story support the role of priests?

THINKING HISTORICALLY

Consider how this primary source supports the division of Indian society into castes, as McNeill discusses in the previous selection. How does this story suggest that the people who wrote the Rig Veda

* VAY duz

Source: "Rig Veda," 10.90, in *Sources of Indian Tradition*, 2nd ed., ed. and rev. Ainslie T. Embree (New York: Columbia University Press, 1988), 18–19.

thought the division of society into four castes was pretty basic? Can you deduce from this source which of the four castes was most likely the originator of the story? Does this support anything else that McNeill said in his interpretation?

Thousand-headed Purusha, thousand-eyed, thousand-footed—he, having pervaded the earth on all sides, still extends ten fingers beyond it.

Purusha alone is all this—whatever has been and whatever is going to be. Further, he is the lord of immortality and also of what grows on account of food.

Such is his greatness; greater, indeed, than this is Purusha. All creatures constitute but one-quarter of him, his three-quarters are the immortal in the heaven.

With his three-quarters did Purusha rise up; one-quarter of him again remains here. With it did he variously spread out on all sides over what eats and what eats not.

From him was Virāj born, from Virāj the evolved Purusha. He, being born, projected himself behind the earth as also before it.

When the gods performed the sacrifice with Purusha as the oblation, then the spring was its clarified butter, the summer the sacrificial fuel, and the autumn the oblation.

The sacrificial victim, namely, Purusha, born at the very beginning, they sprinkled with sacred water upon the sacrificial grass. With him as oblation, the gods performed the sacrifice, and also the Sādhyas [a class of semidivine beings] and the rishis [ancient seers].

From that wholly offered sacrificial oblation were born the verses [ṛc] and the sacred chants; from it were born the meters [chandas]; the sacrificial formula was born from it.

From it horses were born and also those animals who have double rows [i.e., upper and lower] of teeth; cows were born from it, from it were born goats and sheep.

When they divided Purusha, in how many different portions did they arrange him? What became of his mouth, what of his two arms? What were his two thighs and his two feet called?

His mouth became the brāhman; his two arms were made into the rajanya; his two thighs the vaishyas; from his two feet the shūdra was born.

The moon was born from the mind, from the eye the sun was born; from the mouth Indra and Agni, from the breath [prāna] the wind [vāyu] was born.

From the navel was the atmosphere created, from the head the heaven issued forth; from the two feet was born the earth and the quarters (the cardinal directions) from the ear. Thus did they fashion the worlds.

Seven were the enclosing sticks in this sacrifice, thrice seven were the fire-sticks made when the gods, performing the sacrifice, bound down Purusha, the sacrificial victim.

With this sacrificial oblation did the gods offer the sacrifice. These were the first norms [*dharma*] of sacrifice. These greatnesses reached to the sky wherein live the ancient Sādhyas and gods.

3

The Upanishads: Karma and Reincarnation, c. 800–400 B.C.E.

The idea of karma (cause and effect, appropriate consequences) appears in the earliest Upanishads.* Karma meant: "As you sow, so shall you reap." Good karma would be enhanced; bad karma would lead to more bad karma. The universe was a system of complete justice in which all people got what they deserved. The idea that the soul might be reborn in another body may have been an even older idea, but in the Upanishads it combined easily with the idea of karma. That a good soul was reborn in a higher life, or a bad soul in a lower, was perhaps a more material, less subtle, version of the justice of karma. The idea of reincarnation, or the transmigration of souls, united justice with caste.

What effect would these ideas have on people? In what ways would these ideas aid people in gaining a sense of power over their lives? How might these ideas be tools of control? What does "morality" mean in this tradition?

THINKING HISTORICALLY

How does the idea of karma presented in this primary source support McNeill's interpretation of the importance of the caste system in India? Would the idea of reincarnation make caste organization stronger or weaker?

* OO PAH nee shahdz

Source: *Brihad Aranyaka*, IV:4:5–6, in *The Thirteen Principal Upanishads*, ed. and trans. R. E. Hume (Bombay: Oxford University Press, 1954), 140–41. *Chandogya*, V:10:7, in Hume, quoted in *The Hindu Tradition: Readings in Oriental Thought*, ed. Ainslie T. Embree (New York: Vintage, 1966, copyright renewed 1994), 62–63.

According as one acts, according as one conducts himself, so does he become. The doer of good becomes good. The doer of evil becomes evil. One becomes virtuous by virtuous action, bad by bad action.

But people say: "A person is made not of acts, but of desires only." In reply to this I say: As is his desire, such is his resolve; as is his resolve, such the action he performs; what action (*karma*) he performs, that he procures for himself.

On this point there is this verse:—

Where one's mind is attached—the inner self
Goes thereto with action, being attached to it alone.

> *Obtaining the end of his action,*
> *Whatever he does in this world,*
> *He comes again from that world*
> *To this world of action.*

—So the man who desires.

Now the man who does not desire.—He who is without desire, who is freed from desire, whose desire is satisfied, whose desire is the Soul—his breaths do not depart. Being very Brahman, he goes to Brahman.

Accordingly, those who are of pleasant conduct here—the prospect is, indeed, that they will enter a pleasant womb, either the womb of a Brahman, or the womb of a Kshatriya, or the womb of a Vaishya. But those who are of stinking conduct here—the prospect is, indeed, that they will enter a stinking womb, either the womb of a dog, or the womb of a swine, or the womb of an outcaste (*caṇḍāla*).

4

The Upanishads: Brahman and Atman, c. 800–400 B.C.E.

In this selection *Brahman* does not refer to priests or to a specific god. In the late Vedas, or Upanishads, Brahman is all divinity, and all is Brahman. Even the individual soul or *atman* can be one with the universal Brahman, "as the Father of Svetaketu demonstrates to his son through the examples of a banyan tree and salt water." How would ideas like these challenge the caste system?

Source: *Chandogya Upanishad*, in *The Upanishads*, trans. Juan Mascaro (Harmondsworth: Penguin Press, 1965), 113–14.

THINKING HISTORICALLY

McNeill suggests that the Upanishads expressed a religious vision that challenged the power of priests, sacrifice, and caste. How does this selection from the Upanishads support that interpretation?

Great is the Gayatri, the most sacred verse of the Vedas; but how much greater is the Infinity of Brahman! A quarter of his being is this whole vast universe: the other three quarters are his heaven of Immortality. (3.12.5)

There is a Light that shines beyond all things on earth, beyond us all, beyond the heavens, beyond the highest, the very highest heavens. This is the Light that shines in our heart. (3.13.7)

All this universe is in the truth Brahman. He is the beginning and end and life of all. As such, in silence, give unto him adoration.

Man in truth is made of faith. As his faith is in this life, so he becomes in the beyond: with faith and vision let him work.

There is a Spirit that is mind and life, light and truth and vast spaces. He contains all works and desires and all perfumes and all tastes. He enfolds the whole universe, and in silence is loving to all.

This is the Spirit that is in my heart, smaller than a grain of rice, or a grain of barley, or a grain of mustard-seed, or a grain of canary-seed, or the kernel of a grain of canary-seed. This is the Spirit that is in my heart, greater than the earth, greater than the sky, greater than heaven itself, greater than all these worlds.

He contains all works and desires and all perfumes and all tastes. He enfolds the whole universe and in silence is loving to all. This is the Spirit that is in my heart, this is Brahman. (3.14)

"Bring me a fruit from this banyan tree."
"Here it is, father."
"Break it."
"It is broken, Sir."
"What do you see in it?"
"Very small seeds, Sir."
"Break one of them, my son."
"It is broken, Sir."
"What do you see in it?"
"Nothing at all, Sir."

Then his father spoke to him: "My son, from the very essence in the seed which you cannot see comes in truth this vast banyan tree.

Believe me, my son, an invisible and subtle essence is the Spirit of the whole universe. That is Reality. That is Atman. THOU ART THAT."

"Explain more to me, father," said Svetaketu.

"So be it, my son.

Place this salt in water and come to me tomorrow morning."

Svetaketu did as he was commanded, and in the morning his father said to him: "Bring me the salt you put into the water last night."

Svetaketu looked into the water, but could not find it, for it had dissolved.

His father then said: "Taste the water from this side. How is it?"

"It is salt."

"Taste it from the middle. How is it?"

"It is salt."

"Taste it from that side. How is it?"

"It is salt."

"Look for the salt again and come again to me."

The son did so, saying: "I cannot see the salt. I only see water."

His father then said: "In the same way, O my son, you cannot see the Spirit. But in truth he is here.

An invisible and subtle essence is the Spirit of the whole universe. That is Reality. That is Truth. THOU ART THAT." (6.12–14)

5

The Bhagavad Gita: Caste and Self,
c. 1500 B.C.E.

The *Bhagavad Gita** is the best-known work in Hindu religious literature. It is part of a larger epic called the *Mahabharata*,[†] a story of two
feuding families that may have had its origins in India as early as
1500 B.C.E. The *Bhagavad Gita* is a philosophical interlude that inter-
rupts the story just before the great battle between the two families.
It poses some fundamental questions about the nature of life, death,
and proper religious behavior. It begins as the leader of one of the
battling armies, Arjuna, asks why he should fight his friends and relatives on the other side. The answer comes from none other than the
god Krishna, who has taken the form of Arjuna's charioteer.

What is Krishna's answer? What will happen to the people Arjuna
kills? What will happen to Arjuna? What would happen to Arjuna if
he refused to fight the battle? What does this selection tell you about
Hindu ideas of life, death, and the self?

* BUH guh vahd GEE tuh
† mah hah BAH rah tah

Source: *Bhagavad Gita*, trans. Barbara Stoler Miller (New York: Bantam Books, 1986), 31–34, 52, 86–87.

In some ways this work reconciles the conflict in the Upanishads between caste and *atman*. Performing the *dharma*, or duty, of caste is seen as a liberating act. Would the acceptance of this story support or challenge the caste system? Does this primary source support McNeill's interpretation of Indian society?

Lord Krishna

You grieve for those beyond grief,
and you speak words of insight;
but learned men do not grieve
for the dead or the living.

Never have I not existed,
nor you, nor these kings;
and never in the future
shall we cease to exist.

Just as the embodied self
enters childhood, youth, and old age,
so does it enter another body;
this does not confound a steadfast man.

Contacts with matter make us feel
heat and cold, pleasure and pain.
Arjuna, you must learn to endure
fleeting things—they come and go!

When these cannot torment a man,
when suffering and joy are equal
for him and he has courage,
he is fit for immortality.

Nothing of nonbeing comes to be,
nor does being cease to exist;
the boundary between these two
is seen by men who see reality.

Indestructible is the presence
that pervades all this;
no one can destroy
this unchanging reality.

Our bodies are known to end,
but the embodied self is enduring,

indestructible, and immeasurable;
therefore, Arjuna, fight the battle!

He who thinks this self a killer
and he who thinks it killed,
both fail to understand;
it does not kill, nor is it killed.

It is not born,
it does not die;
having been,
it will never not be;
unborn, enduring,
constant, and primordial,
it is not killed
when the body is killed.

Arjuna, when a man knows the self
to be indestructible, enduring, unborn,
unchanging, how does he kill
or cause anyone to kill?

As a man discards
worn-out clothes
to put on new
and different ones,
so the embodied self
discards
its worn-out bodies
to take on other new ones.

Weapons do not cut it,
fire does not burn it,
waters do not wet it,
wind does not wither it.

It cannot be cut or burned;
it cannot be wet or withered;
it is enduring, all-pervasive,
fixed, immovable, and timeless.

It is called unmanifest,
inconceivable, and immutable;
since you know that to be so,
you should not grieve!

If you think of its birth
and death as ever-recurring,

then too, Great Warrior,
you have no cause to grieve!

Death is certain for anyone born,
and birth is certain for the dead;
since the cycle is inevitable,
you have no cause to grieve!

Creatures are unmanifest in origin,
manifest in the midst of life,
and unmanifest again in the end.
Since this is so, why do you lament!

Rarely someone
sees it,
rarely another
speaks it,
rarely anyone
hears it—
even hearing it,
no one really knows it.

The self embodied in the body
of every being is indestructible;
you have no cause to grieve
for all these creatures, Arjuna!

Look to your own duty;
do not tremble before it;
nothing is better for a warrior
than a battle of sacred duty.

The doors of heaven open
for warriors who rejoice
to have a battle like this
thrust on them by chance.

If you fail to wage this war
of sacred duty,
you will abandon your own duty
and fame only to gain evil.

People will tell
of your undying shame,
and for a man of honor
shame is worse than death.

[In this next passage from the *Bhagavad Gita*, Krishna reveals a deeper
meaning to his message to Arjuna. Not only must Arjuna act like a

warrior because that is his caste, but he must also act without regard to the consequences of his action. What does Krishna seem to mean by this? How does one do "nothing at all even when he engages in action"?]

Abandoning attachment to fruits
of action, always content, independent,
he does nothing at all
even when he engages in action.

He incurs no guilt if he has no hope,
restrains his thought and himself,
abandons possessions,
and performs actions with his body only.

Content with whatever comes by chance,
beyond dualities, free from envy,
impartial to failure and success,
he is not bound even when he acts.

When a man is unattached and free,
his reason deep in knowledge,
acting only in sacrifice,
his action is wholly dissolved.

When devoted men sacrifice
to other deities with faith,
they sacrifice to me, Arjuna,
however aberrant the rites.

I am the enjoyer
and the lord of all sacrifices;
they do not know me in reality,
and so they fail.

Votaries of the gods go to the gods,
ancestor-worshippers go to the ancestors,
those who propitiate ghosts go to them,
and my worshippers go to me.

The leaf or flower or fruit or water
that he offers with devotion,
I take from the man of self-restraint
in response to his devotion.

Whatever you do—what you take,
what you offer, what you give,
what penances you perform—
do as an offering to me, Arjuna!

You will be freed from the bonds of action,
from the fruit of fortune and misfortune;
armed with the discipline of renunciation,
your self liberated, you will join me.

I am impartial to all creatures,
and no one is hateful or dear to me;
but men devoted to me are in me,
and I am within them.

If he is devoted solely to me,
even a violent criminal
must be deemed a man of virtue,
for his resolve is right.

His spirit quickens to sacred duty,
and he finds eternal peace;
Arjuna, know that no one
devoted to me is lost.

If they rely on me, Arjuna,
women, commoners, men of low rank,
even men born in the womb of evil,
reach the highest way.

How easy it is then for holy priests
and devoted royal sages—
in this transient world of sorrow,
devote yourself to me!

Keep me in your mind and devotion,
sacrifice to me, bow to me,
discipline yourself toward me,
and you will reach me!

ARISTOTLE

The Athenian Constitution:
Territorial Sovereignty, c. 330 B.C.E.

The process of establishing political authority based on the territorial
state was not achieved at one particular moment in history. Much of
Greek history (indeed, much of world history since the Greeks) witnessed
the struggle of territorial authority over family, blood, and kinship ties.

The process of replacing kinship and tribal alliances with a territorial "politics of place" can, however, be seen in the constitutional reforms attributed to the Athenian noble Cleisthenes* in 508 B.C.E.
Cleisthenes was not a democrat; his reform of Athenian politics was
probably intended to win popular support for himself in his struggle
with other noble families. But the inadvertent results of his reforms
were to establish the necessary basis for democracy: a territorial state
in which commoners as citizens had a stake in government.
A description of those reforms is contained in a document called
"The Athenian Constitution," discovered in Egypt only a hundred
years ago and thought to have been written by the philosopher Aristotle (384–322 B.C.E.) around 330 B.C.E.

Modern scholars doubt that Cleisthenes created the *demes*† (local
neighborhoods) that were the basis of his reforms. Some existed earlier. But by making the *demes* the root of political organization, he undoubtedly undercut the power of dominant families. As *demes* were
given real authority, power shifted from relatives to residents. Also, as
Cleisthenes expanded the number of citizens, the *deme* structure became more "*deme*-ocratic."

Notice how the constitutional reform combined a sense of local,
residential identity with citizenship in a larger city-state by tying city,
country, and coastal *demes* together in each new "tribe." Why were
these new tribes less "tribal" than the old ones? What would be the
modern equivalent of these new tribes? Was democracy possible
without a shift from kinship to territorial or civic identity?

THINKING HISTORICALLY

Territorial sovereignty is something we take for granted. It means the
law of the land. Regardless of the beliefs of our parents or ancestors,
we obey the law of the territory. In the United States, we are bound

* KLYS thuh neez
† deems

Source: Aristotle, "The Athenian Constitution," in *Aristotle, Politics, and the Athenian Constitution*, trans. John Warrington (London: David Campbell Publishers, 1959).

to observe the law of the nation and the law of the state and munici-
pal ordinances. We do not take our own family law with us when we
move from one town or state or country to another. When we go to
Japan, we are bound by Japanese law, even if we are not Japanese. In
the modern world, sovereignty, ultimate authority, is tied to territory.
Because this is so obvious to us in modern society, it is difficult to
imagine that this was not always the case.

Historians have to acknowledge that things they and their societies
take for granted may not have always existed; rather, they have developed throughout history. McNeill's interpretation of the essential difference between India and Greece makes such a leap. Many people
have pointed out the unique Athenian invention of democracy. But
McNeill recognized that the Athenians invented democracy because
they had already invented something more fundamental — territorial
sovereignty, politics, government, citizenship. How does "The Athenian Constitution" support McNeill's interpretation?

The overthrow of the Peisistratid tyranny left the city split into two factions under Isagoras and Cleisthenes respectively. The former, a son of
Tisander, had supported the tyrants; the latter was an Alcmaeonid. Cleisthenes, defeated in the political clubs, won over the people by offering
citizen rights to the masses. Thereupon Isagoras, who had fallen behind
in the race for power, once more invoked the help of his friend Cleomenes
and persuaded him to exorcise the pollution; that is, to expel the Alcmaeonidae, who were believed still to be accursed. Cleisthenes accordingly withdrew from Attica with a small band of adherents, while
Cleomenes proceeded to drive out seven hundred Athenian families. The
Spartan next attempted to dissolve the Council and to set up Isagoras
with three hundred of his supporters as the sovereign authority. The
Council, however, resisted; the populace flew to arms; and Cleomenes
with Isagoras and all their forces took refuge in the Acropolis, to which
the people laid siege and blockaded them for two days. On the third day
it was agreed that Cleomenes and his followers should withdraw. Cleisthenes and his fellow exiles were recalled.

The people were now in control, and Cleisthenes, their leader, was
recognized as head of the popular party. This was not surprising; for the
Alcmaeonidae were largely responsible for the overthrow of the tyrants,
with whom they had been in conflict during most of their rule.

. . . The people, therefore, had every grounds for confidence in Cleisthenes. Accordingly, three years after the destruction of the tyranny, in the
archonship of Isagoras, he used his influence as leader of the popular party
to carry out a number of reforms. (A) He divided the population into ten
tribes instead of the old four. His purpose here was to intermix the members
of the tribes so that more persons might have civic rights; and hence the

advice "not to notice the tribes," which was tendered to those who would examine the lists of the clans. (B) He increased the membership of the Council from 400 to 500, each tribe now contributing fifty instead of one hundred as before. His reason for not organizing the people into *twelve* tribes was to avoid the necessity of using the existing division into trittyes, which would have meant failing to regroup the population on a satisfactory basis. (C) He divided the country into thirty portions—ten urban and suburban, ten coastal, and ten inland—each containing a certain number of demes. These portions he called trittyes, and assigned three of them by lot to each tribe in such a way that each should have one portion in each of the three localities just mentioned. Furthermore, those who lived in any given deme were to be reckoned fellow demesmen. This arrangement was intended to protect new citizens from being shown up as such by the habitual use of family names. Men were to be officially described by the names of their demes; and it is thus that Athenians still speak of one another. Demes had now supplanted the old naucraries,[1] and Cleisthenes therefore appointed Demarchs whose duties were identical with those of the former Naucrari. He named some of the demes from their localities, and others from their supposed founders; for certain areas no longer corresponded to named localities. On the other hand, he allowed everyone to retain his family and clan and religious rites according to ancestral custom. He also gave the ten tribes names which the Delphic oracle had chosen out of one hundred selected national heroes.

7

THUCYDIDES

The Funeral Oration of Pericles, 431 B.C.E.

The most famous statement of Greek loyalty to the city-state is the following account of the funeral speech of the Athenian statesman Pericles in the classic *History of the Peloponnesian War* by the ancient historian Thucydides.* The speech eulogized the Athenian soldiers who had died in the war against Sparta in 431 B.C.E.

---

[1] Forty-eight subdivisions of the old four tribes, each responsible for one galley of the Athenian navy. [Ed.]

* thoo SIH duh deez

Source: *The History of Thucydides*, Book II, trans. Benjamin Jowett (New York: Tandy-Thomas, 1909).

Notice the high value placed on loyalty to Athens and service to the state. Here is the origin of patriotism. Pericles also insists that Athens is a democratic city-state. He praises Athenian freedom as well as public service. Could there be a conflict between personal freedom and public service? If so, how would Pericles resolve such a conflict? You might also notice that Pericles is praising Athenian citizen-soldiers who died defending not their home but the empire. Could there be a conflict between Athenian democracy and the ambitious empire?

THINKING HISTORICALLY

Are the sentiments that Pericles expresses a consequence of territorial sovereignty? Could such sentiments be expressed in defense of caste? Notice how Pericles speaks of ancestors, family, and parents. Do his words suggest any potential conflict between family ties and loyalty to the state? How is Pericles able to convince his audience of the priority of the state over kinship ties? How does this primary source provide evidence for McNeill's interpretation?

I will speak first of our ancestors, for it is right and seemly that now, when we are lamenting the dead, a tribute should be paid to their memory. There has never been a time when they did not inhabit this land, which by their valour they have handed down from generation to generation, and we have received from them a free state. But if they were worthy of praise, still more were our fathers, who added to their inheritance, and after many a struggle transmitted to us their sons this great empire. And we ourselves assembled here today, who are still most of us in the vigour of life, have carried the work of improvement further, and have richly endowed our city with all things, so that she is sufficient for herself both in peace and war. Of the military exploits by which our various possessions were acquired, or of the energy with which we or our fathers drove back the tide of war, Hellenic or Barbarian [non-Greek], I will not speak: for the tale would be long and is familiar to you. But before I praise the dead, I should like to point out by what principles of action we rose to power, and under what institutions and through what manner of life our empire became great. For I conceive that such thoughts are not unsuited to the occasion, and that this numerous assembly of citizens and strangers may profitably listen to them.

Our form of government does not enter into rivalry with the institutions of others. We do not copy our neighbours, but are an example to them. It is true that we are called a democracy, for the administration is in the hands of the many and not of the few. But while the law secures equal justice to all alike in their private disputes, the claim of excellence is also recognised; and when a citizen is in any way distinguished, he is preferred to the public service, not as a matter of privilege, but as the reward of merit. Neither is poverty a bar, but a man may benefit his country whatever be the obscurity of his condition. There is no exclusiveness in our public life, and in our private intercourse we are not suspicious of one another, nor angry with our neighbour if he does what he likes; we do not put on sour looks at him which, though harmless, are not pleasant. While we are thus unconstrained in our private intercourse, a spirit of reverence pervades our public acts; we are prevented from doing wrong by respect for the authorities and for the laws, having an especial regard to those which are ordained for the protection of the injured as well as to those unwritten laws which bring upon the transgressor of them the reprobation of the general sentiment.

And we have not forgotten to provide for our weary spirits many relaxations from toil; we have regular games and sacrifices throughout the year; our homes are beautiful and elegant; and the delight which we daily feel in all these things helps to banish melancholy. Because of the greatness of our city the fruits of the whole earth flow in upon us; so that we enjoy the goods of other countries as freely as of our own.

Then, again, our military training is in many respects superior to that of our adversaries. Our city is thrown open to the world, and we never expel a foreigner or prevent him from seeing or learning anything of which the secret if revealed to an enemy might profit him. We rely not upon management or trickery, but upon our own hearts and hands. And in the matter of education, whereas they from early youth are always undergoing laborious exercises which are to make them brave, we live at ease, and yet are equally ready to face the perils which they face. And here is the proof. . . .

If then we prefer to meet danger with a light heart but without laborious training, and with a courage which is gained by habit and not enforced by law, are we not greatly the gainers? Since we do not anticipate the pain, although, when the hour comes, we can be as brave as those who never allow themselves to rest; and thus too our city is equally admirable in peace and in war. For we are lovers of the beautiful, yet simple in our tastes, and we cultivate the mind without loss of manliness. Wealth we employ, not for talk and ostentation, but when there is a real use for it. To avow poverty with us is no disgrace; the true disgrace is in doing nothing to avoid it. An Athenian citizen does not neglect the state because he takes care of his own household; and even those of us who are engaged in business have a very fair idea of politics. We alone regard a man who takes no interest in public affairs, not as a harmless, but as a useless character; and if few of us are originators, we are all sound judges of policy. The great impediment to action is, in our opinion, not discussion, but the want of that knowledge which is gained by discussion preparatory to action. For we have a peculiar power of thinking before we act and of acting too, whereas other men are courageous from ignorance but hesitate upon reflection. And they are surely to be esteemed the bravest spirits who, having the clearest sense both of the pains and pleasures of life, do not on that account shrink from danger. In doing good, again, we are unlike others; we make our friends by conferring, not by receiving favours. Now he who confers a favour is the firmer friend, because he would fain by kindness keep alive the memory of an obligation; but the recipient is colder in his feelings, because he knows that in requiting another's generosity he will not be winning gratitude but only paying a debt. We alone do good to our neighbours, not upon a calculation of interest, but in the confidence of freedom and in a frank and fearless spirit.

To sum up: I say that Athens is the school of Hellas, and that the individual Athenian in his own person seems to have the power of adapting himself to the most varied forms of action with the utmost versatility and grace. This is no passing and idle word, but truth and fact; and the assertion is verified by the position to which these qualities have raised the state. For in the hour of trial Athens alone among her contemporaries is superior to the report of her. No enemy who comes against her is indignant at the reverses which he sustains at the hands of such a city; no subject complains that his masters are unworthy of him. And we shall assuredly not be without witnesses; there are mighty monuments of our power which will make us the wonder of this and of succeeding ages; we shall not need the praises of Homer or of any other panegyrist whose poetry may please for the moment, although his representation of the facts will not bear the light of day. For we have compelled every land and every sea to open a path for our valour, and have everywhere planted eternal memorials of our friendship and of our enmity. Such is the city of whose sake these men nobly fought and died; they could not bear the thought that she might be taken from them; and every one of us who survive should gladly toil on her behalf.

I have dwelt upon the greatness of Athens because I want to show you that we are contending for a higher prize than those who enjoy none of these privileges, and to establish by manifest proof the merit of these men whom I am now commemorating. Their loftiest praise has been already spoken. For in magnifying the city I have magnified them, and men like them whose virtues made her glorious. And of how few Hellenes can it be said as of them, that their deeds when weighed in the balance have been found equal to their fame! . . . They resigned to hope their unknown chance of happiness; but in the fact of death they resolved to rely upon themselves alone. And when the moment came they were minded to resist and suffer, rather than to fly and save their lives; they ran away from the word of dishonour, but on the battlefield their feet stood fast, and in an instant, at the height of their fortune, they passed away from the scene, not of their fear, but of their glory.

Such was the end of these men; they were worthy of Athens, and the living need not desire to have a more heroic spirit, although they may pray for a less fatal issue. The value of such a spirit is not to be expressed in words. Any one can discourse to you forever about the advantages of a brave defence, which you know already. But instead of listening to him I would have you day by day fix your eyes upon the greatness of Athens, until you become filled with the love of her; and when you are impressed by the spectacle of her glory, reflect that this empire has been acquired by men who knew their duty and had the courage to do it, who in the hour of conflict had the fear of dishonour always present to them, and who, if ever they failed in an enterprise, would not allow their virtues to be lost to their country, but freely gave their lives to her as the fairest offering which they could present at her feast. The sacrifice which they collectively made was individually repaid to them; for they received again each one of himself a praise which grows not old, and the noblest of all sepulchres—I speak not of that in which their remains are laid, but of that in which their glory survives, and is proclaimed always and on every fitting occasion both in word and deed. For the whole earth is the sepulchre of famous men; not only are they commemorated by columns and inscriptions in their own country, but in foreign lands there dwells also an unwritten memorial of them, graven not on stone but in the hearts of men. Make them your examples, and, esteeming courage to be freedom and freedom to be happiness, do not weigh too nicely the perils of war. The unfortunate who has no hope of a change for the better has less reason to throw away his life than the prosperous who, if he survives, is always liable to a change for the worse, and to whom any accidental fall makes the most serious difference. To a man of spirit, cowardice and disaster coming together are far more bitter than death striking him unperceived at a time when he is full of courage and animated by the general hope.

Wherefore I do not now commiserate the parents of the dead who stand here; I would rather comfort them. You know that your life has been passed amid manifold vicissitudes; and that they may be deemed fortunate who have gained most honour, whether an honourable death like theirs, or an honourable sorrow like yours, and whose days have been so ordered that the term of their happiness is likewise the term of their life. I know how hard it is to make you feel this, when the good fortune of others will too often remind you of the gladness which once lightened your hearts. And sorrow is felt at the want of those blessings, not which a man never knew, but which were a part of his life before they were taken from him. Some of you are of an age at which they may hope to have other children, and they ought to bear their sorrow better; not only will the children who may hereafter be born make them forget their own lost ones, but the city will be doubly a gainer. She will not be left desolate, and she will be safer. For a man's counsel cannot have equal weight or worth, when he alone has no children to risk in the general danger. To those of you who have passed their prime, I say: Congratulate yourselves that you have been happy during the greater part of your days; remember that your life of sorrow will not last long, and be comforted by the glory of those who are gone. For the love of honour alone is ever young, and not riches, as some say, but honour is the delight of men when they are old and useless.

To you who are the sons and brothers of the departed, I see that the struggle to emulate them will be an arduous one. For all men praise the dead, and, however pre-eminent your virtue may be, hardly will you be thought, I do not say to equal, but even to approach them. The living have their rivals and detractors, but when a man is out of the way, the honour and good-will which he receives is unalloyed. And, if I am to speak of womanly virtues to those of you who will henceforth be widows, let me sum them up in one short admonition: To a woman not to show more weakness than is natural to her sex is a great glory, and not to be talked about for good or for evil among men.

I have paid the required tribute, in obedience to the law, making use of such fitting words as I had. The tribute of deeds has been paid in part; for the dead have been honourably interred, and it remains only that their children should be maintained at the public charge until they are grown up; this is the solid prize with which, as with a garland, Athens crowns her sons living and dead, after a struggle like theirs. For where the rewards of virtue are greatest, there the noblest citizens are enlisted in the service of the state. And now, when you have duly lamented, everyone his own dead, you may depart.

8

PLATO

The Republic, c. 360 B.C.E.

This selection is from one of the world's most famous books of philosophy. Two events dominated the early life of Plato (428–348 B.C.E.), turning him away from the public life he was expected to lead. Plato was born in the shadow of the Peloponnesian War, which ended with the defeat of Athens in his twenty-third year. Disillusioned with the postwar governments, especially the democracy that condemned his teacher Socrates in 399 B.C.E., Plato forsook the political arena for a life of contemplation.

Source: Plato, *The Republic of Plato*, trans. F. M. Cornford (London: Oxford University Press, 1941), 2–3, 177–79, 227–35.

Plato's philosophical books, called dialogues because of the way they develop ideas from discussion and debate, follow Plato's teacher Socrates around the city-state of Athens. Often they begin, like *The Republic*, with a view of Socrates and other Athenian citizens enjoying the public spaces and festivals of the city. Notice in this introduction how territorial sovereignty creates public places and public activities.

THINKING HISTORICALLY

Plato was neither a democrat nor politically active. Nevertheless, his life and his philosophy exemplify a commitment to the world of what McNeill calls "territorial sovereignty."

A primary source can support a particular viewpoint by espousing it, as Plato espouses the benefits of living in a territorial state or thinking about government. But a source can also provide clues about the society from which it comes. What clues in Plato's text show that his life and the lives of the people around him are shaped by the city-state?

Chapter 1

SOCRATES. I walked down to the Piraeus yesterday with Glaucon, the son of Ariston, to make my prayers to the goddess. As this was the first celebration of her festival, I wished also to see how the ceremony would be conducted. The Thracians, I thought, made as fine a show in the procession as our own people, though they did well enough. The prayers and the spectacle were over, and we were leaving to go back to the city, when from some way off Polemarchus, the son of Cephalus, caught sight of us starting homewards and sent his slave running to ask us to wait for him. The boy caught my garment from behind and gave me the message.

I turned around and asked where his master was.

There, he answered; coming up behind. Please wait.

Very well, said Glaucon; we will.

A minute later Polemarchus joined us, with Glaucon's brother, Adeimantus, and Niceratus, the son of Nicias, and some others who must have been at the procession.

Socrates, said Polemarchus, I do believe you are starting back to town and leaving us.

You have guessed right, I answered.

Well, he said, you see what a large party we are?

I do.

Unless you are more than a match for us, then, you must stay here.

Isn't there another alternative? said I; we might convince you that you must let us go.

How will you convince us, if we refuse to listen?

We cannot, said Glaucon.

Well, we shall refuse; make up your minds to that.

Here Adeimantus interposed: Don't you even know that in the evening there is going to be a torch-race on horseback in honour of the goddess?

On horseback! I exclaimed; that is something new. How will they do it? Are the riders going to race with torches and hand them on to one another?

Just so, said Polemarchus. Besides, there will be a festival lasting all night, which will be worth seeing. We will go out after dinner and look on. We shall find plenty of young men there and we can have a talk. So please stay, and don't disappoint us.

It looks as if we had better stay, said Glaucon.

Well, said I, if you think so, we will.

Accordingly, we went home with Polemarchus.

[At the home of Polemarchus, the participants meet a number of other old friends. After the usual greetings and gossip, the discussion begins in response to Socrates' question, "What is justice?"

Each of the participants poses an idea of justice that Socrates challenges. Then Socrates outlines an ideal state that would be based on absolute justice. In the following selection he is asked how this ideal could ever come about.

Aside from the specifics of Socrates' argument, notice the way in which public issues, for Socrates, are passionate personal concerns.]

Chapter 18

But really, Socrates, Glaucon continued, if you are allowed to go on like this, I am afraid you will forget all about the question you thrust aside some time ago; whether a society so constituted can ever come into existence, and if so, how. No doubt, if it did exist, all manner of good things would come about. I can even add some that you have passed over. Men who acknowledged one another as fathers, sons, or brothers and always used those names among themselves would never desert one another; so they would fight with unequalled bravery. And if their womenfolk went out with them to war, either in the ranks or drawn up in the rear to intimidate the enemy and act as a reserve in case of need, I am sure all this would make them invincible. At home, too, I can see many advantages you have not mentioned. But, since I admit that our commonwealth would have all these merits and any number more, if once it came into existence, you need not describe it in further detail. All we have now to do is to convince ourselves that it can be brought into being and how.

This is a very sudden onslaught, said I; you have no mercy on my shillyshallying. Perhaps you do not realize that, after I have barely escaped the first two waves, the third, which you are now bringing down upon me, is the most formidable of all. When you have seen what it is like and heard my reply, you will be ready to excuse the very natural fears which made me shrink from putting forward such a paradox for discussion.

The more you talk like that, he said, the less we shall be willing to let you off from telling us how this constitution can come into existence; so you had better waste no more time.

Well, said I, let me begin by reminding you that what brought us to this point was our inquiry into the nature of justice and injustice.

True; but what of that?

Merely this: suppose we do find out what justice is, are we going to demand that a man who is just shall have a character which exactly corresponds in every respect to the ideal of justice? Or shall we be satisfied if he comes as near to the ideal as possible and has in him a larger measure of that quality than the rest of the world?

That will satisfy me.

If so, when we set out to discover the essential nature of justice and injustice and what a perfectly just and a perfectly unjust man would be like, supposing them to exist, our purpose was to use them as ideal patterns: we were to observe the degree of happiness or unhappiness that each exhibited, and to draw the necessary inference that our own destiny would be like that of the one we most resembled. We did not set out to show that these ideals could exist in fact.

That is true.

Then suppose a painter had drawn an ideally beautiful figure complete to the last touch, would you think any the worse of him, if he could not show that a person as beautiful as that could exist?

No, I should not.

Well, we have been constructing in discourse the pattern of an ideal state. Is our theory any the worse, if we cannot prove it possible that a state so organized should be actually founded?

Surely not.

That, then, is the truth of the matter. But if, for your satisfaction, I am to do my best to show under what conditions our ideal would have the best chance of being realized, I must ask you once more to admit that the same principle applies here. Can theory ever be fully realized in practice? Is it not in the nature of things that action should come less close to truth than thought? People may not think so; but do you agree or not?

I do.

Then you must not insist upon my showing that this construction we have traced in thought could be reproduced in fact down to the last detail. You must admit that we shall have found a way to meet your demand for realization, if we can discover how a state might be constituted in the closest accordance with our description. Will not that content you? It would be enough for me.

And for me too.

Then our next attempt, it seems, must be to point out what defect in the working of existing states prevents them from being so organized, and what is the least change that would effect a transformation into this type of government—a single change if possible, or perhaps two; at any rate let us make the changes as few and insignificant as may be.

By all means.

Well, there is one change which, as I believe we can show, would bring about this revolution—not a small change, certainly, nor an easy one, but possible.

What is it?

I have now to confront what we called the third and greatest wave. But I must state my paradox, even though the wave should break in laughter over my head and drown me in ignominy. Now mark what I am going to say.

Go on.

Unless either philosophers become kings in their countries or those who are now called kings and rulers come to be sufficiently inspired with a genuine desire for wisdom; unless, that is to say, political power and philosophy meet together, while the many natures who now go their several ways in the one or the other direction are forcibly debarred from doing so, there can be no rest from troubles, my dear Glaucon, for states, nor yet, as I believe, for all mankind; nor can this commonwealth which we have imagined ever till then see the light of day and grow to its full stature. This it was that I have so long hung back from saying; I knew what a paradox it would be, because it is hard to see that there is no other way of happiness either for the state or for the individual.

Socrates, exclaimed Glaucon, after delivering yourself of such a pronouncement as that, you must expect a whole multitude of by no means contemptible assailants to fling off their coats, snatch up the handiest weapon, and make a rush at you, breathing fire and slaughter. If you cannot find arguments to beat them off and make your escape, you will learn what it means to be the target of scorn and derision.

Well, it was you who got me into this trouble.

Yes, and a good thing too. However, I will not leave you in the lurch. You shall have my friendly encouragement for what it is worth; and perhaps you may find me more complaisant than some would be in answering your questions. With such backing you must try to convince the unbelievers.

I will, now that I have such a powerful ally.

[In arguing that philosophers should be kings, Plato (or Socrates) was parting ways with the democratic tradition of Athens. Like other conservative Athenians, he seems to have believed that democracy degenerated into mob rule. The root of this antidemocratic philosophy was the belief that the mass of people was horribly ignorant and only the rare philosopher had true understanding. Plato expressed this idea in one of the most famous passages in the history of philosophy: the parable of the cave.]

Next, said I, here is a parable to illustrate the degrees in which our nature may be enlightened or unenlightened. Imagine the condition of men living in a sort of cavernous chamber underground, with an entrance open to the light and a long passage all down the cave. Here they have been from childhood, chained by the leg and also by the neck, so that they cannot move and can see only what is in front of them, because the chains will not let them turn their heads. At some distance higher up is the light of a fire burning behind them; and between the prisoners and the fire is a track with a parapet built along it, like the screen at a puppet-show, which hides the performers while they show their puppets over the top.

I see, said he.

Now behind this parapet imagine persons carrying along various artificial objects, including figures of men and animals in wood or stone or other materials, which project above the parapet. Naturally, some of these persons will be talking, others silent.

It is a strange picture, he said, and a strange sort of prisoners.

Like ourselves, I replied; for in the first place prisoners so confined would have seen nothing of themselves or of one another, except the shadows thrown by the firelight on the wall of the Cave facing them, would they?

Not if all their lives they had been prevented from moving their heads.

And they would have seen as little of the objects carried past.

Of course.

Now, if they could talk to one another, would they not suppose that their words referred only to those passing shadows which they saw?

Necessarily.

And suppose their prison had an echo from the wall facing them? When one of the people crossing behind them spoke, they could only suppose that the sound came from the shadow passing before their eyes.

No doubt.

In every way, then, such prisoners would recognize as reality nothing but the shadows of those artificial objects.

Inevitably.

Now consider what would happen if their release from the chains and the healing of their unwisdom should come about in this way. Suppose one of them was set free and forced suddenly to stand up, turn his head, and walk with eyes lifted to the light; all these movements would be painful, and he would be too dazzled to make out the objects whose shadows he had been used to see. What do you think he would say, if someone told him that what he had formerly seen was meaningless illusion, but now, being somewhat nearer to reality and turned towards more real objects, he was getting a truer view? Suppose further that he were shown the various objects being carried by and were made to say, in reply to questions, what each of them was. Would he not be perplexed and believe the objects now shown him to be not so real as what he formerly saw?

Yes, not nearly so real.

And if he were forced to look at the firelight itself, would not his eyes ache, so that he would try to escape and turn back to the things which he could see distinctly, convinced that they really were clearer than these other objects now being shown to him?

Yes.

And suppose someone were to drag him away forcibly up the steep and rugged ascent and not let him go until he had hauled him out into the sunlight, would he not suffer pain and vexation at such treatment, and, when he had come out into the light, find his eyes so full of its radiance that he could not see a single one of the things that he was now told were real?

Certainly he would not see them all at once.

He would need, then, to grow accustomed before he could see things in that upper world. At first it would be easiest to make out shadows, and then the images of men and things reflected in water, and later on the things themselves. After that, it would be easier to watch the heavenly bodies and the sky itself by night, looking at the light of the moon and stars rather than the Sun and the Sun's light in the daytime.

Yes, surely.

Last of all, he would be able to look at the Sun and contemplate its nature, not as it appears when reflected in water or any alien medium, but as it is in itself in its own domain.

No doubt.

And now he would begin to draw the conclusion that it is the Sun that produces the seasons and the course of the year and controls everything in the visible world, and moreover is in a way the cause of all that he and his companions used to see.

Clearly he would come at last to that conclusion.

Then if he called to mind his fellow prisoners and what passed for wisdom in his former dwelling-place, he would surely think himself happy in the change and be sorry for them. They may have had a practice of honouring and commending one another, with prizes for the man who had the keenest eye for the passing shadows and the best memory for the order in which they followed or accompanied one another, so that he could make a good guess as to which was going to come next. Would our released prisoner be likely to covet those prizes or to envy the men exalted to honour and power in the Cave? Would he not feel like Homer's Achilles, that he would far sooner "be on earth as a hired servant in the house of a landless man" or endure anything rather than go back to his old beliefs and live in the old way?

Yes, he would prefer any fate to such a life.

Now imagine what would happen if he went down again to take his former seat in the Cave. Coming suddenly out of the sunlight, his eyes would be filled with darkness. He might be required once more to deliver his opinion on those shadows, in competition with the prisoners who had never been released, while his eyesight was still dim and unsteady; and it might take some time to become used to the darkness. They would laugh at him and say that he had gone up only to come back with his sight ruined; it was worth no one's while even to attempt the ascent. If they could lay hands on the man who was trying to set them free and lead them up, they would kill him.

Yes, they would.

Every feature in this parable, my dear Glaucon, is meant to fit our earlier analysis. The prison dwelling corresponds to the region revealed to us through the sense of sight, and the firelight within it to the power of the Sun. The ascent to see the things in the upper world you may take as standing for the upward journey of the soul into the region of the intelligible; then you will be in possession of what I surmise, since that is what you wish to be told. Heaven knows whether it is true; but this, at any rate, is how it appears to me. In the world of knowledge, the last thing to be perceived and only with great difficulty is the essential Form of Goodness. Once it is perceived, the conclusion must follow that, for all things, this is the cause of whatever is right and good; in the visible world it gives birth to light and to the lord of light, while it is itself sovereign in the intelligible world and the parent of intelligence and truth. Without having had a vision of this Form no one can act with wisdom, either in his own life or in matters of state.

So far as I can understand, I share your belief.

Then you may also agree that it is no wonder if those who have reached their height are reluctant to manage the affairs of men. Their souls long to spend all their time in that upper world—naturally enough, if here once more our parable holds true. Nor, again, is it at all strange that one who comes from the contemplation of divine things to the miseries of human life should appear awkward and ridiculous when, with eyes still dazed and not yet accustomed to the darkness, he is compelled, in a law court or elsewhere, to dispute about the shadows of justice or the images that cast those shadows, and to wrangle over the notions of what is right in the minds of men who have never beheld Justice itself.

It is not at all strange.

No; a sensible man will remember that the eyes may be confused in two ways—by a change from light to darkness or from darkness to light; and he will recognize that the same thing happens to the soul. When he sees it troubled and unable to discern anything clearly, instead of laughing thoughtlessly, he will ask whether, coming from a brighter existence, its unaccustomed vision is obscured by the darkness, in which case he will think its condition enviable and its life a happy one; or whether, emerging from the depths of ignorance, it is dazzled by excess of light. If so, he will rather feel sorry for it; or, if he were inclined to laugh, that would be less ridiculous than to laugh at the soul which has come down from the light.

That is a fair statement.

If this is true, then, we must conclude that education is not what it is said to be by some, who profess to put knowledge into a soul which does not possess it, as if they could put sight into blind eyes. On the contrary, our own account signifies that the soul of every man does possess the power of learning the truth and the organ to see it with; and that, just as one might have to turn the whole body round in order that the eye should see light instead of darkness, so the entire soul must be turned away from this changing world, until its eye can bear to contemplate reality and that supreme splendour which we have called the Good. Hence there may well be an art whose aim would be to effect this very thing, the conversion of the soul, in the readiest way; not to put the power of sight into the soul's eye, which already has it, but to ensure that, instead of looking in the wrong direction, it is turned the way it ought to be.

Yes, it may well be so.

It looks, then, as though wisdom were different from those ordinary virtues, as they are called, which are not far removed from bodily qualities, in that they can be produced by habituation and exercise in a soul which has not possessed them from the first. Wisdom, it seems, is certainly the virtue of some diviner faculty, which never loses its power, though its use for good or harm depends on the direction towards which it is turned. You must have noticed in dishonest men with a reputation for sagacity the shrewd glance of a narrow intelligence piercing the objects to which it is directed. There is nothing wrong with their power of vision, but it has been forced into the service of evil, so that the keener its sight, the more harm it works.

Quite true.

And yet if the growth of a nature like this had been pruned from earliest childhood, cleared of those clinging overgrowths which come of gluttony and all luxurious pleasure and, like leaden weights charged with affinity to this mortal world, hang upon the soul, bending its vision downwards; if, freed from these, the soul were turned round towards true reality, then this same power in these very men would see the truth as keenly as the objects it is turned to now.

Yes, very likely.

Is it not also likely, or indeed certain after what has been said, that a state can never be properly governed either by the uneducated who know nothing of truth or by men who are allowed to spend all their days in the pursuit of culture? The ignorant have no single mark before their eyes at which they must aim in all the conduct of their own lives and of affairs of state; and the others will not engage in action if they can help it, dreaming that, while still alive, they have been translated to the Islands of the Blest.

Quite true.

It is for us, then, as founders of a commonwealth, to bring compulsion to bear on the noblest natures. They must be made to climb the ascent to the vision of Goodness, which we called the highest object of knowledge; and, when they have looked upon it long enough, they must not be allowed, as they now are, to remain on the heights, refusing to come down again to the prisoners or to take any part in their labours and rewards, however much or little these may be worth.

Shall we not be doing them an injustice, if we force on them a worse life than they might have?

You have forgotten again, my friend, that the law is not concerned to make any one class specially happy, but to ensure the welfare of the commonwealth as a whole. By persuasion or constraint it will unite the citizens in harmony, making them share whatever benefits each class can contribute to the common good; and its purpose in forming men of that spirit was not that each should be left to go his own way, but that they should be instrumental in binding the community into one.

True, I had forgotten.

You will see, then, Glaucon, that there will be no real injustice in compelling our philosophers to watch over and care for the other citizens. We can fairly tell them that their compeers in other states may quite reasonably refuse to collaborate: there they have sprung up, like a self-sown plant, in despite of their country's institutions; no one has fostered their growth, and they cannot be expected to show gratitude for a care they have never received. "But," we shall say, "it is not so with you. We have brought you into existence for your country's sake as well as for your own, to be like leaders and king-bees in a hive; you have been better and more thoroughly educated than those others and hence you are more capable of playing your part both as men of thought and as men of action. You must go down, then, each in his turn, to live with the rest and let your eyes grow accustomed to the darkness. You will then see a thousand times better than those who live there always; you will recognize every image for what it is and know what it represents, because you have seen justice, beauty, and goodness in their reality; and so you and we shall find life in our commonwealth no mere dream, as it is in most existing states, where men live fighting one another about shadows and quarrelling for power, as if that were a great prize; whereas in truth government can be at its best and free from dissension only where the destined rulers are least desirous of holding office."

Quite true.

Then will our pupils refuse to listen and to take their turns at sharing in the work of the community, though they may live together for most of their time in a purer air?

No; it is a fair demand, and they are fair-minded men. No doubt, unlike any ruler of the present day, they will think of holding power as an unavoidable necessity.

Yes, my friend; for the truth is that you can have a well-governed society only if you can discover for your future rulers a better way of life than being in office; then only will power be in the hands of men who are rich, not in gold, but in the wealth that brings happiness, a good and wise life. All goes wrong when, starved for lack of anything good in their own lives, men turn to public affairs hoping to snatch from thence the happiness they hunger for. They set about fighting for power, and this internecine conflict ruins them and their country. The life of true philosophy is the only one that looks down upon offices of state; and access to power must be confined to men who are not in love with it; otherwise rivals will start fighting. So whom else can you compel to undertake the guardianship of the commonwealth, if not those who, besides understanding best the principles of government, enjoy a nobler life than the politician's and look for rewards of a different kind?

There is indeed no other choice.

■ REFLECTIONS

Caste and territorial sovereignty were alternative but equally effective systems of social organization in the ancient world. Both worked. Both allocated jobs and rewards, arranged marriages and created families, ensured the peace and fought wars. Neither was necessarily more just, tyrannical, expensive, or arbitrary. Yet each system created its own complex world of ideas and behavior.

Caste and territorial sovereignty were not the only bases for identity in the ancient world. In many societies, a person's identity was based on family ties of a different sort than caste. In China, the family lineage, constituting many generations of relatives, was particularly important. Almost every society in human history organized itself around families to a certain extent, and most societies also had a sense of multiple family units called clans or tribes. The Indian caste system was only one variant of these multifamily systems, and some non-Indian societies had divisions resembling castes.

Family, clan, and tribe are still important determinants of identity in the modern world. In some societies, the authority of a tribal leader, clan elder, or family patriarch rivals that of the state. Nevertheless, the modern world is made up of states. We live according to the law of the land, not that of kinship. In the United States, one obeys the laws of the United States, regardless of who one knows. If the police pull you over for driving through a red light, you do not say that your father gave you permission or your uncle ordered you to drive through red lights. In the territory of the United States, you obey the laws of the United States and the particular state in which you find yourself. When a citizen of the United States goes to Canada, he or she must obey the laws of Canada. This is the world of states, of territorial sovereignty.

One of the major transitions in human history in the last five thousand years has been the rise of territorial sovereignty and the supplanting of the authority of the law of the state over the rule of family, clan, tribe, and caste. This is what developed in ancient Greece twenty-five hundred years ago. It did not occur completely and finally with Cleisthenes or even with the rise of Greek democracy in the fifth century B.C.E. Tribal alliances reasserted themselves periodically in Greece and elsewhere, in the Middle Ages and in modern society. The establishment of territorial sovereignty and ultimately of civil society, where political parties replaced tribes, was gradual and interrupted and is still continuing. Aristotle tells us that after Cleisthenes, Greeks took new surnames based on their new civic "tribes." That would have ended the rule of the old family-based tribes, but we know the old tribal names did not disappear. A thorough transition would mean that political parties would express entirely civic goals without a trace of tribal identity, but that too is a process that still continues. In modern Ireland, for instance, one of the political parties, Finn Gael, means literally the tribe of the Gael. In the wake of the U.S. invasion of Iraq in 2003, many Americans have learned how difficult it is to impose a system of territorial sovereignty on a society where tribal identities are strong.

India today is also a modern state in which the law of the land applies to all regardless of caste, family, or tribe. In fact, recent Indian governments have outlawed discrimination based on caste and created affirmative action programs on behalf of Dalits, the outcastes or untouchables. Nevertheless, Indian newspapers still run matrimonial ads that specify caste, though international Web sites often do not.

Modern society encourages us to be many things. Family and caste can still play a role. Religion, ethnicity, national origin, even race are given an importance in modern society that was often absent or irrelevant in ancient societies. But with the civic society produced by territorial sovereignty comes not only citizenship but also a range of chosen identities based on career, education, job, hobbies, friends, and a wide range of living possibilities. These choices can sometimes overwhelm. Sometimes the indelibility of family, caste, or birth can seem a comfort. But over the long term of history, the range and choice of identities seem likely to increase, and more and more of them will likely be voluntary rather than stamped on the birth certificate.

4

Empire and Government
China and Rome, 300 B.C.E.–300 C.E.

■ HISTORICAL CONTEXT

The Chinese and Roman empires of the classical era were similar in many ways. They were roughly contemporaneous. The Chinese Empire began under the Qin dynasty in 221 B.C.E. and continued in revised form through the Han dynasty until 220 C.E. Rome also reached imperial dimensions after 200 B.C.E., recognizing its first emperor in 27 B.C.E. Like China, the Roman Empire was shaken by invading nomads after 200 C.E. Each empire ruled at least fifty million people over an area of one and a half million square miles. (See Maps 4.1 and 4.2.) Both managed to field and maintain enormous armies and tax, govern, and keep the peace for hundreds of years. How did these empires rule and administer such vast areas for so long? In this chapter we explore the management of both empires by studying the actions of emperors and their governments.

When we think of empire we generally presume two things: the rule of a very large territory by a single power and, usually, that this power is held by a single individual who is the emperor of that territory. These elements were simultaneous in China. After centuries in which six kingdoms struggled for dominance, the king of Qin* conquered the remaining independent kingdoms in China and created a single empire with himself as emperor. Known as the First Emperor, the king of Qin created many of the enduring elements of centralized rule. A sense of his enormous power is apparent today thanks to the 1974 discovery of his tomb near his capital Xianyang† with its thousands of life-size terra cotta soldiers. It was

---

* chin
† shin yong

117

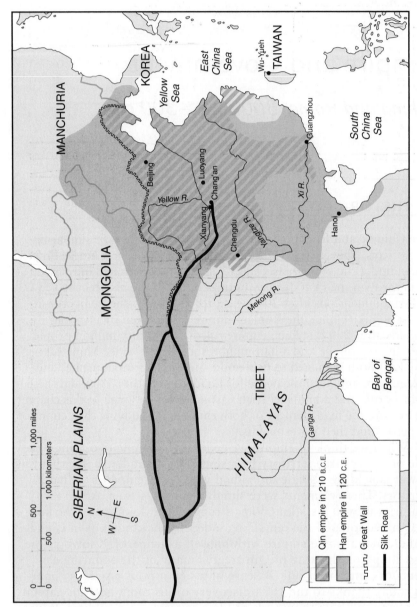

Map 4.1 Imperial China, 210 B.C.E. and 120 C.E.

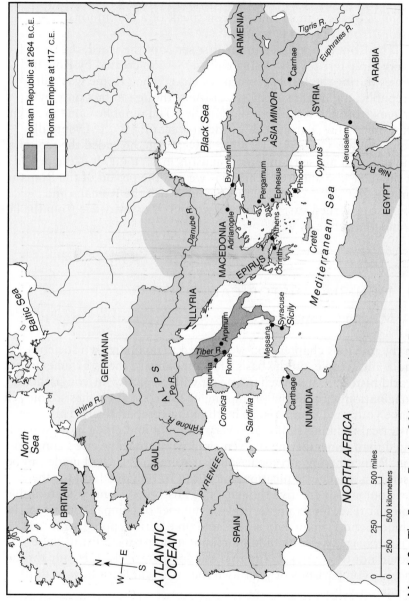

Map 4.2 The Roman Empire, 264 B.C.E. and 117 C.E.

built, the ancient sources tell us, by 700,000 workers, all of whom were buried with their emperor so the site would never be revealed. The Qin dynasty did not last long beyond the death of the first emperor, but the successor Han dynasty continued many of the methods of the Qin so that we can speak of a continuous imperial history from 221 B.C.E. to 220 C.E.

The Roman Empire—in the first sense of the word, the rule of a very large territory by a single power—was created by Roman armies during the last two centuries B.C.E. when Rome was still a republic, a government by the citizens, though in fact only by citizens from the wealthiest old families. The republic came to an end after the civil war at the end of the first century B.C.E. Eventually won by Julius Caesar's adopted son Octavian, he ended the republic and declared himself Emperor Augustus in 27 B.C.E. It is the period of the next few hundred years that we call the period of the Roman Empire, but as we compare the way in which the Romans and Chinese governed vast territories, we will draw evidence from the late Roman Republic as well.

■ THINKING HISTORICALLY

Making Comparisons

In the previous chapter, you were asked to compare two societies, India and Greece, on the basis of a comparative thesis by an eminent world historian. In this chapter, you will exercise your comparative imagination without the prompting of someone else's thesis. You will make your own comparisons by thinking comparatively. This is an historical thinking skill that is very different and much more sophisticated than remembering or even employing someone else's comparison. Remembering a comparison that someone else had made can be useful knowledge acquisition, but it can be only the food for the development of creative thought. The Historical Context section that you just read, for example, offers a number of comparisons of the Chinese and Roman empires—same time period, population, and territory size. We could add more, but memorizing a list of these would not train your ability to think comparatively. It is only through making comparisons of your own that you will learn how to think comparatively.

CONFUCIUS

The Analects, c. 479–221 B.C.E.

Confucius (551–479 B.C.E.), the best-known Chinese philosopher, lived centuries before the creation of a Chinese empire, in an age of competing kingdoms, feudal lords, and feuding families. This period is called the "Age of Warring States" and is also known as an era of competing philosophies, or a "Hundred Schools of Thought." The battle of ideas centered on issues similar to those discussed in the previous chapter on caste in India and the development of territorial sovereignty in Greece. In feudal China, the family, clan, or lineage held society together without much of a state, as was also the case with in India. Territorial states had long conquered and asserted their sovereignty over aristocratic families in many regions. But feudalism died slowly. Even in powerful states like the Zhou[1] Dynasty Kingdom (1046–256 B.C.E.), large feudal families were still able to command the loyalty of numerous clans and thoughtful philosophers. One of these philosophers who wrote in favor of the old-fashioned values of family-based feudal society was Confucius. What were these values? What did Confucius oppose?

THINKING HISTORICALLY

Compare the values that hold a family together with those required by a state. The first emperor of Qin who conquered the other kingdoms and created the empire was not a follower of Confucius. In fact, at one point he had Confucian writings burned. Why might an empire creator be less attracted to the ideas of Confucius? Which ideas expressed in this selection might bother an aggressive conqueror?

On Filial Piety

I, 6. The Master said, "A youth, when at home, should be filial, and, abroad, respectful to his elders. He should be earnest and truthful. He should overflow in love to all, and cultivate the friendship of the good. When he has time and opportunity, after the performance of these things, he should employ them in polite studies."

[1] joe

Source: *The Chinese Classics*, trans. James Legge (New York: John B. Alden, Publisher, 1890), 4, 6, 10, 12, 120, 122, 123, 130.

I, 11. The Master said, "While a man's father is alive, look at the bent of his will; when his father is dead, look at his conduct. If for three years he does not alter from the way of his father, he may be called filial."

II, 7. Ziyou asked what filial piety was. The Master said, "The filial piety nowadays means the support of one's parents. But dogs and horses are also supported—without reverence. What is the difference?"

On Government by Moral Force

I, 5. The Master [Confucius] said, "To rule a country of a thousand chariots, there must be reverent attention to business, and sincerity; economy in expenditure, and love for men; and the employment of the people at the proper seasons."

II, 3. The Master said, "If the people be led by laws, and uniformity sought to be given them by punishments, they will try to avoid the punishment, but have no sense of shame. If they be led by virtue, and uniformity sought to be given them by the rules of propriety, they will have the sense of shame, and moreover will become good."

XII, 11. The Duke Ching, of Ch'i, asked Confucius about government. Confucius replied, "There is government, when the prince is prince, and the minister is minister; when the father is father, and the son is son." "Good!" said the duke, "If, indeed; the prince be not prince, the minister not minister, the father not father, and the son not son, although I have my revenue, can I enjoy it?"

XII, 19. Chi K'ang asked Confucius about government, saying, "What do you say to killing the unprincipled for the good of the principled?" Confucius replied, "Sir, in carrying on your government, why should you use killing at all? Let your evinced desires be for what is good, and the people will be good. The relation between superiors and inferiors is like that between the wind and the grass. The grass must bend, when the wind blows across it."

XIII, 6. The Master said, "When a prince's personal conduct is correct, his government is effective without the issuing of orders. If his personal conduct is not correct, he may issue orders, but they will not be followed."

XIII, 10. The Master said, "If there were (any of the princes) who would employ me, in the course of twelve months, I should have done something considerable. In three years, the government would be perfected."

XIII, 11. The Master said, "'If good men were to govern a country in succession for a hundred years, they would be able to transform the violently bad, and dispense with capital punishments.' True indeed is this saying!"

LAOZI

Daoism: The Way and the Power, c. 400 B.C.E.

The formation of the Chinese Empire in Qin and early Han times centered on the conflict between Confucian and Legalist schools of thought. But there was an earlier Chinese philosophy that resurfaced throughout Chinese history, called Daoism or Taoism.

Laozi (or Lao-tzu or Lao-tze), meaning literally "Old Master," is the name given to an actual or mythical philosopher said to have lived at some point between the sixth and fourth centuries B.C.E. This selection of Daoist (or Taoist) writings from what is called the *Daodejing* (or *Tao-te Ching*)—*The Way and the Power*—contains some of the writings ascribed to Laozi. Originating perhaps as proverbs, fragments of this larger work have been found in a Chinese tomb dating back to 300 B.C.E. But there is little mention of the Daodejing before the Han dynasty, a hundred years later, when it began to invite the variety of interpretations and legions of devotees that it has charmed over the ages.

The Daoist tradition is less ostensibly political than Confucianism; it is also more religious and much more spiritual. Nevertheless, political implications have been drawn from Daoist writings for over two thousand years. What political ideas might you infer from these passages?

THINKING HISTORICALLY

Compare Daoism with Confucianism. Where would they agree? Where would they disagree? Which would make a better set of ideas for running a government or an empire?

PART I

Chapter 2

1. All in the world know the beauty of the beautiful, and in doing this they have (the idea of) what ugliness is; they all know the skill of the skilful, and in doing this they have (the idea of) what the want of skill is.

Source: "The Tao-te Ching," *Sacred Books of the East*, trans. James Legge, ed. Müller, Vol. 39 (Oxford University Press, 1891).

2. So it is that existence and non-existence give birth the one to (the idea of) the other; that difficulty and ease produce the one (the idea of) the other; that length and shortness fashion out the one the figure of the other; that (the ideas of) height and lowness arise from the contrast of the one with the other; that the musical notes and tones become harmonious through the relation of one with another; and that being before and behind give the idea of one following another.

3. Therefore the sage manages affairs without doing anything, and conveys his instructions without the use of speech.

Chapter 3

1. Not to value and employ men of superior ability is the way to keep the people from rivalry among themselves; not to prize articles which are difficult to procure is the way to keep them from becoming thieves; not to show them what is likely to excite their desires is the way to keep their minds from disorder.

2. Therefore the sage, in the exercise of his government, empties their minds, fills their bellies, weakens their wills, and strengthens their bones.

3. He constantly (tries to) keep them without knowledge and without desire, and where there are those who have knowledge, to keep them from presuming to act (on it). When there is this abstinence from action, good order is universal.

Chapter 13

3. Therefore he who would administer the kingdom, honouring it as he honours his own person, may be employed to govern it, and he who would administer it with the love which he bears to his own person may be entrusted with it.

Chapter 18

1. When the Great Tao (Way or Method) ceased to be observed, benevolence and righteousness came into vogue. (Then) appeared wisdom and shrewdness, and there ensued great hypocrisy.

2. When harmony no longer prevailed throughout the six kinships, filial sons found their manifestation; when the states and clans fell into disorder, loyal ministers appeared.

Chapter 19

1. If we could renounce our sageness and discard our wisdom, it would be better for the people a hundredfold. If we could renounce our benevolence and discard our righteousness, the people would again

become filial and kindly. If we could renounce our artful contrivances and discard our (scheming for) gain, there would be no thieves nor robbers.

Chapter 24

He who stands on his tiptoes does not stand firm; he who stretches his legs does not walk (easily). (So), he who displays himself does not shine; he who asserts his own views is not distinguished; he who vaunts himself does not find his merit acknowledged; he who is self-conceited has no superiority allowed to him. Such conditions, viewed from the standpoint of the Tao, are like remnants of food, or a tumour on the body, which all dislike. Hence those who pursue (the course) of the Tao do not adopt and allow them.

Chapter 29

1. If any one should wish to get the kingdom for himself, and to effect this by what he does, I see that he will not succeed. The kingdom is a spirit-like thing, and cannot be got by active doing. He who would so win it destroys it; he who would hold it in his grasp loses it.

Chapter 30

1. He who would assist a lord of men in harmony with the Tao will not assert his mastery in the kingdom by force of arms. Such a course is sure to meet with its proper return.

2. Wherever a host is stationed, briars and thorns spring up. In the sequence of great armies there are sure to be bad years.

3. A skilful (commander) strikes a decisive blow, and stops. He does not dare (by continuing his operations) to assert and complete his mastery. He will strike the blow, but will be on his guard against being vain or boastful or arrogant in consequence of it. He strikes it as a matter of necessity; he strikes it, but not from a wish for mastery.

4. When things have attained their strong maturity they become old. This may be said to be not in accordance with the Tao: and what is not in accordance with it soon comes to an end.

Chapter 31

1. Now arms, however beautiful, are instruments of evil omen, hateful, it may be said, to all creatures. Therefore they who have the Tao do not like to employ them.

2. The superior man ordinarily considers the left hand the most honourable place, but in time of war the right hand. Those sharp weapons

are instruments of evil omen, and not the instruments of the superior man;—he uses them only on the compulsion of necessity. Calm and repose are what he prizes; victory (by force of arms) is to him undesirable. To consider this desirable would be to delight in the slaughter of men; and he who delights in the slaughter of men cannot get his will in the kingdom.

3. On occasions of festivity to be on the left hand is the prized position; on occasions of mourning, the right hand. The second in command of the army has his place on the left; the general commanding in chief has his on the right;—his place, that is, is assigned to him as in the rites of mourning. He who has killed multitudes of men should weep for them with the bitterest grief; and the victor in battle has his place (rightly) according to those rites.

PART II

Chapter 57

1. A state may be ruled by (measures of) correction; weapons of war may be used with crafty dexterity; (but) the kingdom is made one's own (only) by freedom from action and purpose.

2. How do I know that it is so? By these facts:—In the kingdom the multiplication of prohibitive enactments increases the poverty of the people; the more implements to add to their profit that the people have, the greater disorder is there in the state and clan; the more acts of crafty dexterity that men possess, the more do strange contrivances appear; the more display there is of legislation, the more thieves and robbers there are.

3. Therefore a sage has said, 'I will do nothing (of purpose), and the people will be transformed of themselves; I will be fond of keeping still, and the people will of themselves become correct. I will take no trouble about it, and the people will of themselves become rich; I will manifest no ambition, and the people will of themselves attain to the primitive simplicity.'

Chapter 61

1. What makes a great state is its being (like) a low-lying, down-flowing (stream);—it becomes the centre to which tend (all the small states) under heaven.

2. (To illustrate from) the case of all females:—the female always overcomes the male by her stillness. Stillness may be considered (a sort of) abasement.

3. Thus it is that a great state, by condescending to small states, gains them for itself; and that small states, by abasing themselves to a great

state, win it over to them. In the one case the abasement leads to gaining adherents, in the other case to procuring favour.

4. The great state only wishes to unite men together and nourish them; a small state only wishes to be received by, and to serve, the other. Each gets what it desires, but the great state must learn to abase itself.

Chapter 67

1. All the world says that, while my Tao is great, it yet appears to be inferior (to other systems of teaching). Now it is just its greatness that makes it seem to be inferior. If it were like any other (system), for long would its smallness have been known!

2. But I have three precious things which I prize and hold fast. The first is gentleness; the second is economy; and the third is shrinking from taking precedence of others.

3. With that gentleness I can be bold; with that economy I can be liberal; shrinking from taking precedence of others, I can become a vessel of the highest honour. Now-a-days they give up gentleness and are all for being bold; economy, and are all for being liberal; the hindmost place, and seek only to be foremost; — (of all which the end is) death.

4. Gentleness is sure to be victorious even in battle, and firmly to maintain its ground. Heaven will save its possessor, by his (very) gentleness protecting him.

Chapter 80

1. In a little state with a small population, I would so order it, that, though there were individuals with the abilities of ten or a hundred men, there should be no employment of them; I would make the people, while looking on death as a grievous thing, yet not remove elsewhere (to avoid it).

2. Though they had boats and carriages, they should have no occasion to ride in them; though they had buff coats and sharp weapons, they should have no occasion to don or use them.

3. I would make the people return to the use of knotted cords (instead of the written characters).

4. They should think their (coarse) food sweet; their (plain) clothes beautiful; their (poor) dwellings places of rest; and their common (simple) ways sources of enjoyment.

5. There should be a neighbouring state within sight, and the voices of the fowls and dogs should be heard all the way from it to us, but I would make the people to old age, even to death, not have any intercourse with it.

HAN FEI

Legalism, c. 230 B.C.E.

Legalism was the alternative to Confucianism that appealed to the
First Emperor of the Qin dynasty. Han Fei (280–233 B.C.E.) had been
raised on Confucianism but broke with the tradition as he developed
very different ideas about human nature and government. A son of a
noble family from the enemy state of Han, Han Fei fell under suspicion
as an advisor of the Qin king Zheng, who became First Emperor. His
rival had him arrested and poisoned. The following was taken from
the *Han Fei Tzu* (Master Han Fei), as his collected political essays have
become known. What is Han Fei's criticism of Confucianism? How
would you characterize the ideas of Han Fei? How might these ideas
appeal to an empire-builder like the First Emperor?

THINKING HISTORICALLY

To fully understand Han Fei's argument, you need to consider them
in relation to those of Confucius. Compare this document to *The Analects*. Just how different are Han Fei's ideas from those of Confucius?
What aspects of Legalism would you expect empire-builders in history
to find appealing? Think of two very different rulers from history and
compare how they did or did not apply aspects of Legalism to their
rule. Do empires require Legalists? Do they require Moralists?

When the sage rules the state, he does not count on people doing good
of themselves, but employs such measures as will keep them from doing
any evil. If he counts on people doing good of themselves, there will not
be enough such people to be numbered by the tens in the whole country.
But if he employs such measures as will keep them from doing evil, then
the entire state can be brought up to a uniform standard. Inasmuch as
the administrator has to consider the many but disregard the few, he
does not busy himself with morals but with laws.

Evidently, if one should have to count on arrows which are straight
of themselves, there would not be any arrows in a hundred generations;
if one should only count on pieces of wood which are circular of themselves, there would not be any wheels in a thousand generations. Though
in a hundred generations there is neither an arrow that is straight of

Source: *Sources of Chinese Tradition*, comp. William Theodore de Bary et al. (New York:
Columbia University Press, 1963), 1: 127–29, 133–35.

itself nor a wheel that is circular of itself, yet people in every generation ride carts and shoot birds. Why is that? It is because the tools for straightening and bending are used. Though without the use of such tools there might happen to be an arrow straight of itself or a wheel circular of itself, the skilled carpenter will not prize it. Why? Because it is not just one person who wishes to ride, or just one shot that the archers wish to shoot. Similarly, though without the use of rewards and punishments there might happen to be an individual good of himself, the intelligent ruler will not prize him. The reason is that the law of the state must not be sidetracked and government is not for one man. Therefore, the capable prince will not be swayed by occasional virtue, but will pursue a course that will assure certainty. . . .

Now, when witches and priests pray for people, they say: "May you live as long as one thousand and ten thousand years!" . . . [T]here is no sign that even a single day has been added to the age of any man. That is the reason why people despise witches and priests. Likewise, when the Confucianists of the present day counsel the rulers they do not discuss the way to bring about order now, but exalt the achievement of good order in the past. They neither study affairs pertaining to law and government nor observe the realities of vice and wickedness, but all exalt the reputed glories of remote antiquity and the achievements of the ancient kings. Sugar-coating their speech, the Confucianists say: "If you listen to our words, you will be able to become the leader of all feudal lords." Such people are but witches and priests among the itinerant counselors, and are not to be accepted by rulers with principles. Therefore, the intelligent ruler upholds solid facts and discards useless frills. He does not speak about deeds of humanity and righteousness, and he does not listen to the words of learned men.

Those who are ignorant about government insistently say: "Win the hearts of the people." If order could be procured by winning the hearts of the people, then even the wise ministers Yi Yin and Kuan Chung would be of no use. For all that the ruler would need to do would be just to listen to the people. Actually, the intelligence of the people is not to be relied upon any more than the mind of a baby. If the baby does not have his head shaved, his sores will recur; if he does not have his boil cut open, his illness will go from bad to worse. However, in order to shave his head or open the boil someone has to hold the baby while the affectionate mother is performing the work, and yet he keeps crying and yelling incessantly. The baby does not understand that suffering a small pain is the way to obtain a great benefit.

Now, the sovereign urges the tillage of land and the cultivation of pastures for the purpose of increasing production for the people, but they think the sovereign is cruel. The sovereign regulates penalties and increases punishments for the purpose of repressing the wicked, but the people think the sovereign is severe. Again, he levies taxes in cash and in grain to fill up the granaries and treasuries in order to relieve famine and provide for the army, but they think the sovereign is greedy. Finally, he insists upon universal military training without personal favoritism, and urges his forces to fight hard in order to take the enemy captive, but the people think the sovereign is violent. These four measures are methods for attaining order and maintaining peace, but the people are too ignorant to appreciate them. . . .

The literati by means of letters upset laws; the cavaliers[1] by means of their prowess transgress prohibitions. Yet the ruler treats them both with decorum. This is actually the cause of all the disorder. Every departure from the law ought to be apprehended, and yet scholars are nevertheless taken into office on account of their literary learning. Again, the transgression of every prohibition ought to be censured, and yet cavaliers are patronized because of their readiness to draw the sword. Thus, those whom the law reproves turn out to be those whom the ruler employs, and those whom the magistrates suppress are those whom the sovereign patronizes. Thus legal standard and personal inclination as well as ruler and ministers are sharply opposed to each other and all fixed standards are lost. Then, even if there were ten Yellow Emperors,[2] they would not be able to establish any order. Therefore, those who practice humanity and righteousness should not be upheld, for if upheld, they would hinder concrete accomplishments. Again, those who specialize in refinement and learning should not be employed, for if employed, they would disturb the laws. There was in Ch'u an upright man named Kung, who, when his father stole a sheep, reported it to the authorities. The magistrate said: "Put him to death," as he thought the man was faithful to the ruler but disloyal to his father. So the man was apprehended and convicted. From this we can see that the faithful subject of the ruler was an outrageous son to his father. Again, there was a man of Lu who followed his ruler to war, fought three battles, and ran away three times. Confucius interrogated him. The man replied: "I have an old father. Should I die, nobody would take care of him." Confucius regarded him as virtuous in filial piety, commended and exalted him. From this we can see that the dutiful son of the father was a rebellious subject to the ruler. Naturally, following the censure of the honest man by the magistrate, no more culprits in Ch'u were reported to the authorities; and following the reward of the runaway by Confucius, the people of Lu were prone to surrender and run away. The interests of superior and subordinate being so different, it would be hopeless for any ruler to try to exalt the deeds of

---

[1] Horse-mounted soldiers, knights. [Ed.]
[2] Legendary Chinese ruler and culture hero. [Ed.]

private individuals and, at the same time, to promote the public welfare of the state. . . .

Today one cannot count even ten men of devotion and faithfulness, yet official posts in the country are counted by the hundreds. If only men of devotion and faithfulness were appointed to office, there would be an insufficiency of candidates, and in that case guardians of order would be few, while disturbers of peace would be many. Therefore the way of the enlightened sovereign consists in making laws uniform and not depending upon the wisdom of men, in making statecraft firm and not yearning after faithful persons, so that the laws do not fail to function and the multitude of officials will commit neither villainy nor deception. . . .

4

A Record of the Debate on Salt and Iron, 81 B.C.E.

In 81 B.C.E. the Han emperor Zhao held a debate on the economic policies of the preceding Emperor Wu. The debate centered on the question of whether or not the previous emperor's government monopolies, in salt, iron, and liquor, should be continued or abolished. Those in favor of continuing government control were the Legalists, represented by the Imperial Secretary Sang Hongyang. Those in favor of returning the production and distribution of these products to private hands were the Confucians, called the Literati. The following document records the debates between these two sides. What were the arguments in favor of government monopoly? What were the arguments against? In what ways was this also a debate about empire?

THINKING HISTORICALLY

The question of the proper role of government in the economy has been debated down to the present day. How was this salt and iron debate similar to, and different from, recent debates about the role of government in the American or European economy?

Source: *Sources of Chinese Tradition,* compiled by Wm. Theodore de Bary and Irene Bloom, 2nd ed., vol. 1 (New York: Columbia University Press, 1999), 360–64. © 1999 Columbia University Press.

In the sixth year of the era Shiyuan [81 B.C.E.], an imperial edict was issued directing the chancellor and the imperial secretaries to confer with the worthies and literati who had been recommended to the government and to inquire into the grievances and hardships of the people.

The literati responded: We have heard that the way to govern men is to prevent evil and error at their source, to broaden the beginnings of morality, to discourage secondary occupations, and open the way for the exercise of humaneness and rightness. Never should material profit appear as a motive of government. Only then can moral instruction succeed and the customs of the people be reformed. But now in the provinces the salt, iron, and liquor monopolies, and the system of equitable marketing have been established to compete with the people for profit, dispelling rustic generosity and teaching the people greed. Therefore those who pursue primary occupations [farming] have grown few and those following secondary occupations [trading] numerous. As artifice increases, basic simplicity declines; and as the secondary occupations flourish, those that are primary suffer. When the secondary is practiced the people grow decadent, but when the primary is practiced they are simple and sincere. When the people are sincere then there will be sufficient wealth and goods, but when they become extravagant then famine and cold will follow. We recommend that the salt, iron, and liquor monopolies and the system of equitable marketing be abolished so that primary pursuits may be advanced and secondary ones suppressed. This will have the advantage of increasing the profitableness of agriculture.

His Lordship [the Imperial Secretary Sang Hongyang] replied: The Xiongnu have frequently revolted against our sovereignty and pillaged our borders. If we are to defend ourselves, then it means the hardships of war for the soldiers of China, but if we do not defend ourselves properly, then their incursions cannot be stopped. The former emperor [Wu] took pity upon the people of the border areas who for so long had suffered disaster and hardship and had been carried off as captives. Therefore he set up defense stations, established a system of warning beacons, and garrisoned the outlying areas to ensure their protection. But the resources of these areas were insufficient, and so he established the salt, iron, and liquor monopolies and the system of equitable marketing in order to raise more funds for expenditures at the borders. Now our critics, who desire that these measures be abolished, would empty the treasuries and deplete the funds used for defense. They would have the men who are defending our passes and patrolling our walls suffer hunger and cold. How else can we provide for them? Abolition of these measures is not expedient!

His Lordship stated: In former times the peers residing in the provinces sent in their respective products as tribute, but there was much confusion and trouble in transporting them and the goods were often of such poor quality that they were not worth the cost of transportation.

For this reason transportation offices have been set up in each district to handle delivery and shipping and to facilitate the presentation of tribute from outlying areas. Therefore the system is called "equitable marketing." Warehouses have been opened in the capital for the storing of goods, buying when prices are low and selling when they are high. Thereby the government suffers no loss and the merchants cannot speculate for profit. Therefore this is called the "balanced level" [stabilization]. With the balanced level the people are protected from unemployment, and with equitable marketing the burden of labor service is equalized. Thus these measures are designed to ensure an equal distribution of goods and to benefit the people and are not intended to open the way to profit or provide the people with a ladder to crime.

The literati replied: In ancient times taxes and levies took from the people what they were skilled in producing and did not demand what they were poor at. Thus the husbandmen sent in their harvests and the weaving women their goods. Nowadays the government disregards what people have and requires of them what they have not, so that they are forced to sell their goods at a cheap price in order to meet the demands from above. . . . The farmers suffer double hardships and the weaving women are taxed twice. We have not seen that this kind of marketing is "equitable." The government officials go about recklessly opening closed doors and buying everything at will so they can corner all the goods. With goods cornered prices soar, and when prices soar the merchants make their own deals for profit. The officials wink at powerful racketeers, and the rich merchants hoard commodities and wait for an emergency. With slick merchants and corrupt officials buying cheap and selling dear we have not seen that your level is "balanced." The system of equitable marketing of ancient times was designed to equalize the burden of labor upon the people and facilitate the transporting of tribute. It did not mean dealing in all kinds of commodities for the sake of profit.

The Literati Attack Legalist Philosophy

The literati spoke: He who is good with a chisel can shape a round hole without difficulty; he who is good at laying foundations can build to a great height without danger of collapse. The statesman Yi Yin made the ways of Yao and Shun the foundation of the Yin dynasty, and its heirs succeeded to the throne for a hundred generations without break. But Shang Yang made heavy penalties and harsh laws the foundation of the Qin state and with the Second Emperor it was destroyed. Not satisfied with the severity of the laws, he instituted the system of mutual responsibility, made it a crime to criticize the government, and increased corporal punishments until the people were so terrified they did not know where to put their hands and feet. Not content with the manifold taxes and levies, he prohibited the people from using the resources of forests and rivers and made a hundredfold profit on the storage of commodities, while the people were given no chance to voice the slightest objection. Such worship of profit and slight of what is right, such exaltation of power and achievement, lent, it is true, to expansion of land and acquisition of territory. Yet it was like pouring more water upon people who are already suffering from flood and only increasing their distress. You see how Shang Yang opened the way to imperial rule for the Qin, but you fail to see how he also opened for the Qin the road to ruin!

Confucian Literati Ridiculed

His Excellency spoke: . . . Now we have with us over sixty worthy men and literati who cherish the ways of the Six Confucian Arts, fleet in thought and exhaustive in argument. It is proper, gentlemen, that you should pour forth your light and dispel our ignorance. And yet you put all your faith in the past and turn your backs upon the present, tell us of antiquity and give no thought to the state of the times. Perhaps we are not capable of recognizing true scholars. Yet do you really presume with your fancy phrases and attacks upon men of ability to pervert the truth in this manner?

See them [the Confucians] now present us with nothingness and consider it substance, with emptiness and call it plenty! In their coarse gowns and worn shoes they walk gravely along, sunk in meditation as though they had lost something. These are not men who can do great deeds and win fame. They do not even rise above the vulgar masses.

5

NICHOLAS PURCELL

Rome: The Arts of Government, 1988

The evolution of Rome to empire was somewhat different from that of China. In China, the state of Qin formed a unified state by suppressing the independent power of local kings, princes, and nobility. In other words, the First Emperor and the emperors of the Han dynasty brought an end to feudalism.

Source: Nicholas Purcell, "The Arts of Government," in *The Oxford History of the Classical World: The Roman World*, ed. John Boardman, Jasper Griffin, and Oswyn Murray (Oxford: Oxford University Press, 1988), 154, 155, 156, 170–74, 175–77.

Conversely, before Rome became an empire, it was a *republic:* a unified state, not a series of competing feudal powers. The Roman Republic inherited Greek ideas of territorial sovereignty and popular government. But as Roman military power spread beyond Italy, a republican form of government became more and more untenable. Governors had to be sent to conquered provinces, soldiers had to be recruited, and taxes had to be collected from non-Romans. The authority of popular institutions of government was eclipsed first by the aristocratic senate and then by warring generals; the dictator Caesar (47–44 B.C.E.); and finally Octavian, Caesar's nephew and adopted successor, who after 27 B.C.E. declared himself Augustus (Revered) and Imperator (Emperor).

Thus, for at least one hundred years before Rome officially became an empire, it governed vast territories of conquered and allied peoples. The way in which it ruled these subjects after Augustus had been honed by generations of provincial governors and did not change significantly.

In this selection, Nicholas Purcell, a modern historian of Rome, discusses aspects of Roman imperial administration. What does he say about the government of the Roman Empire? What were the strengths and weaknesses of Roman administration?

THINKING HISTORICALLY

How would you compare and contrast Roman administration, as described by Purcell, with Chinese administration of its empire? What are the most important differences? What accounts for these differences? In what respects was Chinese government of its empire superior? In what respects was it not? What other comparative questions does this selection raise in your mind?

"And it came to pass in those days, that there went out a decree from Caesar Augustus, that all the world should be enrolled to be taxed" (Luke 2:1). The evangelist wants to emphasize the centrality in world history of the coming of the Messiah, and accordingly links the birth of Christ to the moment when the power of Rome seemed at its most universal. For him, as often for us, the power of Rome is most potently expressed by reference to its administrative activity. St. Luke, however, was wrong. We know now that no such decree commanded a universal registration of the Roman world, at this time or any other; he exaggerated Roman omnipotence on the basis of the experience of a single province. It remains extremely easy for us too to misunderstand the scope, practice, and effects of Rome's governmental procedures. We mistake patterns of decision-making for policies and take hierarchical sequences of posts for career-structures.

When we find the taking of minutes or the accumulation of archives, we immediately see a bureaucracy. Virtuosity in the public service is confused with professionalism. Recent work has been able to show well how far Rome's administration failed, or could be corrupted or subverted, or simply had no effect but oppression on thousands of provincials. There have been fewer examinations of the way in which the arts of government at which the Romans thought themselves that they excelled actually worked—imposing civilization and peace, leniency to the defeated, and war to the last with the proud. . . .

Roman theories of government were not elaborate; the practice too was simple. Two broad categories cover almost all the activities of Roman rule: settling disputes between communities or individuals, and assembling men, goods, or money—jurisdiction and exaction. Antiquity recognized three main types of authority: magistrate, soldier, and master of a household; and all governmental activity in the Roman Empire can be linked with one of these. The first, deriving from the Greek city, covers both the immemorial officers of the city-state which Rome had been and the magistrates of the hundreds of essentially self-governing cities which made up nearly all the Roman Empire. In a *polis* magistrates ran the military; at Rome the usual citizen militia became under the Empire a permanent, institutionally separate army, whose officers played an ever greater part in government culminating in the militarization of the third century. Finally, in a slave-owning society the type of authority exercised within the household was naturally recognizably different, and also came to be of considerable importance in government. . . . [I]t was always through activities which we would hesitate to call governmental that Roman rule was most effectively maintained: through the involvement of the upper classes in public religion, spectacles, impressive patronage of architecture, philosophy, literature, painting; and in civil benefactions all over the Empire. The civilizing and beneficial effects of this should be remembered as we move on to find the actual administrative and executive structure of the Empire erratic and illiberal.

Rome had from the earliest times enjoyed very close contacts with the Greek world, and had, like most ancient cities, a tripartite political structure of magistrates, council (the Senate), and popular assembly. The importance of the last for our purpose is that its early power produced the uniquely Roman and constitutionally vital concept of *imperium*. The Roman people conferred upon its chosen magistrates the right to command it and the sanctions against disobedience—ever more strictly circumscribed—of corporal and capital punishment of its members. . . .

This is why Rome long retained the habit of dealing with her subjects with the respect deserved by the free, and why Roman rule so long remained indirect. To the end of antiquity most of the cities of the Empire and their territories were ruled by local magistrates many of whose domestic executive actions were taken as if they were independent; indeed they often needed to be reminded that there were limits to the licence they were allowed. Similarly Rome also long tolerated local kings and dynasts, and the survival of these dependent kingdoms and free cities contributed much to the fuzzy informality of the power structure of the Empire before the age of the Antonines.[1] . . .

The search for bureaucracy in the Roman world is vain. We should now look a little more closely at the concern with jurisdiction and exaction which Roman administrators really did have. Then, in conclusion, we can consider in general terms the nature of the governmental process and attempt to discover what really held the empire together.

Because Roman officials spent so much time in jurisdiction it was natural that Roman law should become more complicated and more sophisticated. The natural rule that jurisdiction gravitates to the highest available authority operated to increase the workload of governors, the great prefects at Rome, and the Emperor himself, and to hasten the adoption of Roman law. Even in the reign of Augustus,[2] Strabo[3] can already write that Crete, despite its own venerable legal tradition, had come, like all the provinces, to use the laws of Rome (10.4.22). And the bitterest realism about conditions in the Roman Empire cannot overlook the advantages of the existence of a legal framework to imperial rule, which the Hellenistic kingdoms had lacked, and which offered the Empire's subjects at least the theoretical possibility of redress and restrained the arbitrariness of Rome's rule. Law too grew at Rome with the problems first of city and then of Empire, and legal expertise came to provide an entry to the governing class. Professional legal practice was eventually one of the activities which gave many provincials a place in government, and Roman law was one of the most tenacious legacies of imperial rule—its greatest codification was the product of the eastern Empire under Justinian. There is not space here to recount the gradual evolution of Roman law, but the long accumulation of legal interpretations and precedents in the annual edicts of the praetors,[4] which, when codified by Hadrian,[5] formed the foundation of the legal system, and the role of the Emperor as a source of law and patron of the great jurists of the late second and early third centuries need stressing. For our purposes, however, two connected things are important. First, at Rome there was no question of the separation of

---

[1] 96–192 c.e., period of Roman imperial peace and prosperity; emperors included Trajan (r. 98–117), Hadrian (r. 117–138), and Marcus Aurelius (r. 161–180). [Ed.]

[2] Founder of Roman Empire, first of Julio-Claudian line of emperors; ruled as emperor from 27 b.c.e. to 14 c.e. [Ed.]

[3] Greek geographer and historian (63 b.c.e.–21 c.e.). [Ed.]

[4] Roman officials concerned with jurisdiction (law and administration); originally military; magistrates. [Ed.]

[5] Roman emperor (r. 117–138 c.e.). [Ed.]

judiciary and legislature which is so important a liberal principle to modern political thinkers. The law at Rome was on the whole the creation of judges, not lawgivers. The second point follows from this: legal measures show the same variety, casualness, and lack of generality which we find in Roman administrative decisions, and indeed it is difficult to separate the two. There is no proper ancient equivalent of statute law. The result was that the law was not always sufficiently universal, and the underprivileged might well not reap its benefits. Jewish nationalist writers, for example, compare the hypocrisy of Rome to the ambiguous associations of the unclean pig: "Just as a pig lies down and sticks out its trotters as though to say 'I am clean' [because they are cloven], so the evil empire robs and oppresses while pretending to execute justice."

For the burdens of Roman rule on the Empire were heavy and hated, and much of Roman government was devoted to ensuring their efficacy. The collection of tribute, direct and indirect tax, rents, levies in kind, recruits, protection money, requisitioning, and so on in total amounted to a very heavy oppression, even if the amount of tax formally due was not by comparative standards very high. Roman officials from the highest to the most menial were involved with these matters, and finance was a serious administrative concern. Augustus' great catalogue of his achievements is called in full *Res Gestae et Impensae* ("His Deeds and Expenditure"). And this is undoubtedly the view that most provincials had of the way the Empire worked. A prophecy of Rome's fall concentrated on both the exactions of the ruling power and the—less often discussed but equally odious—drain of manpower to Italy via the slave trade: "the wealth that Rome has received from tributary Asia threefold shall Asia receive again from Rome, which will pay in full the price of its insolent pride. And for each of those who labour in the land of the Italians twenty Italians shall toil in Asia as needy slaves" (*Oracula Sibyllina* 3.350 f.). Given this hostility to the harsh realities of the Empire, and given the amateur nature of Roman government, how was stability achieved?

Communications have been described as the nervous system of the body politic. Compared with what had gone before and what followed the rule of Rome, the frequency of movement and the security of roads and harbours was most impressive (though banditry never completely disappeared even from Italy). The imperial posting system, a creation of Augustus refined over the following centuries, became so huge, authoritative, and elaborate that it represented one of the heaviest burdens on the provincials whose food, animals, and dwellings were constantly being requisitioned for passing officials, as inscriptions from a wide range of places and times bear eloquent witness. But there can be no doubt that the roads and harbours of the Empire were one of the most necessary organs of Roman rule.

The transmission, retrieval, and storage of information is a still more basic ingredient of the stability, durability, and effectiveness of government. [German sociologist] Max Weber called documents the bureaucrat's tools of production. The Roman Empire has won a reputation for bureaucratic sophistication. So what of its documents? . . .

The documents were stored in archive rooms, some of which are known archaeologically. But although papers were kept, there were no filing cabinets, card indexes, reference numbers, registration forms. Collections of documents were made by pasting them together in chronological or — by no means as often as convenience would dictate — in alphabetical order. The codex, the presentation of documents as a book, was occasionally used, but the cartulary, a choice of really important documents for frequent reference, was unknown. Papers were preserved in archives, but it was well known that in most conditions papyrus did not keep well. Why did these things not matter? Because retrieval of documents from the archive was not a particularly urgent consideration in its formation. The tax assessment notice, the letter from the commanding officer, the tax receipt, the birth registration were used only once, in the process of checking a particular tax collection, or implementing a decision. Access to the document *might* be required a second time, but probably only a tiny fraction of all documents was ever looked at twice. The consultation of a document was a serious matter: "for which reason, pious and benevolent Caesar, order that I be given a copy from your *commentarii* as your father intended" says a petitioner to Hadrian. Administrative processes were a favour, a privilege, a wonder, which is why on documents like this, where only what does credit to the purchaser of the inscription appears, what seem to us to be banal details of this kind are recorded in full. So this one actually preserves Hadrian's orders to his secretaries: "Stasimus, Dapenis, publish the decision or opinion from the recorded version (*edite ex forma*)." Authentication was a serious problem, never entirely solved, which helped prevent reliance on documentary authority. The *sardonychus* or imperial signet-ring gave its name to a Palatine department[6]. . . , but there were often rumours that it had fallen into unauthorized hands. The Emperors used codes, but only rather simple ones. One of the principal reasons for the abuse of the public post system was that there was no reliable way of ensuring that only a limited number of people possessed authentic licences to demand hospitality and service. Distribution was another problem. It is very hard for us to imagine how difficult, despite the efficiency of communications, the systematic exchange of documentary information was. A letter of Trajan to Pliny[7] making an important administrative point need never have been known in next door Asia, let alone Germania Inferior. This is perhaps one reason why Pliny's heirs actually published his

---

[6] Department of the palace administration of the Caesars (emperors). [Ed.]

[7] Pliny was an official for the emperor Trajan (r. 98–117 C.E.). The two kept up an extensive correspondence, an example of which is included in selection 8. [Ed.]

correspondence. This difficulty no doubt helped to discourage the formation of any monolithic imperial administrative structure.

Documents, once stored, were of surprisingly little use. Governmental acts could not afford to depend on such an unreliable basis. The archives represented continuity and stability, and were not for regular use. The truth appears well from the story of the disastrous fire of A.D. 192 at Rome, when the central imperial archives of the Palatine were completely destroyed. . . . There is no hint that Roman government was disrupted; but the event was taken as a token that the authority of Rome, embodied in these documents, would weaken. The omen is not so far removed from the association of Rome's universal rule with a census registration at the beginning of the Gospel of St. Luke. . . .

6

CICERO

Letter to His Brother Quintus, 60 B.C.E.

Marcus Tullius Cicero (106–43 B.C.E.) was the most renowned orator and statesman of the late Roman Republic. As a lawyer and champion of the Roman constitution, Cicero fought against tyranny and political corruption, yet he opposed the assassins of Julius Caesar, and in the subsequent civil war he supported Caesar's adopted son, Octavian, against Mark Antony, a move that ultimately cost him his life.

In this selection, Cicero advises his younger brother Quintus (102–43 B.C.E.) who had been re-appointed by the Roman Senate to be magistrate of the Province of Asia on what to expect and how to behave as a Roman official. What advice does he give his brother? What does this advice tell you about the life of a Roman official in the empire? What does it tell you about Roman administration of the empire?

THINKING HISTORICALLY

In what ways was the professional life of Quintus Cicero different from that of a Chinese official? What other comparisons or contrasts between the Roman and Chinese empires does this selection raise in your mind?

Source: *The Letters of Cicero, Vol. I, B.C. 68–52*, trans. Evelyn Shuckburgh (London: George Bell and Sons, 1899).

I. . . . I begin by entreating you not to let your soul shrink and be cast down, nor to allow yourself to be overpowered by the magnitude of the business as though by a wave; but, on the contrary, to stand upright and keep your footing, or even advance to meet the flood of affairs. For you are not administering a department of the state, in which fortune reigns supreme, but one in which a well-considered policy and an attention to business are the most important things. But if I had seen you receiving the prolongation of a command in a great and dangerous war, I should have trembled in spirit, because I should have known that the dominion of fortune over us had been at the same time prolonged. As it is, however, a department of the state has been entrusted to you in which fortune occupies no part, or, at any rate, an insignificant one, and which appears to me to depend entirely on your virtue and self-control. We have no reason to fear, as far as I know, any designs of our enemies, any actual fighting in the field, any revolts of allies, any default in the tribute or in the supply of corn, any mutiny in the army: things which have very often befallen the wisest of men in such a way, that they have been no more able to get the better of the assault of fortune than the best of pilots a violent tempest. You have been granted profound peace, a dead calm: yet if the pilot falls asleep, it may even so overwhelm him, though if he keeps awake it may give him positive pleasure. For your province consists, in the first place, of allies of a race which, of all the world, is the most civilized; and, in the second place, of Citizens, who, either as being publicani are very closely connected with me, or, as being traders who have made money, think that they owe the security of their property to my consulship.

II. But it may be said that among even such men as these there occur serious disputes, many wrongful acts are committed, and hotly contested litigation is the result. As though I ever thought that you had no trouble to contend with! I know that the trouble is exceedingly great, and such as demands the very greatest prudence; but remember that it is prudence much more than fortune on which, in my opinion, the result of your trouble depends. For what trouble is it to govern those over whom you are set, if you do but govern yourself? That may be a great and difficult task to others, and indeed it is most difficult: to you it has always been the easiest thing in the world, and indeed ought to be so, for your natural disposition is such that, even without discipline, it appears capable of self-control; whereas a discipline has, in fact, been applied that might educate the most faulty of characters. But while you resist, as you do, money, pleasure, and every kind of desire yourself, there will, I am to be told, be a risk of your not being able to suppress some fraudulent banker or some rather over-extortionate tax-collector! For as to the Greeks, they will think, as they behold the innocence of your life, that one of the heroes of their history, or a demigod from heaven, has come down into the province. And this I say, not to induce you to act thus, but to make you glad that you are acting or have acted so. It is a splendid thing to have been three years in supreme power in Asia without allowing statue, picture, plate, napery, slave, anyone's good looks, or any offer of money—all of which are plentiful in your province—to cause you to swerve from the most absolute honesty and purity of life. What can be imagined so striking or so desirable as that a virtue, a command over the passions, a self-control such as yours, are not remaining in darkness and obscurity, but have been set in the broad daylight of Asia, before the eyes of a famous province, and in the hearing of all nations and peoples? That the inhabitants are not being ruined by your progresses, drained by your charges, agitated by your approach? That there is the liveliest joy, public and private, wheresoever you come, the city regarding you as a protector and not a tyrant, the private house as a guest and not a plunderer?

III. But in these matters I am sure that mere experience has by this time taught you that it is by no means sufficient to have these virtues yourself, but that you must keep your eyes open and vigilant, in order that in the guardianship of your province you may be considered to vouch to the allies, the citizens, and the state, not for yourself alone, but for all the subordinates of your government. However, you have in the persons of your legati men likely to have a regard for their own reputation. Of these in rank, position, and age Tubero is first; who, I think, particularly as he is a writer of history, could select from his own Annals many whom he would like and would be able to imitate. Allienus, again, is ours, as well in heart and affection, as in his conformity to our principles. I need not speak of Gratidius: I am sure that, while taking pains to preserve his own reputation, his fraternal affection for us makes him take pains for ours also. Your quaestor is not of your own selection, but the one assigned you by lot. He is bound both to act with propriety of his own accord, and to conform to the policy and principles which you lay down. But should any one of these adopt a lower standard of conduct, you should tolerate such behaviour, if it goes no farther than a breach, in his private capacity, of the rules by which he was bound, but not if it goes to the extent of employing for gain the authority which you granted him as a promotion. For I am far from thinking, especially since the moral sentiments of the day are so much inclined to excessive laxity and self-seeking, that you should investigate every case of petty misconduct, and thoroughly examine every one of these persons; but that you should regulate your confidence by the trustworthiness of its recipient. And among such persons you will have to vouch for those whom the Republic has itself given you as companions and assistants in public affairs, at least within the limits which I have before laid down.

IV. In the case, however, of those of your personal staff or official attendants whom you have yourself selected to be about you—who are usually spoken of as a kind of praetor's cohort—we must vouch, not only for their acts, but even for their words. But those you have with you are the sort of men of whom you may easily be fond when they are acting rightly, and whom you may very easily check when they show insufficient regard for your reputation. By these, when you were raw to the work, your frank disposition might possibly have been deceived—for the better a man is the less easily does he suspect others of being bad—now, however, let this third year witness an integrity as perfect as the two former, but still more wary and vigilant. Listen to that only which you are supposed to listen to; don't let your ears be open to whispered falsehoods and interested suggestions. Don't let your signet ring be a mere implement, but, as it were, your second self: not the minister of another's will, but a witness of your own. Let your marshal hold the rank which our ancestors wished him to hold, who, looking upon this place as not one of profit, but of labour and duty, scarcely ever conferred it upon any but their freedmen, whom they indeed controlled almost as absolutely as their slaves. Let the lictor be the dispenser of your clemency, not his own; and let the fasces and axes which they carry before you constitute ensigns rather of rank than of power. Let it, in fact, be known to the whole province that the life, children, fame, and fortunes of all over whom you preside are exceedingly dear to you. Finally, let it be believed that you will, if you detect it, be hostile not only to those who have accepted a bribe, but to those also who have given it. And, indeed, no one will give anything, if it is made quite clear that nothing is usually obtained from you through those who pretend to be very influential with you. Not, however, that the object of this discourse is to make you over-harsh or suspicious towards your staff. For if any of them in the course of the last two years has never fallen under suspicion of rapacity, as I am told about Caesius and Chaerippus and Labeo—and think it true, because I know them—there is no authority, I think, which may not be entrusted to them, and no confidence which may not be placed in them with the utmost propriety, and in anyone else like them. But if there is anyone of whom you have already had reason to doubt, or concerning whom you have made some discovery, in such a man place no confidence, intrust him with no particle of your reputation. . . .

And now, considering the caution and care that I would show in matters of this kind—in which I fear I may be somewhat over-severe—what do you suppose my sentiments are in regard to slaves? Upon these we ought to keep a hold in all places, but especially in the provinces. On this head many rules may be laid down, but this is at once the shortest and most easily maintained—that they should behave during your progresses in Asia as though you were travelling on the Appian way, and not suppose that it makes any difference whether they have arrived at

Tralles or Formiae. But if, again, any one of your slaves is conspicuously trustworthy, employ him in your domestic and private affairs; but in affairs pertaining to your office as governor, or in any department of the state, do not let him lay a finger. For many things which may, with perfect propriety, be in-trusted to slaves, must yet not be so entrusted, for the sake of avoiding talk and hostile remark. But my discourse, I know not how, has slipped into the didactic vein, though that is not what I proposed to myself originally. For what right have I to be laying down rules for one who, I am fully aware, in this subject especially, is not my inferior in wisdom, while in experience he is even my superior? Yet, after all, if your actions had the additional weight of my approval, I thought that they would seem more satisfactory to yourself. Wherefore, let these be the foundations on which your public character rests: first and foremost your own honesty and self-control, then the scrupulous conduct of all your staff, the exceedingly cautious and careful selection in regard to intimacies with provincials and Greeks, the strict and unbending government of your slaves. These are creditable even in the conduct of our private and everyday business: in such an important government, where morals are so debased and the province has such a corrupting influence, they must needs seem divine. Such principles and conduct on your part are sufficient to justify the strictness which you have displayed in some acts of administration, owing to which I have encountered certain personal disputes with great satisfaction, unless, indeed, you suppose me to be annoyed by the complaints of a fellow like Paconius—who is not even a Greek, but in reality a Mysian or Phrygian—or by the words of Tuscenius, a madman and a knave, from whose abominable jaws you snatched the fruits of a most infamous piece of extortion with the most complete justice.

VII. These and similar instances of your strict administration in your province we shall find difficulty in justifying, unless they are accompanied by the most perfect integrity: wherefore let there be the greatest strictness in your administration of justice, provided only that it is never varied from favour, but is kept up with impartiality. But it is of little avail that justice is administered by yourself with impartiality and care, unless the same is done by those to whom you have entrusted any portion of this duty. And, indeed, in my view there is no very great variety of business in the government of Asia: the entire province mainly depends on the administration of justice. In it we have the whole theory of government, especially of provincial government, clearly displayed: all that a governor has to do is to show consistency and firmness enough, not only to resist favouritism, but even the suspicion of it. To this also must be added courtesy in listening to pleaders, consideration in pronouncing a decision, and painstaking efforts to convince suitors of its justice, and to answer their arguments.

Correspondence between Pliny and Trajan, c. 112 C.E.

In 112, the Emperor Trajan* appointed Pliny† the Younger, a highly respected author and senator, to be governor of Bithynia, a Roman province in what is today northwestern Turkey. This was the high point of the Roman Empire, in terms of size and governance (see Map 4.2). Unlike the age of Cicero at the end of the Republic, when the Roman Senate retained power, Romans had grown accustomed to the rule of an emperor and institutions of empire.

General religious tolerance prevailed throughout the Roman Empire, and only Rome as the capital of the empire might require worship of a state god, including, at times, the emperor himself. Christians ran afoul of the law and communal practice not only by refusing the demonstration of loyalty to the state but also by aggressively denying the validity of all other gods—an attitude that many found distasteful. A brief correspondence between Pliny and the Emperor Trajan from about the year 112 C.E. has survived, throwing light on official Roman policy toward Christians of that era. What does Pliny's letter to Trajan tell you about the official Roman policy? What do you think of Trajan's answer? What do these letters tell you about Roman government of the empire?

THINKING HISTORICALLY

Compare this correspondence to Han Fei's essay. How are the two policies similar? What does this correspondence suggest to you about the difference between Roman and Chinese imperial administration?

Pliny to Trajan

It is my custom, Sire, to refer to you in all cases where I am in doubt, for who can better clear up difficulties and inform me? I have never been present at any legal examination of the Christians, and I do not know, therefore, what are the usual penalties passed upon them, or the limits of those penalties, or how searching an inquiry should be made. I have hesitated a great deal in considering whether any distinctions should be

---

* TRAY juhn
† PLIH nee

Source: Pliny the Younger: *Letters*, X.25 ff, from William Stearns Davis, ed., *Readings in Ancient History: Illustrative Extracts from the Sources*, 2 vols. (Boston: Allyn and Bacon, 1912–13), Vol. II: *Rome and the West*, 298–300.

drawn according to the ages of the accused; whether the weak should be punished as severely as the more robust, or whether the man who has once been a Christian gained anything by recanting? Again, whether the name of being a Christian, even though otherwise innocent of crime, should be punished, or only the crimes that gather around it?

In the meantime, this is the plan which I have adopted in the case of those Christians who have been brought before me. I ask them whether they are Christians, if they say "Yes," then I repeat the question the second time, and also a third—warning them of the penalties involved; and if they persist, I order them away to prison. For I do not doubt that—be their admitted crime what it may—their pertinacity and inflexible obstinacy surely ought to be punished.

There were others who showed similar mad folly, whom I reserved to be sent to Rome, as they were Roman citizens. Later, as is commonly the case, the mere fact of my entertaining the question led to a multiplying of accusations and a variety of cases were brought before me. An anonymous pamphlet was issued, containing a number of names of alleged Christians. Those who denied that they were or had been Christians and called upon the gods with the usual formula, reciting the words after me, and those who offered incense and wine before your image—which I had ordered to be brought forward for this purpose, along with the regular statues of the gods—all such I considered acquitted—especially as they cursed the name of Christ, which it is said *bona fide* Christians cannot be induced to do.

Still others there were, whose names were supplied by an informer. These first said they were Christians, then denied it, insisting they had been, "but were so no longer"; some of them having "recanted many years ago," and more than one "full twenty years back." These all worshiped your image and the god's statues and cursed the name of Christ.

But they declared their guilt or error was simply this—on a fixed day they used to meet before dawn and recite a hymn among themselves to Christ, as though he were a god. So far from binding themselves by oath to commit any crime, they swore to keep from theft, robbery, adultery, breach of faith, and not to deny any trust money deposited with them when called upon to deliver it. This ceremony over, they used to depart and meet again to take food—but it was of no special character, and entirely harmless. They also had ceased from this practice after the edict I issued—by which, in accord with your orders, I forbade all secret societies.

I then thought it the more needful to get at the facts behind their statements. Therefore I placed two women, called "deaconesses," under torture, but I found only a debased superstition carried to great lengths, so I postponed my examination, and immediately consulted you. This seems a matter worthy of your prompt consideration, especially as so many people are endangered. Many of all ages and both sexes are put in peril of their lives by their accusers; and the process will go on, for the contagion of this superstition has spread not merely through the free towns, but into the villages and farms. Still I think it can be halted and things set right. Beyond any doubt, the temples—which were nigh deserted—are beginning again to be thronged with worshipers; the sacred rites, which long have lapsed, are now being renewed, and the food for the sacrificial victims is again finding a sale—though up to recently it had almost no market. So one can safely infer how vast numbers could be reclaimed, if only there were a chance given for repentance.

Trajan to Pliny

You have adopted the right course, my dear Pliny, in examining the cases of those cited before you as Christians; for no hard and fast rule can be laid down covering such a wide question. The Christians are not to be hunted out. If brought before you, and the offense is proved, they are to be punished, but with this reservation—if any one denies he is a Christian, and makes it clear he is not, by offering prayer to our gods, then he is to be pardoned on his recantation, no matter how suspicious his past. As for anonymous pamphlets, they are to be discarded absolutely, whatever crime they may charge, for they are not only a precedent of a very bad type, but they do not accord with the spirit of our age.

8

MARCUS AURELIUS
Meditations, c. 167 C.E.

Marcus Aurelius (121–180 C.E.) was both a Roman emperor (161–180 C.E.) and a philosopher. He is numbered the last of the "five good emperors," a line of emperors that began in 96 C.E. and included Trajan. According to the great historian Edward Gibbon, this was an era in which "the Roman Empire was governed by absolute power, under the guidance of wisdom and virtue."[1]

---

[1] Edward Gibbon, *The Decline and Fall of the Roman Empire* (New York: Everyman's Library, 1993), vol. 1, chap. 3, p. 90.

Source: Marcus Aurelius, *Meditations*, trans. George Long, bk. 2, *The Internet Classics Archive*, http://classics.mit.edu/Antoninus/meditations.2.two.html.

Although much of his reign was taken up with wars, Marcus Aurelius also initiated legal reform on behalf of slaves, minors, and widows. As a philosopher, he was an adherent of Stoicism, a set of beliefs aptly summarized in this selection from his *Meditations*, written about 167 C.E. Stoicism originated in Greece in the third century B.C.E. Stoics believed that negative emotions were the result of poor judgment and that wisdom made one immune to pain or misfortune.

In keeping with his Stoic convictions, Marcus Aurelius calls for the mind to regulate the body. Thus it would seem he meant to lead a very controlled and contemplative life. And yet, to be the emperor was to be the most important actor in the Roman world. The historian Dio Cassius tells us that Marcus Aurelius treated his enemies humanely, but the historian also relates stories of the emperor's desire to exterminate an entire enemy people. How might Marcus Aurelius have reconciled his ideas and his actions to produce such varying results?

The years after 165 C.E. were particularly difficult for the emperor and the empire. Roman forces had just defeated the Parthian army, only to return to their homes with a pandemic disease (possibly smallpox or measles) that lasted until about 180 C.E., claiming the lives of as many as five million people, including Marcus Aurelius himself. How might these events have influenced the emperor's philosophy as recorded in the *Meditations*?

THINKING HISTORICALLY

Compare Marcus Aurelius' personal injunctions on how he should act with Confucian ideas as expressed in *The Analects* and Han Fei's Legalist views on government. What sorts of commonalties, if any, do you detect among these three different philosophies? In what ways have these philosophies had a lasting influence? Ask two questions that require you to compare Marcus Aurelius and some aspect of Chinese history. Ask one question that you can answer from what you have read in this chapter and another question which would require research to answer. What sort of research would you have to do in order to answer the second question?

Begin the morning by saying to thyself, I shall meet with the busy-body, the ungrateful, arrogant, deceitful, envious, unsocial. All these things happen to them by reason of their ignorance of what is good and evil. But I who have seen the nature of the good that it is beautiful, and of the bad that it is ugly, and the nature of him who does wrong, that it is akin to me, not only of the same blood or seed, but that it participates in the same intelligence and the same portion of the divinity, I can neither be injured by any of them, for no one can fix on me what is ugly, nor can I be angry with my kinsman, nor hate him, for we are made for co-operation, like feet, like hands, like eyelids, like the rows of the upper and lower teeth. To act against one another then is contrary to nature; and it is acting against one another to be vexed and to turn away.

Whatever this is that I am, it is a little flesh and breath, and the ruling part. Throw away thy books; no longer distract thyself: it is not allowed; but as if thou wast now dying, despise the flesh; it is blood and bones and a network, a contexture of nerves, veins, and arteries. See the breath also, what kind of a thing it is, air, and not always the same, but every moment sent out and again sucked in. The third then is the ruling part: consider thus: Thou art an old man; no longer let this be a slave, no longer be pulled by the strings like a puppet to unsocial movements, no longer either be dissatisfied with thy present lot, or shrink from the future. . . .

Every moment think steadily as a Roman and a man to do what thou hast in hand with perfect and simple dignity, and feeling of affection, and freedom, and justice; and to give thyself relief from all other thoughts. And thou wilt give thyself relief, if thou doest every act of thy life as if it were the last, laying aside all carelessness and passionate aversion from the commands of reason, and all hypocrisy, and self-love, and discontent with the portion which has been given to thee. Thou seest how few the things are, the which if a man lays hold of, he is able to live a life which flows in quiet, and is like the existence of the gods; for the gods on their part will require nothing more from him who observes these things.

Do wrong to thyself, do wrong to thyself, my soul; but thou wilt no longer have the opportunity of honoring thyself. Every man's life is sufficient. But thine is nearly finished, though thy soul reverences not itself but places thy felicity in the souls of others. . . .

How quickly all things disappear, in the universe the bodies themselves, but in time the remembrance of them; what is the nature of all sensible things, and particularly those which attract with the bait of pleasure or terrify by pain, or are noised abroad by vapoury fame; how worthless, and contemptible, and sordid, and perishable, and dead they are. . . .

Though thou shouldst be going to live three thousand years, and as many times ten thousand years, still remember that no man loses any other life than this which he now lives, nor lives any other than this which he now loses. The longest and shortest are thus brought to the same. For the present is the same to all, though that which perishes is not the same; and so that which is lost appears to be a mere moment. For a man cannot lose either the past or the future: for what a man has not, how can anyone take this from him? These two things then thou must bear in mind; the one, that all things from eternity are of like forms and come round in a circle, and that it makes no difference whether a man shall see the same things during a hundred years or two hundred, or an infinite time; and the second, that the longest liver and he who will die soonest lose just the same. For the present is the only thing of which a man can be deprived, if it is true that this is the only thing which he has, and that a man cannot lose a thing if he has it not. . . .

The soul of man does violence to itself, first of all, when it becomes an abscess and, as it were, a tumour on the universe, so far as it can. For to be vexed at anything which happens is a separation of ourselves from nature, in some part of which the natures of all other things are contained. In the next place, the soul does violence to itself when it turns away from any man, or even moves towards him with the intention of injuring, such as are the souls of those who are angry. In the third place, the soul does violence to itself when it is overpowered by pleasure or by pain. Fourthly, when it plays a part, and does or says anything insincerely and untruly. Fifthly, when it allows any act of its own and any movement to be without an aim, and does anything thoughtlessly and without considering what it is, it being right that even the smallest things be done with reference to an end; and the end of rational animals is to follow the reason and the law of the most ancient city and polity.

Of human life the time is a point, and the substance is in a flux, and the perception dull, and the composition of the whole body subject to putrefaction, and the soul a whirl, and fortune hard to divine, and fame a thing devoid of judgment. And, to say all in a word, everything which belongs to the body is a stream, and what belongs to the soul is a dream and vapor, and life is a warfare and a stranger's sojourn, and after-fame is oblivion. What then is that which is able to conduct a man? One thing and only one, philosophy. But this consists in keeping the daemon[1] within a man free from violence and unharmed, superior to pains and pleasures, doing nothing without purpose, nor yet falsely and with hypocrisy, not feeling the need of another man's doing or not doing anything; and besides, accepting all that happens, and all that is allotted, as coming from thence, wherever it is, from whence he himself came; and, finally, waiting for death with a cheerful mind, as being nothing else than a dissolution of the elements of which every living being is compounded. But if there is no harm to the elements themselves in each continually changing into another, why should a man have any apprehension about the change and dissolution of all the elements? For it is according to nature, and nothing is evil which is according to nature.

[1] Spirit. [Ed.]

■ REFLECTIONS

Stoicism might at first thought seem an odd philosophy for an emperor, stranger still as an ideology to direct the governance of an empire. Yet the belief that everything is natural or that resistance is always futile might comfort an emperor, general, or official who feels forced to wage a bloody campaign or annihilate resistant populations. In any case, Stoicism was not the only tool in the armory of Roman rule. Not even the only ideological tool. The great Enlightenment historian Edward Gibbon famously linked Christianity, reputedly a religion of the weak and pacifists, to *The Decline and Fall of the Roman Empire*. If correct, then the martial Roman gods, emperor cults, and state religions might be credited with the growth and maintenance of the empire in its first few hundred years. But the later history of Christianity, the earlier history of Stoicism, and the variable role of Confucianism in China suggest that ideas can be shaped to the needs of different masters and missions.

The more material tools of governance — police, soldiers, officials, laws, forms, and procedures — would seem more practical than the effort to win hearts and minds. So it is striking that Roman officialdom lacked so many of the basic materials of successful administration. Pliny's letter about the Christians is just one example of the many times he found it necessary to refer a minor matter directly to the emperor. Certainly the Chinese emperor was protected from such distractions by layers of bureaucracy and established procedures.

How about the quality of officials? The Chinese made this a top priority through competitive civil service exams designed to select the most gifted and well-prepared students, regardless of their wealth or family connections. Indeed the system was an end run around family, clan, and regional ties: an important part of the effort to supplant feudalism with a uniform state. Officials were, for instance, not assigned to serve in their home areas, where personal connections might pull them away from state responsibilities. Cicero's letter to his brother refers to more complex arrangements in the Roman Empire; some assistant officers are appointed by the state, others are personal allies of the new governor. Cicero also reminds us of the numerous private interests in Roman provinces. He tells his brother to watch out for the *publicani* — private citizens who purchased the right to collect taxes, clearly a public function in the Chinese Empire. Did the wide range of private responsibilities in the Roman Empire increase corruption? Or did its more independent judiciary raise the barrier against corruption? As a lawyer, some of Cicero's most famous trials were prosecutions of corrupt officials. The standard of behavior he expresses to his brother reads like a model for any age, but his words also betray the numerous obstacles to attaining them.

These readings might suggest innumerable comparative questions about the Roman and Chinese empires. Some readings discuss the use of armed force: One might ask why soldiers had higher status in Rome. The Han debate about salt and iron might lead the reader to ask about Rome (which monopolized salt but not iron) or the role of government monopolies in other times and places.

The study of the Roman Empire has always posed comparative questions about more recent empires, especially the British Empire in the nineteenth century and, for many, the global empire of the United States today. The addition of China, or the history of any other empire, helps us see more patterns and ask more questions that might better help us better understand ourselves.

5

Gender, Sex, and Love in Classical Societies

India, China, and the Mediterranean, 500 B.C.E.–550 C.E.

■ HISTORICAL CONTEXT

In the first chapter we saw how male-dominated societies or patriarchies developed, or at the very least strengthened and consolidated, in the wake of plow agriculture, irrigation, and city and state building, beginning about five thousand years ago. In some areas of the world—the Americas, sub-Saharan Africa, and Southeast Asia—patriarchies emerged later or remained less vigorous. Between 500 B.C.E. and 550 C.E., patriarchies flourished in the core areas of early city-societies or "civilizations" in the Mediterranean, India, and China. Historians call this period "classical" because it witnessed the florescence of a number of cultural traditions that are still honored as formative, among them Confucianism, Buddhism, Christianity, and Greco-Roman philosophy. The last chapter illuminated the importance of such philosophical traditions as Confucianism, Legalism, and Stoicism in the period. The next chapter will explore the impact of the great religious traditions of Hinduism, Buddhism, Judaism, and Christianity—all of which were founded or took recognizable form in this period.

This chapter asks about the relationships of men and women in this age of cultural flowering and increasing gender discrimination. What did it mean to be a man or a woman in the classical era? What was the impact of these classical traditions on gender identity? How was being a woman or a man different, and how was it similar, across these classical civilizations? Was it also the classical formative period of our own identities, ideas, and feelings? Or was it ancient history?

153

■ THINKING HISTORICALLY

Asking about Author, Audience, and Agenda

Historical sources, from the simplest laundry list to the most sophisticated work of art, are made by someone for someone to serve a particular purpose. In other words, each has an author, an audience, and an agenda. The better we understand who created a source, its intended reader or viewer, and the reasons it was created, the better we can make sense of the source and the society or culture in which it was produced. In many cases much of this information is not available to us, at least not in the detail we would like. But there are often clues in the source itself that enable us to determine the author, audience, and agenda. In this chapter we will interrogate the sources themselves to find this information.

1

SARAH SHAVER HUGHES AND BRADY HUGHES

Women in the Classical Era, 2005

Sarah and Brady Hughes are modern historians. This selection is part of their essay on the history of women in the ancient world written for a book on the history of women. They write here of the classical era in India, China, Greece, and Rome. All of these were patriarchal societies, but how were they different? The authors also mention Greek Hellenistic society and pre-Roman Etruscan society. How do these two societies round out your understanding of women between 500 B.C.E. and 550 C.E.? What seem to be the conditions or causes that improved the status of women in some societies and in some periods?

THINKING HISTORICALLY

The authors, audience, and agenda in this selection are fairly transparent because it is a secondary source written by modern historians. The authors do not reveal anything of themselves, but their writing is matter-of-fact and dispassionate and shows an effort

Source: Sarah Shaver Hughes and Brady Hughes, "Women in Ancient Civilizations," in *Women's History in Global Perspective*, ed. Bonnie G. Smith (Urbana: University of Illinois Press, published with the American Historical Association, 2005), 2:26–30, 36–39.

to be thorough. All of this is appropriate in an informative essay written for a college-level audience. Note that this essay is part of a book published with the American Historical Association, the national organization of history teachers and scholars. The original essay carried a considerable number of footnotes (sixty-eight notes for a thirty-five-page article), and it lacked the pronunciation and explanatory notes included with this reprinting. Does this suggest a work aimed at scholars, teachers, or students? Does the essay argue a point of scholarship, or does it summarize the scholarly work of others? What other clues in the reading indicate the intended audience and the purpose or agenda of the article?

India

... Women's rights deteriorated after the Vedic* period (1600–800 B.C.E.). No one has been able to prove why this happened. Scholarly interest has focused on women's exclusion from performing Hindu rituals, which was in effect by 500 B.C.E. ... Julia Leslie[1] thinks that women's exclusion resulted from intentional mistranslation of the Vedas[2] by male scholars, as the rituals became more complicated and as the requirement for property ownership was more rigorously enforced at a time when women could not own property.

The falling age of marriage for Indian women is another illustration of their loss of rights. In 400 B.C.E. about sixteen years was a normal age for a bride at marriage; between 400 B.C.E. and 100 C.E. it fell to pre-puberty; and after 100 C.E. pre-puberty was favored. These child marriages also affected women's religious roles. Because girls married before they could finish their education, they were not qualified to perform ritual sacrifices. Furthermore, wives' legal rights eroded. As child wives, they were treated as minors. Then their minority status lengthened until they were lifetime minors as wards of their husbands. Finally, women were prohibited any independence and were always under men's control: their fathers, husbands, or sons. By 100 C.E. Hindu texts defined women with negative characteristics, stating, for example, that women would be promiscuous unless controlled by male relatives. While Indian women were losing their independence, Indian men continued to glorify

---

*VAY dihk

[1] Leslie, "Essence and Existence: Women and Religion in Ancient Indian Text," in *Women's Religious Experience*, ed. Pat Holden (Totawa: Barnes and Noble Books, 1983). Dr. Isobel Julia Leslie (1948–2004), philosopher, historian, and novelist of Indian culture, wrote widely on women in India. [Ed.]

[2] The Vedas (see Chapter 3) were the writings of ancient Indian Hinduism, usually dated as above between 1600 and 800 B.C.E. in origins, though extant texts were written later. [Ed.]

their wives and mothers. A wife was the essence of the home, a man was not complete without a wife, and sons were expected to respect their mothers more than their fathers. As Romila Thapar sums up these contradictions, "The symbol of the woman in Indian culture has been a curious intermeshing of low legal status, ritual contempt, sophisticated sexual partnership, and deification."

One of the causes for this deterioration of women's rights and independence was the increasing rigidity of Hinduism under the influence of the Brahmans.[3] By 600 B.C.E. sects were springing up that opposed Brahman power and ostentatiously omitted some of the Hindu essentials, such as priests, rituals and ceremonies, animal sacrifices, and even caste distinctions.[4] Jainism and Buddhism are two of the sects that have survived. They were especially attractive to women. Jainism, the older religion, gained prominence with the efforts of its last prophet, Mahavira, who lived at the end of the sixth century B.C.E. Jains sought to live without passion and to act "correctly." One could achieve liberation only by living within a monastery or nunnery. Women who sought to join a nunnery found that the Jains had no membership restrictions. Many women entered and found new and exciting roles that were for the first time open to them. . . .

Mahavira's contemporary, Gautama Siddhartha* (the Buddha), began the religion that eventually spread throughout Asia. Among studies of Buddhist women, the early years have been a focus of interest. While Buddhism had no priests, it relied on celibate monks, who were initially homeless, except in the monsoon season, and had to beg for their necessities as they spread their ideas. The Buddha was reluctant to allow women to become nuns. He refused even the women in his family who sought to become nuns until he was reminded repeatedly by his aunt and his disciple Ananda of his stated principle that anyone could attain enlightenment. The Buddha then reluctantly accepted women followers, and they, like monks, eventually lived in their own self-governing celibate monasteries. . . .

China

. . . For Chinese women the ideas of Confucius (551–479 B.C.E.) have been most influential. There is little mention of women in his *Analects*. His neo-Confucian interpreters corrected this omission, however. They made explicit men's desire for a woman's subordination to her family, her husband, and her sons. For example, Lieh Nu Chuan (also known as Liu Hsiang, 80–87

---

*GAW tah moh   sih DAHR thah

[3] Brahmans were priests of the Hindu religion. Because the Vedas enshrined priests as the highest caste, early Hinduism is sometimes called Brahminism. *Brahman* is also used to mean the totality of the divine (God). [Ed.]

[4] Some of these "Hindu essentials" may have actually become Hindu essentials in the Brahman encounter with Buddhism and Jainism after 600 B.C.E. [Ed.]

B.C.E.) wrote *The Biographies of Eminent Chinese Women,* in which he included 125 biographies of women from the peasant class to the emperor's wife, taken from prehistoric legends to the early years of the Han dynasty.

Although the purpose of these biographical sketches was to provide moral instruction in the passive ideals of Confucian womanhood, translator Albert Richard O'Hara's analysis of the women's actions reveals their influence on events that were important to them. The traditional Chinese interpretation of the genre is evident in one of the best known biographies, that of the widowed mother of Mencius (Meng K'o, or Meng-tzu), whose stern supervision and self-sacrifice were shown to have shaped her son's character and philosophy. This tale drives home the point that a woman's highest ambitions should be fulfilled indirectly through the talents of her sons. Pan Chao,[5] a female scholar in the first century C.E., wrote *The Seven Feminine Virtues* as a Confucian manual for girls' behavior. Its prescriptions of humility, meekness, modesty, and hard work continued to be copied by generations of young women until the twentieth century. . . .

Occasionally, imperial women seized power to govern when acting as regent for an underage emperor. Usually regents exercised this power cautiously behind the scenes because there was much opposition to women's open governance. Two famous empresses ruled openly, however, and sought to transfer royal descent to their own natal families. The first, Empress Lu, violated every canon of Confucian femininity. The widow of Gaodi, the first Han emperor (ruled 202–195 B.C.E.), Empress Lu acted swiftly and brutally to eliminate competitors at court during the near-fifteen years of her rule as regent for her son, her grandson, and another adopted infant grandson. By retaining power until her death in 181 B.C.E., she expected that her own nephews would succeed her. Instead, a civil war over the succession ended the period of peaceful prosperity, low taxes, and lessened punishment for crimes that had made her reign popular with the Chinese people. . . .

Greece

Classical Greece has long been admired for its political theories, philosophy, science, and the arts. Until recently, Greek social history was largely ignored. Slavery, homosexuality, and subordination of women are topics once dismissed as insignificant but now recognized as important to understanding the culture. In the classical period there were actually many "Greeces," with distinct societies developing in the citystates of Athens, Sparta, and Thebes. Gender patterns varied considerably among these cities. Sparta's aristocratic women, for example, were often left alone to acquire wealth and some

---

[5] Ban Zhao in selection 2 in this chapter. [Ed.]

autonomy when their mercenary husbands soldiered elsewhere. To some Athenian men such as Aristotle, Spartan women were thought to be despicable, licentious, greedy, and the reason for Sparta's decline.

Aristotle and other Athenian men dominate the discourse from classical Greece. Their male descriptions tell how Athenian society secluded elite women, denigrated and exploited them, and made them the legal dependents of men. Because no women's writings survive, only indirect evidence suggests how Athenian wives escaped their lives of hard work in the isolated, dark rooms that their husbands imagined necessary to preserve their chastity. But as drawn on vases, groups of Athenian women read to one another, spun and wove, shared child care, or talked. Women are shown in public processions and getting water from wells. Bits of documentary records show respectable married women earning their livings as wet nurses, farm workers, and retail vendors. Most records reveal the lives of privileged women, yet many Athenian women were slaves. Exposure of unwanted female babies was one internal source of slaves, for the rescuer of such an infant became her owner. Athenian enslavement of females was exceptional in its celebration of prostitution in literary and artistic records. One explanation for the large number of slave sex workers may be the Athenians' desire to attract sailors and merchants to their port.

Research on women in the Hellenistic period concentrates on Greek women living in Egypt. These women were much more assertive and influential than their sisters in either contemporary Greece or later Rome. Women in the ruling Ptolemaic[6] family often actually ruled Egypt, some as regents, others as queens. Cleopatra VII (69–30 B.C.E.), one of the best-known women in ancient history, guided her country from a tributary position in the Roman Empire into a partnership with Marc Antony that might have led to Egypt's domination of the eastern Mediterranean. Non-elite women had unusual freedom. They owned property (including land), participated in commerce, produced textiles, were educated, and enjoyed careers as artists, poets, and farmers. But some women were slaves. . . .

Rome

As late as the sixth century B.C.E., Rome was dominated by its northern neighbors, the Etruscans. Although no body of Etruscan literature exists, scholars have sought evidence of women's lives from inscriptions and art found in their tombs. Upper-class Etruscan women were more autonomous and privileged than contemporary Greek women. Paintings of husbands

---

[6] The ruling family of Egypt, descended from Alexander the Great's general, Ptolemy, who took power in 323 B.C.E. The Ptolemies ruled for three hundred years until the Roman conquest. The last of the Ptolemies was Cleopatra VII, who ruled briefly with Marc Antony but was conquered by Octavian in 30 B.C.E. and committed suicide. [Ed.]

and wives feasting together horrified Greek males, who only allowed prostitutes to attend their banquets. Etruscan women were not restricted to their homes as Greek women were and attended the games at gymnasiums. In Italy, all women left votive statues of women in sacred places, probably as a fertility offering, but only Etruscan statues included a nursing child, suggesting an affection for children that paralleled the affectionate touching between couples occasionally shown in their art. Finally, Etruscan women had personal names, in contrast to Greek women, who were known first as their fathers' daughters and later as their husbands' wives.

The Romans did not duplicate the autonomy of women in Etruscan society. Roman women legally were constrained within a highly patriarchal agricultural system organized around clans. A father could kill or sell his children into slavery without fear of legal action. Husbands could kill their wives if they were caught in adultery. Women did not speak in public meetings. They could not buy and sell property without their male relatives' approval. Legally treated as minors, women were first the responsibility of their fathers, then of their husbands, and finally of appointed guardians. Rome was a warrior society and a male republic. Men even dominated the state religion, with the exception of the six Vestal Virgins who served as priestesses. Roman society remained staunchly male until conquests brought wealth to Italy in the second century B.C.E. Changes that accompanied the booty of empire gave women a measure of economic and marital independence that is illustrated by the loosening of legal restrictions against women's property ownership.

The paterfamilias, the oldest male in the family, had complete *manus* (legal control) over his children. In marriage, manus passed from the paterfamilias to the new husband. Among other things, that meant the husband then controlled all of his wife's property. Before the first century B.C.E. some Roman marriages were made without transferring manus to the husband; the wife and her property would remain under her father's control, whose approval was theoretically required for the daughter to buy or sell property. Susan Treggiari explains how this enabled many women to gain control over their property:

> Given ancient expectation of life, it is probable that many women were fatherless for a relatively long period of their married lives. The pattern . . . for the middle ranks of Roman society is that girls married in their late teens and men in their mid- to late twenties. If expectation of life at birth is put between twenty and thirty, then 46 percent of fifteen-year-olds had no father left alive. The percentage grows to 59 percent of twenty-year-olds and 70 percent of twenty-five-year-olds. So there is about a 50 percent chance that a woman was already fatherless at the time of her first marriage.

Upon a father's death, manus was transferred to a guardian, and women began to choose as their guardians men who agreed with them.

By the later years of the Roman Republic, therefore, many women bought and sold land as they pleased. Rome's expansion contributed to this change as it fueled a growing market in real and personal property.

In the third century B.C.E., Rome began two centuries of conquests that eventually placed most of the land surrounding the Mediterranean under Roman administration or in the hands of client states. Roman wives farmed while citizen-soldiers of the Republic were on campaigns, sometimes for more than a decade. Successful wars enriched a Roman elite who accumulated estates worked by male and female slaves as small farmers sold their lands and moved to the city with their wives and children. Elite Romans, both men and women, possessed large estates, luxurious urban houses, much rental property, and many slaves. By 50 B.C.E., Rome had a population of approximately one million. Slaves poured into Italy after successful campaigns, when the defeated enemy was enslaved. As the Romans conquered country after country, they brutalized the captured women, enslaving many. Ruling queens in subdued countries were inevitably replaced with either indigenous male elites or Roman officials. Queen Boudicca of Britain, for example, led a revolt that ended in her death in the first century C.E. Queen Zenobia of Palmyra's invasion of the empire in the third century C.E. was so well organized that Roman authors praised her. Cleopatra of Egypt committed suicide when her plan to make Egypt a regional partner of Rome failed.

Roman women did not publicly speak in the Forum (where men debated civic affairs), with the notable exception of Hortensia in 43 B.C.E. She was the spokesperson for a demonstration of wealthy women who protested taxation without representation for civil wars they did not support. Elite women usually indirectly influenced political decisions through networks of politicians' wives. During the civil wars of the first century B.C.E., wives of some tyrants even made temporary political decisions. On a wider scale, middle-class and elite women took advantage of the turmoil at the end of the Republic[7] to acquire businesses, as analysis of Pompeii[8] shows. Prostitution flowered in Rome with the inflow of slaves, both male and female. A small part of the elite lived in the self-indulgent luxury that became famous in literature. In a brief period of two generations at the end of the first century B.C.E., Roman elite women eschewed children and family responsibilities for a glamorous and self-absorbed life of parties and lovers. In this period men and women were openly adulterous. This "café society" flourished in the chaos of civil wars that nearly destroyed the prestige of the elite and killed or exiled many of them.

---

[7] In the second half of the first century B.C.E. [Ed.]

[8] The city of Pompeii was buried in the ashes caused by the eruption of Mount Vesuvius (near modern Naples) in 79 C.E. Because of its instant burial, it is a rich source of information and artifacts from the period. [Ed.]

This era of chaos ended during the reign of the emperor Augustus (ruled 27 B.C.E.–14 C.E.), who sought to stabilize Roman society in part by reducing women's freedoms. Women were criticized for adultery, wearing too much makeup, having immodest dress and conduct, and especially for refusing to have children. Augustus procured laws that intended to remove control of marriage and reproduction from the family and allow the state to regulate marriage and reproduction. He attempted to penalize women between the ages of twenty and fifty and men over the age of twenty-five who did not marry and have children by denying them the right to inherit wealth. Furthermore, women were not to be released from male guardianship until they had three children. The Augustan laws made the state the regulator of private behavior and attempted to raise the birthrate of citizens while accepting some of the social changes that had modified the patriarchal society of the old Roman Republic. Augustus sought political support from conservative males by decreasing the autonomy of women who had less political influence than men.

2

BAN ZHAO

Lessons for Women, c. 100 C.E.

The teachings of Confucius (561–479 B.C.E.) provided the Chinese and other Asian peoples with ideals of private and public conduct. Confucius's teachings emphasized the importance of filial piety, or the duty of children to serve and obey their parents, as well as to exercise restraint and treat others as one would like to be treated (see selection 3 in Chapter 4 for excerpts from Confucius's *Analects*). Ban Zhao* (45–116 C.E.) (Pan Chao in the previous selection) was the leading female Confucian scholar of classical China. Born into a literary family and educated by her mother, she was married at the age of fourteen. After her husband's death she finished writing her brother's history of the Han dynasty and served as imperial historian to Emperor Han Hedi (r. 88–105 C.E.) and as an advisor to the Empress-Dowager Deng.

Ban Zhao is best remembered, however, for her *Lessons for Women*, which she wrote to fill a gap in Confucian literature. With their

*bahn ZHOW

Source: *Pan Chao: Foremost Woman Scholar of China*, trans. Nancy Lee Swann (New York: Century Co., 1932), 82–90.

emphasis on the responsibilities of the son to the father and on the moral example of a good ruler, the writings of Confucius virtually ignored women. Ban Zhao sought to rectify that oversight by applying Confucian principles to the moral instruction of women. What does this piece say about the roles of both men and women? In what ways would Ban Zhao's *Lessons* support Chinese patriarchy? In what ways might they challenge the patriarchy or make it less oppressive for women?

THINKING HISTORICALLY

The author of this primary source provides an unusual bounty of personal autobiographical information in the first section. But why might the modern reader find much of this self-description unconvincing? Similarly, there is a discrepancy between the author's description of her audience and purpose in writing and the modern reader's idea of her audience and agenda. In fact, the introduction (above) and a line by the Hugheses in the previous selection tell you what historians think of the likely audience and agenda for Ban Zhao. What is this discrepancy between the author's presentation and what historians know to be her audience and agenda? How do these discrepancies actually help us better understand the author and, perhaps, Chinese or Confucian classical culture?

I, the unworthy writer, am unsophisticated, unenlightened, and by nature unintelligent, but I am fortunate both to have received not a little favor from my scholarly Father, and to have had a cultured mother and instructresses upon whom to rely for a literary education as well as for training in good manners. More than forty years have passed since at the age of fourteen I took up the dustpan and the broom in the Cao family.[1] During this time with trembling heart I feared constantly that I might disgrace my parents, and that I might multiply difficulties for both the women and the men of my husband's family. Day and night I was distressed in heart, but I labored without confessing weariness. Now and hereafter, however, I know how to escape from such fears.

Being careless, and by nature stupid, I taught and trained my children without system. Consequently I fear that my son Gu may bring disgrace upon the Imperial Dynasty by whose Holy Grace he has unprecedentedly received the extraordinary privilege of wearing the Gold and the Purple,[2] a privilege for the attainment of which by my son, I a humble subject never even hoped. Nevertheless, now that he is a man and able to plan his own life, I need not again have concern for him. But

---

[1] Her husband's family. [Ed.]
[2] Gold seal and purple robe were symbols of high nobility. [Ed.]

I do grieve that you, my daughters, just now at the age for marriage, have not at this time had gradual training and advice; that you still have not learned the proper customs for married women. I fear that by failure in good manners in other families you will humiliate both your ancestors and your clan. I am now seriously ill, life is uncertain. As I have thought of you all in so untrained a state, I have been uneasy many a time for you. At hours of leisure I have composed . . . these instructions under the title, "Lessons for Women." In order that you may have something wherewith to benefit your persons, I wish every one of you, my daughters each to write out a copy for yourself.

From this time on every one of you strive to practice these lessons.

Humility

On the third day after the birth of a girl the ancients observed three customs: first to place the baby below the bed; second to give her a potsherd[3] with which to play; and third to announce her birth to her ancestors by an offering. Now to lay the baby below the bed plainly indicated that she is lowly and weak, and should regard it as her primary duty to humble herself before others. To give her potsherds with which to play indubitably signified that she should practice labor and consider it her primary duty to be industrious. To announce her birth before her ancestors clearly meant that she ought to esteem as her primary duty the continuation of the observance of worship in the home.

These three ancient customs epitomize woman's ordinary way of life and the teachings of the traditional ceremonial rites and regulations. Let a woman modestly yield to others; let her respect others; let her put others first, herself last. Should she do something good, let her not mention it; should she do something bad let her not deny it. Let her bear disgrace; let her even endure when others speak or do evil to her. Always let her seem to tremble and to fear. When a woman follows such maxims as these then she may be said to humble herself before others.

Let a woman retire late to bed, but rise early to duties; let her not dread tasks by day or by night. Let her not refuse to perform domestic duties whether easy or difficult. That which must be done, let her finish completely, tidily, and systematically. When a woman follows such rules as these, then she may be said to be industrious.

Let a woman be correct in manner and upright in character in order to serve her husband. Let her live in purity and quietness of spirit, and attend to her own affairs. Let her love not gossip and silly laughter.

---

[3] A piece of broken pottery. [Ed.]

Let her cleanse and purify and arrange in order the wine and the food for the offerings to the ancestors. When a woman observes such principles as these, then she may be said to continue ancestral worship.

No woman who observes these three fundamentals of life has ever had a bad reputation or has fallen into disgrace. If a woman fails to observe them, how can her name be honored; how can she but bring disgrace upon herself?

Husband and Wife

The Way of husband and wife is intimately connected with Yin and Yang and relates the individual to gods and ancestors. Truly it is the great principle of Heaven and Earth, and the great basis of human relationships. Therefore the "Rites"[4] honor union of man and woman; and in the "Book of Poetry"[5] the "First Ode" manifests the principle of marriage. For these reasons the relationship cannot but be an important one.

If a husband be unworthy, then he possesses nothing by which to control his wife. If a wife be unworthy, then she possesses nothing with which to serve her husband. If a husband does not control his wife, then the rules of conduct manifesting his authority are abandoned and broken. If a wife does not serve her husband, then the proper relationship between men and women and the natural order of things are neglected and destroyed. As a matter of fact the purpose of these two[6] is the same. . . .

Respect and Caution

As Yin and Yang are not of the same nature, so man and woman have different characteristics. The distinctive quality of the Yang is rigidity; the function of the Yin is yielding. Man is honored for strength; a woman is beautiful on account of her gentleness. Hence there arose the common saying: "A man though born like a wolf may, it is feared, become a weak monstrosity; a woman though born like a mouse may, it is feared, become a tiger."

Now for self-culture nothing equals respect for others. To counteract firmness nothing equals compliance. Consequently it can be said that the Way of respect and acquiescence is woman's most important principle of conduct. So respect may be defined as nothing other than holding on to

---

[4] *The Classic of Rites*, one of the five classics of the Confucian canon, believed to be written by Confucius, though the current text dates from the Han dynasty. [Ed.]

[5] *The Classic of Odes.* Also declared one of five classics in the Han dynasty, the *Book of Odes* or *Songs* contains poems from as early as 1000 B.C.E. in the Zhou dynasty, presumed to be edited by Confucius. [Ed.]

[6] The controlling of women by men, and the serving of men by women. [Ed.]

that which is permanent; and acquiescence nothing other than being liberal and generous. Those who are steadfast in devotion know that they should stay in their proper places; those who are liberal and generous esteem others, and honor and serve them.

If husband and wife have the habit of staying together, never leaving one another, and following each other around within the limited space of their own rooms, then they will lust after and take liberties with one another. From such action improper language will arise between the two. This kind of discussion may lead to licentiousness. But of licentiousness will be born a heart of disrespect to the husband. Such a result comes from not knowing that one should stay in one's proper place.

Furthermore, affairs may be either crooked or straight; words may be either right or wrong. Straightforwardness cannot but lead to quarreling; crookedness cannot but lead to accusation. If there are really accusations and quarrels, then undoubtedly there will be angry affairs. Such a result comes from not esteeming others, and not honoring and serving them.

If wives suppress not contempt for husbands, then it follows that such wives rebuke and scold their husbands. If husbands stop not short of anger, then they are certain to beat their wives. The correct relationship between husband and wife is based upon harmony and intimacy, and conjugal love is grounded in proper union. Should actual blows be dealt, how could matrimonial relationship be preserved? Should sharp words be spoken, how could conjugal love exist? If love and proper relationship both be destroyed, then husband and wife are divided.

Womanly Qualifications

A woman ought to have four qualifications: (1) womanly virtue; (2) womanly words; (3) womanly bearing; and (4) womanly work. Now what is called womanly virtue need not be brilliant ability, exceptionally different from others. Womanly words need be neither clever in debate nor keen in conversation. Womanly appearance requires neither a pretty nor a perfect face and form. Womanly work need not be work done more skillfully than that of others.

To guard carefully her chastity; to control circumspectly her behavior; in every motion to exhibit modesty; and to model each act on the best usage, this is womanly virtue.

To choose her words with care; to avoid vulgar language; to speak at appropriate times; and not to weary others with much conversation, may be called the characteristics of womanly words.

To wash and scrub filth away; to keep clothes and ornaments fresh and clean; to wash the head and bathe the body regularly, and to keep the person free from disgraceful filth, may be called the characteristics of womanly bearing.

With whole-hearted devotion to sew and to weave; to love not gossip and silly laughter; in cleanliness and order to prepare the wine and food for serving guests, may be called the characteristics of womanly work.

These four qualifications characterize the greatest virtue of a woman. No woman can afford to be without them. In fact they are very easy to possess if a woman only treasures them in her heart. The ancients had a saying: "Is love afar off? If I desire love, then love is at hand!" So can it be said of these qualifications.

3

VATSYANA

On the Conduct of Wives, Husbands, and Women of the Harem, c. 280–550 C.E.

We know next to nothing about the author of this classic Indian book on *kama* (love, sex, or sensual experience), written between the fourth and sixth centuries C.E. in the Gupta period (c. 280–550 C.E.).[1] What does this selection tell you about classical Indian culture and society, particularly about men, women, and the way they interacted? What does it tell you about sexuality and religion in classical India?

THINKING HISTORICALLY

Vatsyana does not directly tell us anything about himself. Assuming, however, that the translation is faithful to the original, how would you characterize the author's tone and style?

For what kind of people did he write, and what do you think he hoped to accomplish? At the end of the book—a section not included here—the author writes: "The Kama Sutra was composed, according to the precepts of Holy Writ, for the benefit of the world, by Vatsyayana, while leading the life of a religious student, and wholly engaged in the contemplation of the Deity." Does that statement change your idea of the author, his audience, or his agenda in writing the work?

[1] The Gupta period was a period not only of cultural flowering, but also of political expansion. The Gupta Empire covered most of north and central India.

Source: Mallanaga Vatsyana, *The Kama Sutra*, trans. Sir Richard F. Burton (1883), *Internet Sacred Texts Archive*, http://www.sacred-texts.com/sex/kama/kama101.htm.

The causes of re-marrying during the lifetime of the wife are as follows:

- The folly or ill-temper of the wife
- Her husband's dislike to her
- The want of offspring
- The continual birth of daughters
- The incontinence of the husband

From the very beginning, a wife should endeavour to attract the heart of her husband, by showing to him continually her devotion, her good temper, and her wisdom. If however she bears him no children, she should herself toilette her husband to marry another woman. And when the second wife is married, and brought to the house, the first wife should give her a position superior to her own, and look upon her as a sister. In the morning the elder wife should forcibly make the younger one decorate herself in the presence of their husband, and should not mind all the husband's favour being given to her. If the younger wife does anything to displease her husband the elder one should not neglect her, but should always be ready to give her most careful advice, and should teach her to do various things in the presence of her husband. Her children she should treat as her own, her attendants she should look upon with more regard, even than on her own servants, her friends she should cherish with love and kindness, and her relations with great honour.

When there are many other wives besides herself, the elder wife should associate with the one who is immediately next to her in rank and age, and should instigate the wife who has recently enjoyed her husband's favour to quarrel with the present favourite. After this she should sympathize with the former, and having collected all the other wives together, should get them to denounce the favourite as a scheming and wicked woman, without however committing herself in any way. If the favourite wife happens to quarrel with the husband, then the elder wife should take her part and give her false encouragement, and thus cause the quarrel to be increased. If there be only a little quarrel between the two, the elder wife should do all she can to work it up into a large quarrel. But if after all this she finds the husband still continues to love his favourite wife she should then change her tactics, and endeavour to bring about a conciliation between them, so as to avoid her husband's displeasure.

Thus ends the conduct of the elder wife.

The younger wife should regard the elder wife of her husband as her mother, and should not give anything away, even to her own relations, without her knowledge. She should tell her everything about herself, and not approach her husband without her permission.

Whatever is told to her by the elder wife she should not reveal to others, and she should take care of the children of the senior even more than of her own. When alone with her husband she should serve him well, but should not tell him of the pain she suffers from the existence of a rival wife. She may also obtain secretly from her husband some marks of his particular regard for her, and may tell him that she lives only for him, and for the regard that he has for her. She should never reveal her love for her husband, nor her husband's love for her to any person, either in pride or in anger, for a wife that reveals the secrets of her husband is despised by him. As for seeking to obtain the regard of her husband, Gonardiya says, that it should always be done in private, for fear of the elder wife. If the elder wife be disliked by her husband, or be childless, she should sympathize with her, and should ask her husband to do the same, but should surpass her in leading the life of a chaste woman.

Thus ends the conduct of the younger wife towards the elder.

A widow in poor circumstances, or of a weak nature, and who allies herself again to a man, is called a widow remarried.

The followers of Babhravya say that a virgin widow should not marry a person whom she may be obliged to leave on account of his bad character, or of his being destitute of the excellent qualities of a man, she thus being obliged to have recourse to another person. Gonardiya is of opinion that as the cause of a widow's marrying again is her desire for happiness, and as happiness is secured by the possession of excellent qualities in her husband, joined to love of enjoyment, it is better therefore to secure a person endowed with such qualities in the first instance. Vatsyayana however thinks that a widow may marry any person that she likes, and that she thinks will suit her.

At the time of her marriage the widow should obtain from her husband the money to pay the cost of drinking parties, and picnics with her relations, and of giving them and her friends kindly gifts and presents; or she may do these things at her own cost if she likes. In the same way she may wear either her husband's ornaments or her own. As to the presents of affection mutually exchanged between the husband and herself there is no fixed rule about them. If she leaves her husband after marriage of her own accord, she should restore to him whatever he may have given her, with the exception of the mutual presents. If however she is driven out of the house by her husband she should not return anything to him.

After her marriage she should live in the house of her husband like one of the chief members of the family, but should treat the other ladies of the family with kindness, the servants with generosity, and all the friends of the house with familiarity and good temper. She should show that she is better acquainted with the sixty-four arts than the other ladies of the house, and in any quarrels with her husband she should not rebuke him severely but in private do everything that he wishes, and make use of the sixty-four ways of enjoyment. She should be obliging to the other wives of her husband, and to their children she should give presents, behave as their mistress, and make ornaments and playthings for their use. In the friends and servants of her husband she should confide more than in his other wives, and finally she should have a liking for drinking parties, going to picnics, attending fairs and festivals, and for carrying out all kinds of games and amusements.

Thus ends the conduct of a virgin widow remarried.

A woman who is disliked by her husband, and annoyed and distressed by his other wives, should associate with the wife who is liked most by her husband, and who serves him more than the others, and should teach her all the arts with which she is acquainted. She should act as the nurse to her husband's children, and having gained over his friends to her side, should through them make him acquainted of her devotion to him. In religious ceremonies she should be a leader, as also in vows and fasts, and should not hold too good an opinion of herself. When her husband is lying on his bed she should only go near him when it is agreeable to him, and should never rebuke him, or show obstinacy in any way. If her husband happens to quarrel with any of his other wives, she should reconcile them to each other, and if he desires to see any woman secretly, she should manage to bring about the meeting between them. She should moreover make herself acquainted with the weak points of her husband's character, but always keep them secret, and on the whole behave herself in such a way as may lead him to look upon her as a good and devoted wife.

Here ends the conduct of a wife disliked by her husband.

The above sections will show how all the women of the king's seraglio are to behave, and therefore we shall now speak separately only about the king.

The female attendants in the harem . . . should bring flowers, ointments and clothes from the king's wives to the king, and he having received these things should give them as presents to the servants, along with the things worn by him the previous day. In the afternoon the king, having dressed and put on his ornaments, should interview the women of the harem, who should also be dressed and decorated with jewels. Then having given to each of them such a place and such respect as may suit the occasion and as they may deserve, he should carry on with them a cheerful conversation. After that he should see such of his wives as may be virgin widows remarried, and after them the concubines and dancing girls. All of these should be visited in their own private rooms.

When the king rises from his noonday sleep, the woman whose duty it is to inform the king regarding the wife who is to spend the night with him should come to him accompanied by the female attendants of that wife whose turn may have arrived in the regular course, and of her who may have been accidentally passed over as her turn arrived, and of her who may have been unwell at the time of her turn. These attendants should place before the king the ointments and unguents sent by each of these wives, marked with the seal of her ring, and their names and their reasons for sending the ointments should be told to the king. After this the king accepts the ointment of one of them, who then is informed that her ointment has been accepted, and that her day has been settled.[1]

At festivals, singing parties and exhibitions, all the wives of the king should be treated with respect and served with drinks.

But the women of the harem should not be allowed to go out alone, neither should any women outside the harem be allowed to enter it except those whose character is well known. And lastly the work which the king's wives have to do should not be too fatiguing.

Thus ends the conduct of the king towards the women of the harem, and of their own conduct.

A man marrying many wives should act fairly towards them all. He should neither disregard nor pass over their faults, and should not reveal to one wife the love, passion, bodily blemishes and confidential reproaches of the other. No opportunity should be given to any one of them of speaking to him about their rivals, and if one of them should begin to speak ill of another, he should chide her and tell her that she has exactly the same blemishes in her character. One of them he should please by secret confidence, another by secret respect, and another by secret flattery, and he should please them all by going to gardens, by amusements, by presents, by honouring their relations, by telling them secrets, and lastly by loving unions. A young woman who is of a good temper, and who conducts herself according to the precepts of the Holy Writ, wins her husband's attachments, and obtains a superiority over her rivals.

Thus ends the conduct of a husband towards many wives.

---

[1] As kings generally had many wives, it was usual for them to enjoy their wives by turns. But as it happened sometimes that some of them lost their turns owing to the king's absence, or to their being unwell, then in such cases the women whose turns had been passed over, and those whose turns had come, used to have a sort of lottery, and the ointments of all the claimants were sent to the king, who accepted the ointment of one of them, and thus settled the question.

4

PLATO

The Symposium, c. 385 B.C.E.

Plato (428–348 B.C.E.) is certainly the most widely read and most
influential philosopher of classical Greece. The twentieth-century
Platonist A. N. Whitehead famously wrote that all of European philosophy consisted of footnotes to Plato.[1] When we speak of Plato,
however, we also mean Socrates, Plato's teacher. In fact, since Plato's writings consist almost entirely of dialogues (discussions) in
which Plato is absent but Socrates asks questions and elicits
answers and then spells out his own ideas, we have no way of distinguishing the ideas of Plato from those of Socrates. We credit
Plato, however, since he is the author of these thirty-five dialogues
as well as thirteen letters and was the founder of the Athenian
Academy of philosophy.

The Symposium, one of the better-known dialogues, was written
about 385 B.C.E. The subject is a symposium or drinking party in
which the participants eat, drink, and discuss some philosophical
topic — in this case, the meaning of love. This selection contains two
views of love before Socrates speaks. What are those views, and what
do they tell you about the Greek society of the time — particularly
about sexuality and gender? What finally does Socrates say about
love? What does his speech tell you about Greek ideas of men,
women, love, and sex?

THINKING HISTORICALLY

This dialogue, like the others, is a sort of play with its own author,
audience, and agenda. Whose voice is telling the story? What kind of
people make up the "audience" of the dinner party? Why have these
men come together to discuss this topic? What different agenda
might they have had? Of course, even the intended audience of
Plato's written dialogue is very much larger than a few men talking.
For whom do you think he wrote this? What might have been his purpose? Finally, whose ideas are these? If we know little of the biography of Plato, other than that he was the author of these works and
the founder of the Athenian Academy, we know less about Socrates.
Indeed, in some dialogues Socrates raises questions as to whether or
not he expresses his own ideas. How does he suggest that his ideas
may not even be his own in this dialogue?

[1] Alfred North Whitehead, *Process and Reality* (New York: Free Press, 1979), 39.

Source: Plato, *Symposium*, trans. Benjamin Jowett, http://www.ellopos.net/elpenor
/greek-texts/ancient-Greece/plato/plato-symposium.asp.

Regarding audience and agenda, we might assume that the dialogues were to be used for teaching purposes at the Academy, but we have no evidence for that assumption either. To what degree do these uncertainties limit our understanding of classical Greek society and culture? Despite these uncertainties, what can we say—from the internal evidence of the dialogue itself—about the likely audience and agenda of this work?

[Our selection begins as the participants have just finished dinner.]

Then, said Eryximachus, as you are all agreed that drinking is to be voluntary, and that there is to be no compulsion, I move, in the next place, that the flute-girl, who has just made her appearance, be told to go away and play to herself, or, if she likes, to the women who are within. Today let us have conversation instead; and, if you will allow me, I will tell you what sort of conversation. . . .

I think that at the present moment we who are here assembled cannot do better than honor the god Love. If you agree with me, there will be no lack of conversation; for I mean to propose that each of us in turn, going from left to right, shall make a speech in honor of Love. Let him give us the best which he can; and Phaedrus, because he is sitting first on the left hand, and because he is the father of the thought,[1] shall begin. . . .

[Phaedrus:]

Numerous are the witnesses who acknowledge Love to be the eldest of the gods. And not only is he the eldest, he is also the source of the greatest benefits to us. For I know not any greater blessing to a young man who is beginning life than a virtuous lover or to the lover than a beloved youth.[2] For the principle which ought to be the guide of men who would nobly live at principle, I say, neither kindred, nor honor, nor wealth, nor any other motive is able to implant so well as love. Of what am I speaking? Of the sense of honor and dishonor, without which neither states nor individuals ever do any good or great work. And I say that a lover who is detected in doing any dishonorable act, or submitting through cowardice when any dishonor is done to him by another, will be more pained at being detected by his beloved than at being seen by his father, or by his companions, or by anyone else. The beloved too, when he is found in any disgraceful situation, has the same feeling about his

---

[1] Phaedrus had earlier suggested the topic. [Ed.]
[2] Note that this only concerns men and boys. [Ed.]

lover. And if there were only some way of contriving that a state or an army should be made up of lovers and their loves, they would be the very best governors of their own city, abstaining from all dishonor, and emulating one another in honor; and when fighting at each other's side, although a mere handful, they would overcome the world. . . .

[Pausanias:]

If there were only one Love, then what you said would be well enough; but since there are more Loves than one, [we] should have begun by determining which of them was to be the theme of our praises. I will amend this defect; and first of all I would tell you which Love is deserving of praise, and then try to hymn the praiseworthy one in a manner worthy of him. For we all know that Love is inseparable from Aphrodite,[3] and if there were only one Aphrodite there would be only one Love; but as there are two goddesses there must be two Loves.

And am I not right in asserting that there are two goddesses? The elder one, having no mother, who is called the heavenly Aphrodite . . . and the Love who is her fellow-worker is rightly called common, as the other love is called heavenly.[4] . . . The Love who is the offspring of the common Aphrodite is essentially common, and has no discrimination, being such as the meaner sort of men feel, and is apt to be of women as well as of youths, and is of the body rather than of the soul; the most foolish beings are the objects of this love which desires only to gain an end, but never thinks of accomplishing the end nobly, and therefore does good and evil quite indiscriminately. The goddess who is his mother is far younger than the other, and she was born of the union of the male and female, and partakes of both.

But the offspring of the heavenly Aphrodite is derived from a mother in whose birth the female has no part: She is from the male only; this is that love which is of youths, and the goddess being older, there is nothing of wantonness in her. Those who are inspired by this love turn to the male, and delight in him who is the more valiant and intelligent nature; any one may recognize the pure enthusiasts in the very character of their attachments. For they love not boys, but intelligent beings whose reason is beginning to be developed, much about the time at which their beards begin to grow. And in choosing young men to be their companions, they mean to be faithful to them, and pass their whole life in company with them, not to take them in their inexperience, and deceive them, and play

---

[3] The Greek goddess of love and beauty. [Ed.]

[4] Pausanias makes this distinction to account for two Aphrodite origin myths at the time. One is the story of an Aphrodite born in sea foam from her father's discarded genitals—this is the heavenly Aphrodite. Another myth concerns an Aphrodite of common birth. The first accounts for homosexual love, the second for the love between a husband and wife. [Ed.]

the fool with them, or run away from one to another of them. But the love of young boys should be forbidden by law,[5] because their future is uncertain; they may turn out good or bad, either in body or soul, and much noble enthusiasm may be thrown away upon them; in this matter the good are a law to themselves, and the coarser sort of lovers ought to be restrained by force; as we restrain or attempt to restrain them from fixing their affections on women of free birth. These are the persons who bring a reproach on love; and some have been led to deny the lawfulness of such attachments because they see the impropriety and evil of them; for surely nothing that is decorously and lawfully done can justly be censured. . . .

[Finally, it is the turn of Socrates:]

And now, taking my leave of you, I would rehearse a tale of love which I heard from Diotima of Mantineia, a woman wise in this and in many other kinds of knowledge, who in the days of old, when the Athenians offered sacrifice before the coming of the plague, delayed the disease ten years. She was my instructress in the art of love, and I shall repeat to you what she said to me. . . . "Love," she said, "may be described generally as the love of the everlasting possession of the good." "That is most true" [I agreed]. "Then if this be the nature of love, can you tell me further," she said, "what is the manner of the pursuit? What are they doing who show all this eagerness and heat which is called love? And what is the object which they have in view? Answer me." "Nay, Diotima," I replied, "if I had known, I should not have wondered at your wisdom, neither should I have come to learn from you about this very matter." "Well," she said, "I will teach you: The object which they have in view is birth in beauty, whether of body or, soul. . . . And this is the reason why, when the hour of conception arrives, and the teeming nature is full, there is such a flutter and ecstasy about beauty whose approach is the alleviation of the pain of travail. For love, Socrates, is not, as you imagine, the love of the beautiful only." "What then?" "The love of generation and of birth in beauty." "Yes," I said. "Yes, indeed," she replied. "But why of generation?" "Because to the mortal creature, generation is a sort of eternity and immortality," she replied; "and if, as has been already admitted, love is of the everlasting possession of the good, all men will necessarily desire immortality together with good: Wherefore love is of immortality." . . .

". . . [T]he essence of beauty, . . . my dear Socrates, . . . is that life above all others which man should live, in the contemplation of beauty absolute; a beauty which if you once beheld, you would see not to be after the measure of gold, and garments, and fair boys and youths, whose presence now

---

[5] Such love is only appropriate when expressed toward *ephebos* (boys entering manhood, roughly eighteen to twenty years old). It should be against the law if boys are younger. [Ed.]

entrances you; and you and many a one would be content to live seeing them only and conversing with them without meat or drink, if that were possible—you only want to look at them and to be with them. But what if man had eyes to see the true beauty—the divine beauty, I mean, pure and clear and unalloyed, not clogged with the pollutions of mortality and all the colors and vanities of human life—thither looking, and holding converse with the true beauty simple and divine? Remember how in that communion only, beholding beauty with the eye of the mind, he will be enabled to bring forth, not images of beauty, but realities (for he has hold not of an image but of a reality), and bringing forth and nourishing true virtue to become the friend of God and be immortal, if mortal man may. . . ."

5

OVID

The Art of Love, 1 B.C.E.

Ovid (43 B.C.E.–17 C.E.) was one of the leading poets of the culturally rich age of Augustus, the first Roman emperor. Born into a wealthy family, he socialized in imperial circles and practiced law until he gave it up to write poetry. His first major work, *Amores* (Loves), told love stories of the gods and of his own personal life, having been married three times and divorced twice by the age of thirty. Later, in 1 B.C.E., he began publishing the three volumes of his *Ars Amatoria* (Art of Love), the playful guide to seduction included here. Despite the publication of his more respectable poems about the changing forms of gods and nature, *The Metamorphoses*, Ovid was identified with his poems on love and sexuality at a time when Augustus sought to put an end to the loose morality of Roman nobility, including members of his own family. Because of his poetry and a mistake "more serious than murder," he later wrote, Ovid was exiled by Augustus in 8 C.E. to the coast of the Black Sea, where he lived the last decade of his life, pining for the culture and excitement of Rome.

What does this selection tell you about how men and women could behave in Roman society? What does Ovid think of love? How is Ovid's idea of love different from Plato's? Compare Ovid's *Art of Love* with Vatsyana's *Kama Sutra*. What does this selection suggest about the differences in attitudes toward sexuality between Roman society and Greek, Indian, or Chinese society?

Source: Ovid, *The Art of Love*, trans. A. S. Kline, *Poetry in Translation*, http://www.poetryintranslation.com/klineasartoflove.htm.

The author appears loud, front and center in these poems. How would you characterize his voice? He is also fairly explicit about his audience (or audiences), and he suggests various motivations for writing. How would you describe the social class of his intended audience? How does the shift in audience in Book III change your assessment of Ovid's motives? What other reasons might have made him write these poems?

Book I
Part I: His Task

Should anyone here not know the art of love,
read this, and learn by reading how to love.
By art the boat's set gliding, with oar and sail,
by art the chariot's swift: love's ruled by art.

. . .

I sing of safe love, permissible intrigue,
and there'll be nothing sinful in my song.
Now the first task for you who come as a raw recruit
is to find out who you might wish to love.
The next task is to make sure that she likes you:
the third, to see to it that the love will last.
That's my aim, that's the ground my chariot will cover:
that's the post my thundering wheels will scrape.

Part II: How to Find Her

While you're still free, and can roam on a loose rein,
pick one to whom you could say: "You alone please me."
She won't come falling for you out of thin air:
the right girl has to be searched for: use your eyes.

. . .

If you'd catch them very young and not yet grown,
real child-brides will come before your eyes:
if it's young girls you want, thousands will please you.
You'll be forced to be unsure of your desires:
if you delight greatly in older wiser years,
here too, believe me, there's an even greater crowd.

. . .

Part IV: Or at the Theatre

But hunt for them, especially, at the tiered theatre:
that place is the most fruitful for your needs.

There you'll find one to love, or one you can play with,
one to be with just once, or one you might wish to keep.
As ants return home often in long processions,
carrying their favourite food in their mouths,
or as the bees buzz through the flowers and thyme,
among their pastures and fragrant chosen meadows,
so our fashionable ladies crowd to the famous shows:
my choice is often constrained by such richness.
They come to see, they come to be seen as well:
the place is fatal to chaste modesty.

. . .

Part V: Or at the Races, or the Circus

Don't forget the races, those noble stallions:
the Circus holds room for a vast obliging crowd.
No need here for fingers to give secret messages,
nor a nod of the head to tell you she accepts:
You can sit by your lady: nothing's forbidden,
press your thigh to hers, as you can do, all the time:
and it's good the rows force you close, even if you don't like it,
since the girl is touched through the rules of the place.
Now find your reason for friendly conversation,
and first of all engage in casual talk.
Make earnest enquiry whose those horses are:
and rush to back her favourite, whatever it is.
When the crowded procession of ivory gods goes by,
you clap fervently for Lady Venus[1]:
if by chance a speck of dust falls in the girl's lap,
as it may, let it be flicked away by your fingers:
and if there's nothing, flick away the nothing:
let anything be a reason for you to serve her.
If her skirt is trailing too near the ground,
lift it, and raise it carefully from the dusty earth:
Straightaway, the prize for service, if she allows it,
is that your eyes catch a glimpse of her legs.

. . .

Part IX: How to Win Her

So far, riding her unequal wheels, the Muse has taught you
where you might choose your love, where to set your nets.

---

[1] Roman goddess of love; origins in Latin goddess of vegetation and Greek Aphrodite.
[Ed.]

Now I'll undertake to tell you what pleases her,
by what arts she's caught, itself a work of highest art.

. . .

Part X: First Secure the Maid

But to get to know your desired-one's maid
is your first care: she'll smooth your way.
See if she's close to her mistress's thoughts,
and has plenty of true knowledge of her secret jests.
Corrupt her with promises, and with prayers:
you'll easily get what you want, if she wishes.
She'll tell the time (the doctors would know it too)
when her mistress's mind is receptive, fit for love.
Her mind will be fit for love when she luxuriates
in fertility,[2] like the crop on some rich soil.

. . .

Part XVII: Tears, Kisses, and Take the Lead

And tears help: tears will move a stone:
let her see your damp cheeks if you can.
If tears (they don't always come at the right time)
fail you, touch your eyes with a wet hand.
What wise man doesn't mingle tears with kisses?
Though she might not give, take what isn't given.
Perhaps she'll struggle, and then say "you're wicked":
struggling she still wants, herself, to be conquered.
Only, take care her lips aren't bruised by snatching,
and that she can't complain that you were harsh.

. . .

Book II
Part XX: The Task's Complete . . . But Now . . .

. . .

I've given you weapons: Vulcan[3] gave Achilles his:
excel with the gifts you're given, as he excelled.
But whoever overcomes an Amazon[4] with my sword,
write on the spoils "Ovid was my master."
Behold, you tender girls ask for rules for yourselves:
well yours then will be the next task for my pen!

---

[2] Recent studies confirm increased desire at the point of ovulation, but Ovid knew only the Roman (and general ancient) association of women and earth, passion and flowering. [Ed.]

[3] Roman god of fire; forged the shield of the warrior Achilles. [Ed.]

[4] Mythic tribe of warrior women. [Ed.]

Book III
Part I: It's Time to Teach You Girls

I've given the Greeks arms, against Amazons: arms remain,
to give to you Penthesilea,[5] and your Amazon troop.
Go equal to the fight: let them win, those who are favoured
by Venus, and her Boy, who flies through all the world.
It's not fair for armed men to battle with naked girls:
that would be shameful, men, even if you win.
Someone will say: "Why add venom to the snake,
and betray the sheepfold to the rabid she-wolf?"
Beware of loading the crime of the many onto the few:
let the merits of each separate girl be seen.

. . .

Only playful passions will be learnt from me:
I'll teach girls the ways of being loved.
Women don't brandish flames or cruel bows:
I rarely see men harmed by their weapons.
Men often cheat: it's seldom tender girls,
and, if you check, they're rarely accused of fraud.

. . .

What destroyed you all, I ask? Not knowing how to love:
your art was lacking: love lasts long through art.
You still might lack it now: but, before my eyes,
stood Venus herself, and ordered me to teach you.
She said to me, then: "What have the poor girls done,
an unarmed crowd betrayed to well-armed men?
Two books of *their* tricks have been composed:
let this lot too be instructed by your warnings." . . .

. . .

Part IV: Make-Up, but in Private

How near I was to warning you, no rankness of the wild goat
under your armpits, no legs bristling with harsh hair!
But I'm not teaching girls from the Caucasian hills,
or those who drink your waters, Mysian Caicus.[6]
So why remind you not to let your teeth get blackened,
by being lazy, and to wash your face each morning in water?

---

[5] In Greek mythology Penthesilea was queen of the Amazons (the warrior women). [Ed.]

[6] Caucasian hills and Mysian Caicus suggest unrefined people from wild areas: the rugged mountains of the Caucusus and the swirling waters of the Caicus River in Roman Asia (northwest Turkey). [Ed.]

You know how to acquire whiteness with a layer of powder:
she who doesn't blush by blood, indeed, blushes by art.
You make good the naked edges of your eyebrows,
and hide your natural cheeks with little patches.

. . .

Still, don't let your lover find cosmetic bottles . . .

. . .

Part XIV: Use Jealousy and Fear

Let all be betrayed: I've unbarred the gates to the enemy:
and let my loyalty be to treacherous betrayal.
What's easily given nourishes love poorly:
mingle the odd rejection with welcome fun.
Let him lie before the door, crying: "Cruel entrance!,"
pleading very humbly, threatening a lot too.
We can't stand sweetness: bitterness renews our taste:

. . .

Also when the lover you've just caught falls into the net,
let him think that only he has access to your room.
Later let him sense a rival, the bed's shared pact:
remove these arts, and love grows old.
The horse runs swiftly from the starting gate,
when he has others to pass, and others follow.
Wrongs relight the dying fires, as you wish:
See (I confess!), I don't love unless I'm hurt.

Part XVIII: And So to Bed

To have been taught more is shameful: but kindly Venus
said: "What's shameful is my particular concern."
Let each girl know herself: adopt a reliable posture
for her body: one layout's not suitable for all.
She who's known for her face, lie there face upwards:
let her back be seen, she whose back delights.

. . .

Woman, feel love, melted to your very bones,
and let both delight equally in the thing.
Don't leave out seductive coos and delightful murmurings,
don't let wild words be silent in the middle of your games.
You to whom nature denies sexual feeling,
pretend to sweet delight with artful sounds.
Unhappy girl, for whom that sluggish place is numb,
which man and woman equally should enjoy.

Only beware when you feign it, lest it shows:
create belief in your movements and your eyes.
When you like it, show it with cries and panting breath:
Ah! I blush, that part has its own secret signs.
She who asks fondly for a gift after love's delights,
can't want her request to carry any weight.
Don't let light into the room through all the windows:
it's fitting for much of your body to be concealed.

The game is done: time to descend, you swans,
you who bent your necks beneath my yoke.
As once the boys, so now my crowd of girls
inscribe on your trophies "Ovid was my master."

6

Depictions of Gender in Classical Societies, c. 500 B.C.E.–300 C.E.

The images shown here offer examples of how artists and craftsmen depicted gender in classical Greece, China, India, and Egypt. The first image (Figure 5.1) comes from a kouros, which was a freestanding figure of a young man, usually nude and beardless—an art form that developed in Archaic or early Greece. Our image would have appeared on the face of a platform that supported the kouros. It would have stood in a cemetery testifying to the athletic abilities and virility of the deceased. What does this art form tell you about early Greek society?

Figure 5.1 Base of a funerary kouros with six athletes, 510–500 B.C.E.
Source: National Museum of Archaeology. © BeBa / Iberfoto / The Image Works.

Figure 5.2   Qin Dynasty pottery warrior from tomb of Ch'in Shih-Huang-Ti, 210 B.C.E.

Source: © AAAC/Topham/The Image Works.

Thousands of the full size warriors shown in Figure 5.2, made of baked clay and painted in military uniform but with individual features, were placed in the underground entrance to the tomb of the first Qin emperor and then buried. They were only recently discovered as the location of the tomb was kept secret. It is said that 700,000 workmen constructed the tomb and then were killed to conceal it. In what ways was Qin China like Greece? In what ways was it like the ancient kingdoms of Mesopotamia?

The third image, Figure 5.3, comes from a frieze that most likely decorated a Buddhist temple or monastery in India. It probably would have been one of a number of panels that told stories about the life of the Buddha. This panel tells the story of Sundarananda, the brother of the Buddha, who adored his lovely wife Sundari (Beautiful). Here we see him and a maid help Sundari dress. We see how beautiful she is and how attentive he is. The next panels might have shown the rest of the story: the arrival of the Buddha at Sundarananda's house eager to convert him and take him away from domestic desires; Sundari spitting on the floor saying "you better be back before that dries" as Sundarananda with begging bowl in hand leaves, looking back longingly; the Buddha bringing his brother to heaven to show him the 500 maidens who are waiting his arrival,

Figure 5.3 Sundarananda help-
ing Sundari dress, Kushan period,
first century B.C.E.

Source: DeAgostini / SuperStock.

followed by a trip to hell to show him the boiling pot being prepared
to cook him after his 500 years in heaven. The message of the tale is
that heaven and hell are part of the cycle of life, of desire and loss,
loving and losing. The only solution is release from it all: Even from
beautiful Sundari. How does the image convey this message? What
does it suggest about the roles of men and women?

Figure 5.4 is one of hundreds of excavated portraits of both men
and women from the Fayum or desert oasis area in central Egypt that
were made to adorn the coffin of the mummified individual. The tradition of a portrait on the mummy dates back to Pharaonic Egypt,
but these examples of almost photographic realism stem from the
artistic developments of Hellenistic Greece, some of whose artists
and elite settled in Roman Egypt. What does the look and attire of
this woman suggest to you? How does it reinforce what you have
read about women in Hellenistic Egypt?

THINKING HISTORICALLY

Who would have been the "audience" for these different works of art?
Which works seem to be intended more for men than women? Which
of these reflect patriarchal values? How? What were the purposes of
these different art forms? What message would a cemetery full of

Figure 5.4 Portrait of a Fayum woman with large gold necklace, Roman Egypt, first century B.C.E.– third century C.E.

Source: Detroit Institute of Arts, USA / Gift of Julius H. Haass / Bridgeman Images.

figures such as that of the athletes shown in Figure 5.1 convey to Greek men? What would it convey to Greek women? How might a funerary statue for an Athenian woman differ? What do you think viewers were supposed to feel when looking at the Indian frieze shown in Figure 5.3? How does this differ from the message suggested by the warrior figure from the Qin Dynasty? Does this image convey a different message to men than it does to women, and if so, how?

Figure 5.4, like most other Fayum portraits, shows a person who is neither old nor decrepit. They were probably painted when the person was still very much alive. Given the obvious purpose, how would you sit today for your coffin portrait? Would your expression be like that of this woman? How is the agenda of this portrait similar to, or different from, the others here in document 6? How are the audiences similar or different?

■ REFLECTIONS

Over thirty years ago the historian Joan Kelly ignited the study of women's history with an essay that asked: "Did Women Have a Renaissance?" Questioning whether the great eras in men's history were also great eras for women, she found that men's achievements often came at the expense of women. We have seen how the urban revolution fit this pattern. The rise of cities, the creation of territorial states, the invention of writing, and the development of complex societies, all beginning about five thousand years ago, accompanied the development of patriarchal institutions and ideas. Similarly, the rise of classical cultures, cities, and states about twenty-five hundred years ago seems to have cemented patriarchy. The great religious and philosophical traditions of the classical era emerged with the new states. Some, like Chinese Legalism, voiced support for the new order; others, like Confucianism, evoked an older feudal order that was fading. In China neither the statist nor feudal philosophy brought relief to women, though in the hands of someone like Ban Zhao, Confucianism might be shaped to strengthen the bonds between husband and wife as well as the more traditional male-centered bonds. Indian state building of the classical age similarly pitted a renewed patriarchal Brahmanism against emerging Buddhist and other reforming movements for greater social equality. But by the time of the Gupta era, patriarchal Brahmanism had won the day, creating a world for the upper-caste Hindu male secure enough to not require the sexual repression of all women. The upper-class Greek classical patriarchy enjoyed similar assurances.

History is a method of investigation as well as a subject matter. Historians use various methods, some of which we have included in our "Thinking Historically" sections. But beyond these, history is a general method as well. Historians historicize. We make things historical that were previously thought to have no history. We find that some aspects of life that were generally thought to be eternal or unchanging actually have changed over the course of time. They have a history. This chapter shows how ideas of love and gender are historical rather than always and everywhere the same. To see that different cultures have developed or emphasized different ideas of love is not to rule out any role for biology or human nature, but it is to recognize that our emotions are also learned, perhaps more than we thought.

In addition to love, we have learned to historicize gender identity. Male and female stereotypes that held sway into the mid-twentieth century have long been undermined by historical studies of gender, psychological studies, sensitivity training, and public law. We recognize that personality traits stereotypically thought to be "masculine" or "feminine" can be learned. They do not seem to be coded to a male or female anatomy. In this and previous chapters we have also historicized sexuality to the degree that we have seen different ideas about sex and the sacred, and different customs related to sex in different societies. Homosexuality raises the possibility of a more sweeping historicizing of sexuality. Is it possible that the percentage of homosexuals or heterosexuals in society also varies historically? Is same-sex or opposite-sex preference also historical? Are we taught to be "gay" or "straight"? These questions are prompted, of course, by our study of classical Greece, mainly Athens, and, for that matter, a small class of intellectuals in that city-state. Their influence very likely goes far beyond their numbers. We have no way of knowing if Athens contained a higher proportion of homosexuals or bisexuals than other societies. In fact, these may be the wrong questions. It may be that *heterosexuality* and *homosexuality* are also historical constructs. These modern words and the concepts they entail, based as they are on post-Greek religious traditions (Judaic, Christian, and Islamic) that oppose and moralize the difference, may miss what the Greeks meant and felt. For them, these liaisons had more to do with education than lifestyle, they were often more spiritual than physical, and physical penetration had more to do with social standing than gender. For most of these Greeks, it would make more sense to speak of *bisexuality* rather than *homosexuality*, except that bisexuality implies a combination of two extremes they probably did not see. The world has been constantly changing, and so too have the words we use to describe it.

6

From Tribal to Universal Religion

Hindu-Buddhist and Judeo-Christian Traditions, 1000 B.C.E.—100 C.E.

■ HISTORICAL CONTEXT

From 1000 B.C.E. to 100 C.E. two major religious traditions, one centered in the Middle East and the other in northern India, split into at least four major religious traditions, so large that today they are embraced by a majority of the inhabitants of the world. Both of the two original traditions, Hinduism and Judaism, were in 1000 B.C.E. highly restricted in membership. Neither sought converts but instead ministered to members of their own tribe and castes. This chapter explores how these two essentially inward-looking religions created universal religions, open to all. It is a story not only of the emergence of Christianity and Buddhism but also of the development of modern Judaic and Hindu religions.

Remarkably, both of these traditions moved from tribal to universal religions; even more remarkable are the common elements, given their different routes along that path. While Hinduism cultivated a psychological approach to spiritual enlightenment out of a religion based on caste, Brahman priests, and offerings to innumerable deities, Judaism developed an abiding faith in a universal historical providence after the repeated conquest of a local temple administered by a tribal priesthood. In both transitions, traditions of sacrifice, ritual, worldly prosperity, and inherited status diminished, to be replaced by ideas of universal salvation from this world.

Understanding how religions change or evolve is especially difficult because of the tendency of religious adherents to emphasize the timelessness of their truths. Fortunately, religious commitment and belief do not require a denial of historical change. Indeed, many adherents have found strength in all manifestations of the sacred—the specific and historical as well as the universal and eternal.

Whether motives are primarily religious or secular, however, the historical study of religion offers a useful window on understanding large-scale changes in human behavior. Since religions tend to conserve, repeat, and enshrine, change is more gradual than in many other aspects of human thought and behavior: fashion, say, or technology. Thus, when religions develop radically new ideas or institutions, we can learn much about human resistance and innovation by studying the circumstances.

As you read the selections in this chapter, notice over the course of the first millennium B.C.E. how both core religions created new faiths and reformed the old. Notice also the fundamentally different ways these two great religious traditions changed. Finally, observe how the later offspring religions, Buddhism and Christianity, preached ideas that were already current, but not dominant, in the "parental" traditions.

▨ THINKING HISTORICALLY

Detecting Change in Primary Sources

Because religions typically prefer conservation over innovation, changes are often grafted onto old formulations. Historians who want to understand when and how change occurred must sometimes look at primary sources to uncover new ideas and ways of doing things that have been assimilated into the tradition.

The easiest way to see change in primary sources is to compare a number of them composed in different historical periods. However, sometimes we are able to see examples of change in a single document. A written source may, for instance, originate in more than one oral account, and the writer may combine them both even though one is later than the other and they represent different ideas. A manuscript might also pick up errors or updates as it is rewritten for the next generation. We will see examples of both of these changes and others in the documents in this chapter.

Hinduism: Svetasvatara Upanishad, c. 400 B.C.E.

In Chapter 3, selections from the Hindu Vedas and Upanishads help introduce some basic ideas in Hinduism: the belief that animals and human castes were created out of the primal sacrifice of the god Purusha in the Vedas, the complementary ideas of karma and reincarnation in the Upanishads, and, last, the identification of Brahman and *atman* (God and self), also in the Upanishads.

Take a look at the same selections again to understand the changing nature of Hinduism from the earliest Vedas to the latest Upanishads. For example, we see in Chapter 3, selection 2, the interest of the authors of the Vedas in defining and justifying caste differences and the supremacy of the Brahman priests as masters of sacrifice, prayers, rituals, and sacred hymns.

The authors of the Upanishads were less interested in sacrifice and priestly rituals and more absorbed by philosophical questions. Thus, Chapter 3, selection 3, on karma and reincarnation, spells out the idea of justice and a philosophy of nature that reflects the interests of a later settled society. Finally, selection 4 on the identity of Brahman and *atman* reflects an even more meditative Upanishad that virtually ignores the role of priests. This meditative tradition may have existed in early Hinduism, but there is far more evidence of its expression in the Upanishads (after 800 B.C.E.) than in the earlier Vedas.

The *Svetasvatara** Upanishad selection included here reflects an additional step along the path from the religion of priests, sacrifice, and caste obligation to individualized spirituality. Here the idea of the transmigration of souls from one body to another in an endless cycle of reincarnations — an idea that developed after the Vedas — is challenged by the idea that the individual who seeks Brahman might break out of the wheel of life. How would this idea of escaping reincarnation diminish the power of Brahman priests? How does it minimize the importance of caste and karma?

THINKING HISTORICALLY

Recognizing changes in the Hindu tradition is more difficult than in the Judaic tradition. The literature of Judaism is full of historical references: names of historical figures and even dates. Hindu sacred literature, as you can tell from this brief introduction, shows virtually

* sveh tah SVAH tah ruh

Source: *Svetasvatara* Upanishad in *The Upanishads: The Breath of the Eternal*, trans. Swami Prabhavananda and Frederick Manchester (Hollywood: The Vedanta Society of Southern California, 1948; New York: Mentor Books, 1957), 118–21.

no interest in historical names and dates. Because time in India was conceived as cyclical, rather than linear, and the cycles of the Indian time scheme were immense, determining the exact time an event occurred was less important in Hindu thought than understanding its eternal meaning.

Consequently, our analysis of the changes in Hinduism is more logical than chronological. We can therefore speak of a long-term historical process even though we cannot date each step.

The oldest of the thirteen universally recognized Upanishads, all of which were composed between 800 and 400 B.C.E., are the Brihad Aranyaka and the Chandogya (from which selections 3 and 4 in Chapter 3 are taken). The *Svetasvatara* is one of the last of the thirteen, composed closer to 400 B.C.E. What is the idea of time suggested by this Upanishad?

This vast universe is a wheel. Upon it are all creatures that are subject to birth, death, and rebirth. Round and round it turns, and never stops. It is the wheel of Brahman. As long as the individual self thinks it is separate from Brahman, it revolves upon the wheel in bondage to the laws of birth, death, and rebirth. But when through the grace of Brahman it realizes its identity with him, it revolves upon the wheel no longer. It achieves immortality.

He who is realized by transcending the world of cause and effect, in deep contemplation, is expressly declared by the scriptures to be the Supreme Brahman. He is the substance, all else the shadow. He is the imperishable. The knowers of Brahman know him as the one reality behind all that seems. For this reason they are devoted to him. Absorbed in him, they attain freedom from the wheel of birth, death, and rebirth.

The Lord supports this universe, which is made up of the perishable and the imperishable, the manifest and the unmanifest. The individual soul, forgetful of the Lord, attaches itself to pleasure and thus is bound. When it comes to the Lord, it is freed from all its fetters.

Mind and matter, master and servant—both have existed from beginningless time. The Maya which unites them has also existed from beginningless time. When all three—mind, matter, and Maya—are known as one with Brahman, then is it realized that the Self is infinite and has no part in action. Then is it revealed that the Self is all.

Matter is perishable. The Lord, the destroyer of ignorance, is imperishable, immortal. He is the one God, the Lord of the perishable and of all souls. By meditating on him, by uniting oneself with him, by identifying oneself with him, one ceases to be ignorant.

Know God, and all fetters will be loosed. Ignorance will vanish. Birth, death, and rebirth will be no more. Meditate upon him and transcend physical consciousness. Thus will you reach union with the lord of the universe. Thus will you become identified with him who is One without a second. In him all your desires will find fulfillment.

The truth is that you are always united with the Lord. But you must *know* this. Nothing further is there to know. Meditate, and you will realize that mind, matter, and Maya (the power which unites mind and matter) are but three aspects of Brahman, the one reality.

Fire, though present in the firesticks, is not perceived until one stick is rubbed against another. The Self is like that fire: It is realized in the body by meditation on the sacred syllable OM.[1]

Let your body be the stick that is rubbed, the sacred syllable OM the stick that is rubbed against it. Thus shall you realize God, who is hidden within the body as fire is hidden within the wood.

Like oil in sesame seeds, butter in cream, water in the river bed, fire in tinder, the Self dwells within the soul. Realize him through truthfulness and meditation.

Like butter in cream is the Self in everything. Knowledge of the Self is gained through meditation. The Self is Brahman. By Brahman is all ignorance destroyed.

To realize God, first control the outgoing senses and harness the mind. Then meditate upon the light in the heart of the fire—meditate, that is, upon pure consciousness as distinct from the ordinary consciousness of the intellect. Thus the Self, the Inner Reality, may be seen behind physical appearance.

[1] Sacred symbol for God and the sound chanted in meditation. [Ed.]

2

Buddhism: Gotama's Discovery, c. 500–100 B.C.E.

Gotama Siddhartha* (c. 563–483 B.C.E.), known to history as the Buddha, was the son of a Hindu Kshatriya prince in northern India. This selection tells a traditional story about his youth. Because his father was warned by "Brahman soothsayers" that young Gotama would leave his home to live among the seekers in the forest, his father kept the boy distracted in the palace, the sufferings of people outside hidden from him. This selection begins when the prince, or *rāja*, finally agrees to let Gotama tour outside the palace.

*GAH tah mah   sih DAHR thah

Source: "The Life of Gotama the Buddha," trans. E. H. Brewster, in Clarence H. Hamilton, *Buddhism* (1926; reprint, New York: The Bobbs-Merrill Company, 1952), 6–11.

What does Gotama discover? What seems to be the meaning of these discoveries for him? How is his subsequent thought or behavior similar to that of other Hindus in the era? How is the message of this story similar to the lessons of the Upanishads?

THINKING HISTORICALLY

None of the stories we have of the Buddha was written during his lifetime. For some four hundred years, stories of the Buddha were passed by word of mouth before they were put into writing. Can you see any signs in this story that it was memorized and told orally? When the stories were finally written down, some were no doubt more faithful to the Buddha's actual words and experience than others. What elements in this story would most likely reflect the experience of Gotama? What parts of the story would most likely be added later by people who worshiped the Buddha?

Now the young lord Gotama, when many days had passed by, bade his charioteer make ready the state carriages, saying: "Get ready the carriages, good charioteer, and let us go through the park to inspect the pleasaunce."[1] "Yes, my lord," replied the charioteer, and harnessed the state carriages and sent word to Gotama: "The carriages are ready, my lord; do now what you deem fit." Then Gotama mounted a state carriage and drove out in state into the park.

Now the young lord saw, as he was driving to the park, an aged man as bent as a roof gable, decrepit, leaning on a staff, tottering as he walked, afflicted and long past his prime. And seeing him Gotama said: "That man, good charioteer, what has he done, that his hair is not like that of other men, nor his body?"

"He is what is called an aged man, my lord."

"But why is he called aged?"

"He is called aged, my lord, because he has not much longer to live."

"But then, good charioteer, am I too subject to old age, one who has not got past old age?"

"You, my lord, and we too, we all are of a kind to grow old; we have not got past old age."

"Why then, good charioteer, enough of the park for today. Drive me back hence to my rooms."

"Yea, my lord," answered the charioteer, and drove him back. And he, going to his rooms, sat brooding sorrowful and depressed, thinking, "Shame then verily be upon this thing called birth, since to one born old age shows itself like that!"

[1] A garden. [Ed.]

Thereupon the rāja sent for the charioteer and asked him: "Well, good charioteer, did the boy take pleasure in the park? Was he pleased with it?"

"No, my lord, he was not."

"What then did he see on his drive?"

(And the charioteer told the rāja all.)

Then the rāja thought thus: We must not have Gotama declining to rule. We must not have him going forth from the house into the homeless state. We must not let what the brāhman soothsayers spoke of come true.

So, that these things might not come to pass, he let the youth be still more surrounded by sensuous pleasures. And thus Gotama continued to live amidst the pleasures of sense.

Now after many days had passed by, the young lord again bade his charioteer make ready and drove forth as once before. . . .

And Gotama saw, as he was driving to the park, a sick man, suffering and very ill, fallen and weltering in his own water, by some being lifted up, by others being dressed. Seeing this, Gotama asked: "That man, good charioteer, what has he done that his eyes are not like others' eyes, nor his voice like the voice of other men?"

"He is what is called ill, my lord."

"But what is meant by ill?"

"It means, my lord, that he will hardly recover from his illness."

"But am I too, then, good charioteer, subject to fall ill; have I not got out of reach of illness?"

"You, my lord, and we too, we are all subject to fall ill; we have not got beyond the reach of illness."

"Why then, good charioteer, enough of the park for today. Drive me back hence to my rooms." "Yea, my lord," answered the charioteer, and drove him back. And he, going to his rooms, sat brooding sorrowful and depressed, thinking: Shame then verily be upon this thing called birth, since to one born decay shows itself like that, disease shows itself like that.

Thereupon the rāja sent for the charioteer and asked him: "Well, good charioteer, did the young lord take pleasure in the park and was he pleased with it?"

"No, my lord, he was not."

"What did he see then on his drive?"

(And the charioteer told the rāja all.)

Then the rāja thought thus: We must not have Gotama declining to rule; we must not have him going forth from the house to the homeless state; we must not let what the brāhman soothsayers spoke of come true.

So, that these things might not come to pass, he let the young man be still more abundantly surrounded by sensuous pleasures. And thus Gotama continued to live amidst the pleasures of sense.

Now once again, after many days . . . the young lord Gotama . . . drove forth.

And he saw, as he was driving to the park, a great concourse of people clad in garments of different colours constructing a funeral pyre. And seeing this he asked his charioteer: "Why now are all those people come together in garments of different colours, and making that pile?"

"It is because someone, my lord, has ended his days."

"Then drive the carriage close to him who has ended his days."

"Yea, my lord," answered the charioteer, and did so. And Gotama saw the corpse of him who had ended his days and asked: "What, good charioteer, is ending one's days?"

"It means, my lord, that neither mother, nor father, nor other kinsfolk will now see him, nor will he see them."

"But am I too then subject to death, have I not got beyond reach of death? Will neither the rāja, nor the ranee, nor any other of my kin see me more, or shall I again see them?"

"You, my lord, and we too, we are all subject to death; we have not passed beyond the reach of death. Neither the rāja, nor the ranee, nor any other of your kin will see you any more, nor will you see them."

"Why then, good charioteer, enough of the park for today. Drive me back hence to my rooms."

"Yea, my lord," replied the charioteer, and drove him back.

And he, going to his rooms, sat brooding sorrowful and depressed, thinking: Shame verily be upon this thing called birth, since to one born the decay of life, since disease, since death shows itself like that!

Thereupon the rāja questioned the charioteer as before and as before let Gotama be still more surrounded by sensuous enjoyment. And thus he continued to live amidst the pleasures of sense.

Now once again, after many days . . . the lord Gotama . . . drove forth.

And he saw, as he was driving to the park, a shaven-headed man, a recluse, wearing the yellow robe. And seeing him he asked the charioteer, "That man, good charioteer, what has he done that his head is unlike other men's heads and his clothes too are unlike those of others?"

"That is what they call a recluse, because, my lord, he is one who has gone forth."

"What is that, 'to have gone forth'?"

"To have gone forth, my lord, means being thorough in the religious life, thorough in the peaceful life, thorough in good action, thorough in meritorious conduct, thorough in harmlessness, thorough in kindness to all creatures."

"Excellent indeed, friend charioteer, is what they call a recluse, since so thorough is his conduct in all those respects, wherefore drive me up to that forthgone man."

"Yea, my lord," replied the charioteer and drove up to the recluse. Then Gotama addressed him, saying, "You master, what have you done that your head is not as other men's heads, nor your clothes as those of other men?"

"I, my lord, am one who has gone forth."

"What, master, does that mean?"

"It means, my lord, being thorough in the religious life, thorough in the peaceful life, thorough in good actions, thorough in meritorious conduct, thorough in harmlessness, thorough in kindness to all creatures."

"Excellently indeed, master, are you said to have gone forth since so thorough is your conduct in all those respects." Then the lord Gotama bade his charioteer, saying: "Come then, good charioteer, do you take the carriage and drive it back hence to my rooms. But I will even here cut off my hair, and don the yellow robe, and go forth from the house into the homeless state."

"Yea, my lord," replied the charioteer, and drove back. But the prince Gotama, there and then cutting off his hair and donning the yellow robe, went forth from the house into the homeless state.

Now at Kapilavatthu, the rāja's seat, a great number of persons, some eighty-four thousand souls, heard of what prince Gotama had done and thought: Surely this is no ordinary religious rule, this is no common going forth, in that prince Gotama himself has had his head shaved and has donned the yellow robe and has gone forth from the house into the homeless state. If prince Gotama has done this, why then should not we also? And they all had their heads shaved and donned the yellow robes; and in imitation of the Bodhisat [Buddha][2] they went forth from the house into the homeless state. So the Bodhisat went forth from the house into the homeless state. So the Bodhisat went up on his rounds through the villages, towns, and cities accompanied by that multitude.

Now there arose in the mind of Gotama the Bodhisat, when he was meditating in seclusion, this thought: That indeed is not suitable for me that I should live beset. 'Twere better were I to dwell alone, far from the crowd.

So after a time he dwelt alone, away from the crowd. Those eighty-four thousand recluses went one way, and the Bodhisat went another way.

Now there arose in the mind of Gotama the Bodhisat, when he had gone to his place and was meditating in seclusion, this thought: Verily, this world had fallen upon trouble—one is born, and grows old, and dies, and falls from one state, and springs up in another. And from the suffering, moreover, no one knows of any way to escape, even from decay and death. O, when shall a way of escape from this suffering be made known—from decay and from death?

[2] Here the author clearly means the Buddha, but the term *Bodhisat* or *Bodhisattva* came to designate a kind of Buddhist saint who helped others achieve salvation in the later Mahayana school of Buddhism. [Ed.]

3

Buddhism and Caste,
c. 500–100 B.C.E.

This story, part of the Buddhist canon that was written between one hundred and four hundred years after Buddha's death, tells of a confrontation between the Buddha and Brahmans, members of the Hindu priestly caste. Such an encounter would have been common as Brahmans and Buddhists confronted each other during the Maurya Empire (321–184 B.C.E.), which included the great Buddhist convert, King Ashoka (304–232 B.C.E.). (A Brahman reaction set in during the following Shunga dynasty, and Buddhism almost vanished from India.) How would you expect most Brahmans to react to the Buddha's opposition to caste? Would some Brahmans be persuaded by the Buddha's arguments? How and why might Buddhism have a wider appeal than Hinduism?

THINKING HISTORICALLY

What signs do you see in the document that it was not written during the lifetime of the Buddha? Notice the mention of Greece and the dialogue style of this selection. If, as some scholars have suggested, there may be Greek influence here, which Greek writer would they be referring to (see Chapter 3)? How might this Greek influence help us find an approximate date for this writing?

Once when the Lord was staying at Sāvatthī there were five hundred brāhmans from various countries in the city . . . and they thought: "This ascetic Gautama preaches that all four classes are pure. Who can refute him?"

At that time there was a young brāhman named Assalāyana in the city . . . a youth of sixteen, thoroughly versed in the Vedas . . . and in all brāhmanic learning. "He can do it!" thought the brāhmans, and so they asked him to try; surrounded by a crowd of brāhmans, he went to the Lord, and, after greeting him, sat down and said:

"Brāhmans maintain that only they are the highest class, and the others are below them. They are white, the others black; only they are pure, and not the others. Only they are the true sons of Brahmā, born from his mouth, born of Brahmā, creations of Brahmā, heirs of Brahmā. Now what does the worthy Gautama say to that?"

"Do the brāhmans really maintain this, Assalāyana, when they're born of women just like anyone else, of brāhman women who have their periods and conceive, give birth and nurse their children, just like any other women?"

Source: *The Buddhist Tradition in India, China and Japan*, ed. William Theodore de Bary (New York: Random House, 1969), 49–51.

"For all you say, this is what they think. . . ."

"Have you ever heard that in the lands of the Greeks and Kambojas and other peoples on the borders there are only two classes, masters and slaves, and a master can become a slave and vice versa?"

"Yes, I've heard so."

"And what strength or support does that fact give to the brāhmans' claim?"

"Nevertheless, that is what they think."

"Again if a man is a murderer, a thief, or an adulterer, or commits other grave sins, when his body breaks up on death does he pass on to purgatory if he's a kshatriya,[1] vaishya,[2] or shūdra,[3] but not if he's a brāhman?"

"No, Gautama. In such a case the same fate is in store for all men, whatever their class."

"And if he avoids grave sin, will he go to heaven if he's a brāhman, but not if he's a man of the lower classes?"

"No, Gautama. In such a case the same reward awaits all men, whatever their class."

"And is a brāhman capable of developing a mind of love without hate or ill-will, but not a man of the other classes?"

"No, Gautama. All four classes are capable of doing so."

"Can only a brāhman go down to a river and wash away dust and dirt, and not men of the other classes?"

"No, Gautama, all four classes can."

"Now suppose a king were to gather together a hundred men of different classes and to order the brāhmans and kshatriyas to take kindling wood of sāl, pine, lotus, or sandal, and light fires, while the lowclass folk did the same with common wood. What do you think would happen? Would the fires of the high-born men blaze up brightly . . . and those of the humble fail?"

"No, Gautama. It would be alike with high and lowly. . . . Every fire would blaze with the same bright flame." . . .

"Suppose there are two young brāhman brothers, one a scholar and the other uneducated. Which of them would be served first at memorial feasts, festivals, and sacrifices, or when entertained as guests?"

"The scholar, of course; for what great benefit would accrue from entertaining the uneducated one?"

"But suppose the scholar is ill-behaved and wicked, while the uneducated one is well-behaved and virtuous?"

"Then the uneducated one would be served first, for what great benefit would accrue from entertaining an ill-behaved and wicked man?"

---

[1] KSHAH tree uh   Warrior. [Ed.]

[2] VYS yuh   Free peasant, artisan, or producer. [Ed.]

[3] SHOO druh   Serf. [Ed.]

"First, Assalāyana, you based your claim on birth, then you gave up birth for learning, and finally you have come round to my way of thinking, that all four classes are equally pure!"

At this Assalāyana sat silent . . . his shoulders hunched, his eyes cast down, thoughtful in mind, and with no answer at hand.

4

Mahayana Buddhism: The Lotus Sutra, c. 100 C.E.

Written in India in the first or early second century C.E., the Lotus Sutra became one of the favorite Buddhist scriptures in China, Japan, and other Mahayana Buddhist countries. This very brief section from the sutra tells of the Buddha's death ("passing into extinction" or nirvana). The goal of all Buddhists, like the Buddha himself, was a state of consciousness called *bodhi* (enlightenment, or awakening) that brought a release from the suffering of the world and the attainment of ultimate peace, called nirvana. After the Buddha achieved this state, two Buddhist schools developed concerning the issue of how others might attain nirvana. One, the Theravada, said you had to emulate the hard, ascetic life of the Buddha. Another, the Mahayana, said it was easier and open to everyone because you could pray for help.

Mahayana Buddhism developed alongside but in opposition to Theravada (or Orthodox) Buddhism in its home in India. Theravada Buddhism (still practiced in Southeast Asia) was the more exacting and orthodox form of Buddhism; it encouraged all young men to emulate the Buddha by becoming monks, practicing rigorous discipline begging for their food, and studying the classic texts. Mahayana Buddhism means "the Greater Vehicle" because it could appeal to a greater range of people. Central to Mahayana Buddhism is the idea of a Bodhisattva—a Buddha-type who is capable of achieving nirvana but who, instead, helps others reach enlightenment. Thus, one can pray to a Bodhisattva to achieve salvation. Mahayana Buddhism spread through China and North Asia, offering a less demanding avenue to salvation than Theravada Buddhism because, instead of renouncing the everyday world and becoming a monk or a nun, one could continue a normal life while worshiping at temples and making offerings to the Buddha and various Bodhisattvas.

Source: *The Lotus Sutra*, translated by the Buddhist Text Translation Society, Mahayana Buddhists sutras in English at http://www.cttbusa.org/lotus/lotus1_1.asp.

Which ideas of this sutra make Buddhism more universal or offer "salvation" to a broader audience than monks, nuns, and other religious specialists?

THINKING HISTORICALLY

Some words and ideas in this document are "pre-Buddha" and some are "post-Buddha." That is, some words and ideas could be found in a Hindu text before the Buddha was born. Others seem to come from a world after the Buddha has died. Which words or ideas fit into one or the other of these categories? How can you distinguish between what might have happened at the time of the Buddha's death and what was probably added some time later? How are the ideas expressed in this sutra different from the ideas attributed to the Buddha in previous selections from this chapter? What might account for these differences? How did the early Buddhists who composed this sutra transform the Buddha as seeker of enlightenment into the Buddha as object of worship?

I recall that in ages past,
Limitless, countless aeons ago,
There appeared a Buddha, one honored among people
By the name of Brightness of Sun-Moon-Lamp,
That World Honored One[1] proclaimed the Dharma,[2]
Taking limitless living beings across,
Causing countless millions of Bodhisattvas
To enter the wisdom of the Buddhas.

Before that Buddha had left home,
The eight royal sons born to him,
Seeing the Great Sage leave his home,
Also followed him to practice Brahman conduct.

The Buddha then spoke a Great Vehicle[3]
Sutra by the name of Limitless Principles;
Amidst the assembly, and for their sake,
He set it forth in extensive detail.
When the Buddha had finished speaking the Sutra,
Seated in the Dharma-seat,

[1] The Buddha. [Ed.]
[2] The Law. [Ed.]
[3] *Mahayana* literally means "Great Vehicle." [Ed.]

He sat in full lotus[4] and entered the Samadhi[5]
Called the Station of Limitless Principles.
From the heavens fell a rain of Mandarava flowers,[6]
And heavenly drums of themselves did sound,
While all the gods, dragons, ghosts and spirits,
Made offerings to the Honored One;
And, within all the Buddha lands,
There occurred a mighty trembling.
The light emitted from between the Buddha's brows
Manifested all these rare events.

The light illumined to the east
Eighteen thousand Buddha lands,
Revealing the places of living beings'
Karmic retributions of birth and death.
Seen, too, were Buddha lands adorned
With a multitude of gems,
The color of lapis lazuli[7] and crystal,
Illumined by the Buddha's light.
Seen as well were gods and people,
Dragons, spirits, and Yaksha[8] Hordes,
Gandharvas and Kinnaras,[9]
Each making offering to the Buddha. . . .

The Buddha, having spoken The Dharma Flower[10]
And caused the assembly to rejoice,
Later, on that very day,
Announced to the host of gods and humans;
"The meaning of the real mark of all Dharmas
Has already been spoken for all of you,
And now at midnight, I
shall enter into Nirvana.
You should single-heartedly advance with vigor,
And avoid laxness, for
Buddhas are difficult indeed to meet,
Encountered but once in a million aeons."

---

[4] Yoga position on folded legs. [Ed.]

[5] Highest state of consciousness reached in meditation. [Ed.]

[6] Bright scarlet flowers associated with the story of an Indian princess. [Ed.]

[7] Rare blue stone. [Ed.]

[8] Indian nature spirits, often tree spirits, imagined in human form. [Ed.]

[9] Ancient tribal peoples or music spirits. [Ed.]

[10] The words that lead to the flowering of the Law; the Buddha's last words; sometimes refers to this Lotus Sutra itself. [Ed.]

All of the disciples of the World Honored One
Hearing of the Buddha's entry into Nirvana,
Each harbored grief and anguish,
"Why must the Buddha take extinction so soon?"
The sagely Lord, the Dharma King,
Then comforted the limitless multitude:
"After my passage into extinction,
None of you should worry or fear,
For the Bodhisattva Virtue Treasury,[11]
With respect to the non-outflow mark of reality,[12]
In heart has penetrated it totally;
He will next become a Buddha,
By the name of Pure Body, and
Will also save uncounted multitudes.

That night the Buddha passed into extinction,
As a flame dies once its fuel has been consumed.
The Sharira[13] were divided up,
And limitless stupas[14] built.
The Bhikshus and Bhikshuni,[15]
Their number like the Ganges' sands,
Redoubled their vigor in advancing
In their quest for the unsurpassed path.

[11] The name of the first Bodhisattva. [Ed.]
[12] He understands the true reality. [Ed.]
[13] The bones of the Buddha after cremation. [Ed.]
[14] Temples, usually built over a bone or other relic of the Buddha. [Ed.]
[15] Ordained nuns and monks. [Ed.]

5

Judaism and the Bible: History, Laws, and Psalms, c. 850–600 B.C.E.

Just as the caste-based Hinduism of ancient India gave rise to universal Buddhism after 500 B.C.E., so did the Judaism of the Hebrew tribe of Abraham give birth to universalist Christianity. Judaism was already an ancient religion by the time of Jesus and the birth of

Source: Gen. 1:1–31, 2:1–25, 17:1–14; Exod. 19:1–9, 20:1–18; Lev. 1:1–9; Ps. 23:1–6; Amos 5:21–24. All biblical selections are from the New International Version.

Christianity. It traced its roots back (perhaps two thousand years) to Abraham himself, who, according to tradition, made a contract (or covenant) with God to worship him and him alone.

This commitment to one god, and one god only, was a development unique to the history of Judaism. The worship of various ancestral and nature spirits was common practice among hunting-gathering and agricultural peoples. Early cities added numerous local protectors and, in some cases, a pantheon of deities presented in myth and legend. The Bronze Age empires were probably the first to imagine a single ruler of the heavens — an obvious parallel to the role of the emperor on Earth. The Egyptians for a brief moment (around 1300 B.C.E.) preached the singularity of god, in this case the sun god Aton, but that was soon renounced. Persian Zoroastrianism imagined competing gods of light and darkness, each supreme in his realm, an idea that was to leave its mark in Persian-occupied Jerusalem. But the idea of a single creator of the universe — and no other gods — was new to the ancient Hebrews.

Since such a belief was unusual, the descendants of Abraham had difficulty accepting it. In their wanderings throughout the land of the Tigris and Euphrates rivers, from Abraham's native Ur to Egypt and Palestine, the Jews came into contact with many different religious beliefs; some were even tempted by foreign gods. However, by around 1300 B.C.E., Abraham's descendants had escaped Egyptian domination, crossed the Red Sea, and with the help of Moses renewed their covenant with God in the Ten Commandments. Even then, stories were told of Jews who worshiped the Golden Calf and other idols and of the displeasure of the God of Abraham. "I am a jealous God," he told his people. "You shall have no other gods before me."

Such is the story told in the books of the Hebrew Bible,[1] written after the Jews settled in Jerusalem and the surrounding area sometime after 1000 B.C.E. The Hebrew Bible not only recounts the story of the people of Abraham but also takes its story back ages before the patriarch, stretching back to the beginning of the world and forward to the period of Jewish kingdoms after 900 B.C.E., when kings Saul, David, and Solomon ruled large parts of what is today Israel, Palestine, and Jordan. The Hebrew Bible included their histories, the laws of the two Jewish kingdoms Judah and Israel, and various other writings (songs, poetry called psalms, philosophy, and stories of prophecy).

As you read these first selections from the Bible (Genesis, Exodus, Leviticus, Psalms, Amos), note how they are similar to, and different from, the Vedas and Upanishads of Hinduism. How, for instance, is

---

[1] *Hebrew Bible* refers to the books in the Bible that were written in Hebrew. Christians call these books the Old Testament. The first five books of the Bible are called the Torah by Jews. [Ed.]

the Bible's story of the beginning of the world different from the Hindus' creation story of the sacrifice of Purusha? Why might an understanding of history be more important to the Jews than it was to the Hindus? Compare the role of morality in the religion of Jews and Hindus. In what sense is the morality of Judaism universal and that of Hinduism caste based? How is the Judaic emphasis on morality also different from Buddhist ideas?

THINKING HISTORICALLY

Since the books of the Hebrew Bible were composed over a long period of time, from about 900 B.C.E. to about 165 B.C.E., we might expect to see changes in emphasis, especially since this period was such a tumultuous one in Jewish history. The immediate descendants of Abraham were a nomadic pastoral people — shepherds, Psalm 23 reminds us — though this beautiful psalm attributed to King David was written in an urban, monarchal stage of Jewish history. Leviticus, too, echoes an earlier pastoral life when animal sacrifice, and the worship by shepherds generally, was still practiced.

When did morality replace sacrifice as the sign of respect to the God of Abraham? Was it around 1300 B.C.E., the traditional date for the reception by Moses of the Ten Commandments? Or is the existence of Leviticus, perhaps five hundred years later, a sign that sacrifice was still practiced? The sentiments of Amos (783–743 B.C.E.) suggest that the Jews later rejected not only animal sacrifice but also moral obedience that was not truly felt.

When did monotheism (the belief in one god) become unequivocal, unquestioned? Since this was a new idea, there must have been a time when it wasn't held. Some scholars see signs of an earlier polytheism (belief in many gods) in the book of Genesis itself. For instance, in Genesis 3:5 we find "ye shall be as gods," and Genesis 3:22 reads "And the Lord God said: Behold the man has become like one of us."

Certainly the beginning of Genesis is no-nonsense monotheism, majestically so: "In the beginning God created the heavens and the earth." But scholars have pointed out that this opening is followed by another story of origin, beginning at Chapter 2, Verse 4, that not only tells the story over again, but does so without the intense declarative monotheism. They date this document at about 850 B.C.E. and the section from 1:1 to 2:3 at about 650 B.C.E. Compare the language in Genesis 1 to 2:3 with the section that begins at 2:4. Which selection from Genesis seems more idealized, which more like a report? Which version would probably be closer to the oral storytelling tradition? Which reflects the style of a sophisticated, urban, philosophical culture? Which term is more monotheistic: *God* or *Lord God*?

If we can see increased emphasis on monotheism from 850 to 650 B.C.E., we might also see in these selections the transition from the religion of a tribe of shepherds to that of a political kingdom. What evidence do you see that a pastoral religion of animal sacrifice became a religion of law, or even internalized morality?

Finally, notice that there is no heaven here—no afterlife. God promised Abraham land and prosperity. The ideas of a last judgment, heaven and hell, and salvation became important in Christianity, but we will explore the development of these ideas in Judaism in the second century B.C.E.

Genesis 1

The Beginning

1 In the beginning God created the heavens and the earth.

2 Now the earth was formless and empty, darkness was over the surface of the deep, and the Spirit of God was hovering over the waters.

3 And God said, "Let there be light," and there was light. 4 God saw that the light was good, and He separated the light from the darkness. 5 God called the light "day," and the darkness he called "night." And there was evening, and there was morning—the first day.

6 And God said, "Let there be an expanse between the waters to separate water from water." 7 So God made the expanse and separated the water under the expanse from the water above it. And it was so. 8 God called the expanse "sky." And there was evening, and there was morning—the second day.

9 And God said, "Let the water under the sky be gathered to one place, and let dry ground appear." And it was so. 10 God called the dry ground "land," and the gathered waters he called "seas." And God saw that it was good.

11 Then God said, "Let the land produce vegetation: seed-bearing plants and trees on the land that bear fruit with seed in it, according to their various kinds." And it was so. 12 The land produced vegetation: plants bearing seed according to their kinds and trees bearing fruit with seed in it according to their kinds. And God saw that it was good. 13 And there was evening, and there was morning—the third day.

14 And God said, "Let there be lights in the expanse of the sky to separate the day from the night, and let them serve as signs to mark seasons and days and years, 15 and let them be lights in the expanse of the sky to give light on the earth." And it was so. 16 God made two great lights—the greater light to govern the day and the lesser light to govern the night. He also made the stars. 17 God set them in the expanse of the sky to give light on the earth, 18 to govern the day and the night, and to

separate light from darkness. And God saw that it was good. 19 And there was evening, and there was morning—the fourth day.

20 And God said, "Let the water teem with living creatures, and let birds fly above the earth across the expanse of the sky." 21 So God created the great creatures of the sea and every living and moving thing with which the water teems, according to their kinds, and every winged bird according to its kind. And God saw that it was good. 22 God blessed them and said, "Be fruitful and increase in number and fill the water in the seas, and let the birds increase on the earth." 23 And there was evening, and there was morning—the fifth day.

24 And God said, "Let the land produce living creatures according to their kinds: livestock, creatures that move along the ground, and wild animals, each according to its kind." And it was so. 25 God made the wild animals according to their kinds, the livestock according to their kinds, and all the creatures that move along the ground according to their kinds. And God saw that it was good.

26 Then God said, "Let us make man in our image, in our likeness, and let them rule over the fish of the sea and the birds of the air, over the livestock, over all the earth, and over all the creatures that move along the ground."

27 So God created man in his own image,
    in the image of God he created him;
    male and female he created them.

28 God blessed them and said to them, "Be fruitful and increase in number; fill the earth and subdue it. Rule over the fish of the sea and the birds of the air and over every living creature that moves on the ground."

29 Then God said, "I give you every seed-bearing plant on the face of the whole earth and every tree that has fruit with seed in it. They will be yours for food. 30 And to all the beasts of the earth and all the birds of the air and all the creatures that move on the ground—everything that has the breath of life in it—I give every green plant for food." And it was so.

31 God saw all that he had made, and it was very good. And there was evening, and there was morning—the sixth day.

Genesis 2

1 Thus the heavens and the earth were completed in all their vast array.

2 By the seventh day God had finished the work he had been doing; so on the seventh day he rested from all his work. 3 And God blessed the seventh day and made it holy, because on it he rested from all the work of creating that he had done.

Adam and Eve

4 This is the account of the heavens and the earth when they were created.

When the LORD God made the earth and the heavens—5 and no shrub of the field had yet appeared on the earth and no plant of the field had yet sprung up, for the LORD God had not sent rain on the earth and there was no man to work the ground, 6 but streams came up from the earth and watered the whole surface of the ground—7 the LORD God formed the man from the dust of the ground and breathed into his nostrils the breath of life, and the man became a living being.

8 Now the LORD God had planted a garden in the east, in Eden; and there he put the man he had formed. 9 And the LORD God made all kinds of trees grow out of the ground—trees that were pleasing to the eye and good for food. In the middle of the garden were the tree of life and the tree of the knowledge of good and evil.

10 A river watering the garden flowed from Eden; from there it was separated into four headwaters. 11 The name of the first is the Pishon; it winds through the entire land of Havilah, where there is gold. 12 (The gold of that land is good; aromatic resin and onyx are also there.) 13 The name of the second river is the Gihon; it winds through the entire land of Cush. 14 The name of the third river is the Tigris; it runs along the east side of Asshur. And the fourth river is the Euphrates.

15 The LORD God took the man and put him in the Garden of Eden to work it and take care of it. 16 And the LORD God commanded the man, "You are free to eat from any tree in the garden; 17 but you must not eat from the tree of the knowledge of good and evil, for when you eat of it you will surely die."

18 The LORD God said, "It is not good for the man to be alone. I will make a helper suitable for him."

19 Now the LORD God had formed out of the ground all the beasts of the field and all the birds of the air. He brought them to the man to see what he would name them; and whatever the man called each living creature, that was its name. 20 So the man gave names to all the livestock, the birds of the air and all the beasts of the field.

But for Adam no suitable helper was found. 21 So the LORD God caused the man to fall into a deep sleep; and while he was sleeping, he took one of the man's ribs and closed up the place with flesh. 22 Then the LORD God made a woman from the rib he had taken out of the man, and he brought her to the man.

23 The man said,

"This is now bone of my bones
and flesh of my flesh;
she shall be called 'woman,'
for she was taken out of man."

24 For this reason a man will leave his father and mother and be united to his wife, and they will become one flesh.

25 The man and his wife were both naked, and they felt no shame.

Genesis 17

The Covenant of the Circumcision

1 When Abram was ninety-nine years old, the LORD appeared to him and said, "I am God Almighty; walk before me and be blameless. 2 I will confirm my covenant between me and you and will greatly increase your numbers."

3 Abram fell facedown, and God said to him, 4 "As for me, this is my covenant with you: You will be the father of many nations. 5 No longer will you be called Abram; your name will be Abraham, for I have made you a father of many nations. 6 I will make you very fruitful; I will make nations of you, and kings will come from you. 7 I will establish my covenant as an everlasting covenant between me and you and your descendants after you for the generations to come, to be your God and the God of your descendants after you. 8 The whole land of Canaan, where you are now an alien, I will give as an everlasting possession to you and your descendants after you; and I will be their God."

9 Then God said to Abraham, "As for you, you must keep my covenant, you and your descendants after you for the generations to come. 10 This is my covenant with you and your descendants after you, the covenant you are to keep: Every male among you shall be circumcised. 11 You are to undergo circumcision, and it will be the sign of the covenant between me and you. 12 For the generations to come every male among you who is eight days old must be circumcised, including those born in your household or bought with money from a foreigner—those who are not your offspring. 13 Whether born in your household or bought with your money, they must be circumcised. My covenant in your flesh is to be an everlasting covenant. 14 Any uncircumcised male, who has not been circumcised in the flesh, will be cut off from his people; he has broken my covenant. . . ."

Exodus 19

At Mount Sinai

1 In the third month after the Israelites left Egypt—on the very day—they came to the Desert of Sinai. 2 After they set out from Rephidim, they entered the Desert of Sinai, and Israel camped there in the desert in front of the mountain.

3 Then Moses went up to God, and the LORD called to him from the mountain and said, "This is what you are to say to the house of Jacob and what you are to tell the people of Israel: 4 'You yourselves have seen what I did to Egypt, and how I carried you on eagles' wings and brought you to myself. 5 Now if you obey me fully and keep my covenant, then out of all nations you will be my treasured possession. Although the whole earth is mine, 6 you will be for me a kingdom of priests and a holy nation.' These are the words you are to speak to the Israelites."

7 So Moses went back and summoned the elders of the people and set before them all the words the LORD had commanded him to speak. 8 The people all responded together, "We will do everything the LORD has said." So Moses brought their answer back to the LORD.

9 The LORD said to Moses, "I am going to come to you in a dense cloud, so that the people will hear me speaking with you and will always put their trust in you." Then Moses told the LORD what the people had said.

Exodus 20

The Ten Commandments

1 And God spoke all these words:

2 "I am the LORD your God, who brought you out of Egypt, out of the land of slavery.

3 "You shall have no other gods before me.

4 "You shall not make for yourself an idol in the form of anything in heaven above or on the earth beneath or in the waters below. 5 You shall not bow down to them or worship them; for I, the LORD your God, am a jealous God, punishing the children for the sin of the fathers to the third and fourth generation of those who hate me, 6 but showing love to a thousand [generations] of those who love me and keep my commandments.

7 "You shall not misuse the name of the LORD your God, for the LORD will not hold anyone guiltless who misuses his name.

8 "Remember the Sabbath day by keeping it holy. 9 Six days you shall labor and do all your work, 10 but the seventh day is a Sabbath to the LORD your God. On it you shall not do any work, neither you, nor your son or daughter, nor your manservant or maidservant, nor your animals, nor the alien within your gates. 11 For in six days the LORD made the heavens and the earth, the sea, and all that is in them, but he rested on the seventh day. Therefore the LORD blessed the Sabbath day and made it holy.

12 "Honor your father and your mother, so that you may live long in the land the LORD your God is giving you.

13 "You shall not murder.

14 "You shall not commit adultery.

15 "You shall not steal.

16 "You shall not give false testimony against your neighbor.

17 "You shall not covet your neighbor's house. You shall not covet your neighbor's wife, or his manservant or maidservant, his ox or donkey, or anything that belongs to your neighbor."

18 When the people saw the thunder and lightning and heard the trumpet and saw the mountain in smoke, they trembled with fear.

Leviticus 1

The Burnt Offering

1 The LORD called to Moses and spoke to him from the Tent of Meeting. He said, 2 "Speak to the Israelites and say to them: 'When any of you brings an offering to the LORD, bring as your offering an animal from either the herd or the flock.

3 "'If the offering is a burnt offering from the herd, he is to offer a male without defect. He must present it at the entrance to the Tent of Meeting so that it will be acceptable to the LORD. 4 He is to lay his hand on the head of the burnt offering, and it will be accepted on his behalf to make atonement for him. 5 He is to slaughter the young bull before the LORD, and then Aaron's sons the priests shall bring the blood and sprinkle it against the altar on all sides at the entrance to the Tent of Meeting. 6 He is to skin the burnt offering and cut it into pieces. 7 The sons of Aaron the priest are to put fire on the altar and arrange wood on the fire. 8 Then Aaron's sons the priests shall arrange the pieces, including the head and the fat, on the burning wood that is on the altar. 9 He is to wash the inner parts and the legs with water, and the priest is to burn all of it on the altar. It is a burnt offering, an offering made by fire, an aroma pleasing to the LORD. . . .' "

Psalm 23

A Psalm of David

1 The LORD is my shepherd, I shall not be in want.

2 He makes me lie down in green pastures,
    he leads me beside quiet waters,

3 he restores my soul.
    He guides me in paths of righteousness
    for his name's sake.

4 Even though I walk
   through the valley of the shadow of death,[1]
   I will fear no evil,
   for you are with me;
   your rod and your staff,
   they comfort me.

5 You prepare a table before me
   in the presence of my enemies.
   You anoint my head with oil;
   my cup overflows.

6 Surely goodness and love will follow me
   all the days of my life,
   and I will dwell in the house of the LORD
   forever.

Amos 5

21 "I hate, I despise your religious feasts;
   I cannot stand your assemblies.

22 Even though you bring me burnt offerings and grain offerings,
   I will not accept them.
   Though you bring choice fellowship offerings,
   I will have no regard for them.

23 Away with the noise of your songs!
   I will not listen to the music of your harps.

24 But let justice roll on like a river,
   righteousness like a never-failing stream!"

[1] Or *through the darkest valley.* [Ed.]

6

Judaism and the Bible: Prophecy and the Apocalypse, c. 600–165 B.C.E.

The golden days of Jewish kings were not to last. Powerful empires rose up to challenge and dominate the Jews: the Assyrians in 800 B.C.E., the Babylonians around 600 B.C.E., then the Medes, the Persians, the armies of Alexander the Great, his successor states — ruled by his generals and their descendants — and then the Romans after 64 B.C.E. The Babylonians were among the worst of the invaders. They conquered Jerusalem, destroyed the temple, and brought Jews as hostages to Babylon. In 538 B.C.E. Cyrus, king of the Persians, allowed Jews to return to Jerusalem and even rebuild the temple. But the Jews never regained their kingdom or independence (except for brief periods), and the Greek Seleucid* rulers after Alexander proved to be intolerant of non-Greek forms of worship.

Ironically, it was during this period of conquest and dispersal that Judaism began to develop the elements of a universal religion. The Babylonian destruction of the temple and population transfer made the religion of Yahweh less dependent on place. Virtually all religions of the ancient world were bound to a particular place, usually the sacred temple where the god was thought to reside. Judaism remained a religion of the descendants of Abraham and his son Israel, and the period after 600 B.C.E. was one of intense cultivation of that identity. But much of the Hebrew Bible was composed in exile, as a way of recalling a common history, reaffirming a common identity, and predicting a common destiny. The prophets foresaw a brighter future or explained how the violation of the covenant had brought God's wrath on the people.

One of the great prophets of the exile and the postexile period was Daniel, described as one of the young men who was brought to Babylon by Nebuchadnezzar,† conqueror of Jerusalem in 586 B.C.E. The Book of Daniel begins by recounting that conquest. In Babylon Nebuchadnezzar asked Daniel to reveal the meaning of a dream. You will read his response below.

Daniel is the first to foretell of an apocalyptic end to history and the first to envision personal immortality. Previous prophets had predicted a new independent kingdom of Judah or God's punishment of his people, but Daniel prophesied that God would come down to reign on Earth forever, judging the living and the dead for all eternity. These ideas — an end to history, the Last Judgment, the Kingdom of

*sel OO sihd
†neh boo kuhd NEH zur

Source: Dan. 2:31–45, 11:28–45, 12:1–13. New International Version.

God, eternal life or damnation—became more important later in
Christianity than in Judaism, where these notions never entered the
mainstream. But their appearance in Daniel shows the way in which
Judaic ideas became more universal over the course of the first
millennium B.C.E. Why would Daniel's ideas open the Judaic tradition
to non-Jews or people not descended from Abraham? How would
Daniel's prophecy affect his contemporaries? How would it affect you?

THINKING HISTORICALLY

When did the idea of an afterlife enter Judaism? To answer this
question we have to date the Book of Daniel, which is a bit more
complex than it would seem. As mentioned, the book is presented
as the prophecy of a Daniel who was taken from Jerusalem to Babylon
around 586 B.C.E. But the author of the book knows considerably
more about the period toward the end of his prophecy (180–165
B.C.E.) than about the third to sixth century B.C.E. This discrepancy and
the use of second-century Hebrew and Aramaic have led biblical
scholars to conclude that the Book of Daniel is prophecy after the
fact, or a book of history presented as prophecy. Detailed footnotes
have been added to this selection to show that the author's references
to very specific events of the second century, especially the time of
Antiochus IV (r. 175–163 B.C.E.), would have been easily recognized by
a contemporary audience. So the author lived sometime in this
period. He recounts the unhappy story of the conquests of the Jews by
successive empires: from the Babylonian (627–550 B.C.E.) and Median
(612–550 B.C.E.) to the Persian (550–330 B.C.E.) to the Greek under
Alexander (330–323 B.C.E.) to the Seleucids (Alexander's successors),
including Antiochus (312–63 B.C.E.). This is the meaning of the gold,
silver, bronze, iron, and clay ages. When the author then speaks of the
signs of the last days, he distinctly sees the acts of Antiochus IV as the
turning point that will bring about God's eternal kingdom. Antiochus
pressured the Jews to accept Greek gods. In 168 B.C.E. he polluted the
temple in Jerusalem by slaughtering pigs on the altar and then erecting
a statue of the Greek god Zeus. This is the event that the author pre-
dicts will bring on God's last judgment. Many Jews must have felt that
the desecration of the holy temple was such a world-changing event.
In fact, the acts of Antiochus also sparked a Jewish revolt under the
Macabees, who eventually defeated Antiochus in 163 B.C.E. and
restored an independent Jewish state.

What would be the purpose of presenting this prophecy? What
would be the advantage of presenting it as the writing of someone
who had lived hundreds of years earlier? How can we know that the
Book of Daniel was written after 168 but before 163 B.C.E.? When
and why would the author of the Book of Daniel have predicted that

the end of the world would occur 1,290 days (about 3½ years) after an event in 168 B.C.E.? When and why would the author have written, "Blessed is the one who waits . . . 1,335 days"?

Daniel 2 [Daniel Interprets the Dream of Nebuchadnezzar]

31 "You looked, O king, and there before you stood a large statue—an enormous, dazzling statue, awesome in appearance. 32 The head of the statue was made of pure gold, its chest and arms of silver, its belly and thighs of bronze, 33 its legs of iron, its feet partly of iron and partly of baked clay. 34 While you were watching, a rock was cut out, but not by human hands. It struck the statue on its feet of iron and clay and smashed them. 35 Then the iron, the clay, the bronze, the silver and the gold were broken to pieces at the same time and became like chaff on a threshing floor in the summer. The wind swept them away without leaving a trace. But the rock that struck the statue became a huge mountain and filled the whole earth.

36 "This was the dream, and now we will interpret it to the king. 37 You, O king, are the king of kings. The God of heaven has given you dominion and power and might and glory; 38 in your hands he has placed mankind and the beasts of the field and the birds of the air. Wherever they live, he has made you ruler over them all. You are that head of gold.

39 "After you, another kingdom[1] will rise, inferior to yours. Next, a third kingdom, one of bronze,[2] will rule over the whole earth. 40 Finally, there will be a fourth kingdom,[3] strong as iron—for iron breaks and smashes everything—and as iron breaks things to pieces, so it will crush and break all the others. 41 Just as you saw that the feet and toes were partly of baked clay and partly of iron, so this will be a divided kingdom;[4] yet it will have some of the strength of iron in it, even as you saw iron mixed with clay. 42 As the toes were partly iron and partly clay, so this kingdom will be partly strong and partly brittle. 43 And just as you saw the iron mixed with baked clay, so the people will be a mixture[5] and will not remain united, any more than iron mixes with clay.

[1] Media, or the Mede Empire; Iranians who shared rule with Neo-Babylonians (Chaldeans) and were seen as successors in the Middle East to 550 B.C.E. [Ed.]

[2] Persia, 550–330 B.C.E. [Ed.]

[3] Greek empire of Alexander the Great, 330–323 B.C.E. [Ed.]

[4] The Middle Eastern portion of Alexander's empire was divided after his death in 323 B.C.E. by his generals: Seleucus in Palestine and Syria and Ptolemy in Egypt. The kingdom of the Seleucids (iron) was stronger than that of the Ptolemies (clay). These two dynasties lasted until conquered by Rome and Persian Parthia. [Ed.]

[5] Probably refers to mixing of peoples and cultures in Alexander's and his successors' empire. [Ed.]

44 "In the time of those kings, the God of heaven will set up a kingdom that will never be destroyed, nor will it be left to another people. It
will crush all those kingdoms and bring them to an end, but it will itself
endure forever. 45 This is the meaning of the vision of the rock cut out
of a mountain, but not by human hands — a rock that broke the iron, the
bronze, the clay, the silver and the gold to pieces.

"The great God has shown the king what will take place in the
future. The dream is true and the interpretation is trustworthy."

Daniel 11 [Daniel Sees the End of the Age of Iron and Clay]

28 "The king[6] of the North will return to his own country[7] with
great wealth, but his heart will be set against the holy covenant.[8] He will
take action against it and then return to his own country.

29 "At the appointed time he will invade the South again,[9] but this
time the outcome will be different from what it was before. 30 Ships of
the western coastlands[10] will oppose him, and he will lose heart. Then he
will turn back and vent his fury against the holy covenant. He will return
and show favor to those who forsake[11] the holy covenant.

31 "His armed forces will rise up to desecrate the temple fortress
and will abolish the daily sacrifice. Then they will set up the abomination that causes desolation.[12] 32 With flattery he will corrupt those who
have violated the covenant, but the people who know their God will
firmly resist him.

33 "Those who are wise will instruct many, though for a time they
will fall by the sword or be burned or captured or plundered. 34 When
they fall, they will receive a little help,[13] and many who are not sincere
will join them.[14] 35 Some of the wise will stumble, so that they may be
refined, purified and made spotless until the time of the end, for it will
still come at the appointed time.

---

[6] Antiochus IV, the Seleucid emperor from 175 to 164 B.C.E., ruled Palestine, Syria, and
Alexander's eastern empire, which included Jerusalem. [Ed.]

[7] Antiochus IV returned to Jerusalem after his first war with Egypt, 170 B.C.E. [Ed.]

[8] Antiochus stole temple treasures and massacred many Jews, 169 B.C.E. [Ed.]

[9] The second war of Antiochus IV with Egypt in 168 B.C.E. was not successful. [Ed.]

[10] Cyprus. Here it means ships of Romans, generally, who blocked him. [Ed.]

[11] Jews like Jason the high priest, who favored Greek customs. [Ed.]

[12] The army of Antiochus broke down the temple walls, desecrated the interior, and
installed Greek statues. [Ed.]

[13] While many Jews chose martyrdom, some received the help of Judas Maccabeus, leader
of the opposition to Antiochus. [Ed.]

[14] Some of the followers of Judas Maccabeus were insincere. [Ed.]

The King Who Exalts Himself

36 "The king will do as he pleases. He will exalt and magnify himself above every god[15] and will say unheard-of things against the God of gods. He will be successful until the time of wrath is completed, for what has been determined must take place. 37 He will show no regard for the gods of his fathers or for the one desired by women, nor will he regard any god, but will exalt himself above them all. 38 Instead of them, he will honor a god of fortresses; a god unknown to his fathers he will honor with gold and silver, with precious stones and costly gifts. 39 He will attack the mightiest fortresses with the help of a foreign god and will greatly honor those who acknowledge him. He will make them rulers over many people and will distribute the land at a price.

40 "At the time of the end the king of the South[16] will engage him in battle, and the king of the North will storm out against him with chariots and cavalry and a great fleet of ships. He will invade many countries and sweep through them like a flood. 41 He will also invade the Beautiful Land. Many countries will fall, but Edom, Moab and the leaders of Ammon will be delivered from his hand. 42 He will extend his power over many countries; Egypt will not escape. 43 He will gain control of the treasures of gold and silver and all the riches of Egypt, with the Libyans and Nubians in submission. 44 But reports from the east and the north[17] will alarm him, and he will set out in a great rage to destroy and annihilate many. 45 He will pitch his royal tents between the seas at the beautiful holy mountain.[18] Yet he will come to his end,[19] and no one will help him."

Daniel 12

The End Times

1 "At that time Michael,[20] the great prince who protects your people, will arise. There will be a time of distress such as has not happened from the beginning of nations until then. But at that time your people—everyone whose name is found written in the book—will be delivered. 2 Multitudes who sleep in the dust of the earth will awake: some to everlasting life, others to shame and everlasting contempt. 3 Those who are wise will shine like the brightness of the heavens, and

---

[15] Antiochus had himself declared "Epiphanes," or God Manifest. [Ed.]

[16] Ptolemy VI Philometor (Egypt) initiated the third Egyptian war, against Antiochus. [Ed.]

[17] Antiochus spent his last year in war with Armenia and Parthia (Persia). [Ed.]

[18] In Palestine. [Ed.]

[19] Antiochus IV died at Tabae in Persia in 163 B.C.E. [Ed.]

[20] Protective angel of Israel. [Ed.]

those who lead many to righteousness, like the stars for ever and ever. 4 But you, Daniel, close up and seal the words of the scroll until the time of the end. Many will go here and there to increase knowledge."

5 Then I, Daniel, looked, and there before me stood two others, one on this bank of the river and one on the opposite bank. 6 One of them said to the man clothed in linen, who was above the waters of the river, "How long will it be before these astonishing things are fulfilled?"

7 The man clothed in linen, who was above the waters of the river, lifted his right hand and his left hand toward heaven, and I heard him swear by him who lives forever, saying, "It will be for a time, times and half a time. When the power of the holy people has been finally broken, all these things will be completed."

8 I heard, but I did not understand. So I asked, "My lord, what will the outcome of all this be?"

9 He replied, "Go your way, Daniel, because the words are closed up and sealed until the time of the end. 10 Many will be purified, made spotless and refined, but the wicked will continue to be wicked. None of the wicked will understand, but those who are wise will understand.

11 "From the time that the daily sacrifice is abolished and the abomination that causes desolation is set up, there will be 1,290 days. 12 Blessed is the one who waits for and reaches the end of the 1,335 days.

13 "As for you, go your way till the end. You will rest, and then at the end of the days you will rise to receive your allotted inheritance."

7

The Christian Bible: Jesus According to Matthew, c. 70 C.E.

The ideas first enunciated in Daniel—the coming end of the world or the Kingdom of God, the Last Judgment, individual immortality or life after death—were to become central to the branch of Judaism that produced Christianity. Along with Judaic monotheism and the insistence of the prophets (like Amos) on internalized morality, the idea of personal responsibility and eternal salvation or damnation gave Christianity an appeal that would eventually reach far beyond the children of Abraham.

In this selection from the Christian New Testament, the evangelist Matthew recounts Jesus speaking of the apocalypse with a note of urgency. Like Daniel, Jesus speaks of the signs that the end is at hand.

Source: Matt. 24:1–41. New International Version.

Yet, in the same chapter, sometimes in the same paragraph, Matthew recounts Jesus telling his listeners that there is plenty of time before the end.

What accounts for this apparent contradiction? If you were in the audience listening to Jesus, which idea would motivate you more — that the end of the world is rapidly approaching or that it is generations away? If you were taking notes for the daily newspaper, which message would get the headline? If you were writing a history of Jesus for future generations, which message would you emphasize?

THINKING HISTORICALLY

Matthew wrote his gospel about forty years after Jesus died. If he had been among those who heard Jesus speak, he took a long time to write it down. It is more likely that the author of this gospel is a second-generation evangelist, drawing on an earlier source, now lost. He may have had access to an earlier eyewitness account or to a collection of sayings of Jesus.

We know that Matthew updated the words of Jesus for the benefit of those Christians living after 70 c.e. Notice, for example, Matthew's reference to Daniel in 24:15: Jesus tells his listeners that when they see the abomination of the temple of which Daniel spoke, they should flee into the mountains to prepare for the end. But we know today that Daniel was speaking of the desecration of the temple by Antiochus IV in 168 b.c.e. Matthew, unaware of the historical context of Daniel and writing after the Roman destruction of the temple in 70 c.e., believed that Roman destruction was the event Daniel was predicting. So Matthew updates the message of Jesus for future generations by including the temple destruction for the readers of his gospel ("let the reader understand"). This is one of the ways we know that Matthew's text was written after 70 c.e. Jesus would not have referred to an event that was for his audience forty years into the future and expect his audience to understand his reference. In addition to the Daniel reference, which parts of this selection are most likely the written updates of Matthew? Which statements are most likely the actual spoken words of Jesus?

Matthew 24

Signs of the End of the Age

1 Jesus left the temple and was walking away when his disciples came up to him to call his attention to its buildings. 2 "Do you see all these things?" he asked. "I tell you the truth, not one stone here will be left on another; every one will be thrown down."

3 As Jesus was sitting on the Mount of Olives, the disciples came to him privately. "Tell us," they said, "when will this happen, and what will be the sign of your coming and of the end of the age?"

4 Jesus answered: "Watch out that no one deceives you. 5 For many will come in my name, claiming, 'I am the Christ,' and will deceive many. 6 You will hear of wars and rumors of wars, but see to it that you are not alarmed. Such things must happen, but the end is still to come. 7 Nation will rise against nation, and kingdom against kingdom. There will be famines and earthquakes in various places. 8 All these are the beginning of birth pains.

9 "Then you will be handed over to be persecuted and put to death, and you will be hated by all nations because of me. 10 At that time many will turn away from the faith and will betray and hate each other, 11 and many false prophets will appear and deceive many people. 12 Because of the increase of wickedness, the love of most will grow cold, 13 but he who stands firm to the end will be saved. 14 And this gospel of the kingdom will be preached in the whole world as a testimony to all nations, and then the end will come.

15 "So when you see standing in the holy place 'the abomination that causes desolation,' spoken of through the prophet Daniel — let the reader understand — 16 then let those who are in Judea flee to the mountains. 17 Let no one on the roof of his house go down to take anything out of the house. 18 Let no one in the field go back to get his cloak. 19 How dreadful it will be in those days for pregnant women and nursing mothers! 20 Pray that your flight will not take place in winter or on the Sabbath. 21 For then there will be great distress, unequaled from the beginning of the world until now — and never to be equaled again. 22 If those days had not been cut short, no one would survive, but for the sake of the elect those days will be shortened. 23 At that time if anyone says to you, 'Look, here is the Christ!' or, 'There he is!' do not believe it. 24 For false Christs and false prophets will appear and perform great signs and miracles to deceive even the elect — if that were possible. 25 See, I have told you ahead of time.

26 "So if anyone tells you, 'There he is, out in the desert,' do not go out; or, 'Here he is, in the inner rooms,' do not believe it. 27 For as lightning that comes from the east is visible even in the west, so will be the coming of the Son of Man. 28 Wherever there is a carcass, there the vultures will gather.

29 "Immediately after the distress of those days

'the sun will be darkened,
and the moon will not give its light;
the stars will fall from the sky,
and the heavenly bodies will be shaken.'

30 "At that time the sign of the Son of Man will appear in the sky, and all the nations of the earth will mourn. They will see the Son of Man

coming on the clouds of the sky, with power and great glory. 31And he will send his angels with a loud trumpet call, and they will gather his elect from the four winds, from one end of the heavens to the other.

32 "Now learn this lesson from the fig tree: As soon as its twigs get tender and its leaves come out, you know that summer is near. 33 Even so, when you see all these things, you know that it is near, right at the door. 34 I tell you the truth, this generation will certainly not pass away until all these things have happened. 35 Heaven and earth will pass away, but my words will never pass away.

The Day and Hour Unknown

36 "No one knows about that day or hour, not even the angels in heaven, nor the Son, but only the Father. 37 As it was in the days of Noah, so it will be at the coming of the Son of Man. 38 For in the days before the flood, people were eating and drinking, marrying and giving in marriage, up to the day Noah entered the ark; 39 and they knew nothing about what would happen until the flood came and took them all away. That is how it will be at the coming of the Son of Man. 40 Two men will be in the field; one will be taken and the other left. 41 Two women will be grinding with a hand mill; one will be taken and the other left."

8

Paul, Letters, c. 50 C.E.

Paul of Tarsus (d. c. 65 C.E.), born with the name Saul in a Jewish community in what is today southeastern Turkey, was educated in the Hellenistic Greek culture of his time. As a young man, according to his testimony, he persecuted the followers of Jesus until, about the year 33, on the road to Damascus he was thrown from his horse, blinded, and reprimanded by God for his actions. From then on, Paul became the most vigorous missionary of Jesus, traveling throughout the Mediterranean converting nonbelievers and corresponding with communities of fellow followers. In contrast to the followers of Jesus in Jerusalem, Paul spread his gospel to others who were neither Jewish nor had known Jesus, believing that the message of the life, death, and resurrection of Jesus transcended any particular national community. In these selections from his letters to communities of Jesus followers throughout the Mediterranean, Paul emphasizes

Source: Rom. 2:25–29; 1 Cor. 15:1–8; Eph. 1:1–10, 2:1–10. New International Version.

certain ideas that opened up the religion to non-Jews and aided its spread to new communities. What are these ideas? How would these new ideas or emphases make the early church of Jesus universal in its appeal and potential membership?

THINKING HISTORICALLY

As a Jew, Paul would have been familiar with the Hebrew Bible in Greek translation, though it had not yet been codified in its present form. He would also have had access to stories about Jesus, though the gospels that we have in Greek had not yet been written. How different is Paul's message about Jesus from the message that later appeared in the gospel according to Matthew? How similar is it? Is Paul more interested in presenting the message *of* Jesus or the message *about* Jesus?

Romans 2

25 Circumcision has value if you observe the law, but if you break the law, you have become as though you had not been circumcised. 26 If those who are not circumcised keep the law's requirements, will they not be regarded as though they were circumcised? 27 The one who is not circumcised physically and yet obeys the law will condemn you who, even though you have the written code and circumcision, are a lawbreaker.

28 A man is not a Jew if he is only one outwardly, nor is circumcision merely outward and physical. 29 No, a man is a Jew if he is one inwardly; and circumcision is circumcision of the heart, by the Spirit, not by the written code. Such a man's praise is not from men, but from God.

1 Corinthians 15

The Resurrection of Christ

1 Now, brothers, I want to remind you of the gospel I preached to you, which you received and on which you have taken your stand. 2 By this gospel you are saved, if you hold firmly to the word I preached to you. Otherwise, you have believed in vain.

3 For what I received I passed on to you as of first importance: that Christ died for our sins according to the Scriptures, 4 that he was buried, that he was raised on the third day according to the Scriptures, 5 and that he appeared to Peter, and then to the Twelve. 6 After that, he appeared to more than five hundred of the brothers at the same time, most of whom are still living, though some have fallen asleep. 7 Then he

appeared to James, then to all the apostles, 8 and last of all he appeared to me also, as to one abnormally born.[1]

Ephesians 1

1 Paul, an apostle of Christ Jesus by the will of God,
To the saints in Ephesus, the faithful in Christ Jesus:
2 Grace and peace to you from God our Father and the Lord Jesus Christ.

Spiritual Blessings in Christ

3 Praise be to the God and Father of our Lord Jesus Christ, who has blessed us in the heavenly realms with every spiritual blessing in Christ. 4 For he chose us in him before the creation of the world to be holy and blameless in his sight. In love 5 he predestined us to be adopted as his sons through Jesus Christ, in accordance with his pleasure and will—6 to the praise of his glorious grace, which he has freely given us in the One he loves. 7 In him we have redemption through his blood, the forgiveness of sins, in accordance with the riches of God's grace 8 that he lavished on us with all wisdom and understanding. 9 And he made known to us the mystery of his will according to his good pleasure, which he purposed in Christ, 10 to be put into effect when the times will have reached their fulfillment—to bring all things in heaven and on earth together under one head, even Christ. . . .

Ephesians 2

Made Alive in Christ

1 As for you, you were dead in your transgressions and sins, 2 in which you used to live when you followed the ways of this world and of the ruler of the kingdom of the air, the spirit who is now at work in those who are disobedient. 3 All of us also lived among them at one time, gratifying the cravings of our sinful nature and following its desires and thoughts. Like the rest, we were by nature objects of wrath. 4 But because of his great love for us, God, who is rich in mercy, 5 made us alive with Christ even when we were dead in transgressions—it is by grace you have been saved. 6 And God raised us up with Christ and seated us with him in the heavenly realms in Christ Jesus, 7 in order that in the

---

[1] Refers to vision on road to Damascus after death of Jesus—an event out of normal time. [Ed.]

coming ages he might show the incomparable riches of his grace, expressed in his kindness to us in Christ Jesus. 8 For it is by grace you have been saved, through faith—and this not from yourselves, it is the gift of God—9 not by works, so that no one can boast. 10 For we are God's workmanship, created in Christ Jesus to do good works, which God prepared in advance for us to do.

■ REFLECTIONS

The layers of revision are etched more sharply in the book of Daniel in the Hebrew Bible and Matthew in the New Testament of the Bible than in the Hindu and Buddhist documents because dates, chronology, and time sequences were far more important to the Judeo-Christian tradition. It was, and is, a tradition committed to the belief that God works in time; that there is a beginning, middle, and end to things; and that it is crucially important for humans to know where they are in the providential timeline. A modern skeptic might be bothered by the way the author or authors of Daniel turn history into prophecy. But for the Jews of the 160s B.C.E., the need to get the dates right and be ready for the end of days was far more important than checking who predicted what when.

Ironically, the precise prophecy of Daniel transcended its historical moorings when it was used by the author of Matthew in an effort to update the prophecy of Jesus, and it has been used regularly by every generation since with a different "king of the south" and new supporting cast. But if the Judeo-Christian tradition has left a legacy of apocalyptic warnings and millennial musings, it has also given us the interest and the tools that have shaped this chapter. The need to date, to find the actual words, to peel away the layers of rust that obfuscate an authentic past—that is a fine legacy indeed.

We have seen how Hinduism produced Buddhism and how Judaism generated Christianity, but neither Hinduism nor Judaism ended two thousand years ago. In fact, both "parental" religions underwent profound changes as well. Both became more universal, less dependent on particular places or people, and less limited to caste, region, or tribe.

We saw in the Upanishads how, around 500 B.C.E., Hinduism became almost monotheistic in its worship of Brahman. Similarly, about three hundred years later, Hindu devotional cults that centered on two of the other deities of the Hindu pantheon (Vishnu—especially in his incarnation as Krishna—and Shiva) developed. Reread the last eight stanzas of the *Bhagavad Gita* (written about 200 B.C.E.) in Chapter 3 to see how the worship of Vishnu/Krishna became enormously appealing to masses of Indian people.

At about the time of Jesus, Judaism also underwent a transformation that has continued until this day. A process that began with the destruction of the first temple and the captivity in Babylon in the sixth century B.C.E.—the development of a Judaism independent of a particular temple or place—was revived after the Romans destroyed the second temple in 70 C.E. The Roman conquest created a more global Judaism than the Babylonian conquest. Judaism became a religion of rabbis (teachers) rather than of temple priests and guardians. So great was this transformation of Judaism that one might argue, with Alan Segal in *Rebecca's Children*, that "the time of Jesus marks the birth of not one but two great religions in the West, Judaism and Christianity. . . . So great is the contrast between previous Jewish religious systems and rabbinism."[1]

---

[1] Alan F. Segal, *Rebecca's Children: Judaism and Christianity in the Roman World* (Cambridge: Harvard University Press, 1986), 1.

7

The Spread of Universal Religions

Afro-Eurasia, 100–1000 C.E.

■ HISTORICAL CONTEXT

From their beginnings, Buddhism and Christianity were less tribal and more universal than their parental religions, Hinduism and Judaism, because they offered universal salvation to their followers. The teachings of Jesus and the Buddha emphasized personal religious experience over the dictates of caste, ancestry, and formal law, making their ideas more likely to spread beyond their cultures of origin. Both religions, however, had relatively small followings at the deaths of their founders. How, then, did they win millions of converts within the next few hundred years? Similarly, how did Islam, founded in 622, spread from the Arabian peninsula to embrace the Berbers of North Africa, the Visigoths of Spain, Syrians, Persians, Turks, Central Asians, Indians, and even the western Chinese by 750? What was happening throughout Eurasia that explained these successes? In this chapter we explore how both an array of powerful and charismatic individuals and specific economic, political, and social conditions helped to broaden the appeal of the salvation religions and find larger audiences for their gospels.

The previous chapter explored the rise of universal religions. Paul of Tarsus almost singlehandedly separated Jesus from his Jewish roots, presenting him as the Son of God who was sacrificed for the sins of humankind, not just a prophet or messiah (king) of the Jewish people. Similarly, Mahayana Buddhists taught that Buddha was more than a teacher and spiritual guide whom one could imitate; he was a savior, responsive to prayer and worship. In addition, the devout could appeal to numerous Christian saints or Buddhist Bodhisattvas for help in achieving salvation.

Religious leaders weren't the only ones spreading faith; merchants and traders (occupations of the Prophet Muhammad) also played a crucial role. The spread of universal faiths and common cultures over great distances owed much to the expansive roads and maritime transport of the Roman and Chinese empires, as well as the Persian, Central Asian, and Indian states in between (see Map 7.1 on p. 226). But it was also a product of the Silk Road, or Roads, that connected China with Rome by land and sea after 100 B.C.E. The expansion of the great religious traditions was the work of merchants as well as monks; statues of gods traveled in camel caravans, and holy images were carried on rolls of silk.

Contact alone, however, is not enough to explain why people converted to Christianity, Buddhism, and Islam. The appeals to salvation beyond this world testified to difficult times. Nomadic pastoral peoples undermined the stability of empires already weakened by public debt, class antagonisms, dwindling crop yields, and disease. Populations declined from 200 to 800 C.E. and did not reach earlier levels again until about 1000 C.E. in Europe and China. People sought spiritual reassurance as well as economic alliances that would protect them in uncertain times. When those in power adopted new religions, it often benefited others to follow their lead, and thus a network of influence for new religious movements was secured.

▪ THINKING HISTORICALLY

Understanding Continuity and Change

Thinking historically involves thinking about the way things do and do not change over time. In this chapter we will be looking at Christianity, Buddhism, and Islam as they expand, and we will ask how they bring change to the regions, people, and customs where they make converts. We will also ask how the religions themselves change as they expand. Only when we can see exactly what has changed, and what has remained constant—known as continuities—can we begin to understand the causes of change.

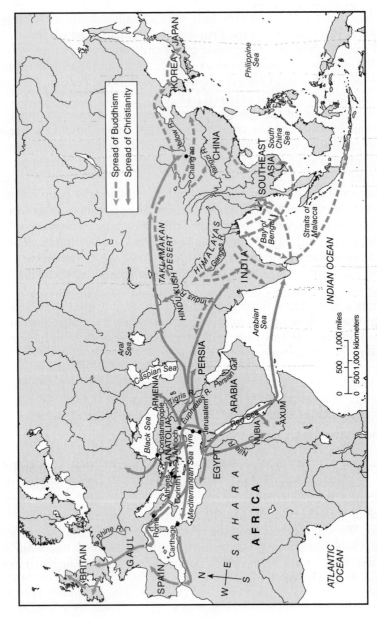

Map 7.1 The Spread of Early Christianity and Buddhism.

1

SHLOMO SAND

The Invention of the Jewish People, 2009

It is a common belief that Judaism is a religion into which one is
born. Conversions are infrequent and not even encouraged by some
orthodox groups. We saw in the last chapter that Judaism was indeed
an inherited national religion for the people of ancient Palestine. But
in the Hellenistic period (after Alexander the Great and his successors
spread Greek culture throughout the Middle East), some schools of
Judaism embraced a more global view of their place in the world. We
saw different manifestations of such universalism in the teachings of
Daniel, Jesus, and, especially, Paul. But maybe Paul was neither as
unique nor such a break with Judaism as is usually maintained.

In this selection by an Israeli historian we are asked to consider the
possibility that Christianity was not the only branch of Judaism that
converted large numbers of people in the centuries of the Roman Empire. What is the argument of Shlomo Sand? What is his evidence?
What do you think of his conclusion?

THINKING HISTORICALLY

Sand makes a number of startling claims for both continuity and
change. What claims of change does he make for the spread of
the Jewish and Christian religions? What claim of continuity does he
make for both religions? Why is a religion based on belief that one
chooses to convert to more open to changes than a religion that one
is born into?

The popularity of Judaism before and after the Common Era spread
beyond the Mediterranean region. In *Antiquities of the Jews*, Josephus
tells the fabulous story of the conversion to Judaism in the first century
CE of the rulers of Adiabene (Hadyab). As this conversion is described in
other sources, there is no reason to doubt its broad outline.

The kingdom of Adiabene was in the north of the Fertile Crescent,
roughly corresponding to today's Kurdistan and Armenia. Jewish proselytizing led to the conversion of the kingdom's much-loved heir to the
throne, Izates, as well as his mother Helena, herself an important person-
age in the kingdom. They were persuaded to convert by a merchant
named Hananiah, who assured the prince that it was enough to observe

Source: Shlomo Sand, *The Invention of the Jewish People*, trans. Yael Lotan (London: Verso, 2009), 165–73, 176.

the precepts without being circumcised. However, when the prince ascended the throne, a stricter Jewish preacher, a Galilean named Eleazar, demanded that he circumcise himself in order to complete his conversion, and Izates complied. Josephus reports that the ruling dynasty's conversion annoyed Adiabene's nobility, some of whom tried to rebel. But Izates succeeded in suppressing and eliminating his pagan enemies, and when his brother Monobazus II (Monobaz) succeeded him, he too converted to Judaism, along with the rest of the royal family. Queen Helena, accompanied by her son, went on a pilgrimage to Jerusalem, where she helped the Judeans to survive a severe drought, and she was buried in the holy city in a grand "royal tomb" built for her. The sons of Izates also went to the holy city in the center of Judea to be educated in the faith. . . .

The kingdom of Adiabene was the first political entity outside Judea to convert to Judaism, but it was not the last. Nor was it the only one to give rise to an important Jewish community that would survive until modern times.

If Alexander's conquests created an open Hellenistic sphere, Rome's expansion and her enormous empire completed the process. Henceforth, all the cultural centers around the Mediterranean basin would undergo the dynamism of blending and the forging of new phenomena. The littorals[1] grew closer, and the passage from the eastern to the western end became easier and faster. This emerging world opened a fresh perspective for the spread of Judaism; at its high point there, Judaism was professed by 7 to 8 percent of all the empire's inhabitants. The word "Jew" ceased to denote the people of Judea, and now included the masses of proselytes and their descendants.

At the height of Judaism's expansion, in the early third century CE, Cassius Dio described this significant historical development, asserting: "I do not know how this title [Jews] came to be given to them, but it applies also to all the rest of mankind, although of alien race, who affect their customs." His near contemporary, the Christian theologian Origen, wrote: "The noun *ioudaios* is not the name of an *ethnos*, but of a choice [in the manner of life]. For if there be someone not from the nation of the Jews, a gentile, who accepts the ways of the Jews and becomes a proselyte, this person would properly be called a *Ioudaios*." * . . .

As the rate of conversion to Judaism intensified, so did the government's disquiet and the resentment on the part of many Latin intellectuals.

---

* ee oo DAH yos
[1] Coasts. [Ed.]

The great Roman poet Horace made a humorous reference to the Jewish missionary drive in one of his poems: "like the Jews, we [the poets] will force you to come over to our numerous party." The philosopher Seneca thought the Jews were a damned people, because "the customs of this accursed race have gained such influence that they are now received throughout all the world. The vanquished have given laws to their victors." The historian Tacitus, no lover of Jews, was even more acerbic about the converts to Judaism:

> The most degraded out of other races, scorning their national beliefs, brought to them their contributions and presents. This augmented the wealth of the Jews . . . Circumcision was adopted by them as a mark of difference from other men. Those who come over to their religion adopt the practice, and have this lesson first instilled into them, to despise all gods, to disown their country, and set at nought parents, children, and brethren.

Juvenal, the author of the *Satires*, written in the early second century CE, was especially sarcastic. He did not hide his disgust at the wave of Judaization sweeping over many good Romans, and ridiculed the process of conversion that had become popular in his time:

> Some who have had a father who reveres the Sabbath, worship nothing but the clouds, and the divinity of the heavens, and see no difference between eating swine's flesh, from which their father abstained, and that of man; and in time they take to circumcision. Having been wont to flout the laws of Rome, they learn and practise and revere the Jewish law, and all that Moses committed to his secret tome, forbidding to point out the way to any not worshipping the same rites, and conducting none but the circumcised to the desired fountain. For all which the father was to blame, who gave up every seventh day to idleness, keeping it apart from all the concerns of life.

At the end of the second century, Celsus, a philosopher known for his dislike of the Christians, was much less hostile to the Jews. But as the conversions grew apace, and the old religions were abandoned, he became openly antagonistic toward the proselytized masses, stating, "If, then, in these respects the Jews were carefully to preserve their own law, they are not to be blamed for so doing, but those persons rather who have forsaken their own usages, and adopted those of the Jews."

This mass phenomenon annoyed the authorities in Rome and upset a good many of the capital's prominent literati. It upset them because Judaism became seductive to broad circles. All the conceptual and intellectual elements that would make for the future appeal of Christianity and its eventual triumph were present in this transient success of Judaism; traditional, conservative Romans felt the danger and voiced their concern in various ways.

The crisis of the hedonistic culture, the absence of an integrating belief in collective values, and the corruption infecting the administration of the imperial government appeared to call for tighter normative systems and a firmer ritual framework—and the Jewish religion met those needs. The Sabbath rest, the concept of reward and punishment, the belief in an afterlife, and above all the transcendent hope of resurrection were enticing features that persuaded many people to adopt the Jewish faith.

Furthermore, Judaism also offered a rare communal feeling that the spreading imperial world, with its corrosive effects on old identities and traditions, seemed to lack. It was not easy to follow the new set of commandments, but joining the chosen people, the holy nation, also conferred a precious sense of distinction, a fair compensation for the effort. The most intriguing element of this process was its gender aspect—it was the women who led the large-scale movement of Judaization.

Josephus's story about Damascus noted that Judaism was especially popular among the city's women, and as we have seen, Queen Helena of Adiabene had a decisive role in the conversion of the royal family. In the New Testament, we are told, Saul of Tarsus, known as Paul, had a disciple who was "the son of a certain woman which was a Jewess and believed, but his father *was* a Greek" (Acts 16:1). In Rome, too, the women were drawn more readily to Judaism. The poet Martial, who came from Iberia, made fun of the women who observed the Sabbath. Epigraphic material[2] from the Jewish catacombs names as many female converts as male. Especially notable is the inscription about Veturia Paulla, who was renamed Sarah after her conversion and became the "mother" of two synagogues. Fulvia (wife of Saturninus)—on whose account, according to Josephus, Jews were expelled in the year 19 CE—was a full convert. Pomponia Graecina, the wife of the famous commander Aulus Plautius, who conquered Britain, was put on trial and divorced by her husband for her devotion to the Jewish (or possibly the Christian) faith. Poppaea Sabina, the emperor Nero's second wife, made no secret of her tendency to Judaism. These women and many other matrons spread the Jewish faith in Rome's upper classes. There is evidence that Judaism was also becoming popular among the lower urban classes, as well as among the soldiers and freed slaves. From Rome, Judaism spilled over to parts of Europe annexed by the Roman Empire, such as the Slavic and Germanic lands, southern Gaul and Spain.

The pivotal role of women in proselytization might indicate a particular female interest in the religion's personal laws, such as the early

[2] Inscriptions. [Ed.]

rules of personal purification, which were preferred to the common pagan customs. Possibly it was also due to the fact that women did not have to undergo circumcision, which was a difficult requirement that deterred many would-be male converts. In the second century CE, after Hadrian prohibited all circumcision, the emperor Antoninus Pius permitted the Jews to circumcise their sons, but forbade males who were not children of Jews to do it. This was another reason that, parallel with the increase of converts, there was a growing category of "God-fearers"—probably an adaptation of the biblical term "fearers of Yahweh" (*sebomenoi* in Greek; *metuentes* in Latin).

These were semi-converts—people who formed broad peripheries around the Jewish community, took part in its ceremonies, attended the synagogues, but did not keep all the commandments. Josephus mentions them several times, and describes Nero's wife as God-fearing. The term is also found in many extant synagogue inscriptions as well as Roman catacombs. The New Testament confirms their massive presence. For example: "And there were dwelling at Jerusalem Jews, devout men, out of every nation under heaven" (Acts 2:5). When Paul reached Antioch, he entered a synagogue on the Sabbath and began his sermon with the words, "Men of Israel, and ye that fear God, give audience" (Acts 13:16). In case some of his hearers were puzzled by this address, he said further: "Men *and* brethren, children of the stock of Abraham, and whosoever among you feareth God, to you is the word of this salvation sent" (13:26). The text goes on: "Now when the congregation was broken up, many of the Jews and religious proselytes followed Paul and Barnabas" (13:43). The next week, a row broke out between zealous Jews and the two successful preachers—"But the Jews stirred up the devout and honourable women, and the chief men of the city, and raised persecution against Paul and Barnabas, and expelled them out of their coasts" (13:50). The two missionaries went on their way and reached the city of Philippi in Macedonia. There, "we sat down, and spake unto the women which resorted *thither*. And a certain woman . . . whose heart the Lord opened . . . was baptized, and her household" (Acts 16:13–15).

It was precisely in these gray areas, between troubled paganism and partial or full conversion to Judaism, that Christianity made headway. Carried by the momentum of proliferating Judaism and the flourishing varieties of religious syncretism, an open and more flexible belief system arose that skillfully adapted to those who accepted it. It is amazing to what extent the followers of Jesus, the authors of the New Testament, were conscious of the two competing marketing policies. The Gospel of Matthew offers additional testimony to outright Jewish missionizing as well as its limitation: "Woe unto you, scribes and Pharisees, hypocrites! for ye compass sea and land to make one proselyte; and when he is made, ye make him twofold more the child of hell than yourselves" (Matt. 23:15).

This was, of course, the criticism of experienced, professional preachers about the strict commandments from which they were distancing themselves. These new preachers were better at interpreting the sensitivities of the shaky polytheistic world, and knew how to offer it a more sophisticated, user-friendly approach to the monotheistic deity. . . .

In this lively culture of God-fearers, partial converts, full converts, Christian Jews, and born Jews, canceling commandments while preserving the belief in the one god was a revolutionary move of liberation and alleviation. For the spreading monotheism to withstand persecution and external opposition, it had to loosen the exclusivist tendency that lingered in it from the time of Ezra and Nehemiah.[3] In the rising Christian world, there was greater equality between new and established members, and there was even some preference for the "poor in spirit," namely the newcomers. The young religion discarded the element of privileged genealogy—now limited to Jesus as the son of God—and opted for a more sublime genealogy, that of the messianic-universal telos: "There is neither Jew nor Greek, there is neither bond nor free, there is neither male nor female: for ye are all one in Christ Jesus. And if ye *be* Christ's, then are ye Abraham's seed and heirs according to the promise" (Gal. 3: 28–9)

It was Paul who completed the transformation of "Israel in the flesh" into "Israel in the spirit," an idea that conformed with the open and flexible policy of identities that increasingly characterized the Roman Empire. It was not surprising that this dynamic monotheistic movement, which introduced the idea of charity and compassion for all (and the resurrection of at least one person), eventually triumphed over paganism, and cast it into the rubbish bin of history throughout Europe.

[3] Fifth century B.C.E. [Ed.]

2

EUSEBIUS
Life of Constantine, c. 339

Christians in the Roman Empire were generally subject to greater persecution than Jews. Judaism in Palestine was considered a national religion, and thus free from Roman interference, but monotheists,

Source: P. Schaff and H. Wace, eds., *The Library of Nicene and Post-Nicene Fathers*, vol. I, *Church History, Life of Constantine, Oration in Praise of Constantine* (New York: The Christian Literature Company, 1890), 489–91.

whether Jews or Christians, who flouted Roman state religion and sought converts to do the same, were to be challenged. The degree that challenge should take was not always clear to Roman administrators, as Pliny's letter to the Emperor Trajan demonstrates (see document 4.7). Nevertheless, state persecution was the standard response during the first three centuries, occurring first and perhaps most viciously under Emperor Nero (37–68 C.E.) and then continuing intermittently thereafter.

If Christians were persecuted by Roman officials and emperors, and despised by the thoughtful and powerful elite of Roman society, how then did Christianity ever succeed? Part of the answer lies in the location of these Christians. They were more concentrated in urban than rural areas (the Latin word *pagan* meant "rural" before it meant "unchristian") and managed to gain significant advocates among the powerful elite.

Perhaps the most powerful urban, elite advocate for Christianity was the Roman emperor Constantine (288–337 C.E.). The emperor's historian Eusebius* (260–339 C.E.) recognized both the importance of the emperor and the role of the empire in the success of Christianity in winning the Roman Empire:

At the same time one universal power, the Roman Empire arose and flourished, while the enduring and implacable hatred of nation against nation was now removed; and as the knowledge of one god and one way of religion and salvation, even the doctrine of Christ, was made known to all mankind; so at the same time the entire dominion of the Roman Empire being invested in a single sovereign, profound peace reigned throughout the world. And thus, by the express appointment of the same God, two roots of blessing, the Roman Empire and the doctrine of Christian piety, sprang up together for the benefit of men.[1]

Prior to his rule as emperor, Constantine ruled the imperial lands of Gaul and Britain as a Caesar. In 312 C.E., Constantine (r. 306–337) was about to invade Italy and try to gain the throne of the western empire by defeating Maxentius, who ruled Rome. In his *Life of Constantine*, Eusebius, who knew the emperor, tells a story about events prior to the invasion that must have circulated at the time to explain Constantine's support of Christianity. What reasons does Eusebius give for Constantine's adoption of Christianity? What does this story suggest about Constantine's knowledge of Christianity before his conversion? What does it suggest about the way people chose religions at this time?

* yoo SAY bee uhs
[1] Eusebius, *Oration in Praise of Constantine*, xv, 4. [Ed.]

THINKING HISTORICALLY

We think of conversion as a transforming experience. However, a close reading of this selection shows little change in Constantine himself. Other sources confirm this. Constantine continued the gladiator displays that had been so offensive to Christians, left memorials to other deities, and ruled brutally. But if adopting Christianity was more of a political than spiritual mission for Constantine, he nevertheless carried it out forcefully. He styled himself an Old Testament King David, rebuilt Jerusalem, unified the eastern and western halves of the Roman Empire (which had been split under the previous emperor for administrative purposes), and commandeered the church by holding councils, persecuting "heresies," and enforcing a uniform dogma that transformed the church from a marginalized cult protest to prominence in the governance of the empire. How was the Christianity that Constantine embraced different from that known to Paul or Pliny?

Being convinced, however, that he needed some more powerful aid than his military forces could afford him, on account of the wicked and magical enchantments which were so diligently practiced by the tyrant [Maxentius], he sought Divine assistance, deeming the possession of arms and a numerous soldiery of secondary importance, but believing the cooperating power of Deity invincible and not to be shaken. He considered, therefore, on what God he might rely for protection and assistance. While engaged in this enquiry, the thought occurred to him, that, of the many emperors who had preceded him, those who had rested their hopes in a multitude of gods, and served them with sacrifices and offerings, had in the first place been deceived by flattering predictions, and oracles which promised them all prosperity, and at last had met with an unhappy end, while not one of their gods had stood by to warn them of the impending wrath of heaven; while one alone [Constantine's father][2] who had pursued an entirely opposite course, who had condemned their error, and honored the Supreme God during his whole life, had found him to be the Saviour and Protector of his empire, and the Giver of every good thing. Reflecting on this, and well weighing the fact that they who had trusted in many gods had also fallen by manifold forms of death,

___

[2] Eusebius claims that Constantine's father, Constantius, was a Christian, though he appeared to be pagan. [Ed.]

without leaving behind them either family or offspring, stock, name, or memorial among men: while the God of his father had given to him, on the other hand, manifestations of his power and very many tokens: and considering farther that those who had already taken arms against the tyrant, and had marched to the battle-field under the protection of a multitude of gods, had met with a dishonorable end (for one of them had shamefully retreated from the contest without a blow, and the other, being slain in the midst of his own troops, became, as it were, the mere sport of death); reviewing, I say, all these considerations, he judged it to be folly indeed to join in the idle worship of those who were no gods, and after such convincing evidence, to err from the truth; and therefore felt it incumbent on him to honor his father's God alone.

Accordingly he called on Him with earnest prayer and supplications that he would reveal to him who He was, and stretch forth His right hand to help him in his present difficulties. And while he was thus praying with fervent entreaty, a most marvelous sign appeared to him from heaven, the account of which it might have been hard to believe had it been related by any other person. But since the victorious emperor himself long afterwards declared it to the writer of this history, when he was honored with his acquaintance and society, and confirmed his statement by an oath, who could hesitate to accredit the relation, especially since the testimony of after-time has established its truth? He said that about noon, when the day was already beginning to decline, he saw with his own eyes the trophy of a cross of light in the heavens, above the sun, and bearing the inscription, CONQUER BY THIS. At this sight he himself was struck with amazement, and his whole army also, which followed him on this expedition, and witnessed the miracle.

He said, moreover, that he doubted within himself what the import of this apparition could be. And while he continued to ponder and reason on its meaning, night suddenly came on; then in his sleep the Christ of God appeared to him with the same sign which he had seen in the heavens, and commanded him to make a likeness of that sign which he had seen in the heavens, and to use it as a safeguard in all engagements with his enemies.

At the dawn of day he arose, and communicated the marvel to his friends: and then, calling together the workers in gold and precious stones, he sat in the midst of them, and described to them the figure of the sign he had seen, bidding them represent it in gold and precious stones. And this representation I myself have had an opportunity of seeing. . . .

The emperor constantly made use of this sign of salvation as a safeguard against every adverse and hostile power, and commanded that others similar to it should be carried at the head of all his armies.

These things were done shortly afterwards. But at the time above specified, being struck with amazement at the extraordinary vision, and resolving to worship no other God save Him who had appeared to him, he sent for those who were acquainted with the mysteries of His doctrines, and enquired who that God was, and what was intended by the sign of the vision he had seen.

They affirmed that He was God, the only begotten Son of the one and only God: that the sign which had appeared was the symbol of immortality, and the trophy of that victory over death which He had gained in time past when sojourning on earth. They taught him also the causes of His advent, and explained to him the true account of His incarnation. Thus he was instructed in these matters, and was impressed with wonder at the divine manifestation which had been presented to his sight. Comparing, therefore, the heavenly vision with the interpretation given, he found his judgment confirmed; and, in the persuasion that the knowledge of these things had been imparted to him by Divine teaching, he determined thenceforth to devote himself to the reading of the inspired writings.

3

Christianity in China:
The Nestorian Monument, 781

This selection is part of an inscription found on a ten-foot stone in China. It was inscribed in Aramaic and Chinese in 781 by Nestorian Christian missionaries in China who came from Syria. In Syria, Nestorian Christian beliefs were not very different from those of other Christians. They believed that Jesus had both a human and divine nature but emphasized the human side of Jesus more than other Christians. From Syria, Nestorians brought Christianity to Persia and Central Asia, reaching China by at least 635. What does the emperor's proclamation suggest about the way Christianity came to China? Why did the emperor support it?

THINKING HISTORICALLY

How is the message of this inscription different from that of Jesus, Paul, or other early Christians (see Chapter 6)? What words or ideas in this document show the influence of Confucian or Daoist thought? What expected Christian words or ideas are missing from this document? What do these changes tell you about Christianity in China? What seems to have remained constant, and what seems to have changed?

Source: Charles F. Horne, ed., *The Sacred Books and Early Literature of the East*, vol. XII, *Medieval China* (New York: Parke, Austin, & Lipscomb, 1917), 381–92. Modernized by Jerome S. Arkenberg. Internet East Asian History Sourcebook, http://legacy.fordham.edu /halsall/eastasia/781nestorian.asp.

"Behold the unchangeably true and invisible, who existed through all eternity without origin; the far-seeing perfect intelligence, whose mysterious existence is everlasting; operating on primordial substance he created the universe, being more excellent than all holy intelligences, inasmuch as he is the source of all that is honorable. This is our eternal true lord God, triune[1] and mysterious in substance. He appointed the cross as the means for determining the four cardinal points,[2] he moved the original spirit, and produced the two principles of nature;[3] the somber void[4] was changed, and heaven and earth were opened out; the sun and moon revolved, and day and night commenced; having perfected all inferior objects, he then made the first man; upon him he bestowed an excellent disposition, giving him in charge the government of all created beings; man, acting out the original principles of his nature, was pure and unostentatious;[5] his unsullied and expansive mind was free from the least inordinate desire; until Satan introduced the seeds of falsehood,[6] to deteriorate his purity of principle; the opening thus commenced in his virtue gradually enlarged, and by this crevice in his nature was obscured and rendered vicious; hence three hundred and sixty-five sects followed each other in continuous track,[7] inventing every species of doctrinal complexity; while some pointed to material objects as the source of their faith,[8] others reduced all to vacancy, even to the annihilation of the two primeval principles,[9] some sought to call down blessings by prayers and supplications,[10] while others by an assumption of excellence held

[1] The idea of the Trinity, that God consisted of three persons—Father, Son, and Holy Spirit—became orthodox in the fourth century, after the Council at Nicaea (325) declared that the Father and Son were of the same substance. Ironically, this council defeated the Arian emphasis on the humanity of Jesus, which was closer to the view of Nestorian Christianity. The Council of Nicaea was called by Constantine to unify Christian belief; Nicaea (modern Iznik, Turkey) was the capital of Bithnia, where Pliny governed, attempted urban renewal, and met Christians in the first century. [Ed.]

[2] The Chinese character for the number 10 is a cross. So this could be translated as "he appointed the Chinese figure for 10 as the means for determining the four cardinal points" of the compass: north, east, south, and west. One translator suggests that this is a whimsical way of saying that this God created all the universe; that is, he is not just a god of a mountain or stream. [Ed.]

[3] Probably refers to the Nestorian idea that the two natures of Christ, human and divine, were conjoined. A church council at Ephesus in 431 held that they became one nature, causing some Nestorians to split and move eastward. The Chinese may have thought of two natures as yin and yang. [Ed.]

[4] This void may be closer to Daoism or Buddhism. [Ed.]

[5] Compare this sentence to Genesis. [Ed.]

[6] May refer to the temptation of Adam. [Ed.]

[7] May refer to mankind cast out of paradise. [Ed.]

[8] Possibly a criticism of the Buddhist idea of the world as maya, or illusion. [Ed.]

[9] May refer to the Daoist idea of emptiness. [Ed.]

[10] May refer to ancestor worship. [Ed.]

themselves up as superior to their fellows;[11] their intellects and thoughts continually wavering, their minds and affections incessantly on the move, they never obtained their vast desires, but being exhausted and distressed they revolved in their own heated atmosphere; till by an accumulation of obscurity they lost their path, and after long groping in darkness they were unable to return. Thereupon, our Trinity being divided in nature, the illustrious and honorable Messiah,[12] veiling his true dignity, appeared in the world as a man; angelic powers promulgated the glad tidings, a virgin gave birth to the Holy One in Syria; a bright star announced the felicitous event, and Persians observing the splendor came to present tribute; the ancient dispensation, as declared by the twenty-four holy men [the writers of the Old Testament], was then fulfilled, and he laid down great principles for the government of families and kingdoms; he established the new religion of the silent[13] operation of the pure spirit of the Triune; he rendered virtue subservient to direct faith; he fixed the extent of the eight boundaries,[14] thus completing the truth and freeing it from dross; he opened the gate of the three constant principles,[15] introducing life and destroying death; he suspended the bright sun[16] to invade the chambers of darkness, and the falsehoods of the devil were thereupon defeated; he set in motion the vessel of mercy[17] by which to ascend to the bright mansions, whereupon rational beings were then released, having thus completed the manifestation of his power, in clear day he ascended to his true station.[18]

Twenty-seven sacred books [the number in the New Testament] have been left, which disseminate intelligence by unfolding the original transforming principles. By the rule for admission, it is the custom to apply the water of baptism,[19] to wash away all superficial show and to cleanse and purify the neophytes. As a seal, they hold the cross, whose influence is reflected in every direction, uniting all without distinction.

---

[11] May refer to Confucians. [Ed.]

[12] "Second Person of the Trinity" may be a better translation, since there is no Chinese for "Messiah." [Ed.]

[13] Recalls the Daoist idea that the sage conveys wisdom without words. [Ed.]

[14] Perhaps the eight beatitudes in Matthew ("Blessed are the . . . ," etc.), as opposed to the Buddha's eight-fold path. [Ed.]

[15] Some translate this as three virtues: faith, hope, and charity. Followers of Persian Manichaenism would understand it as the three Permanences of the Almighty: his Light, Strength, and Goodness. [Ed.]

[16] Possible reference to crucifixion (though, if so, very veiled). Probable intent is that followers will recognize meaning but nonbelievers won't be put off by the idea of a God who was executed and died. [Ed.]

[17] Christ's death on the cross, like the sacrifice of a Bodhisattva (a vessel of mercy). [Ed.]

[18] Reference to Christ ascending into heaven. [Ed.]

[19] Baptism, or immersion in water as a rite of purification, was practiced in Judaism, but in early Christianity it became associated with being a Christian. [Ed.]

As they strike the wood, the fame of their benevolence is diffused abroad; worshiping toward the east, they hasten on the way to life and glory; they preserve the beard to symbolize their outward actions, they shave the crown to indicate the absence of inward affections; they do not keep slaves, but put noble and mean all on an equality; they do not amass wealth, but cast all their property into the common stock; they fast, in order to perfect themselves by self-inspection; they submit to restraints, in order to strengthen themselves by silent watchfulness; seven times a day they have worship and praise for the benefit of the living and the dead; once in seven days they sacrifice, to cleanse the heart and return to purity.

It is difficult to find a name to express the excellence of the true and unchangeable doctrine; but as its meritorious operations are manifestly displayed, by accommodation it is named the Illustrious Religion.[20] Now without holy men,[21] principles cannot become expanded; without principles, holy men cannot become magnified; but with holy men and right principles, united as the two parts of a signet, the world becomes civilized and enlightened.

In the time of the accomplished Emperor Tai-tsung, the illustrious and magnificent founder of the dynasty, among the enlightened and holy men who arrived was the most-virtuous Olopun,[22] from the country of Syria. Observing the azure clouds, he bore the true sacred books; beholding the direction of the winds,[23] he braved difficulties and dangers. In the year of our Lord 635 he arrived at Chang-an; the Emperor sent his Prime Minister, Duke Fang Hiuen-ling; who, carrying the official staff to the west border, conducted his guest into the interior; the sacred books were translated in the imperial library, the sovereign investigated the subject in his private apartments; when becoming deeply impressed with the rectitude and truth of the religion, he gave special orders for its dissemination.

In the seventh month of the year A.D. 638 the following imperial proclamation was issued:

"Right principles have no invariable name, holy men have no invariable station; instruction is established in accordance with the locality, with the object of benefiting the people at large. The greatly virtuous Olopun, of the kingdom of Syria, has brought his sacred books

[20] This sentence is full of phrases from the *Tao Te Ching*. [Ed.]

[21] Some translators prefer "ruler" to "holy men," suggesting that this was a flattering call for the Chinese emperor to help spread the religion. [Ed.]

[22] Identified as Raban in some translations, the Nestorian monk who brought Christianity. [Ed.]

[23] Reference (not translated here) to the sound of winds in musical tubes refers to the Chinese form of divination. [Ed.]

and images from that distant part, and has presented them at our chief capital. Having examined the principles of this religion, we find them to be purely excellent and natural; investigating its originating source, we find it has taken its rise from the establishment of important truths; its ritual is free from perplexing expressions, its principles will survive when the framework is forgot; it is beneficial to all creatures; it is advantageous to mankind. Let it be published throughout the Empire, and let the proper authority build a Syrian church in the capital in the I-ning May,[24] which shall be governed by twenty-one priests. When the virtue of the Chau Dynasty declined, the rider on the azure ox ascended to the west;[25] the principles of the great Tang becoming resplendent, the Illustrious breezes have come to fan the East."

Orders were then issued to the authorities to have a true portrait of the Emperor taken; when it was transferred to the wall of the church, the dazzling splendor of the celestial visage irradiated the Illustrious portals. The sacred traces emitted a felicitous influence, and shed a perpetual splendor over the holy precincts. According to the Illustrated Memoir of the Western Regions, and the historical books of the Han and Wei dynasties, the kingdom of Syria reaches south to the Coral Sea; on the north it joins the Gem Mountains; on the west it extends toward the borders of the immortals and the flowery forests; on the east it lies open to the violent winds and tideless waters. The country produces fire-proof cloth,[26] life-restoring incense,[27] bright moon-pearls,[28] and night-luster gems. Brigands and robbers are unknown, but the people enjoy happiness and peace. None but Illustrious laws prevail; none but the virtuous are raised to sovereign power. The land is broad and ample, and its literary productions are perspicuous and clear. . . .

[The following is in Syriac at the foot of the stone.]

"In the year of the Greeks one thousand and ninety-two [781 C.E.], the Lord Jazedbuzid, Priest and Vicar-episcopal of Cumdan the royal city, son of the enlightened Mailas, Priest of Balkh a city of Turkestan, set up this tablet, whereon is inscribed the Dispensation of our Redeemer, and the preaching of the apostolic missionaries to the King of China."

---

[24] I-ning quarter of Chang-an was west where Persian and Central Asian merchants were concentrated. [Ed.]

[25] Evokes story told of Lao Tze riding an ox into the west at the end of his life. The point of this sentence, which was probably not part of the imperial proclamation, is that the Nestorian faith prospered after the end of the dynasty. [Ed.]

[26] Probably asbestos. [Ed.]

[27] Probably a balsam said to revive plague victims; used medicinally and in mummification. [Ed.]

[28] Likely oysters. [Ed.]

Buddhism in China:
The Disposition of Error, Fifth or Sixth Century

When Buddhist monks traveled from India to China, they came to a culture with different philosophical and religious traditions. In China, ancestor worship, which did not exist for Indians who believed in reincarnation, was a very important religious tradition. The leading Chinese philosopher Confucius said very little about religion but stressed the need for respect: sons to fathers (filial piety), wives to husbands, children to parents, students to teachers, youngsters to elders, everyone to the emperor, the living to the deceased. More spiritual and meditative was the religion developed by the followers of a contemporary of Confucius, Laozi,* whose *Daodejing* (The Way and the Power) prescribed the peace that came from an acceptance of natural flows and rhythms. "Practice nonaction" was the Daoist method.

The Disposition of Error is a Buddhist guide for converting the Chinese. While the author and date are uncertain, this kind of tract was common under the Southern Dynasties (420–589 C.E.). The author uses a frequently-asked-questions (FAQ) format that enables us to see what the Chinese — mainly Confucian — objections were to Buddhism, as well as what they considered good Buddhist answers.

What were the main Chinese objections to Buddhism? Why were Buddhist ideas of death and rebirth such a stumbling block for Chinese Confucians? Were Confucian ideas about care of the body and hair only superficial concerns, or did they reflect basic differences between Confucianism and Buddhism? What did the Buddhists expect to be the main appeal of their religion?

THINKING HISTORICALLY

This Buddhist missionary's guide to converting the Chinese offers a unique window on both the continuities of Chinese tradition and the possibilities of change. We can see continuities in those Chinese beliefs and styles that the Buddhist monks accept, adopt, or attempt to work within. Note the style of presentation in this guide, for instance. Compare it to the *Analects* of Confucius and the Buddhist documents you have read. Is an FAQ format closer to Confucian or Buddhist

*low TSAY

Source: Hung-ming Chi, in Taishō daizōkyō, LII, 1–7, quoted in William Theodore de Bary, ed., *The Buddhist Tradition in India, China and Japan* (New York: Random House, 1969), 132–37.

style? Note also the different ways in which Confucian and Buddhist documents refer to an authority to solve a problem. Does this document follow Confucian or Buddhist style?

Why Is Buddhism Not Mentioned in the Chinese Classics?

The questioner said: If the way of the Buddha is the greatest and most venerable of ways, why did Yao, Shun, the Duke of Chou, and Confucius not practice it? In the Five Classics one sees no mention of it. You, sir, are fond of the *Book of Odes* and the *Book of History*, and you take pleasure in rites and music. Why, then, do you love the way of the Buddha and rejoice in outlandish arts? Can they exceed the Classics and commentaries and beautify the accomplishments of the sages? Permit me the liberty, sir, of advising you to reject them.

Mou Tzu said: All written works need not necessarily be the words of Confucius, and all medicine does not necessarily consist of the formulae of [the famous physician] P'ien-ch'üeh. What accords with principle is to be followed, what heals the sick is good. The gentleman-scholar draws widely on all forms of good, and thereby benefits his character. Tzu-kung [a disciple of Confucius] said, "Did the Master have a permanent teacher?" Yao served Yin Shou, Shun served Wuch'eng, the Duke of Chou learned from Lü Wang, and Confucius learned from Lao Tzu. And none of these teachers is mentioned in the Five Classics. Although these four teachers were sages, to compare them to the Buddha would be like comparing a white deer to a unicorn, or a swallow to a phoenix. Yao, Shun, the Duke of Chou, and Confucius learned even from such teachers as these. How much less, then, may one reject the Buddha, whose distinguishing marks are extraordinary and whose superhuman powers know no bounds! How may one reject him and refuse to learn from him? The records and teachings of the Five Classics do not contain everything. Even if the Buddha is not mentioned in them, what occasion is there for suspicion?

Why Do Buddhist Monks Do Injury to Their Bodies?

The questioner said: The *Classic of Filial Piety* says, "Our torso, limbs, hair, and skin we receive from our fathers and mothers. We dare not do them injury." When Tseng Tzu was about to die, he bared his hands and feet.[1] But now the monks shave their heads. How this violates the sayings of the sages and is out of keeping with the way of the filially pious! . . .

---

[1] To show he had preserved them intact from all harm.

Mou Tzu said: . . . Confucius has said, "He with whom one may follow a course is not necessarily he with whom one may weigh its merits." This is what is meant by doing what is best at the time. Furthermore, the *Classic of Filial Piety* says, "The kings of yore possessed the ultimate virtue and the essential Way." T'ai-po cut his hair short and tattooed his body, thus following of his own accord the customs of Wu and Yüeh and going against the spirit of the "torso, limbs, hair, and skin" passage.[2] And yet Confucius praised him, saying that his might well be called the ultimate virtue.

Why Do Monks Not Marry?

The questioner said: Now of felicities there is none greater than the continuation of one's line, of unfilial conduct there is none worse than childlessness. The monks forsake wife and children, reject property and wealth. Some do not marry all their lives. How opposed this conduct is to felicity and filial piety! . . .

Mou Tzu said: . . . Wives, children, and property are the luxuries of the world, but simple living and inaction are the wonders of the Way. Lao Tzu has said, "Of reputation and life, which is dearer? Of life and property, which is worth more?" . . . Hsü Yu and Ch'ao-fu dwelt in a tree. Po I and Shu Ch'i starved in Shou-yang, but Confucius praised their worth, saying, "They sought to act in accordance with humanity and they succeeded in acting so." One does not hear of their being illspoken of because they were childless and propertyless. The monk practices the Way and substitutes that for the pleasures of disporting himself in the world. He accumulates goodness and wisdom in exchange for the joys of wife and children.

Death and Rebirth

The questioner said: The Buddhists say that after a man dies he will be reborn. I do not believe in the truth of these words. . . .

Mou Tzu said: . . . The spirit never perishes. Only the body decays. The body is like the roots and leaves of the five grains, the spirit is like the seeds and kernels of the five grains. When the roots and leaves come forth they inevitably die. But do the seeds and kernels perish? Only the body of one who has achieved the Way perishes. . . .

Someone said: If one follows the Way one dies. If one does not follow the Way one dies. What difference is there?

---

[2] Uncle of King Wen of the Chou who retired to the barbarian land of Wu and cut his hair and tattooed his body in barbarian fashion, thus yielding his claim to the throne to King Wen.

Mou Tzu said: You are the sort of person who, having not a single day of goodness, yet seeks a lifetime of fame. If one has the Way, even if one dies one's soul goes to an abode of happiness. If one does not have the Way, when one is dead one's soul suffers misfortune.

Why Should a Chinese Allow Himself to Be Influenced by Indian Ways?

The questioner said: Confucius said, "The barbarians with a ruler are not so good as the Chinese without one." Mencius criticized Ch'en Hsiang for rejecting his own education to adopt the ways of [the foreign teacher] Hsü Hsing, saying, "I have heard of using what is Chinese to change what is barbarian, but I have never heard of using what is barbarian to change what is Chinese." You, sir, at the age of twenty learned the way of Yao, Shun, Confucius, and the Duke of Chou. But now you have rejected them, and instead have taken up the arts of the barbarians. Is this not a great error?

Mou Tzu said: . . . What Confucius said was meant to rectify the way of the world, and what Mencius said was meant to deplore one-sidedness. Of old, when Confucius was thinking of taking residence among the nine barbarian nations, he said, "If a gentleman-scholar dwells in their midst, what baseness can there be among them?" . . . The Commentary says, "The north polar star is in the center of heaven and to the north of man." From this one can see that the land of China is not necessarily situated under the center of heaven. According to the Buddhist scriptures, above, below, and all around, all beings containing blood belong to the Buddha-clan. Therefore I revere and study these scriptures. Why should I reject the Way of Yao, Shun, Confucius, and the Duke of Chou? Gold and jade do not harm each other, crystal and amber do not cheapen each other. You say that another is in error when it is you yourself who err.

Why Must a Monk Renounce Worldly Pleasures?

The questioner said: Of those who live in the world, there is none who does not love wealth and position and hate poverty and baseness, none who does not enjoy pleasure and idleness and shrink from labor and fatigue. . . . But now the monks wear red cloth, they eat one meal a day, they bottle up the six emotions, and thus they live out their lives. What value is there in such an existence?

Mou Tzu said: Wealth and rank are what man desires, but if he cannot obtain them in a moral way, he should not enjoy them. Poverty and mean-ness are what man hates, but if he can only avoid them by departing from the Way, he should not avoid them. Lao Tzu has said, "The five colors make men's eyes blind, the five sounds make men's ears deaf, the five flavors dull the palate, chasing about and hunting make men's minds mad, possessions difficult to acquire bring men's conduct to an impasse. The sage acts for his belly, not for his eyes." Can these words possibly be vain? Liu-hsia Hui would not exchange his way of life for the rank of the three highest princes of the realm. Tuankan Mu would not exchange his for the wealth of Prince Wen of Wei. . . . All of them followed their ideas, and cared for nothing more. Is there no value in such an existence?

Does Buddhism Have No Recipe for Immortality?

The questioner said: The Taoists say that Yao, Shun, the Duke of Chou, and Confucius and his seventy-two disciples did not die, but became immortals. The Buddhists say that men must all die, and that none can escape. What does this mean?

Mou Tzu said: Talk of immortality is superstitious and unfounded; it is not the word of the sages. Lao Tzu says, "Even Heaven and earth cannot be eternal. How much the less can man!" Confucius says, "The wise man leaves the world, but humanity and filial piety last forever." I have observed the six arts and examined the commentaries and records. According to them, Yao died, Shun had his [death place at] Mount Ts'ang-wu, Yü has his tomb on K'uai-chi, Po I and Shu Ch'i have their grave in Shou-yang. King Wen died before he could chastise Chou, King Wu died without waiting for King Ch'eng to grow up. We read of the Duke of Chou that he was reburied, and of Confucius that [shortly before his death] he dreamed of two pillars. [As for the disciples of Confucius], Po-yü died before his father, of Tzu Lu it is said that his flesh was chopped up and pickled.

5

Selections from the Quran, Seventh Century

In the centuries following the expansion of Christianity and Buddhism, a new monotheistic salvation religion, Islam, originated in Arabia and spread rapidly among Arab polytheists as well as to many Jews and Christians along ancient trade routes (see Map 7.2). The new faith centered on the Quran (or Koran), which is said by Islamic believers, or Muslims, to be the word of God as spoken by the Angel Gabriel to the Prophet Muhammad about 610. Muhammad then

Source: Chapters 1, 91, 109, and 112: *Approaching the Qur'an: The Early Revelations*, trans. Michael Sells (Ashland, OR: White Cloud Press, 1999), 42, 108, 128, 136. Chapters 2 and 4: *The New On-Line Translation of the Qur'an*, the Noor Foundation, http://islamusa.org/.

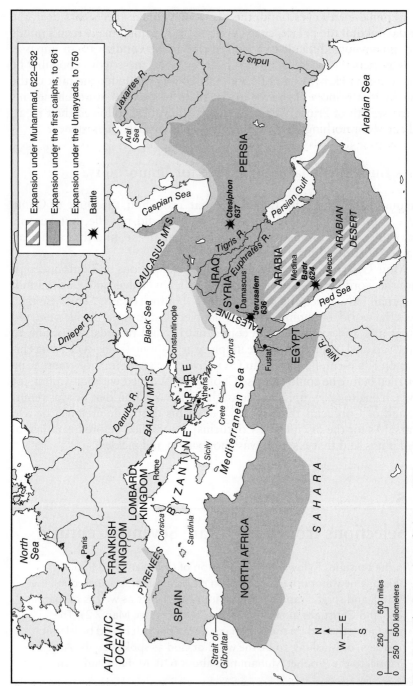

Map 7.2 The Expansion of Islam to 750 C.E.

recited these words so that others could memorize them or write them down. After Muhammad's death (632), these writings and memories were gathered together to form the Quran (literally "Recitation").

The chapters (or *surahs*) of the Quran, 114 in all, are organized primarily by length, with the longest first, and in reverse chronological order. This means that the earliest pieces, which are among the shortest, are found at the end of the book. We begin with the first, an exception to this length rule, *surah* 1, "The Opening," followed in rough chronology by a few of the earliest *surahs*: numbers 99, 109, and 112. We conclude with excerpts from the later *surahs*, number 2, "The Cow,"[1] and number 4, "Women." What beliefs do these *surahs* convey? How are they similar to, and different from, the beliefs of Judaism and Christianity? Which messages of the Quran would be effective in aiding the expansion of the religion?

THINKING HISTORICALLY

The early *surahs* (those with higher numbers) almost certainly reflect the concerns of early Islam. What are these concerns? The later *surahs* (such as 2 and 4) were probably written after Muhammad, threatened by the ruling tribes, had fled Mecca and taken control of the government of Medina. They may even have been written after Muhammad's death when his successors struggled with problems of governance. Judging from these later chapters, what kinds of issues most concerned leaders of the Muslim community? How did the message or emphasis change from the early to the later *surahs*? What would account for such a change?

Surah 1
The Opening

In the name of God
   the Compassionate the Caring
Praise be to God
   lord sustainer of the worlds
the Compassionate the Caring
master of the day of reckoning
To you we turn to worship
   and to you we turn in time of need

---

[1] The title "The Cow" refers to verses 67–73 in *surah* 2 of the Quran (not included here), which tell of a dispute between Moses and the Israelites. After Moses tells the Israelites that God wants them to sacrifice a cow, they hesitate by asking a number of questions as to what kind of cow. The Muslim meaning is that one should submit to God, not debate his commands. [Ed.]

Guide us along the road straight
the road of those to whom you are giving
   not those with anger upon them
   not those who have lost the way

Surah 99
The Quaking

In the Name of God the Compassionate the Caring

When the earth is shaken, quaking
When the earth bears forth her burdens
And someone says "What is with her?"
At that time she will tell her news
As her lord revealed her
At that time people will straggle forth
   to be shown what they have done
Whoever does a mote's weight good will see it
Whoever does a mote's weight wrong will see it

Surah 109
Those Who Reject the Faith

In the Name of God the Compassionate the Caring

Say: You who reject the faith
I do not worship what you worship
and you do not worship what I worship
I am not a worshipper of what you worship
You are not a worshipper of what I worship
A reckoning for you and a reckoning for me

Surah 112
Sincerity / Unity

In the Name of God the Compassionate the Caring

Version 1
   Say he is God, one
   God forever
   Not begetting, unbegotten,
      and having as an equal none

Version 2
   Say he is God, one
   God the refuge

Not begetting, unbegotten,
 and having as an equal none

Version 3
 Say he is God, one
 God the rock
 Not begetting, unbegotten,
  and having as an equal none

Surah 2
The Cow

Section 22

177. It is not the sole virtue that you turn your faces to the east or the west but true virtue is theirs, who believe in Allâh, the Last Day, the angels, the Book, and in the Prophets, and who give away their wealth (and substance) out of love for Him, to the near of kin, the orphans, the needy, the wayfarer and to those who ask (in charity) and in ransoming the slaves; and who observe the Prayer, who go on presenting the *Zakât* (the purifying alms) and those who always fulfill their pledges and agreements when they have made one, and those who are patiently persevering in adversity and distress and (steadfast) in times of war. It is these who have proved truthful (in their promises and in their faith) and it is these who are strictly guarded against evil.

178. O you who believe! equitable retaliation has been ordained for you in (the matter of) the slain. (Everyone shall pay for his own crime), the freeman (murderer) for the freeman (murdered), and the slave (murderer) for the slave (murdered), and the female (murderer) for the female (murdered), but who has been granted any remission by his (aggrieved) brother (or family) then pursuing (of the matter) shall be done with equity and fairness, and the payment (of the blood money) to him (the heir) should be made in a handsome manner. This is an alleviation from your Lord and a mercy. But he who exceeds the limits after this (commandment), for him is a grievous punishment.

179. O people of pure and clear wisdom! your very life lies in (the law of) equitable retaliation, (you have been so commanded) so that you may enjoy security.

180. It has been prescribed for you at the time of death to any one of you, that if the (dying) person is leaving considerable wealth behind, to make a will to his parents and the near of kin to act with equity and fairness. This is an obligation incumbent on those who guard against evil.

181. He who alters it (the will) after he has heard it, (should know that) it is those that alter it who shall bear the burden of sin. Allâh indeed is All-Hearing, All-Knowing.

182. If anyone apprehends that the testator is partial or follows a sinful course there will be no blame on him provided he sets things right (and so brings about reconciliation) between them (the parties concerned under the will). Surely, Allâh is Great Protector, Ever Merciful.

Section 23

183. O you who believe! you are bound to observe fasting as those before you (followers of the Prophets) were bound, so that you may guard against evil.

184. (You are required to fast) for a prescribed number of days. But if anyone of you is sick or is on a journey he shall fast (to make up) the prescribed number in other days. And for those who are able to fast is an expiation (as thanksgiving) the feeding of a poor person (daily for the days of fasting). And he who volunteers (extra) good, (will find that) it is even better for him. And that you observe fasting is better for you, if you only know.

185. The (lunar) month of *Ramadzân* is that in which the Qur'ân (started to be) revealed as a guidance for the whole of mankind with its clear evidences (providing comprehensive) guidance and the Discrimination (between right and wrong). Therefore he who shall witness the month, should fast (for full month) during it, but he who is sick or is on a journey shall fast (to make up) the prescribed number in other days. Allâh wishes facility for you and does not wish hardship for you. (This facility is given to you) that you may complete the number (of required fasts) and you may exalt the greatness of Allâh for His having guided you, and that you may render thanks (to Him)....

187. (Though during Fasting you must abstain from all the urges of nature including the sexual urge) it is made lawful for you on the nights of the fasts to approach and lie with your wives (for sexual relationship). They are (a sort of) garment for you and you are (a sort of) garment for them. Allâh knows that you have been doing injustice to yourselves (by restricting conjugal relations with your wives even at night), so He turned to you with mercy and provided you relief; now enjoy their company (at night during *Ramadzân*) and seek what Allâh has ordained for you. Eat and drink till the white streak of the dawn becomes distinct to you from the black streak (of the darkness), then complete the fast till nightfall. And you shall not lie with them (your wives) while you perform *I'tikâf* (while you are secluding in the mosque for prayer and devotion to God). These are the limits (imposed) by Allâh so do not approach these (limits). Thus does Allâh explain His commandments for people that they may become secure against evil....

Section 24

190. And fight in the cause of Allâh those who fight and persecute you, but commit no aggression. Surely, Allâh does not love the aggressors.

191. And slay them (the aggressors against whom fighting is made incumbent) when and where you get the better of them, in disciplinary way, and turn them out whence they have turned you out. (Killing is bad but) lawlessness is even worse than carnage. But do not fight them in the precincts of *Masjid al-Harâm* (the Holy Mosque at Makkah) unless they fight you therein. Should they attack you (there) then slay them. This indeed is the recompense of such disbelievers.

192. But if they desist (from aggression) then, behold, Allâh is indeed Great Protector, Ever Merciful.

193. And fight them until persecution is no more and religion is (freely professed) for Allâh. But if they desist (from hostilities) then (remember) there is no punishment except against the unjust (who still persist in persecution). . . .

195. And spend in the cause of Allâh and do not cast yourselves into ruin with your own hands, and do good to others, and verily Allâh loves the doers of good to others.

196. Accomplish the _Hajj_* (the Greater Pilgrimage to Makkah) and the 'Umrah (the minor pilgrimage) for the sake of Allâh. But if you are kept back, then (offer) whatever sacrifice is easily available, and do not shave your heads (as is prescribed for the Pilgrims) till the offering reaches its destination (in time, or place). And whosoever of you is sick and has an ailment of his head (necessitating shaving before time) then he should make an expiation either by fasting or alms-giving or by making a sacrifice. When you are in peaceful conditions then he, who would avail himself of the 'Umrah (a visit to the Ka'bah or a minor _Hajj_) together with the _Hajj_ (the Greater Pilgrimage and thus performs _Tammattu'_) should make whatever offering is easily available; and whosoever finds none (for an offering) should fast for three days during (the days of) the pilgrimage and (for) seven (days) when he returns (home)—these are ten complete (days of fasting in all). This is for him whose family does not reside near the _Masjid al-Harâm_ (the Holy Mosque at Makkah). Take Allâh as a shield, and know that Allâh is Severe in retribution (if you neglect your duties).

Section 25

197. The months of performing the _Hajj_ are well Known; so whoever undertakes to perform the _Hajj_ in them (should remember that) there is (to be) no obscenity, nor abusing, nor any wrangling during the (time of) _Hajj_. And whatever good you do Allâh knows it. And take provisions for yourselves. Surely, the good of taking provision is

*HAH juh

guarding (yourselves) against the evil (of committing sin and begging). Take Me alone as (your) shield, O people of pure and clear wisdom!

198. There is no blame on you that you seek munificence from your Lord (by trading during the time of *Hajj*). When you pour forth (in large numbers) from 'Arafât then glorify Allâh (with still more praises) near *Mash'aral-Harâm* (Holy Mosque in *Muzdalifah*), and remember Him (with gratitude) as He has guided you, though formerly you were certainly amongst the astray. . . .

Surah 4
Women

Section 1

1. O you people! take as a shield your Lord Who created you from a single being. The same stock from which He created the man He created his spouse, and through them both He caused to spread a large number of men and women. O people! regard Allâh with reverence in Whose name you appeal to one another, and (be regardful to) the ties of relationship (particularly from the female side). Verily, Allâh ever keeps watch over you.

2. And give the orphans their property and substitute not (your) worthless things for (their) good ones, nor consume their property mingling it along with your own property, for this indeed is a great sin.

3. And if (you wish to marry them and) you fear that you will not be able to do justice to the orphan girls then (marry them not, rather) marry of women (other than these) as may be agreeable to you, (you may marry) two or three or four (provided you do justice to them), but if you fear that you will not be able to deal (with all of them) equitably then (confine yourselves only to) one, or (you may marry) that whom your right hands possess (your female captives of war). That is the best way to avoid doing injustice.

4. And give the women their dowers unasked, willingly and as agreed gift. But if they be pleased to remit you a portion thereof, of their own free will, then take it with grace and pleasure.

Section 2

11. Allâh prescribes (the following) law (of inheritance) for your children. For male is the equal of the portion of two females; but if they be all females (two or) more than two, for them is two thirds of what he (the deceased) has left; and if there be only one, for her is the half and for his parents, for each one of the two is a sixth of what he has left, if he (the deceased) has a child; but if he has no child and his parents only be

his heirs, then for the mother is one third (and the rest two thirds is for the father); but if there be (in addition to his parents) his brothers (and sisters) then there is one sixth for the mother after (the payment of) any bequest he may have bequeathed or (still more important) of any debt (bequests made by the testator and his debts shall however be satisfied first). Your fathers and your children, you do not know which of them deserve better to benefit from you. (This) fixing (of portions) is from Allâh. Surely, Allâh is All-Knowing, All-Wise.

12. And for you is half of that which your wives leave behind, if they have no child; but if they have a child, then for you is one fourth of what they leave behind, after (the payment of) any bequest they may have bequeathed or (still more important) of any (of their) debt. And for them (your wives) is one fourth of what you leave behind if you have no child; but if you leave a child, then, for them is an eighth of what you leave after (the payment of) any bequest you have bequeathed or (still more important) of any debt. And if there be a man or a woman whose heritage is to be divided and he (or she—the deceased) has no child and he (or she) has (left behind) a brother or a sister then for each one of the twain is a sixth; but if they be more than one then they are (equal) sharers in one third after the payment of any bequest bequeathed or (still more important) of any debt (provided such bequest made by the testator and the debt) shall be without (any intent of) being harmful (to the interests of the heirs). This is an injunction from Allâh, and Allâh is All-Knowing, Most Forbearing.

13. These are the limits (of the law imposed) by Allâh, and who obeys Allâh and His Messenger He will admit them into Gardens served with running streams; therein they shall abide for ever; and that is a great achievement.

14. But whoso disobeys Allâh and His Messenger and transgresses the limits imposed by Him He will make him enter Fire where he shall abide long, and for him is a humiliating punishment.

15. As to those of your women who commit sexual perversity, call in four of you to witness against them, and if they bear witness then confine them to their houses, until death overtakes them or Allâh makes for them a way out.

16. And if two of your males commit the same (act of indecency), then punish them both, so if they repent and amend (keeping their conduct good) then turn aside from them, verily Allâh is Oft-Returning (with compassion), Ever Merciful.

RICHARD C. FOLTZ

The Islamization of the Silk Road, 1999

In the following selection Foltz, a modern historian of religion, explores the early history of Islam and its spread east of the Mediterranean. Placing the rise of Islam solidly within the Arab traditions of trading and raiding, Foltz distinguishes between the initial development of unified Arab rule and the subsequent spread of Islamic religious culture. He argues that the "convert or die" idea that pervades the history of Islam is largely mythic and that early Muslim rulers actually discouraged conversion. According to Foltz, what role did economics play in early Muslim expansion? How did Islam spread so widely and so quickly, and what was the nature of this early growth? How did non-Arabs who converted to Islam change it?

THINKING HISTORICALLY

What economic and political forces does Foltz emphasize? What continuities does Foltz suggest? What roles did individuals play in the conversion process? What similarities were there between the spread of Buddhism, Christianity, and Islam?

No religious tradition in world history favored trade as much as did Islam. The Prophet Muhammad himself was a businessman by profession. While in his twenties he became employed by a wealthy merchant woman of Mecca, Khadija, and made his reputation by successfully carrying out a trade mission to Syria; Khadija married him soon after.

Sometime around 610 of the common era, Muhammad, who liked to spend time alone meditating in the mountains outside Mecca, began hearing voices during the course of these retreats. At first he began to doubt his own sanity, but Khadija persuaded him that these voices might be divine in nature and should be listened to. Gradually Muhammad came to believe he was receiving revelations from God, calling upon him to "rise and warn" his fellow Meccans that the time had come to mend their ways.

Source: Richard C. Foltz, *Religions of the Silk Road: Overland Trade and Cultural Exchange from Antiquity to the Fifteenth Century* (New York: St. Martin's Press, 1999), 89–93, 95–97.

Mecca was a desert town with little to subsist on apart from its trade. Successful merchants must have been its wealthiest inhabitants. Many of the revelations Muhammad received dealt with social injustice, which was clearly a problem in Mecca at that time. His message found a growing audience of sympathetic ears, while it increasingly alienated the social classes who were the target of his criticism. Before long certain powerful residents of Mecca were making life difficult for Muhammad and his followers.

In 622 the citizens of Yathrib, a town some two hundred twenty miles to the north of Mecca, were involved in factional disputes they could not resolve. Hearing of Muhammad's reputation for fairness and piety, they invited him to come and arbitrate. He accepted. Sending most of his followers ahead of him, the Prophet of Islam put his affairs in order and finally left his hometown, an event known to Muslims as the *hijra*, or migration, which marks the beginning of the Islamic calendar.

Once in Yathrib, the Muslims were not only no longer persecuted, they enjoyed special status. From their new power base they launched raids (Ar. *Razzia*) on Meccan-bound caravans, at the same time enriching their own treasury while inflicting damage on their former persecutors. After several battles with the Meccans, the Muslims were able to negotiate the right to return to Mecca for the traditional Arabian pilgrimage to the sacred *ka' ba* stone; by 628 Mecca was under Muslim control.

Raiding caravans was an established part of the economic life of Arabia. The only rule was that one couldn't raid clan members or groups with whom one had made a nonaggression pact. With the successes of the Muslims growing from year to year, eventually all the tribes of the Arabian peninsula sent emissaries to Muhammad in order to seek such pacts. Their professions of loyalty were described by later Muslim writers as "submission," which in Arabic is *islam*. Small wonder that these sources, and the non-Muslim histories based on them, interpret this as meaning all the Arabian tribes had accepted the new religion.

Understanding this term "submission" in its more restricted literal sense, however, more easily explains what happened upon the Prophet's death in 632: Most of the Arabian tribes rebelled. Later Muslim sources refer to these as rebellions of "apostasy." A simpler interpretation would be that the rebel parties simply saw their nonaggression pacts as having been rendered null and void by the Prophet's passing.

The Muslims immediately chose a successor, or caliph (from Middle Pers. *Khalifa*), Abu Bakr, under whose leadership the various Arab tribes were forced to resubmit. Since the Arabian economy required the component of raiding, and since according to the nonaggression pacts no one in Arabia could legitimately be raided, the Muslims were forced to launch forays beyond the Arabian peninsula into Byzantine and Persian territory.

Their success in defeating the armies of both empires probably surprised many of the Muslims as much as it did their imperial enemies.

It is important to recognize the economic aspect of Muslim expansion, driven by the ancient Arabian tradition of raiding. While in hindsight both Muslims and non-Muslims have read into this early expansion a large element of religious zeal, the Arab armies of the time were simply doing what they were naturaly acculturated to do, what the economic conditions of their homeland had always constrained them to do. What had changed was that, for the first time, all the Arab groups of the peninsula had excluded for themselves the possibility of raiding other Arab groups. They were forced, therefore, to raid elsewhere. Their new religious self-concept may indeed have inspired them by giving divine meaning to their increasing successes, but other factors were at work as well.

Iranians, in the form of Medes, Achemenians, Parthians, and Sasanians, had been vying with Athenian, Seleucid, and Roman Greeks for hegemony in western Asia for over a millennium. By the seventh century both the Sasanian Persian and Byzantine Greek empires were exhausted and decadent. Neither treated their subject peoples in Mesopotamia, Syria, or Egypt with anything that could be called benevolence. In many locations townspeople threw open the gates to the Arabs and welcomed them as liberators. The Muslims were, in fact, no more foreign in most of the lands they conquered than had been the previous rulers, and at first they were less exploitative.

By the 660s, however, the ruling Arab family, the Umayyads, had set themselves up in Damascus in very much the mold of the Byzantine governors they had dislodged. Throughout the subsequent decades non-Muslims came to chafe under the new regime. Many Arab Muslims, furthermore, resented the imperial manner and "un-Islamic" lifestyles of the Umayyads, many of whom had taken to drinking and debauchery in the best Roman tradition.

But the group which was to bring about the Umayyads' downfall and, in doing so, forever change the very nature of Islam as a cultural tradition was the non-Arabs who chose to adopt the Islamic religion.

Initially and throughout the Umayyad period, the Arabs had seen Islam as a religion belonging to them; their subjects, likewise, referred to Islam as "the Arab religion" (al-din al-'arab). The Quran enjoined Muslims to spread Muslim *rule* throughout the world but laid down no requirement to spread the faith itself. The original impulse of holy war (jihad) was that no Muslim should be constrained to live under the rule of infidels. Once a given locality agreed to submit to Muslim authority and pay the poll tax (jizya) levied on protected communities (dhimmis, usually "peoples of the Book," i.e., Christians and Jews), there was no further need for coercion on either side.

In fact, Arab Muslims had strong reasons *not* to want non-Arabs to join the faith, since conversion directly affected both their sources of income and the spread of its distribution among Muslims. Conversely, there were numerous reasons why non-Muslims might wish to join the ruling group, which could most obviously be symbolized by adopting their faith. Despite some apparent resistance from the Arab elite, by the early eighth century non-Arab converts were probably beginning to out-number Arab Muslims.

Islam had attempted to eliminate class and racial distinctions, but even during the Prophet's lifetime this goal was never met. Early con-verts and their descendants often felt entitled to greater status and privi-lege than later converts, and members of aristocratic families never forgot who came from humble ones. Tribal and clan loyalties affected government appointments and led to rivalries.

Often these rivalries developed power bases in garrison towns where particular factions were dominant. Local governors, therefore, usually had more or less personal armies at their ready disposal. In areas where the Arabs were quartered among non-Arab majority populations, there was increasing pressure from converts to be treated on equal footing with Arab Muslims.

The problem was that a non-Arab, even after converting to Islam, had no tribal affiliation which could provide him an identity within Arab society. A solution to this was devised whereby an Arab Muslim could take a non-Arab convert under his wing as a "client" (*mawla*), making the convert a sort of honorary tribal member. Of course, such clients were at the mercy of the individual who sponsored them.

Over time this inequality between Arab and non-Arab Muslims became a major pretext for various parties disaffected with Umayyad rule. Not surprisingly it was in eastern Iran, at the fringes of Umayyad power, that a rebel movement capable of overthrowing the central gov-ernment and completely reshaping Muslim society took place.

In addition to complaints about the un-Islamic character of the Umayyad elite and the inequalities between Arab and non-Arab Mus-lims, the anti-Umayyad movement could draw on the issue of the very legitimacy of Umayyad rule. The first Umayyad caliph, Mu'awiya, had assumed power by refusing to recognize the selection of the Prophet's nephew and son-in-law, Ali, as fourth caliph. A significant minority of Muslims felt that leadership should be sought in charismatic authority passed down through the Prophet's line. For the "partisans of Ali" (*shi' at Ali*), the Umayyads (and indeed the first three caliphs) had been usurp-ers from the outset.

All of these antigovernment impulses came together in the so-called Abbasid revolution of 749 to 751, in which a Khurasan-based Muslim army rallied behind an Iranian general, Abu Muslim, in the name of an Arab descendant of the Prophet's uncle Abbas. The rebels succeeded in wresting power from the Umayyads, moved the capital to Mesopotamia, and began setting up a new Islamic administration on the Sasanian imperial model. . . .

As with any case of mass cultural conversion, the Islamization of Central Asia was a complex process which occurred on more than one level. The first, and most visible, level was the spread of political power. It is worth noting that the spread of a particular religion's rule is not identical with the spread of faith, although historians have often written as if it were.

Muslim rule over the western half of the Silk Road came fairly early and was established, albeit through a period of false starts and occasional reversals, by the mid-eighth century. Muslims thereafter controlled much of trans-Asian trade, which became the second major factor in the Islamization of Central Asian culture. Gradually a third factor, the influence of charismatic Muslim preachers, entered into the process.

The reality of Muslim rule could no longer be reasonably ignored once the numerous eighth-century attempts to rally behind local, non-Islamic religious figures had all failed. Politics was therefore an initial influence encouraging Central Asians to abandon their native cultural traditions and join the growing world culture of Islamic civilization. It appears, however, that the only local rulers, especially those who had raised arms against the Muslims, were ever subjected to the convert-or-die alternative that has so long been the stereotype characterizing the spread of Islam. Other people, at least at first, would have embraced the faith of their new rulers for other reasons, in certain cases no doubt spiritual ones.

One of the most commonly cited incentives to religio-cultural conversion is the pursuit of patronage. Anyone directly dependent on the government for his livelihood might sense advantages in joining the cultural group of his patrons and accepting the norms and values of that ruling group. To a large extent, converts to Islam do appear to have held onto their preconquest positions, and being a Muslim increased one's chances of attaining a new or better one.

A second and probably greater influence affecting Islamization was the Muslim domination of commercial activity. A businessman could feel that becoming a Muslim would facilitate contacts and cooperation with other Muslim businessmen both at home and abroad; he would also benefit from favorable conditions extended by Muslim officials and from the Islamic laws governing commerce.

The presence of Muslim rule and the increasing Muslim dominance of trade meant that Islamization came first in the urban areas along the Silk Road and only in later centuries spread to the countryside. The gradual Islamization of the nomadic Turkic peoples of Central and Inner Asia was at first directly tied to their increasing participation in the oasis-based Silk Road trade in the tenth century, accelerated by the political activities of three Turkic Muslim dynasties—the Qarakhanids, the Ghaznavids, and the Seljuks—and supplemented by the proselytizing efforts of Muslim missionaries.

The third major factor accounting for the Islamization of the Silk Road, which follows those of politics and economics, is assimilation. Whatever the reasons for one's converting to Islam, Islamization occurs most profoundly (and irrevocably) among the succeeding generation, since the convert's children in principle will be raised within the father's new community, not his original one. Furthermore, although a Muslim man may marry a non-Muslim woman, Islamic law requires that the children of a mixed marriage be raised as Muslims. However, . . . it may be safe to assume that aspects of pre-Islamic local religion survived through transmission by non-Muslim wives of Muslims.

7

Peace Terms with Jerusalem, 636

The early expansion of Islam was far more rapid and more forceful than the expansion of Christianity and Buddhism. By 636, Arab armies had conquered many of the lands previously held by the Byzantine and Persian empires. Merchants and holy men would spread the faith even farther afield at a later stage. But by 750 an Arab-dominated Muslim government controlled North Africa, the Arabian peninsula, and significant portions of Eurasia from the Strait of Gibraltar to the western borders of India and China. (See Map 7.2 on p. 246.)

How much of this early expansion was military conquest and how much religious conversion? To help us answer this question, we look at an early peace treaty after the conquest of Jerusalem from the Byzantine Empire (known then as the Roman Empire, but ruled from Constantinople).

As the Arabian force for Judeo-Christian monotheism, Muslims had a strong sentimental attachment to Jerusalem. In the first years of the faith, Muhammad and his followers prayed facing Jerusalem, Al Quds (the Holy City, as it is still called in Arabic). In 624, after only modest Jewish conversions, Mecca was substituted as the *qibla* or direction to face for prayer. At the time of Muhammad's death (632), his followers

Source: "Peace Terms with Jerusalem (636)," in *Islam from the Prophet Muhammad to the Conquest of Constantinople*, ed. and trans. Bernard Lewis, vol. I, *Politics and War* (New York: Harper & Row, 1974), 235–36. Originally published in Al Tabari, *Tarik al-Rusulcwa'l muluk*, vol. I (Leiden: Brill), 2405–6.

controlled most of Arabia. His successor (or *caliph*), Abu Bakr
(r. 632–634), regained control of the tribes that tried to withdraw
from the alliance after the Prophet's death and turned to the conquest
of Iraq and Syria. The second caliph, Umar (r. 634–644), negotiated
the surrender of the Byzantine forces that controlled Jerusalem after
the defeat of Byzantine armies in 636. This document, written by the
caliph and directed to the Christian community of Jerusalem, set the
terms for continued Christian presence in the city. Many of these
terms were continuations of past practice. One of the terms included
jizya, which was a tax or tribute that non-Muslims paid Muslim governments for protection. This document also reinstates the expulsion
of Jews from Jerusalem, a policy first instated under Roman administration and later continued under the Byzantine Christian administration, though Umar later allowed Jews to reside in the city.

Other Muslim sources tell us that the inhabitants of Jerusalem
appealed to Umar to take control of Jerusalem. What evidence
do you see in these terms that would make that story plausible?
What would both sides, Muslim and Christian, seem to gain
by these terms?

THINKING HISTORICALLY

If this peace treaty were observed as written, what would have changed
in Jerusalem? What would have remained the same? Are these changes
mainly religious or political? To what extent, if any, does Muslim
control of Jerusalem suggest Jewish or Christian conversions to Islam?

In the name of God the Merciful and the Compassionate.

This is the safe-conduct accorded by the servant of God Umar, the
Commander of the Faithful, to the people of Aelia [Jerusalem].[1]

He accords them safe-conduct for their persons, their property, their
churches, their crosses, their sound and their sick, and the rest of their
worship.

Their churches shall neither be used as dwellings nor destroyed.
They shall not suffer any impairment, nor shall their dependencies, their
crosses, nor any of their property.

---

[1] Aelia Capitolina was the name given to Jerusalem by Roman emperor Hadrian after he
suppressed the second Jewish revolt in 132–135 (the first revolt was 66–70). He also expelled
Jews from the city and banned them from living there. The Christian Byzantines continued this
policy. Thus, this was a concession to Christians. Umar later let the Jews return to Jerusalem.
In the seventh century one could be both a Jew and a Muslim. [Ed.]

No constraint shall be exercised against them in religion nor shall any harm be done to any among them.

No Jew shall live with them in Aelia.

The people of Aelia must pay the *jizya*[2] in the same way as the people of other cities.

They must expel the Romans[3] and the brigands from the city. Those who leave shall have safe-conduct for their persons and property until they reach safety. Those who stay shall have safe-conduct and must pay the *jizya* like the people of Aelia.

Those of the people of Aelia who wish to remove their persons and effects and depart with the Romans and abandon their churches and their crosses shall have safe-conduct for their persons, their churches, and their crosses, until they reach safety.

The country people who were already in the city before the killing of so-and-so may, as they wish, remain and pay the *jizya* the same way as the people of Aelia or leave with the Romans or return to their families. Nothing shall be taken from them until they have gathered their harvest.

This document is placed under the surety of God and the protection [*dhimma*] of the Prophet, the Caliphs and the believers, on condition that the inhabitants of Aelia pay the *jizya* that is due from them.

Witnessed by Khālid ibn al-Wald, 'Amr ibn al-Āṣ, 'Abd al-Raḥmān ibn 'Awf, Muāwiya ibn Abī Sufyān, the last of whom wrote this document in the year 15 [636].

[2] A tax on non-Muslims in return for exemption from the *zakat* tax on Muslims and military service. [Ed.]

[3] Byzantine soldiers and officials. [Ed.]

8

Epic of Sundiata, Thirteenth Century

This is a brief selection from one of the great epics of West Africa. In a culture without a system of written notation, stories like this were told by griots — specialists with prodigious memories. Most of these griots worked in the courts of kings, learning, like their fathers before

Source: *Sunjata: A West African Epic of the Mande Peoples*, trans. David C. Conrad and narrated by Djanka Tassey Condé (Indianapolis, IN: Hackett, 2004), 17–19 (lines 420–93).

them, to tell the story of their patron's family. The *Epic of Sundiata* is
the account of one of the great families of the Mande people. The
Epic centers on Sundiata Keita (c. 1217–1255), who founded the Mali
Empire. Our selection is drawn from the story of Maghan Konfara,
Sundiata's father, and tells of his conversion to Islam. It begins with
the declaration of a visitor, Manjan Bereté, after Maghan Konfara
has asked to marry his sister. What does this story add to your
understanding of religious conversions and the spread of salvation
religions?

THINKING HISTORICALLY

A single conversion would seem to bring far less change than the conquest of a city. Yet, as we have seen, the conversion of a king might
have consequences as profound as the conquest of a kingdom. What
sort of changes would you expect to occur after this conversion? We
are also used to thinking of religious conversion as a momentous
change for the individual who experiences it, not the casual affair
depicted here. What, if anything, does this story tell you about the
history of internal or psychological change?

[The visitor declares:]

"We are Bereté.
It was our ancestor who planted a date farm for the Prophet
          at Mecca
That was the beginning of our family identity.
When the date farm was planted for the Prophet,
He blessed our ancestor.
He said everyone should leave us alone:
Bè anu to yè, and that is why they call us Bereté.
No man of Manden will tell you
That we originated the Bereté family identity.
It was the Prophet who said we should be set apart,
That nobody's foolishness should trouble us.
Bè anu to yè, everyone should leave us alone.
Thus we became the Bereté.
From that time up to today,
We have not done anything other than the Prophet's business.
This place[1] has already become impious

---

[1] Maghan Konfara's place, Konfara, Farakoro, or more generally the land of the Mande
(modern southwest Mali). [Ed.]

Because of your lack of attention to Islam.
So how can I give you my little sister?
I did not come from Farisi[2] for that purpose,
So I will not give you my little sister."
"Aaah," said Simbon,[3] "Give her to me.
If you want wealth, I will give you wealth."
(You heard it?)
"If you not give her to me,
I will take her for myself,
Because you are not in your home, you are in my home."
When Manjan Bereté was told this, he said,
"If you take my sister for yourself, I will go back to Farisi.
I will go and get Suraka[4] warriors to come and destroy Manden
If you take my little sister by force."
Simbon said, "You just do that.
If you go back to Farisi to get warriors,
You might come and destroy Manden.
But by then your sister will be pregnant,
I will have a child by then.
Even if I die, it will still be my child."
(You heard it?)
He said, "I have taken her."
He took her.
"If you call for wealth, I will give you wealth.
If you call for the sword, I will agree to that.
I have the power, you have no power, you are in my place."

Manjan Bereté packed up his books and went back to Farisi.
He went and told his fathers and brothers,
"The Mande *mansa*[5] that I went to visit,
He has used his chiefly power to take my little sister from me."
His fathers and brothers said, "Ah, Manjan Bereté,
Your youth has betrayed you.
You carry the sacred book.
Go back and tell the Mande people,
Tell Simbon,
That if he is in love with your younger sister,
You will give him both her and the book.
Tell him 'If you convert, and become another like me,

---

[2] Fars, Persia. [Ed.]
[3] Speaks for Maghan Konfara. [Ed.]
[4] Arab, Moor, or North African warriors. [Ed.]
[5] King. [Ed.]

So that we can proselytize together,
I will give you my younger sister,
But if you refuse to convert, I will go for my warriors.'
If he does not convert, come back and we will give you warriors.
If he agrees to convert, that is what you went for."

Manjan Bereté returned to Farakoro.
After he explained to Simbon,
Maghan Konfara said, "What your father said,
That your youth betrayed you, is true.
If you had done what he said in the first place,
You would not have returned to Farisi.
All I want is a child, no matter what the cost.
I agree to what you propose.
Since you have requested that I convert,
I agree."
They shaved his head, and together they read the Koran.
After reading the Koran,
Manjan Bereté gave his little sister to Maghan Konfara.

■ REFLECTIONS

The expansion of the great universal religions continued well beyond
1000. In fact, it continues today. We live in a world of about two
hundred nation-states, but two-thirds of the world's people follow only
three religions: Christianity, Islam, and Buddhism. We return to the
question that opened this chapter: What enabled these particular
religions to convert so many?

We noted here, and in the previous chapter, that many of the
religions of this period were book or text based. The Bible and Quran
were said by many to be given by God. The stories of the Buddha also
took on an aura of authority that must have enhanced their appeal.
Most people could not read or write, of course, but the great religions
created writing-based bureaucracies, educators, and thinkers who
ensured the dissemination of the sacred scripture, eternal truths, and
revered tales. The stories of the life of Jesus were carved into the walls
of the Christian churches, etched into the colored glass of the
windows, and told and reenacted in the religious rite of the Eucharist,
which celebrated the last supper of Jesus. Statues of the Buddha of
every size and description were carved and placed for worship in
temples throughout Asia. Five times a day, the Muslim call to prayer
reverberated from the minarets that spiked the skyline from Morocco

to Malacca, and from Tashkent to Timbuktu. One did not have to be able to read in order to pray.

The learned devised, collected, or correlated these texts, often insisting they were the words of the founder, spoken by God or engraved in stone. Then they and their successors explained and interpreted them, often turning intractable prose into metaphor, amending failed prophecies, and inventing myths to suit current politics.

Our readings suggest that the decision to adopt a particular religion was often more political than theological. Kings and emperors made the decision, often with the same degree of calculation whether they were defending state cults, like Trajan (document 4.7); embracing radical challenges, like Constantine; or simply negotiating a marriage, like Sundiata's father. Universal religions and imperial systems fit well together because it was easier for the emir or emperor to work with a unified set of religious values and only universal religions allowed new converts. Example and influence probably played a greater role than conquest. The spread of Islam was the most obvious conquest in this period (as Christianity was later), but the image of Muslims forcing others to convert or die was largely a projection of later Christian crusaders. Recent historical research reveals a rapid military conquest by traditional Arab raiding armies followed later by a gradual process of conversion. Many conquered people, like the Jews of Jerusalem, viewed the Arab armies as liberators. In general, Arab rule was remote and indirect. Normally, the Arabs left earlier structures in control, sometimes making the collection of tribute more efficient, even more lenient. Arab Muslim conquerors were not highly motivated in winning converts because mass conversions would limit the *jizya*, the head tax that only non-Muslims paid. A study by the historian Richard Bulliet shows that Iranians adopted Muslim names (a sign of conversion) gradually a hundred years after the conquest of 648 and that the number of Iranian Muslims increased over the next few hundred years at rates that can be charted on a standard bell curve, the same way any new style or technology rises and then levels off close to saturation.

Distinguishing change and continuity is a historical skill useful in understanding any historical document, period, process, or place. It helps us pose questions, not give simplistic answers like "religion x was continuous, but religion y changed." Everything changes to some degree. It is relative change or constancy that we are after. How fast, how sudden, what specifically changed, and what continued pretty much as before? And what can we learn from asking these questions?

If Judaism was a universal religion that converted large populations from North Africa to Central Asia in the years before and after the fall of Rome, then its continuity, like that of the other universal religions, is in belief and tradition, not ethnicity or place. If the continuity of Islam stretches back to a more widespread Judaism than previously thought, then it makes sense to think of a Judeo-Christian-Islamic tradition, to recognize the apocalyptic theme that pulses through it, and to see the continuity between Islam and Nestorian Christianity, as well as the seal of a new prophecy. On the other hand, a post-Nestorian Christianity in Tang China that neither mentions Jesus nor explains the symbolism of the cross, but instead speaks in the metaphors of the Dao, may tell us more about the continuity of Chinese cultural traditions than of Christianity. Lessons like these are not only interesting in their own right. They might have also been useful for later generations of empire builders, colonial settlers, missionaries, and diplomats.

8

Migrations, Trade, and Travel

The Movement of People, Goods, and Ideas in Eurasia, Africa, and the Pacific, 3000 B.C.E.—1350 C.E.

■ HISTORICAL CONTEXT

We tend to think of immigration issues as very current, and indeed they are. But human migration is an old story. In fact, the movement of peoples is the oldest story of human history, going back to the migrations of early humans out of Africa two million to a hundred thousand years ago.

By 3000 B.C.E. all of the continents except Antarctica had been occupied by humans for at least 10,000 years, agriculture had spread in parts of all of those areas, and many were dotted by cities and organized into states. However, over the course of the next thousand years, three major migrations began to reshape the core of Eurasia, most of sub-Saharan Africa, and much of Southeast Asia and the Pacific. These were the formative population movements of the last five thousand years: the Indo-European impact on Eurasia, the Bantu expansion of central and southern Africa, and the Austronesian migration to Southeast Asia and later Polynesian settlement of the Pacific.

After considering these long-term migrations, two of which—the Bantu and Polynesian—continued into the Middle Ages, we will refocus on the Medieval era. Here we will look at a process of migration of people, plants, technologies, and ideas from Southeast Asia northward through Eurasia, a process our author and historian, Lynda Shaffer, calls "Southernization." This was a process not only of migrations but also the establishment of trading networks and religious missions that often developed hand in hand.

Finally we will read some of the travel accounts of two of the great travelers of the Medieval era. The first, from about 400 C.E., is the Chinese monk Faxian who traveled to India to obtain writings and relics of the Buddha. The other, from about 1350, is the great Muslim traveler Ibn Battuta who traveled from Morocco to China. Together they provide close-ups of travel and trade at the beginning and end of the Middle Ages. We will also read one of the great tools consulted by traders.

■ THINKING HISTORICALLY

Sifting Factors

By "sifting factors," I mean distinguishing political, economic, social, and cultural features of sources, facts, events, or subjects. These four aspects of life, paralleling four major specialties of historians, don't cover everything under the Sun. But if we use them broadly enough, we have a useful model for bringing order to the past. In the context of this chapter, the political will also include diplomatic (a field of history that is sometimes independent); economic will include the study of trade, business, money, poverty, and similar subjects; and social will include demography or demographic history, the study of peoples — as in migrations. Other subjects of social history are family, gender, education, marriage, social class, and status. Under culture, we will include religion, ideas, styles, music, art, philosophy, science, literature, and popular culture.

From the preceding, you can see that these are not hard-and-fast categories. Some might say religious history, for example, should be separate from cultural history because religion includes social behavior as much as ideas. Others might like a separate category for technology; otherwise, do we place it under science and, therefore, culture? And what about work, war, or marriage? How would you categorize these conditions? The problem is that human behavior is too complex to put everything in four neat boxes. But like historians, we have to organize the chaos of information in order to make any sense of it. Therefore, we will be systematic in categorizing the material in this chapter by political, economic, social, and cultural factors. The best way to proceed might be to mark a page with four columns labeled P, E, S, and C, and then list items mentioned in the readings in one, or more if appropriate, of these columns.

1

PATRICK MANNING

Austronesian, Indo-European, and Bantu Migrations, 2005

In this selection, a modern world historian who is a specialist in African and migration history, sketches out the three great long migrations between 3000 B.C.E. and the first millennium C.E. The Austronesians of Southeast Asia and Oceania were themselves descended from people who migrated from Yunan in southwest China to Taiwan. From there the Austronesians brought their culture to Southeast Asia and the islands of New Guinea and the Bismarck Archipelago of the southwestern Pacific. There assimilation eventually produced the people we call Polynesians, who settled the islands of the Pacific in the first millennium C.E. The Indo-Europeans, or Aryans, traveled with their horses and chariots from the grasslands north of the Black Sea and Caspian Sea in what is today southern Russia eastward through Europe to the Atlantic and southwestward to India over the period from 3000 B.C.E. to 1500 B.C.E. The Bantu people migrated south and east from Cameroon in West Africa, assimilating with forest dwellers in the south and East Africans before settling much of southern Africa.

What are the different ways in which these migrations occurred? In what ways were they similar? How might these migrations be considered early steps of globalization?

THINKING HISTORICALLY

Historians normally consider migration to be part of the study of demography, the study of human populations — a part of social history. In these three cases, however, much of the evidence for the movement of people comes from the study of language. Such terms as *Austronesian, Polynesian, Indo-European*, and *Bantu* are names for related languages. Thus, the evidence for the movement or changes in language usage is dependent on the work of philologists who study literary sources and linguists who study language. In terms of our distinction among political, social, economic, and cultural history, which factor(s) would be most appropriate in studying this aspect of the historical record?

Notice how Manning's migration history also contains evidence of foods and other subjects. What are these subjects? Under which of the four categories would you classify them?

Source: Patrick Manning, *Migrations in World History* (New York: Routledge, 2005), 80–84.

The human habit of migration, by small and large groups, made itself felt in this era [after 3000 B.C.E.] as in previous times. The difference is that after 3000 BCE migrations are easier to document in detail because of the availability of written records. Still, some of the most significant migratory movements of this era are documented by linguistic and archaeological evidence rather than through written records. In this section I will describe migrations that linked rural areas to each other, and which in so doing led to significant change in world population distribution, and to opening of new linkages among populations.

Migrations in Southeast Asia, in this period as in earlier times, set trends affecting much of the eastern hemisphere. Sino-Tibetan-speakers, with an ancestral homeland in the deep valleys to the east of the Himalayas, had periodically sent migrants out in various directions. . . . In the period leading up to 3000 BCE, the Tibetan plateau yielded to new technology, including domestication of the yak (a high-altitude relative of cattle), and the Tibetan population and language took shape. In the same period, Burmese-speakers moved south along the Salween and Irrawaddy valleys and occupied lands up to the shores of the Indian Ocean.

Meanwhile the neighboring Austric family of languages, with an ancestral homeland only slightly further lower in the same valleys, also spread from Yunnan in various directions, especially to the south and the east. The Austric languages, spoken in an area overlapping Sino-Tibetan languages, were nonetheless distinct. Most speakers of these languages remained on the Southeast Asian mainland, where today they predominate in the nations of Vietnam, Thailand, Laos, and Cambodia. The northern range of the Austric homeland, over time, came to be shared with southward-moving groups of Chinese-speakers.

Best documented, however, are the migrations of those among the speakers of Austric languages who left the mainland and populated the islands of Southeast Asia and the Pacific. [See Map 8.1.] The ancestors of Austronesian-speakers had developed a homeland downriver from Yunnan, with advanced rice production, but also with boats. These canoes with outriggers for stability may have been developed in the inland rivers, but when fitted with sails they proved to have special benefits for oceanic travel. After crossing the strait of over 100 kilometers to Taiwan, the developing Austronesian populations were then able to sail with shorter crossings north along the chain of islands leading to Okinawa and toward Japan, and south to the Philippines. This migration began in about 3000 BCE, or perhaps somewhat before that time. Setting up farms of rice, yams, chickens, and pigs as well as harvesting the sea, Austronesian-speakers settled throughout the Indonesian archipelago and even moved northwest to the Malayan mainland.

Some of the Austronesians headed further west, and their languages survive in Madagascar—where languages are most closely related to

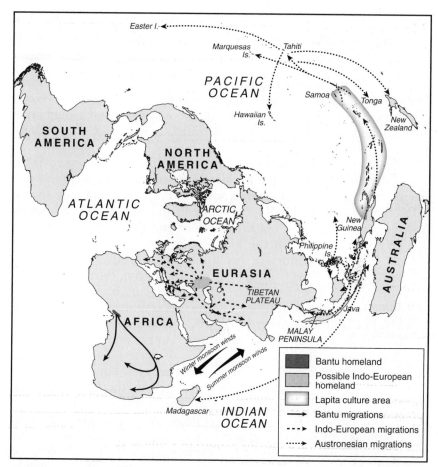

Map 8.1 Bantu, Indo-European, and Austronesian Migrations.

languages of Borneo. These mariners appear to have made their travels at the beginning of the Common Era or perhaps even earlier. They thus appear to have been sailing the Indian Ocean at the same time as Greek, Roman, Indian, and Persian ships were sailing the same waters. This is also the era that Lynda Shaffer has called "Southernization," in which Indonesian and Indian mariners knit together the whole Indian Ocean.

Austronesian-speakers spreading into Taiwan, the Philippines, and the Indonesian archipelago encountered local populations who, presumably, spoke Indo-Pacific languages and lived by fishing, hunting, and gathering. (Language-distribution studies indicate that the Indo-Pacific languages once covered a huge area, including most of Indonesia and areas of the eastern Indian Ocean, as well as islands surrounding New Guinea, and Tasmania as well.) The Austronesian-speakers, with their economy relying on rice and yams, became more populous and absorbed the Indo-Pacific-speakers until they got to Papua New Guinea and the Bismarck Archipelago, where Indo-Pacific-speakers had long since developed agriculture relying on taro, bananas, sugar cane, and other crops. The Papuans were too numerous to be absorbed by the visitors. The incoming Austronesian-speakers, however, were able to establish a firm presence in the coastal areas of New Guinea and neighboring islands. The stage was set for intermarriage, an exchange of traditions, and development of a new tradition.

Out of this social crucible came populations that occupied lands across the far reaches of the Pacific. These populations were the sole groups to inhabit the area now known as Polynesia, and they shared with other groups the lands of Micronesia and Melanesia. They speak Austronesian languages, but their culture and their genetic composition rely substantially on the Indo-Pacific-speaking peoples of New Guinea. This culture thrived beginning about 3000 BCE along the northern coast of New Guinea and the neighboring Bismarck Islands. By 1000 BCE these settlers had reached Tonga and Samoa, thousands of kilometers to the southeast. Rice lost its importance among these farmers, but Southeast Asian yams, chickens, and pigs combined with Papuan taro and bananas and with seafood to provide a varied cuisine. The development of a characteristic style of pottery known as Lapita marks the archaeological remains of these peoples. Equally important was the double-hulled sailing craft developed by the Lapita peoples, which eased the sailing of the high seas. The Polynesian double-hulled vessels had stability, speed, maneuverability, and the capacity to hold large numbers of sailors and supplies for long voyages. With these vessels, navigation skills could be developed to a high level. Without writing or instruments, but with intensive observation of stars, winds, the currents, and the patterns of birds, mariners of the Pacific were able to develop pinpoint navigation.

From their homeland, Polynesian mariners reached the Marquesas Islands, from which they were able to carry out voyages of discovery north to Hawaii, east to Easter Island, and south to New Zealand. It is likely even that these mariners reached and settled on the coast of South America. The evidence is indirect but, I find, convincing. There they learned to cultivate sweet potatoes from the peoples of the Peruvian coast, and brought cuttings with them to the islands. Ultimately, the sweet potato made possible the development of a large Polynesian population on the islands of New Zealand—a region where the normal Polynesian crops, especially taro, could not thrive. These Lapita societies maintained an active trade network until about 500 CE, then allowed it to decline. In the western Pacific, however, the network of rapid connection among islands through double-hulled and outrigger canoes continued to the nineteenth century.

Meanwhile, at the opposite, western fringe of the Austronesian diaspora, the occupation of Madagascar and the Comoros may have been parallel to that of Polynesia and Micronesia in two fashions. First, Austronesian-speaking mariners led in the settlement. Second, it may be that Austronesian connection with East African populations led to a social and biological synthesis that distinguished this stage of migration from those before it. That is, we may seek an East African equivalent to the Lapita homeland of the Pacific. In each case, the argument is that cross-community exchanges may have been important even in migrations that appear from a distance to be a massive colonization effort.

At about the time when the Austronesian mariners began their voyages, Indo-European-speakers in the steppes north of the Black Sea took steps beyond their practice of hunting horses and were able to domesticate them. The result soon led to horse-drawn chariots and then to mounted warriors, especially among Indo-European speakers but also among neighboring groups speaking Altaic or Semitic languages. Horses, harnessed to two-wheeled chariots, became a potent military force, and were associated with the expansion of several Indo-European-speaking groups, including the Hittites of the Anatolian peninsula. Among the eastern groups of Indo-European languages were the Indo-Iranian languages. [See Map 8.1.]

This expansion of Indo-European horse-keepers was a development subsequent to the spread of agriculture throughout Eurasia, which had begun several thousand years earlier. The Indo-Iranian subgroup of Indo-Europeans filtered into Iran and, in a related movement, into north India. Those in Iran gave rise to the religious tradition of Zoroaster and then to the Achaemenid dynasty that created the first large empire. Those in India brought the religious poetry known as the Vedas.

Horses spread beyond Indo-European-speakers soon enough. Speakers of Altaic languages, also reliant on horses (and, in the opinion of some, the first to domesticate them), moved periodically from the East and Central Asian homelands far to the west and somewhat to the south. The Avars and Scythians were such groups in the first millennium BCE, and were followed in the fifth century CE by the Xiongnu in the east and the Huns in the west. Domestication of camels—both in Central Asia and in Arabia—took place in the first millennium CE.

At much the same time as the Aryan migrations into Iran and India, another set of movements remade the map of a similarly sized region of Africa. This was the dispersal of Bantu-speakers into Central and eastern Africa. [See Map 8.1.] Their style of movement, however, was on foot rather than by chariot, and warfare appears to have been less important than farming in their expansion. They were farmers like the Aryans, but lacked horses. They slowly advanced into the forests that are now Cameroon and Congo, displacing and absorbing previous inhabitants in a fashion parallel to that of the Austronesians and the Aryans. When Bantu migrants reached the highland areas of East Africa late in the first millennium BCE, they encountered other farming groups. There, as had been the case in Melanesia, a more complex set of interactions and a new set of innovations developed. Through combination with peoples from Afroasiatic and perhaps Nilo-Saharan language groups, the Bantu-speakers adopted cattle, sheep, and millet, and expanded more rapidly into eastern and southern Africa.

To show that these three stories of rural migration were not only similar but connected, we need only return to the Austronesian voyages to the western Indian Ocean. On the eastern coast of Africa, Austronesian-speakers introduced bananas, Asian yams, the music of xylophones, and outrigger canoes. The first three of these innovations spread across the African continent from hand to hand; bananas were of particular impor-tance in the valleys and highlands of Bantu-speaking Central Africa, where they became a crop of first importance.

By the same token, the Austronesian migrants had to pass through Indian waters on their way to East Africa, and surely camped and settled at several points along the coast, probably as merchants. Along the coasts of north India and Iran, they would therefore have encountered Indo-Iranian-speakers whose ancestors had entered the region over a thousand years earlier.

2

LYNDA NORENE SHAFFER

Southernization, 1994

The author of this selection began her career as a historian of China, but she is currently a world historian, having published books on Native American, Southeast Asian, and Chinese history. Shaffer coins the term *Southernization* to suggest that *Westernization* was preceded by an earlier "southern" process of technological expansion that eventu-ally made Westernization possible. Which of her examples of South-ernization do you find most important in changing the world? Which least significant? Did India and Indian Ocean societies of the early Middle Ages play a role like that of the West today?

Source: Lynda Norene Shaffer, "Southernization," *Journal of World History* 5 (Spring 1994): 1–21.

THINKING HISTORICALLY

The mark of an excellent piece of scholarship in world history is the way the author integrates various states, empires, regions, even continents into a single narrative. At its best, this integration allows us to see patterns that were not visible from the viewpoint of a single state, region, or area. Notice the range of political entities (from cities to dynasties) that Shaffer mentions. Plot the political entities that Shaffer mentions on a timeline of your own creation and then survey them in a historical atlas.

Good historical writing also makes connections of another kind: connections between different aspects of life, often using the broad categories of politics, economics, society, and culture. Specialists often address these topics individually, and such specialized study is often the best way to approach an enormous body of source material. A historian of science or mathematics, for example, has enough to do just focusing on his or her area of specialization. But once some of this specialist work is done, it becomes possible for a generalist to see if there are connections that might be made between different branches of study, be it Indian mathematical innovation and the spread of pomegranates or mastering the monsoon winds. A work of historical integration like Shaffer's has jumped the boundaries not only of political, economic, social, and cultural history but also the boundaries of numerous subgroups: the history of food, technology, science, climate, and religion, to name a few. The best way to see what factors an author has used is to deconstruct her analysis: List all of these categories and sub-categories that Shaffer uses and note the examples of each she gives in the text.

The term *Southernization* is a new one. It is used here to refer to a multifaceted process that began in Southern Asia and spread from there to various other places around the globe. The process included so many interrelated strands of development that it is impossible to do more here than sketch out the general outlines of a few of them. Among the most important that will be omitted from this discussion are the metallurgical, the medical, and the literary. Those included are the development of mathematics; the production and marketing of subtropical or tropical spices; the pioneering of new trade routes; the cultivation, processing, and marketing of southern crops such as sugar and cotton; and the development of various related technologies.

The term *Southernization* is meant to be analogous to *Westernization*. Westernization refers to certain developments that first occurred in western Europe. Those developments changed Europe and eventually spread to other places and changed them as well. In the same way, southernization changed Southern Asia and later spread to other areas, which then underwent a process of change.

Southernization was well under way in Southern Asia by the fifth century C.E., during the reign of India's Gupta kings (320–535 C.E.). It was by that time already spreading to China. In the eighth century various elements characteristic of Southernization began spreading through the lands of the Muslim caliphates. Both in China and in the lands of the caliphate, the process led to dramatic changes, and by the year 1200 it was beginning to have an impact on the Christian Mediterranean. One could argue that within the Northern Hemisphere, by this time the process of Southernization had created an Eastern Hemisphere characterized by a rich south and a north that was poor in comparison. And one might even go so far as to suggest that in Europe and its colonies, the process of Southernization laid the foundation for Westernization.

The Indian Beginning

Southernization was the result of developments that took place in many parts of southern Asia, both on the Indian subcontinent and in Southeast Asia. By the time of the Gupta kings, several of its constituent parts already had a long history in India. Perhaps the oldest strand in the process was the cultivation of cotton and the production of cotton textiles for export. Cotton was first domesticated in the Indus River valley some time between 2300 and 1760 B.C.E., and by the second millennium B.C.E., the Indians had begun to develop sophisticated dyeing techniques. During these early millennia Indus River valley merchants are known to have lived in Mesopotamia, where they sold cotton textiles.

In the first century C.E. Egypt became an important overseas market for Indian cottons. By the next century there was a strong demand for these textiles both in the Mediterranean and in East Africa, and by the fifth century they were being traded in Southeast Asia. The Indian textile trade continued to grow throughout the next millennium. Even after the arrival of European ships in Asian ports at the turn of the sixteenth century, it continued unscathed. According to one textile expert, "India virtually clothed the world" by the mid-eighteenth century. The subcontinent's position was not undermined until Britain's Industrial Revolution, when steam engines began to power the production of cotton textiles.

Another strand in the process of Southernization, the search for new sources of bullion, can be traced back in India to the end of the Mauryan Empire (321–185 B.C.E.). During Mauryan rule Siberia had been India's main source of gold, but nomadic disturbances in Central Asia disrupted the traffic between Siberia and India at about the time that the Mauryans fell. Indian sailors then began to travel to the Malay peninsula and the islands of Indonesia in search of an alternative source, which they most likely "discovered" with the help of local peoples who knew the sites. (This is generally the case with bullion discoveries, including those made by Arabs and Europeans.) What the Indians (and others later on) did do was introduce this gold to international trade routes.

The Indians' search for gold may also have led them to the shores of Africa. Although its interpretation is controversial, some archaeological evidence suggests the existence of Indian influence on parts of East Africa as early as 300 C.E. There is also one report that gold was being sought in East Africa by Ethiopian merchants, who were among India's most important trading partners.

The sixth-century Byzantine geographer Cosmas Indicopleustes described Ethiopian merchants who went to some location inland from the East African coast to obtain gold. "Every other year they would sail far to the south, then march inland, and in return for various made-up articles they would come back laden with ingots of gold." The fact that the expeditions left every other year suggests that it took two years to get to their destination and return. If so, their destination, even at this early date, may have been Zimbabwe. The wind patterns are such that sailors who ride the monsoon south as far as Kilwa can catch the return monsoon to the Red Sea area within the same year. But if they go beyond Kilwa to the Zambezi River, from which they might go inland to Zimbabwe, they cannot return until the following year.

Indian voyages on the Indian Ocean were part of a more general development, more or less contemporary with the Mauryan Empire, in which sailors of various nationalities began to knit together the shores of the "Southern Ocean," a Chinese term referring to all the waters from the South China Sea to the eastern coast of Africa. During this period there is no doubt that the most intrepid sailors were the Malays, peoples who lived in what is now Malaysia, Indonesia, the southeastern coast of Vietnam, and the Philippines.

Sometime before 300 B.C.E. Malay sailors began to ride the monsoons, the seasonal winds that blow off the continent of Asia in the colder months and onto its shores in the warmer months. Chinese records indicate that by the third century B.C.E. "Kunlun" sailors, the Chinese term for the Malay seamen, were sailing north to the southern coasts of China. They may also have been sailing west to India, through the straits now called Malacca and Sunda. If so they may have been the first to establish contact between India and Southeast Asia.

Malay sailors had reached the eastern coast of Africa at least by the first century B.C.E., if not earlier. Their presence in East African waters is testified to by the peoples of Madagascar, who still speak a Malayo-Polynesian language. Some evidence also suggests that Malay sailors had settled in the Red Sea area. Indeed, it appears that they were the first to develop a long-distance trade in a southern spice. In the last centuries B.C.E., if not earlier, Malay sailors were delivering cinnamon from South China Sea ports to East Africa and the Red Sea.

By about 400 C.E. Malay sailors [Polynesians] could be found two-thirds of the way around the world, from Easter Island to East Africa. They rode the monsoons without a compass, out of sight of land, and often at latitudes below the equator where the northern pole star cannot be seen. They navigated by the wind and the stars, by cloud formations, the color of the water, and swell and wave patterns on the ocean's surface. They could discern the presence of an island some thirty miles from its shores by noting the behavior of birds, the animal and plant life in the water, and the swell and wave patterns. Given their manner of sailing, their most likely route to Africa and the Red Sea would have been by way of the island clusters, the Maldives, the Chagos, the Seychelles, and the Comoros.

Malay ships used balance lug sails, which were square in shape and mounted so that they could pivot. This made it possible for sailors to tack against the wind, that is, to sail into the wind by going diagonally against it, first one way and then the other. Due to the way the sails were mounted, they appeared somewhat triangular in shape, and thus the Malays' balance lug sail may well be the prototype of the triangular lateen, which can also be used to tack against the wind. The latter was invented by both the Polynesians to the Malays' east and by the Arabs to their west, both of whom had ample opportunity to see the Malays' ships in action.

It appears that the pepper trade developed after the cinnamon trade. In the first century C.E. Southern India began supplying the Mediterranean with large quantities of pepper. Thereafter, Indian merchants could be found living on the island of Socotra, near the mouth of the Red Sea, and Greek-speaking sailors, including the anonymous author of the *Periplus of the Erythraean Sea*,[1] could be found sailing in the Red Sea and riding the monsoons from there to India.

Indian traders and shippers and Malay sailors were also responsible for opening up an all-sea route to China. The traders' desire for silk drew them out into dangerous waters in search of a more direct way to its source. By the second century C.E. Indian merchants could make the trip by sea, but the route was slow, and it took at least two years to make a round trip. Merchants leaving from India's eastern coast rounded the shores of the Bay of Bengal. When they came to the Isthmus of Kra, the narrowest part of the Malay peninsula, the ships were unloaded, and the goods were portaged across to the Gulf of Thailand. The cargo was then reloaded on ships that rounded the gulf until they reached Funan, a kingdom on what is now the Kampuchea [Cambodia]-Vietnam

---

[1] Written about 60 C.E. [Ed.]

border. There they had to wait for the winds to shift, before embarking upon a ship that rode the monsoon to China.

Some time before 400 C.E. travelers began to use a new all-sea route to China, a route that went around the Malay peninsula and thus avoided the Isthmus of Kra portage. The ships left from Sri Lanka and sailed before the monsoon, far from any coasts, through either the Strait of Malacca or the Strait of Sunda into the Java Sea. After waiting in the Java Sea port for the winds to shift, they rode the monsoon to southern China. The most likely developers of this route were Malay sailors, since the new stopover ports were located within their territories.

Not until the latter part of the fourth century, at about the same time as the new all-sea route began to direct commercial traffic through the Java Sea, did the fine spices—cloves, nutmeg, and mace—begin to assume importance on international markets. These rare and expensive spices came from the Moluccas, several island groups about a thousand miles east of Java. Cloves were produced on about five minuscule islands off the western coast of Halmahera; nutmeg and mace came from only a few of the Banda Islands, some ten islands with a total area of seventeen square miles, located in the middle of the Banda Sea. Until 1621 these Moluccan islands were the only places in the world able to produce cloves, nutmeg, and mace in commercial quantities. The Moluccan producers themselves brought their spices to the international markets of the Java Sea ports and created the market for them.

It was also during the time of the Gupta kings, around 350 C.E., that the Indians discovered how to crystallize sugar. There is considerable disagreement about where sugar was first domesticated. Some believe that the plant was native to New Guinea and domesticated there, and others argue that it was domesticated by Southeast Asian peoples living in what is now southern China. In any case, sugar cultivation spread to the Indian subcontinent. Sugar, however, did not become an important item of trade until the Indians discovered how to turn sugarcane juice into granulated crystals that could be easily stored and transported. This was a momentous development, and it may have been encouraged by Indian sailing, for sugar and clarified butter (ghee) were among the dietary mainstays of Indian sailors.

The Indians also laid the foundation for modern mathematics during the time of the Guptas. Western numerals, which the Europeans called Arabic since they acquired them from the Arabs, actually come from India. (The Arabs call them Hindi numbers.) The most significant feature of the Indian system was the invention of the zero as a number concept. The oldest extant treatise that uses the zero in the modern way is a mathematical appendix attached to Aryabhata's text on astronomy, which is dated 499 C.E.

The Indian zero made the place-value system of writing numbers superior to all others. Without it, the use of this system, base ten or otherwise, was fraught with difficulties and did not seem any better than alternative systems. With the zero the Indians were able to perform calculations rapidly and accurately, to perform much more complicated calculations, and to discern mathematical relationships more aptly. These numerals and the mathematics that the Indians developed with them are now universal—just one indication of the global significance of Southernization.

As a result of these developments India acquired a reputation as a place of marvels, a reputation that was maintained for many centuries after the Gupta dynasty fell. As late as the ninth century Amr ibn Bahr al Jahiz (c. 776–868), one of the most influential writers of Arabic, had the following to say about India:

> As regards the Indians, they are among the leaders in astronomy, mathematics—in particular, they have Indian numerals—and medicine; they alone possess the secrets of the latter, and use them to practice some remarkable forms of treatment. They have the art of carving statues and painted figures. They possess the game of chess, which is the noblest of games and requires more judgment and intelligence than any other. They make Kedah swords, and excel in their use. They have splendid music. . . . They possess a script capable of expressing the sounds of all languages, as well as many numerals. They have a great deal of poetry, many long treatises, and a deep understanding of philosophy and letters; the book *Kalila wa-Dimna* originated with them. They are intelligent and courageous. . . . Their sound judgment and sensible habits led them to invent pins, cork, toothpicks, the drape of clothes, and the dyeing of hair. They are handsome, attractive, and forbearing; their women are proverbial; and their country produces the matchless Indian aloes which are supplied to kings. They were the originators of the science of *fikr*, by which a poison can be counteracted after it has been used, and of astronomical reckoning, subsequently adopted by the rest of the world. When Adam descended from Paradise, it was to their land that he made his way.

The Southernization of China

These Southern Asian developments began to have a significant impact on China after 350 C.E. The Han dynasty had fallen in 221 C.E., and for more than 350 years thereafter China was ruled by an ever-changing collection of regional kingdoms. During these centuries Buddhism became increasingly important in China, Buddhist monasteries spread throughout the disunited realm, and cultural exchange between India and China grew accordingly. By 581, when the Sui dynasty reunited the empire, processes associated with Southernization had already had a major impact on China. The influence of Southernization continued during the T'ang (618–906) and Sung (960–1279) dynasties. One might even go so far as to suggest that the process of Southernization underlay the revolutionary social, political, economic, and technological developments of the T'ang and Sung.

The Chinese reformed their mathematics, incorporating the advantages of the Indian system, even though they did not adopt the Indian numerals at that time. They then went on to develop an advanced mathematics, which was flourishing by the time of the Sung dynasty. Cotton and indigo became well established, giving rise to the blueblack peasant garb that is still omnipresent in China. Also in the Sung period the Chinese first developed cotton canvas, which they used to make a more efficient sail for ocean-going ships.

Although sugar had long been grown in some parts of southern China it did not become an important crop in this region until the process of Southernization was well under way. The process also introduced new varieties of rice. The most important of these was what the Chinese called Champa rice, since it came to China from Champa, a Malay kingdom located on what is now the southeastern coast of Vietnam. Champa rice was a drought-resistant, early ripening variety that made it possible to extend cultivation up well-watered hillsides, thereby doubling the area of rice cultivation in China. . . .

In southern China the further development of rice production brought significant changes in the landscape. Before the introduction of Champa rice, rice cultivation had been confined to lowlands, deltas, basins, and river valleys. Once Champa rice was introduced and rice cultivation spread up the hillsides, the Chinese began systematic terracing and made use of sophisticated techniques of water control on mountain slopes. Between the mid-eighth and the early twelfth century the population of southern China tripled, and the total Chinese population doubled. According to Sung dynasty household registration figures for 1102 and 1110—figures that Sung dynasty specialists have shown to be reliable—there were 100 million people in China by the first decade of the twelfth century.

Before the process of Southernization, northern China had always been predominant, intellectually, socially, and politically. The imperial center of gravity was clearly in the north, and the southern part of China was perceived as a frontier area. But Southernization changed this situation dramatically. By 600, southern China was well on its way to becoming the most prosperous and most commercial part of the empire. The most telling evidence for this is the construction of the Grand Canal, which was completed around 610, during the Sui dynasty. Even though the rulers of the Sui had managed to put the pieces of the empire back together in 581 and rule the whole of China again from a single northern capital, they were dependent on the new southern crops. Thus it is no coincidence that this dynasty felt the need to build a canal that could deliver southern rice to northern cities.

The T'ang dynasty, when Buddhist influence in China was especially strong, saw two exceedingly important technological innovations—the invention of printing and gunpowder. These developments may also be linked to Southernization. Printing seems to have developed within the walls of Buddhist monasteries between 700 and 750, and subtropical Sichuan was one of the earliest centers of the art. The invention of gunpowder in China by Taoist alchemists in the ninth century may also be related to the linkages between India and China created by Buddhism. In 644 an Indian monk identified soils in China that contained saltpeter and demonstrated the purple flame that results from its ignition. As early as 919 C.E. gunpowder was used as an igniter in a flamethrower, and the tenth century also saw the use of flaming arrows, rockets, and bombs thrown by catapults. The earliest evidence of a cannon or bombard (1127) has been found in Sichuan, quite near the Tibetan border, across the Himalayas from India.

By the time of the Sung the Chinese also had perfected the "south-pointing needle," otherwise known as the compass. Various prototypes of the compass had existed in China from the third century B.C.E., but the new version developed during the Sung was particularly well suited for navigation. Soon Chinese mariners were using the south-pointing needle on the oceans, publishing "needle charts" for the benefit of sea captains, and following "needle routes" on the Southern Ocean.

Once the Chinese had the compass they, like Columbus, set out to find a direct route to the spice markets of Java and ultimately to the Spice Islands in the Moluccas. Unlike Columbus, they found them. They did not bump into an obstacle, now known as the Western Hemisphere, on their way, since it was not located between China and the Spice Islands. If it had been so situated, the Chinese would have found it some 500 years before Columbus.

Cities on China's southern coasts became centers of overseas commerce. Silk remained an important export, and by the T'ang dynasty it had been joined by a true porcelain, which was developed in China sometime before 400 C.E. China and its East Asian neighbors had a monopoly on the manufacture of true porcelain until the early eighteenth century. Many attempts were made to imitate it, and some of the resulting imitations were economically and stylistically important. China's southern ports were also exporting to Southeast Asia large quantities of ordinary consumer goods, including iron hardware, such as needles, scissors, and cooking pots. Although iron manufacturing was concentrated in the north, the large quantity of goods produced was a direct result of the size of the market in southern China and overseas. Until the British Industrial Revolution of the eighteenth century, no other place ever equaled the iron production of Sung China.

The Muslim Caliphates

In the seventh century C.E., Arab cavalries, recently converted to the new religion of Islam, conquered eastern and southern Mediterranean shores that had been Byzantine (and Christian), as well as the [Persian] Sassanian empire (Zoroastrian) in what is now Iraq and Iran. In the eighth century they went on to conquer Spain and Turko-Iranian areas of Central Asia, as well as northwestern India. Once established on the Indian frontier, they became acquainted with many of the elements of Southernization.

The Arabs were responsible for the spread of many important crops, developed or improved in India, to the Middle East, North Africa, and Islamic Spain. Among the most important were sugar, cotton, and citrus fruits. Although sugarcane and cotton cultivation may have spread to Iraq and Ethiopia before the Arab conquests, only after the establishment of the caliphates did these southern crops have a major impact throughout the Middle East and North Africa.

The Arabs were the first to import large numbers of enslaved Africans in order to produce sugar. Fields in the vicinity of Basra, at the northern end of the Persian Gulf, were the most important sugar-producing areas within the caliphates, but before this land could be used, it had to be desalinated. To accomplish this task, the Arabs imported East African (Zanj) slaves. This African community remained in the area, where they worked as agricultural laborers. The famous writer al Jahiz, whose essay on India was quoted earlier, was a descendant of Zanj slaves. In 869, one year after his death, the Zanj slaves in Iraq rebelled. It took the caliphate fifteen years of hard fighting to defeat them, and thereafter Muslim owners rarely used slaves for purposes that would require their concentration in large numbers.

The Arabs were responsible for moving sugarcane cultivation and sugar manufacturing westward from southern Iraq into other relatively arid lands. Growers had to adapt the plant to new conditions, and they had to develop more efficient irrigation technologies. By 1000 or so sugarcane had become an important crop in the Yemen; in Arabian oases; in irrigated areas of Syria, Lebanon, Palestine, Egypt, and the Mahgrib; in Spain; and on Mediterranean islands controlled by Muslims. By the tenth century cotton also had become a major crop in the lands of the caliphate, from Iran and Central Asia to Spain and the Mediterranean islands. Cotton industries sprang up wherever the plant was cultivated, producing for both local and distant markets. . . .

Under Arab auspices, Indian mathematics followed the same routes as the crops. Al-Kharazmi (c. 780–847) introduced Indian mathematics to the Arabic-reading world in his *Treatise on Calculation with the Hindu Numerals*, written around 825. Mathematicians within the caliphates then could draw upon the Indian tradition, as well as the Greek and Persian. On this foundation Muslim scientists of many nationalities, including al-Battani (d. 929), who came from the northern reaches of the Mesopotamian plain, and the Persian Omar Khayyám (d. 1123), made remarkable advances in both algebra and trigonometry.

The Arab conquests also led to an increase in long-distance commerce and the "discovery" of new sources of bullion. Soon after the Abbasid caliphate established its capital at Baghdad, the caliph al-Mansur (r. 745–75) reportedly remarked, "This is the Tigris; there is no obstacle between us and China; everything on the sea can come to us." By this time Arab ships were plying the maritime routes from the Persian Gulf to China, and they soon outnumbered all others using these routes. By the ninth century they had acquired the compass (in China, most likely), and they may well have been the first to use it for marine navigation, since the Chinese do not seem to have used it for this purpose until after the tenth century.

. . . [Similarly,] the Arabs "pioneered" or improved an existing long-distance route across the Sahara, an ocean of sand rather than water. Routes across this desert had always existed, and trade and other contacts between West Africa and the Mediterranean date back at least to the Phoenician period. Still, the numbers of people and animals crossing this great ocean of sand were limited until the eighth century when Arabs, desiring to go directly to the source of the gold,[2] prompted an expansion of trade across the Sahara. Also during the eighth century Abdul al-Rahman, an Arab ruler of Morocco, sponsored the construction of wells on the trans-Saharan route from Sijilmasa to Wadidara to facilitate this traffic. This Arab "discovery" of West African gold eventually doubled the amount of gold in international circulation. East Africa, too, became a source of gold for the Arabs. By the tenth century Kilwa had become an important source of Zimbabwean gold.

Developments after 1200: The Mongolian Conquest and the Southernization of the European Mediterranean

By 1200 the process of Southernization had created a prosperous south from China to the Muslim Mediterranean. Although mathematics, the pioneering of new ocean routes, and "discoveries" of bullion are not inextricably connected to locations within forty degrees of the equator, several crucial elements in the process of Southernization were closely linked to latitude. Cotton generally does not grow above the fortieth parallel. Sugar, cinnamon, and pepper are tropical or subtropical crops,

---

[2] One of the sources of gold was the area called the "gold coast" of Africa, south of the Sahara centered in what is today Ghana. [Ed.]

and the fine spices will grow only on particular tropical islands. Thus for many centuries the more southern parts of Asia and the Muslim Mediterranean enjoyed the profits that these developments brought, while locations that were too far north to grow these southern crops were unable to participate in such lucrative agricultural enterprises.

The process of Southernization reached its zenith after 1200, in large part because of the tumultuous events of the thirteenth century. During that century in both hemispheres there were major transformations in the distribution of power, wealth, and prestige. In the Western Hemisphere several great powers went down. Cahokia (near East St. Louis, Illinois), which for three centuries had been the largest and most influential of the Mississippian mound-building centers, declined after 1200, and in Mexico Toltec power collapsed. In the Mediterranean the prestige of the Byzantine empire was destroyed when Venetians seized its capital in 1204. From 1212 to 1270 the Christians conquered southern Spain, except for Granada. In West Africa, Ghana fell to Sosso, and so did Mali, one of Ghana's allies. But by about 1230 Mali, in the process of seeking its own revenge, had created an empire even larger than Ghana's. At the same time Zimbabwe was also becoming a major power in southern Africa.

The grandest conquerors of the thirteenth century were the Central Asians. Turkish invaders established the Delhi sultanate in India. Mongolian cavalries devastated Baghdad, the seat of the Abbasid caliphate since the eighth century, and they captured Kiev, further weakening Byzantium. By the end of the century they had captured China, Korea, and parts of mainland Southeast Asia as well.

Because the Mongols were pagans at the time of their conquests, the western Europeans cheered them on as they laid waste to one after another Muslim center of power in the Middle East. The Mongols were stopped only when they encountered the Mamluks of Egypt at Damascus. In East Asia and Southeast Asia only the Japanese and the Javanese were able to defeat them. The victors in Java went on to found Majapahit, whose power and prestige then spread through maritime Southeast Asia.

Both hemispheres were reorganized profoundly during this turmoil. Many places that had flourished were toppled, and power gravitated to new locales. In the Eastern Hemisphere the Central Asian conquerors had done great damage to traditional southern centers just about everywhere, except in Africa, southern China, southern India, and maritime Southeast Asia. At the same time the Mongols' control of overland routes between Europe and Asia in the thirteenth and early fourteenth centuries fostered unprecedented contacts between Europeans and peoples from those areas that had long been southernized. Marco Polo's long sojourn in Yüan Dynasty China is just one example of such interaction.

Under the Mongols overland trade routes in Asia shifted north and converged on the Black Sea. After the Genoese helped the Byzantines to retake Constantinople from the Venetians in 1261, the Genoese were granted special privileges of trade in the Black Sea. Italy then became directly linked to the Mongolian routes. Genoese traders were among the first and were certainly the most numerous to open up trade with the Mongolian states in southern Russia and Iran. In the words of one Western historian, in their Black Sea colonies they "admitted to citizenship" people of many nationalities, including those of "strange background and questionable belief," and they "wound up christening children of the best ancestry with such uncanny names as Saladin, Hethum, or Hulugu."

Such contacts contributed to the Southernization of the Christian Mediterranean during this period of Mongolian hegemony. Although European conquerors sometimes had taken over sugar and cotton lands in the Middle East during the Crusades, not until some time after 1200 did the European-held Mediterranean islands become important exporters. Also after 1200 Indian mathematics began to have a significant impact in Europe. Before that time a few western European scholars had become acquainted with Indian numerals in Spain, where the works of al-Kharazmi, al-Battani, and other mathematicians had been translated into Latin. Nevertheless, Indian numerals and mathematics did not become important in western Europe until the thirteenth century after the book *Liber abaci* (1202), written by Leonardo Fibonacci of Pisa (c. 1170–1250), introduced them to the commercial centers of Italy. Leonardo had grown up in North Africa (in what is now Bejala, Algeria), where his father, consul over the Pisan merchants in that port, had sent him to study calculation with an Arab master.

In the seventeenth century, when Francis Bacon observed the "force and virtue and consequences of discoveries," he singled out three technologies in particular that "have changed the whole face and state of things throughout the world." These were all Chinese inventions—the compass, printing, and gunpowder. All three were first acquired by Europeans during this time of hemispheric reorganization.

It was most likely the Arabs who introduced the compass to Mediterranean waters, either at the end of the twelfth or in the thirteenth century. Block printing, gunpowder, and cannon appeared first in Italy in the fourteenth century, apparently after making a single great leap from Mongolian-held regions of East Asia to Italy. How this great leap was accomplished is not known, but the most likely scenario is one suggested by Lynn White Jr., in an article concerning how various other Southern (rather than Eastern) Asian technologies reached western Europe at about this time. He thought it most likely that they were introduced by "Tatar" slaves, Lama Buddhists from the frontiers of China whom the Genoese purchased in Black Sea marts and delivered to Italy. By 1450 when this trade reached its peak, there were thousands of these Asian slaves in every major Italian city. . . .

The Rise of Europe's North

The rise of the north, or more precisely, the rise of Europe's northwest, began with the appropriation of those elements of Southernization that were not confined by geography. In the wake of their southern European neighbors, they became partially southernized, but they could not engage in all aspects of the process due to their distance from the equator. Full Southernization and the wealth that we now associate with northwestern Europe came about only after their outright seizure of tropical and subtropical territories and their rounding of Africa and participation in Southern Ocean trade. . . .

Even though the significance of indigenous developments in the rise of northwestern Europe should not be minimized, it should be emphasized that many of the most important causes of the rise of the West are not to be found within the bounds of Europe. Rather, they are the result of the transformation of western Europe's relationships with other regions of the Eastern Hemisphere. Europe began its rise only after the thirteenth-century reorganization of the Eastern Hemisphere facilitated its Southernization, and Europe's northwest did not rise until it too was reaping the profits of Southernization. Thus the rise of the North Atlantic powers should not be oversimplified so that it appears to be an isolated and solely European phenomenon, with roots that spread no farther afield than Greece. Rather, it should be portrayed as one part of a hemisphere-wide process, in which a northwestern Europe ran to catch up with a more developed south—a race not completed until the eighteenth century.

FAXIAN

Travel on the Silk Road and Seas, c. 400

Faxian (or Fa-Hien as rendered here) was a Chinese Buddhist monk who traveled from Chang'an China to India beginning in 399 in search of holy books and relics of the Buddha. He did not return until 414. It took him six years to reach central India and he spent another six years in India, visiting places where the Buddha had lived, collecting stories about the Buddha, and gathering holy books and art.

Source: *A Record of Buddhist Kingdoms: Being an Account of the Chinese Monk Fa-Hien of His Travels in India and Ceylon* (A.D. 399–414) *in Search of the Buddhist Books of Discipline*, trans. James Legge (Oxford at the Clarendon Press, 1886), 10–22, 111–16.

This selection comes from Faxian's account of his travels. The first four chapters describe his travel on the Silk Road from Chang'an to Khotan in far Western China; the last chapter describes his sea voyages home from Sri Lanka to Java and from Java to China. This sea route was sometimes called a southern silk road.

The Silk Road proper was a land route from Eastern China — Chang'an or Xian or Beijing — to Western China, and then on to Central Asia and the Mediterranean. It developed in the early Han Empire, the story goes, as a way for the Chinese to secure Central Asian horses in exchange for silk. Faxian's interests have nothing to do with horses or silk, and we can tell from his description that the route had as much to do with religion as trade. What does this selection tell you about Faxian and Chinese Buddhism? What does it tell you about travel at the beginning of the fifth century?

THINKING HISTORICALLY

This is a source that can be read for many different purposes. It is crucial to an understanding of the history of Buddhism in China, an important topic of religious and cultural history. Some of that, especially Faxian's description of the Buddhist kingdom of Khotan, is included here. But, for the most part, we have excluded Faxian's thoughts on Buddhism. This is because we are reading this source for a different purpose — to understand travel, especially long-distance travel in this period. Historians do this all of the time. We comb sources for information that might have been incidental to the author. Choose a few topics that you would like to know more about: food, social class, or something else that appears in the text. Then sift through the text to find mentions of this subject. Gather the information, sort it according to the four key factors of political, economic, social, and cultural history, and then see if you can use it to draw some conclusion or make some statement.

Chapter I: From Ch'ang-Gan to the Sandy Desert

After starting from Ch'ang-gan, they passed through Lung, and came to the kingdom of K'een-kwei, where they stopped for the summer retreat. When that was over, they went forward to the kingdom of Now-t'an, crossed the mountain of Yang-low, and reached the emporium of Chang-yih. There they found the country so much disturbed that travelling on the roads was impossible for them. Its king, however, was very attentive to them, kept them (in his capital), and acted the part of their danapati.[1]

---

[1] Patron. [Ed.]

Here they met with Che-yen, Hwuy-keen, Sang-shao, Pao-yun, and Sang-king; and in pleasant association with them, as bound on the same journey with themselves, they passed the summer retreat (of that year) together, resuming after it their travelling, and going on to T'un-hwang, (the chief town) in the frontier territory of defence extending for about 80 le from east to west, and about 40 from north to south. Their company, increased as it had been, halted there for some days more than a month, after which Fa-hien and his four friends started first in the suite of an envoy, having separated (for a time) from Pao-yun and his associates.

Le Hao, the prefect of T'un-hwang, had supplied them with the means of crossing the desert (before them), in which there are many evil demons and hot winds. (Travelers) who encounter them perish all to a man. There is not a bird to be seen in the air above, nor an animal on the ground below. Though you look all round most earnestly to find where you can cross, you know not where to make your choice, the only mark and indication being the dry bones of the dead (left upon the sand).

Chapter II: On to Shen-Shen and Thence to Khoten

After travelling for seventeen days, a distance we may calculate of about 1500 le, (the pilgrims) reached the kingdom of Shen-shen, a country rugged and hilly, with a thin and barren soil. The clothes of the common people are coarse, and like those worn in our land of Han, some wearing felt and others coarse serge or cloth of hair;—this was the only difference seen among them. The king professed (our) Law, and there might be in the country more than four thousand monks, who were all students of the hinayana.[2] The common people of this and other kingdoms (in that region), as well as the sramans,[3] all practice the rules of India, only that the latter do so more exactly, and the former more loosely. So (the travellers) found it in all the kingdoms through which they went on their way from this to the west, only that each had its own peculiar barbarous speech. (The monks), however, who had (given up the worldly life) and quitted their families, were all students of Indian books and the Indian language. Here they stayed for about a month, and then proceeded on their journey, fifteen days walking to the north-west bringing them to the country of Woo-e. In this also there were more than four thousand monks, all students of the hinayana. They were very strict in their rules, so that sramans from the territory of Ts'in were all unprepared for their regulations. Fa-hien, through the management of Foo Kung-sun, /maitre

[2] Orthodox; strictly followed asceticism of the Buddha. [Ed.]
[3] Monks or nuns. [Ed.]

d'hotellerie/, was able to remain (with his company in the monastery where they were received) for more than two months, and here they were rejoined by Pao-yun and his friends. (At the end of that time) the people of Woo-e neglected the duties of propriety and righteousness, and treated the strangers in so niggardly a manner that Che-yen, Hwuy-keen, and Hwuy-wei went back towards Kao-ch'ang, hoping to obtain there the means of continuing their journey. Fa-hien and the rest, however, through the liberality of Foo Kung-sun, managed to go straight forward in a south-west direction. They found the country uninhabited as they went along. The difficulties which they encountered in crossing the streams and on their route, and the sufferings which they endured, were unparalleled in human experience, but in the course of a month and five days they succeeded in reaching Yu-teen.[4]

Chapter III: Khoten. Processions of Images. The King's New Monastery

Yu-teen is a pleasant and prosperous kingdom, with a numerous and flourishing population. The inhabitants all profess our Law, and join together in its religious music for their enjoyment. The monks amount to several myriads, most of whom are students of the mahayana.[5] They all receive their food from the common store. Throughout the country the houses of the people stand apart like (separate) stars, and each family has a small tope[6] reared in front of its door. The smallest of these may be twenty cubits high, or rather more. They make (in the monasteries) rooms for monks from all quarters, the use of which is given to travelling monks who may arrive, and who are provided with whatever else they require.

The lord of the country lodged Fa-hien and the others comfortably, and supplied their wants, in a monastery called Gomati, of the mahayana school. Attached to it there are three thousand monks, who are called to their meals by the sound of a bell. When they enter the refectory, their demeanour is marked by a reverent gravity, and they take their seats in regular order, all maintaining a perfect silence. No sound is heard from their alms-bowls and other utensils. When any of these pure men require food, they are not allowed to call out (to the attendants) for it, but only make signs with their hands.

---

[4] Yu-teen, here also called Khoten, is now called the ancient Buddhist kingdom of Khotan. Conquered by Tibet in 670 and by Muslims in 1006. It is now the largely Muslim city of Hotan. [Ed.]

[5] Less orthodox and more open to public participation and worship than Hinayana. While Hinayana was more successful in Southeast Asia, Mahayana won over Tibet, China, Mongolia, Japan, Korea, and northern Vietnam. [Ed.]

[6] Bell-shaped dome structure similar to a miniature stupa or Buddhist temple. [Ed.]

Hwuy-king, Tao-ching, and Hwuy-tah set out in advance towards the country of K'eeh-ch'a; but Fa-hien and the others, wishing to see the procession of images, remained behind for three months. There are in this country four great monasteries, not counting the smaller ones. Beginning on the first day of the fourth month, they sweep and water the streets inside the city, making a grand display in the lanes and byways. Over the city gate they pitch a large tent, grandly adorned in all possible ways, in which the king and queen, with their ladies brilliantly arrayed, take up their residence (for the time).

The monks of the Gomati monastery, being mahayana students, and held in great reverence by the king, took precedence of all others in the procession. At a distance of three or four le from the city, they made a four-wheeled image car, more than thirty cubits high, which looked like the great hall (of a monastery) moving along. The seven precious substances[7] were grandly displayed about it, with silken streamers and canopies hanging all around. The (chief) image[8] stood in the middle of the car, with two Bodhisattvas[9] in attendance upon it, while devas[10] were made to follow in waiting, all brilliantly carved in gold and silver, and hanging in the air. When (the car) was a hundred paces from the gate, the king put off his crown of state, changed his dress for a fresh suit, and with bare feet, carrying in his hands flowers and incense, and with two rows of attending followers, went out at the gate to meet the image; and, with his head and face (bowed to the ground), he did homage at its feet, and then scattered the flowers and burnt the incense. When the image was entering the gate, the queen and the brilliant ladies with her in the gallery above scattered far and wide all kinds of flowers, which floated about and fell promiscuously to the ground. In this way everything was done to promote the dignity of the occasion. The carriages of the monasteries were all different, and each one had its own day for the procession. (The ceremony) began on the first day of the fourth month, and ended on the fourteenth, after which the king and queen returned to the palace.

Seven or eight le to the west of the city there is what is called the King's New Monastery, the building of which took eighty years, and extended over three reigns. It may be 250 cubits in height, rich in elegant carving and inlaid work, covered above with gold and silver, and finished throughout with a combination of all the precious substances. Behind the tope there has been built a Hall of Buddha, of the utmost

[7] Sanskrit phrase translated by Chinese to mean precious stones: usually gold, silver, lapis lazuli, rock crystal, rubies, diamonds, or emeralds, and agate. [Ed.]

[8] The Buddha. [Ed.]

[9] Buddhist saints of the Mahayana tradition. People who postponed their own nirvana to help others. [Ed.]

[10] Spirits. [Ed.]

magnificence and beauty, the beams, pillars, venetianed doors, and windows being all overlaid with gold-leaf. Besides this, the apartments for the monks are imposingly and elegantly decorated, beyond the power of words to express. Of whatever things of highest value and preciousness the kings in the six countries on the east of the (Ts'ung) range of mountains are possessed, they contribute the greater portion (to this monastery), using but a small portion of them themselves.

Chapter IV: Through the Ts'ung or "Onion" Mountains to K'eeh-Ch'a

When the processions of images in the fourth month were over, Sang-shao, by himself alone, followed a Tartar who was an earnest follower of the Law, and proceeded towards Kophene. Fa-hien and the others went forward to the kingdom of Tsze-hoh, which it took them twenty-five days to reach. Its king was a strenuous follower of our Law, and had (around him) more than a thousand monks, mostly students of the mahayana. Here (the travellers) abode fifteen days, and then went south for four days, when they found themselves among the Ts'ung-ling mountains, and reached the country of Yu-hwuy, where they halted and kept their retreat. When this was over, they went on among the hills for twenty-five days, and got to K'eeh-ch'a[11] there rejoining Hwuy-king and his two companions. . . .

Chapter XL: Disastrous Passage to Java; and Thence to China

Fa-hien abode in this country two years; and, in addition (to his acquisitions in Patna), succeeded in getting a copy of the Vinaya-pitaka of the Mahisasakah (school); the Dirghagama and Samyuktagama (Sutras); and also the Samyukta-sanchaya-pitaka;—all being works unknown in the land of Han. Having obtained these Sanskrit works, he took passage in a large merchantman, on board of which there were more than 200 men, and to which was attached by a rope a smaller vessel, as a provision against damage or injury to the large one from the perils of the navigation. With a favourable wind, they proceeded eastwards for three days, and then they encountered a great wind. The vessel sprang a leak and the water came in. The merchants wished to go to the small vessel; but the men on board it, fearing that too many would come, cut the connecting rope. The merchants were greatly alarmed, feeling their risk of

[11] Probably in Ladak, northwest India. [Ed.]

instant death. Afraid that the vessel would fill, they took their bulky goods and threw them into the water. Fa-hien also took his pitcher and washing-basin, with some other articles, and cast them into the sea; but fearing that the merchants would cast overboard his books and images, he could only think with all his heart of Kwan-she-yin,[12] and commit his life to (the protection of) the church of the land of Han,[13] (saying in effect), "I have travelled far in search of our Law. Let me, by your dread and supernatural (power), return from my wanderings, and reach my resting-place!"

In this way the tempest continued day and night, till on the thirteenth day the ship was carried to the side of an island, where, on the ebbing of the tide, the place of the leak was discovered, and it was stopped, on which the voyage was resumed. On the sea (hereabouts) there are many pirates, to meet with whom is speedy death. The great ocean spreads out, a boundless expanse. There is no knowing east or west; only by observing the sun, moon, and stars was it possible to go forward. If the weather were dark and rainy, (the ship) went as she was carried by the wind, without any definite course. In the darkness of the night, only the great waves were to be seen, breaking on one another, and emitting a brightness like that of fire, with huge turtles and other monsters of the deep (all about). The merchants were full of terror, not knowing where they were going. The sea was deep and bottomless, and there was no place where they could drop anchor and stop. But when the sky became clear, they could tell east and west, and (the ship) again went forward in the right direction. If she had come on any hidden rock, there would have been no way of escape.

After proceeding in this way for rather more than ninety days, they arrived at a country called Java-dvipa,[14] where various forms of error and Brahmanism are flourishing, while Buddhism in it is not worth speaking of. After staying there for five months, (Fa-hien) again embarked in another large merchantman, which also had on board more than 200 men. They carried provisions for fifty days, and commenced the voyage on the sixteenth day of the fourth month. Fa-hien kept his retreat on board the ship. They took a course to the north-east, intending to fetch Kwang-chow. After more than a month, when the night-drum had sounded the second watch, they encountered a black wind and tempestuous rain, which threw the merchants and passengers into consternation. Fa-hien again with all his heart directed his thoughts to Kwan-she-yin and the monkish communities of the land of Han; and, through their dread and mysterious protection, was preserved to

---

[12] Chinese goddess of compassion and mercy. [Ed.]

[13] China. [Ed.]

[14] India established first kingdom in Java c. 78. [Ed.]

day-break. After day-break, the Brahmans deliberated together and said, "It is having this Sramana on board which has occasioned our misfortune and brought us this great and bitter suffering. Let us land the bhikshu[15] and place him on some island-shore. We must not for the sake of one man allow ourselves to be exposed to such imminent peril." A patron of Fa-hien, however, said to them, "If you land the bhikshu, you must at the same time land me; and if you do not, then you must kill me. If you land this Sramana, when I get to the land of Han, I will go to the king, and inform against you. The king also reveres and believes the Law of Buddha, and honours the bhikshus." The merchants hereupon were perplexed, and did not dare immediately to land (Fa-hien).

At this time the sky continued very dark and gloomy, and the sailing-masters looked at one another and made mistakes. More than seventy days passed (from their leaving Java), and the provisions and water were nearly exhausted. They used the salt-water of the sea for cooking, and carefully divided the (fresh) water, each man getting two pints. Soon the whole was nearly gone, and the merchants took counsel and said, "At the ordinary rate of sailing we ought to have reached Kwang-chow, and now the time is passed by many days;—must we not have held a wrong course?" Immediately they directed the ship to the north-west, looking out for land; and after sailing day and night for twelve days, they reached the shore on the south of mount Lao,[16] on the borders of the prefecture of Ch'ang-kwang, and immediately got good water and vegetables. They had passed through many perils and hardships, and had been in a state of anxious apprehension for many days together; and now suddenly arriving at this shore, and seeing those (well-known) vegetables, the lei and kwoh, they knew indeed that it was the land of Han. Not seeing, however, any inhabitants nor any traces of them, they did not know whereabouts they were. Some said that they had not yet got to Kwang-chow, and others that they had passed it. Unable to come to a definite conclusion, (some of them) got into a small boat and entered a creek, to look for some one of whom they might ask what the place was. They found two hunters, whom they brought back with them, and then called on Fa-hien to act as interpreter and question them. Fa-hien first spoke assuringly to them, and then slowly and distinctly asked them, "Who are you?" They replied, "We are disciples of Buddha?" He then asked, "What are you looking for among these hills?" They began to lie, and said, "To-morrow is the fifteenth day of the seventh month. We wanted to get some peaches to present[17] to Buddha." He asked further, "What country

---

[15] Buddhist monk. [Ed.]

[16] Near modern Qingdao. [Ed.]

[17] They probably said they were Buddhists to please the monk, Faxian, but realizing that Buddhists don't hunt they said they were looking for peaches. [Ed.]

is this?" They replied, "This is the border of the prefecture of Ch'ang-kwang, a part of Ts'ing-chow under the (ruling) House of Tsin." When they heard this, the merchants were glad, immediately asked for (a portion of) their money and goods, and sent men to Ch'ang-kwang city.

The prefect Le E was a reverent believer in the Law of Buddha. When he heard that a Sramana had arrived in a ship across the sea, bringing with him books and images, he immediately came to the seashore with an escort to meet (the traveller), and receive the books and images, and took them back with him to the seat of his government. On this the merchants went back in the direction of Yang-chow; (but) when (Fa-hien) arrived at Ts'ing-chow, (the prefect there) begged him (to remain with him) for a winter and a summer. After the summer retreat was ended, Fa-hien, having been separated for a long time from his (fellow-)masters, wished to hurry to Ch'ang-gan; but as the business which he had in hand was important, he went south to the Capital;[18] and at an interview with the masters (there) exhibited the Sutras and the collection of the Vinaya (which he had procured).

After Fa-hien set out from Ch'ang-gan, it took him six years to reach Central India; stoppages there extended over (other) six years; and on his return it took him three years to reach Ts'ing-chow. The countries through which he passed were a few under thirty. From the sandy desert westwards on to India, the beauty of the dignified demeanour of the monkhood and of the transforming influence of the Law was beyond the power of language fully to describe; and reflecting how our masters had not heard any complete account of them, he therefore (went on) without regarding his own poor life, or (the dangers to be encountered) on the sea upon his return, thus incurring hardships and difficulties in a double form. He was fortunate enough, through the dread power of the three Honoured Ones,[19] to receive help and protection in his perils; and therefore he wrote out an account of his experiences, that worthy readers might share with him in what he had heard and said.

---

[18] Probably not Chang'an, but Nanjing, the capital of the southern Jin/Tsin under a different name.

[19] Buddha, Law, and Monkhood. [Ed.]

IBN BATTUTA
Travels, 1354

Ibn Battuta (1304–1369), a Muslim Berber from Tangier Morocco left to make the pilgrimage to Mecca at the age of twenty-one, a journey of sixteen months. He did not return for another twenty-four years. Instead he joined a caravan of returning pilgrims to Iraq and continued on over the years to Persia, Afghanistan, India, and China. Including later travels to sub-Saharan Africa, he covered about 75,000 miles, probably more than anyone else had ever done before the age of steam.

In this selection from his account of his travels, the *Rihla* or *Journey*, he describes his entry into India and some of his experiences in the city of Delhi (here rendered as Dilhi) under the Muslim ruler Muhammad bin Tughluq in 1334. What does this selection tell you about travel in India at the time? What does it tell you about Ibn Battuta? In what ways has travel changed? In what ways is it similar?

THINKING HISTORICALLY

This selection from the *Rihla* was chosen because of what it tells us about travel, usually classified as a sub-category of social history. Even this selection, however, could be read for information about political, economic, or cultural history. Explain how.

North-Western India

Banj Ab is one of the greatest rivers on earth. It rises in flood in the hot season, and the inhabitants of that country sow at the time of its flood, just as the people of Egypt do during the Nile flood. This river is the frontier of the territories of the exalted Sultan Muhammad Shah, king of Hind and Sind.

When we reached this river the officials of the intelligence service came to us and wrote a report about us. From the province of Sind to the sultan's capital, the city of Dihli, it is fifty days' journey, but when the intelligence officers write to the sultan from Sind the letter reaches him in five days by the postal service.

Source: *The Travels of Ibn Battutah*, abridged, introduced, and annotated by Tim Mackintosh-Smith (New York: Picador, 2002), 149–51, 155–57, 187–90, 199; trans. by Sir Hamilton Gibb and C. F. Beckinham (Hakluyt Society, 1958, 2000).

Description of the Barid[1]

The service of couriers on foot has within the space of each mile three relays. The manner of its organization is as follows. At every third of a mile there is an inhabited village, outside which there are three pavilions. In these sit men girded up ready to move off, each of whom has a rod two cubits long with copper bells at the top. When a courier leaves the town he takes the letter in the fingers of one hand and the rod with the bells in the other, and runs with all his might. The men in the pavilions, on hearing the sound of the bells, get ready to meet him and when he reaches them one of them takes the letter in his hand and passes on, running with all his might and shaking his rod until he reaches the next relay, and so they continue until the letter reaches its destination. This post is quicker than the mounted post, and they often use it to transport fruits from Khurasan which are regarded as great luxuries in India; the couriers put them on woven baskets like plates and carry them with great speed to the sultan. In the same way they transport the principal criminals; they place each man on a stretcher and run carrying the stretcher on their heads. Likewise they bring the sultan's drinking water when he resides at Dawlat Abad, carrying it from the river Gang [Ganges], to which the Hindus go on pilgrimage and which is at a distance of forty days' journey from there.

When the intelligence officials write to the sultan informing him of those who arrive in his country, the letter is written with the utmost precision and fulness of description. They report to him that a certain man has arrived of such-and-such appearance and dress, and note the number of his party, slaves and servants and beasts, his behaviour both on the move and at rest, and all his doings, omitting no details relating to all of these. When the newcomer reaches the town of Multan, which is the capital of Sind, he stays there until the sultan's order is received regarding his entry and the degree of hospitality to be extended to him. A man is honoured in that country only according to what may be seen of his actions, conduct, and zeal, since no one there knows anything of his family or parentage. The king of India, the Sultan Abu'l-Mujahid Muhammad Shah, makes a practice of honouring strangers and showing affection to them and singling them out for governorships or high dignities of state. The majority of his courtiers, palace officials, ministers of state, judges, and relatives by marriage are foreigners, and he has issued a decree that foreigners are to be called in his country by the title of Aziz [Honourable], so that this has become a proper name for them.

Every person proceeding to the court of this king must needs have a gift ready to present to him in person, in order to gain his favour. The

[1] Postal service. [Ed.]

sultan requites him for it by a gift many times its value. We shall have much to tell later on about the presents made to him by foreigners. When people became familiar with this habit of his, the merchants in Sind and India began to furnish each person who came to visit the sultan with thousands of dinars as a loan, and to supply him with whatever he might desire to offer as a gift or for his own use, such as riding animals, camels and goods. They place both their money and their persons at his service, and stand before him like attendants. When he reaches the sultan, he receives a magnificent gift from him and pays off his debts and his dues to them in full. So they ran a flourishing trade and made vast profits, and it became an established usage amongst them. On reaching Sind I followed this practice and bought horses, camels, white slaves and other goods from the merchants. I had already bought in Ghaznah from an Iraqi merchant about thirty horses and a camel with a load of arrows, for this is one of the things presented to the sultan. This merchant went off to Khurasan and on returning later to India received his money from me. He made an enormous profit through me and became one of the principal merchants. I met him many years later, in the city of Aleppo, when the infidels had robbed me of everything I possessed, but I received no kindness from him. . . .

From Ujah I travelled to the city Multan, the capital of the land of Sind and residence of its ruling amir. On the road to Multan and ten miles distant from it is the river called Khusru Abad, a large river that cannot be crossed except by boat. At this point the goods of all who pass are subjected to a rigorous examination and their baggage searched. Their practice at the time of our arrival was to take a quarter of everything brought in by the merchants, and to exact a duty of seven dinars for every horse. When we set about the crossing of this river and the baggage was examined, the idea of having my baggage searched was very disagreeable to me, for though there was nothing much in it, it seemed a great deal in the eyes of the people, and I did not like having it looked into. By the grace of God Most High there arrived on the scene one of the principal officers on behalf of Qutb al-Mulk, the governor of Multan, who gave orders that I should not be subjected to examination or search. And so it happened, and I gave thanks to God for the mercies which He had vouchsafed me. We spent that night on the bank of the river and next morning were visited by the postmaster. I was introduced to him and went in his company to visit the governor of Multan.

The Governor of Multan and the Ordering of Affairs at His Court

The Governor of Multan is Qutb al-Mulk, one of the greatest and most excellent of the amirs. When I entered his presence, he rose to greet me, shook my hand, and bade me sit beside him. I presented him with a white slave, a horse, and some raisins and almonds. These are among the greatest gifts that can be made to them, since they do not grow in their land but are imported from Khurasan. This governor in his public audience sat on a large carpeted dais, having the qadi and the preacher beside him. To right and left of him were ranged the commanders of the troops, and armed men stood at his back, while the troops were passed in review before him. They had a number of bows there, and when anyone comes desiring to be enrolled in the army as an archer he is given one of the bows to draw. They differ in stiffness and his pay is graduated according to the strength he shows in drawing them. For anyone desiring to be enrolled as a trooper there is a target set up; he puts his horse into a run and tries to hit it with his lance. There is a ring there too, suspended to a low wall; the candidate puts his horse into a run until he comes level with the ring, and if he lifts it off with his lance he is accounted among them a good horseman. For those wishing to be enrolled as mounted archers, there is a ball placed on the ground; each man gallops towards it and shoots at it, and his pay is proportioned to his accuracy in hitting it.

Two months after we reached Multan two of the sultan's chamberlains arrived in the town. They had instructions to arrange for the journey to Dihli of all those who had come on one mission or another. They came to me together and asked me why I had come to India. I told them that I had come to enter permanently the service of Khund Alam ['Master of the World'], namely the sultan, this being how he is called in his dominions. He had given orders that no one coming from Khurasan should be allowed to enter India unless he came with the intention of staying there. So when I told them that I had come to stay they summoned the qadi and notaries and drew up a contract binding me and those of my company who wished to remain in India, but some of them refused to take this engagement.

We then set out on the journey to the capital, which is forty days' march from Multan through continuously inhabited country. The first town we entered was the city of Abuhar, which is the first of these lands of Hind, a small but pretty place with a large population, and with flowing streams and trees. . . .

We continued our journey from the city of Abuhar across open country extending for a day's journey. On its borders are formidable mountains, inhabited by Hindu infidels who frequently hold up parties of travellers. Of the inhabitants of India the majority are infidels. Some of them are subjects under Muslim rule; others of them are rebels and warriors, who maintain themselves in the fastness of the mountains and plunder travelers. . . .

Account of the Sultan's Arrival and Our Meeting with Him

On the fourth of Shawwal [8th June 1334] the sultan alighted at a castle called Tilbat, seven miles from the capital, and the vizier ordered us to go out to him. We set out, each man with his present of horses, camels, fruits of Khurasan, Egyptian swords, mamluks, and sheep brought from the land of the Turks, and came to the gate of the castle where all the newcomers were assembled. They were then introduced before the sultan in order of precedence and were given robes of linen, embroidered in gold. When my turn came I entered and found the sultan seated on a chair. At first I took him to be one of the chamberlains until I saw him with the chief of the royal intimates, whom I had come to know during the sultan's absence. The chamberlain made obeisance and I did so too. After this the chief of the intimate courtiers said to me, 'Bismillah, Mawlana Badr al-Din,' for in India they used to call me Badr al-Din, and mawlana [Our Master] is a title given to all scholars. I approached the sultan, who took my hand and shook it, and continuing to hold it addressed me most affably, saying in Persian, 'This is a blessing; your arrival is blessed; be at ease, I shall be compassionate to you and give you such favours that your fellow-countrymen will hear of it and come to join you.' Then he asked me where I came from and I said to him, 'From the land of the Maghrib.' He said to me, 'The land of Abd al-Mu'min?' and I said, 'Yes.' Every time he said any encouraging word to me I kissed his hand, until I had kissed it seven times, and after he had given me a robe of honour I withdrew.

Account of the Sultan's Entry into His Capital

On the day following that on which we went out to the sultan each one of us was given a horse from the sultan's stables, with a richly ornamented saddle and bridle, and when the sultan mounted for the entry into his capital we rode in the front part of the procession together with the Grand Qadi Sadr al-Jahan. The elephants were decorated and paraded in front of the sultan, with standards fixed on them and sixteen parasols, some of them gilded and some set with precious stones. Over the sultan's head there was displayed a parasol of the same kind and in front of him was carried the ghashiyah, which is a saddle-cloth studded with gems. On some of the elephants there were mounted small military catapults, and when the sultan came near the city parcels of gold and silver coins mixed together were thrown from these machines. The men on foot in front of the sultan and the other persons present scrambled for the money, and they kept on scattering it until the procession reached the palace. There marched before him thousands of foot-soldiers, and wooden pavilions covered with silk fabrics were constructed with singing girls in them, as we have already related.

After his entry into the city the sultan used to summon us to eat in his presence and would enquire how we fared and address us most affably. He said to us one day, 'You have honoured as by your coming and we cannot sufficiently reward you. The elder amongst you is in the place of my father, the man of mature age is my brother, and the young man like my son. There is in my kingdom nothing greater than this city of mine and I give it to you,' whereupon we thanked him and invoked blessings upon him.

One day he sent two of his high officers to us to say, 'The Master of the World says to you, "Whoever amongst you is capable of undertaking the function of vizier or secretary or commander or judge or professor or shaikh, I shall appoint to that office."' Everyone was silent at first, for what they were wanting was to gain riches and return to their countries. Then one of the officers said to me in Arabic, 'What do you say, *ya say-yidi?*' (The people of that country never address an Arab except by the title of sayyid, and it is by this title that the sultan himself addresses him, out of respect for the Arabs.) I replied, 'Vizierships and secretaryships are not my business, but as to qadis and shaikhs, that is my occupation, and the occupation of my fathers before me. And as for military commands, you know that the non-Arabs were converted to Islam only at the point of the sword of the Arabs.' The sultan was pleased when he heard what I said.

He was at the time in the Thousand Columns eating a meal, and he sent for us and we are in his presence as he was eating. We then withdrew to the outside of the Thousand Columns and my companions sat down, while I retired on account of a boil which prevented me from sitting. When the sultan summoned us a second time my companions presented themselves and made excuses to him on my behalf. I came back after the afternoon prayer and I performed the sunset and night prayers in the audience hall. The chamberlain then came out and summoned us. I went in and found the sultan of the terrace of the palace with his back leaning on the royal couch, the Vizier Khwajah Jahan before him, and the 'great king' Qabulah standing there upright. When I saluted him the 'great king' said to me, 'Do homage, for the Master of the World has appointed you qadi of the royal city of Dihli and has fixed your stipend at 12,000 dinars a year, and assigned to you village to that amount, and commanded for you 12,000 dinars in cash, which you shall draw from the treasury tomorrow (if God will), and has given you a horse with its saddle and bridle and has ordered you to be invested with a *maharibi* robe of honour,' that is, a robe which has on its breast and on its back the figure of a *mihrab*. So I did homage and when he had taken me by the hand and presented me before the sultan, the sultan said to me, 'Do not think that the office of qadi of Dihli is one of the minor functions; it is the highest of functions in our estimation.' I understood what he said though I could not speak in Persian fluently, but the sultan understood Arabic although he could not speak it fluently, so I said to him, 'O Master, I belong to the school of Malik and these people are Hanafis, and I do not know the language.' He replied, 'I have appointed two substitutes for you; they will be guided by your advice and you will be the one who signs all the documents, for you are in the place of a son to us,' to which I replied, 'Nay, but your slave and your servant.' He said to me in Arabic with humility and friendly kindness, 'No, but you are our lord and master.' . . .

Account of His Command to Me to Proceed to China on Embassy

When I had completed forty days the sultan sent me saddled horses, slave girls and boys, robes and a sum of money, so I put on the robes and went to him. I had a quilted tunic of blue cotton which I wore during my retreat, and as I put it off and dressed in the sultan's robes I upbraided myself. Ever after, when I looked at that tunic, I felt a light within me, and it remained in my possession until the infidels despoiled me of it on the sea. When I presented myself before the sultan, he showed me greater favour than before, and said to me, 'I have expressly sent for you to go as my ambassador to the king of China, for I know your love of travel and sight-seeing.' He then provided me with everything I required, and appointed certain other persons to accompany me, as I shall relate presently.

5

FRANCESCO BALDUCCI PEGOLOTTI

Merchant Handbook, 1343

Francesco Balducci Pegolotti (c. 1290–1347) was a businessman employed by the Bardi Company of Florence. In that capacity, he worked in London, Antwerp, and Cyprus. While he did not travel to China himself, he learned much about the routes and terms of trade in Asia from those who did travel there for the merchant companies of Florence, Genoa, and Venice. Between 1335 and 1343 he compiled that information for the *Merchant Handbook* that is excerpted here. The route he discusses leads from north of the Black Sea to northwest of the Caspian Sea, north into the Khanate of the Golden Horde, and then across to what is today Uzbekistan and Kazakhstan into China along one of the silk roads.

Notice that this is the period of Mongol supremacy in Asia. What does this selection tell you about business travel in this period? What does it tell you about trade on the silk roads? What role did the Mongols play?

Source: Henry Yule and Henri Cordier, trans. and ed., *Cathay and the Way Thither, Being a Collection of Medieval Notices of China*, Vol. III (London: Hakluyt Society, 1866), 287–95. Spelling modernized and Americanized.

Most of this, like the previous selections, might be broadly classified as social history. But trade is also economic history. What could an economic historian learn from this selection? If you were writing a cultural history, what might you draw from this account?

Information Regarding the Journey to Cathay, for Such As Will Go by Tana and Come Back with Goods

In the first place, from Tana to Gintarchan may be twenty-five days with an ox-wagon, and from ten to twelve days with a horse-wagon. On the road you will find plenty of Mongols, that is to say, of armed men. And from Gittarchan to Sara may be a day by river, and from Sara to Saracanco, also by river, eight days. You can do this either by land or by water; but by water you will be at less charge for your merchandize.

From Saracanco to Organci may be twenty days journey in camel-wagon. It will be well for anyone travelling with merchandize to go to Organci, for in that city there is a ready sale for goods. From Organci to Oltrarre is thirty-five to forty days in camel-wagons. But if when you leave Saracanco you go direct to Oltrarre, it is a journey of fifty days only, and if you have no merchandize it will be better to go this way than to go by Organci.

From Oltrarre to Armalec is forty-five days' journey with pack-asses, and every day you find Mongols. And from Armalec to Camexu is seventy days with asses, and from Camexu until you come to a river called [Grand Canal?] . . . is forty-five days on horseback; and then you can go down the river to Cassai, and there you can dispose of the *sommi* of silver that you have with you, for that is a most active place of business. After getting to Cassai you carry on with the money which you get for the *sommi* of silver which you sell there; and this money is made of paper, and is called *balishi*. And four pieces of this money are worth one *sommo* of silver in the province of Cathay. And from Cassai to Garnalec [Beijing], which is the capital city of the country of Cathay, is thirty days' journey.

Things Needful for Merchants Who Desire to Make the Journey to Cathay Above Described

In the first place, you must let your beard grow long and not shave. And at Tana you should furnish yourself with a dragoman [translator/guide]. And you must not try to save money in the matter of dragomen by taking a bad one instead of a good one. For the additional wages of the good one will not cost you so much as you will save by having him. And besides the dragoman it will be well to take at least two good men servants, who are acquainted with the Cumanian [Central Asian] tongue. And if the merchant likes to take a woman with him from Tana, he can do so; if he does not like to take one there is no obligation, only if he does take one he will be kept much more comfortably than if he does not take one. Howbeit, if he do take one, it will be well that she be acquainted with the Cumanian tongue as well as the men.

And from Tana travelling to Gittarchan you should take with you twenty-five days' provisions, that is to say, flour and salt fish, for as to meat you will find enough of it at all the places along the road. And so also at all the chief stations noted in going from one country to another in the route, according to the number of days set down above, you should furnish yourself with flour and salt fish; other things you will find in sufficiency, and especially meat.

The road you travel from Tana to Cathay is perfectly safe, whether by day or by night, according to what the merchants say who have used it. Only if the merchant, in going or coming, should die upon the road, everything belonging to him will become the perquisite of the lord of the country in which he dies, and the officers of the lord will take possession of all. And in like manner if he die in Cathay. But if his brother be with him, or an intimate friend and comrade calling himself his brother, then to such an one they will surrender the property of the deceased, and so it will be rescued.

And there is another danger: this is when the lord of the country dies, and before the new lord who is to have the lordship is proclaimed; during such intervals there have sometimes been irregularities practiced on the Franks, and other foreigners. (They call *Franks* all the Christians of these parts from Romania westward.) And neither will the roads be safe to travel until the other lord be proclaimed who is to reign in room of him who is deceased.

Cathay is a province which contained a multitude of cities and towns. Among others there is one in particular, that is to say the capital city, to which is great resort of merchants, and in which there is a vast amount of trade; and this city is called Cambalec. And the said city hath a circuit of one hundred miles, and is all full of people and bourses [markets] and of dwellers in the said city.

You may calculate that a merchant with a dragoman, and with two men servants, and with goods to the value of twenty-five thousand golden florins, should spend on his way to Cathay from sixty to eighty *sommi* of silver, and not more if he manage well; and for all the road back again from Cathay to Tana, including the expenses of living and the pay of servants, and all other charges, the cost will be about five *sommi* per head of pack animals, or something less. And you may reckon the *sommo* to be worth five golden florins. You may reckon also that each ox-wagon will require one ox, and will carry ten cantars Genoese weight; and the camel-wagon will require three camels, and will carry thirty cantars Genoese weight; and the horse-wagon will require one horse, and will commonly carry six and half cantars of silk, at 250 Genoese pounds to the cantar [a Genoese pound was apparently about 12 ounces]. And a bale of silk may be reckoned at between 110 and 115 Genoese pounds.

You may reckon also that from Tana to Sara the road is less safe than on any other part of the journey; and yet even when this part of the road is at its worst, if you are some sixty men in the company you will go as safely as if you were in your own house.

Anyone from Genoa or from Venice, wishing to go to the places above-named, and to make the journey to Cathay, should carry linens with him, and if he visit Organci he will dispose of these well. In Organci he should purchase *sommi* of silver, and with these he should proceed without making any further investment, unless it be some bales of the very finest stuffs which go in small bulk, and cost no more for carriage than coarser stuffs would do.

Merchants who travel this road can ride on horseback or on asses, or mounted in any way that they list to be mounted.

Whatever silver the merchants may carry with them as far as Cathay the lord of Cathay will take from them and put into his treasury. And to merchants who thus bring silver they give that paper money of theirs in exchange. This is of yellow paper, stamped with the seal of the lord aforesaid. And this money is called *balishi*; and with this money you can readily buy silk and all other merchandize that you have a desire to buy. And all the people of the country are bound to receive it. And yet you shall not pay a higher price for your goods because your money is of paper. And of the said paper money there are three kinds, one being worth more than another, according to the value which has been established for each by that lord.

And you may reckon that you can buy for one *sommo* of silver nineteen or twenty pounds of Cathay silk, when reduced to Genoese weight, and that the *sommo* should weigh eight and a half ounces of Genoa, and should be of the alloy of eleven ounces and seventeen deniers to the pound.

You may reckon also that in Cathay you should get three or three and a half pieces of damasked silk for a *sommo*; and from three and a half to five pieces of *nacchetti* of silk and gold, likewise for a *sommo* of silver.

■ REFLECTIONS

The Greek philosopher Heraclitus famously said that you can't step into the same river twice. (He could have said you can't step into the *same* river once!) The waters are always changing so no two trips are the same. Travel is always to some degree a step into the unknown. Our selection from Ibn Battuta only hinted at the many adventures and misadventures that awaited him: the escapes from bandits, ambush, drowning, and public execution; the number of times he was robbed of everything but his prayer rug or the clothes he wore, the loss of the royal treasures with which he had been entrusted. We also only touched on the wide range of his positive experiences: the prestigious offices and responsibilities, the wives and fortunes that were given him as he traveled from one world to another. The long title of the *Rihla* captures the positive: *A Gift to Those Who Contemplate the Wonders of Cities and the Marvels of Travelling*. A devout Muslim who begins his journey on a pilgrimage to Mecca and makes detours throughout to visit "great saints," and holy men, Ibn Battuta is also the first modern traveler. Whether traveling alone, surrounded by an entourage, or escorted by a sultan's cavalry, Ibn Battuta is on his own, following his nose, looking for new wonders and marvels. He tries on new identities, sires families, administers kingdoms, and then discards them, traveling on as the winds change.

A thousand years earlier Faxian also began a pilgrimage. He too suffered dangerous terrain, bandit-infested roads, overcrowded leaky ships, bone-crushing accommodations, and life-threatening attacks. He too rejoiced in his travels—at the discovery of the Buddhist kingdom of Khotan and, in pages we did not include, of marvelous discoveries of Buddhist texts, encounters at Buddhist monasteries and hospitals, and immersion in the Buddha's world. Unlike Ibn Battuta, Faxian remained a pilgrim throughout. The long title of his *Record* underlines his single-mindedness: *A Record of Buddhist Kingdoms, Being an Account by the Chinese Monk Faxian of his Travels in India and Ceylon in Search of the Buddhist Books of Discipline*. There was no room in Faxian's travels for diversion or a change of plans. He might spend another month to witness a Buddhist festival, but he was not about to choose a different home, occupation, or identity. For Faxian, travel was a necessary path to his goal. For Ibn Battuta and innumerable travelers since, the path was the goal.

Were the paths of the fourteenth century safer, smoother, or better tended than they had been a thousand years before? In some places they were, but changes were likely more a consequence of local or recent circumstances than long-term improvement. The Sultan's fleet-footed postal service may have been the envy of some, but, except for the shorter runs, it was no more advanced than the first marathon almost two thousand years before. The roads of India were as dangerous as they had ever been, in part because the rule of the Sultan was recently unraveling. They had been better under the Guptas a thousand years before. If there were technological changes occurring that would eventually nurture the modern independent traveler, it is hard to see them in the dirt roads or pirate-infested open seas of the fourteenth century.

In what ways were the travelers of the Middle Ages different from the individuals who took part in the great migrations of the previous millennia? We have virtually no information to reconstruct the lives of individual Indo-European or Bantu travelers. Evidence suggests movement of families, clans, or tribes, not individuals. Migrations were also normally gradual, measurable in miles per generation. The great Polynesian migrations often spanned great distances and each colonization of a new island began with a small group. But this too was a process of gradual settlement over the course of many generations. In one respect Polynesian colonization into the Pacific was unique: Since the deep Pacific islands were empty of human inhabitants, colonization was essentially a one-way process. By contrast, the Indo-European, Bantu, and even early Austronesian migrations created assimilated and hybrid cultures and societies.

Lynda Shaffer's essay on "Southernization" reminds us that all of these movements involved more than people. Languages and cultures, even seeds and technologies, could move while some people stayed in place. In fact, as Patrick Manning explains, much of our evidence for the movement of people is based on the evidence of the movement of language. In modern India, Hindu nationalists have made much of this fact in an attempt to preserve an ancestry free of West Asian foreigners. But prior to the modern era of telegraph, radio, television, and the Internet no cultural expansion occurred without the physical movement of people. The process of Southernization created a zone of intercommunication that included Brahmin priests who brought the Vedas to Cambodia, Arab merchants in East Africa, mace planters in the Moluccas, and Chinese monks who followed the footsteps of Faxian. In some respects, Ibn Battuta was also part of that process, aiding the spread of Islam, six hundred years after it had conquered Silk Road cities like Faxian's paradise of Buddhist Khotan, and at the moment that it was extending the faith to the islands that would become Indonesia, the world's most populous Muslim-majority nation today, and the place from which Faxian took the summer southern winds back to China.

9
_____

Love, Sex, and Marriage

Medieval Europe and Asia, 400–1350

■ HISTORICAL CONTEXT

Most people in modern society share a common ideal about love, sex, and marriage. That ideal is that love, sex, and marriage are, and should be, a unified and exclusive experience. We might boil this down to a set of simple injunctions: You should marry the one you love, and love the one you marry; you should not love others more; you should have sex only with the one you love and marry. To say this is our ideal is not to say we always live up to it; rather, it is to say that we feel we ought to, and when we do not, we feel guilt, remorse, or disappointment with ourselves. In some parts of modern society, this ideal has recently been rejected, replaced by a culture of "hook-ups" or casual sex, but even then the rejected ideal casts a long shadow. A postlove culture is not a nonlove culture: It bears the marks of what it seeks to replace.

Historically, this love-culture ideal is relatively new. The idea that marriage should be based on love was hardly viable in societies where parents arranged marriages (as they did until very recently in most societies). Nor was sexual pleasure an intrinsic element. Most societies regulated women's sexual activity, but not men's. Patriarchal societies often made little association between sexuality and either marriage or love.

The modern idea of romantic love owes much to the idea of romance that developed in Europe in the Middle Ages. We have other ideas of love, to be sure: friendship, religious love, parental love, among others. But when we read love stories, watch romantic films or plays, or listen to love songs, we draw on the ideas and images of medieval romance. We begin this chapter by studying this European set of ideas because it is the origin of much of what we mean when we use the word *love* today. We might be surprised, however, to see how little such love had to do with marriage or even sex. Next we look at two cultures of love—in India and Japan, about the same time period—that are in some ways similar and in some ways different. Finally, for another perspective, we read ideas about sex from a Chinese visitor to medieval Cambodia.

■ THINKING HISTORICALLY

Analyzing Cultural Differences

In the previous chapter, we distinguished among the economic, social, political, and cultural aspects of a society. In this chapter we will examine cultural aspects alone. Actually, culture is never alone, any more than is economics, politics, or social behavior. Culture is nothing less than all our thoughts and feelings and the way we express them by the way we walk, talk, dream, and read history books. Every culture encompasses a wide variety of ideas and behavior at any one time, making it difficult to argue that a certain idea or behavior defines the culture as a whole. Nevertheless, if there were no commonalities there could be no culture.

Initially our focus is on love, the idea of romantic love or courtly love, that was "cultivated" in medieval Europe (and perhaps also in India and Japan). This is preeminently a cultural product. Sex we think of as biological, and marriage is certainly a social institution, but we will look at sex as driven as much by the psyche as the body, and we will touch on the way people thought about marriage. Therefore, we will be making cultural comparisons. We will ask how each culture thought about love, sex, and marriage, and how each culture did or did not put them together. You may be struck by how varied cultures can be. For some, a conclusion of human relativity is disconcerting; but it might also be seen as a testament to human invention and capacity. In any case, the exercise in making comparisons is a fundamental skill in navigating any of our worlds.

KEVIN REILLY

Love in Medieval Europe, India, and Japan, 1997

We hesitantly introduce this piece as a secondary source. It might be
better called a tertiary source because it is based so much on the
work of others and is part of a chapter in a college textbook.
Nevertheless, it sets the stage for our discussion about love. The
selection begins with the classic argument that romantic love was a
product of medieval Europe, originating in the troubadour tradition
of southern France around the twelfth century. The story of Ulrich
von Liechtenstein, although probably not typical, details all the
facets of the new idea of love, as well as the courts of chivalry that
developed its code of behavior. What, according to this interpretation,
are the elements of romantic love? How is it similar to, or different
from, other kinds of love? How does it relate to sex and marriage?
How is the medieval Indian tradition of *bhakti* different from
European romantic love? How were medieval Hindu ideas of sex
different from Christian ideas of sex? How was the Japanese idea of
love during the Heian* period (794–1185) different from European
romantic love? How was it similar?

THINKING HISTORICALLY

One way to understand what makes one culture different from another
is to discount the extreme behavior at the fringes and focus on what
most people think or do. But another way is to compare the extremes
of one culture with the extremes of another, on the assumption that
the extremists of any culture will magnify the culture's main trait. You
might think of Ulrich von Liechtenstein as an extreme example of
medieval European ideas of romantic love. A question to ask after
you read about other societies is: Could there have been an Ulrich
elsewhere? Could medieval India or Japan have produced an Ulrich?
If not, why not?

Notice also that this selection highlights particular social classes
as well as particular cultures. How do cultures and classes interact to
form the ideal of romantic love in Europe and something both similar
and different in Japan?

* hay AHN

Source: Kevin Reilly, *The West and the World*, 3rd ed. (Princeton, NJ: Markus Wiener, 1997),
279–80, 282–83, 287–92.

In the Service of Woman

In the twelfth century the courtly love tradition of the troubadours traveled north into France and Germany, and it became a guide to behavior for many young knights.

We are lucky to have the autobiography of one of these romantic knights, a minor noble who was born in Austria about 1200. His name was Ulrich von Liechtenstein, and he called his autobiography, appropriately enough, *In the Service of Woman*.[1]

At an early age Ulrich learned that the greatest honor and happiness for a knight lay in the service of a beautiful and noble woman. He seems to have realized, at least subconsciously, that true love had to be full of obstacles and frustrations in order to be spiritually ennobling. So at the age of twelve Ulrich chose as the love of his life a princess. She was a perfect choice: Far above him socially, she was also older than Ulrich and already married. Ulrich managed to become a page in her court so that he could see her and touch the same things that she touched. Sometimes he was even able to steal away to his room with the very water that she had just washed her hands in, and he would secretly drink it.

By the age of seventeen Ulrich had become a knight and took to the countryside to joust in the tournaments wearing the lady's colors. Finally after a number of victories, Ulrich gained the courage to ask his niece to call on the lady and tell her that he wanted to be a distant, respectful admirer. The princess would have none of it. She told Ulrich's niece that she was repulsed by Ulrich's mere presence, that he was low class and ugly — especially with that harelip of his. On hearing her reply Ulrich was overjoyed that she had noticed him. He went to have his harelip removed, recuperated for six weeks, and wrote a song to the princess. When the lady heard of this she finally consented to let Ulrich attend a riding party she was having, suggesting even that he might exchange a word with her if the opportunity arose. Ulrich had his chance. He was next to her horse as she was about to dismount, but he was so tongue-tied that he couldn't say a word. The princess thought him such a boor that she pulled out a lock of his hair as she got off her horse.

Ulrich returned to the field for the next three years. Finally the lady allowed him to joust in her name, but she wouldn't part with as much as a ribbon for him to carry. He sent her passionate letters and songs that he had composed. She answered with insults and derision. In one letter the princess derided Ulrich for implying that he had lost a finger while fighting for her when he had actually only wounded it slightly. Ulrich responded by having a friend hack off the finger and send it to the lady in a green velvet case. The princess was evidently so impressed with the

---

[1] Paraphrased from Morton Hunt, *The Natural History of Love* (New York: Alfred A. Knopf, 1959), 132–39. Quotations from Hunt.

power that she had over Ulrich that she sent back a message that she would look at it every day—a message that Ulrich received as he had the others—"on his knees, with bowed head and folded hands."

More determined than ever to win his lady's love, Ulrich devised a plan for a spectacular series of jousts, in which he challenged all comers on a five-week trip. He broke eight lances a day in the service of his princess. After such a showing, the princess sent word that Ulrich might at last visit her, but that he was to come disguised as a leper and sit with the other lepers who would be there begging. The princess passed him, said nothing, and let him sleep that night out in the rain. The following day she sent a message to Ulrich that he could climb a rope to her bedroom window. There she told him that she would grant no favors until he waded across the lake; then she dropped the rope so that he fell into the stinking moat.

Finally, after all of this, the princess said that she would grant Ulrich her love if he went on a Crusade in her name. When she learned that he was making preparations to go, she called it off and offered her love. After almost fifteen years Ulrich had proved himself to the princess.

What was the love that she offered? Ulrich doesn't say, but it probably consisted of kisses, an embrace, and possibly even a certain amount of fondling. Possibly more, but probably not. That was not the point. Ulrich had not spent fifteen years for sex. In fact, Ulrich had not spent fifteen years to win. The quest is what kept him going. His real reward was in the suffering and yearning. Within two years Ulrich was after another perfect lady.

Oh yes. We forgot one thing. Ulrich mentions that in the middle of his spectacular five-week joust, he stopped off for three days to visit the wife and kids. He was married? He was married. He speaks of his wife with a certain amount of affection. She was evidently quite good at managing the estate and bringing up the children. But what were these mundane talents next to the raptures of serving the ideal woman? Love was certainly not a part of the "details of crops, and cattle, fleas and fireplaces, serfs and swamp drainage."[2] In fact, Ulrich might expect that his wife would be proud of him if she knew what he was up to. The love of the princess should make Ulrich so much more noble and esteemed in his wife's eyes.

Courtly Love

The behavior of Ulrich von Liechtenstein reflected in exaggerated form a new idea of love in the West. Historians have called it "courtly love" because it developed in the courts of Europe, where noble ladies and knights of "quality" came together. For the first time since the Greeks a man could idealize a woman, but only if he minimized her sexuality. The evidence is overwhelming that these spiritual affairs would ideally never be consummated.

[2] Morton Hunt.

It is difficult for us to understand how these mature lords and ladies could torture themselves with passionate oaths, feats of endurance, and fainting spells when they heard their lover's name or voice, in short the whole repertoire of romance, and then refrain from actually consummating that love. Why did they insist on an ideal of "pure love" that allowed even naked embraces but drew the line at intercourse, which they called "false love"? No doubt the Christian antipathy for sex was part of the problem. Earlier Christian monks had practiced a similar type of *agape*;[3] Christianity had always taught that there was a world of difference between love and lust. The tendency of these Christian men to think of their ladies as replicas of the Virgin Mother also made sex inappropriate, if not outright incestuous.

But these lords and ladies were also making a statement about their "class" or good breeding. They were saying (as did Sigmund Freud almost a thousand years later) that civilized people repress their animal lust. They were distinguishing themselves from the crude peasants and soldiers around them who knew only fornication and whoring and raping. They were cultivating their emotions and their sensitivity, and priding themselves on their self-control. They were privileged (as members of the upper class) to know that human beings were capable of loyalty and love and enjoying beauty without behaving like animals. They were telling each other that they were refined, that they had "class." . . .

Further, despite the new romanticized view of the woman (maybe because of it), wives were just as excluded as they had always been. Noble, uplifting love, genuine romantic love, could not be felt for someone who swept the floor any more than it could be felt *by* someone whose life was preoccupied with such trivia. The lords and one of their special ladies, Marie, the countess of Champagne, issued the following declaration in 1174:

> We declare and we hold as firmly established that love cannot exert its power between two people who are married to each other. For lovers give each other everything freely, under no compulsion of necessity, but married people are in duty bound to give in to each other's desires and deny themselves to each other in nothing.[4]

The Court of Love

The proclamation was one of many that were made by the "courts of love" that these lords and ladies established in order to settle lovers' quarrels—and to decide for themselves the specifics of the new morality. . . .

No one did more to formulate these rules than Andreas Capellanus. Andreas not only summarized the numerous cases that came before the court, but he used these decisions to write a manual of polite, courtly

---

[3] Greek for a spiritual love. [Ed.]

[4] Andreas Capellanus, *Tractatus de Amore*, 1:6, 7th Dialogue. Quoted in Hunt, 143–44.

love. He called his influential book *A Treatise on Love and Its Remedy*, a title that indicated his debt to Sappho and the Greek romantic idea of love as a sickness. Andreas, however, did not think that he was advocating a "romantic" idea of love. The word was not even used in his day. He considered himself to be a modern twelfth-century Ovid—merely updating the Roman's *Art of Love*. He called himself Andreas the Lover and, like Ovid, considered himself an expert on all aspects of love.

But Andreas only used the same word as Ovid. The similarity ended there. The "aspects" of love that Andreas taught concerned the loyalty of the lovers, courteous behavior, the spiritual benefits of "pure love," the importance of gentleness, the subservience of the man to his lover, and the duties of courtship. There is none of Ovid's preoccupation with the techniques of seduction. Andreas is not talking about sex. In fact, he clearly advises against consummating the relationship.

Ovid made fun of infatuation and silly emotional behavior, but urged his readers to imitate such sickness in order to get the woman in bed. Andreas valued the passionate emotional attachment that Ovid mocked. Sincerity and honesty were too important to Andreas to dream of trickery, deceit, or pretense. Love, for Andreas, was too noble an emotion, too worthy a pursuit, to be put on like a mask. In short, the Roman had been after sexual gratification; the Christian wanted to refine lives and cleanse souls. They both called it love, but Andreas never seemed to realize that they were not talking the same language.

A Medieval Indian Alternative: Mystical Eroticism

Sometimes the best way to understand our own traditions is to study those of a different culture. It is difficult, for instance, for us to see Christian sexual morality as unusual because it has shaped our culture to such a great extent.

There have been alternatives, however. One of the most remarkable was the Indian ecstatic religion of the Middle Ages. Some medieval temple sculpture was erotic. The temples at Khajuraho and Orissa are full of sexual imagery: sensuous nudes and embracing couples. Similarly, the popular story *Gita Govinda* of the twelfth century tells of the loves of the god Krishna. He is shown scandalizing young women, dancing deliriously, and bathing with scores of admirers. Krishna's erotic appeal is a testament to his charisma. He is

> divine in proportion to his superiority as a great lover. . . . Worshippers were encouraged to commit excesses during festivals as the surest way to achieve . . . ecstasy, the purging climax of the orgiastic feast, the surmounting of duality.[5]

[5] Richard Lannoy, *The Speaking Tree: A Study of Indian Culture and Society* (Oxford: Oxford University Press, 1971), 64.

Among the most popular forms of medieval Hindu worship were the *bhakti* cults, which originated in devotion to Krishna in the *Bhagavad Gita*. *Bhakti* cults underline the difference between Indian and European devotion. While the Christian church discouraged spiritual love that might easily lead to "carnal love," the Indian *bhakti* sects encouraged rituals of ecstasy and sensual love precisely because they obliterated moral distinctions. The ecstatic union with the divine Krishna, Vishnu, or Shiva enabled the worshiper to transcend the limitations of self and confining definitions of good and evil.

Thus, Indian ecstatic religion sought sexual expression as a path to spiritual fulfillment. It is interesting that the word *bhakti* meant sex as well as worship, while we use the word "devotion" to mean worship and love. Hindu eroticism had nothing to do with the private expression of romantic love. In fact, it was the opposite. While romantic love depended on the development of the individual personality and the cultivation of individual feelings, *bhakti* depended on the loss of self in the sexual act.

Bhakti cults differed from the European courtly love tradition in one other important respect. They were not expressions of upper-class control. They were popular expressions of religious feeling. In essence they were directed against the dominating *brahman* and *kshatriya* castes because they challenged the importance of caste distinctions altogether. The ecstatic communion with the deity that they preached was open to all, regardless of caste. They appealed even to women and untouchables, as well as to farmers and artisans.

As Christianity did in Europe, popular Hinduism of the Middle Ages replaced a classical formal tradition with a spiritual passion. Ovid's *Art of Love* and the *Kama Sutra* were mechanical, passionless exercises for tired ruling classes. Both India and Europe turned to more emotionally intense religious experiences in the Middle Ages. . . . But the differences between Christian courtly love and *bhakti* cults were also profound. In India, sexual passion was an avenue to spiritual salvation. In Christian Europe sexual passion was at best a dead end, and at worst a road to hell.

Polygamy, Sexuality, and Style: A Japanese Alternative

At the same time that feudal Europe was developing a code of chivalry that romanticized love and almost desexualized marriage, the aristocracy of feudal Japan was evolving a code of polygamous sexuality without chivalry and almost without passion. We know about the sexual lives of Japanese aristocrats between 950 and 1050—the apex of the Heian period—through a series of remarkable novels and diaries, almost all of which were written by women. These first classics of Japanese literature, like *The Tale of Genji* and *The Pillow Book*, were written by women because Japanese men were still writing the "more important" but less-informative laws and theological studies in Chinese (just as Europeans still wrote in a Latin that was very different from the everyday spoken language).

When well-born Japanese in the Heian court spoke of "the world" they were referring to a love affair, and the novels that aristocratic women like Murasaki Shikibu or Sei Shonagon had time to compose in the spoken language were full of stories of "the world."

In *The World of the Shining Prince* Ivan Morris distinguishes three types of sexual relationships between men and women of the Heian aristocracy. (Homosexuality among the court ladies was "probably quite common," he writes, "as in any society where women were obliged to live in continuous and close proximity," but male homosexuality among "warriors, priests, and actors" probably became prevalent in later centuries.) The first type of heterosexual relationship was between the male aristocrat and his "principal wife." She was often several years older than her boy-husband and frequently served more as a guardian than as a bride. She was always chosen for her social standing, usually to cement a political alliance between ruling families. Although the match must frequently have been loveless, her status was inviolate; it was strictly forbidden, for instance, for a prince to exalt a secondary wife to principal wife. Upon marriage the principal wife would normally continue to live with her family, visited by her husband at night, until he became the head of his own household on the death or retirement of his father. Then the principal wife would be installed with all of her servants and aides as the head of the north wing of her husband's residence. An aristocratic woman (but never a peasant woman) might also become a secondary wife or official concubine. If she were officially recognized as such (much to the pleasure of her family), she might be moved into another wing of the official residence (leading to inevitable conflicts with the principal wife and other past and future secondary wives), or she might be set up in her own house. The arrangements were virtually limitless. The third and most frequent type of sexual relationship between men and women was the simple (or complex) affair—with a lady at court, another man's wife or concubine, but usually with a woman of a far lower class than the man. Ivan Morris writes of this kind of relationship:

> Few cultured societies in history can have been as tolerant about sexual relations as was the world of *The Tale of Genji.* Whether or not a gentleman was married, it redounded to his prestige to have as many affairs as possible; and the palaces and great mansions were full of ladies who were only too ready to accommodate him if approached in the proper style. From reading the *Pillow Book* we can tell how extremely commonplace these casual affairs had become in court circles, the man usually visiting the girl at night behind her screen of state and leaving her at the crack of dawn.[6]

[6] Ivan Morris, *The World of the Shining Prince: Court Life in Ancient Japan* (Baltimore: Penguin Books, 1969), 237.

That emphasis on "the proper style" is what distinguishes the sexuality of medieval Japan from that of ancient Rome, and reminds us of the medieval European's display of form—the aristocracy's mark of "class." Perhaps because the sexuality of the Heian aristocracy was potentially more explosive than the repressed rituals of European chivalry, style was that much more important. Polygamous sexuality could be practiced without tearing the society apart (and destroying aristocratic dominance in the process) only if every attention were given to style. Listen, for instance, to what the lady of *The Pillow Book* expected from a good lover:

> A good lover will behave as elegantly at dawn as at any other time. He drags himself out of bed with a look of dismay on his face. The lady urges him on: "Come, my friend, it's getting light. You don't want anyone to find you here." He gives a deep sigh, as if to say that the night has not been nearly long enough and that it is agony to leave. Once up, he does not instantly pull on his trousers. Instead he comes close to the lady and whispers whatever was left unsaid during the night. Even when he is dressed, he still lingers, vaguely pretending to be fastening his sash.
>
> Presently he raises the lattice, and the two lovers stand together by the side door while he tells her how he dreads the coming day, which will keep them apart; then he slips away. The lady watches him go, and this moment of parting will remain among her most charming memories.
>
> Indeed, one's attachment to a man depends largely on the elegance of his leave-taking. When he jumps out of bed, scurries about the room, tightly fastens his trouser-sash, rolls up the sleeves of his Court cloak, over-robe, or hunting costume, stuffs his belongings into the breast of his robe and then briskly secures the outer sash—one really begins to hate him.[7]

The stylistic elegance of the lover's departure was one of the principal themes of Heian literature. Perhaps no situation better expressed the mood of the Japanese word *aware** (a word that was used over a thousand times in *The Tale of Genji*), which meant the poignant or the stylishly, even artistically, sorrowful—a style of elegant resignation. The word also suggests the mood of "the lady in waiting" and even the underlying anguish and jealousy of a precariously polygamous existence for the women consorts and writers of the Japanese feudal age. . . .

Aristocracies have behaved in similar ways throughout the world, and throughout history. They demonstrate their "class" or "good breeding"

---

* ah wa ray

[7] *The Pillow Book of Sei Shonagon*, trans. Ivan Morris (Baltimore: Penguin Books, 1971), 49–50.

with elaborate rituals that differentiate their world from the ordinary. But the example of aristocratic Heian Japan a thousand years ago points to some of the differences between Japanese and Christian culture. The Japanese developed rituals of courtship and seduction for the leisured few that were sexually satisfying and posed no threat to marriage. They were rituals that showed artistic refinement rather than sexual "purity" or chastity. They could be sexual because Japanese culture did not disparage sexuality. Rather it disparaged lack of "taste." The affair did not threaten marriage because the culture did not insist on monogamy. The new sexual interest could be carried on outside or inside the polygamous estate of the Japanese aristocrat. Perhaps the main difference, then, is that the Japanese aristocrat invented stylized sex rather than romantic love.

2

ULRICH VON LIECHTENSTEIN

The Service of Ladies, 1255

This selection is drawn from Ulrich von Liechtenstein's own account of his adventures. After over ten years of service, as a page and then a distant admirer, in 1226, von Liechtenstein undertook a spectacular series of jousts to impress and win his lady, the princess. In the course of a five-week itinerary in northern Italy and southern German-speaking areas in which he took on all comers, he claims to have broken 307 lances. In the first part of this selection, he details his preparation for the traveling tournament. In the second part, he tells of a brief interruption in his jousting for a stop at home. What does this selection tell you about von Liechtenstein's ideas of love and marriage?

THINKING HISTORICALLY

Sometimes the best entry point for analyzing cultural differences is to begin with the surprising or incomprehensible. If we can refrain from merely dismissing what seems beyond the pale, this can be an opportunity to understand how cultures can be truly different from our own.

Source: Ulrich von Liechtenstein, *The Service of Ladies*, trans. J. W. Thomas (Suffolk, England, and Rochester, NY: The Boydell Press, 2004; published by arrangement with University of North Carolina Press, Chapel Hill, 1969), 46–49, 85–86.

Even a moderately careful reading of the two selections from von Liechtenstein's autobiography should evoke some surprise. In the first selection, von Liechtenstein sketches a visual image of himself on horseback that is far from our expectations. Imagine what he must have looked like. Imagine how others must have seen him. Recognizing that this was not some Halloween prank, that others proceeded to joust with him rather than laugh him out of town, we are forced to rethink what his outfit and presentation meant to him and those in his society. The recognition that the meaning of an act (like donning women's clothing) could be vastly different in Europe of the thirteenth century from what it is today offers the entry to comparative analysis.

We may also note that there are many things in von Liechtenstein's description of love that are not at all surprising. This may be because they have become second nature to our own society. Certainly some of the elements of romantic love, which were fresh in von Liechtenstein's day, have become clichés in modern film and television. What do you make of the elements of this story that are familiar? What do you make of those that surprise you?

"My service must be God's command.
Now let me tell you what I've planned.
I'll take on woman's dress and name
and thus disguised will strive for fame.
Sweet God protect me and sustain!
I'll travel with a knightly train
up to Bohemia from the sea.
A host of knights shall fight with me.

"This very winter I shall steal
out of the land and shall conceal
my goal from everyone but you.
I'll travel as a pilgrim who
to honor God is bound for Rome
(no one will question this at home).
I'll stop in Venice and shall stay
in hiding till the first of May.

"I'll carefully remain unseen
but deck myself out like a queen;
it should be easy to acquire
some lovely feminine attire
which I'll put on—now hear this last—
and when St. George's day is past,
the morning afterwards, I'll ride
(I pray that God is on my side)

"from the sea to Mestre, near
by Venice. He who breaks a spear
with me to serve, by tourneying,
his lady fair will get a ring
of gold and it will be quite nice.
I'll give it to him with this advice,
that he present it to his love,
the one he's in the service of.

"Messenger, I'll make the trip
so there will never be a slip
and no one possibly can guess
whose form is hid beneath the dress.
For I'll be clad from head to toe
in woman's garb where'er I go,
fully concealed from people's eyes.
They'll see me only in disguise.

"If you would please me, messenger,
then travel once again to her.
Just tell her what I have in mind
and ask if she will be so kind
as to permit that I should fight
throughout this journey as her knight.
It's something she will not repent
and I'll be glad of her assent."

He rode at once to tell her this
and swore upon his hope of bliss
my loyalty would never falter,
that I was true and would not alter.
He told my plan in full detail
and said, "My lady, should you fail
to let him serve and show your trust
in him, it wouldn't seem quite just."

"Messenger," she spoke, "just let
him have this message, don't forget.
This trip, if I have understood
you right, will surely do him good
and he will win a rich reward
in praise from many a lady and lord.
Whether it helps with me or not,
from others he will gain a lot."

The messenger was pleased and sure.
He found me by the river Mur
at Liechtenstein where I was then.
'T was nice to have him there again.
I spoke, "O courtly youth, now tell
me if the lady's feeling well.
For, if my darling's doing fine,
then shall rejoice this heart of mine."

He spoke, "She's fair and happy too;
she bade me bring this word to you
about your journey. If you should
go through with it 't will do you good
and, whether it helps with her or not,
from others you will gain a lot.
She certainly supports your aim
and says that you'll be rich in fame."

. . .

I got to Venice without delay
and found a house in which to stay,
right on the edge of town, a place
where none would ever see my face
who might have recognized me there.
I was as cautious everywhere
and all the winter long I hid.
But let me tell you what I did:

I had some woman's clothing made
to wear throughout the masquerade.
They cut and sewed for me twelve skirts
and thirty fancy lady's shirts.
I bought two braids for my disguise,
the prettiest they could devise,
and wound them with some pearls I got
which didn't cost an awful lot.

I bade the tailors then prepare
three velvet cloaks for me to wear,
all white. The saddles too on which
the master labored, stitch by stitch,
were silver white. As for a king
was made the saddle covering,
long and broad and gleaming white.
The bridles all were rich and bright.

The tailors sewed for every squire
(there were a dozen) white attire.
A hundred spears were made for me
and all as white as they could be.
But I need not continue so,
for all I wore was white as snow
and everything the squires had on
was just as white as any swan.

My shield was white, the helmet too.
I had them make ere they were through
a velvet cover for each steed
as armor. These were white, indeed,
as was the battle cape which I
should wear for jousting by and by,
the cloth of which was very fine.
I was quite pleased to call it mine.

At last I had my horses sent
to me (none knew just where they went)
and got some servants, as I'd planned,
each native to a foreign land.
They carefully did not let slip
a thing about my coming trip
and I took heed that those who came
to serve me never learned my name.

. . .

They rode toward me with armor on;
I had not waited long to don
a rich and splendid battle dress.
Von Ringenberg with full success
broke off a spear on me. The one
I jousted with when this was done
I knocked down backwards off his horse,
which made him feel ashamed, of course.

The spears I broke then numbered four.
On the field had come no more
with armor on and lance in hand
and so I stopped. At my command
the servants gave six rings away.
I sought the inn where I should stay
and found a pretty hostel there;
I got some other things to wear.

I changed my clothing under guard,
and then the hostel door was barred.
I took with me a servant who
would not say anything, I knew.
We stole away without a sound
and rode with joy to where I found
my dearest wife whom I adore;
I could not ever love her more.

She greeted me just as a good
and loving woman always should
receive a husband she holds dear.
That I had come to see her here
had made her really very pleased.
My visit stilled her grief and eased
her loneliness. We shared our bliss,
my sweet and I, with many a kiss.

She was so glad to see her knight,
and I had comfort and delight
till finally the third day came;
to give me joy was her sole aim.
When dawn appeared it was the third.
I dressed, an early mass was heard,
I prayed God keep me from transgressing,
and then received a friendly blessing.

Right after that I took my leave,
lovingly, you may believe,
and rode with joyful heart to where
I'd left my servants unaware.
I entered Gloggnitz hastily
and found them waiting there for me,
prepared to journey on again.
At once we left the city then.

We rode to Neunkirchen gaily decked
and were received as I'd expect
of those whose manners are refined.
Each knight was courteous and kind
who waited there with spear and shield.
When I came riding on the field
I found them all prepared, adorned
with trappings no one would have scorned.

Nine waited there, not more nor less,
to joust with me, in battle dress.
I saw them and it wasn't long
till I'd donned armor, bright and strong.
The first to come I'd heard much of;
his great desire was ladies' love.
It was Sir Ortold von Graz, a name
already widely known to fame.

All that he wore was of the best.
The good man cut me in the chest
so strong and skilful was his joust;
through shield and armor went the thrust.
When I beheld the wound indeed
and saw that it began to bleed
I hid it quickly with my coat
before the other knights took note.

I broke nine lances there in haste
and found my inn. I dared not waste
much time before I got in bed.
I sent nine rings of golden red
to each of them who with his spear
had earned from me a present here.
My injuries were deftly bound
by a doctor whom my servants found.

3

ANDREAS CAPELLANUS
The Art of Courtly Love, 1184–1186

Andreas Capellanus (Andreas the Chaplain) compiled this guide to
courtly love between 1184 and 1186. He probably intended his
book to update Ovid's *Art of Love*, as discussed in selection 1, but
his approach reflects many of the new ideas of love circulating
among the upper classes of Europe in the twelfth century. Andreas
says that love is suffering, but also that it is wonderful. What does
he mean? Compare his ideas about sex and marriage to those of

Source: Andreas Capellanus, *The Art of Courtly Love*, trans. John J. Parry (New York: Columbia University Press, 1990), 28–30, 31–32, 159, 161–62, 163–64, 177, 184–86.

Ulrich von Liechtenstein. The bishop of Paris condemned Andreas's ideas in 1277, but do they seem religious or Christian in any way? Notice the author's attention to passion and proper behavior. What does Andreas think is the proper relationship between passionate love and marriage? What is his attitude toward sexuality? Homosexuality?

THINKING HISTORICALLY

Compare this idea of "character" with that of the Japanese (discussed in the first selection). What does Andreas think of multiple partners? Compare this attitude with those of other cultures. How do the ideas of Andreas the Chaplain on love and marriage compare to those of a modern Christian chaplain?

Introduction to the Treatise on Love

We must first consider what love is, whence it gets its name, what the effect of love is, between what persons love may exist, how it may be acquired, retained, increased, decreased, and ended, what are the signs that one's love is returned, and what one of the lovers ought to do if the other is unfaithful.

What Love Is

Love is a certain inborn suffering derived from the sight of and excessive meditation upon the beauty of the opposite sex, which causes each one to wish above all things the embraces of the other and by common desire to carry out all of love's precepts in the other's embrace.

That love is suffering is easy to see, for before the love becomes equally balanced on both sides there is no torment greater, since the lover is always in fear that his love may not gain its desire and that he is wasting his efforts. He fears, too, that rumors of it may get abroad, and he fears everything that might harm it in any way, for before things are perfected a slight disturbance often spoils them. If he is a poor man, he also fears that the woman may scorn his poverty; if he is ugly, he fears that she may despise his lack of beauty or may give her love to a more handsome man; if he is rich, he fears that his parsimony in the past may stand in his way. To tell the truth, no one can number the fears of one single lover. This kind of love, then, is a suffering which is felt by only one of the persons and may be called "single love." But even after both are in love the fears that arise are just as great, for each of the lovers fears that what he has acquired with so much effort may be lost through the effort of someone else, which is certainly much worse for a man than if, having no hope, he sees that his efforts are accomplishing nothing, for it is worse to lose the things you are seeking than to be deprived of a gain you merely hope for. The lover fears, too, that he may offend his loved one in some way; indeed he fears so many things that it would be difficult to tell them.

That this suffering is inborn I shall show you clearly, because if you will look at the truth and distinguish carefully you will see that it does not arise out of any action; only from the reflection of the mind upon what it sees does this suffering come. For when a man sees some woman fit for love and shaped according to his taste, he begins at once to lust after her in his heart; then the more he thinks about her the more he burns with love, until he comes to a fuller meditation. Presently he begins to think about the fashioning of the woman and to differentiate her limbs, to think about what she does, and to pry into the secrets of her body, and he desires to put each part of it to the fullest use. Then after he has come to this complete meditation, love cannot hold the reins, but he proceeds at once to action; straightway he strives to get a helper to find an intermediary. He begins to plan how he may find favor with her, and he begins to seek a place and a time opportune for talking; he looks upon a brief hour as a very long year, because he cannot do anything fast enough to suit his eager mind. It is well known that many things happen to him in this manner. This inborn suffering comes, therefore, from seeing and meditating. Not every kind of meditation can be the cause of love, an excessive one is required; for a restrained thought does not, as a rule, return to the mind, and so love cannot arise from it.

Between What Persons Love May Exist

Now, in love you should note first of all that love cannot exist except between persons of opposite sexes. Between two men or two women love can find no place, for we see that two persons of the same sex are not at all fitted for giving each other the exchanges of love or for practicing the acts natural to it. Whatever nature forbids, love is ashamed to accept. . . .

What the Effect of Love Is

Now it is the effect of love that a true lover cannot be degraded with any avarice. Love causes a rough and uncouth man to be distinguished for his handsomeness; it can endow a man even of the humblest birth with nobility of character; it blesses the proud with humility; and the man in love becomes accustomed to performing many services gracefully for everyone. O what a wonderful thing is love, which makes a man shine with so many virtues and teaches everyone, no matter who he is, so many good traits of character! There is another thing about love that we should not praise in few words: it adorns a man, so to speak, with the virtue of chastity, because he who shines with the light of one love can hardly think of embracing another woman, even a beautiful one. For when he thinks deeply of his beloved the sight of any other woman seems to his mind rough and rude. . . .

If One of the Lovers Is Unfaithful to the Other

If one of the lovers should be unfaithful to the other, and the offender is the man, and he has an eye to a new love affair, he renders himself wholly unworthy of his former love, and she ought to deprive him completely of her embraces. . . .

But what if he should be unfaithful to his beloved—not with the idea of finding a new love, but because he has been driven to it by an irresistible passion for another woman? What, for instance, if chance should present to him an unknown woman in a convenient place or what if at a time when Venus is urging him on to that which I am talking about he should meet with a little strumpet or somebody's servant girl? Should he, just because he played with her in the grass, lose the love of his beloved? We can say without fear of contradiction that just for this a lover is not considered unworthy of the love of his beloved unless he indulges in so many excesses with a number of women that we may conclude that he is overpassionate. But if whenever he becomes acquainted with a woman he pesters her to gain his end, or if he attains his object as a result of his efforts, then rightly he does deserve to be deprived of his former love, because there is strong presumption that he has acted in this way with an eye toward a new one, especially where he has strayed with a woman of the nobility or otherwise of an honorable estate. . . .

But I know that once when I sought advice I got the answer that a true lover can never desire a new love unless he knows that for some definite and sufficient reason the old love is dead; we know from our own experience that this rule is very true. We have fallen in love with a woman of the most admirable character, although we have never had, or hope to have, any fruit of this love. For we are compelled to pine away for love of a woman of such lofty station that we dare not say one word about it, nor dare we throw ourself upon her mercy, and so at length we are forced to find our body shipwrecked. But although rashly and without foresight we have fallen into such great waves in this tempest, still we cannot think about a new love or look for any other way to free ourself.

But since you are making a special study of the subject of love, you may well ask whether a man can have a pure love for one woman and a mixed or common love with another. We will show you, by an unanswerable argument, that no one can feel affection for two women in this fashion. For although pure love and mixed love may seem to be very different things, if you will look at the matter properly you will see that pure love, so far as its substance goes, is the same as mixed love and comes from the same feeling of the heart. The substance of the love is the same in each case, and only the manner and form of loving are different, as this illustration will make clear to you. Sometimes we see a man with a desire to drink his wine unmixed, and at another time his appetite prompts him to drink only water or wine and water mixed; although his appetite manifests itself differently, the substance of it is the same and unchanged. So likewise when two people have long been united by pure love and afterwards desire to practice mixed love, the substance of the love remains the same in them, although the manner and form and the way of practicing it are different. . . .

The Rules of Love

Let us come now to the rules of love, and I shall try to present to you very briefly those rules which the King of Love[1] is said to have proclaimed with his own mouth and to have given in writing to all lovers. . . .

I. Marriage is no real excuse for not loving.
II. He who is not jealous cannot love.
III. No one can be bound by a double love.
IV. It is well known that love is always increasing or decreasing.
V. That which a lover takes against the will of his beloved has no relish.
VI. Boys do not love until they arrive at the age of maturity.
VII. When one lover dies, a widowhood of two years is required of the survivor.
VIII. No one should be deprived of love without the very best of reasons.
IX. No one can love unless he is impelled by the persuasion of love.
X. Love is always a stranger in the home of avarice.
XI. It is not proper to love any woman whom one should be ashamed to seek to marry.
XII. A true lover does not desire to embrace in love anyone except his beloved.
XIII. When made public love rarely endures.
XIV. The easy attainment of love makes it of little value; difficulty of attainment makes it prized.
XV. Every lover regularly turns pale in the presence of his beloved.
XVI. When a lover suddenly catches sight of his beloved his heart palpitates.

[1] King Arthur of Britain. [Ed.]

XVII.	A new love puts to flight an old one.
XVIII.	Good character alone makes any man worthy of love.
XIX.	If love diminishes, it quickly fails and rarely revives.
XX.	A man in love is always apprehensive.
XXI.	Real jealousy always increases the feeling of love.
XXII.	Jealousy, and therefore love, are increased when one suspects his beloved.
XXIII.	He whom the thought of love vexes, eats and sleeps very little.
XXIV.	Every act of a lover ends in the thought of his beloved.
XXV.	A true lover considers nothing good except what he thinks will please his beloved.
XXVI.	Love can deny nothing to love.
XXVII.	A lover can never have enough of the solaces of his beloved.
XXVIII.	A slight presumption causes a lover to suspect his beloved.
XXIX.	A man who is vexed by too much passion usually does not love.
XXX.	A true lover is constantly and without intermission possessed by the thought of his beloved.
XXXI.	Nothing forbids one woman being loved by two men or one man by two women.

4

Locales of Love: Tournament and Temple, Eleventh and Fourteenth Centuries

Here we compare images of love from Medieval Christian Europe and Hindu India. The first image is taken from a German illustrated songbook, the *Codex Manesse*, from about 1300. The second is a photograph of statues on a Hindu temple in Khajuraho, India, which was built around 1000. How do these images reflect different attitudes toward love? Are there any similarities between European courtly love and the Indian tradition of *bhakti* (p. 315)?

THINKING HISTORICALLY

To determine whether or not these images accurately reflect differences between medieval European and Indian cultures, rather than just random instances that could be found in any culture, we should ask how representative they are. How common or (on the other hand) unusual is it to see an association of attentive young ladies with knights, horses, swords, and tournaments in European art? Are there similarities between the image from the *Codex Manesse* and Ulrich's love story? Compare the physical signs of love in the Khajuraho image with the story *Gita Govinda* (p. 314). In what ways are they similar? In what ways are they different?

Figure 9.1　Scene from the *Codex Manesse*.

Source: De Agostini / A. Dagli Orti / Getty Images.

Figure 9.2   Statues on a Hindu temple in Khajuraho.

Source: Richard Ashworth/Robert Harding World Imagery/Getty Images.

OMAR KHAYYÁN

The Rubáiyát, c. 1100

Omar Khayyám was a Persian scientist and mathematician who lived
at the end of the eleventh and the beginning of the twelfth century.
These verses, attributed to Khayyám but communicated to most of
the English-speaking world through this 1859 translation by Edward
FitzGerald, reflect the sophisticated, cosmopolitan world of Islam
around 1100. What do you learn about Islamic society and culture
from these verses? What do you learn about ideas of love and
marriage in the medieval Muslim world?

THINKING HISTORICALLY

While verses from this work have graced greeting cards and filled the
pages of inspirational books, their deeper meanings are complex.
They derive from a tradition of Islam, particularly strong in Persia,
called Sufism. Sufis are Muslim mystics, seers, who strive to recognize
God's presence in everything. The love professed in these verses is the
love of God; the "Thee" and "Thy" refer to God.

    Muslim Sufis are, of course, not the only people to speak of the
love of God. After reading this selection, try to think of a document
in your own cultural tradition that expresses similar ideas of religious
love. If you want to determine if such ideas are universal (found
in all cultures), general (found in many cultures), or unusual (found
in few cultures), where will you look for comparable documents?
You have already read many religious selections in this volume. Do
any of them help you understand how common or unusual this
document is?

I

Wake! For the Sun, who scatter'd into flight
The Stars before him from the Field of Night,
    Drives Night along with them from Heav'n, and strikes
The Sultán's Turret with a Shaft of Light.

Source: Omar Khayyám, *Rubáiyát of Omar Khayyám*, trans. Edward FitzGerald (New York:
St. Martin's Press, 1983), 53, 54, 56–60, 62, 66–67, 70, 74, 76, 84, 87, 90–95, 104.

II

Before the phantom of False morning died,
Methought a Voice within the Tavern cried,
   "When all the Temple is prepared within,
Why nods the drowsy Worshipper outside?"

IV

Now the New Year reviving old Desires,
The thoughtful Soul to Solitude retires,
   Where the WHITE HAND OF MOSES on the Bough
Puts out, and Jesus from the Ground suspires.

VII

Come, fill the Cup, and in the fire of Spring
Your Winter-garment of Repentance fling:
   The Bird of Time has but a little way
To flutter—and the Bird is on the Wing.

VIII

Whether at Naishápúr or Babylon,
Whether the Cup with sweet or bitter run,
   The Wine of Life keeps oozing drop by drop,
The Leaves of Life keep falling one by one.

IX

Each Morn a thousand Roses brings, you say;
Yes, but where leaves the Rose of Yesterday?
   And this first Summer month that brings the Rose
Shall take Jamshýd and Kaikobád away.

XI

With me along the strip of Herbage strown
That just divides the desert from the sown,
   Where name of Slave and Sultán is forgot—
And Peace to Mahmúd on his golden Throne!

XII

A Book of Verses underneath the Bough,
A Jug of Wine, a Loaf of Bread—and Thou
    Beside me singing in the Wilderness—
Oh, Wilderness were Paradise enow!

XIII

Some for the Glories of This World; and some
Sigh for the Prophet's Paradise to come;
    Ah, take the Cash, and let the Credit go,
Nor heed the rumble of a distant Drum!

XVI

The Worldly Hope men set their Hearts upon
Turns Ashes—or it prospers; and anon,
    Like Snow upon the Desert's dusty Face,
Lighting a little hour or two—is gone.

XVII

Think, in this batter'd Caravanserai
Whose Portals are alternate Night and Day,
    How Sultán after Sultán with his Pomp
Abode his destined Hour, and went his way.

XXIV

Ah, make the most of what we yet may spend,
Before we too into the Dust descend;
    Dust into Dust, and under Dust to lie
Sans Wine, sans Song, sans Singer, and—sans End!

XXV

Alike lot those who for To-DAY prepare,
And those that after some To-MORROW stare,
    A Muezzín from the Tower of Darkness cries
"Fools! your Reward is neither Here nor There."

XXXII

There was the Door to which I found no Key;
There was the Veil through which I might not see:
    Some little talk awhile of ME and THEE
There was—and then no more of THEE and ME.

XXXVII

For I remember stopping by the way
To watch a Potter thumping his wet Clay:
    And with its all-obliterated Tongue
It murmur'd—"Gently, Brother, gently, pray!"

XXXVIII

And has not such a Story from of Old
Down Man's successive generations roll'd
    Of such a clod of saturated Earth
Cast by the Maker into Human mould?

XLII

And if the Wine you drink, the Lip you press
End in what All begins and ends in—Yes;
    Think then you are To-DAY what YESTERDAY
You were—To-MORROW you shall not be less.

LV

You know, my Friends, with what a brave Carouse
I made a Second Marriage in my house;
    Divorced old barren Reason from my Bed
And took the Daughter of the Vine to Spouse.

LX

The mighty Mahmúd, Allah-breathing Lord
That all the misbelieving and black Horde
    Of Fears and Sorrows that infest the Soul
Scatters before him with his whirlwind Sword.

LXIV

Strange, is it not? that of the myriads who
Before us pass'd the door of Darkness through,
   Not one returns to tell us of the Road,
Which to discover we must travel too.

LXVI

I sent my Soul through the Invisible,
Some letter of that After-life to spell:
   And by and by my Soul return'd to me,
And answer'd "I Myself am Heav'n and Hell."

LXVII

Heav'n but the Vision of fulfill'd Desire,
And Hell the Shadow from a Soul on fire,
   Cast on the Darkness into which Ourselves,
So late emerged from, shall so soon expire.

LXIX

But helpless Pieces of the Game He plays
Upon this Chequer-board of Nights and Days;
   Hither and thither moves, and checks, and slays,
And one by one back in the Closet lays.

LXXI

The Moving Finger writes; and, having writ,
Moves on: nor all your Piety nor Wit
   Shall lure it back to cancel half a Line,
Nor all your Tears wash out a Word of it.

LXXIII

With Earth's first Clay They did the Last Man knead;
And there of the Last Harvest sow'd the Seed:
   And the first Morning of Creation wrote
What the Last Dawn of Reckoning shall read.

LXXXVII

Whereat some one of the loquacious Lot—
I think a Súfi pipkin—waxing hot—
  "All this of Pot and Potter—Tell me then,
Who is the Potter, pray, and who the Pot?"

6

MURASAKI SHIKIBU

The Tale of Genji, c. 1000

The *Tale of Genji* is, by some measures, the world's first novel. It was written by Murasaki Shikibu, a woman at the Japanese court, probably in the first decade after the year 1000. During the Heian period (794–1185) of Japanese history, women in the Japanese aristocracy differentiated their culture from the Chinese one that had dominated it since the seventh century.

In *The Tale of Genji* we also see signs of multiple marriages and numerous lovers, consorts, and courtesans among the Heian aristocracy. The emperor had been married but preferred a lower-class courtesan, Lady Kiritsubo, who died shortly after giving birth to Genji. Lady Kokiden, a more powerful mistress of the emperor, ensured that her son, Suzku, would outrank Genji as the next emperor. She forced the emperor to make Genji a commoner and to make him go into exile. After Lady Kiritsubo's death, the despondent emperor met a princess, Fujitsubo, who reminded him of Kiritsubo. She became the emperor's favorite as well as the love of her stepson, Genji, who returned from exile. Fujitsubo bore the emperor a son whom everyone but she and Genji knew to be the emperor's, and that son became the Heir Apparent. Genji, cut off from intimate contact with Fujitsubo, and uninterested in his wife, played lover and patron to the young Murasaki, who bore him a future emperor, and carried out various affairs and liaisons—one of which is described in this selection. What does this relationship between Genji and one of the younger sisters of Kokiden tell you about sex, love, and marriage in upper-class Heian society?

This selection also reveals much about the culture of the Japanese court. Notice the cultivation of music, dance, and poetry among the

Source: Murasaki Shikibu, *The Tale of Genji*, trans. Royall Tyler (New York: Penguin Books, 2001), 155–61.

court nobility. What, if anything, does this display of sensitivity have to do with ideas of love and marriage? What signs do you see here of the persistence of Chinese culture in Heian Japan?

Also, notice the absence of monogamy in the court. The emperor is married but has taken in turn three consorts: Kokiden, Kiritsubo, and now Fujitsubo. What is the relationship between marriage and sex in this society? What does that tell you about the mores of the time?

THINKING HISTORICALLY

Would you call this a story of romantic love? In what ways is the love Lady Murasaki describes similar to, or different from, the love Andreas Capellanus describes in selection 3? What aspects of Heian Japanese culture are different from the culture of medieval Europe? Is the dominant upper-class idea of love in Japan during this period different from that of Europe? How is this Japanese idea of love and marriage different from that of India?

A little past the twentieth of the second month, His Majesty held a party to honor the cherry tree before the Shishinden.[1] To his left and right were enclosures for the Empress and the Heir Apparent, whose pleasure it was to be present according to his wishes. The Kokiden Consort took offense whenever Her Majesty received such respect, but she came, for she would not have missed the event.

It was a lovely day, with a bright sky and birdsong to gladden the heart, when those who prided themselves on their skill—Princes, senior nobles, and all—drew their rhymes and began composing Chinese verses. As usual, Genji's very voice announcing, "I have received the character 'spring,'" resembled no other. The Secretary Captain came next. He was nervous about how he might look, after Genji, but he maintained a pleasing composure, and his voice rang out with impressive dignity. Most of the rest appeared tense and self-conscious. Naturally, those belonging to the lesser ranks were even more in awe of the genius of His Majesty and the Heir Apparent, which stood out even then, when so many others excelled at that sort of thing. They advanced in dread across the immaculate expanse of the broad court, only to make a painful labor of their simple task. . . .

When the time came to declaim the poems, the Reader could not get on with Genji's because the gathering repeated and commented admiringly on every line. Even the Doctors were impressed. His Majesty was undoubtedly pleased, since to him Genji was the glory of every such occasion.

---

[1] The main hall at the Kyoto Imperial Palace. [Ed.]

The Empress wondered while she contemplated Genji's figure how the Heir Apparent's mother could dislike him so, and she lamented that she herself liked him all too well.

"If with common gaze I could look upon that flower just as others do,
why should it occur to me to find in him any flaw?"

she murmured. One wonders how anyone could have passed on words meant only for herself.

The festival ended late that night. Once the senior nobles had withdrawn, once the Empress and the Heir Apparent were gone and all lay quiet in the beauty of brilliant moonlight, Genji remained drunkenly unwilling to grant that the night was over. His Majesty's gentlewomen all being asleep, he stole off toward the Fujitsubo, in case fortune should favor him at this odd hour, but the door through which he might have approached her was locked, and so he went on, sighing but undeterred, to the long aisle of the Kokiden, where he found the third door open. Hardly anyone seemed to be about, since the Consort had gone straight to wait on His Majesty. The door to the inner rooms was open, too. There was no sound.

This is how people get themselves into trouble, he thought, stepping silently up into the hall. Everyone must be asleep. But could it be? He heard a young and pretty voice, surely no common gentlewoman's, coming his way and singing, "Peerless the night with a misty moon . . ." He happily caught her sleeve.

"Oh, don't! Who are you?" She was obviously frightened.

"You need not be afraid.

That you know so well the beauty of the deep night leads me to assume
you have with the setting moon nothing like a casual bond!"

With this he put his arms around her, lay her down, and closed the door. Her outrage and dismay gave her delicious appeal.

"A man—there is a man here!" she cried, trembling.

"I may do as I please, and calling for help will not save you. Just be still!"

She knew his voice and felt a little better. She did not want to seem cold or standoffish, despite her shock. He must have been quite drunk, because he felt he must have her, and she was young and pliant enough that she probably never thought seriously of resisting him.

She pleased him very much, and he was upset to find daybreak soon upon them. She herself seemed torn. "Do tell me your name!" he pleaded. "How can I keep in touch with you? Surely you do not want this to be all!"

With sweet grace she replied,

"If with my sad fate I were just now to vanish, would you really
come—ah, I wonder!—seeking me over grassy wastes of moor?"

"I understand. Please forgive me.

While I strove to learn in what quarter I should seek my
dewdrop's dwelling, wind, I fear, would be blowing out across
the rustling moors.

We might be frank with each other. Or would you prefer to evade me?"

He had no sooner spoken than gentlewomen began rising noisily, and there was much coming and going between the Kokiden and His Majesty's apartments. They were both in peril. He merely gave her his fan as a token, took hers, and went away.

Some of the many women at the Kiritsubo were awake. "He certainly keeps up his secret exploring, doesn't he!" they whispered, poking each other and pretending all the while to be asleep.

He came in and lay down, but he stayed awake. What a lovely girl! She must be one of the Consort's younger sisters—the fifth or sixth, I suppose, since she had not known a man before.[2] . . . It was all very difficult, and he was unlikely to find out which one she was even if he tried. She did not seem eager to break it off, though—so why did she not leave me any way to correspond with her? These ruminations of his no doubt confirmed his interest in her, but still, when he thought of *her*, he could not help admiring how superbly inaccessible she was in comparison.

The second party was to be today, and he was busy from morning to night. He played the *sō no koto*. The event was more elegant and amusing than the one the day before. Dawn was near when Fujitsubo went to wait on His Majesty.

Desperate to know whether she of the moon at dawn would now be leaving the palace, he set the boundlessly vigilant Yoshikiyo and Koremitsu to keep watch. When he withdrew from His Majesty's presence, they gave him their report. "Several carriages have just left from the north gate, where they were waiting discreetly," they said. "Relatives of His Majesty's ladies were there, and when the Fourth Rank Lieutenant and the Right Controller rushed out to see the party off, we gathered that it must have been the Kokiden Consort who was leaving. Several other quite distinguished ladies were obviously in the party, too. There were three carriages in all."

Genji's heart beat fast. How was he to learn which one she was? What if His Excellency her father found out and made a great fuss over him? That would be highly unwelcome, as long as he still knew so little about her. At any rate, he could not endure his present ignorance, and he lay in an agony of frustration about what to do. He thought fondly of his young lady. How bored she must be, and probably dejected as well, since he had not seen her for days!

The keepsake fan was a triple cherry blossom layered one with a misty moon reflected in water painted on its colored side—not an

---

[2] Genji's brother. [Ed.]

original piece of work but welcome because so clearly favored by its owner. Her talk of "grassy wastes of moor" troubled him, and he wrote on the fan, which he then kept with him,

"All that I now feel, I have never felt before, as the moon at dawn melts away before my eyes into the boundless heavens." . . .

The lady of the misty moon remembered that fragile dream with great sadness. Her father had decided that her presentation to the Heir Apparent was to take place in the fourth month, and the prospect filled her with despair. Meanwhile her lover, who thought he knew how to pursue her if he wished, had not yet actually found out which sister she was, and besides, he hesitated to associate himself with a family from which he had nothing but censure. Then, a little after the twentieth of the third month, the Minister of the Right held an archery contest attended by many senior nobles and Princes and followed immediately by a party for the wisteria blossoms.

The cherry blossom season was over, but two of His Excellency's trees must have consented to wait, for they were in late and glorious bloom. He had had his recently rebuilt residence specially decorated for the Princesses' donning of the train. Everything was in the latest style, in consonance with His Excellency's own florid taste.

His Excellency had extended an invitation to Genji as well, one day when they met at court, and Genji's failure to appear disappointed him greatly, for to his mind this absence cast a pall over the gathering. . . .

Genji dressed with great care, and the sun had set by the time he arrived to claim his welcome.

He wore a grape-colored train-robe under a cherry blossom dress cloak of sheer figured silk. Among the formal cloaks worn by everyone else, his costume displayed the extravagant elegance of a Prince, and his grand entry was a sensation. The very blossoms were abashed, and the gathering took some time to regain its animation.

He played beautifully, and it was quite late by the time he left again, on the pretext of having drunk so much that he was not well. The First and Third Princesses were in the main house, and he went to sit by the door that opened from there toward the east. The lattice shutters were up, and all the women were near the veranda, since this was the corner where the wisteria was blooming. Their sleeves spilled showily under the blinds as though for the New Year's mumming, but Genji disapproved and only found his thoughts going to Fujitsubo.

"I felt unwell to begin with," he said, "and then I was obliged to drink until now I am quite ill. May I be allowed to hide in Their Highnesses' company, if it is not too forward of me to ask?" He thrust himself halfway through the blind in the double doorway.

"Oh, no, please!" one cried. "Surely it is for little people like us to claim protection from the great!"

Genji saw that these ladies, although not of commanding rank, were not ordinary young gentlewomen either. Their stylish distinction was clear. The fragrance of incense hung thickly in the air, and the rustling of silks conveyed ostentatious wealth, for this was a household that preferred modish display to the deeper appeal of discreet good taste. The younger sister had no doubt taken possession of the doorway because Their Highnesses wished to look out from there.

He should not have accepted the challenge, but it pleased him, and he wondered with beating heart which one she was. "Alas," he sang as innocently as could be, still leaning against a pillar, "my fan is mine no more, for I have met with woe . . ."

"What a very odd man from Koma!" The one who answered seemed not to understand him.

Another said nothing but only sighed and sighed. He leaned toward her, took her hand through her standing curtain, and said at a guess,

> *"How sadly I haunt the slope of Mount Irusa, where the crescent sets, yearning just to see again the faint moon that I saw then!*

Why should that be?"

This must have been too much for her, because she replied,

> *"Were it really so that your heart goes straight and true, would you lose your way even in the dark of night, when no moon is in the sky?"*

Yes, it was her voice. He was delighted, though at the same time . . .

7

ZHOU DAGUAN

Sex in the City of Angkor, 1297

Angkor, the great Kymer or Cambodian civilization of the Middle Ages, originated in the early ninth century. At its zenith in the twelfth and thirteenth centuries, its empire included the southern halves of modern Laos and Thailand as well as all of modern Cambodia. In 1296 Zhou Daguan was sent on a mission to Cambodia by the Mongol emperor of China, Temur Khan, the grandson and successor of Kubilai Khan. He stayed in the recently completed capital, which

Source: Zhou Daguan, *A Record of Cambodia: The Land and Its People*, trans. Peter Harris (Chiang Mai, Thailand: Silkworm Books, 2007), 54–59.

still stands today as Angkor Thom, and wrote his record of the country and its people. This is a brief selection from what remains of that account. What does it tell you about family life and attitudes toward sex and sexuality in Angkor?

THINKING HISTORICALLY

Zhou Daguan makes no comparisons with other cultures, but implicit in almost every statement is a comparison with his own Chinese culture. What surprises him? What does he find strange or even offensive? What do his responses tell us about the differences between Chinese and Cambodian customs or ideas regarding sex and love? Compare Cambodian ideas about sex with those in Europe, Japan, and India. What do you think explains these differences? What seems to be the impact of different religions on a culture's attitudes toward sex and sexuality?

6
The People

The one thing people know about southern barbarians is that they are coarse, ugly, and very black. I know nothing at all about those living on islands in the sea or in remote villages, but this is certainly true of those in the ordinary localities. When it comes to the women of the palace and women from the *nanpeng*—that is, the great houses—there are many who are as white as jade, but that is because they do not see the light of the sun.

Generally, men and women alike wrap a cloth around their waist, but apart from that they leave their smooth chests and breasts uncovered. They wear their hair in a topknot and go barefoot. This is the case even with the wives of the king.

The king has five wives, one principal wife and one for each of the four cardinal points. Below them, I have heard, there are four or five thousand concubines and other women of the palace. They also divide themselves up by rank. They only go out of the palace on rare occasions.

Every time I went inside the palace to see the king, he always came out with his principal wife, and sat at the gold window in the main room. The palace women lined up by rank in two galleries below the window. They moved to and fro to steal looks at us, and I got a very full view of them. Any family with a female beauty is bound to have her summoned into the palace.

At the lower level there are also the so-called *chenjialan*, servant women who come and go providing services inside the palace and number at least a thousand or two. In their case they all have husbands and live mixed in among ordinary people. They shave back the hair on the top of their head, which gives them the look of northerners with their "open canal" partings.[1] They paint the area with vermilion, which they also paint on to either side of their temples. In this way they mark themselves out as being *chenjialan*. They are the only women who can go into the palace; no one else below them gets to go in. There is a continuous stream of them on the roads in front of and behind the inner palace.

Apart from wearing their hair in a topknot, ordinary women do not have ornaments in their hair like pins or combs. They just wear gold bracelets on their arms and gold rings on their fingers. The *chenjialan* and the women in the palace all wear them too. Men and women usually perfume themselves with scents made up of a mixture of sandalwood, musk, and other fragrances.

Every family practices Buddhism.

There are a lot of effeminate men in the country who go round the markets every day in groups of a dozen or so. They frequently solicit the attentions of Chinese in return for generous gifts. It is shameful and wicked.

7

Childbirth

As soon as they give birth the local women prepare some hot rice, mix it with salt, and put it into the entrance of the vagina. They usually take it out after a day and a night. Because of this, women do not fall sick when they are giving birth, and usually contract so as to be like young girls again.

When I first heard this I was surprised by it, and seriously doubted whether it was true. Then a girl in the family I was staying with gave birth to a child, and I got a full picture of what happened to her. The day after the birth, she took up the baby right away and went to bathe in the river with it. It was a truly amazing thing to see.

Then again, I have often heard people say that the local women are very lascivious, so that a day or two after giving birth they are immediately coupling with their husbands. If a husband doesn't meet his wife's wishes he will be abandoned right away, as Zhu Maichen[2] was. If the husband happens to have work to do far away, if it is only for a few nights that is all right, but if it is for more than ten nights or so the wife will say, "I'm not a ghost—why am I sleeping alone?" This is how strong their sexual feelings are. That said, I have heard that there are some who exercise self-restraint.

---

[1] Hair pulled back to show a wide part, which is then painted red. [Ed.]

[2] A Han dynasty folktale of a poor scholar, Zhu Maichen, whose wife left him for another man. [Ed.]

The women age very quickly indeed, the reason being that they marry and have children young. A twenty- or thirty-year-old woman is like a Chinese woman of forty or fifty.

8
Young Girls

When a family is bringing up a daughter, her father and mother are sure to wish her well by saying, "May you have what really matters — in future may you marry thousands and thousands of husbands!"

When they are seven to nine years old — if they are girls from wealthy homes — or only when they are eleven — if they come from the poorest families — girls have to get a Buddhist monk or a Daoist to take away their virginity, in what is called *zhentan*.

So every year, in the fourth month of the Chinese calendar, the authorities select a day and announce it countrywide. The families whose daughters should be ready for *zhentan* let the authorities know in advance. The authorities first give them a huge candle. They make a mark on it, and arrange for it to be lit at dusk on the day in question. When the mark is reached the time for *zhentan* has come.

A month, fifteen days, or ten days beforehand, the parents have to choose a Buddhist monk or a Daoist. This depends on where the Buddhist and Daoist temples are. The temples often also have their own clients. Officials' families and wealthy homes all get the good, saintly Buddhist monks in advance, while the poor do not have the leisure to choose.

Wealthy and noble families give the monks wine, rice, silk and other cloth, betel nuts, silverware, and the like, goods weighing as much as a hundred piculs and worth two or three hundred ounces of Chinese silver. The smallest amount a family gives weighs ten to forty piculs, depending on how thrifty the family is.

The reason poor families only start dealing with the matter when their girls reach eleven is simply that it is hard for them to manage these things. Some wealthy families do also give money for poor girls' *zhentan*, which they call doing good work. Moreover in any one year a monk can only take charge of one girl, and once he has agreed to and accepted the benefits, he cannot make another commitment.

On the night in question a big banquet with drums and music is laid on for relatives and neighbors. A tall canopy is put up outside the entrance to the house, and various clay figurines of people and animals are laid out on top of it. There can be ten or more of these, or just three or four — or none at all in the case of poor families. They all have to do with events long ago, and they usually stay up for seven days before people start taking them down.

At dusk the monk is met with palanquin, parasol, drums, and music and brought back to the house. Two pavilions are put up, made of colorful silk. The girl sits inside one, and the monk inside the other. You can't understand what he's saying because the drums and music are making so much noise—on that night the night curfew is lifted. I have heard that when the time comes the monk goes into a room with the girl and takes away her virginity with his hand, which he then puts into some wine. Some say the parents, relatives and neighbors mark their foreheads with it, others say they all taste it. Some say the monk and the girl have sex together, others say they don't. They don't let Chinese see this, though, so I don't really know.

Toward dawn the monk is seen off again with palanquin, parasol, drums, and music. Afterward silk, cloth, and the like have to be given to the monk to redeem the body of the girl. If this is not done the girl will be the property of the monk for her whole life and won't be able to marry anyone else.

The instance of this that I saw took place early on the sixth night of the fourth month of the year *dingyou* in the Dade reign period (1297).

Before this happens, the parents always sleep together with their daughter; afterward, she is excluded from the room and goes wherever she wants without restraint or precaution. When it comes to marriage, there is a ceremony with the giving of gifts, but it is just a simple, easygoing affair. There are many who get married only after leading a dissolute life, something local custom regards as neither shameful nor odd.

On a *zhentan* night up to ten or more families from a single alley may be involved. On the city streets people are out meeting Buddhist monks and Daoists, going this way and that, and the sounds of drums and music are everywhere.

9
Slaves

Family slaves are all savages purchased to work as servants. Most families have a hundred or more of them; a few have ten or twenty; only the very poorest have none at all. The savages are people from the mountains. They have their own way of categorizing themselves, but are commonly called "thieving Zhuang." When they come to the city, none of them dares go in and out of people's homes. They are so despised that if there is a quarrel between two city dwellers, it only takes one of them to be called a Zhuang for hatred to enter into the marrow of his bones. . . .

The males and females mate together, but the master would never have reason to have intercourse with them. Sometimes a Chinese who comes to Cambodia and has long been single will act carelessly, but as soon as he has had relations with one of them the master will hear of it, and the following day he will refuse to sit with the Chinese, on the grounds that he has come into contact with a savage.

Sometimes one of them will have intercourse with an outsider, to the point of becoming pregnant and having a baby. But the master won't try and find out where it is from, since the mother has no status and he will profit from the child, who can eventually become his slave.

■ REFLECTIONS

Cultural comparisons, formerly a staple of historical studies, have come under harsh criticism in recent years, and for good reason. The ambitious general histories and philosophical anthropologies written at the beginning of the twentieth century were full of gross generalizations about the "essence" of various cultures and the advantages of one civilization over another. These grand overviews, predating serious empirical studies of African, Asian, and Latin American societies, invariably argued that such "premodern," or "traditional," societies lacked some critical cultural attribute honed in Europe that enabled Europeans to conquer the world after 1500. It goes without saying that these sweeping interpretations were written by Europeans and their North American descendants.

The comparative history of love got caught up in the academic whirlwind of historians and anthropologists, who, in seeking to explain European expansion, industrialization, and modernization, argued that conjugal love—the nonromantic familial variety—created family units in Europe and America that were different from those in other parts of the world. They saw the Western family as the stimulus of modern society. Some also found the Western practices of dating, mate choosing, and individual decision making unique.

Toward the end of the twentieth century, in a postcolonial age that had grown skeptical of Western claims of objectivity, cultural comparisons were seen for what they often were—thinly veiled exercises in self-aggrandizement and implicit rationales for Western domination. For example, Western scientific racism, in which some Western anthropologists and scientists divided the world by cranial sizes, nose width, or culture-bound intelligence tests (always putting themselves on top), lost favor after its rationale was exposed as the foundation for the horrific genocides of World War II.

There is a growing debate about the strategy of explaining Western growth and dominance by looking for Western traits that non-Western cultures lacked. But whether or not such a strategy is wise, we would be foolish to stop trying to compare cultures. Cultures are rich repositories of human thought and behavior; they differ over time and across the globe; and the process of comparison is essential to learning and creating knowledge. In any case, historical comparisons should not be about establishing which culture is better or worse. Culture, almost by definition, is good for the particular society in which it arises. That people in different parts of the world have found different ways of dealing with the same human conditions should not surprise us. To call some better than others is meaningless.

What we can learn from cultural comparison is something about the malleability of human nature and the range of options available to us. We also learn much about ourselves when we peer at another face in the mirror. The differences leap out at us over time as well as space. In some ways, Ulrich's mirror is as foreign as Genji's. In other ways, it is not. In response to an age of prejudice and cultural stereotyping, many well-intentioned people choose to deny or celebrate cultural differences. A far wiser course is to understand what these differences reveal about our world and us.

10

Muslim, Christian, and Jewish Encounters

Afro-Eurasia, 1000–1300

■ HISTORICAL CONTEXT

The great monotheistic religions of Afro-Eurasia — Islam, Christianity, and Judaism — came into frequent contact in the centuries after 1000, as they continue to do today. They had more than their belief in one God in common. Christianity and Judaism shared the same birthplace in Jerusalem. Islam began less than 800 miles away on the Arabian Peninsula. Islam also held Jerusalem as its second most important city. In fact, the Prophet Muhammad initially called the faithful to pray facing Jerusalem, only later choosing Mecca. Christians and Muslims accepted the Hebrew Bible as the word of God; Muslims also accepted the Christian New Testament as divinely inspired. For Muslims, Jesus was another prophet in a long line of religious leaders that stretched back to Moses and Abraham. All three faiths believed that God used his prophets to guide mankind, and all believed God planned a future kingdom for the faithful. Thus, while Jews did not accept Jesus, and Christians did not accept Muhammad, all three faiths believed in the commandments of Moses, the stories of the Bible, and the coming of an Apocalypse, a Last Judgment, and a Kingdom of God.

So why couldn't they get along? Well, we will see that they often did. Still, conflicts occurred, and sometimes metastasized. The belief held by all three of these groups that there is only one God, the creator of the universe, means we are all brothers and sisters. But monotheists can be particularly troubled by brothers and sisters who mistake God's word, fail to follow it, or in some way reject who they consider to be the One and Only God.

Polytheists may follow many gods and many ways of doing things: Agriculturalists could worship Earth Mothers and Sky Fathers; ancients from Gilgamesh to Augustus worshiped a panoply of gods and goddesses; Hindus generally respected the thousands of gods or pathways to divinity; Chinese Daoists could worship the Buddha and follow Confucian principles. But monotheists were often more doctrinaire and less tolerant. They were more eager to spread the word. Christians and Muslims (though not Jews in this period) tried to convert others to their faith, sometimes by force.

So if monotheism could lead to universalism or tribalism, brotherhood or sibling rivalry, toleration or persecution, what prompted the expression of one or the other tendency? To answer this, we have to look at the particular events and their background of causes.

■ THINKING HISTORICALLY

Understanding Causes

Historians often distinguish between long-term causes and immediate or proximate causes. This is a loose distinction: Long-term causes can be more or less long term. To say that monotheism is a cause of conflict, for instance, is to emphasize a very long time indeed — back at least two thousand years, if not the three to four thousand years that the Bible infers. Proximate causes are also elastic in length of time before the event. They can be anything from a recent change like a developing famine or economic crisis to yesterday's speech or a declaration of war. Proximate causes often refer to individuals and individual actions, whereas long-term causes usually refer to social forces, traditions, or other slowly changing processes.

History is a process of continual change. Nothing remains eternally the same. Generally, slow changes are better explained by long-term causes, and sudden changes are better explained by proximate causes. In this chapter, we will try to explain both long-term developments, like Christian anti-Semitism, and short-term events, like the First Crusade (between 1095 and 1099). You will be asked to think about causes in both the long and short term. You will also be encouraged to reflect on the meaning of causation and the value of causal explanation.

SHELOMO DOV GOITEIN

Interfaith Relations in Muslim North Africa (1000–1300), 1969

This is a secondary source by a modern historian, but it is based on a trove of primary sources that have a history worth telling. In the Middle Ages, a Jewish tradition that said Hebrew was the language of God led at least some Jewish communities to ensure that no written material in Hebrew was destroyed. Instead, any bit of writing was deposited in a large silo-shaped structure called a *geniza*. Goitein's six-volume *Mediterranean Society* is based on the modern discovery of a thousand years of written notes, books, letters, and all other writings that were deposited in the Geniza in Cairo from 870 to the nineteenth century. The writers were all Jews, but the material is so extensive that it provides a unique window on all of Cairo. This particular selection is from the beginning of Goitein's discussion of interfaith relations.

What does Goitein say about the relations among Jews, Muslims, and Christians in Cairo in this period? What pieces of writing from the Geniza illustrate his summary?

THINKING HISTORICALLY

Goitein paints a picture of communities living side by side in relative forbearance, if not mutual engagement. What seem to be the long- or short-term causes of this accommodation? What might be the social, religious, or political forces that bring about or maintain the peace?

Interfaith relations in the Middle Ages should not be compared with those in our own times. Owing to the religious character of medieval society, the religious minorities formed a state within the state, by law as well as in fact. The group consciousness of the members of the various religions was similar to that of modern nations. The adherents of another faith were not necessarily enemies, but certainly foreigners. The contrast went even deeper. Since each of the three monotheistic religions claimed to be the sole possessor of the full truth, the very existence of other religions was a challenge or even an offense.

In view of these facts, the modern term "discrimination" can be applied to the Middle Ages only in a qualified sense. When an alien today is treated

Source: S. D. Goitein, *Mediterranean Society, Vol. II* (Berkeley: University of California Press, 1969), 273–78.

differently from a citizen, for example, if he is not permitted to be gainfully employed, he is not being discriminated against, but is so treated because he does not share the financial and other responsibilities of citizens or permanent residents. Similarly, Christians and Jews under Islam regarded it as natural, albeit burdensome, that certain restrictions were imposed on them by the Muslim community in the midst of which they lived, but to which they did not belong. They, too, discriminated against Muslims. Thus, as a rule, they would certainly not feel themselves obliged to provide for the poor of the Muslims or to ransom their captives.

On the other hand, the minority groups lived in closest proximity to the majority and were bound up with it by the same economy and by being subjects of the same government. They shared similar burdens and were exposed to a similar fate. This made the situation complicated and markedly different from the mutual relationships of the members of modern nations. The Muslim, Christian, and Jewish communities each formed a nation, *umma*, in itself, but in every country they shared a homeland, *watan*, in common. Both concepts were of highest practical and emotional significance, as the Geniza letters show. While it was natural, however, to be treated differently as a member of another religion, it was revolting to be discriminated against as a permanent resident of the same country.

This dichotomy in the relationship of a medieval minority group toward the surrounding majority is beautifully expressed in this passage from a letter of the Jewish judge of Barqa (eastern Libya), written in Alexandria. He had intended to make the pilgrimage to the Holy City, but, as usual, the ways in Palestine were unsafe, the winter was cold, and our judge was clearly homesick. Traveling conditions could not have been too bad at that time, for the addressee, who lived in Old Cairo, was indeed setting out for Jerusalem. In view of this, the writer felt somehow apologetic, explaining at length (in a letter sent a short time before the one containing the passage translated below) why his return to Barqa was urgently needed. Before leaving Alexandria for the West he wrote again. After extending greetings to various dignitaries in Jerusalem whom the addressee was supposed to meet and settling some business matters (for the judge, as was usual with pilgrims, had also done some trading on his way), he continues: "On this very day a big caravan is setting out for Barqa under the command of Ibn Shibl. I have booked in it for myself and for my goods at the price of 3 dinars, and have already paid the fare. Most of the travelers are Barqis. They have promised me to be considerate with regard to the watering places and the keeping of the Sabbath and similar matters. For in the whole caravan there is not a single Jew besides myself. Notwithstanding, I confide in God that everything will work out fine according to his will." Besides demonstrating his confidence in God it was clearly the fact that he traveled in the company of compatriots who gave the lonely Jew the feeling that he was safe. . . .

Group consciousness made itself felt in many direct and indirect ways. Spiritual life centered entirely on religion (in contrast with scientific studies, which were interdenominational, but confined to limited circles). Economic and legal transactions were made as far as possible within the religious group. Many business letters and legal documents reflect this situation. Whenever a commodity was ordered from overseas or out of town with no business friend available for supervising its transport, the letter would state whether it should be carried by Jews only, or by trustworthy gentiles as well. . . .

Intermarriage of course was proscribed by both the Church and the Synagogue, while Islam permitted a Muslim to marry a Christian woman or a Jewess. No such occurrence, however, is reported or referred to in our documents. The second Fatimid caliph of Egypt, al-'Aziz (975–996), had, among others, a Christian wife, but in such cases the female partner normally accepted the religion of the husband. Because of his dietary laws, a Muslim would not partake of a meal in a Christian family, nor a Jew anywhere outside his community. One should also bear in mind that in a Christian or Jewish house even a casual visitor would be offered a glass of wine, while at least the Muslim middle class would shun such an open display of disregard for the prohibitions of their religion. . . .

Unlike Europe, where the Jews formed a single and exceedingly small group within a foreign environment, in Islam the detrimental effects of segregation were mitigated by the existence of two minority groups, which, during the Geniza period, were still sizable and influential even on the conduct of the state.

2

BISHOP OF SPEYER
Grant to the Jews, 1084

Jews lived in Europe as early as Roman times, although more moved into northern Europe after the tribal invasions of the fourth and fifth centuries emptied Roman cities and brought an end to the Western Roman Empire. By 1000, there were a few settlements of Jews along the Rhine River in what is today Germany. This document explains

Source: W. Altmann and E. Bernheim, eds., *Ausgeuvahlte Urkunden zur Erlauterung der Verfassungsge schichte Deutschlands im Mitzelalter* (Berlin: Weidmannsche Buchhandlung, 1904), p. 156, reprinted in Roy C. Cave and Herbert H. Coulson, *A Source Book for Medieval Economic History* (Milwaukee: Bruce Publishing Co., 1936; reprint ed., New York: Biblo & Tannen, 1965), pp. 101–02.

the settlement of a Jewish colony in the city of Speyer. What did the Bishop of Speyer grant to the Jews? How does this document show peaceful accommodation, and how does it show tension between the Christian and Jewish communities?

THINKING HISTORICALLY

What parts of this text show the reasons or factors behind Christian/ Jewish cooperation? What parts explain possible causes of hostility?

In the name of the Holy and Indivisible Trinity, I, Rudiger, surnamed Huozmann, Bishop of Speyer,

When I made the villa of Speyer into a town, thought I would increase the honor I was bestowing on the place if I brought in the Jews. Therefore I placed them outside the town and some way off from the houses of the rest of the citizens, and, lest they should be too easily disturbed by the insolence of the citizens, I surrounded them with a wall. Now the place of their habitation which I acquired justly (for in the first place I obtained the hill partly with money and partly by exchange, while I received the valley by way of gift from some heirs) that place, I say, I transferred to them on condition that they pay annually three and a half pounds of the money of Speyer for the use of the brethren. I have granted also to them within the district where they dwell, and from that district outside the town as far as the harbor, and within the harbor itself, full power to change gold and silver, and to buy and sell what they please. And I have also given them license to do this throughout the state. Besides this I have given them land of the church for a cemetery with rights of inheritance. This also I have added that if any Jew should at any time stay with them he shall pay no thelony. Then also just as the judge of the city hears cases between citizens, so the chief rabbi shall hear cases which arise between the Jews or against them. But if by chance he is unable to decide any of them they shall go to the bishop or his chamberlain. They shall maintain watches, guards, and fortifications about their district, the guards in common with our vassals. They may lawfully employ nurses and servants from among our people. Slaughtered meat which they may not eat according to their law they may lawfully sell to Christians, and Christians may lawfully buy it. Finally, to round out these concessions, I have granted that they may enjoy the same privileges as the Jews in any other city of Germany.

Lest any of my successors diminish this gift and concession, or constrain them to pay greater taxes, alleging that they have usurped these privileges, and have no episcopal warrant for them, I have left this charter as a suitable testimony of the said grant. And that this may never be forgotten, I have signed it, and confirmed it with my seal as may be seen, below. Given on September 15th, 1084, etc.

3

FULCHER OF CHARTRES

The First Crusade: Pope Urban's Speech at Clermont, c. 1095–1127

Relations between Christians and Muslims fluctuated by time and place. Early Muslim conquests from 622 to 750 came at the cost of Christian territory in the Byzantine Empire, North Africa, and Spain. Christian communities in the Persian Sassanid Empire, which had been weakened by constant war with the Byzantines, were also conquered. The boundaries between Christian and Muslim territories stabilized around 750, until a new Muslim force, the Seljuk Turks, came out of Central Asia to threaten both older Muslim regimes and the remains of the Byzantine Empire in what is now called (after the Seljuk Turks) Turkey. By the end of the eleventh century, the Seljuks held Baghdad and Jerusalem, and they threatened the capital of the Byzantine Empire at Constantinople. In response in 1095, the Byzantine Emperor Alexis sent ambassadors to Pope Urban II to ask for help in defending Constantinople.

Fulcher of Chartres picks up our story from there. Fulcher's perspective was that of a Christian with little knowledge of the world beyond France, but he was there in Clermont and likely gives us a reliable account of the pope's speech and its immediate reception. What, in addition to the Seljuk Turks, was on the pope's mind? What problems of Christian society concerned him?

THINKING HISTORICALLY

Leaders who call for war do not always reveal their uppermost reasons in their public appeals. Urban says nothing here about an appeal from Emperor Alexis. He doesn't direct his listeners to the defense of Constantinople. Fulcher suggests that the ultimate goal was Jerusalem (although he was writing after 1099 when the Christians had, in fact, already conquered Jerusalem). Another source suggests that Pope Urban might have been swayed by a man called Peter the Hermit, who alleged that he had been prevented from visiting Christian holy places in Jerusalem.

We may never know all of the causes of the First Crusade, and we certainly should not rely on only one source to make a judgment. Nevertheless, what does this single source suggest about the reasons for Pope Urban's call? Whether he wanted Christians to defend Jerusalem, fight the Seljuks in the Byzantine Empire, or conquer Jerusalem, what did he hope to gain?

Source: *The First Crusade: The Chronicle of Fulcher of Chartres and Other Source Materials*, 2nd ed., ed. Edward Peters (Philadelphia: University of Pennsylvania Press, 1998), 49–55.

I. The Council of Clermont

1. In the year 1095 from the Lord's Incarnation, with Henry reigning in Germany as so-called emperor,[1] and with Philip as king in France, manifold evils were growing in all parts of Europe because of wavering faith. In Rome ruled Pope Urban II, a man distinguished in life and character, who always strove wisely and actively to raise the status of the Holy Church above all things.

2. He saw that the faith of Christianity was being destroyed to excess by everybody, by the clergy as well as by the laity. He saw that peace was altogether discarded by the princes of the world, who were engaged in incessant warlike contention and quarreling among themselves. He saw the wealth of the land being pillaged continuously. He saw many of the vanquished, wrongfully taken prisoner and very cruelly thrown into foulest dungeons, either ransomed for a high price or, tortured by the triple torments of hunger, thirst, and cold, blotted out by a death hidden from the world. He saw holy places violated; monasteries and villas burned. He saw that no one was spared of any human suffering, and that things divine and human alike were held in derision.

3. He heard, too, that the interior regions of Romania, where the Turks ruled over the Christians, had been perniciously subjected in a savage attack.[2] Moved by long-suffering compassion and by love of God's will, he descended the mountains to Gaul, and in Auvergne he called for a council to congregate from all sides at a suitable time at a city called Clermont. Three hundred and ten bishops and abbots, who had been advised beforehand by messengers, were present.

4. Then, on the day set aside for it, he called them together to himself and, in an eloquent address, carefully made the cause of the meeting known to them. In the plaintive voice of an aggrieved Church, he expressed great lamentation, and held a long discourse with them about the raging tempests of the world, which have been mentioned, because faith was undermined.

5. One after another, he beseechingly exhorted them all, with renewed faith, to spur themselves in great earnestness to overcome the Devil's devices and to try to restore the Holy Church, most unmercifully weakened by the wicked, to its former honorable status.

[1] Henry IV (1056–1106). Fulcher uses the term "so-called emperor," since Henry was not recognized as rightful emperor by adherents of Gregory VII and Urban II.
[2] This refers to the Seljuk conquest of Anatolia, probably to Manzikert, 1071.

II. The Decree of Pope Urban in the Council

1. "Most beloved brethren," he said, "by God's permission placed over the whole world with the papal crown, I, Urban, as the messenger of divine admonition, have been compelled by an unavoidable occasion to come here to you servants of God. I desired those whom I judged to be stewards of God's ministries to be true stewards and faithful, with all hypocrisy rejected.

2. "But with temperance in reason and justice being remote, I, with divine aid, shall strive carefully to root out any crookedness or distortion which might obstruct God's law. For the Lord appointed you temporarily as stewards over His family to serve it nourishment seasoned with a modest savor. Moreover, blessed will you be if at last the Overseer find you faithful.

3. "You are also called shepherds; see that you are not occupied after the manner of mercenaries. Be true shepherds, always holding your crooks in your hands; and sleeping not, guard on every side the flock entrusted to you.

4. "For if through your carelessness or negligence, some wolf seizes a sheep, you doubtless will lose the reward prepared for you by our Lord. Nay, first most cruelly beaten by the whips of the lictors,[3] you afterwards will be angrily cast into the keeping of a deadly place.

5. "Likewise, according to the evangelical sermon, you are the 'salt of the earth.' But if you fail, it will be disputed wherewith it was salted. O how much saltiness, indeed, is necessary for you to salt the people in correcting them with the salt of wisdom, people who are ignorant and panting with desire after the wantonness of the world; so that, unsalted, they might not be rotten with sins and stink whenever the Lord might wish to exhort them.

6. "For if because of the sloth of your management, He should find in them worms, that is, sin, straightway, He will order that they, despised, be cast into the dungheap. And because you could not make restoration for such a great loss, He will banish you, utterly condemned in judgment, from the familiarity of His love.

7. "It behooves saltiness of this kind to be wise, provident, temperate, learned, peace-making, truth-seeking, pious, just, equitable, pure. For how will the unlearned be able to make men learned, the intemperate make temperate, the impure make them pure? If one despises peace, how will he appease? Or if one has dirty hands, how will he be able to wipe the filth off another one defiled? For it is read, 'If the blind lead the blind, both shall fall into a ditch.'[4]

---

[3] Enforcers. Latin term for imperial bodyguards. [Ed.]
[4] Matthew 15:14.

8. "Set yourselves right before you do others, so that you can blamelessly correct your subjects. If you wish to be friends of God, gladly practice those things which you feel will please Him.

9. "Especially establish ecclesiastical affairs firm in their own right, so that no simoniac[5] heresy will take root among you. Take care lest the vendors and moneychangers, flayed by the scourges of the Lord, be miserably driven out into the narrow streets of destruction.

10. "Uphold the Church in its own ranks altogether free from all secular power. See that the tithes of all those who cultivate the earth are given faithfully to God; let them not be sold or held back.

11. "Let him who has seized a bishop be considered an outlaw. Let him who has seized or robbed monks, clerics, nuns and their servants, pilgrims, or merchants, be excommunicated. Let the robbers and burners of homes and their accomplices, banished from the Church, be smitten with excommunication.

12. "It must be considered very carefully, as Gregory says, by what penalty he must be punished who seizes other men's property, if he who does not bestow his own liberally is condemned to Hell. For so it happened to the rich man in the well-known Gospel, who on that account was not punished because he had taken away the property of others, but because he had misused that which he had received.

13. "And so by these iniquities, most beloved, you have seen the world disturbed too long; so long, as it was told to us by those reporting, that perhaps because of the weakness of your justice in some parts of your provinces, no one dares to walk in the streets with safety, lest he be kidnapped by robbers by day or thieves by night, either by force or trickery, at home or outside.

14. "Wherefore the Truce,[6] as it is commonly called, now for a long time established by the Holy Fathers, must be renewed. In admonition, I entreat you to adhere to it most firmly in your own bishopric. But if anyone affected by avarice or pride breaks it of his own free will, let him be excommunicated by God's authority and by the sanction of the decrees of this Holy Council."

III. The Pope's Exhortation Concerning the Expedition to Jerusalem

1. These and many other things having been suitably disposed of, all those present, both clergy and people, at the words of Lord Urban, the Pope, voluntarily gave thanks to God and confirmed by a faithful

---

[5] Buying or selling church offices. [Ed.]

[6] Truce of God—Cessation of all feuds from Wednesday evening to Monday morning in every week and during church festivals, ordered by the Church in 1041. This was proclaimed anew at the Council of Clermont.

promise that his decrees would be well kept. But straightway he added that another thing not less than the tribulation already spoken of, but even greater and more oppressive, was injuring Christianity in another part of the world, saying:

2. "Now that you, O sons of God, have consecrated yourselves to God to maintain peace among yourselves more vigorously and to uphold the laws of the Church faithfully, there is work to do, for you must turn the strength of your sincerity, now that you are aroused by divine correction, to another affair that concerns you and God. Hastening to the way, you must help your brothers living in the Orient, who need your aid for which they have already cried out many times.

3. "For, as most of you have been told, the Turks, a race of Persians,[7] who have penetrated within the boundaries of Romania[8] even to the Mediterranean to that point which they call the Arm of Saint George[9] in occupying more and more of the lands of the Christians, have overcome them, already victims of seven battles, and have killed and captured them, have overthrown churches, and have laid waste God's kingdom. If you permit this supinely for very long, God's faithful ones will be still further subjected.

4. "Concerning this affair, I, with suppliant prayer—not I, but the Lord—exhort you, heralds of Christ, to persuade all of whatever class, both knights and footmen, both rich and poor, in numerous edicts, to strive to help expel that wicked race from our Christian lands before it is too late.

5. "I speak to those present, I send word to those not here; moreover, Christ commands it. Remission of sins will be granted for those going thither, if they end a shackled life either on land or in crossing the sea, or in struggling against the heathen. I, being vested with that gift from God, grant this to those who go.

6. "O what a shame, if a people, so despised, degenerate, and enslaved by demons would thus overcome a people endowed with the trust of almighty God, and shining in the name of Christ! O how many evils will be imputed to you by the Lord Himself, if you do not help those who, like you, profess Christianity!

7. "Let those," he said, "who are accustomed to wage private wars wastefully even against Believers, go forth against the Infidels in a battle worthy to be undertaken now and to be finished in victory. Now, let those, who until recently existed as plunderers, be soldiers of Christ; now, let those, who formerly contended against brothers and relations,

[7] Really Seljuk Turks who conquered lands from east to west by way of Persia.

[8] Fulcher uses the term *Romania* to refer to the Anatolian as well as to the European provinces of the Byzantine Empire, but here, of course, he means the Anatolian. The Seljuks called the state which they founded here *Rum*.

[9] An eleventh-century term for the Bosporus, since it ran by St. George's monastery near Byzantium. [Ed.]

rightly fight barbarians; now, let those, who recently were hired for a few pieces of silver, win their eternal reward. Let those, who wearied themselves to the detriment of body and soul, labor for a twofold honor. Nay, more, the sorrowful here will be glad there, the poor here will be rich there, and the enemies of the Lord here will be His friends there.

8. "Let no delay postpone the journey of those about to go, but when they have collected the money owed to them and the expenses for the journey, and when winter has ended and spring has come, let them enter the crossroads courageously with the Lord going on before."

IV. The Bishop of Puy and the Events after the Council

1. After these words were spoken, the hearers were fervently inspired. Thinking nothing more worthy than such an undertaking, many in the audience solemnly promised to go, and to urge diligently those who were absent. There was among them one Bishop of Puy, Ademar by name, who afterwards, acting as vicar-apostolic, ruled the whole army of God wisely and thoughtfully, and spurred them to complete their undertaking vigorously.

2. So, the things that we have told you were well established and confirmed by everybody in the Council. With the blessing of absolution given, they departed; and after returning to their homes, they disclosed to those not knowing, what had taken place. As it was decreed far and wide throughout the provinces, they established the peace, which they call the Truce, to be upheld mutually by oath.

3. Many, one after another, of any and every occupation, after confession of their sins and with purified spirits, consecrated themselves to go where they were bidden.

4. Oh, how worthy and delightful to all of us who saw those beautiful crosses, either silken or woven of gold, or of any material, which the pilgrims sewed on the shoulders of their woolen cloaks or cassocks by the command of the Pope, after taking the vow to go. To be sure, God's soldiers, who were making themselves ready to battle for His honor, ought to have been marked and fortified with a sign of victory. And so by embroidering the symbol [of the cross] on their clothing in recognition of their faith, in the end they won the True Cross itself. They imprinted the ideal so that they might attain the reality of the ideal.

5. It is plain that good meditation leads to doing good work and that good work wins salvation of the soul. But, if it is good to mean well, it is better, after reflection, to carry out the good intention. So, it is best to win salvation through action worthy of the soul to be saved. Let each and everyone, therefore, reflect upon the good, that he makes better in fulfillment, so that, deserving it, he might finally receive the best, which does not diminish in eternity.

6. In such a manner Urban, a wise man and reverenced,
  Meditated a labor, whereby the world florescenced.[10]

For he renewed peace and restored the laws of the Church to their former standards; also he tried with vigorous instigation to expel the heathen from the lands of the Christians. And since he strove to exalt all things of God in every way, almost everyone gladly surrendered in obedience to his paternal care.

[10] Blossomed. [Ed.]

4

Chronicle of Solomon bar Simson, c. 1140

Jews and Christians lived in relative harmony in Western Europe for the first thousand years of Christianity. St. Augustine's view that Jews were the living embodiments of Old Testament Law, and his admonition that they should not be persecuted, shaped Christian thinking about Jews. Jews often lived in separate areas, similar to later ghettos, but there are accounts of Christians and Jews sharing in family celebrations and public events. One source of increasing tension came from the role of Jews as a more mercantile, educated, and entrepreneurial population. Christian restrictions on Jewish ownership of land led many Jews to invest in trade, finance, and education (even educating their daughters). Consequently, as monarchies grew stronger after 1000, kings and princes employed Jews as lawyers, doctors, accountants, administrators, and moneylenders. Christians were also moneylenders, but they were less successful and generally charged higher interest rates. Jewish moneylenders became easy scapegoats for kings and aristocrats in debt over their heads, rising Christian competitors, and the highly impressionable class of struggling, indebted poor.

Two other factors shifted the balance from peaceful accommodation to hostility after 1000, and they are both revealed in the previous reading: church reform and the Crusade. The kind of church reform that Urban II called for was part of a larger effort by the papacy to end not only corrupt behavior but also to weed out false doctrines and heresies: to purify the church spiritually as well as materially.

Source: "Chronicle of Solomon bar Simson," in *The Jews and the Crusaders: The Hebrew Chronicles of the First and Second Crusades*, ed. and trans. Shlomo Eidelberg (Madison: University of Wisconsin Press, 1977), 21–26.

The impact of the Crusade, or at least one impact of the Crusade, is described in the following selection by Solomon bar Simson. We know nothing else about the author. What do you know about him from the text? How would you describe what he recounts?

THINKING HISTORICALLY

How does the author explain the events that occurred? How would you explain the causes? What, if anything, has changed since 1084?

I will now recount the event of this persecution in other martyred communities as well—the extent to which they clung to the Lord, God of their fathers, bearing witness to His Oneness to their last breath.

In the year four thousand eight hundred and fifty-six, the year one thousand twenty-eight of our exile, in the eleventh year of the cycle Ranu, the year in which we anticipated salvation and solace, in accordance with the prophecy of Jeremiah: "Sing with gladness for Jacob, and shout at the head of the nations," etc.—this year turned instead to sorrow and groaning, weeping and outcry. Inflicted upon the Jewish People were the many evils related in all the admonitions; those enumerated in Scripture as well as those unwritten were visited upon us.

At this time arrogant people, a people of strange speech, a nation bitter and impetuous, Frenchmen and Germans, set out for the Holy City, which had been desecrated by barbaric nations, there to seek their house of idolatry and banish the Ishmaelites and other denizens of the land and conquer the land for themselves. They decorated themselves prominently with their signs, placing a profane symbol—a horizontal line over a vertical one—on the vestments of every man and woman whose heart yearned to go on the stray path to the grave of their Messiah. Their ranks swelled until the number of men, women, and children exceeded a locust horde covering the earth; of them it was said: "The locusts have no king [yet go they forth all of them by bands]."[1] Now it came to pass that as they passed through the towns where Jews dwelled, they said to one another: "Look now, we are going a long way to seek out the profane shrine and to avenge ourselves on the Ishmaelites, when here, in our very midst, are the Jews—they whose forefathers murdered and crucified him for no reason. Let us first avenge ourselves on them and exterminate them from among the nations so that the name of Israel will no longer be remembered, or let them adopt our faith and acknowledge the offspring of promiscuity."

When the Jewish communities became aware of their intentions, they resorted to the custom of our ancestors, repentance, prayer, and charity. The hands of the Holy Nation turned faint at this time, their

---

[1] Proverbs 30:27. [Ed.]

hearts melted, and their strength flagged. They hid in their innermost rooms to escape the swirling sword. They subjected themselves to great endurance, abstaining from food and drink for three consecutive days and nights, and then fasting many days from sunrise to sunset, until their skin was shriveled and dry as wood upon their bones. And they cried out loudly and bitterly to God.

But their Father did not answer them; He obstructed their prayers, concealing Himself in a cloud through which their prayers could not pass, and He abhorred their tent, and He removed them out of His sight—all of this having been decreed by Him to take place "in the day when I visit"; and this was the generation that had been chosen by Him to be His portion, for they had the strength and the fortitude to stand in His Sanctuary, and fulfill His word, and sanctify His Great Name in His world. It is of such as these that King David said: "Bless the Lord, ye angels of His, ye almighty in strength, that fulfil His word," etc.

That year, Passover fell on Thursday, and the New Moon of the following month, Iyar, fell on Friday and the Sabbath. On the eighth day of Iyar, on the Sabbath, the foe attacked the community of Speyer and murdered eleven holy souls who sanctified their Creator on the holy Sabbath and refused to defile themselves by adopting the faith of their foe. There was a distinguished, pious woman there who slaughtered herself in sanctification of God's Name. She was the first among all the communities of those who were slaughtered. The remainder were saved by the local bishop without defilement [i.e., baptism], as described above.

On the twenty-third of Iyar they attacked the community of Worms.[2] The community was then divided into two groups; some remained in their homes and others fled to the local bishop seeking refuge. Those who remained in their homes were set upon by the steppe-wolves who pillaged men, women, and infants, children, and old people. They pulled down the stairways and destroyed the houses, looting and plundering; and they took the Torah Scroll, trampled it in the mud, and tore and burned it. The enemy devoured the children of Israel with open maw.

Seven days later, on the New Moon of Sivan—the very day on which the Children of Israel arrived at Mount Sinai to receive the Torah—those Jews who were still in the court of the bishop were subjected to great anguish. The enemy dealt them the same cruelty as the first group and put them to the sword. The Jews, inspired by the valor of their brethren, similarly chose to be slain in order to sanctify the Name before the eyes of all, and exposed their throats for their heads to be severed for the glory of the Creator. There were also those who took their own lives, thus fulfilling the verse: "The mother was dashed in pieces with her children."[3] Fathers fell upon their sons, being slaughtered upon one another, and they slew one another—each man his kin, his wife and children;

---

[2] Town in the Holy Roman Empire (now Germany). [Ed.]
[3] Hosea 10:14. [Ed.]

bridegrooms slew their betrothed, and merciful women their only children. They all accepted the divine decree wholeheartedly and, as they yielded up their souls to the Creator, cried out: "Hear, O Israel, the Lord is our God, the Lord is One." The enemy stripped them naked, dragged them along, and then cast them off, sparing only a small number whom they forcibly baptized in their profane waters. The number of those slain during the two days was approximately eight hundred—and they were all buried naked. It is of these that the Prophet Jeremiah lamented: "They that were brought up in scarlet embrace dunghills."[4] I have already cited their names above. May God remember them for good.

[4] Lamentations 4:5. [Ed.]

5

IBN AL-ATHIR

A Muslim History of the First Crusade, 1231

Ibn al-Athir[1] (1160–1233) was one of the great Muslim historians. His multivolume history was for all intents a world history, from the time of Adam to his present. An ethnic Kurd, he spent most of his life in Mosul, Iraq, but he also lived in Aleppo and Damascus in Syria, where he fought for the army of Saladin. For his early history he borrowed heavily from the works of earlier Muslim historians.

What does the author's account suggest about Muslim attitudes toward Christians? In what ways were Muslims and Christians allies? In what ways were they enemies?

THINKING HISTORICALLY

When we are asking about the causes of something, we must decide when that something began. How is Ibn al-Athir's periodization different from that of Fulcher? If we begin the story when Ibn al-Athir does, how does that change the story? Which of the events described here would be likely to increase the enmity between Christians and Muslims?

[1] IH buhn ahl AH tuhr

Source: Francesco Gabrieli, *Arab Historians of the Crusades*, trans. E. J. Costello. Islamic World Series (Berkeley: University of California Press, 1969), 3–7.

The power of the Franks first became apparent when in the year 478/1085–86 they invaded the territories of Islām and took Toledo and other parts of Andalusia, as was mentioned earlier. Then in 484/1091 they attacked and conquered the island of Sicily and turned their attention to the African coast. Certain of their conquests there were won back again but they had other successes, as you will see.

In 490/1097 the Franks attacked Syria. This is how it all began: Baldwin, their King,[1] a kinsman of Roger the Frank who had conquered Sicily, assembled a great army and sent word to Roger saying: 'I have assembled a great army and now I am on my way to you, to use your bases for my conquest of the African coast. Thus you and I shall become neighbours.'

Roger called together his companions and consulted them about these proposals. 'This will be a fine thing both for them and for us!' they declared, 'for by this means these lands will be converted to the Faith!' At this Roger raised one leg and farted loudly, and swore that it was of more use than their advice. 'Why?' 'Because if this army comes here it will need quantities of provisions and fleets of ships to transport it to Africa, as well as reinforcements from my own troops. Then, if the Franks succeed in conquering this territory they will take it over and will need provisioning from Sicily. This will cost me my annual profit from the harvest. If they fail they will return here and be an embarrassment to me here in my own domain. As well as all this Tamīm[2] will say that I have broken faith with him and violated our treaty, and friendly relations and communications between us will be disrupted. As far as we are concerned, Africa is always there. When we are strong enough, we will take it.'

He summoned Baldwin's messenger and said to him: 'If you have decided to make war on the Muslims your best course will be to free Jerusalem from their rule and thereby win great honour. I am bound by certain promises and treaties of allegiance with the rulers of Africa.' So the Franks made ready and set out to attack Syria.

Another story is that the Fatimids of Egypt were afraid when they saw the Seljuqids extending their empire through Syria as far as Gaza, until they reached the Egyptian border and Atsiz[3] invaded Egypt itself. They therefore sent to invite the Franks to invade Syria and so protect Egypt from the Muslims.[4] But God knows best.

When the Franks decided to attack Syria they marched east to Constantinople, so that they could cross the straits and advance into Muslim

---

[1] Baldwin is a mythical character, compounded of the various Baldwins of Flanders and Jerusalem; or else the first Baldwin is mistakenly thought to have been already a king in the West.

[2] The Zirid amīr of Tunisia Tamīm ibn Muʿizz.

[3] A general of the Seljuqid Sultan Malikshāh, who in 1076 attacked Egypt from Palestine.

[4] Of course the Fatimids were also Muslims, but they were Shiʿa and so opposed to the rest of *sunni* Islām.

territory by the easier, land route. When they reached Constantinople, the Emperor of the East refused them permission to pass through his domains. He said: 'Unless you first promise me Antioch, I shall not allow you to cross into the Muslim empire.' His real intention was to incite them to attack the Muslims, for he was convinced that the Turks, whose invincible control over Asia Minor he had observed, would exterminate every one of them. They accepted his conditions and in 490/1097 they crossed the Bosphorus at Constantinople. Iconium and the rest of the area into which they now advanced belonged to Qilij Arslān ibn Sulaimān ibn Qutlumísh, who barred their way with his troops. They broke through in rajab 490/July 1097, crossed Cilicia, and finally reached Antioch, which they besieged.

When Yaghi Siyān, the ruler of Antioch, heard of their approach, he was not sure how the Christian people of the city would react, so he made the Muslims go outside the city on their own to dig trenches, and the next day sent the Christians out alone to continue the task. When they were ready to return home at the end of the day he refused to allow them. 'Antioch is yours,' he said, 'but you will have to leave it to me until I see what happens between us and the Franks.' 'Who will protect our children and our wives?' they said. 'I shall look after them for you.' So they resigned themselves to their fate, and lived in the Frankish camp for nine months, while the city was under siege.

Yaghi Siyān showed unparalleled courage and wisdom, strength and judgment. If all the Franks who died had survived they would have overrun all the lands of Islām. He protected the families of the Christians in Antioch and would not allow a hair of their heads to be touched.

After the siege had been going on for a long time the Franks made a deal with one of the men who were responsible for the towers. He was a cuirass-maker called Ruzbih whom they bribed with a fortune in money and lands. He worked in the tower that stood over the river-bed, where the river flowed out of the city into the valley. The Franks sealed their pact with the cuirass-maker, God damn him! and made their way to the water-gate. They opened it and entered the city. Another gang of them climbed the tower with ropes. At dawn, when more than 500 of them were in the city and the defenders were worn out after the night watch, they sounded their trumpets. Yaghi Siyān woke up and asked what the noise meant. He was told that trumpets had sounded from the citadel and that it must have been taken. In fact the sound came not from the citadel but from the tower. Panic seized Yaghi Siyān and he opened the city gates and fled in terror, with an escort of thirty pages. His army commander arrived, but when he discovered on enquiry that Yaghi Siyān had fled, he made his escape by another gate. This was of great help to the Franks, for if he had stood firm for an hour, they would have been wiped out. They entered the city by the gates and sacked it, slaughtering all the Muslims they found there. This happened in jumada I (491/April/May

1098). As for Yaghi Siyān, when the sun rose he recovered his self control and realized that his flight had taken him several *farsakh*[5] from the city. He asked his companions where he was, and on hearing that he was four *farsakh* from Antioch he repented of having rushed to safety instead of staying to fight to the death. He began to groan and weep for his desertion of his household and children. Overcome by the violence of his grief he fell fainting from his horse. His companions tried to lift him back into the saddle, but they could not get him to sit up, and so left him for dead while they escaped. He was at his last gasp when an Armenian shepherd came past, killed him, cut off his head and took it to the Franks at Antioch.

The Franks had written to the rulers of Aleppo and Damascus to say that they had no interest in any cities but those that had once belonged to Byzantium. This was a piece of deceit calculated to dissuade these rulers from going to the help of Antioch.

[5] One *farsakh* is about four miles.

6

IBN AL-ATHIR

The Conquest of Jerusalem, c. 1231

In this selection from Ibn al-Athir's history, he takes the story of the First Crusade from the Western conquest of Aleppo to the Crusaders' conquest of Jerusalem. Notice, however, that the Seljuk control of Jerusalem was challenged before the Christian armies arrived. What does this part of the history tell you about relations between Christians and Muslims in 1098 and 1099?

THINKING HISTORICALLY

If you were to date the rise of Christian-Muslim enmity from the period of the First Crusade, the pertinent period, year, or event might vary for Christians and Muslims. At what point between 1095 and 1099 did Christians become anti-Muslim? When were Muslims likely to become anti-Christian? How were the triggers of each response different?

Source: Francesco Gabrieli, ed., *Arab Historians of the Crusades: Selected and Translated from the Arabic Sources*, ed. and trans. E. J. Costello. Islamic World Series (Berkeley: University of California Press, 1969), 10–12.

Taj ad-Daula Tutūsh was the Lord of Jerusalem but had given it as a feoff to the amīr Suqmān ibn Artūq the Turcoman. When the Franks defeated the Turks at Antioch the massacre demoralized them, and the Egyptians, who saw that the Turkish armies were being weakened by desertion, besieged Jerusalem under the command of al-Afdal ibn Badr al-Jamali. Inside the city were Artūq's sons, Suqmān and Ilghazi, their cousin Sunij and their nephew Yaquti. The Egyptians brought more than forty siege engines to attack Jerusalem and broke down the walls at several points. The inhabitants put up a defense, and the siege and fighting went on for more than six weeks. In the end the Egyptians forced the city to capitulate, in Sha'bān 491 [August 1098]. Suqmān, Ilghazi, and their friends were well treated by al-Afdal, who gave them large gifts of money and let them go free. They made for Damascus and then crossed the Euphrates. Suqmān settled in Edessa and Ilghazi went on into Iraq. The Egyptian governor of Jerusalem was a certain Iftikhār ad-Daula, who was still there at the time of which we are speaking.

After their vain attempt to take Acre by siege, the Franks moved on to Jerusalem and besieged it for more than six weeks. They built two towers, one of which, near Sion, the Muslims burnt down, killing everyone inside it. It had scarcely ceased to burn before a messenger arrived to ask for help and to bring the news that the other side of the city had fallen. In fact Jerusalem was taken from the north on the morning of Friday 22 Sha'bān 492 [July 15, 1099]. The population was put to the sword by the Franks, who pillaged the area for a week. A band of Muslims barricaded themselves into the Oratory of David and fought on for several days. They were granted their lives in return for surrendering. The Franks honoured their word, and the group left by night for Ascalon. In the Masjid al-Aqsa the Franks slaughtered more than 70,000 people, among them a large number of Imams and Muslim scholars, devout and ascetic men who had left their homelands to live lives of pious seclusion in the Holy Place. The Franks stripped the Dome of the Rock of more than forty silver candelabra, each of them weighing 3,600 drams, and a great silver lamp weighing forty-four Syrian pounds, as well as a hundred and fifty smaller silver candelabra and more than twenty gold ones, and a great deal more booty. Refugees from Syria reached Baghdād in Ramadan,[1] among them the qadi Abu Sa'd al-Hárawi. They told the Caliph's ministers a story that wrung their hearts and brought tears to their eyes. On Friday they went to the Cathedral Mosque and begged for help, weeping so that their hearers wept with them as they described the sufferings of the Muslims in that Holy City:

---

[1] The holy month of Ramadan, the month of fasting. [Ed.]

the men killed, the women and children taken prisoner, the homes pillaged. Because of the terrible hardships they had suffered, they were allowed to break the fast. . . .

It was the discord between the Muslim princes, as we shall describe, that enabled the Franks to overrun the country. Abu l-Muzaffar al-Abiwardi composed several poems on this subject, in one of which he says:

> We have mingled blood with flowing tears, and there is no room
>   left in us for Pity.
> To shed tears is a man's worst weapon when the swords stir up the
>   embers of war.
> Sons of Islām, behind you are battles in which heads rolled at
>   your feet.
> Dare you slumber in the blessed shade of safety, where life is as
>   soft as an orchard flower?
> How can the eye sleep between the lids at a time of disasters that
>   would waken any sleeper?
> While your Syrian brothers can only sleep on the backs of their
>   chargers, or in vultures' bellies!
> Must the foreigners feed on our ignominy, while you trail behind
>   you the train of a pleasant life, like men whose world is at peace?
> When blood has been spilt, when sweet girls must for shame hide
>   their lovely faces in their hands!
> When the white swords' points are red with blood, and the iron of
>   the brown lances is stained with gore!
> At the sound of sword hammering on lance young children's hair
>   turns white.
> This is war, and the man who shuns the whirlpool to save his life
>   shall grind his teeth in penitence.
> This is war, and the infidel's sword is naked in his hand, ready to
>   be sheathed again in men's necks and skulls.
> This is war, and he who lies in the tomb at Medina seems to raise
>   his voice and cry: "O sons of Hashim!
> I see my people slow to raise the lance against the enemy: I see the
>   Faith resting on feeble pillars.
> For fear of death the Muslims are evading the fire of battle, refus-
>   ing to believe that death will surely strike them."
> Must the Arab champions then suffer with resignation, while the
>   gallant Persians shut their eyes to their dishonour?

Letter from a Jewish Pilgrim in Egypt, 1100

This is a letter from an Egyptian Jew who wanted to travel to
Jerusalem between 1098 and 1100, but he was continually
frustrated by events there. What were those frustrations? What
does the writer's description of, and response to, those frustrations
tell you about his attitude toward Muslims and Christians? How
does the writer compare the Egyptian conquest of Jerusalem with
that of the Crusaders?

THINKING HISTORICALLY

What long-term factors of daily life suggested here would have likely
led this Jew to be more or less comfortable with Muslims? What
immediate experiences described here would have increased or
lessened those feelings?

In Your Name, You Merciful.

If I attempted to describe my longing for you, my Lord, my brother
and cousin,—may God prolong your days and make permanent your
honour, success, happiness, health, and welfare; and . . . subdue your
enemies—all the paper in the world would not suffice. My longing
will but increase and double, just as the days will grow and double.
May *the Creator of the World* presently make us meet together in joy
when I return under His guidance to my homeland *and to the inheritance of my Fathers* in complete happiness, *so that we rejoice and be
happy through His great mercy and His vast bounty; and thus may be
His will*!

You may remember, my Lord, that many years ago I left our country to seek God's mercy and help in my poverty, to behold Jerusalem
and return thereupon. However, when I was in Alexandria God brought
about circumstances which caused a slight delay. Afterwards, however,
"the sea grew stormy," and many armed bands made their appearance
in Palestine; "*and he who went forth and he who came had no peace,*"
so that hardly one survivor out of a whole group came back to us from
Palestine and told us that scarcely anyone could save himself from
those armed bands, since they were so numerous and were gathered

---

Source: S. D. Goitein, trans., "Contemporary Letters on the Capture of Jerusalem by the Crusaders," *Journal of Jewish Studies* 3, no. 4 (1952): 162–77.

round . . . every town. There was further the journey through the desert, among [the bedouins] and whoever escaped from the one, fell into the hands of the other. Moreover, mutinies [spread throughout the country and reached] even Alexandria, so that we ourselves were besieged several times and the city was ruined; . . . the end however *was good*, for the Sultan—may God bestow glory upon his victories—conquered the city and caused justice to abound in it in a manner unprecedented in the history of any king in the world; not even a dirham was looted from anyone. Thus I had come to hope that because of his justice and strength God would give the land into his hands, and I should thereupon go to Jerusalem in safety and tranquility. For this reason I proceeded from Alexandria to Cairo, in order to start [my journey] from there.

When, however, God had given Jerusalem, the blessed, into his hands this state of affairs continued for too short a time to allow for making a journey there. The Franks arrived and killed everybody in the city, whether of *Ishmael or of Israel*; and the few who survived the slaughter were made prisoners. Some of these have been ransomed since, while others are still in captivity in all parts of the world.

Now, all of us had anticipated that our Sultan—may God bestow glory upon his victories—would set out against them [the Franks] with his troops and chase them away. But time after time our hope failed. Yet, to this very present moment we do hope that God will give his [the Sultan's] enemies into his hands. For it is inevitable that the armies will join in battle this year; and, if God grants us victory through him [the Sultan] and he conquers Jerusalem—and so it may be, with God's will—I for one shall not be amongst those who will linger, but shall go there to behold the city; and shall afterwards return straight to you—if God wills it. My salvation is in God, for this [is unlike] the other previous occasions [of making a pilgrimage to Jerusalem]. God, indeed, will exonerate me, since at my age I cannot afford to delay and wait any longer; I want to return home under any circumstances, if I still remain alive—whether I shall have seen Jerusalem or have given up the hope of doing it—both of which are possible.

You know, of course, my Lord, what has happened to us in the course of the last five years: the plague, the illnesses, and ailments have continued unabated for four successive years. As a result of this the wealthy became impoverished and a great number of people died *of the plague*, so that entire families perished in it. I, too, was affected with a grave illness, from which I recovered only about a year ago; then I was taken ill the following year so that (on the margin) for four years I have remained. . . . He who has said: *The evil diseases of Egypt* . . . he who hiccups does not live . . . ailments and will die . . . otherwise . . . will remain alive.

8

Ecclesia and Synagoga, c. 1230

For the first thousand years of Christianity, most Christians followed the view of Augustine that Jews, as the receivers of the Old Testament, were the "living letters of the Law"; as such, they deserved respect and were not to be persecuted. Medieval Christian paintings made no distinction between Jews and Christians in appearance. But Christian attitudes toward Jews became increasingly hostile during the Crusades and the simultaneous papal campaigns to clarify Christian doctrine and punish heresy.

One of the traditional medieval Christian ways of portraying the relationship between Christianity and Judaism was to personify each as a beautiful woman beside the cross at the crucifixion. The woman who personified the Church (Ecclesia in Latin) stood to the right of the Jesus, with a chalice that caught the blood flowing from a wound caused by the lance of a Roman soldier. The other was a personification of Judaism, or the people of the Synagogue (Synagoga in Latin). She was also young and beautiful, but she stood at the left of the dying Jesus, often looking away.

This selection shows the next development of Ecclesia and Synagoga imagery: statues on each side of the main entrance to a church (Figures 10.1 and 10.2), in this case the thirteenth-century cathedral in Strassburg. How can you tell which is Ecclesia and which is Synagoga? What symbols are used to indicate their identities? How does the artist show increased criticism of Judaism? How does the artist still show respect for Judaism?

THINKING HISTORICALLY

St. Paul in a letter to the Greeks of Corinth wrote (II Corinthians 3:13–16)

13 We are not like Moses, who would put a veil over his face to prevent the Israelites from seeing the end of what was passing away.

14 But their minds were made dull, for to this day the same veil remains when the old covenant is read. It has not been removed, because only in Christ is it taken away.

15 Even to this day when Moses is read, a veil covers their hearts.

16 But whenever anyone turns to the Lord, the veil is taken away.

How might this passage have influenced the artist in depicting Synagoga?

Earlier images of Synagoga do not show this influence. What could be the cause of that?

Figure 10.1 Statue of Ecclesia.
Source: Foto Marburg / Art Resource, NY.

Figure 10.2 Statue of Synagoga.
Source: © Bildarchiv Monheim GmbH / Alamy Stock Photo.

■ REFLECTIONS

Historians study change. We ask how things change. We also ask about continuity (how things remain the same), but only because we know nothing remains the same forever. We try to find the causes of particular changes and periods of continuity. Understanding causation is perhaps the skill most intrinsic to the study of history.

We have seen that Christians were not always hostile to Jews, nor were all Christians hostile toward Muslims, even in the period of the First Crusade. We have seen Muslims and Jews living amicably side by side, Jews invited to live with and protected by Christian bishops; and we have seen cases of violent antagonism.

To recognize this diversity is only a start, however. Nothing is learned by throwing up one's hands and declaring the diversity of human nature. Human nature tells us nothing about human history. The study of history calls us to pose more useful questions: How should we weigh Pope Urban's political versus religious motives for launching the Crusade? Why did the German city of Speyer invite Jews in 1084 and then allow them to be killed by Crusaders in 1095? What changed in Speyer between 1084 and 1095? How do we account for the cooperation between Muslim and Christian armies described by Ibn al-Athir? When did Muslim hostility to Christians harden? Was it the Christian massacre of Muslims in Jerusalem in 1095? Why did Jews seem comfortable with Muslim rule?

Even when we cannot answer these questions definitively, we have left the realm of intractable conflict for an examination of possibilities: possible explanations of the past and possible solutions in the future.

11

Raiders of Steppe and Sea: Vikings and Mongols

Eurasia and the Atlantic, 900–1350

■ HISTORICAL CONTEXT

Ever since the first urban settlements emerged five thousand years ago, they have been at risk of attack. The domestication of the horse and the development of sailing ships about four thousand years ago increased that risk. Much of ancient history is the story of the conflict between settled peoples and raiders on horseback or sailors on fleet ships. Eventually—between the third and fifth centuries C.E.—the great empires of Rome and Han dynasty China succumbed to raiding nomadic tribes from Central Asia. As nomadic peoples settled themselves, new waves of raiders appeared.

In the previous chapter, we explored the impact of the Seljuk Turks who conquered cities in the Middle East that had been taken hundreds of years earlier by Arab armies on horseback. At about the same time as the Turks emerged from Central Asia to threaten settlements south of the great Eurasian steppe grasslands, a new force from the north, Viking raiders on sailing ships, burst across the northern seas to attack the coastal enclaves and river cities of Europe and what came to be known in their wake as Russia. As generations oscillated between raiding and trading, new waves of Norsemen explored the edges of known waters to plant new settlements as far west as Iceland, Greenland, and North America. (See Map 11.1.) Who were these people? What did they hope to accomplish? How were they different from the land-raiders who preceded them?

At about the time that the Vikings were becoming farmers and settlers in their conquered lands, around the year 1200, the Eurasian steppe exploded with its last and largest force of nomadic tribesmen

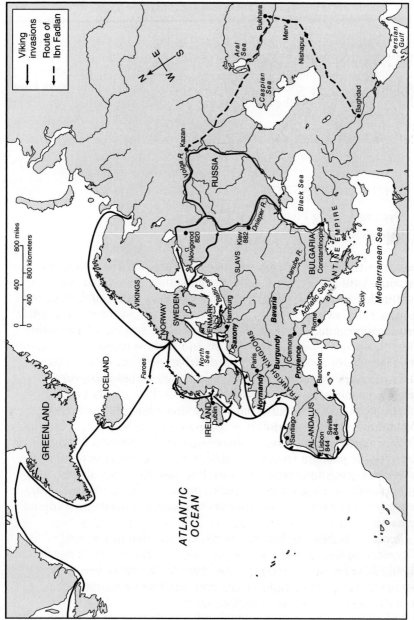

Map 11.1 Viking Invasions and Voyages of the Ninth and Tenth Centuries.

on horseback: the Mongols. Between the election of Genghis Khan*
(c. 1162–1227) as the Khan of Khans in 1206 and the pandemic
plague known as the Black Death of 1346–1350 (or the end of the
Mongol Yuan dynasty in China in 1368), the Mongols swept across
Eurasia and created the largest empire the world had ever seen. (See
Map 11.2.) Who were the Mongols? What made them so successful?
How were they similar to, and different from, the Norsemen?

What was the impact of these raiding peoples on settled societies?
How did they change each other? How did they change themselves? How
did they create some of the conditions necessary for the modern world to
come into being?

■ THINKING HISTORICALLY

Distinguishing Historical Understanding from Moral Judgments

The ancient Greeks called non-Greeks "barbarians" (because their
languages contained "bar-bar"-like sounds that seemed foreign,
untutored, and, thus, uncivilized). Since then the terms *barbarian* and
civilized have been weighted with the same combination of descriptive
and moral meaning. In the nineteenth century it was even fashionable
among historians and anthropologists to use these terms to distinguish
between nomadic peoples and settled, urban peoples. As our first
reading (and perhaps modern common sense) makes clear, rural or
nomadic people are not necessarily less "moral" than city people;
technological development is hardly the same thing as moral
development (or the opposite).

What connection, if any, is there between history and morality?
Stories of the past are frequently used to celebrate or condemn past
individuals or groups. Sometimes we find past behavior shocking or
reprehensible. Is it logical or proper to make moral judgments about
the past? Can historians find answers to moral questions by studying
the past?

Perhaps the place to begin is by recognizing that just as the "is" is
different from the "ought," so too the "was" is different from the
"should have been." Historians must begin by finding out what was. Our
own moral values may lead us to ask certain questions about the past,
but the historian's job is only to find out what happened. We will see in
the following selections how difficult it has been for past observers to
keep their own moral judgments from coloring their descriptions of

* geng GIHZ kahn

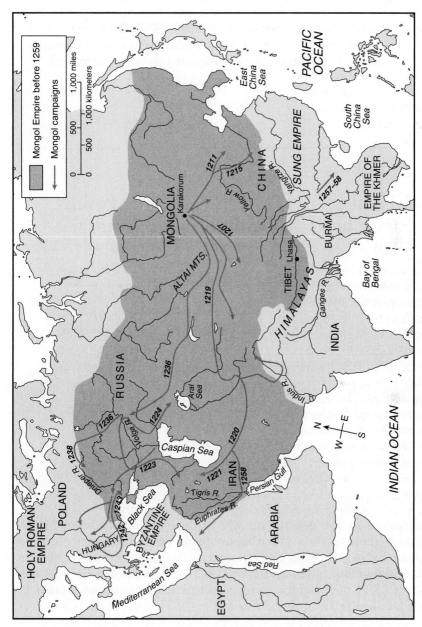

Map 11.2 Mongol Invasions of the Thirteenth Century.

peoples and events they found disagreeable. This part of our study may help us realize how our own moral feelings affect our responses.

Then, assuming we have established the facts fairly, can our moral sentiments legitimately come into play? As "consumers" of history, readers, and thinking people, we cannot avoid making judgments about the past. Under what conditions are such judgments fair, helpful, or appropriate? We will explore this much larger and more complex question in this chapter.

GREGORY GUZMAN

Were the Barbarians a Negative or Positive Factor in Ancient and Medieval History? 1988

Gregory Guzman is a modern world historian. In this essay he asks some questions about the peoples who have been called "barbarians." How were the lives of pastoral nomads different from those of settled people? How did the horse shape life on the steppe? How effective were these herders as rulers of settled societies? What were the achievements of the pastoral nomads?

THINKING HISTORICALLY

Why, according to Guzman, have most histories of the barbarians made them look bad? How have city people or historians let their own prejudices block an appreciation of the achievements of pastoralists?

According to the general surveys of ancient and medieval history found in most textbooks, barbarian peoples and/or primitive savages repeatedly invaded the early Eurasian civilized centers in Europe, the Middle East, India, and China. All accounts of the early history of these four civilizations contain recurrent references to attacks by such familiar and famous barbarians as the Hittites, Hyksos, Kassites,

Source: Gregory Guzman, "Were the Barbarians a Negative or Positive Factor in Ancient and Medieval History?" *The Historian* 50 (August 1988): 558–72.

Aryans, Scythians, Sarmatians, Hsiung-nu, Huns, Germans, Turks, and Mongols, and they also record the absorption and assimilation of these Inner Asian barbarian hordes into the respective cultures and lifestyles of the more advanced coastal civilizations. The early sources generally equate the barbarians with chaos and destruction. The barbarians are presented as evil and despicable intruders, associated only with burning, pillaging, and slaughtering, while the civilized peoples are portrayed as the good and righteous forces of stability, order, and progress.

But it must be remembered that most of these early sources are not objective; they are blatantly one-sided, biased accounts written by members of the civilized societies. Thus, throughout recorded history, barbarians have consistently received bad press—bad PR to use the modern terminology. By definition, barbarians were illiterate, and thus they could not write their own version of events. All written records covering barbarian-civilized interaction came from the civilized peoples at war with the barbarians—often the sedentary peoples recently defeated and overwhelmed by those same barbarians. Irritated and angered coastal historians tended to record and emphasize only the negative aspects of their recent interaction with the barbarians. These authors tended to condemn and denigrate the way their barbarian opponents looked and to associate them with the devil and evil, rather than to report with objectivity what actually happened. For example, the Roman historian Ammianus Marcellinus, whose description is distorted by hatred and fear, described the barbarians as "two-footed beasts, seemingly chained to their horses from which they take their meat and drink, never touching a plough and having no houses." While living in Jerusalem, St. Jerome also left a vivid description of the Huns who ". . . filled the whole earth with slaughter and panic alike as they flittered hither and thither on their swift horses. . . . They were at hand everywhere before they were expected; by their speed they outstripped rumor, and they took pity neither upon religion nor rank nor age nor wailing childhood. Those who had just begun to live were compelled to die. . . ."

Such reports obviously made the barbarians look bad, while their nomadic habits and practices, which differed from those of the sedentary coastal peoples, were clearly portrayed as inferior and less advanced: the incarnation of evil itself. These horror-filled and biased descriptions were not the accounts of weak and defenseless peoples. Rather, they were written by the citizens of the most advanced and powerful states and empires in Europe, the Middle East, India, and China. The individual barbarian tribes were, nevertheless, able to attack and invade these strong and well-organized civilized states with relative impunity— pillaging and killing almost at will.

Several important questions, not addressed by the ancient and medieval historians, need to be answered here. Who were these barbarians? Why and how did they manage to repeatedly defeat and overwhelm so easily the wealthiest and most advanced civilizations of the day? And why were they so vehemently condemned and hated in recorded history, if these barbarian Davids were able to consistently defeat such mighty Goliath civilized centers? Since the rich and populous civilized states enjoyed tremendous advantages in the confrontations, why have the barbarians so often been denied the popular role of the underdog?

In the process of answering those questions, this study would like to suggest that maybe the barbarians were not really the "bad guys." While they may not deserve to be called the "good guys," they made a much more positive contribution to human civilization than presented in the grossly distorted written sources. The barbarians deserve much more credit than they have been given, for they created a complex pastoral lifestyle as an alternative to sedentary agriculture, and in that achievement they were not subhuman savages only out to loot, pillage, and destroy. As this study will show, the barbarians played a much more positive and constructive role in the development and diffusion of early human history than that with which they are usually credited.

Before proceeding further, it is necessary to identify these much-maligned barbarians and describe how their way of life and their basic practices differed from those of the sedentary coastal peoples in order to better evaluate the barbarian role and its impact on the history of humanity.

In terms of identity, the barbarians were the steppe nomads of Inner Asia or Central Eurasia. This area represents one of the toughest and most inhospitable places in the world in which to survive. The climate of the interior of the large Eurasian landmass is not moderated by the distant seas, resulting in extremes of climate, of hot and cold, wet and dry. It is an area of ice, forest, desert, and mountains—with bitter winds, dust, and poor soil. Unlike the coastal regions with their dependable moisture and warmth, the soil of Inner Asia was too cold, poor, and dry for agriculture; thus the sedentary urban lifestyle of the coastal civilized centers was not an option in the Eurasian heartland. The people living there had to be tough to endure such a hostile environment, where they constantly fought both nature and other people for survival.

Due to necessity, the people of Inner Asia were nomads, wandering in search of food and pasture, and they became herdsmen, shepherds, and warriors. These steppe nomads, the barbarians of recorded history, were frequently nothing more than migrants looking for new homes; these people needed little encouragement to seek safety, security, and better living conditions in the warm, rich, and fertile coastal civilization centers. Thus the steppe barbarians were not always savage marauders coming only to loot and pillage. Many of the so-called barbarian invaders constituted a surplus population which harsh Inner Asia could not support, or they represented whole tribes being pushed out of their ancestral homeland by stronger tribes behind them. At any rate, these repeated waves of nomadic peoples leaving the steppes soon encountered the coastal civilizations.

These Inner Asian barbarians were more or less harmless outsiders until the horse dramatically changed their lifestyle on the vast steppes. They adopted the pastoral system as the best way of providing for basic needs. The natural pasture provided by the steppe grassland proved ideal for grazing large herds and flocks of animals. Soon their whole life revolved around their animals; they became shepherds, herders, and keepers of beasts. . . .

The dominant feature of this emerging barbarian pastoralism was its mounted nature; it was essentially a horse culture by 1000 B.C. At first small horses were kept only for food and milk, but bigger horses eventually led to riding. Once an accomplished fact, mounted practices dramatically changed the lifestyle of the barbarian steppe peoples. Horseback riding made the tending of scattered herds faster and less tiring, and it enlarged the size of herds while increasing the range of pastoral movement. It also made possible, when necessary, the total migration of entire tribes and clans. Mastery of the horse reduced the vast expanses of steppe pasturage to more manageable proportions. Steppe nomads moved twice a year between traditional winter and summer pastures; the spring and fall were spent moving between the necessary grazing grounds. All peoples and possessions moved with regularity; the nomads became used to living in the saddle, so to speak.

The horse thus became the center of pastoral life on the steppes. The barbarian nomads could literally live off their animals which provided meat, milk, and hides for clothing, coverings, boots, etc. Tools and weapons were made from the bones and sinews, and dried dung was used as fuel. The barbarians ate, sold, negotiated, slept, and took care of body functions in the saddle. . . . These mounted practices led to the emergence of the centaur motif in Middle Eastern art, as the civilized people tended to view the horse and rider as one inseparable unit.

Military action also became an integral part of nomadic steppe life. Warfare was simply cavalry action by the pastoral herdsmen who served as soldiers for the duration of the conflict. Steppe military service differed little from the normal, on-the-move pastoral life. Large-scale steppe alliances were hard to organize and even harder to hold together among the independent nomads. Such temporary alliances, called hordes, rose swiftly to great strength and power, but they usually declined and disintegrated just as quickly.

At any rate, these barbarian nomads were tough and hardy warriors. The horse gave them speed and mobility over both the light and heavily armed infantry of the civilized centers, but for this speed and mobility the barbarians gave up any type of defensive armor. They learned to guide their horses with their knees, since both arms needed to be free for the bow and arrow, their primary offensive weapon. . . .

Early civilized armies had no cavalry. The famous Macedonian phalanx and the formidable Roman legions contained only light and heavily armed infantry. At first these brave foot soldiers had no tactical maneuvers to face and contain a barbarian cavalry charge. Even more devastating was the storm of arrows raining down upon them long before they could engage in the traditional hand-to-hand combat. The formidable steppe cavalry thus subjected civilized defenses to continuous pressure. Every nomad with a horse and bow was a potential frontline soldier who was tough, resourceful, and ferocious, whereas only a small percentage of the civilized population was equipped and trained for war. The nomadic lifestyle and the speed of the horse eliminated the need for expensive and heavy metal armor and its accompanying technological skills. Cavalry tactics gave an initial military advantage to the barbarians and the mounted horsemen won most of the early battles. The best defense against barbarian cavalry was an insurmountable obstacle, a wall. . . .

Since they had the military advantage of cavalry tactics, the steppe nomads attacked and conquered various coastal civilizations with regularity. In a typical conquest, the victorious barbarians were the new military/political rulers. These new rulers possessed strengths obvious to all. The barbarians had vigorous and dynamic leadership; good, able, and charismatic leadership had been needed to organize the independent nomads into an effective horde in the first place. The new rulers had the complete loyalty of their followers; their group identity based on common blood and ancestors resulted in an intense personal and individual allegiance and commitment.

The first century after the initial conquest was usually an era of dynamic leadership, good government, and economic prosperity, as nomadic strengths mixed with the local advances and practices of that civilization. The new ruling family was often a fusion of the best of both sides as the barbarian victors married into the previous ruling dynasty. This brought forth an age of powerful and successful rulers, and produced an era of energetic leadership, good government, low taxes, agricultural revival, and peace. . . .

After this early period of revitalized and dynamic rule, slow decline usually set in. Royal vigor and ability sank as the rulers became soft, both mentally and physically. Without physical exercise and self-discipline, the rulers became overindulgent, instantly acquiring everything they wanted—excessive amounts of food or drink, harems, puppets, and yes-men as advisers. At the same time court rivalries and internal divisiveness began to emerge once the strong unity required for the conquest was no longer needed. A rivalry that often arose was between the ruler and various groups of his followers. . . . His steppe horsemen began to give first loyalty to their new family land rather than to their individual leader who was now weak, impaired, and soft. Such internal rivalries weakened the central government and led to chaos and civil wars. Thus, a civilized center was ripe for the next series of invasions and conquest. . . .

The barbarians can and should be viewed as representing a dynamic and vital element in human history for they periodically revived many stagnating coastal civilizations. Many of these sedentary centers flourished, growing rich and powerful. In the process they also became conservative, settled into a fixed routine. Preferring the status quo, they tended to use old answers and ways to face new problems and issues, and as a consequence they lost the vitality and flexibility required for healthy and progressive growth.

The barbarians were active and dynamic. In their conquests of civilized centers, they frequently destroyed and eliminated the old and outdated and preserved and passed on only the good and useful elements. Sometimes, the mounted invaders also introduced new ideas and practices. Some of these new barbarian innovations (horseback riding, archery, trousers, and boots, etc.) fused with the good and useful practices of the sedentary peoples. . . . The ongoing encounters with barbarian strangers inevitably fostered innovation and progress in the civilized centers. . . .

It can be argued that barbarians also played a positive role in the spread and diffusion of civilization itself. The four major Eurasian civilization centers were separated from each other by deserts, mountains, and the vast expanses of the steppe heartland of Inner Asia. In its early stages each civilization was somewhat isolated from the others. Overland trade and contact was possible only through the barbarian steppe highway which stretched over five thousand miles across Eurasia, from Hungary to Manchuria. There was little early sea contact between the four sedentary centers, as naval travel was longer and more dangerous than the overland routes.

Thus the steppe barbarians were the chief agency through which the ideas and practices of one civilization were spread to another before 1500 A.D. According to [historian] William H. McNeill, there was much conceptual diffusion carried along the steppe highway by the barbarians. Writing originated in the ancient Middle East. The concept, not the form, of writing then spread eastward from the Middle East, as the Indian and Chinese forms and characters were significantly different than Middle Eastern cuneiform. The making and use of bronze and chariots also spread from the Middle East to Europe, India, and China. Chariots were introduced to China, on the eastern end of the steppe highway, a few centuries after their appearance in the Middle East. Needless to say, this type of early cultural diffusion is difficult to document with any degree of certainty, but enough evidence exists to make it highly probable, even if not scientifically provable.

The late medieval period provides even more examples of cultural diffusion via the movement of barbarians along the Inner Asian steppe highway. The great Eurasian *Pax Mongolica*[1] opened the way for much cultural cross-fertilization in the late-thirteenth and early-fourteenth centuries. Chinese inventions like gunpowder and printing made their way to the Middle East and Europe in this period. Records show that Chinese artillerymen accompanied the Mongol armies into the Middle East. Papal envoys like John of Plano Carpini and William of Rubruck traveled to the Mongol capital of Karakorum in the 1240s and 1250s. In the 1280s, Marco Polo brought with him from Kublai Khan's court in China a Mongol princess to be the bride of the Mongol Khan of Persia. . . .

This cultural interaction and exchange between Eurasian coastal civilizations ended with the collapse of the Mongol Khanates in Persia and China in the mid-fourteenth century. The barbarian Mongols, therefore, provided the last period of great cultural cross-fertilization before the modern age.

Historical evidence that exists enables one to argue that the barbarian nomads played an active and positive role in the history of mankind. The barbarian invaders revitalized stagnant and decaying civilizations and were responsible for a certain amount of cultural diffusion between emerging ancient and medieval civilizations. The traditional portrayal of barbarians as mere marauders and destroyers is misleading and incorrect. Unfortunately this is the usual role they are given when historians center their study of the past narrowly on the civilized centers and the biased written sources produced by those peoples. All too often historians tend to adopt and reflect the biases and values of their subjects under study, and thus continue to denigrate and condemn all barbarians without objectively evaluating their real contributions to human development. The study of the steppe nomads, the barbarians, is just as valid a topic for historical analysis as the traditional study of coastal sedentary civilizations. Only by knowing and understanding the pastoral barbarian can historians accurately evaluate the constant interaction between the two lifestyles and come to understand the full picture of humanity's early growth and development in the ancient and medieval periods of Eurasian history.

[1] Mongolian Peace, after the *Pax Romana*, or Roman Peace. [Ed.]

IBN FADLAN

The Viking Rus, 922

In 921 the Muslim caliph of Baghdad sent Ibn Fadlan* on a mission
to the king of the Bulgars.[1] The Muslim king of the Bulgars may have
been looking for an alliance with the caliph of Baghdad against the
Khazars, sandwiched between them just west of the Caspian Sea.
North and west of the Bulgars was the area that became Ukraine and
Russia. The Volga River, which had its source in the Ural Mountains,
flowed south through this land into the Caspian Sea. In the eighth
and ninth centuries this area was inhabited by various tribes, many of
which spoke early Slavic languages. At some point these tribes were
united under the command of a people called the Rus. The origins of
the Rus are disputed, but most experts believe that they were either
Vikings or the descendants of Vikings and Slavs.

Ibn Fadlan provides our earliest description of these Rus (or
Northmen, as he calls them here), whom he encountered on the
Volga near the modern city of Kazan during his trip to the Bulgar
king. (See Map 11.1 on p. 377 for his route.) They or their ancestors
had sailed downriver from the Baltic Sea on raiding and trading
expeditions. What does Ibn Fadlan tell us about these Scandinavian
raiders who gave their name to Russia?

THINKING HISTORICALLY

Notice Ibn Fadlan's moral judgments about the Viking Rus. Notice
your own moral judgments. How are Ibn Fadlan's judgments different from your own? What do you think accounts for those
differences?

I saw how the Northmen had arrived with their wares, and pitched their
camp beside the Volga. Never did I see people so gigantic; they are tall as
palm trees, and florid and ruddy of complexion. They wear neither cami-
soles nor *chaftans*,[2] but the men among them wear a garment of rough

---

* IH buhn fahd LAHN
[1] These Bulgars, with a Muslim king, had recently been forced north of the Caspian Sea
(while other Bulgars moved west to what is today Bulgaria where they were converted to
Christianity by Byzantium). [Ed.]
[2] Probably means no fine or fitted tops or robes; but see later description of funeral. [Ed.]

Source: Albert Stanborough Cook, "Ibn Fadlan's Account of Scandinavian Merchants on the
Volga in 922," *Journal of English and Germanic Philology* 22, no. 1 (1923): 56–63.

cloth, which is thrown over one side, so that one hand remains free. Every one carries an axe, a dagger, and a sword, and without these weapons they are never seen. Their swords are broad, with wavy lines, and of Frankish make. From the tip of the finger-nails to the neck, each man of them is tattooed with pictures of trees, living beings, and other things. The women carry, fastened to their breast, a little case of iron, copper, silver, or gold, according to the wealth and resources, of their husbands. Fastened to the case they wear a ring, and upon that a dagger, all attached to their breast. About their necks they wear gold and silver chains. If the husband possesses ten thousand dirhems, he has one chain made for his wife; if twenty thousand, two; and for every ten thousand, one is added. Hence it often happens that a Scandinavian woman has a large number of chains about her neck. Their most highly prized ornaments consist of small green shells, of one of the varieties which are found in [the bottoms of] ships. They make great efforts to obtain these, paying as much as a dirhem for such a shell, and stringing them as a necklace for their wives.

They are the filthiest race that God ever created. They do not wipe themselves after going to stool, nor wash themselves after a nocturnal pollution, any more than if they were wild asses.

They come from their own country, anchor their ships in the Volga, which is a great river, and build large wooden houses on its banks. In every such house there live ten or twenty, more or fewer. Each man has a couch, where he sits with the beautiful girls he has for sale. Here he is as likely as not to enjoy one of them while a friend looks on. At times several of them will be thus engaged at the same moment, each in full view of the others. Now and again a merchant will resort to a house to purchase a girl, and find her master thus embracing her, and not giving over until he has fully had his will.

Every morning a girl comes and brings a tub of water, and places it before her master. In this he proceeds to wash his face and hands, and then his hair, combing it out over the vessel. Thereupon he blows his nose, and spits into the tub, and, leaving no dirt behind, conveys it all into this water. When he has finished, the girl carries the tub to the man next [to] him, who does the same. Thus she continues carrying the tub from one to another till each of those who are in the house has blown his nose and spit into the tub, and washed his face and hair.

As soon as their ships have reached the anchorage, every one goes ashore, having at hand bread, meat, onions, milk, and strong drink, and betakes himself to a high, upright piece of wood, bearing the likeness of a human face; this is surrounded by smaller statues, and behind these there are still other tall pieces of wood driven into the ground. He advances to the large wooden figure, prostrates himself before it, and thus addresses it: "O my Lord, I am come from a far country, bringing with me so and so many girls, and so and so many pelts of sable" [or, marten]; and when he has thus enumerated all his merchandise, he continues, "I have brought thee this present," laying before the wooden statue what he has brought, and saying: "I desire thee to bestow upon me a purchaser who has gold and silver coins, who will buy from me to my heart's content, and who will refuse none of my demands." Having so said, he departs. If his trade then goes ill, he returns and brings a second, or even a third present. If he still continues to have difficulty in obtaining what he desires, he brings a present to one of the small statues, and implores its intercession, saying: "These are the wives and daughters of our lord." Continuing thus, he goes to each statue in turn, invokes it, beseeches its intercession, and bows humbly before it. If it then chances that his trade goes swimmingly, and he disposes of all his merchandise, he reports: "My lord has fulfilled my desire; now it is my duty to repay him." Upon this, he takes a number of cattle and sheep, slaughters them, gives a portion of the meat to the poor, and carries the rest before the large statue and the smaller ones that surround it, hanging the heads of the sheep and cattle on the large piece of wood which is planted in the earth. When night falls, dogs come and devour it all. Then he who has so placed it exclaims: "I am well pleasing to my lord; he has consumed my present."

If one of their number falls sick, they set up a tent at a distance, in which they place him, leaving bread and water at hand. Thereafter they never approach nor speak to him, nor visit him the whole time, especially if he is a poor person or a slave. If he recovers and rises from his sick bed, he returns to his own. If he dies, they cremate him; but if he is a slave they leave him as he is till at length he becomes the food of dogs and birds of prey.

If they catch a thief or a robber, they lead him to a thick and lofty tree, fasten a strong rope round him, string him up, and let him hang until he drops to pieces by the action of wind and rain.

I was told that the least of what they do for their chiefs when they die, is to consume them with fire. When I was finally informed of the death of one of their magnates, I sought to witness what befell. First they laid him in his grave—over which a roof was erected—for the space of ten days, until they had completed the cutting and sewing of his clothes. In the case of a poor man, however, they merely build for him a boat, in which they place him, and consume it with fire. At the death of a rich man, they bring together his goods, and divide them into three parts. The first of these is for his family; the second is expended for the garments they make; and with the third they purchase strong drink, against the day when the girl resigns herself to death, and is burned with her master. To the use of wine they abandon themselves in mad fashion, drinking it day and night; and not seldom does one die with the cup in his hand.

When one of their chiefs dies, his family asks his girls and pages: "Which one of you will die with him?" Then one of them answers, "I." From the time that he [or she] utters this word, he is no longer free: should he wish to draw back, he is not permitted. For the most part, however, it is the girls that offer themselves. So, when the man of whom I spoke had died, they asked his girls, "Who will die with him?" One of them answered, "I." She was then committed to two girls, who were to keep watch over her, accompany her wherever she went, and even, on occasion, wash her feet. The people now began to occupy themselves with the dead man — to cut out the clothes for him, and to prepare whatever else was needful. During the whole of this period, the girl gave herself over to drinking and singing, and was cheerful and gay.

When the day was now come that the dead man and the girl were to be committed to the flames, I went to the river in which his ship lay, but found that it had already been drawn ashore. Four corner-blocks of birch and other woods had been placed in position for it, while around were stationed large wooden figures in the semblance of human beings. Thereupon the ship was brought up, and placed on the timbers above mentioned. In the mean time the people began to walk to and fro, uttering words which I did not understand. The dead man, meanwhile, lay at a distance in his grave, from which they had not yet removed him. Next they brought a couch, placed it in the ship, and covered it with Greek cloth of gold, wadded and quilted, with pillows of the same material. There came an old crone, whom they call the angel of death, and spread the articles mentioned on the couch. It was she who attended to the sewing of the garments, and to all the equipment; it was she, also, who was to slay the girl. I saw her; she was dark, . . . thickset, with a lowering countenance.

When they came to the grave, they removed the earth from the wooden roof, set the latter aside, and drew out the dead man in the loose wrapper in which he had died. Then I saw that he had turned quite black, by reason of the coldness of that country. Near him in the grave they had placed strong drink, fruits, and a lute; and these they now took out. Except for his color, the dead man had not changed. They now clothed him in drawers, leggings, boots, and a *kurtak* and *chaftan* of cloth of gold, with golden buttons, placing on his head a cap made of cloth of gold, trimmed with sable! Then they carried him into a tent placed in the ship, seated him on the wadded and quilted covering, supported him with the pillows, and, bringing strong drink, fruits, and basil, placed them all beside him. Then they brought a dog, which they cut in two, and threw into the ship; laid all his weapons beside him; and led up two horses which they chased until they were dripping with sweat, whereupon they cut them in pieces with their swords, and threw the flesh into the ship. Two oxen were then brought forward, cut in pieces, and flung into the ship. Finally they brought a cock and a hen, killed them, and threw them in also.

The girl who had devoted herself to death meanwhile walked to and fro, entering one after another of the tents which they had there. The occupant of each tent lay with her, saying, "Tell your master, 'I [the man] did this only for love of you.'"

When it was now Friday afternoon, they led the girl to an object which they had constructed, and which looked like the framework of a door. She then placed her feet on the extended hands of the men, was raised up above the framework, and uttered something in her language, whereupon they let her down. Then again they raised her, and she did as at first. Once more they let her down, and then lifted her a third time, while she did as at the previous times. They then handed her a hen, whose head she cut off and threw away; but the hen itself they cast into the ship. I inquired of the interpreter what it was that she had done. He replied: "The first time she said, 'Lo, I see here my father and mother'; the second time, 'Lo, now I see all my deceased relatives sitting'; the third time, 'Lo, there is my master, who is sitting in Paradise. Paradise is so beautiful, so green. With him are his men and boys. He calls me, so bring me to him.'" Then they led her away to the ship.

Here she took off her two bracelets, and gave them to the old woman who was called the angel of death, and who was to murder her. She also drew off her two anklets, and passed them to the two servingmaids, who were the daughters of the so-called angel of death. Then they lifted her into the ship, but did not yet admit her to the tent. Now men came up with shields and staves, and handed her a cup of strong drink. This she took, sang over it, and emptied it. "With this," so the interpreter told me, "she is taking leave of those who are dear to her." Then another cup was handed her, which she also took, and began a lengthy song. The crone admonished her to drain the cup without lingering, and to enter the tent where her master lay. By this time, as it seemed to me, the girl had become dazed [or, possibly, crazed]; she made as though she would enter the tent, and had brought her head forward between the tent and the ship, when the hag seized her by the head, and dragged her in. At this moment the men began to beat upon their shields with the staves, in order to drown the noise of her outcries, which might have terrified the other girls, and deterred them from seeking death with their masters in the future. Then six men followed into the tent, and each and every one had carnal companionship with her. Then they laid her down by her master's side, while two of the men seized her by the feet and two by the hands. The old woman known as the angel of death now knotted a rope around her neck, and handed the ends to two of the men to pull. Then with a broad-bladed dagger she smote her between the ribs, and drew the blade forth while the two men strangled her with the rope till she died.

The next of kin to the dead man now drew near, and, taking a piece of wood, lighted it, and walked backwards toward the ship holding the stick in one hand, with the other placed upon his buttocks (he being naked), until the wood which had been piled under the ship was ignited. Then the others came up with staves and firewood, each one carrying a stick already lighted at the upper end, and threw it all on the pyre. The pile was soon aflame, then the ship, finally the tent, the man, and the girl, and everything else in the ship. A terrible storm began to blow up, and thus intensified the flames, and gave wings to the blaze.

At my side stood one of the Northmen, and I heard him talking with the interpreter, who stood near him. I asked the interpreter what the Northman had said, and received this answer: "'You Arabs,' he said, 'must be a stupid set! You take him who is to you the most revered and beloved of men, and cast him into the ground, to be devoured by creeping things and worms. We, on the other hand, burn him in a twinkling, so that he instantly, without a moment's delay, enters into Paradise.' At this he burst out into uncontrollable laughter, and then continued: 'It is the love of the Master [God] that causes the wind to blow and snatch him away in an instant.'" And, in very truth, before an hour had passed, ship, wood, and girl had with the man, turned to ashes.

Thereupon they heaped over the place where the ship had stood something like a rounded hill, and erecting on the centre of it a large birchen post, wrote on it the name of the deceased, along with that of the king of the Northmen. Having done this, they left the spot.

Eirik's Saga, c. 1260

Scandinavian seafarers spread out in all directions in the tenth century. While Swedes and Finns sailed down the rivers of Russia to the Black and Caspian seas, Danes conquered and colonized from England down the coast of France into the Mediterranean as far as Italy, North Africa, and Arabia. The Vikings of Norway sailed mainly westward, colonizing Iceland, Greenland, and North America (certainly Newfoundland but likely farther south). The Norsemen discovered Iceland in about 860 and began settlement some fourteen years later. By 930, Iceland contained the families and retainers of many lords who fled western Norway to escape the conquering Harald Fairhair.

Eirik the Red (950–1003) came to Iceland with his family in 960 after his father had to flee Norway because of "some killings." In turn, Eirik was exiled from Iceland in 982 after he committed murder in the heat of two quarrels. Exile meant searching for a settlement

Source: "Eirik's Saga," in *The Vinland Sagas: The Norse Discovery of America*, trans. and introduction by Magnus Magnusson and Hermann Palsson (Harmondsworth, Middlesex, England: Penguin Books, 1965), 75–78.

even farther west, leading Eirik to Greenland. Although not the first
to see or land in Greenland, Eirik established the first colony there.

Insofar as it captures the oral tradition, this excerpt from "Eirik's
Saga," written about 1260, gives us an idea of Viking thought in
the tenth century. What kind of world does it portray? How does it
contribute to your understanding of the Viking expansion?

THINKING HISTORICALLY

How does this internal view of Viking society inevitably change
our moral perspective from that of an outsider? How might the
differences between Ibn Fadlan and this author lead to different
moral perspectives?

There was a warrior king called Olaf the White, who was the son of
King Ingjald. Olaf went on a Viking expedition to the British Isles, where
he conquered Dublin and the adjoining territory and made himself king
over them. He married Aud the Deep-Minded, the daughter of Ketil Flat-
Nose; they had a son called Thorstein the Red.

Olaf was killed in battle in Ireland, and Aud and Thorstein the Red
then went to the Hebrides. There Thorstein married Thurid, the daughter of Eyvind the Easterner; they had many children.

Thorstein the Red became a warrior king, and joined forces with
Earl Sigurd the Powerful, together they conquered Caithness, Suther-
land, Ross, and Moray, and more than half of Argyll. Thorstein ruled
over these territories as king until he was betrayed by the Scots and
killed in battle.

Aud the Deep-Minded was in Caithness when she learned of Thorstein's death; she had a ship built secretly in a forest, and when it was
ready she sailed away to Orkney. There she gave away in marriage Groa,
daughter of Thorstein the Red.

After that, Aud set out for Iceland; she had twenty freeborn men aboard
her ship. She reached Iceland and spent the first winter with her brother
Bjorn at Bjarnarhaven. Then she took possession of the entire Dales district
between Dogurdar River and Skraumuhlaups River, and made her home at
Hvamm. She used to say prayers at Kross Hills; she had crosses erected
there, for she had been baptized and was a devout Christian.

Many well-born men, who had been taken captive in the British Isles
by Vikings and were now slaves, came to Iceland with her. One of them
was called Vifil; he was of noble descent. He had been taken prisoner in
the British Isles and was a slave until Aud gave him his freedom.

When Aud gave land to members of her crew, Vifil asked her why
she did not give him some land like the others. Aud replied that it was of
no importance, and said that he would be considered a man of quality

wherever he was. She gave him Vifilsdale, and he settled there. He married, and had two sons called Thorbjorn and Thorgeir; they were both promising men, and grew up with their father.

Eirik Explores Greenland

There was a man called Thorvald, who was the father of Eirik the Red. He and Eirik left their home in Jaederen because of some killings and went to Iceland. They took possession of land in Hornstrands, and made their home at Drangar. Thorvald died there, and Eirik the Red then married Thjodhild, and moved south to Haukadale; he cleared land there and made his home at Eirikstead, near Vatnshorn.

Eirik's slaves started a landslide that destroyed the farm of a man called Valthjof, at Valthjofstead; so Eyjolf Saur, one of Valthjof's kinsmen, killed the slaves at Skeidsbrekkur, above Vatnshorn. For this, Eirik killed Eyjolf Saur; he also killed Hrafn the Dueller, at Leikskalar. Geirstein and Odd of Jorvi, who were Eyjolf's kinsmen, took action over his killing, and Eirik was banished from Haukadale.

Eirik then took possession of Brok Island and Oxen Island, and spent the first winter at Tradir, in South Island. He lent his benchboards to Thorgest of Breidabolstead. After that, Eirik moved to Oxen Island, and made his home at Eirikstead. He then asked for his benchboards back, but they were not returned; so Eirik went to Breidabolstead and seized them. Thorgest pursued him, and they fought a battle near the farmstead at Drangar. Two of Thorgest's sons and several other men were killed there.

After this, both Eirik and Thorgest maintained a force of fighting-men at home. Eirik was supported by Styr Thorgrimsson, Eyjolf of Svin Island, Thorbjorn Vifilsson, and the sons of Thorbrand of Alptafjord; Thorgest was supported by Thorgeir of Hitardale, Aslak of Langadale and his son Illugi, and the sons of Thord Gellir.

Eirik and his men were sentenced to outlawry at the Thorsness Assembly. He made his ship ready in Eiriksbay, and Eyjolf of Svin Island hid him in Dimunarbay while Thorgest and his men were scouring the islands for him.

Thorbjorn Vifilsson and Styr and Eyjolf accompanied Eirik out beyond the islands, and they parted in great friendship; Eirik said he would return their help as far as it lay within his power, if ever they had need of it. He told them he was going to search for the land that Gunnbjorn, the son of Ulf Crow, had sighted when he was driven westwards off course and discovered the Gunnbjarnar Skerries; he added that he would come back to visit his friends if he found this country.

Eirik put out to sea past Snæfells Glacier, and made land near the glacier that is known as Blaserk. From there he sailed south to find out if the country were habitable there. He spent the first winter on Eiriks Island, which lies near the middle of the Eastern Settlement. In the spring he went to Eiriksfjord, where he decided to make his home. That summer he explored the wilderness to the west and gave names to many landmarks there. He spent the second winter on Eiriks Holms, off Hvarfs Peak. The third summer he sailed all the way north to Snæfell and into Hrafnsfjord, where he reckoned he was farther inland than the head of Eiriksfjord. Then he turned back and spent the third winter on Eiriks Island, off the mouth of Eiriksfjord.

He sailed back to Iceland the following summer and put in at Breidafjord. He stayed the winter with Ingolf of Holmlatur. In the spring he fought a battle with Thorgest of Breidabolstead and was defeated. After that a reconciliation was arranged between them.

That summer Eirik set off to colonize the country he had discovered; he named it *Greenland*, for he said that people would be much more tempted to go there if it had an attractive name.

YVO OF NARBONA
The Mongols, 1243

Within a couple of generations after 1206, a nomadic tribe of herders from the grasslands of Central Asia created a mounted army that conquered an expanse from the Pacific coast of Asia to Eastern Europe. With the conquest of the Islamic caliphate at Baghdad in 1258 and Song dynasty China by 1276, Mongols ruled about a hundred million people, having killed about thirty million others. They ruled almost a third of the human population and the largest land empire the world had ever known. Who were they? How did they manage such a feat? What were its costs?

To help answer some of those questions, we have a selection from a letter written in 1243 from one Yvo of Narbona[1] (we know nothing

---

[1] Narbona, or Narbonne, was a Mediterranean port city in what is today southern France.

Source: Samuel Purchas, *Hakluytus Posthumus or Purchas His Pilgrimes: Contayning a History of the World, in Sea voyages & lande-Trauells, by Englishmen & others* [*with* Purchas his Pilgrimage or Relations of the world*]* (London: William Stanley for Henrie Featherstone 1625–26), 5 vols., 183–87. Spelling modernized and Americanized.

else about him) to the archbishop of Bordeaux, France. Yvo has just witnessed the conquest of Hungary by a Mongol army. He describes what he saw and also relates the account of an Englishman (also unknown, even by name) who worked for the Mongols as an interpreter before he escaped amidst the Mongol withdrawal from Hungary. What does this document tell us about the Mongols? What does it suggest about the reasons for their rapid expansion? What does it suggest about their impact?

THINKING HISTORICALLY

No people before modern times received greater condemnation than the Mongols. Their negative reputation originated in the writings of their victims almost immediately after Genghis Khan expanded Mongol power into China and Central Asia in the 1210s and 1220s. The second-generation Mongol onslaught on Russia and Europe had a similar impact. Here we get an eyewitness account of the Mongol invasion of Hungary in 1241. Actually, we have two accounts: The tale of an Englishman who served as interpreter for the Mongols is contained within the letter of Yvo, who was also a witness. Which of these two witnesses is more objective, or less moralistic? What examples do you see of either witness judging rather than describing? What descriptions do not seem factually based? What examples do you see of either witness interpreting Mongol behavior in a favorable light?

Part of an Epistle written by one Yvo of Narbona unto the Archbishop of Bordeaux, containing the confession of an Englishman as touching the barbarous demeanor of the Tartars,[2] which had lived long among them, and was drawn along perforce with them in their expedition against Hungary: Recorded by Mathew Paris in the year of our Lord 1243.

The Lord therefore being provoked to indignation, by reason of this and other sins committed among us Christians, is become, as it were, a destroying enemy, and a dreadful avenger.[3] This I may justly affirm to be true, because a huge nation, and a barbarous and inhumane people, whose law is lawless, whose wrath is furious, even the rod of God's anger, overruns and utterly wastes infinite countries, cruelly abolishing

---

[2] The Mongols were misidentified as "Tatars" (another central Asian people), which then became "Tartars," probably to suggest people of "Tartarus," the underground place of punishment in Greek mythology, that is, devils. [Ed.]

[3] Like the prophets of ancient Israel, Christians interpreted invasions as God's punishment for their sins. [Ed.]

all things where they come, with fire and sword. And this present summer, the foresaid nation, being called Tartars, departing out of Hungary,[4] which they had surprised by treason, laid siege unto the very same town, wherein I myself abode, with many thousands of soldiers: neither were there in the said town on our part above 50 men of war, whom, together with 20 crossbows, the captain had left in garrison. All these, out of certain high places, beholding the enemies vast army, and abhorring the beastly cruelty of Anti-Christ his accomplices, signified forthwith unto their governor, the hideous lamentations of his Christian subjects, who suddenly being surprised in all the province adjoining, without any difference or respect of condition, fortune, sex, or age, were by manifold cruelties, all of them destroyed:[5] with whose carcasses, the Tartarian chieftains, and their brutish and savage followers, glutting themselves, as with delicious cakes, left nothing for vultures but the bare bones. And a strange thing it is to consider, that the greedy and ravenous vultures disdained to prey upon any of the relics, which remained. Old and deformed women they gave, as it were for daily sustenance, unto their Cannibals:[6] the beautiful devoured they not, but smothered them lamenting and scratching, with forced and unnatural ravishments. Like barbarous miscreants, they quelled virgins unto death, and cutting off their tender paps[7] to present for dainties unto their magistrates, they engorged themselves with their bodies.[8]

. . . In the meantime crying from the top of a high mountain, the Duke of Austria, the King of Bohemia, the Patriarch of Aquileia, the Duke of Carinthia, and (as some report) the Earl of Baden, with a mighty power, and in battle array, approaching towards them, that accursed crew immediately vanished,[9] and all those Tartarian vagabonds retired themselves into the distressed and vanquished land of Hungary; who as they came suddenly, so they departed also on the sudden: which their celerity[10] caused all men to stand in horror and astonishment of them. But of the said fugitives, the prince of Dalmatia took eight: one of which number the Duke of

---

[4] The Mongols invaded Hungary in 1241 under Batu Khan, the grandson of Genghis Khan. They withdrew in the spring of 1242 because of the death of Ogodei, the successor to Genghis, to return to Mongolia to choose the next Great Khan. [Ed.]

[5] The Mongols normally spared women and children. In this case they killed all the captives before returning to Mongolia. [Ed.]

[6] The charge of cannibalism is contested by modern historians. The Mongols would sometimes eat horse meat, mice, lice, and the afterbirth of foals, but the eating of human flesh was a rare occurrence, confined to threats of starvation. [Ed.]

[7] Breasts. [Ed.]

[8] Rape was common among all medieval armies, as was the selection of young women for slaves or harems, but the charges of cutting off their breasts are almost certainly fictional since that would make captured women less valuable. [Ed.]

[9] A classic Mongol tactic was a pretended retreat followed by an ambush, but this may refer to the return to Mongolia. [Ed.]

[10] Speed. [Ed.]

Austria knew to be an English man, who was perpetually banished out of the Realm of England, in regard of certain notorious crimes by him committed. This fellow, on the behalf of the most tyrannical king of the Tartars, had been twice, as a messenger and interpreter, with the king of Hungary, menacing and plainly foretelling the mischief which afterward happened, unless he would submit himself and his kingdom unto the Tartars yoke. Well, being allured by our Princes to confess the truth, he made such oaths and protestations, as (I think) the devil himself would have been trusted for. First therefore he reported of himself, that presently after the time of his banishment, namely about the 30th year of his age, having lost all that he had in the city of Acon[11] at dice, even in the midst of Winter, being compelled by ignominious hunger, wearing nothing about him but a shirt of sack, a pair of shoes, and a hair cap only, being shaven like a fool, and uttering an uncouth noise as if he had been dumb, he took his journey, and so travelling many countries, and finding in divers places friendly entertainment, he prolonged his life in this manner for a season, albeit every day by rashness of speech, and inconstancy of heart, he endangered himself to the devil. At length, by reason of extreme travail, and continual change of air and of meats in Chaldea,[12] he fell into a grievous sickness insomuch that he was weary of his life. Not being able therefore to go forward or backward, and staying there a while to refresh himself, he began (being somewhat learned) to commend to writing those words which he heard spoken, and within a short space, so aptly to pronounce, and to utter them himself, that he was reputed for a native member of that country: and by the same dexterity he attained to many languages. This man the Tartars having intelligence of by their spies, drew him perforce into their society: and being admonished by an oracle or vision, to challenge dominion over the whole earth, they allured him by many rewards to their faithful service, by reason that they wanted Interpreters. But concerning their manners and superstitions, of the disposition and stature of their bodies, of their country and manner of fighting etc., he protested the particulars following to be true: namely, that they were above all men, covetous, hasty, deceitful, and merciless: notwithstanding, by reason of the rigor and extremity of punishments to be inflicted upon them by their superiors, they are restrained from brawling, and from mutual strife and contention. The ancient founders and fathers of their tribes, they call by the name of gods,[13] and at certain set times they do celebrate solemn feasts unto them, many of them being particular, and but four only general. They

---

[11] Acre, in modern north-coastal Israel. Captured by the Crusaders in 1104 and again in 1191. Stronghold of Crusader state until 1291 fall to Mamluks. [Ed.]

[12] Mesopotamia; modern Iraq. [Ed.]

[13] Might refer to elements of ancestor worship in traditional Mongol belief system of Tengriism, which also included elements of shamanism, animism, and totenism, but Genghis Khan recognized the numerous religions of Central Asia (including Christianity, Buddhism, and Islam) and so maintained religious tolerance. [Ed.]

think that all things are created for themselves alone. They esteem it no offense to exercise cruelty against rebels. They are hardy and strong in the breast, lean and pale-faced, rough and hug-shouldered, having flat and short noses, long and sharp chins, their upper jaws are low and declining, their teeth long and thin, their eye-brows extending from their foreheads down to their noses, their eyes inconstant and black, their countenances writhen and terrible, their extreme joints strong with bones and sinews, having thick and great thighs, and short legs, and yet being equal unto us in stature: for that length which is wanting in their legs, is supplied in the upper parts of their bodies. Their country in old time was a land utterly desert and waste,[14] situated far beyond Chaldea, from whence they have expelled lions, bears, and such like untamed beasts, with their bows, and other engines. Of the hides of beasts being tanned, they use to shape for themselves light but yet impenetrable armor. They ride fast bound unto their horses, which are not very great in stature, but exceedingly strong, and maintained with little provender.[15] They used to fight constantly and valiantly with javelins, maces, battle-axes, and swords. But especially they are excellent archers, and cunning warriors with their bows. Their backs are slightly armed, that they may not flee. They withdraw not themselves from the combat till they see the chief standard of their general give back. Vanquished, they ask no favor, and vanquishing, they show no compassion. They all persist in their purpose of subduing the whole world under their own subjection, as if they were but one man, and yet they are more than millions in number.[16] They have 60,000 couriers, who being sent before upon light horses to prepare a place for the army to encamp in, will in the space of one night gallop three days journey. And suddenly diffusing themselves over a whole province, and surprising all the people thereof unarmed, unprovided, dispersed, they make such horrible slaughters, that the king or prince of the land invaded, cannot find people sufficient to wage battle against them, and to withstand them. They delude all people and princes of regions in time of peace, pretending that for a cause, which indeed is no cause. Sometimes they say that they will make a voyage to Cologne to fetch home the three wise kings into their own country;[17] sometimes to punish the avarice and pride of the Romans,[18] who oppressed

---

[14] Bordered by desert in the south and forests in the north, the steppe is relatively treeless and dry but with ample grass for grazing. [Ed.]

[15] Food. [Ed.]

[16] A likely exaggeration. Probably more like a million. Individual armies like Batu's probably numbered something like 30,000. Total forces of 500,000 might have been possible. All Mongol men rode in battle. All enemies were killed or enslaved. At its height the Mongol Empire might have ruled 100 million people. On the other hand, Mongol rule depleted the population of that empire by tens of millions. [Ed.]

[17] Cologne, in modern Germany. A medieval legend told of how the three kings who visited Jesus were reburied together in St. Peter's church in Cologne. [Ed.]

[18] "Romans" is a general term for Christians of Western Europe. [Ed.]

them in times past;[19] sometimes to conquer barbarous and Northern nations; sometimes to moderate the fury of the Germans[20] with their own meek mildness; sometimes to learn warlike feats and stratagems of the French; sometimes for the finding out of fertile ground to suffice their huge multitudes; sometimes again in derision they say that they intend to go on pilgrimage to St. James of Galicia.[21] In regard of which slights and collusions certain indiscreet governors concluding a league with them, have granted them free passage through their territories, which leagues notwithstanding being violated, were an occasion of ruin and destruction unto the governors, etc.

[19] May refer to the Roman Empire or to Christian Crusades, or it may conflate both. [Ed.]
[20] The German Teutonic Knights fought Crusades to Christianize the Baltic, Poland, and Hungary in the thirteenth century. [Ed.]
[21] Santiago De Compostela, in northwest Spain; a pilgrimage site, said to be the burial place of St. James. [Ed.]

5

The Secret History of the Mongols, c. 1240

This Mongol account records the early years of Mongol expansion under Genghis Khan, the founder of the empire. Born Temujin in 1155 or 1167, this son of a minor tribal chieftain attracted the support of Mongol princes in the years between 1187 and 1206 through a series of decisive military victories over other tribes and competing Mongol claimants to the title of Great Khan.

The Mongols were illiterate before the time of Genghis Khan, who adopted the script of the Uighurs,* one of the more literate peoples of the steppe. Thus *The Secret History* was written in Mongolian with Uighur letters. The only surviving version is a fourteenth-century Chinese translation. The author is unknown, but the book provides detailed accounts of the early years of Temujin and ends with the reign of his son and successor, Ogodei, in 1228 — only a year after his father's death.

* WEE gurs

Source: Adapted by K. Reilly from R. P. Lister, *Genghis Khan* (New York: Barnes & Noble, 1993), 166–76. While this volume is a retelling of the almost indecipherable *The Secret History of the Mongols* in Lister's own words, the selections that follow simplify without contextualizing or explaining the original work. More scholarly editions, translated and edited by Francis Woodman Cleaves (Cambridge, MA: Harvard University Press, 1982) and Paul Kahn (San Francisco: North Point Press, 1984), are less accessible.

Because so much about the Mongols was written by their literate enemies, *The Secret History* is an invaluable resource: It is clearly an "insider's" account of the early years of Mongol expansion. Although it includes mythic elements—it begins with the augury of the birth of a blue wolf to introduce Genghis Khan—*The Secret History* is, without doubt, an authentic representation of a Mongol point of view.

In this selection, you will read the Mongol account of an important Mongol victory over the Naiman, a neighboring Turkic- or Mongol-speaking people, in 1204. What does the account tell you about the lives of steppe nomads like the Naiman and Mongols? What does this selection tell you about the sources of Mongol military strength?

THINKING HISTORICALLY

What moral values does this selection reveal? Do the Mongols think of themselves as "moral" people? Is the author-historian interested in describing what happened objectively or in presenting an unblemished, sanitized view?

In what ways does this written Mongol history make you more sympathetic to the Mongols? Notice that the selection begins with an "inside" view of the Mongol's enemy, the Naiman. How informed and fair does the Mongol author seem to be toward the Naiman? Do you think the Mongol authors described the Naiman more accurately than Chinese or Europeans described the Mongols?

Tayang Khan of the Naiman

When the news was brought to [the Naiman] Tayang Khan that someone claiming to be Ong Khan had been slain at the Neikun watercourse, his mother, Gurbesu, said: "Ong Khan was the great Khan of former days. Bring his head here! If it is really he, we will sacrifice to him."

She sent a message to Khorisu, commanding him to cut the head off and bring it in. When it was brought to her, she recognised it as that of Ong Khan. She placed it on a white cloth, and her daughter-in-law carried out the appropriate rites. . . . A wine-feast was held and stringed instruments were played. Gurbesu, taking up a drinking-bowl, made an offering to the head of Ong Khan.

When the sacrifice was made to it, the head grinned.

"He laughs!" Tayang Khan cried. Overcome by religious awe, he flung the head on the floor and trampled on it until it was mangled beyond recognition.

The great general Kokse'u Sabrakh was present at these ceremonies, and observed them without enthusiasm. It was he who had been the only Naiman general to offer resistance to Temujin and Ong Khan on their expedition against Tayang Khan's brother Buyiruk.

"First of all," he remarked, "you cut off the head of a dead ruler, and then you trample it into the dust. What kind of behaviour is this? Listen to the baying of those dogs: It has an evil sound. The Khan your father, Inancha Bilgei, once said: 'My wife is young, and I, her husband, am old. Only the power of prayer has enabled me to beget my son, this same Tayang. But will my son, born a weakling, be able to guard and hold fast my common and evil-minded people?'

"Now the baying of the dogs seems to announce that some disaster is at hand. The rule of our queen, Gurbesu, is firm; but you, my Khan, Torlukh Tayang, are weak. It is truly said of you that you have no thought for anything but the two activities of hawking and driving game, and no capacity for anything but these."

Tayang Khan was accustomed to the disrespect of his powerful general, but he was stung into making a rash decision.

"There are a few Mongols in the east. From the earliest days this old and great Ong Khan feared them, with their quivers; now they have made war on him and driven him to death. No doubt they would like to be rulers themselves. There are indeed in Heaven two shining lights, the sun and the moon, and both can exist there; but how can there be two rulers here on earth? Let us go and gather those Mongols in."

His mother Gurbesu said: "Why should we start making trouble with them? The Mongols have a bad smell; they wear black clothes. They are far away, out there; let them stay there. Though it is true," she added, "that we could have the daughters of their chieftains brought here; when we had washed their hands and feet, they could milk our cows and sheep for us."

Tayang Khan said: "What is there so terrible about them? Let us go to these Mongols and take away their quivers."

"What big words you are speaking," Kokse'u Sabrakh said. "Is Tayang Khan the right man for it? Let us keep the peace."

Despite these warnings, Tayang Khan decided to attack the Mongols. It was a justifiable decision; his armies were stronger, but time was on Temujin's side. Tayang sought allies, sending a messenger to Alakhu Shidigichuri of the Onggut, in the south, the guardians of the ramparts between Qashin and the Khingan. "I am told that there are a few Mongols in the east," he said. "Be my right hand! I will ride against them from here, and we will take their quivers away from them."

Alakhu's reply was brief: "I cannot be your right hand." He in his turn sent a message to Temujin. "Tayang Khan of the Naiman wants to come and take away your quivers. He sent to me and asked me to be his right hand. I refused. I make you aware of this, so that when he comes your quivers will not be taken away."[1]

---

[1] Temujin, grateful for this warning, sent him five hundred horses and a thousand sheep. His friendship with Alakhu was valuable to him at a later time.

War against the Naiman

When he received Alakhu's message Temujin, having wintered near Guralgu, was holding one of his immense roundups of game on the camel-steppes of Tulkinche'ut, in the east. The beasts had been encircled by the clansmen and warriors; the chieftains were gathered together, about to begin the great hunt.

"What shall we do now?" some of them said to each other. "Our horses are lean at this season."

. . . The snow had only lately left the steppe; the horses had found nothing to graze on during these recent months. Their ribs stuck out and they lacked strength.

The Khan's youngest brother, Temuga, spoke up. . . .

"How can that serve as an excuse," he said, "that the horses are lean? My horses are quite fat enough. How can we stay sitting here, when we receive a message like that?"

Prince Belgutai spoke. . . .

"If a man allows his quivers to be taken away during his lifetime, what kind of an existence does he have? For a man who is born a man, it is a good enough end to be slain by another man, and lie on the steppe with his quiver and bow beside him. The Naiman make fine speeches, with their many men and their great kingdom. But suppose, having heard their fine speeches, we ride against them, would it be so difficult to take their quivers away from them? We must mount and ride; it is the only thing to do."

Temujin was wholly disposed to agree with these sentiments. He broke off the hunt, set the army in motion, and camped near Ornu'u on the Khalkha. Here he paused for a time while he carried out a swift reorganization of the army. A count was held of the people; they were divided up into thousands, hundreds, and tens, and commanders of these units were appointed. Also at this time he chose his personal bodyguards, the seventy day-guards and eighty night-guards.

Having reorganised the army, he marched away from the mountainside of Ornu'u on the Khalkha, and took the way of war against the Naiman.

The spring of the Year of the Rat [1204] was by now well advanced. During this westward march came the Day of the Red Disc, the sixteenth day of the first moon of summer. On this day, the moon being at the full, the Khan caused the great yak's-tail banner to be consecrated, letting it be sprinkled with fermented mare's milk, with the proper observances.

They continued the march up the Kerulen, with Jebe and Khubilai in the van. When they came on to the Saari steppes, they met with the first scouts of the Naiman. There were a few skirmishes between the Naiman and Mongol scouts; in one of these, a Mongol scout was captured, a man riding a grey horse with a worn saddle. The Naiman studied this horse with critical eyes, and thought little of it. "The Mongols' horses are inordinately lean," they said to each other.

The Mongol army rode out on to the Saari steppes, and began to deploy themselves for the forthcoming battle. . . . Dodai Cherbi, one of the newly appointed captains, put a proposal before the Khan.

"We are short in numbers compared to the enemy; besides this, we are exhausted after the long march, our horses in particular. It would be a good idea to settle in this camp, so that our horses can graze on the steppe, until they have had as much to eat as they need. Meanwhile, we can deceive the enemy by making puppets and lighting innumerable fires. For every man, we will make at least one puppet, and we will burn fires in five places. It is said that the Naiman people are very numerous, but it is rumored also that their king is a weakling, who has never left his tents. If we keep them in a state of uncertainty about our numbers, with our puppets and our fires, our geldings can stuff themselves till they are fat."

The suggestion pleased Temujin, who had the order passed on to the soldiers to light fires immediately. Puppets were constructed and placed all over the steppe, some sitting or lying by the fires, some of them even mounted on horses.

At night, the watchers of the Naiman saw, from the flanks of the mountain, fires twinkling all over the steppe. They said to each other: "Did they not say that the Mongols were very few? Yet they have more fires than there are stars in Heaven."

Having previously sent to Tayang Khan news of the lean grey horse with the shabby saddle, they now sent him the message: "The warriors of the Mongols are camped out all over the Saari steppes. They seem to grow more numerous every day; their fires outnumber the stars."

When this news was brought to him from the scouts, Tayang Khan was at the watercourse of Khachir. He sent a message to his son Guchuluk.

"I am told that the geldings of the Mongols are lean, but the Mongols are, it seems, numerous. Once we start fighting them, it will be difficult to draw back. They are such hard warriors that when several men at once come up against one of them, he does not move an eyelid; even if he is wounded, so that the black blood flows out, he does not flinch. I do not know whether it is a good thing to come up against such men.

"I suggest that we should assemble our people and lead them back to the west, across the Altai; and all the time, during this retreat, we will fight off the Mongols as dogs do, by running in on them from either side as they advance. Our geldings are too fat; in this march we shall make them lean and fit. But the Mongols' lean geldings will be brought to such a state of exhaustion they will vomit in the Mongols' faces."

On receiving this message, Guchuluk Khan, who was more warlike than his father, said: "That woman Tayang has lost all his courage, to speak such words. Where does this great multitude of Mongols come from? Most of the Mongols are with Jamukha, who is here with us. Tayang speaks like this because fear has overcome him. He has never been farther from his tent than his pregnant wife goes to urinate. He has never dared to go so far as the inner pastures where the knee-high calves are kept." So he expressed himself on the subject of his father, in the most injurious and wounding terms.

When he heard these words, Tayang Khan said: "I hope the pride of this powerful Guchuluk will not weaken on the day when the clash of arms is heard and the slaughter begins. Because once we are committed to battle against the foe, it will be hard to disengage again."

Khorisu Beki, a general who commanded under Tayang Khan, said: "Your father, Inancha Bilgei, never showed the back of a man or the haunch of a horse to opponents who were just as worthy as these. How can you lose your courage so early in the day? We would have done better to summon your mother Gurbesu to command over us. It is a pity that Kokse'u Sabrakh has grown too old to lead us. Our army's discipline has become lax. For the Mongols, their hour has come. It is finished! Tayang, you have failed us." He belted on his quiver and galloped off.

Tayang Khan grew angry. "All men must die," he said. "Their bodies must suffer. It is the same for all men. Let us fight, then."

So, having created doubt and dismay, and lost the support of some of his best leaders, he decided to give battle. He broke away from the watercourse of Khachir, marched down the Tamir, crossed the Orkhon and skirted the eastern flanks of the mountain Nakhu. When they came to Chakirma'ut, Temujin's scouts caught sight of them and brought back the message: "The Naiman are coming!"

The Battle of Chakirma'ut

When the news was brought to Temujin he said: "Sometimes too many men are just as big a handicap as too few."

Then he issued his general battle orders. "We will march in the order 'thick grass,' take up positions in the 'lake' battle order, and fight in the manner called 'gimlet.' "[2] He gave Kasar the command of the main army, and appointed Prince Otchigin to the command of the reserve horses, a special formation of great importance in Mongol warfare.

The Naiman, having advanced as far as Chakirma'ut, drew themselves up in a defensive position on the foothills of Nakhu, with the mountain behind them. . . . The Mongols forced their scouts back on to the forward lines, and then their forward lines back on to the main army, and drove tightly knit formations of horsemen again and again into the Naiman ranks. The Naiman, pressed back on themselves, could do nothing but retreat gradually up the mountain. Many of their men . . . hardly had the chance to fight at all, but were cut down in an immobile mass of men as soon as the Mongols reached them.

---

[2] These were the names of various tactical disciplines in which he had drilled his army.

Tayang Khan, with his advisers, also retreated up the mountain as the day advanced. From the successive spurs to which they climbed, each one higher than the last, they could see the whole of this dreadful disaster as it took place below them.

Jamukha was with Tayang Khan. . . .

"Who are those people over there," Tayang Khan asked him, "who throw my warriors back as if they were sheep frightened by a wolf, who come huddling back to the sheepfold?"

Jamukha said: "My *anda*[3] Temujin has four hounds whom he brought up on human flesh, and kept in chains. They have brows of copper, snouts like chisels, tongues like bradawls, hearts of iron, and tails that cut like swords. They can live on dew, and ride like the wind. On the day of battle they eat the flesh of men. You see how, being set loose, they come forward slavering for joy. Those two are Jebe and Khubilai; those two are Jelmei and Subetai. That is who those four hounds are.". . .

"Who is it coming up there in the rear," Tayang Khan asked him, "who swoops down on our troops like a ravening falcon?"

"That is my *anda* Temujin. His entire body is made of sounding copper; there is no gap through which even a bodkin could penetrate. There he is, you see him? He advances like an eagle about to seize his prey. You said formerly that if you once set eyes on the Mongols you would not leave so much of them as the skin of a lamb's foot. What do you think of them now?"

By this time the chieftains were standing on a high spur. Below them, the great army of the Naiman, Jamukha's men with them, were retreating in confusion, fighting desperately as the Mongols hemmed them in.

"Who is that other chieftain," Tayang asked Jamukha, "who draws ever nearer us, in a dense crowd of men?"

"Mother Hoelun brought up one of her own sons on human flesh. He is nine feet tall; he eats a three-year-old cow every day. If he swallows an armed man whole, it makes no difference to his appetite. When he is roused to anger, and lets fly with one of his *angqu'a* [forked] arrows, it will go through ten or twenty men. His normal range is a thousand yards; when he draws his bow to its fullest extent, he shoots over eighteen hundred yards. He is mortal, but he is not like other mortals; he is more than a match for the serpents of Guralgu. He is called Kasar."

They were climbing high up the mountain now, to regroup below its summit. Tayang Khan saw a new figure among the Mongols.

"Who is that coming up from the rear?" he asked Jamukha.

"That is the youngest son of Mother Hoelun. He is called Otchigin [Odeigin] the Phlegmatic. He is one of those people who go to bed early and get up late. But when he is behind the army, with the reserves, he does not linger; he never comes too late to the battle lines."

---

[3] Sworn brother, blood brother, declared ally.

"We will climb to the peak of the mountain," Tayang Khan said.

Jamukha, seeing that the battle was lost, slipped away to the rear and descended the mountain, with a small body of men. One of these he sent to Temujin with a message. "Say this to my *anda*. Tayang Khan, terrified by what I have told him, has completely lost his senses. He has retreated up the mountain as far as he can. He could be killed by one harsh word. Let my *anda* take note of this: They have climbed to the top of the mountain, and are in no state to defend themselves any more. I myself have left the Naiman."

Since the evening was drawing on, Temujin commanded his troops in the forefront of the attack to draw back. Bodies of men were sent forward on the wings, east and west, to encircle the summit of Mount Nakhu. There they stood to arms during the night. During the night, the Naiman army tried to break out of the encircling ring. Bodies of horsemen plunged down the mountainside in desperate charges; many fell and were trampled to death, the others were slain. In the first light they were seen lying about the mountain in droves, like fallen trees. Few were left defending the peak; they put up little resistance to the force sent up against them.

6

IBN AL-ATHIR

The Mongols, c. 1231

The great Muslim historian Ibn al-Athir (1160–1233), whose history of the First Crusade we excerpted in the previous chapter, actually lived through the early period of the Mongol invasion. Like many of his contemporaries he saw these events in biblical terms. In this selection he refers to the Mongols as Tatars, a common word at the time for the Turkic-speaking people subjugated by the Mongols and a word that evoked classical Tartarus, a realm of Hades, or Hell.

If you peel away the biblical allusions, what did the Mongols actually do, according to the author? How would you compare their conquests to those of the Vikings or others you have read about?

Source: Edward G. Browne, *A Literary History of Persia* (Cambridge: Cambridge University Press, 1902), Vol. II, 427–31.

THINKING HISTORICALLY
How might Ibn al-Athir's use of biblical language be unfair to the
Mongols? Does it make his writing less objective? Can you point to
places in the text where he is too moralistic or judgmental regarding
the Mongols?

For some years I continued averse from mentioning this event, deeming
it so horrible that I shrank from recording it and ever withdrawing one
foot as I advanced the other. To whom, indeed, can it be easy to write the
announcement of the death-blow of Islam and the Muslims, or who is
he on whom the remembrance thereof can weigh lightly? O would that
my mother had not born me or that I had died and become a forgotten
thing ere this befell! Yet, withal a number of my friends urged me to set
it down in writing, and I hesitated long, but at last came to the conclusion
that to omit this matter could serve no useful purpose.

I say, therefore, that this thing involves the description of the
greatest catastrophe and the most dire calamity (of the like of which
days and nights are innocent) which befell all men generally, and the
Muslims in particular; so that, should one say that the world, since
God Almighty created Adam until now, has not been afflicted with
the like thereof, he would but speak the truth. For indeed history does
not contain anything which approaches or comes near unto it. For of
the most grievous calamities recorded was what Nebuchadnezzar
inflicted on the children of Israel by his slaughter of them and his
destruction of Jerusalem; and what was Jerusalem in comparison to
the countries which these accursed miscreants destroyed, each city of
which was double the size of Jerusalem? Or what were the children
of Israel compared to those whom these slew? For verily those whom
they massacred in a single city exceeded all the children of Israel.
Nay, it is unlikely that mankind will see the like of this calamity, until
the world comes to an end and perishes, except the final outbreak of
Gog and Magog.[1]

For even Antichrist will spare such as follow him, though he destroy
those who oppose him, but these Tatars spared none, slaying women and
men and children, ripping open pregnant women and killing unborn
babes. Verily to God do we belong, and unto Him do we return, and
there is no strength and no power save in God, the High, the Almighty,
in face of this catastrophe, whereof the sparks flew far and wide, and the
hurt was universal; and which passed over the lands like clouds driven

[1] From Book of Ezekiel associated with idea of apocalypse.

by the wind. For these were a people who emerged from the confines of China, and attacked the cities of Turkestan, like Kashghar and Balasaghun, and thence advanced on the cities of Transoxiana, such as Samarqand, Bukhara and the like, taking possession of them, and treating their inhabitants in such wise as we shall mention; and of them one division then passed on into Khurasan, until they had made an end of taking possession, and destroying, and slaying, and plundering, and thence passing on to Ray, Hamadan and the Highlands, and the cities contained therein, even to the limits of Iraq, whence they marched on the towns of Adharbayjan and Arraniyya, destroying them and slaying most of their inhabitants, of whom none escaped save a small remnant; and all this in less than a year; this is a thing whereof the like has not been heard. And when they had finished with Adharbayjan and Arraniyya, they passed on to Darband-i-Shirwan, and occupied its cities, none of which escaped save the fortress wherein was their King; wherefore they passed by it to the countries of the Lan and the Lakiz and the various nationalities which dwell in that region, and plundered, slew, and destroyed them to the full. And thence they made their way to the lands of Qipchaq, who are the most numerous of the Turks, and slew all such as withstood them, while the survivors fled to the fords and mountain-tops, and abandoned their country, which these Tatars overran. All this they did in the briefest space of time, remaining only for so long as their march required and no more.

Another division, distinct from that mentioned above, marched on Ghazna and its dependencies, and those parts of India, Sistan and Kirman which border thereon, and wrought therein deeds like unto the other, nay, yet more grievous. Now this is a thing the like of which ear has not heard; for Alexander, concerning whom historians agree that he conquered the world, did not do so with such swiftness, but only in the space of about ten years; neither did he slay, but was satisfied that men should be subject to him. But these Tatars conquered most of the habitable globe, and the best, the most flourishing and most populous part thereof, and that whereof the inhabitants were the most advanced in character and conduct, in about a year; nor did any country escape their devastations which did not fearfully expect them and dread their arrival.

Moreover they need no commissariat, nor the conveyance of supplies, for they have with them sheep, cows, horses, and the like quadrupeds, the flesh of which they eat, naught else. As for their beasts which they ride, these dig into the earth with their hoofs and eat the roots of plants, knowing naught of barley. And so, when they alight anywhere, they have need of nothing from without. As for their religion, they worship the sun when it rises, and regard nothing as unlawful, for they eat all beasts, even dogs, pigs, and the like; nor do they recognize the marriage-tie, for several men are in marital relations with one woman, and if a child is born, it knows not who is its father.

Therefore Islam and the Muslims have been afflicted during this period with calamities wherewith no people hath been visited. These Tatars (may God confound them!) came from the East, and wrought deeds which horrify all who hear of them, and which you shall, please God, see set forth in full detail in their proper connection. And of these was the invasion of Syria by the Franks (may God curse them!) out of the West, and their attack on Egypt, and occupation of the port of Damietta therein, so that Egypt and Syria were like to be conquered by them, but for the grace of God and the help which He vouchsafed us against them, as we have mentioned under the year 614 (A.D. 1217–1218). Of these, moreover, was that the sword was drawn between those who escaped from these two foes, and strife was rampant, as we have also mentioned: and verily unto God do we belong and unto Him do we return! We ask God to vouchsafe victory to Islam and the Muslims, for there is none other to aid, help, or defend the True Faith. But if God intends evil to any people, naught can avert it, nor have they any ruler save Him. As for these Tatars, their achievements were only rendered possible by the absence of any effective obstacle; and the cause of this absence was that Muhammad Khwarazmshah had overrun the lands, slaying and destroying their Kings, so that he remained alone ruling over all these countries; wherefore, when he was defeated by the Tatars, none was left in the lands to check those or protect these, that so God might accomplish a thing which was to be done.

It is now time for us to describe how they first burst forth into the lands. Stories have been related to me, which the hearer can scarcely credit, as to the terror of the Tatars, which God Almighty cast into men's hearts; so that it is said that a single one of them would enter a village or a quarter wherein were many people, and would continue to slay them one after another, none daring to stretch forth his hand against this horseman. And I have heard that one of them took a man captive, but had not with him any weapon wherewith to kill him; and he said to his prisoner, "Lay your head on the ground and do not move," and he did so, and the Tatar went and fetched his sword and slew him therewith. Another man related to me as follows: "I was going," said he, "with seventeen others along a road, and there met us a Tatar horseman, and bade us bind one another's arms. My companions began to do as he bade them, but I said to them, 'He is but one man; wherefore, then, should we not kill him and flee?' They replied, 'We are afraid.' I said, 'This man intends to kill you immediately; let us therefore rather kill him, that perhaps God may deliver us.' But I swear by God that not one of them dared to do this, so I took a knife and slew him, and we fled and escaped." And such occurrences were many.

7

JOHN OF PLANO CARPINI
History of the Mongols, 1245–1250

Genghis Khan united the tribes of the steppe and conquered northern China, capturing Peking by 1215. He then turned his armies against the West, conquering the tribes of Turkestan and the Khorezmian Empire, the great Muslim power of Central Asia, by 1222 and sending an army around the Caspian Sea into Russia. In 1226, he turned again to the East, subduing and destroying the kingdom of Tibet before he died in 1227. One historian, Christopher Dawson, summarizes the career of Genghis Khan this way:

> In spite of the primitive means at his disposal, it is possible that [Genghis Khan] succeeded in destroying a larger portion of the human race than any modern expert in total warfare. Within a dozen years from the opening of his campaign against China, the Mongol armies had reached the Pacific, the Indus, and the Black Sea, and had destroyed many of the great cities in India. For Europe especially, the shock was overwhelming.[1]

European fears intensified in 1237 as the principal Mongol armies under Batu Khan systematically destroyed one Russian city after another. In April 1241, one Mongol army destroyed a combined force of Polish and German armies, while another defeated the Hungarian army and threatened Austria. In 1245, desperate to learn as much as possible about Mongol intentions, Pope Innocent IV sent a mission to the Mongols. For this important task, he sent two Franciscan monks — one of whom was John of Plano Carpini — with two letters addressed to the Emperor of the Tartars (a compounded error that changed the Tatars, the Mongols' enemy, into the denizens of Tartarus, or Hell).

In May, the barefoot sixty-five-year-old Friar John reached Batu's camp on the Volga River, from which he was relayed to Mongolia by five fresh horses a day in order to reach the capital at Karakorum in time for the installation of the third Great Khan, Guyuk (r. 1246–1248) in July and August.

---

[1] From Christopher Dawson, ed., *Mission to Asia*, p. xii.

Source: John of Plano Carpini, "History of the Mongols," in *Mission to Asia: Narratives and Letters of the Franciscan Missionaries in Mongolia and China in the Thirteenth and Fourteenth Centuries*, trans. a nun of Stanbrook Abbey, ed. Christopher Dawson (1955; reprint, New York: Harper & Row, 1966), 60–69.

In this selection from his *History of the Mongols,* John writes of his arrival in Mongolia for the installation of Guyuk (here written as Cuyuc). In what ways does John's account change or expand your understanding of the Mongols? Was John a good observer? How does he compensate for his ignorance (as an outside observer) of Mongol society and culture? In what ways does he remain a victim of his outsider status?

How was Mongol society similar to, and different from, Viking society? Compare the role of women in Mongol and Viking societies.

THINKING HISTORICALLY

How would you characterize John's moral stance toward the Mongols? How is his judgment of the Mongols different from that of Yvo of Narbona, and what might account for that difference? Consider your own moral judgment, if any, of the Mongols. How is it related to your historical understanding?

... On our arrival Cuyuc had us given a tent and provisions, such as it is the custom for the Tartars to give, but they treated us better than other envoys. Nevertheless we were not invited to visit him for he had not yet been elected, nor did he yet concern himself with the government. The translation of the Lord Pope's letter, however, and the things I had said had been sent to him by Bati. After we had stayed there for five or six days he sent us to his mother where the solemn court was assembling. By the time we got there a large pavilion had already been put up made of white velvet, and in my opinion it was so big that more than two thousand men could have got into it. Around it had been erected a wooden palisade, on which various designs were painted. On the second or third day we went with the Tartars who had been appointed to look after us and there all the chiefs were assembled and each one was riding with his followers among the hills and over the plains round about.

On the first day they were all clothed in white velvet, on the second in red — that day Cuyuc came to the tent — on the third day they were all in blue velvet, and on the fourth in the finest brocade. In the palisade round the pavilion were two large gates, through one of which the Emperor alone had the right to enter and there were no guards placed at it although it was open, for no one dare enter or leave by it; through the other gate all those who were granted admittance entered and there were guards there with swords and bows and arrows. . . . The chiefs went about everywhere armed and accompanied by a number of their men, but none, unless their group of ten was complete, could go as far as the horses; indeed those who attempted to do so were severely beaten.

There were many of them who had, as far as I could judge, about twenty marks' worth of gold on their bits, breastplates, saddles, and cruppers. The chiefs held their conference inside the tent and, so I believe, conducted the election. All the other people however were a long way away outside the aforementioned palisade. There they remained until almost midday and then they began to drink mare's milk and they drank until the evening, so much that it was amazing to see. We were invited inside and they gave us mead as we would not take mare's milk. They did this to show us great honour, but they kept on plying us with drinks to such an extent that we could not possibly stand it, not being used to it, so we gave them to understand that it was disagreeable to us and they left off pressing us.

Outside were Duke Jerozlaus of Susdal in Russia and several chiefs of the Kitayans and Solangi, also two sons of the King of Georgia, the ambassador of the Caliph of Baghdad, who was a Sultan, and more than ten other Sultans of the Saracens, so I believe and so we were told by the stewards. There were more than four thousand envoys there, counting those who were carrying tribute, those who were bringing gifts, the Sultans and other chiefs who were coming to submit to them, those summoned by the Tartars and the governors of territories. All these were put together outside the palisade and they were given drinks at the same time, but when we were outside with them we and Duke Jerozlaus were always given the best places. I think, if I remember rightly, that we had been there a good four weeks when, as I believe, the election took place; the result however was not made public at that time; the chief ground for my supposition was that whenever Cuyuc left the tent they sang before him and as long as he remained outside they dipped to him beautiful rods on the top of which was scarlet wool, which they did not do for any of the other chiefs. They call this court the Sira Orda.

Leaving there we rode all together for three or four leagues to another place, where on a pleasant plain near a river among the mountains another tent had been set up, which is called by them the Golden Orda, it was here that Cuyuc was to be enthroned on the feast of the Assumption of Our Lady. . . .

At that place we were summoned into the presence of the Emperor, and Chingay the protonotary wrote down our names and the names of those who had sent us, also the names of the chief of the Solangi and of others, and then calling out in a loud voice he recited them before the Emperor and all the chiefs. When this was finished each one of us genuflected four times on the left knee and they warned us not to touch the lower part of the threshold. After we had been most thoroughly searched for knives and they had found nothing at all, we entered by a door on the east side, for no one dare enter from the west with the sole exception of the Emperor or, if it is a chief's tent, the chief; those of lower rank do not pay much attention to such things. This was the first time since Cuyuc had been made Emperor that we had entered his tent in his presence. He also received all the envoys in that place, but very few entered his tent.

So many gifts were bestowed by the envoys there that it was marvellous to behold—gifts of silk, samite, velvet, brocade, girdles of silk threaded with gold, choice furs, and other presents. The Emperor was also given a sunshade or little awning such as is carried over his head, and it was all decorated with precious stones. . . .

Leaving there we went to another place where a wonderful tent had been set up all of red velvet, and this had been given by the Kitayans; there also we were taken inside. Whenever we went in we were given mead and wine to drink, and cooked meat was offered us if we wished to have it. A lofty platform of boards had been erected, on which the Emperor's throne was placed. The throne, which was of ivory, was wonderfully carved and there was also gold on it, and precious stones, if I remember rightly, and pearls. Steps led up to it and it was rounded behind. Benches were also placed round the throne, and here the ladies sat in their seats on the left; nobody, however, sat on the right, but the chiefs were on benches in the middle and the rest of the people sat beyond them. Every day a great crowd of ladies came.

Finally, after some time, John was to be brought again before the Emperor. When he heard from them that we had come to him he ordered us to go back to his mother, the reason being that he wished on the following day to raise his banner against the whole of the Western world—we were told this definitely by men who knew . . .—and he wanted us to be kept in ignorance of this. On our return we stayed for a few days, then we went back to him again and remained with him for a good month, enduring such hunger and thirst that we could scarcely keep alive, for the food provided for four was barely sufficient for one, moreover, we were unable to find anything to buy, for the market was a very long way off. If the Lord had not sent us a certain Russian, by name Cosmas, a goldsmith and a great favourite of the Emperor, who supported us to some extent, we would, I believe, have died, unless the Lord had helped us in some other way. . . .

After this the Emperor sent for us, and through Chingay his protonotary told us to write down what we had to say and our business, and give it to him. We did this and wrote out for him all that we said earlier to Bati. . . . A few days passed by; then he had us summoned again and told us through Kadac, the procurator of the whole empire, in the presence of Bala and Chingay his protonotaries and many other scribes, to say all we had to say: We did this willingly and gladly. Our interpreter on this as on the previous occasion was Temer, a knight of Jerozlaus': and there were also present a cleric who was with him and another cleric who was with the Emperor. On this occasion we were asked if there were any people with the Lord Pope who understood the writing of the Russians or Saracens or even of the Tartars. We gave answer that we used neither the

Ruthenian nor Saracen writing; there were however Saracens in the country but they were a long way from the Lord Pope; but we said that it seemed to us that the most expedient course would be for them to write in Tartar and translate it for us, and we would write it down carefully in our own script and we would take both the letter and the translation to the Lord Pope. Thereupon they left us to go to the Emperor.

On St. Martin's day we were again summoned, and Kadac, Chingay, and Bala, the aforementioned secretaries, came to us and translated the letter for us word by word. When we had written it in Latin, they had it translated so that they might hear a phrase at a time, for they wanted to know if we had made a mistake in any word. When both letters were written, they made us read it once and a second time in case we had left out anything. . . .

It is the custom for the Emperor of the Tartars never to speak to a foreigner, however important he may be, except through an intermediary, and he listens and gives his answer, also through the intermediary. Whenever his subjects have any business to bring before Kadac, or while they are listening to the Emperor's reply, they stay on their knees until the end of the conversation, however important they may be. It is not possible nor indeed is it the custom for anyone to say anything about any matter after the Emperor has declared his decision. This Emperor not only has a procurator and protonotaries and secretaries, but all officials for dealing with both public and private matters, except that he has no advocates, for everything is settled according to the decision of the Emperor without the turmoil of legal trials. The other princes of the Tartars do the same in those matters concerning them.

The present Emperor may be forty or forty-five years old or more; he is of medium height, very intelligent, and extremely shrewd, and most serious and grave in his manner. He is never seen to laugh for a slight cause nor to indulge in any frivolity, so we were told by the Christians who are constantly with him. The Christians of his household also told us that they firmly believed he was about to become a Christian, and they have clear evidence of this, for he maintains Christian clerics and provides them with supplies of Christian things; in addition he always has a chapel before his chief tent and they sing openly and in public and beat the board for services after the Greek fashion like other Christians, however big a crowd of Tartars or other men be there. The other chiefs do not behave like this.

. . . on the feast of St. Brice [November 13th], they gave us a permit to depart and a letter sealed with the Emperor's seal, and sent us to the Emperor's mother. She gave each of us a fox-skin cloak, which had the fur outside and was lined inside, and a length of velvet; our Tartars stole a good yard from each of the pieces of velvet and from the piece given to our servant they stole more than half. This did not escape our notice, but we preferred not to make a fuss about it.

We then set out on the return journey.

■ REFLECTIONS

The great Chinese artist Zheng Sixiao (1241–1318) continued to paint his delicate Chinese orchids in the years after the Mongol defeat of the Sung dynasty, under the alien rule of Kublai Khan (r. 1260–1294), the fifth Great Khan and the founder of the Mongol Yuan dynasty of China. But when Zheng was asked why he always painted the orchids without earth around their roots, he replied that the earth had been stolen by the barbarians.

Just as it would be a mistake to see a fifth-generation Mongol ruler like Kublai as a barbarian, it would also be a mistake to assume that Zheng's hardened resistance remained the norm. In fact, a younger generation of artists found opportunity and even freedom in Kublai's China. Kublai appointed some of the most famous Chinese painters of his era to positions of government—Ministries of War, Public Works, Justice, Personnel, Imperial Sacrifices—actively recruiting the bright young men, artists and intellectuals, for his government. While some painters catered to the Mongol elite's inclination for paintings of horses, others relished the wider range of subjects allowed by a regime free of highly cultivated prejudices.

If conquest invariably brings charges of barbarism, it also eventually turns to issues of government and administration. Administrators need officials. Though Kublai Khan abolished the Chinese civil service examination system because it would have forced him to rely on Chinese officials, the Chinese language, and an educational system based on the Chinese classics, he actively sought ways of governing that were neither too Chinese nor too Mongolian. Typically, he promulgated a Chinese alphabet that was based on Tibetan, hoping that its phonetic symbols would make communication easier and less classical. Many of his achievements were unintended. While his officials continued to use Chinese characters and the Uighur script, the Yuan dynasty witnessed a flowering of literary culture, including theater and novels. For some, no doubt, the wind from the steppe blew away the dust and cobwebs that had accumulated for too long.

Our judgment of the Mongols depends to a great extent on the period of Mongol history we consider. But while it is easy to condemn Genghis Khan and the initial conquests and praise the later enlightened governance, two considerations come to mind. First, in the great sweep of history, many "barbarians" became benign, even indulgent, administrators. Second, the Mongols were not unique in making that transition.

Before the Mongols, the Vikings had already made the transition from raiding to trading and from conquering to colonizing. In fact, the Vikings had always been farmer-sailors who were as hungry for land as for plunder. Unlike the Mongols who were born on horses, continually picking up and remaking camp in new pastureland, the Vikings became nomadic in emergencies when a search for new settlements was necessary.

The memory of Viking assaults also faded faster than that of the Mongols. The Viking Rus had the Mongols to thank. The Rus of Viking cities like Novgorod became the national heroes of anti-Mongol Russian legend, eventually becoming the Russians. In Europe, too, the descendants of Vikings helped establish new national identities. The last great Viking king, Harald the Hard Ruler, "Thunderbolt of the North," won back his father's crown as king of Norway in 1047, after preparing himself in Russian trading cities and Byzantine courts. He had married a Russian princess and fought for the Byzantines in Asia Minor, Jerusalem, and the Caucasus Mountains. In 1066, this king of Norway lost his control of England when he was killed by an English earl. A few days later the new English king was killed by William Duke of Normandy, a Viking son who had previously conquered much of France. Norman rule was to last over a hundred years, from 1066 to 1215, and create a new English identity.

At the end of the day, history is neither moral nor immoral. History is what happened, for better or worse, and moralistic history is generally bad history. The Vikings and Mongols of our period were no more morally frozen in time than were the Christian and Muslim Crusaders of the same era who visited such violence upon each other.

Just as the role of nomads and settlers changes over time, so does the degree to which a people are particularly aggressive or peaceful. It is hard to imagine a more fearful people than the Mongols of the thirteenth century or the Vikings of the tenth century. Yet modern Scandinavia, Iceland, and Mongolia are among the most peaceful places on the planet.

12

The Black Death

Afro-Eurasia, 1346–1350

■ HISTORICAL CONTEXT

The Mongol peace that made the Persian Ilkhanid dynasty (1256–1353) and the Chinese Yuan dynasty (1279–1368) sister empires nurtured a level of economic exchange and artistic communication greater than in the most cosmopolitan days of the early Roman/Han Silk Road. But the new caravan routes that spanned Central Asia could carry microbes as well as people. The plague that had long been endemic in country rats spread by fleas to city rats and other animals, including humans. As early as 1346, travelers reported millions killed in China, Central Asia, and the Middle East. In Europe and Egypt, approximately a third of the population perished. In some cities, the death toll was greater than half. This pandemic plague of 1346–1350 is sometimes called the Black Death, after the discolored wounds it caused.

■ THINKING HISTORICALLY

Considering Cause and Effect

The study of history, like the practice of medicine, is a process of understanding the causes of certain effects. In medicine the effects are diseases or good health; in history they are more varied events. Nevertheless, understanding the causes of things is central to both disciplines. For medical specialists the goal of understanding causes is implicitly a part of the process of improving health or finding a cure. Historians rarely envision "cures" for social ills, but many believe that an understanding of cause and effect can improve society's chances of avoiding undesirable outcomes in favor of more helpful ones.

Still, the most hopeful medical researcher or historian would agree that the process of relating cause and effect, of finding causes and explaining effects, is fraught with difficulties. There is first the problem of precisely defining the effect to be explained. Next there is the need to find possible causes in past events (though medical specialists often have the advantage of replicating the past by experiment). Then there is the need to establish a connection between the past event and the current condition (avoiding the logical fallacy *post hoc ergo propter hoc*: "after this, therefore because of this"). We will explore some of those difficulties in this chapter.

MARK WHEELIS

Biological Warfare at the 1346 Siege of Caffa, 2002

We are used to thinking of biological warfare as a recently developed threat. This article, published in a journal for public health professionals, suggests a longer history. According to the author, how and where did the Black Death originate? What was the significance of the Mongol siege of the northern Black Sea port of Caffa in 1346? The author draws on the contemporary account of the Black Death by Gabriele de' Mussis. On what points does he agree and disagree with de' Mussis?

THINKING HISTORICALLY

The author of this selection, a professor of microbiology at the University of California, was trained as a bacterial physiologist and geneticist, but for more than the last ten years his research has concentrated on the history and control of biological weapons. Notice how he uses both medical and historical ways of explaining causes. In medicine and science, the study of causes is called etiology. Give an example from the reading of an etiological explanation of the Black Death. The author also offers historical explanations of causes. Give examples of these. How are the etiological and historical similar and different?

Source: Mark Wheelis, "Biological Warfare at the 1346 Siege of Caffa," *Emerging Infectious Diseases* 8, no. 9 (September 2002): 971–75. The journal is published by the U.S. Centers for Disease Control and Prevention (C.D.C.), Atlanta, and is also available online at http://www.nc.cdc.gov/eid/article/8/9/01-0536_article.

The Black Death, which swept through Europe, the Near East, and North Africa in the mid-fourteenth century, was probably the greatest public health disaster in recorded history and one of the most dramatic examples ever of emerging or reemerging disease. Europe lost an estimated one-quarter to one-third of its population, and the mortality in North Africa and the Near East was comparable. China, India, and the rest of the Far East are commonly believed to have also been severely affected, but little evidence supports that belief.

A principal source on the origin of the Black Death is a memoir by the Italian Gabriele de' Mussis. This memoir has been published several times in its original Latin and has recently been translated into English (although brief passages have been previously published in translation). This narrative contains some startling assertions: that the Mongol army hurled plague-infected cadavers into the besieged Crimean city of Caffa, thereby transmitting the disease to the inhabitants; and that fleeing survivors of the siege spread plague from Caffa to the Mediterranean Basin. If this account is correct, Caffa should be recognized as the site of the most spectacular incident of biological warfare ever, with the Black Death as its disastrous consequence. After analyzing these claims, I have concluded that it is plausible that the biological attack took place as described and was responsible for infecting the inhabitants of Caffa; however, the event was unimportant in the spread of the plague pandemic.

Origin of the Fourteenth-Century Pandemic

The disease that caused this catastrophic pandemic has, since Hecker,[1] generally been considered to have been a plague, a zoonotic disease caused by the gram-negative bacterium *Yersinia pestis*, the principal reservoir for which is wild rodents. The ultimate origin of the Black Death is uncertain—China, Mongolia, India, central Asia, and southern Russia have all been suggested. Known fourteenth-century sources are of little help; they refer repeatedly to an eastern origin, but none of the reports is firsthand. Historians generally agree that the outbreak moved west out of the steppes north of the Black and Caspian Seas, and its spread through Europe and the Middle East is fairly well documented. [See Map 12.1.] However, despite more than a century of speculation about an ultimate origin further east, the requisite scholarship using Chinese and central Asian sources has yet to be done. In any event, the Crimea[2] clearly played a pivotal role as the proximal source from which the Mediterranean Basin was infected.

---

[1] Justus Friedrich Karl Hecker (1795–1850), German physician who founded the study of disease in history. See *The Black Death: The Dancing Mania*. See also selection 4 of this chapter. [Ed.]

[2] The peninsula that juts into the Black Sea from the north (modern Ukraine); Caffa was one of its port cities. [Ed.]

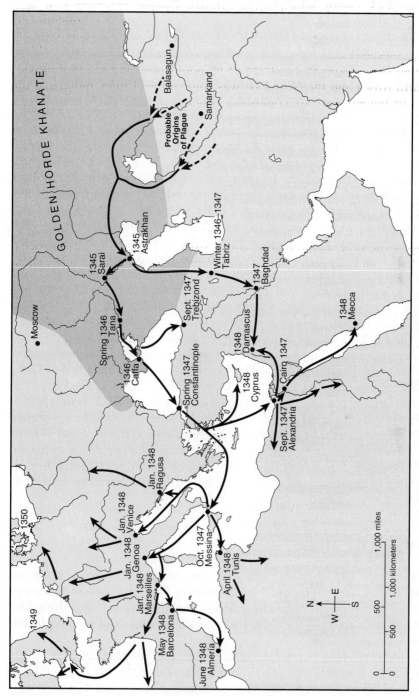

Map 12.1 Tentative Chronology of the Initial Spread of Plague in the Mid-Fourteenth Century.

Historical Background to the Siege of Caffa

Caffa (now Feodosija, Ukraine) was established by Genoa in 1266 by agreement with the Kahn of the Golden Horde. It was the main port for the great Genoese merchant ships, which connected there to a coastal shipping industry to Tana (now Azov, Russia) on the Don River. Trade along the Don connected Tana to Central Russia, and overland caravan routes linked it to Sarai and thence to the Far East.

Relations between Italian traders and their Mongol hosts were uneasy, and in 1307 Toqtai, Kahn of the Golden Horde, arrested the Italian residents of Sarai, and besieged Caffa. The cause was apparently Toqtai's displeasure at the Italian trade in Turkic slaves (sold for soldiers to the Mameluke Sultanate). The Genoese resisted for a year, but in 1308 set fire to their city and abandoned it. Relations between the Italians and the Golden Horde remained tense until Toqtai's death in 1312.

Toqtai's successor, Özbeg, welcomed the Genoese back, and also ceded land at Tana to the Italians for the expansion of their trading enterprise. By the 1340s, Caffa was again a thriving city, heavily fortified within two concentric walls. The inner wall enclosed 6,000 houses, the outer 11,000. The city's population was highly cosmopolitan, including Genoese, Venetian, Greeks, Armenians, Jews, Mongols, and Turkic peoples.

In 1343 the Mongols under Janibeg (who succeeded Özbeg in 1340) besieged Caffa and the Italian enclave at Tana following a brawl between Italians and Muslims in Tana. The Italian merchants in Tana fled to Caffa (which, by virtue of its location directly on the coast, maintained maritime access despite the siege). The siege of Caffa lasted until February 1344, when it was lifted after an Italian relief force killed 15,000 Mongol troops and destroyed their siege machines. Janibeg renewed the siege in 1345 but was again forced to lift it after a year, this time by an epidemic of plague that devastated his forces. The Italians blockaded Mongol ports, forcing Janibeg to negotiate, and in 1347 the Italians were allowed to reestablish their colony in Tana.

Gabriele de' Mussis

Gabriele de' Mussis, born circa 1280, practiced as a notary in the town of Piacenza, over the mountains just north of Genoa. [Nineteenth-century Italian historian] Tononi summarizes the little we know of him. His practice was active in the years 1300–1349. He is thought to have died in approximately 1356.

Although [the German historian] Henschel thought de' Mussis was present at the siege of Caffa, Tononi asserts that the Piacenza archives contain deeds signed by de' Mussis spanning the period 1344 through the first half of 1346. While this does not rule out travel to Caffa in late

1346, textual evidence suggests that he did not. He does not claim to have witnessed any of the Asian events he describes and often uses a passive voice for descriptions. After describing the siege of Caffa, de' Mussis goes on to say, "Now it is time that we passed from east to west to discuss all the things which we ourselves have seen. . . ."

The Narrative of Gabriele de' Mussis

The de' Mussis account is presumed to have been written in 1348 or early 1349 because of its immediacy and the narrow time period described. The original is lost, but a copy is included in a compilation of historical and geographic accounts by various authors, dating from approximately 1367. The account begins with an introductory comment by the scribe who copied the documents: "In the name of God, Amen. Here begins an account of the disease or mortality which occurred in 1348, put together by Gabrielem de Mussis of Piacenza."

The narrative begins with an apocalyptic speech by God, lamenting the depravity into which humanity has fallen and describing the retribution intended. It goes on:

". . . In 1346, in the countries of the East, countless numbers of Tartars and Saracens were struck down by a mysterious illness which brought sudden death. Within these countries broad regions, far-spreading provinces, magnificent kingdoms, cities, towns and settlements, ground down by illness and devoured by dreadful death, were soon stripped of their inhabitants. An eastern settlement under the rule of the Tartars called Tana, which lay to the north of Constantinople and was much frequented by Italian merchants, was totally abandoned after an incident there which led to its being besieged and attacked by hordes of Tartars who gathered in a short space of time. The Christian merchants, who had been driven out by force, were so terrified of the power of the Tartars that, to save themselves and their belongings, they fled in an armed ship to Caffa, a settlement in the same part of the world which had been founded long ago by the Genoese.

"Oh God! See how the heathen Tartar races, pouring together from all sides, suddenly invested the city of Caffa and besieged the trapped Christians there for almost three years. There, hemmed in by an immense army, they could hardly draw breath, although food could be shipped in, which offered them some hope. But behold, the whole army was affected by a disease which overran the Tartars and killed thousands upon thousands every day. It was as though arrows were raining down from heaven to strike and crush the Tartars' arrogance. All medical advice and attention was useless; the Tartars died as soon as the signs of disease appeared on their bodies: swellings in the armpit or groin caused by coagulating humours, followed by a putrid fever.

"The dying Tartars, stunned and stupefied by the immensity of the disaster brought about by the disease, and realizing that they had no hope of escape, lost interest in the siege. But they ordered corpses to be placed in catapults[3] and lobbed into the city in the hope that the intolerable stench would kill everyone inside.[4] What seemed like mountains of dead were thrown into the city, and the Christians could not hide or flee or escape from them, although they dumped as many of the bodies as they could in the sea. And soon the rotting corpses tainted the air and poisoned the water supply, and the stench was so overwhelming that hardly one in several thousand was in a position to flee the remains of the Tartar army. Moreover one infected man could carry the poison to others, and infect people and places with the disease by look alone. No one knew, or could discover, a means of defense.

"Thus almost everyone who had been in the East, or in the regions to the south and north, fell victim to sudden death after contracting this pestilential disease, as if struck by a lethal arrow which raised a tumor on their bodies. The scale of the mortality and the form which it took persuaded those who lived, weeping and lamenting, through the bitter events of 1346 to 1348—the Chinese, Indians, Persians, Medes, Kurds, Armenians, Cilicians, Georgians, Mesopotamians, Nubians, Ethiopians, Turks, Egyptians, Arabs, Saracens, and Greeks (for almost all the East has been affected)—that the last judgement had come.

". . . As it happened, among those who escaped from Caffa by boat were a few sailors who had been infected with the poisonous disease. Some boats were bound for Genoa, others went to Venice and to other Christian areas. When the sailors reached these places and mixed with the people there, it was as if they had brought evil spirits with them: every city, every settlement, every place was poisoned by the contagious pestilence, and their inhabitants, both men and women, died suddenly. And when one person had contracted the illness, he poisoned his whole family even as he fell and died, so that those preparing to bury his body were seized by death in the same way. Thus death entered through the windows, and as cities and towns were depopulated their inhabitants mourned their dead neighbours."

The account closes with an extended description of the plague in Piacenza, and a reprise of the apocalyptic vision with which it begins.

---

[3] Technically trebuchets, not catapults. Catapults hurl objects by the release of tension on twisted cordage; they are not capable of hurling loads over a few dozen kilograms. Trebuchets are counter-weight-driven hurling machines, very effective for throwing ammunition weighing a hundred kilos or more.

[4] Medieval society lacked a coherent theory of disease causation. Three notions coexisted in a somewhat contradictory mixture: 1) disease was a divine punishment for individual or collective transgression; 2) disease was the result of "miasma," or the stench of decay; and 3) disease was the result of person-to-person contagion.

Commentary

In this narrative, de' Mussis makes two important claims about the siege of Caffa and the Black Death: that plague was transmitted to Europeans by the hurling of diseased cadavers into the besieged city of Caffa and that Italians fleeing from Caffa brought it to the Mediterranean ports.

Biological Warfare at Caffa

De' Mussis's account is probably secondhand and is uncorroborated; however, he seems, in general, to be a reliable source, and as a Piacenzian he would have had access to eyewitnesses of the siege. Several considerations incline me to trust his account: this was probably not the only, nor the first, instance of apparent attempts to transmit disease by hurling biological material into besieged cities; it was within the technical capabilities of besieging armies of the time; and it is consistent with medieval notions of disease causality.

Tentatively accepting that the attack took place as described, we can consider two principal hypotheses for the entry of plague into the city: it might, as de' Mussis asserts, have been transmitted by the hurling of plague cadavers; or it might have entered by rodent-to-rodent transmission from the Mongol encampments into the city.

Diseased cadavers hurled into the city could easily have transmitted plague, as defenders handled the cadavers during disposal. Contact with infected material is a known mechanism of transmission; for instance, among 284 cases of plague in the United States in 1970–1995 for which a mechanism of transmission could be reasonably inferred, 20 percent were thought to be by direct contact. Such transmission would have been especially likely at Caffa, where cadavers would have been badly mangled by being hurled, and many of the defenders probably had cut or abraded hands from coping with the bombardment. Very large numbers of cadavers were possibly involved, greatly increasing the opportunity for disease transmission. Since disposal of the bodies of victims in a major outbreak of lethal disease is always a problem, the Mongol forces may have used their hurling machines as a solution to their mortuary problem, in which case many thousands of cadavers could have been involved. De' Mussis's description of "mountains of dead" might have been quite literally true.

Thus it seems plausible that the events recounted by de' Mussis could have been an effective means of transmission of plague into the city. The alternative, rodent-to-rodent transmission from the Mongol encampments into the city, is less likely. Besieging forces must have camped at least a kilometer away from the city walls. This distance is necessary to have a healthy margin of safety from arrows and artillery and to provide space for logistical support and other military activities between the encampments and the front lines. Front-line location must have been approximately 250–300 m from the walls; trebuchets are known from modern reconstruction to be capable of hurling 100 kg more than 200 m, and historical sources claim 300 m as the working range of large machines. Thus, the bulk of rodent nests associated with the besieging armies would have been located a kilometer or more away from the cities, and none would have likely been closer than 250 m. Rats are quite sedentary and rarely venture more than a few tens of meters from their nest. It is thus unlikely that there was any contact between the rat populations within and outside the walls.

Given the many uncertainties, any conclusion must remain tentative. However, the considerations above suggest that the hurling of plague cadavers might well have occurred as de' Mussis claimed, and if so, that this biological attack was probably responsible for the transmission of the disease from the besiegers to the besieged. Thus, this early act of biological warfare, if such it were, appears to have been spectacularly successful in producing casualties, although of no strategic importance (the city remained in Italian hands, and the Mongols abandoned the siege).

Crimea as the Source of European and Near Eastern Plague

There has never been any doubt that plague entered the Mediterranean from the Crimea, following established maritime trade routes. Rat infestations in the holds of cargo ships would have been highly susceptible to the rapid spread of plague, and even if most rats died during the voyage, they would have left abundant hungry fleas that would infect humans unpacking the holds. Shore rats foraging on board recently arrived ships would also become infected, transmitting plague to city rat populations.

Plague appears to have been spread in a stepwise fashion, on many ships rather than on a few [see Map 12.1], taking over a year to reach Europe from the Crimea. This conclusion seems fairly firm, as the dates for the arrival of plague in Constantinople and more westerly cities are reasonably certain. Thus de' Mussis was probably mistaken in attributing the Black Death to fleeing survivors of Caffa, who should not have needed more than a few months to return to Italy.

Furthermore, a number of other Crimean ports were under Mongol control, making it unlikely that Caffa was the only source of infected ships heading west. And the overland caravan routes to the Middle East from Serai and Astrakhan insured that plague was also spreading south (Map 12.1), whence it would have entered Europe in any case. The siege of Caffa and its gruesome finale thus are unlikely to have been seriously implicated in the transmission of plague from the Black Sea to Europe.

Conclusion

Gabriele de' Mussis's account of the origin and spread of plague appears to be consistent with most known facts, although mistaken in its claim that plague arrived in Italy directly from the Crimea. His account of biological attack is plausible, consistent with the technology of the time, and it provides the best explanation of disease transmission into besieged Caffa. This thus appears to be one of the first biological attacks recorded and among the most successful of all time.

However, it is unlikely that the attack had a decisive role in the spread of plague to Europe. Much maritime commerce probably continued throughout this period from other Crimean ports. Overland caravan routes to the Middle East were also unaffected. Thus, refugees from Caffa would most likely have constituted only one of several streams of infected ships and caravans leaving the region. The siege of Caffa, for all of its dramatic appeal, probably had no more than anecdotal importance in the spread of plague, a macabre incident in terrifying times.

Despite its historical unimportance, the siege of Caffa is a powerful reminder of the horrific consequences when disease is successfully used as a weapon. The Japanese use of plague as a weapon in World War II and the huge Soviet stockpiles of *Y. pestis* prepared for use in an all-out war further remind us that plague remains a very real problem for modern arms control, six and a half centuries later.

2

GABRIELE DE' MUSSIS
Origins of the Black Death, c. 1348

Gabriele de' Mussis (d. 1356) was a lawyer who lived in the northern Italian city of Piacenza. The previous reading introduced you to de' Mussis and the importance of his history of the Black Death. Since Wheelis quoted abundantly from the story of the siege of Caffa, we pick up the story in de' Mussis's words regarding the spread of the plague to Europe, where, as he wrote, he had direct evidence. How would you rate de' Mussis as an eyewitness observer? According to his evidence, how did the Black Death spread in Italy? How deadly was it?

Source: *The Black Death*, trans. and ed. Rosemary Horrox (Manchester, England: Manchester University Press, 1994), 18–26.

THINKING HISTORICALLY

As in the previous selection, there are two causal chains in this account, but in this case they are not medical and historical. Rather, reminiscent of the readings on the First Crusade, they are divine and human chains of causation. What, according to the author, were the divine or religious causes of the Black Death? What were the human, physical, or scientific causes? What remedies does each type of cause call for?

Now it is time that we passed from east to west, to discuss all the things which we ourselves have seen, or known, or consider likely on the basis of the evidence, and, by so doing, to show forth the terrifying judgements of God. Listen everybody, and it will set tears pouring from your eyes. For the Almighty has said: "I shall wipe man, whom I created, off the face of the earth. Because he is flesh and blood, let him be turned to dust and ashes. My spirit shall not remain among man."

—"What are you thinking of, merciful God, thus to destroy your creation and the human race; to order and command its sudden annihilation in this way? What has become of your mercy; the faith of our fathers; the blessed virgin, who holds sinners in her lap; the precious blood of the martyrs; the worthy army of confessors and virgins; the whole host of paradise, who pray ceaselessly for sinners; the most precious death of Christ on the cross and our wonderful redemption? Kind God, I beg that your anger may cease, that you do not destroy sinners in this way, and, because you desire mercy rather than sacrifice, that you turn away all evil from the penitent, and do not allow the just to be condemned with the unjust."

—"I hear you, sinner, dropping words into my ears. I bid you weep. The time for mercy has passed. I, God, am called to vengeance. It is my pleasure to take revenge on sin and wickedness. I shall give my signs to the dying, let them take steps to provide for the health of their souls."

As it happened, among those who escaped from Caffa by boat were a few sailors who had been infected with the poisonous disease. Some boats were bound for Genoa, others went to Venice and to other Christian areas. . . .

—"We Genoese and Venetians bear the responsibility for revealing the judgements of God. Alas, once our ships had brought us to port we went to our homes. And because we had been delayed by tragic events, and because among us there were scarcely ten survivors from a thousand sailors, relations, kinsmen and neighbours flocked to us from all sides. But, to our anguish, we were carrying the darts of death. While they hugged and kissed us we were spreading poison from our lips even as we spoke."

When they returned to their own folk, these people speedily poisoned the whole family, and within three days the afflicted family would succumb to the dart of death. Mass funerals had to be held and there was not enough room to bury the growing numbers of dead. Priests and doctors, upon whom most of the care of the sick devolved, had their hands full in visiting the sick and, alas, by the time they left they too had been infected and followed the dead immediately to the grave. Oh fathers! Oh mothers! Oh children and wives! For a long time prosperity preserved you from harm, but one grave now covers you and the unfortunate alike. You who enjoyed the world and upon whom pleasure and prosperity smiled, who mingled joys with follies, the same tomb receives you and you are handed over as food for worms. Oh hard death, impious death, bitter death, cruel death, who divides parents, divorces spouses, parts children, separates brothers and sisters. We bewail our wretched plight. The past has devoured us, the present is gnawing our entrails, the future threatens yet greater dangers. What we laboured to amass with feverish activity, we have lost in one hour.

Where are the fine clothes of gilded youth? Where is nobility and the courage of fighters, where the mature wisdom of elders and the regal throng of great ladies, where the piles of treasure and precious stones? Alas! All have been destroyed; thrust aside by death. To whom shall we turn, who can help us? To flee is impossible, to hide futile. Cities, fortresses, fields, woods, highways and rivers are ringed by thieves — which is to say by evil spirits, the executioners of the supreme Judge, preparing endless punishments for us all.

We can unfold a terrifying event which happened when an army was camped near Genoa. Four of the soldiers left the force in search of plunder and made their way to Rivarolo on the coast, where the disease had killed all the inhabitants. Finding the houses shut up, and no one about, they broke into one of the houses and stole a fleece which they found on a bed. They then rejoined the army and on the following night the four of them bedded down under the fleece. When morning comes it finds them dead. As a result everyone panicked, and thereafter nobody would use the goods and clothes of the dead, or even handle them, but rejected them outright.

Scarcely one in seven of the Genoese survived. In Venice, where an inquiry was held into the mortality, it was found that more than 70 percent of the people had died, and that within a short period 20 out of 24 excellent physicians had died. The rest of Italy, Sicily, and Apulia and the neighbouring regions maintain that they have been virtually emptied of inhabitants. The people of Florence, Pisa, and Lucca, finding themselves bereft of their fellow residents, emphasise their losses. The Roman Curia at Avignon, the provinces on both sides of the Rhône, Spain, France, and the Empire cry up their griefs and disasters — all of which makes it extraordinarily difficult for me to give an accurate picture.

By contrast, what befell the Saracens can be established from trustworthy accounts. In the city of Babylon alone (the heart of the Sultan's power), 480,000 of his subjects are said to have been carried off by disease in less than three months in 1348—and this is known from the Sultan's register which records the names of the dead, because he receives a gold bezant for each person buried. I am silent about Damascus and his other cities, where the number of dead was infinite. In the other countries of the East, which are so vast that it takes three years to ride across them and which have a population of 10,000 for every one inhabitant of the west, it is credibly reported that countless people have died.

Everyone has a responsibility to keep some record of the disease and the deaths, and because I am myself from Piacenza I have been urged to write more about what happened there in 1348. . . .

I don't know where to begin. Cries and laments arise on all sides. Day after day one sees the Cross and the Host[1] being carried about the city, and countless dead being buried. The ensuing mortality was so great that people could scarcely snatch breath. The living made preparations for their burial, and because there was not enough room for individual graves, pits had to be dug in colonnades and piazzas, where nobody had ever been buried before. It often happened that man and wife, father and son, mother and daughter, and soon the whole household and many neighbours, were buried together in one place. The same thing happened in Castell' Arquato and Viguzzolo and in the other towns, villages, cities, and settlements, and last of all in the Val Tidone, where they had hitherto escaped the plague.

Very many people died. One Oberto de Sasso, who had come from the infected neighbourhood around the church of the Franciscans, wished to make his will and accordingly summoned a notary and his neighbours as witnesses, all of whom, more than sixty of them, died soon after. At this time the Dominican friar Syfredo de Bardis, a man of prudence and great learning who had visited the Holy Sepulchre, also died, along with 23 brothers of the same house. There also died within a short time the Franciscan friar Bertolino Coxadocha of Piacenza, renowned for his learning and many virtues, along with 24 brothers of the same house, nine of them on one day; seven of the Augustinians; the Carmelite friar Francesco Todischi with six of his brethren; four of the order of Mary; more than sixty prelates and parish priests from the city and district of Piacenza; many nobles; countless young people; numberless women, particularly those who were pregnant. It is too distressing to recite any more, or to lay bare the wounds inflicted by so great a disaster.

---

[1] The consecrated Eucharistic wafer. The reference is to priests taking the last sacrament to the dying. [Ed.]

Let all creation tremble with fear before the judgement of God. Let human frailty submit to its creator. May a greater grief be kindled in all hearts, and tears well up in all eyes as future ages hear what happened in this disaster. When one person lay sick in a house no one would come near. Even dear friends would hide themselves away, weeping. The physician would not visit. The priest, panic-stricken, administered the sacraments with fear and trembling.

Listen to the tearful voices of the sick: "Have pity, have pity, my friends. At least say something, now that the hand of God has touched me."

"Oh father, why have you abandoned me? Do you forget that I am your child?"

"Mother, where have you gone? Why are you now so cruel to me when only yesterday you were so kind? You fed me at your breast and carried me within your womb for nine months."

"My children, whom I brought up with toil and sweat, why have you run away?"

Man and wife reached out to each other, "Alas, once we slept happily together but now are separated and wretched."

And when the sick were in the throes of death, they still called out piteously to their family and neighbours, "Come here. I'm thirsty, bring me a drink of water. I'm still alive. Don't be frightened. Perhaps I won't die. Please hold me tight, hug my wasted body. You ought to be holding me in your arms."

At this, as everyone else kept their distance, somebody might take pity and leave a candle burning by the bed head as he fled. And when the victim had breathed his last, it was often the mother who shrouded her son and placed him in the coffin, or the husband who did the same for his wife, for everybody else refused to touch the dead body. . . .

I am overwhelmed, I can't go on. Everywhere one turns there is death and bitterness to be described. The hand of the Almighty strikes repeatedly, to greater and greater effect. The terrible judgement gains in power as time goes by.

—What shall we do? Kind Jesus, receive the souls of the dead, avert your gaze from our sins and blot out all our iniquities.

We know that whatever we suffer is the just reward of our sins. Now, therefore, when the Lord is enraged, embrace acts of penance, so that you do not stray from the right path and perish. Let the proud be humbled. Let misers, who withheld alms from the poor, blush for shame. Let the envious become zealous in almsgiving. Let lechers put aside their filthy habits and distinguish themselves in honest living. Let the raging and wrathful restrain themselves from violence. Let gluttons temper their appetites by fasting. Let the slaves of sloth arise and dress themselves in good works. Let adolescents and youths abandon their present delight in following fashion. Let there be good faith and equity among judges, and respect for the law among merchants. Let pettifogging lawyers study and grow wise before they put pen to paper. Let members of religious orders abandon hypocrisy. Let the dignity of prelates be put to better use. Let all of you hurry to set your feet on the way of salvation. And let the overweening vanity of great ladies, which so easily turns into voluptuousness, be bridled. It was against their arrogance that Isaiah inveighed: "Because the daughters of Sion are haughty, and have walked with stretched out necks and wanton glances of their eyes, and made a noise as they walked with their feet, and moved in a set pace. . . . Thy fairest men also shall fall by the sword: and thy valiant ones in battle. And her gates shall lament and mourn: and she shall sit desolate on the ground" [Isaiah 3.16–26]. This was directed against the pride of ladies and young people.

For the rest, so that the conditions, causes, and symptoms of this pestilential disease should be made plain to all, I have decided to set them out in writing. Those of both sexes who were in health, and in no fear of death, were struck by four savage blows to the flesh. First, out of the blue, a kind of chilly stiffness troubled their bodies. They felt a tingling sensation, as if they were being pricked by the points of arrows. The next stage was a fearsome attack which took the form of an extremely hard, solid boil. In some people this developed under the armpit and in others in the groin between the scrotum and the body. As it grew more solid, its burning heat caused the patients to fall into an acute and putrid fever, with severe headaches. As it intensified its extreme bitterness could have various effects. In some cases it gave rise to an intolerable stench. In others it brought vomiting of blood, or swellings near the place from which the corrupt humour arose: on the back, across the chest, near the thigh. Some people lay as if in a drunken stupor and could not be roused. Behold the swellings, the warning signs sent by the Lord.[2] All these people were in danger of dying. Some died on the very day the illness took possession of them, others on the next day, others—the majority—between the third and fifth day. There was no known remedy for the vomiting of blood. Those who fell into a coma, or suffered a swelling or the stink of corruption very rarely escaped. But from the fever it was sometimes possible to make a recovery. . . .

Truly, then was a time of bitterness and grief, which served to turn men to the Lord. I shall recount what happened. A warning was given by a certain holy person, who received it in a vision, that in cities, towns and other settlements, everyone, male and female alike, should gather in their parish church on three consecutive days and, each with a lighted candle in their hand, hear with great devotion the mass of the Blessed Anastasia, which is normally performed at dawn on Christmas day, and they should humbly beg for mercy, so that they might be delivered from the disease through the merits of the holy mass. Other people sought deliverance

---

[2] A pun: *bulla* is a swelling, but it is also the word for the papal seal, and hence for a papal document (or bull). De' Mussis is playing on the idea of the swelling characteristic of the plague being God's seal, notifying the victim of his imminent fate. [Ed.]

through the mediation of a blessed martyr; and others humbly turned to other saints, so that they might escape the abomination of disease. For among the aforesaid martyrs, some, as stories relate, are said to have died from repeated blows, and it was therefore the general opinion that they would be able to protect people against the arrows of death. Finally, in 1350, the most holy Pope Clement ordained a general indulgence, to be valid for a year, which remitted penance and guilt to all who were truly penitent and confessed. And as a result a numberless multitude of people made the pilgrimage to Rome, to visit with great reverence and devotion the basilicas of the blessed apostles Peter and Paul and St John.

Oh, most dearly beloved, let us therefore not be like vipers, growing ever more wicked, but let us rather hold up our hands to heaven to beg for mercy on us all, for who but God shall have mercy on us? With this, I make an end. May the heavenly physician heal our wounds—our spiritual rather than our bodily wounds. To whom be the blessing and the praise and the glory for ever and ever, Amen.

3

GIOVANNI BOCCACCIO

The Plague in Florence: From the *Decameron*, c. 1350

Giovanni Boccaccio* (1313–1375) was a poet in Florence, Italy, when the plague struck in 1348. His *Decameron*[†] is a collection of a hundred tales based on his experiences during the plague years. This selection is drawn from the Introduction. What does Boccaccio add to your understanding of the Black Death?

THINKING HISTORICALLY

Compare Boccaccio's treatment of divine and human causes of the plague. Boccaccio not only muses on the causes of the plague; he also sees the plague as the cause of new forms of behavior. What were the behavioral effects of the plague according to Boccaccio?

* boh KAH chee oh
[†] deh KAM uh rahn

Source: Giovanni Boccaccio, *Decameron*, trans. G. H. McWilliam (Harmondsworth, England: Penguin, 1972), 50–58.

I say, then, that the sum of thirteen hundred and forty-eight years had elapsed since the fruitful Incarnation of the Son of God, when the noble city of Florence, which for its great beauty excels all others in Italy, was visited by the deadly pestilence. Some say that it descended upon the human race through the influence of the heavenly bodies, others that it was a punishment signifying God's righteous anger at our iniquitous way of life. But whatever its cause, it had originated some years earlier in the East, where it had claimed countless lives before it unhappily spread westward, growing in strength as it swept relentlessly on from one place to the next.

In the face of its onrush, all the wisdom and ingenuity of man were unavailing. Large quantities of refuse were cleared out of the city by officials specially appointed for the purpose, all sick persons were forbidden entry, and numerous instructions were issued for safeguarding the people's health, but all to no avail. Nor were the countless petitions humbly directed to God by the pious, whether by means of formal processions or in any other guise, any less ineffectual. For in the early spring of the year we have mentioned, the plague began, in a terrifying and extraordinary manner, to make its disastrous effects apparent. It did not take the form it had assumed in the East, where if anyone bled from the nose it was an obvious portent of certain death. On the contrary, its earliest symptom, in men and women alike, was the appearance of certain swellings in the groin or the armpit, some of which were egg-shaped whilst others were roughly the size of the common apple. Sometimes the swellings were large, sometimes not so large, and they were referred to by the populace as *gavòccioli*. From the two areas already mentioned, this deadly *gavòcciolo* would begin to spread, and within a short time it would appear at random all over the body. Later on, the symptoms of the disease changed, and many people began to find dark blotches and bruises on their arms, thighs, and other parts of the body, sometimes large and few in number, at other times tiny and closely spaced. These, to anyone unfortunate enough to contract them, were just as infallible a sign that he would die as the *gavòcciolo* had been earlier, and as indeed it still was.

Against these maladies, it seemed that all the advice of physicians and all the power of medicine were profitless and unavailing. Perhaps the nature of the illness was such that it allowed no remedy; or perhaps those people who were treating the illness (whose numbers had increased enormously because the ranks of the qualified were invaded by people, both men and women, who had never received any training in medicine), being ignorant of its causes, were not prescribing the appropriate cure. At all events, few of those who caught it ever recovered, and in most cases death occurred within three days from the appearance of the symptoms we have described, some people dying more rapidly than others, the majority without any fever or other complications.

But what made this pestilence even more severe was that whenever those suffering from it mixed with people who were still unaffected, it would rush upon these with the speed of a fire racing through dry or oily substances that happened to be placed within its reach. Nor was this the full extent of its evil, for not only did it infect healthy persons who conversed or had any dealings with the sick, making them ill or visiting an equally horrible death upon them, but it also seemed to transfer the sickness to anyone touching the clothes or other objects which had been handled or used by its victims. . . .

Some people were of the opinion that a sober and abstemious mode of living considerably reduced the risk of infection. They therefore formed themselves into groups and lived in isolation from everyone else. Having withdrawn to a comfortable abode where there were no sick persons, they locked themselves in and settled down to a peaceable existence, consuming modest quantities of delicate foods and precious wines and avoiding all excesses. They refrained from speaking to outsiders, refused to receive news of the dead or sick, and entertained themselves with music and whatever other amusements they were able to devise.

Others took the opposite view, and maintained that an infallible way of warding off this appalling evil was to drink heavily, enjoy life to the full, go round singing and merrymaking, gratify all of one's cravings whenever the opportunity offered, and shrug the whole thing off as one enormous joke. Moreover, they practised what they preached to the best of their ability, for they would visit one tavern after another, drinking all day and night to immoderate excess; or alternatively (and this was their more frequent custom), they would do their drinking in various private houses, but only in the ones where the conversation was restricted to subjects that were pleasant or entertaining. Such places were easy to find, for people behaved as though their days were numbered, and treated their belongings and their own persons with equal abandon. Hence most houses had become common property, and any passing stranger could make himself at home as naturally as though he were the rightful owner. But for all their riotous manner of living, these people always took good care to avoid any contact with the sick.

In the face of so much affliction and misery, all respect for the laws of God and man had virtually broken down and been extinguished in our city. For like everybody else, those ministers and executors of the laws who were not either dead or ill were left with so few subordinates that they were unable to discharge any of their duties. Hence everyone was free to behave as he pleased.

There were many other people who steered a middle course between the two already mentioned, neither restricting their diet to the same degree as the first group, nor indulging so freely as the second in drinking and other forms of wantonness, but simply doing no more than satisfy their appetite. Instead of incarcerating themselves, these people moved about freely, holding in their hands a posy of flowers, or fragrant herbs, or one of a wide range of spices, which they applied at frequent intervals to their nostrils, thinking it an excellent idea to fortify the brain with smells of that particular sort; for the stench of dead bodies, sickness, and medicines seemed to fill and pollute the whole of the atmosphere.

Some people, pursuing what was possibly the safer alternative, callously maintained that there was no better or more efficacious remedy against a plague than to run away from it. Swayed by this argument, and sparing no thought for anyone but themselves, large numbers of men and women abandoned their city, their homes, their relatives, their estates, and their belongings, and headed for the countryside, either in Florentine territory or, better still, abroad. It was as though they imagined that the wrath of God would not unleash this plague against men for their iniquities irrespective of where they happened to be, but would only be aroused against those who found themselves within the city walls; or possibly they assumed that the whole of the population would be exterminated and that the city's last hour had come.

Of the people who held these various opinions, not all of them died. Nor, however, did they all survive. On the contrary, many of each different persuasion fell ill here, there, and everywhere, and having themselves, when they were fit and well, set an example to those who were as yet unaffected, they languished away with virtually no one to nurse them. It was not merely a question of one citizen avoiding another, and of people almost invariably neglecting their neighbours and rarely or never visiting their relatives, addressing them only from a distance; this scourge had implanted so great a terror in the hearts of men and women that brothers abandoned brothers, uncles their nephews, sisters their brothers, and in many cases wives deserted their husbands. But even worse, and almost incredible, was the fact that fathers and mothers refused to nurse and assist their own children, as though they did not belong to them.

Hence the countless numbers of people who fell ill, both male and female, were entirely dependent upon either the charity of friends (who were few and far between) or the greed of servants, who remained in short supply despite the attraction of high wages out of all proportion to the services they performed. Furthermore, these latter were men and women of coarse intellect and the majority were unused to such duties, and they did little more than hand things to the invalid when asked to do so and watch over him when he was dying. And in performing this kind of service, they frequently lost their lives as well as their earnings.

As a result of this wholesale desertion of the sick by neighbours, relatives, and friends, and in view of the scarcity of servants, there grew up a practice almost never previously heard of, whereby when a woman fell ill, no matter how gracious or beautiful or gently bred she might be, she raised no objection to being attended by a male servant, whether he was young or not. Nor did she have any scruples about showing him every part of her body as freely as she would have displayed it to a woman, provided that the nature of her infirmity required her to do so; and this explains why those women who recovered were possibly less chaste in the period that followed.

Moreover a great many people died who would perhaps have survived had they received some assistance. And hence, what with the lack of appropriate means for tending the sick, and the virulence of the plague, the number of deaths reported in the city whether by day or night was so enormous that it astonished all who heard tell of it, to say nothing of the people who actually witnessed the carnage. . . .

As for the common people and a large proportion of the bourgeoisie, they presented a much more pathetic spectacle, for the majority of them were constrained, either by their poverty or the hope of survival, to remain in their houses. Being confined to their own parts of the city, they fell ill daily in their thousands, and since they had no one to assist them or attend to their needs, they inevitably perished almost without exception. Many dropped dead in the open streets, both by day and by night, whilst a great many others, though dying in their own houses, drew their neighbours' attention to the fact more by the smell of their rotting corpses than by any other means. And what with these, and the others who were dying all over the city, bodies were here, there, and everywhere. . . .

[T]here were no tears or candles or mourners to honour the dead; in fact, no more respect was accorded to dead people than would nowadays be shown towards dead goats. For it was quite apparent that the one thing which, in normal times, no wise man had ever learned to accept with patient resignation (even though it struck so seldom and unobtrusively), had now been brought home to the feeble-minded as well, but the scale of the calamity caused them to regard it with indifference.

Such was the multitude of corpses (of which further consignments were arriving every day and almost by the hour at each of the churches), that there was not sufficient consecrated ground for them to be buried in, especially if each was to have its own plot in accordance with long-established custom. So when all the graves were full, huge trenches were excavated in the churchyards, into which new arrivals were placed in their hundreds, stowed tier upon tier like ships' cargo, each layer of corpses being covered over with a thin layer of soil till the trench was filled to the top.

But rather than describe in elaborate detail the calamities we experienced in the city at that time, I must mention that, whilst an ill wind was blowing through Florence itself, the surrounding region was no less badly affected. In the fortified towns, conditions were similar to those in the city itself on a minor scale; but in the scattered hamlets and the countryside proper, the poor unfortunate peasants and their families had no physicians or servants whatever to assist them, and collapsed by the wayside, in their fields, and in their cottages at all hours of the day and night, dying more like animals than human beings. Like the townspeople, they too grew apathetic in their ways, disregarded their affairs, and neglected their possessions. Moreover, they all behaved as though each day was to be their last, and far from making provision for the future by tilling their lands, tending their flocks, and adding to their previous labours, they tried in every way they could think of to squander the assets already in their possession. Thus it came about that oxen, asses, sheep, goats, pigs, chickens, and even dogs (for all their deep fidelity to man) were driven away and allowed to roam freely through the fields, where the crops lay abandoned and had not even been reaped, let alone gathered in. And after a whole day's feasting, many of these animals, as though possessing the power of reason, would return glutted in the evening to their own quarters without any shepherd to guide them.

But let us leave the countryside and return to the city. What more remains to be said, except that the cruelty of heaven (and possibly, in some measure, also that of man) was so immense and so devastating that between March and July of the year in question, what with the fury of the pestilence and the fact that so many of the sick were inadequately cared for or abandoned in their hour of need because the healthy were too terrified to approach them, it is reliably thought that over a hundred thousand human lives were extinguished within the walls of the city of Florence? Yet before this lethal catastrophe fell upon the city, it is doubtful whether anyone would have guessed it contained so many inhabitants.

4

Causes According to College of Physicians, Paris, c. 1348

Justus Hecker (1795–1850) was a German physician and writer who pioneered the study of the history of disease and medicine. While his interpretations are dated, his access to primary sources is still valuable. The French source presented in this selection appeared in

---

Source: Quoted by J. F. C. (Justus Friedrich Carl) Hecker, in *The Black Death* (in German) (1832) trans. B. G. Babington (1888).

his *The Black Death in the 14th century: from the sources by physicians and non-physicians.*

What, according to the College of Physicians in Paris, were the causes of the plague? What precautions did they urge people to take? How was their advice similar to, or different from, that of the people of Florence as described by Bocaccio?

THINKING HISTORICALLY

In their declaration, the College of Physicians in Paris concentrate on astrology and natural science (the role of earth, air, fire, and water) to understand causation. How do they use these two systems to explain causes and precautions? What similarities are there with our contemporary systems of explanation?

We, the Members of the College of Physicians, of Paris, have, after mature consideration and consultation on the present mortality, collected the advice of our old masters in the art, and intend to make known the causes of this pestilence, more clearly than could be done according to the rules and principles of astrology and natural science; we, therefore, declare as follows:

It is known that in India, and the vicinity of the Great Sea, the constellations which combated the rays of the sun, and the warmth of the heavenly fire, exerted their power especially against that sea, and struggled violently with its waters. Hence, vapors often originate which envelope the sun, and convert his light into darkness. These vapors alternately rose and fell for twenty-eight days; but at last, sun and fire acted so powerfully upon the sea, that they attracted a great portion of it to themselves, and the waters of the ocean arose in the form of vapor; thereby the waters were in some parts, so corrupted, that the fish which they contained, died. Those corrupted waters, however, the heat of the sun could not consume, neither could other wholesome water, hail or snow, and dew, originate there from. On the contrary, this vapor spread itself through the air in many places on the earth, and enveloped them in fog.

Such was the case all over Arabia, in a part of India; in Crete; in the plains and valleys of Macedonia, in Hungary; Albania and Sicily. Should the same thing occur in Sardinia, not a man will be left alive; and the like will continue, so long as the sun remains in the sign of Leo, on all the islands and adjoining countries to which this corrupted sea-wind extends, or has already extended from India. If the inhabitants of those parts do not employ and adhere to the following, or similar means and precepts, we announce to them inevitable death — except the grace of Christ preserve their lives.

We are of opinion, that the constellations, with the aid of Nature, strive, by virtue of their divine might, to protect and heal the human race; and to this end, in union with the rays of the sun, acting through the power of fire, endeavor to break through the mist. Accordingly, within the next ten days, and until the 17th of the ensuing month of July, this mist will be converted into a stinking deleterious rain, whereby the air will be much purified. Now, as soon as this rain announces itself, by thunder or hail, every one of you should protect himself from the air; and, as well before as after the rain, kindle a large fire of vine-wood, green laurel, or other green wood; worm-wood and chamomile should also be burnt in great quantity in the market places, in other densely inhabited localities, and in the houses. Until the earth is again completely dry, and for three days afterwards, no one ought to go abroad in the fields. During this time the diet should be simple, and people should be cautious in avoiding exposure in the cool of the evening, at night, and in the morning. Poultry and water-fowl, young pork, old beef, and fat meat, in general, should not be eaten; but on the contrary, meat of a proper age, of a warm and dry nature, by no means, however, heating and exciting. Broth should be taken, seasoned with ground pepper, ginger and cloves, especially by those who are accustomed to live temperately, and are yet choice in their diet. Sleep in the day-time is detrimental; it should be taken at night until sunrise, or somewhat longer. At breakfast, one should drink little; supper should be taken an hour before sunset, when more may be drunk than in the morning. Clear light wine, mixed with a fifth or sixth part of water, should be used as a beverage. Dried or fresh fruits with wine are not injurious; but highly so without it. Beet-root and other vegetables, whether eaten pickled or fresh, are hurtful; on the contrary, spicy pot-herbs, as sage or rosemary, are wholesome. Cold, moist, watery food is, in general, prejudicial. Going out at night, and even until three o'clock in the morning, is dangerous, on account of the dew. Only small river fish should be used. Too much exercise is hurtful. The body should be kept warmer than usual, and thus protected from moisture and cold. Rain-water must not be employed in cooking, and everyone should guard against exposure to wet weather. If it rain, a little fine treacle should be taken after dinner. Fat people should not sit in the sunshine. Good clear wine should be selected and drunk often, but in small quantities, by day. Olive-oil, as an article of food, is fatal. Equally injurious are fasting or excessive abstemiousness, anxiety of mind, anger, and excessive drinking. Young people, in autumn especially, must abstain from all these things, if they do not wish to run a risk of dying of dysentery. In order to keep the body properly open, an enema, or some other simple means, should be employed, when necessary. Bathing is injurious. Men must preserve chastity as they value their lives. Everyone should impress this on his recollection, but especially those who reside on the coast, or upon an island into which the noxious wind has penetrated.

Images of the Black Death, Fourteenth and Fifteenth Centuries

Contemporary accounts testify to the plague's terrifying physical, social, and psychological impact. Images from the period document the ravages of the epidemic as well, sometimes in gruesome detail. The engraving in Figure 12.1, for example, shows a plague victim covered in the dark blotches characteristic of the disease. The town in the background appears to be going up in flames while lightning flares in the sky above. What else do you think is going on in this image?

Figure 12.1   The Black Death, 1348.

Source: Private Collection / Bridgeman Images.

Figure 12.2 Flagellants, from a fifteenth-century chronicle from Constance, Switzerland.

Source: Bettmann/© Corbis.

Figures 12.2 and 12.3 show two well-documented phenomena of the plague years: The first depicts a group of flagellants, members of a movement who wandered from town to town beating themselves with whips studded with iron nails in an effort to do penance for the sins they believed had brought on the plague. Written accounts confirm many elements in this picture: Flagellants usually carried crosses or banners with crosses on them, wore long pleated skirts, and went around bare-chested, the better to make their scourging as painful as possible. Figure 12.3 illustrates a similar impulse toward punishment as a means of coping with the plague, but this time the violence is directed outward, against Jews, so often the scapegoats in troubled times. Baseless accusations that Jews poisoned wells to spread the plague resulted in many such attacks against them during the period.

THINKING HISTORICALLY

What can these images tell us about fourteenth-century people's beliefs about the possible causes — medical or religious — of the plague? Do the images suggest a greater belief in medical or religious causes? Think about the social and religious changes wrought by the plague recounted in the de' Mussis and Boccaccio readings. What evidence, if any, do you see in these images of these changes?

Figure 12.3   The burning of Jews in an early printed woodcut.
Source: © Mary Evans Picture Library / Alamy Stock Photo.

 6

AHMAD AL-MAQRIZI

The Plague in Cairo, Fifteenth Century

Ahmad al-Maqrizi* (1364–1442) became a historian after pursuing a career as an administrator in post-plague Cairo. Although he wrote his history of the plague period more than fifty years after the event, he probably had access to contemporary sources that are now lost to us. Compare al-Maqrizi's account of the plague in Cairo with the prior accounts of the plague in Italy. How was the experience of the Black Death in Cairo similar to, and different from, the experience in Florence?

* ahk MAHD ahl mah KREE zee

Source: John Aberth, *The Black Death: The Great Mortality of 1348–1350, A Brief History with Documents* (Boston: Bedford/St. Martin's, 2005), 84–87.

THINKING HISTORICALLY

Like Boccaccio, al-Maqrizi devotes more attention to the effects than to the causes of the Black Death. What effects were similar in Florence and Cairo? Al-Maqrizi discusses certain effects that were not mentioned in the Italian accounts. Which, if any, of these effects do you think also probably occurred in Italy?

In January 1349, there appeared new symptoms that consisted of spitting up of blood. The disease caused one to experience an internal fever, followed by an uncontrollable desire to vomit; then one spat up blood and died. The inhabitants of a house were stricken one after the other, and in one night or two, the dwelling became deserted. Each individual lived with this fixed idea that he was going to die in this way. He prepared for himself a good death by distributing alms; he arranged for scenes of reconciliation and his acts of devotion multiplied. . . .

By January 21, Cairo had become an abandoned desert, and one did not see anyone walking along the streets. A man could go from the Port Zuwayla to Bāb al-Nasr[1] without encountering a living soul. The dead were very numerous, and all the world could think of nothing else. Debris piled up in the streets. People went around with worried faces. Everywhere one heard lamentations, and one could not pass by any house without being overwhelmed by the howling. Cadavers formed a heap on the public highway, funeral processions were so many that they could not file past without bumping into each other, and the dead were transported in some confusion. . . .

One began to have to search for readers of the Koran for funeral ceremonies, and a number of individuals quit their usual occupations in order to recite prayers at the head of funeral processions. In the same way, some people devoted themselves to smearing crypts with plaster; others presented themselves as volunteers to wash the dead or carry them. These latter folk earned substantial salaries. For example, a reader of the Koran took ten *dirhams*.[2] Also, hardly had he reached the oratory when he slipped away very quickly in order to go officiate at a new [funeral]. Porters demanded 6 *dirhams* at the time they were engaged, and then it was necessary to match it [at the grave]. The gravedigger demanded fifty *dirhams* per grave. Most of the rest of these people died without having taken any profit from their gains. . . . Also families kept their dead on the bare ground, due to the impossibility of having them

---

[1] This was apparently the busiest boulevard in medieval Cairo.
[2] A silver coin used in the Muslim world.

interred. The inhabitants of a house died by the tens and, since there wasn't a litter ready to hand, one had to carry them away in stages. Moreover, some people appropriated for themselves without scruple the immovable and movable goods and cash of their former owners after their demise. But very few lived long enough to profit thereby, and those who remained alive would have been able to do without. . . .

Family festivities and weddings had no more place [in life]. No one issued an invitation to a feast during the whole time of the epidemic, and one did not hear any concert. The *vizier*[3] lifted a third of what he was owed from the woman responsible [for collecting] the tax on singers. The call to prayer was canceled in various places, and in the exact same way, those places [where prayer] was most frequent subsisted on a *muezzin*[4] alone. . . .

The men of the [military] troop and the cultivators took a world of trouble to finish their sowing [of fields]. The plague emerged at the end of the season when the fields were becoming green. How many times did one see a laborer, at Gaza, at Ramleh, and along other points of the Syrian littoral,[5] guide his plow being pulled by oxen suddenly fall down dead, still holding in his hands his plow, while the oxen stood at their place without a conductor.

It was the same in Egypt: When the harvest time came, there remained only a very small number of *fellahs*.[6] The soldiers and their valets left for the harvest and attempted to hire workers, promising them half of the crop, but they could not find anyone to help them reap it. They loaded the grain on their horses, did the mowing themselves, but, being powerless to carry out the greatest portion of the work, they abandoned this enterprise.

The endowments[7] passed rapidly from hand to hand as a consequence of the multiplicity of deaths in the army. Such a concession passed from one to the other until the seventh or eighth holder, to fall finally [into the hands] of artisans, such as tailors, shoemakers, or public criers, and these mounted the horse, donned the [military] headdress, and dressed in military tunics.

Actually, no one collected the whole revenue of his endowment, and a number of holders harvested absolutely nothing. During the flooding of the Nile[8] and the time of the sprouting of vegetation, one could procure a laborer only with difficulty: On half the lands only did the harvest

---

[3] The chief minister of the caliph, or leader of the Muslim community.

[4] An official of the mosque who called the faithful to prayer from the minaret.

[5] The coastal plain of southern Palestine, where the most fertile land was located.

[6] Arabic word for ploughman or tiller, which also denoted the peasantry of Egypt and is the origin of the modern term *fellahin*.

[7] Mamluk commanders and elite soldiers, like their Ayyubid predecessors, were paid out of the revenues of land grants, known as *iqtas* (similar to fiefs in Europe). With the dearth of labor caused by the Black Death, it became far more difficult to extract income from these estates.

[8] This usually took place between September and November of every year.

reach maturity. Moreover, there was no one to buy the green clover [as feed] and no one sent their horses to graze over the field. This was the ruin of royal properties in the suburbs of Cairo, like Matarieh, Hums, Siryaqus, and Bahtit. In the canton [administrative district] of Nay and Tanan, 1,500 *feddans*[9] of clover were abandoned where it stood: No one came to buy it, either to pasture their beasts on the place or to gather it into barns and use it as fodder.

The province of Upper Egypt was deserted, in spite of the vast abundance of cultivable terrain. It used to be that, after the land surface was cultivated in the territory of Asyūt,[10] 6,000 individuals were subject to payment of the property tax; now, in the year of the epidemic [1348–1349], one could not count on more than 106 contributors. Nevertheless, during this period, the price of wheat did not rise past fifteen *dirhams* per *ardeb*.[11]

Most of the trades disappeared, for a number of artisans devoted themselves to handling the dead, while the others, no less numerous, occupied themselves in selling off to bidders [the dead's] movable goods and clothing, so well that the price of linen and similar objects fell by a fifth of their real value, at the very least, and still further until one found customers. . . .

Thus the trades disappeared: One could no longer find either a water carrier, or a laundress, or a domestic. The monthly salary of a groom rose from thirty *dirhams* to eighty. A proclamation made in Cairo invited the artisans to take up their old trades, and some of the recalcitrants reformed themselves. Because of the shortage of men and camels, a goatskin of water reached the price of eight *dirhams*, and in order to grind an *ardeb* of wheat, one paid fifteen *dirhams*.

■ REFLECTIONS

It might seem that there would be little more we could learn about a plague that occurred over 650 years ago. But that is not the case. Historians are constantly asking new questions about the past, sometimes armed with new sources of information or new techniques of investigation. One recent line of inquiry has centered on the causes of the disease. In *The Black Death and the Transformation of the West* (Harvard University Press, 1997), David Herlihy questions whether the Black Death was in fact the plague. His student, Samuel K. Cohn Jr., answers a vigorous "no." Cohn's *The Black Death Transformed: Disease and Culture in Early Renaissance Europe* (Arnold, 2003) argues that

---

[9] A *feddan* is equivalent to 1.038 acres.
[10] Located along the Nile in Upper Egypt, about midway between Cairo and Aswan.
[11] An *ardeb* is equivalent to 5.62 bushels.

the disease resembled a viral infection rather than the bacterium *Yersinia pestis* that causes the plague. Cohn writes that the Black Death, like the flu pandemic of 1918, was highly contagious, moved very rapidly, apparently on droplets in the air, taking enormous casualties. By contrast, the last wave of plague, which originated in Hong Kong in 1894 (and from which *Y. pestis* was identified), traveled slowly as it was transferred by fleas from rats to humans, infecting only those who were bitten, and killing only about 3 percent of those exposed. Further, Cohn points out, we do not hear of rats and fleas in the accounts of the Black Death. He adds that twentieth-century plague deaths in India and Manchuria continued year after year, providing no immunity from exposure, whereas the Black Death occurred only in the summer of 1348 (when incidentally the hot, dry weather meant few fleas) and then again for about one year every decade, causing fewer and fewer fatalities, except for children—who had no immunity. This would seem to be a good case for DNA testing. In fact, recent DNA studies have revealed the existence of Yersinia pestis at a number of European Black Death sites. The debate continues.

Scholars have also explored the dimensions of the Black Death beyond Europe. Until recently, the subject was a virtual monopoly of European historians, but we can now ask about the Black Death in Egypt and the Middle East. Stuart J. Borsch, in *The Black Death in Egypt and England: A Comparative Study* (University of Texas Press, 2005), asks about longer-term consequences: Why did Europe recover and thrive after 1350 whereas the economy of Egypt began a long decline? He finds the answer in the differences between the landholding systems of English peasants, who prospered as their numbers declined, and the disinterested absentee landlords of the Egyptian Mamluk regime (1250–1517), who just cut their losses and left. Other factors may account for the long-term economic decline of Egypt and other Muslim regimes in contrast to the revival of Christian Europe. Religious explanations were more common in Christian Europe in 1348 than they were in Muslim Egypt, where secular explanations outnumbered religious ones. Yet this imbalance was reversed in later years. After 1350 Europeans increasingly described the event in secular terms, crediting individual doctors and medical treatments rather than supernatural factors for their survival. The Islamic world of the Middle East moved in the opposite direction after 1350, becoming less secular and more religious. Cohn offers the rise of secular humanism in the European Renaissance as further evidence that the Black Death was like a flu that abated as people developed immunity and therefore felt more confident about human effort; but a similar response to the same disease did not occur in Egypt or the Middle East, more generally.

We still do not know how global the Black Death was. We trace its origins to Central Asia because we have no anecdotal or literary evidence for China or India. But we know that the population of China declined drastically from about 1200 to 1400[1] and that India was part of the Eurasian zone of shared diseases and immunities. We also do not know if the Black Death penetrated beyond the Sahara or up the Nile to sub-Saharan Africa. So there is still a lot more to learn, even to answer today's questions.

[1] In 1400 the Chinese population was actually about the same as it had been in 1200, but in both the previous and the subsequent 200-year period, it increased by 40–50 percent. A continuous population increase between 1200 and 1400 would have added about 150 million people. But this was also the period of the Mongol conquest and the revolt against the Mongols that ushered in the Ming dynasty, both extraordinary killers.

13

Students and Education

The World, 800–1400

■ HISTORICAL CONTEXT

Cultures perpetuate themselves by educating new students every generation. Students are taught the language of the culture as well as its norms, values, history, and expectations. They are taught how to conform to the culture, perform some useful role in the society, and continue the process as they raise the next generation. This process has been carried out since the urban revolution 5,000 years ago. It has been managed by governmental or religious organizations in formal settings designed for the purpose of education. Today we call them schools, colleges, universities, institutes, and academies, but we might also include other places where formal instruction is offered like the military, monasteries, and prisons.

The colleges and universities of today are here to teach students more than just the skills needed for a career—they help students think about their place in the world and the kind of life they might lead. As a reader of this book, you are probably a student in one of these educational institutions.

As you will see, these goals of a liberal arts education are very different from the educational goal of earlier societies. In order to understand how your own education is slated to be different from—and similar to—earlier ideas of education, we will look at students and their educations over the long course of human history. We'll start from before the age of writing and continue to the age of the liberal arts university.

As you read the following sources, notice how cultures, societies, governments, institutions, and establishments create systems of education to perpetuate themselves. Essentially, they want students to learn about and to accept and continue the way things are. But also notice how education can subvert these intentions. This creates a tension that you might feel in your own education.

■ THINKING HISTORICALLY

Texts and Contexts

Historians are always emphasizing context. Perhaps because we immerse ourselves in the rich tapestry of particulars, we fear the misunderstanding that comes from taking events out of context. To give an example, you would have limited understanding of the European Christian flagellants shown in the last chapter (p. 442) if you did not see them in the context of the Black Death.

Just as events must be seen in context, so must texts. Both primary and secondary sources arise in a particular period, to answer particular questions, or engage particular needs, because of particular things going on. We know more about a source by understanding the larger context in which it is composed and appears.

Sometimes contextual elements are visible in the text. Sometimes not. We will explore this issue in the following selections. Keep in mind that everything, every text, has many contexts. Each time we see a new context, we find an added meaning or point of view. Context may reveal bias, but more frequently it simply adds information that deepens our understanding.

In addition to asking about the context in which the source is composed, we will ask about the context in which the source presents its subject. How does the source contextualize its subject?

1

H. J. FISHER

Islam, Literacy, and Education in the Sudan, 1977

The invention of writing in the first cities 5,000 years ago may have caused the greatest changes in the way people were educated, but the author of this selection suggests that the expected changes did not always happen when writing was introduced. What was expected? When did it occur? When did it not occur? Why?

Source: H. J. Fisher, "The Eastern Maghrib and the Central Sudan" in *The Cambridge History of Africa: From c. 1050 to c. 1600*, Vol. 3 (London: Cambridge University Press, 1977), 320–24.

The author also describes the education of societies in central Sudanic Africa (the grasslands south of the Sahara Desert and north of the equatorial forests) after the introduction of Islam and literacy in the ninth century.

THINKING HISTORICALLY

This is from a book on African history, yet the author of this chapter chose to put that history in the larger context of the history of literacy and began with an unflattering comparison with the ancient Greeks. Since the publication of this book in 1977, historians have urged the study of African history on its own terms. Does the emphasis on literacy or the Greek comparison miss that mark? If so, is it instructive anyway? In what ways does the author give an account of African history on its own terms?

A pair of anthropologists, looking recently at the effects of literacy, and basing their generalizations chiefly upon evidence drawn from ancient Greece, suggest that writing down some of the main elements in the cultural tradition of a particular society brought about an awareness of two things: of the past as different from the present; and of the inherent inconsistencies in the picture of life as it was inherited by the individual from the cultural tradition in its recorded form. Such tension had not arisen in a society employing only oral tradition, for there 'structural amnesia' operated to bring the past more closely into line with the present: that is to say, those elements of the past which ceased to be relevant for an understanding of contemporary society were forgotten; the record of the past, as preserved in living memory, being constantly remodelled in order to keep it closely meshed with the present. The double awareness aroused by literacy, on the contrary, led to 'scepticism, not only about the legendary past, but about received ideas about the universe as a whole'. Individuals were 'impelled to a much more conscious, comparative and critical, attitude to the accepted world picture, and notably to the notions of God, the universe and the past'. These particular aspects of the Greek experience are markedly absent from Muslim development in the central Sudan, and indeed throughout all black Africa. Several reasons, according to the anthropologists' argument, explain why the effect of Muslim literacy has been different: its relatively narrower distribution, the continuation of teaching methods more suited to an oral than to a literary tradition, concentration upon a holy book in a foreign language (as Arabic was for most, though admittedly not all, in the central Sudan), but most of all the close association between literacy and Islam as an exclusive, all-embracing religion. 'It is above all the predominantly religious character of literacy that, here as elsewhere, prevented the medium from fulfilling its promise.'

This is perhaps an unnecessarily gloomy conclusion. The central Sudan in the period from 1050 to 1600 was not situated, as ancient Greece had been, at a crossroads of the civilized world. Rather it was perched, somewhat precariously, at the far end of perilous routes. The primary theme of the area and period is . . . the pattern of penetration, carrying ideas, organizations and people across the Sahara and further and further afield, but always with one eye over the shoulder lest the lines of communication become overextended and break. Literacy made its most important contribution just at this point, a guarantee that essential lifelines with the heritage of the Muslim heartlands would not be severed. A kind of holding operation took priority.

The anthropologists lamented that Muslim black Africa, hog-tied by religion, restricted the 'explosive potentialities' of literacy to results far 'less radical' than obtained elsewhere. Yet, taking a longer view, it is clear that Muslim literacy did have a dramatic impact. Aloma, at the very end of our period, was one of the first rulers in the central Sudan to show the double awareness of which the anthropologists speak: he seems to have known well enough that the past, of the great days of Islam, was vastly different from the present, of corrupt and mixed Muslim practice, which he saw around him; and, similarly, he knew that any individual's experience in the central Sudan in his day would have been largely inconsistent with the recorded cultural traditions of Islam. Turning to still later periods, awareness of these tensions between past and present became even more compelling for men such as Usuman dan Fodio. The reaction of the concerned Muslim of the central Sudan, however, was in a sense the mirror image of that found in ancient Greece: the Greeks used the present to refine their understanding of the past, while in the central Sudan it was the past—and the ideals of Islam there enshrined—that was used to reform and re-order the present.

One further point may be made about literacy before education in the narrower sense is discussed. The anthropologists stress its association with 'the notion of the world of knowledge as transcending political units'. This was of critical importance in black Africa, though Muslims there would have spoken of the authority of God and His law—equally given universality of application by its expression in written form—rather than of 'the world of knowledge'. The 'transcending of political units' is also reproduced in black Africa, where it has taken two forms: one, and usually first, the creation of larger states incorporating various smaller traditional units, all of which recognize, more or less, even if only in the payment of tax or tribute, that Islam has superior claims; and secondly, the appeal, often revolutionary, of the reformers to the obedience demanded by God, overriding that of even these larger states, even of those among them that patronized these very reformers.

Muslim education, throughout black Africa, began with the simple Koranic school, often no more than a group of children on the porch of their teacher's house during the rainy season, or around a bonfire at dawn and dusk during the dry one. The pupil's essential equipment was his writing board, on which were written portions of the Koran for him to memorize, or, as it might be in the case of longer passages, simply to learn to read fluently. A song about Humai, the eleventh-century ruler of Kanem, describes him thus:

Whose writing slate is made of 'kabwi' wood:
At night [a warrior] on a coal-black horse;
but when day dawns he [is to be seen] with his Koran in his hand.

The board became a popular simile: a Shuwa love-song likens the shoulders of a pretty girl to the board of the Prophet Moses, from which he said his prayers. The standard of education might be very low, pupils learning to recite, in barbaric accent and without understanding, a few snatches of the Koran. The water with which the writing was washed from the slates might be drunk—perhaps a literal fulfilment of the verse of the Prophet Jeremiah, 'Thy words were found, and I did eat them'—or used otherwise as medicine.

Pupils often performed menial tasks, domestic or on the farm, for their teacher. The story of the Tubu schoolboy Issa shows what this might involve. Issa feared to go away, even to a more celebrated teacher, lest he should have to guard the well at watering-time, draw water, fill the waterskins, water the calves, take the animals to pasture and have no time to study all the rainy season and part of the dry. Persuaded at last to go, Issa stayed only a week; then he stole a camel, covered two days' journey in a single night, and came home. Although the system was open to occasional abuse, as Issa evidently thought, it often worked well, and had the advantages that even a student from a poor family could, so to speak, earn his way, and that pupils were prepared for that peasant or pastoral life which, for most, was the only opportunity open to them. The Koranic schools were closely integrated with the local communities, and often served purposes much like those of the initiation schools of traditional pagan societies. A glimpse of the Koranic school's place in society comes from Ghadames in 1610. The Ottoman commander from Tunis was advancing upon the city, which had refused his request for slaves and other tribute. The Ghadamsi children, while their parents prepared to resist, paraded through the streets and mosques, carrying their slates and calling upon God to help them.

Beyond memorization of the Koran was the second main sphere of the traditional Islamic curriculum, in which the student learnt the Arabic language, and went on to work with subjects such as grammar, rhetoric, jurisprudence, logic, Koranic commentary, the traditions of the Prophet and the sources of the law. Such studies were usually centred on particular books. Each book would be read, sometimes even memorized; commentaries on the book would be examined; and the chain of authorities, from the original author or first commentator down to the student's present teacher, would be learnt. After mastering each book, or subject, the student received from his teacher an *ijāza*, or licence, indicating that the student himself was now competent to teach that subject to others.

The basic pattern in both stages, the memorization of the Koran and advanced studies, was one of master-seeking, the pupil moving from one teacher to another, from one place to another. Particularly for younger pupils, teachers might be their own relatives—a father, an uncle, an elder brother. But even for the young it was generally felt better to leave home. A Bornu song tells of a mother sending her son away to study, for even though his father is a cleric, a child with its mother cannot study. Teachers also moved about, sometimes with their pupils. In many cases, the pioneer Muslim missionary in any particular area is remembered primarily as a teacher. . . .

Loyalties established between teacher and pupil were often close and lasting, and where the individuals on both sides were, or became, persons of authority, such connections might be very influential. A Hausa folktale tells of a teacher who prayed for the special wishes of his four pupils: one for a lovely wife, one for wealth, one for high office and one for wisdom. Later, the teacher visited them all, and found the pupil who had been blessed with wisdom surrounded by clerics learning from him. When the visitor arrived, these students left, and the visitor and his former pupil talked all through the night. This simple story accurately illustrates a strong social bond between Muslims in the central Sudan.

ICHISADA MIYAZAKI
The Chinese Civil Service Exam, 1976

The Chinese civil service examination system originated fourteen hundred years ago, making it the first in the world. As a device for ensuring government by the brightest young men, regardless of class or social standing, it may be viewed as one of the world's earliest democratic systems. It was not perfect. Like democratic systems in the West only two hundred years ago, it excluded women. The system also put enormous pressure on young boys of ambitious families.

Source: Ichisada Miyazaki, *China's Examination Hell*, trans. Conrad Schirokauer (New York: Weatherhill, 1976), 13–17, 111–16.

This selection consists of two passages from a book by a noted modern Japanese historian of China. The first passage concerns the elaborate early preparations for the exams. The second section presents an evaluation of the system.

What were the purposes of the Chinese examination system? How did it perpetuate the Chinese state and Chinese culture? Compare the impact of literacy on Chinese education with that of literacy in the central Sudan. To what extent did the Chinese system achieve what the previous author called the potential of literacy?

THINKING HISTORICALLY

Notice how this study of Chinese students and education is placed in the context of Chinese society and government policy. In what social and political contexts did the examination system change? Compare this reading with the previous selection. How is the issue of writing and literacy presented in this selection, and how does this differ from the context provided in the previous document?

Preparing for the Examinations

Competition for a chance to take the civil service examinations began, if we may be allowed to exaggerate only a little, even before birth. On the back of many a woman's copper mirror the five-character formula "Five Sons Pass the Examinations" expressed her heart's desire to bear five successful sons. Girls, since they could not take the examinations and become officials but merely ran up dowry expenses, were no asset to a family; a man who had no sons was considered to be childless. People said that thieves warned each other not to enter a household with five or more girls because there would be nothing to steal in it. The luckless parents of girls hoped to make up for such misfortune in the generation of their grandchildren by sending their daughters into marriage equipped with those auspicious mirrors.

Prenatal care began as soon as a woman was known to be pregnant. She had to be very careful then, because her conduct was thought to have an influence on the unborn child, and everything she did had to be right. She had to sit erect, with her seat and pillows arranged in exactly the proper way, to sleep without carelessly pillowing her head on an arm, to abstain from strange foods, and so on. She had to be careful to avoid unpleasant colors, and she spent her leisure listening to poetry and the classics being read aloud. These preparations were thought to lead to the birth of an unusually gifted boy.

If, indeed, a boy was born the whole family rejoiced, but if a girl arrived everyone was dejected. On the third day after her birth it was the custom to place a girl on the floor beneath her bed, and to make her grasp a tile and a pebble so that even then she would begin to form a lifelong habit of submission and an acquaintance with hardship. In contrast, in early times when a boy was born arrows were shot from an exorcising bow in the four directions of the compass and straight up and down. In later times, when literary accomplishments had become more important than the martial arts, this practice was replaced by the custom of scattering coins for servants and others to pick up as gifts. Frequently the words "First-place Graduate" were cast on those coins, to signify the highest dreams of the family and indeed of the entire clan.

It was thought best for a boy to start upon his studies as early as possible. From the very beginning he was instructed almost entirely in the classics, since mathematics could be left to merchants, while science and technology were relegated to the working class. A potential grand official must study the Four Books, the Five Classics, and other Confucian works, and, further, he must know how to compose poems and write essays. For the most part, questions in civil service examinations did not go beyond these areas of competence.

When he was just a little more than three years old, a boy's education began at home, under the supervision of his mother or some other suitable person. Even at this early stage the child's home environment exerted a great effect upon his development. In cultivated families, where books were stacked high against the walls, the baby sitter taught the boy his first characters while playing. As far as possible these were characters written with only a few strokes.

First a character was written in outline with red ink on a single sheet of paper. Then the boy was made to fill it in with black ink. Finally he himself had to write each character. At this stage there was no special need for him to know the meanings of the characters.

After he had learned in this way to hold the brush and to write a number of characters, he usually started on the *Primer of One Thousand Characters*. This is a poem that begins:

> Heaven is dark, earth is yellow,
> The universe vast and boundless . . .

It consists of a total of two hundred and fifty lines, and since no character is repeated, it provided the student with a foundation of a thousand basic ideograms.

Upon completing the *Primer,* a very bright boy, who could memorize one thing after another without difficulty, would go on to a history text called *Meng Ch'iu (The Beginner's Search)* and then proceed to the Four Books and the Five Classics normally studied in school. If rumors of such a prodigy reached the capital, a special "tough examination" was held, but often such a precocious boy merely served as a plaything for adults and did not accomplish much in later life. Youth examinations were popular during the Sung dynasty, but declined and finally were eliminated when people realized how much harm they did to the boys.

Formal education began at about seven years of age (or eight, counting in Chinese style). Boys from families that could afford the expense were sent to a temple, village, communal, or private school staffed by former officials who had lost their positions, or by old scholars who had repeatedly failed the examinations as the years slipped by. Sons of rich men and powerful officials often were taught at home by a family tutor in an elegant small room located in a detached building, which stood in a courtyard planted with trees and shrubs, in order to create an atmosphere conducive to study.

A class usually consisted of eight or nine students. Instruction centered on the Four Books, beginning with the *Analects,* and the process of learning was almost entirely a matter of sheer memorization. With their books open before them, the students would parrot the teacher, phrase by phrase, as he read out the text. Inattentive students, or those who amused themselves by playing with toys hidden in their sleeves, would be scolded by the teacher or hit on the palms and thighs with his fan-shaped "warning ruler." The high regard for discipline was reflected in the saying, "If education is not strict, it shows that the teacher is lazy."

Students who had learned how to read a passage would return to their seats and review what they had just been taught. After reciting it a hundred times, fifty times while looking at the book and fifty with the book face down, even the least gifted would have memorized it. At first the boys were given twenty to thirty characters a day, but as they became more experienced they memorized one, two, or several hundred each day. In order not to force a student beyond his capacity, a boy who could memorize four hundred characters would be assigned no more than two hundred. Otherwise he might become so distressed as to end by detesting his studies.

Along with the literary curriculum, the boys were taught proper conduct, such as when to use honorific terms, how to bow to superiors and to equals, and so forth — although from a modern point of view their training in deportment may seem somewhat defective, as is suggested by the incident concerning a high-ranking Chinese diplomat in the late Ch'ing dynasty who startled Westerners by blowing his nose with his fingers at a public ceremony.

It was usual for a boy to enter school at the age of eight and to complete the general classical education at fifteen. The heart of the curriculum was the classics. If we count the number of characters in the classics that the boys were required to learn by heart, we get the following figures:

Analects	11,705
Mencius	34,685
Book of Changes	24,107
Book of Documents	25,700
Book of Poetry	39,234
Book of Rites	99,010
Tso Chuan	196,845

The total number of characters a student had to learn, then, was 431,286. . . . They required exactly six years of memorizing, at the rate of two hundred characters a day.

After the students had memorized a book, they read commentaries, which often were several times the length of the original text, and practiced answering questions involving passages selected as examination topics. On top of all this, other classical, historical, and literary works had to be scanned, and some literary works had to be examined carefully, since the students were required to write poems and essays modeled upon them. Anyone not very vigorous mentally might well become sick of it all halfway through the course.

Moreover, the boys were at an age when the urge to play is strongest, and they suffered bitterly when they were confined all day in a classroom as though under detention. Parents and teachers, therefore, supported a lad, urging him on to "become a great man!" From ancient times, many poems were composed on the theme, "If you study while young, you will get ahead." The Sung emperor Chen-tsung wrote such a one:

> To enrich your family, no need to buy good land:
> Books hold a thousand measures of grain.
> For an easy life, no need to build a mansion:
> In books are found houses of gold.
> Going out, be not vexed at absence of followers:
> In books, carriages and horses form a crowd.
> Marrying, be not vexed by lack of a good go-between:
> In books there are girls and faces of jade.
> A boy who wants to become a somebody
> Devotes himself to the classics, faces the window, and reads.

In later times this poem was criticized because it tempted students with the promise of beautiful women and riches, but that was the very reason it was effective.

Nonetheless, in all times and places students find shortcuts to learning. Despite repeated official and private injunctions to study the Four Books and Five Classics honestly, rapid-study methods were devised with the sole purpose of preparing candidates for the examinations. Because not very many places in the classics were suitable as subjects for examination questions, similar passages and problems were often repeated. Aware of this, publishers compiled collections of examination answers, and a candidate who, relying on these compilations, guessed successfully during the course of his own examinations could obtain a good rating without having worked very hard. But if he guessed wrong he faced unmitigated disaster because, unprepared, he would have submitted so bad a paper that the officials could only shake their heads and fail him. Reports from perturbed officials caused the government to issue frequent prohibitions of the publication of such collections of model answers, but since it was a profitable business with a steady demand, ways of issuing them surreptitiously were arranged, and time and again the prohibitions rapidly became mere empty formalities.

An Evaluation of the Examination System

Did the examination system serve a useful purpose? . . .

The purpose of instituting the examinations, some fourteen hundred years ago under the Sui rulers, was to strike a blow against government by the hereditary aristocracy, which had prevailed until then, and to establish in its place an imperial autocracy. The period of disunion lasting from the third to the sixth century was the golden age of the Chinese aristocracy: during that time it controlled political offices in central and local governments. . . .

The important point in China, as in Japan, was that the power of the aristocracy seriously constrained the emperor's power to appoint officials. He could not employ men simply on the basis of their ability, since any imperial initiative to depart from the traditional personnel policy evoked a sharp counterattack from the aristocratic officials. This was the situation when the Sui emperor, exploiting the fact that he had reestablished order and that his authority was at its height, ended the power of the aristocracy to become officials merely by virtue of family status. He achieved this revolution when he enacted the examination system (and provided that only its graduates were to be considered qualified to hold government office), kept at hand a reserve of such officials, and made it a rule to use only them to fill vacancies in central and local government as they occurred. This was the origin of the examination system.

The Sui dynasty was soon replaced by the T'ang, which for the most part continued the policies of its predecessor. Actually, as the T'ang was in the process of winning control over China, a new group of aristocrats appeared who hoped to transmit their privileges to their descendants. To deal with this problem the emperor used the examination system and favored its *chin-shih*[1] trying to place them in important posts so that he could run the government as he wished. The consequence was strife between the aristocrats and the *chin-shih*, with the contest gradually turning in favor of the latter. Since those who gained office simply through their parentage were not highly regarded, either by the imperial government or by society at large, career-minded aristocrats, too, seem

---

[1] Highest degree winner. [Ed.]

to have found it necessary to enter officialdom through the examination system. Their acceptance of this hard fact meant a real defeat for the aristocracy.

The T'ang can be regarded as a period of transition from the aristocratic government inherited from the time of the Six Dynasties to the purely bureaucratic government of future regimes. The examination system made a large contribution to what was certainly a great advance for China's society, and in this respect its immense significance in Chinese history cannot be denied. Furthermore, that change was begun fourteen hundred years ago, at about the time when in Europe the feudal system had scarcely been formed. In comparison, the examination system was immeasurably progressive, containing as it did a superb idea the equal of which could not be found anywhere else in the world at that time.

This is not to say that the T'ang examination system was without defects. First, the number of those who passed through it was extremely small. In part this was an inevitable result of the limited diffusion of China's literary culture at a time when printing had not yet become practical and hand-copied books were still both rare and expensive, thus restricting the number of men able to pursue scholarly studies. Furthermore, because the historical and economic roots of the new bureaucratic system were still shallow, matters did not always go smoothly and sometimes there were harsh factional conflicts among officials. The development of those conflicts indicates that they were caused by the examination system itself and constituted a second serious defect.

As has been indicated, a master-disciple relationship between the examiner and the men he passed was established, much like that between a political leader and his henchmen, while the men who passed the examination in the same year considered one another as classmates and helped one another forever after. When such combinations became too strong, factions were born.

These two defects of the examination system were eliminated during the Sung regime. For one thing, the number of men who were granted degrees suddenly rose, indicating a similar rise in the number of candidates. This was made possible by the increase in productive power and the consequent accumulation of wealth, which was the underlying reason that Chinese society changed so greatly from the T'ang period to the Sung. A new class appeared in China, comparable to the bourgeoisie in early modern Europe. In China this newly risen class concentrated hard on scholarship, and with the custom of this group, publishers prospered mightily. The classic books of Buddhism and Confucianism were printed; the collected writings of contemporaries and their discourses and essays on current topics were published; and the government issued an official gazette, so that in a sense China entered upon an age of mass communications. As a result learning was so widespread that candidates for the examinations came from virtually every part of the land, and the government could freely pick the best among them to form a reserve of officials.

In the Sung dynasty the system of conducting the examinations every three years was established. Since about three hundred men were selected each time, the government obtained an average of one hundred men a year who were qualified for the highest government positions. Thus the most important positions in government were occupied by *chin-shih*, and no longer were there conflicts between men who differed in their preparatory backgrounds, such as those between *chin-shih* and *non–chin-shih* that had arisen in the T'ang period.

Another improvement made during the Sung period was the establishment of the palace examination as the apex of the normal examination sequence. Under the T'ang emperors the conduct of the examinations was completely entrusted to officials, but this does not mean that emperors neglected them, because they were held by imperial order. It even happened that Empress Wu (r. 684–705) herself conducted the examinations in an attempt to win popularity. . . .

The position of the emperor in the political system changed greatly from T'ang times to Sung. No longer did the emperor consult on matters of high state policy with two or three great ministers deep in the interior of the palace, far removed from actual administrators. Now he was an autocrat, directly supervising all important departments of government and giving instructions about every aspect of government. Even minor matters of personnel needed imperial sanction. Now the emperor resembled the pivot of a fan, without which the various ribs of government would fall apart and be scattered. The creation of the palace examination as the final examination, given directly under the emperor's personal supervision, went hand in hand with this change in his function in the nation's political machinery and was a necessary step in the strengthening of imperial autocracy.

Thus, the examination system changed, along with Chinese society as a whole. Created to meet an essential need, it changed in response to that society's demand. It was most effective in those early stages when, first in the T'ang period, it was used by the emperor to suppress the power of the aristocracy, and then later, in the Sung period, when the cooperation of young officials with the *chin-shih* was essential for the establishment of imperial autocracy. Therefore, in the early Sung years *chin-shih* enjoyed very rapid promotion; this was especially true of the first-place *chin-shih*, not a few of whom rose to the position of chief councilor in fewer than ten years.

Regulations of Buddhist Monks in a Japanese Mountain School, 818

Buddhism came to Japan from China between the second and sixth centuries. By the time of the Heian Period (794–1185), there were numerous Buddhist sects, some of which exerted considerable power from monasteries. There were even armies of monks.

This selection, our first primary source of the chapter, comes from a monastery overlooking the Heian capital-city Kyoto from Mt. Hiei. The monastery was established by the monk Saicho to teach Mahayana Buddhism. This form of Buddhism emphasized the universal accessibility of salvation through the training of Bodhisat-tvas. Saicho had the support of the emperor in moving away from the many Theravada monasteries around the old capital of Nara. These monasteries had become so powerful they were able to challenge the power of the state. Saicho's monastery on Mt. Hiei was formed to commit a unified Buddhist community to the state and emperor. Initially, better students often left the cold mountain for the richer monastic culture of Nara; that was why Saicho demanded a twelve-year residency. Eventually, however, Mt. Hiei was able to draw the sons of nobility as it became the monastery best placed to train the next generation of "treasures" or teachers of the nation. Notice how the document refers to both Buddhist Law and the nation. What might this suggest about the role of the state or government in this essentially religious education? What would be the benefits and the drawbacks of education here? How is education in this monastery similar to, and different from, that of Confucian China and Muslim Africa as described in the previous two selections?

THINKING HISTORICALLY

A curriculum, catalog of courses, or list of student rules, like any text, can best be understood in context. For Mt. Hiei, there was the context of the battle with the monasteries of Nara, the well-established intellectual powerhouse of the old regime that the Heian dynasty was succeeding. Closely tied to this conflict was that between the more

Source: *Sources of Japanese Traditions: From Earliest Times to 1600*, 2nd ed., Vol. I, compiled by Wm. Theodore de Bary et al. (New York: Columbia University Press, 2001), 147–49.

open Mahayana doctrine and the more elitist orthodoxy of Hinayana or Theravada Buddhism. Why might an establishment be more likely to hold the Theravada belief that only the few could achieve enlightenment? Why might a challenger to the establishment be more likely to teach the Mahayana position that salvation was open to all?

A similar debate was waged between those who believed that Buddhist doctrine was clear and understandable and those who believed it was esoteric — secrets known only to a few. After the death of Saicho, who emphasized the understandable doctrine, Mt. Hiei brought in scholars more interested in esoteric knowledge. Why was that period more likely to attract the sons of nobility?

1. Twelve regular students of the Tendai sect will be appointed for terms of six years each. Each year as two places fall vacant, they are to be replaced by two new students.

The method of examining students will be as follows. All Tendai teachers will assemble in the Seminary Hall and there examine candidates on their recitations of the Lotus and Golden Light Sūtras. When a student passes the examinations, his family name and the date of the examination will be reported to the government.

Students who have completed six years of study will be examined in the above manner. Students who fail to complete the course will not be examined. If any students withdraw, their names, together with those of the candidates for their places, should be reported to the government.

2. Regular students must provide their own clothing and board. Students who possess the proper mental ability and whose conduct is excellent but who cannot provide their own clothing and board shall be furnished by the monastery with a document authorizing them to seek alms throughout the county for their expenses.

3. If a regular student's character does not accord with the monastic discipline and he does not obey the regulations, a report will be made to the government requesting his replacement in accordance with the regulations.

4. Regular students are required to receive the Mahāyāna initiation during the year of their ordination. After the ceremony, they shall remain for twelve years within the gates of the monastery engaged in study and practice. During the first six years, the study of the sūtras under a master will be their major occupation, with meditation and the observance of discipline their secondary pursuits. Two-thirds of their time will be devoted to Buddhism and the remaining third to the Chinese classics. An extensive study of the sūtras will be their duty, and teaching others about Buddhism, their work. During the second six years in residence, meditation and the observance of discipline will be their chief occupation, and the study of the sūtras their secondary pursuit. In the practice of Calming and Contemplation (*shikan*) students will be required to observe the four forms of meditation and in the esoteric practice will be required to recite the three sūtras.

5. The names of Tendai students at the Ichijō Shikan Monastery on Mount Hiei, whether students with annual grants or privately enrolled, should not be removed from the rolls of temples with which they were originally affiliated. For the purposes of receiving provisions, they should nevertheless be assigned to one of the wealthy temples in Omi. In keeping with Mahāyāna practice, alms will be sought throughout the country to provide them with summer and winter robes. With the material needs of their bodies thus taken care of, they will be able to continue their studies without interruption. Once admitted to the monastery, it will be a fast rule for these students that a thatched hut will serve as their quarters and bamboo leaves as their seats.[1] They will value but slightly their own lives, reverencing the Law. They will strive to perpetuate the Law eternally and to safeguard the nation.

6. If ordained monks who belong to other sects and are not recipients of annual appointments wish of their own free will to spend twelve years on the mountain in order to study the two courses [of study or practice], their original temple affiliation and the name of their master, together with documents from this monastery, must be deposited in the government office. When they have completed twelve years of study, they will be granted the title of master of the Law as in the case of the annual appointees of the Tendai sect. If they should fail to live up to the regulations, they are to be returned to the temple with which were originally affiliated.

7. The request will be made that the court bestow the title of great master of the Law on students who have remained twelve years on the mountain and have studied and observed the disciplines in strict adherence to the regulations. The request will be made that the court bestow the title master of the Law on students who, although they may not be accomplished in their studies, have spent twelve years on the mountain without ever having left it.

If any members of the sect fail to observe the regulations and do not remain on the mountain or if, in spite of their having remained on the mountain, they have been guilty of numerous infractions of the Law or have failed to remain the full period, they will be removed permanently from the official register of the Tendai sect and returned to the temple with which they were originally affiliated.

8. Two lay attendants will be appointed to this Tendai monastery to supervise it alternately and to keep out robbers, liquor, and women. Thus the Buddhist Law will be upheld and the nation safeguarded.

The above eight articles are for the maintenance of the Buddhist Law and the benefit of the nation. They should serve the way of goodness.

The imperial assent is respectfully requested.

Saichō, the Monk who formerly sought the Law in China [September 30, 818].

---

[1] That is, they will lead a life of poverty.

4

KING T'AEJO
Founding Edict, Korea, 1392

Like Japan, Korea also adopted both Buddhism and Confucianism from China. King T'aejo was the founder of the Korean Choson (or Joseon) Dynasty (1392–1897), which replaced the Goryeo (or Koryo) Dynasty (918–1392). One of the ways the new dynasty took hold was with the help of intellectuals and officials who were supporters of a "new" or Neo-Confucian movement. The previous Goryeo Dynasty had a Buddhist focus. Notice the importance of education in the founding edict of the dynasty. How would Confucian education be different from Buddhist education? What signs do you see here of King T'aejo's embrace of Confucianism? What would be the advantages of this education over that of the Buddhist monastery in the previous selection? How would the new education system help the king undercut the power of the old aristocratic families?

THINKING HISTORICALLY

A "founding edict" of a new king *may* tell us what he wanted, but it cannot be taken as a summary of what he accomplished (any more than a modern presidential inaugural address could). For that, we need to know the context in which the edict was presented. What sort of documents would you want to examine to see how much of King T'aejo's edict was carried out in his lifetime, or in the period of his dynasty?

The king issued the following edict to all the officials and the people:
The king announces:
It is Heaven which created all the people of the earth, Heaven which ordaines their rulers, Heaven which nurtured them to share life with each other, and Heaven which governed them so as to enjoy peace with one another. There have been both good and bad rulers, and there have been times when people followed their rulers willingly and other times when they turned against them. Some have been blessed with the Mandate of Heaven and others have lost it. This is a principle that has remained constant.

Source: *Sources of Korean Tradition, Volume One: From Early Times to the Sixteenth Century*, eds. Peter H. Lee and Wm. Theodore de Bary (New York: Columbia University Press, 1997), 272–74.

On the sixteenth of the seventh month of the twenty-fifth year in the reign of the Hung-wu Emperor [1392], the Privy Council and all ranks of officials together urged me to take the throne, saying: "After King Kongmin died leaving no legitimate heir the doom of the Koryŏ dynasty was sealed. Although King Kongyang [1389–1392] was empowered temporarily to take charge of state affairs, he was confused and broke the law, causing many people to rebel and even his own relatives to turn against him, and he was incapable of preserving and protecting the ancestral shrines and institutions. How could anyone restore what Heaven has abandoned? The ancestral shrines and institutions should only be entrusted to one who is worthy, and the throne must not be left vacant for long. People's minds are all looking up to your meritorious achievements and virtue, and you should accept the throne to rectify the situation, thereby satisfying the people's desire."

Fearful that I lack both virtue and capacity to assume the awesome responsibilities, I declined the offer of the throne repeatedly. But I am told that the people's wishes are such that Heaven's will is clearly manifested in them and that no one should refuse the wishes of the people, for to do so is to act contrary to the will of Heaven. Because the people insisted so steadfastly, I yielded finally to their will and ascended the throne. Now that we are at the threshold of a new beginning, I must show abundant grace, and I hereby announce the following policies for the benefit of the people.

As for the civil and the military examinations, I will not abandon one in favor of the other. Let more students be chosen for the Royal Confucian Academy in the capital and the county schools in order to promote scholarship and train men of talent. The original purpose of the examination system was to recruit men of talent for the state. With the practice of calling the examiners "masters" and the candidates "disciples," the system of impartial selection has been replaced by a system of private favors. This does not accord with the original purpose of the law. From now on, the registrar of the Royal Confucian Academy in the capital and the governors of each province will select those students in their schools who are bright in the classics and of good character; they will certify their age, clan, and three ancestors and record the classics they have mastered; and then they will send them to the director of the Royal Confucian Academy. The students will then be examined on their knowledge of the classics, and those who did well on the Four Books and the Five Classics[1] as well as the *Comprehensive Mirror for Aid in Governance* will be ranked according to the degree of their mastery. Those who pass this first stage of the examination will be sent to the Ministry of Rites for the second stage, where they will be tested on their ability to compose documentary prose, memorials, and rhyme-prose. They will

[1] The authoritative books of Confucianism. [Ed.]

then be examined at the final stage on problem essays. Of those who are successful in all three stages of examination, thirty-three men will be selected. They will then be forwarded to the Ministry of Personnel for appointment to an office according to their abilities.

The Military Training Administration will be in charge of instruction in military matters. Candidates will be instructed in the seven military classics as well as marksmanship and horsemanship, and they will then be ranked according to their mastery of the classics and their skill as marksmen and horsemen. Thirty-three finalists will be awarded the military degree in the manner of awarding the civil examination degree. Their names then will be sent to the Ministry of War for official appointment.

The cardinal rituals of our state are the rites of capping, marriage, funerals, and ancestor worship. In order for human relations to be harmonized and customs to be rectified, let the Ministry of Rites carefully research the classics and codes, deliberate on past practices, and then establish regulations for the rituals.

We cannot overemphasize the importance of the magistrates, whose duties involve direct dealing with the people. The Privy Council, the Censorate, and the Six Ministries will recommend those whom they know to be just, fair, upright, and capable of appointments as magistrates. After thirty months in office, those whose records are outstanding will be promoted. If any fail to live up to expectations, those who recommended them will bear the blame.

Because of the importance of morals and customs, we should encourage loyal ministers, filial sons, righteous husbands, and faithful wives. Let local officials seek out such people and recommend them for preferential treatment and further advancement and for memorial arches to commemorate their virtuous deeds.

The king should place importance on extending sympathy and providing relief to aged widowers and widows, orphans, and the childless. All local officials should assist those who are hungry and destitute within their jurisdiction and should give them exemption from corvée duties.

Toward the end of Koryŏ, there was no unified system of criminal justice. The Ministry of Punishments, the constabulary, and the detention halls all meted out punishments on their own. These were not always appropriate. Henceforth the Ministry of Punishments will be in charge of the criminal code, litigation, and criminal investigations and punishments. The constabulary, on the other hand, will be in charge of patrolling, catching thieves, and maintaining order. At present, when the Ministry of Punishments renders judgment in a case, the culprit is invariably stripped of his writ of appointment and forced to resign his post, even if the offense is only punishable by flogging, and guilt is attached to his descendants. This is not the way the sage-kings meant it to be.

5

MURASAKI SHIKIBU

The Tale of Genji: Chinese Literacy among Japanese Women, c. 1000

This selection from Murasaki Shikibu's *The Tale of Genji* reveals the attitudes of some of her male contemporaries toward educated women. In Heian Japan, educational opportunities for women were limited. Nunneries had been numerous in the previous Nara period, but they declined markedly by 1000. Those that remained were increasingly run by men, and they generally offered ordination rather than education. The better monasteries, like Mt. Hiei, banned all women. Only at the apex of society did aristocratic women, like Lady Murasaki, receive a classical education. How is the combined gender and class divide reflected in this selection?

THINKING HISTORICALLY

There are numerous contexts that can help us understand this selection. One context, possibly reflected in the decline of nunneries and nuns, is the declining status of women in Heian society compared with earlier periods. Some scholars see the increasing influence of Chinese Confucianism as responsible. What evidence do you see for this in the text?

Chinese was the classical language for the Japanese in the Heian period, much like Latin was in medieval Europe. In both cases, it was being supplanted in popular conversation by more inventive native languages—Japanese and European languages. In the case of Heian Japan, this native language was turned into a literary form by women, who were discouraged from learning Chinese. It was considered too complex, classical, and masculine for them. In fact, *The Tale of Genji* is a prime example of this forging of Japanese into a literary language. It is why the first Japanese novel was written by a woman; men suffered the limitations of a language too formal and foreign to use creatively. How is this context reflected in the text?

"Come," the Secretary Captain urged the Aide of Ceremonial, "you must have a good story. Let us hear it!"

"How could your lordships take an interest in anything that a nobody like me might have to say?" But the Secretary Captain only

Source: Murasaki Shikibu, *The Tale of Genji*, trans. Royall Tyler (New York: Penguin Books, 2001), 33–35.

muttered, "Come, come," and kept at him until after due thought he began. "I was still a student at the Academy when I knew a brilliant woman. Like the one the Chief Equerry wanted, you could talk over public affairs with her, her grasp of how to live life was penetrating, and on any topic her daunting learning simply left nothing further to add.

"It all started when I was visiting a certain scholar's home to pursue my studies. Having gathered that he had several daughters, I seized a chance to make this one's acquaintance, which he had no sooner discovered than in he came, bearing wine cups and declaiming insinuatingly, 'Hark while I sing of two roads in life . . .' I had no such wish, but I still managed somehow to go on seeing her, in order not to offend him.

"She was very good to me. Even while we lay awake at night, she would pursue my edification or instruct me in matters beneficial to a man in government service, and no note from her was ever marred by a single one of those *kana* letters, being couched in language of exemplary formality.[1] What with all this I could not have left her, because it was she who taught me how to piece together broken-backed Chinese poems and such, and for that I remain eternally grateful. As to making her my dear wife, however, a dunce like me could only have been embarrassed to have her witness his bumbling efforts. Your lordships undoubtedly need that sort of conjugal tutelage even less than I did. All this was foolish of me, I agree, and I should have forgone my involvement with her, but sometimes destiny just draws you on. I suppose the men are really the foolish ones."

"But what an extraordinary woman!" The Secretary Captain wanted to get him to finish. The Aide of Ceremonial knew he would have to, but he still wrinkled up his nose before complying.

"Well, I had not been to see her for a long time when for some reason I went again. She was not in her usual room; instead she spoke to me through an absurd screen. Is she jealous, then? I wondered, at once amused by this nonsense and perfectly conscious that this might be just the chance I was looking for. But no, my paragon of learning was not one to indulge in frivolous complaints. She knew the world and its ways too well to be upset with me. Instead she briskly announced, 'Having lately been prostrate with a most vexing indisposition, I have for medicinal purposes been ingesting *Allium sativum*,[2] and my breath, I fear, is too noxious to allow me to entertain you in my normal fashion. However, while I cannot address you face-to-face, I hope that you will communicate to me any services you may wish me to perform on your behalf.'

---

[1] Women wrote mainly in the phonetic *kana* script, men in more or less accomplished Chinese. This avoidance of *kana* (her letters are entirely in Chinese characters) creates a strangely formal, masculine effect.

[2] Garlic.

"It was an imposing oration. What could I possibly answer? I just said, 'Very well,' got up, and started out. I suppose she had been hoping for something better, because she called after me, 'Do return when the odor has abated!' I hated to pretend I had not heard her, but this was no time to waver, and besides, the smell really was rather overpowering, so in desperation I glanced back at her and replied,

> 'When the spider's ways this evening gave fair
> > warning I would soon arrive,
> how strange of you to tell me, Come after my garlic days!

What kind of excuse is that?'
"I fled once the words were out, only to hear behind me,

> 'If I meant to you enough that you came to me each and every night,
> Why should my garlic days so offend your daintiness?'

Oh, yes, she was very quick with her tongue," the Aide calmly concluded.

The appalled young gentlemen assumed that he must have made up his story, and they burst into laughter. "There cannot be any such woman!" cried the Secretary Captain. "You might as well have made friends with a demon. It is too weird!" He snapped his fingers and glared at the Aide in mute outrage. "Come," he finally insisted, "you will have to do better!"

However, the Aide stood fast. "How do you expect me to improve on that?" he said.

"I cannot stand the way mediocrities, men or women, so long to show off all the tiny knowledge they may possess," the Chief Equerry put in. "There is nothing at all attractive about having absorbed weighty stuff like the Three Histories and the Five Classics, and besides, why should anyone, just because she is a woman, be completely ignorant of what matters in this world, public or private? A woman with any mind at all is bound to retain many things, even if she does not actually study. So she writes cursive Chinese characters after all and crams her letters more than half full of them, even ones to other women, where they are hopelessly out of place, and you think, Oh no! If only she could be more feminine! She may not have meant it that way, but the letter still ends up being read to her correspondent in a stiff, formal tone, and it sounds as though that was what she had meant all along. A lot of senior gentle-women do that sort of thing, you know."

WALTER DE MERTON
Merton College Statutes, 1264

Merton College in England was one of the first three Oxford colleges founded in the thirteenth century. All were founded as self-governing institutions (a particularly European form), but all were also religious institutions. This document is the founding charter of the college, written by its founder, Walter de Merton (1205–1277). He was the Bishop of Rochester and chancellor to King Henry III. He donated not only the land and buildings for the college but also the endowment that would fund it. How would you compare the rules of Merton College with those of the Japanese Buddhist Mountain School at Mt. Hiei? How would you compare the roles of the founders of each institution? Which curriculum is more prescriptive? Which is likely to allow more independent thought?

THINKING HISTORICALLY

We might ask the same questions here that we asked about the previous readings. As with the *Regulations of Buddhist Monks in a Japanese Mountain School*, we wonder about the reliability of regulations to describe actual behavior. And like King T'aejo's *Founding Edict*, this clearly reflects the wishes of one man, the founder of the college. Just as the origins of Mt. Hiei must be understood in the context of the numerous Theravada Buddhist monasteries of Nara, so too must Merton be understood in a larger context. Merton became a model for other Oxford colleges, and its autonomy helped ensure that Oxford would consist of other independent and autonomous colleges. How does this difference reflect differing roles of the state compared with that of private groups or individuals in Japan and England?

The house shall be called the House of the Scholars of Merton, and it shall be the residence of the Scholars for ever.

There shall be a constant succession of scholars devoted to the study of letters, who shall be bound to employ themselves in the study of Arts or Philosophy, the Canons or Theology. Let there also be one member of the collegiate body, who shall be a grammarian, and must entirely devote himself to the study of grammar; let him have the care of the students in grammar, and to him also let the more advanced have recourse without a blush, when doubts arise in their faculty.

The number of the Scholars is to be dependent on the means of the House itself; and each individual is to receive fifty shillings, and no more,

Source: The Oxford Book of Oxford, ed. Jan Morris (Oxford: Oxford University Press, 1978), 20–22.

annually, the payments to be at fitting seasons, yet so that they shall receive every week a certain proportion for their commons.

The House is to have a Superior, who is always to be denominated the Warden, and who must be a man of circumspection in spiritual and temporal affairs; and all persons, as well Scholars as ministers of the altar, brethren, managers, and bailiffs, are to obey and look up to him as their Superior.

Some of the discreetest of the Scholars to be selected; and they, in subordination to the Warden, and in the character of his coadjutors, must undertake the care of the younger sort, and see to their proficiency in study and good behaviour. There is to be one person in every chamber, where Scholars are resident, of more mature age than the others, who is to make his report of their morals and advancement in learning to the Warden.

The Scholars who are appointed to the duty of studying in the House are to have a common table, and a dress as nearly alike as possible.

The members of the College must all be present together, as far as their leisure serves, at the canonical hours and celebration of masses on holy and other days. Four ministers of the altar, or three at fewest, who are to be in priest's orders, and who must wear a respectable and suitable attire, shall be in constant residence within the House.

The Scholars are to have a reader at meals, and in eating together they are to observe silence, and to listen to what is read.

In their chambers, they must abstain from noise and interruption of their fellows; and when they speak they must use the Latin language.

Also the Scholars are carefully to observe the following injunction: that no one shall become burdensome to his fellows by introducing strangers, or even near relatives, in order that the quiet or the rest may not be disturbed by these means, and so altercations and quarrels arise; but as they were admitted to the support of the College out of charity, so must they all live meekly in fellowship, without burdening each other, but sharing all things fairly.

Care and a diligent solicitude shall be taken that no persons be admitted but those who are of good conduct, chaste, peaceable, humble, indigent, of ability for study, and desirous of improvement. Among those, however, who are to be admitted and to receive this gratuitous support, those persons who are of my own kin are to be the chief and first.

If a Scholar shall be clearly found guilty, by competent witnesses or other conclusive evidence, before the Superior, assisted by six or seven of the Seniors of the House, of perjury, sacrilege, theft, or robbery, homicide, adultery, or other lapse of the flesh, or beating a Fellow, or the Warden, which is worse, the whole commission of such an offence, even for the first time, shall suffice to show him most worthy of expulsion from the House. But if a suspicion only of some grave crime shall arise against him, or if he shall commit any one of the lighter offences, as for instance, some trifling act of disobedience, he is to be reproved by an admonition, thrice repeated. But in case he slight this thrice repeated warning, he is to be expelled from the House without hope of restoration, and to remain for ever in that state of expulsion.

A Scrutiny shall be holden in the House by the Warden and the Seniors, and all the Scholars there present, three times in the year; a diligent enquiry is to be instituted into the life, conduct, morals, and progress in learning, of each and all; and what requires correction then is to be corrected, and excesses are to be visited with condign punishment.

The Warden, upon receiving notice from the Senior [or Vice-Warden] and the Scholars, is once a year, to convene, on a day certain, all the stewards and brethren of their manors and possessions, to some one of the manors or places: and then a diligent enquiry is to be instituted by the said Senior and Scholars into the life, conduct and morals of the Warden, stewards and brethren; and thereupon, after the accounts of each have been audited, delinquencies are to be severely punished, but all the persons who are found to have acted with prudence and fidelity are to be continued in their former administrations.

I also enjoin the Scholars above all things, in God's name and by their hopes of happiness both in this life and the next, that in all things, and above all things, they ever observe unity, and mutual charity, peace, concord and love.

Codex Mendoza: Aztec Discipline and Education, c. 1535

The *Codex Mendoza* is one of a number of Aztec books made after the Spanish conquest of 1521. These books retained the pictorial style of earlier Aztec folded screens but added Spanish lettering since they were intended for a Spanish audience. The *Codex Mendoza*, named after the Spanish governor who commissioned it in 1535, contained sections on Aztec history and everyday life.

This page shows how young Aztec boys and girls, ages eleven to fourteen, were disciplined and educated. How did the Aztec writers indicate the age of the child? Note how the author used drawings of tortillas to indicate food rations for each age. What evidence do you see for the idea that Aztecs trained their children to tolerate hunger? At what age were boys and girls punished by having to inhale the smoke of hot chillies? How was the training of boys different from that of girls? How was it similar?

THINKING HISTORICALLY

We need a larger context to avoid seeing this page as a summary of Aztec education. This page only deals with the training of children, ages eleven to fourteen, by parents. All children were also educated in Aztec traditions in schools called "Houses of Song" between the ages

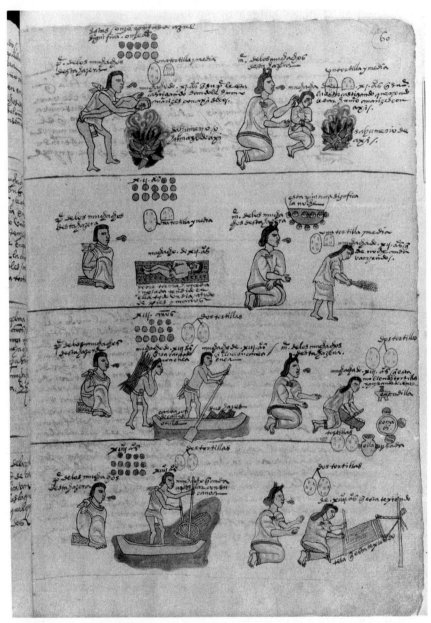

Figure 13.1 Page from the *Codex Mendoza*.
Source: Heritage / SuperStock.

of twelve and fifteen. After that, boys were placed either in military academies to become soldiers or in monasteries to become priests and officials. With some exceptions, commoners became soldiers and the sons of the nobility received the more academic religious education. Why, then, does this page tell us more about Aztec culture than about Aztec education? What does it tell us about Aztec culture?

■ REFLECTIONS

It can be tempting to suggest that human education has gone from teaching *what* to think to teaching *how* to think. Certainly the great educations in holy books (perhaps even including Confucius) were intended to pass on the revealed truths to the uninitiated. Students were taught what to think and what to do. In some cases, as in the Sudan where revelation was in a foreign language, memorization was considered more important than understanding.

Chinese Confucian education depended on more than memory. The readings in Confucius and the other classics were sufficiently varied to open up space for discussion and interpretation. While the Civil Service Exam rewarded recall more than thought, the rich body of readings provided an abundance of "case studies" that would help graduates think through and solve the daily problems of a magistrate or official.

Buddhist education also relied on scriptural records, but even the sayings attributed directly to the Buddha lacked the authority of the Quran. Buddhists had no obligation to *believe*, or even *accept* the Buddha's ideas. They might worship the Buddha, but they could worship other figures as well. Only half the curriculum for the young monks on Mt. Hiei was reading, in any case. The other half consisted of meditation, a discipline that taught a highly sophisticated psychological awareness.

These are all formidable skills, but teaching *how* to think is a step beyond retrieving quotes, solving practical problems, and gaining psychological insights. It is knowing how to find relevant information, rather than just the ability to quote. It is the ability to *pose* theoretical, as well as practical, problems. And it is the ability to turn insight into questions or theory.

Questioning is crucial, and the questioning has to be authentic. That is why the clash between two all-encompassing systems of knowledge like Christianity and Greek science contributed so effectively to the development of education in the West.

One of the larger contexts of the selections in this chapter is the world of book-based, urban religions. That is also the world that established patriarchy. It is no wonder, then, that educators of the great holy books paid scant attention to the education of women. Women who escaped those limitations, like Murasaki Shikibu, revealed the colossal cultural loss in silencing half the population. The Aztec division of labor by gender was common after the urban revolution: women inside, men outside. The Aztecs, perhaps uniquely, continued to educate women until the age of fifteen. But like the other societies studied here, the Aztecs failed to cultivate "inside knowledge" from then on.

Today, the mantra of education is "Teach students how to think." Phrases like critical thinking, independent thinking, student-directed education, learning assessment, and thinking skills fill education journals, faculty meetings, Department of Education memos, and course syllabi. Still, there is formidable resistance. Faculty want to tell students what they know. Students want to know what will be on the exam. Lists go up on whiteboards to be memorized. Even controversy is easily summarized in textbooks; debates are explained with PowerPoint pros and cons. So to say that human education has evolved from teaching *what* to think to teaching *how* to think may be more of a wish than a reality.

14

Environment, Culture, and Technology

Europe, Asia, and Oceania, 500–1500

■ HISTORICAL CONTEXT

Everyone knows that the world has changed drastically since the Middle Ages. And most people would agree that the most important and far-reaching changes have occurred in the fields of ecology, technology, and science. Global population has grown tenfold. The world has become a single ecological unit where microbes, migrants, and money travel everywhere at jet speed. In most parts of the world, average life expectancy has doubled; cities have mushroomed, supplanting farm and pasture. Machines have replaced the labor of humans and animals. Powers that were only imagined in the Middle Ages—elixirs to cure disease, energy to harness rivers, machines that could fly—are now commonplace. Other aspects of life—among them religion, political behavior, music, and art—have also evolved, but even these were affected significantly by advances in modern science and technology.

Have the changes been for good or ill? The signs of environmental stress are visible everywhere. The North Pole floats in the summer. Ten-thousand-year-old glaciers are disappearing. The oceans are rising two to four inches every ten years. Our atmosphere contains more carbon gasses than it has for at least 650,000 years. The stored energy of millions of years burns to service the richest members of a couple of generations. Ancient aquifers are drained to water the lawns of desert cities.

Precisely what change or changes occurred? When did the cycle of change begin, and what caused it? We will examine these questions here. You will read some substantial answers. These explanations of long-term change differ most markedly in how they explain the roots of the transformation. Lynn White Jr. defines the transformation to modernity in largely technological and ecological terms but emphasizes the role of cultural causes. Though a historian of medieval European technology, he focuses on the role of medieval European religion: Christianity. Jared Diamond writes of cultural failures to meet new natural and technological crises. Diamond, a professor of geography with numerous specializations in fields like physiology, evolutionary biology, and biogeography, warns that our contemporary ecological problems are very similar to earlier tragedies that ended in a failure of will. Terry Hunt and J. R. McNeill challenge this assessment and, in the process, offer alternative explanations of our environmental problems.

■ THINKING HISTORICALLY

Evaluating Grand Theories

Big questions deserve big answers—or at least grand theories. Here we consider grand theories about the origins of our technological transformation and ecological difficulties, the links between environmental decline and the growth of technology and science, and the role of Western (European and American) economic growth in undermining the environment. Grand theories are especially speculative. They give us much to question and challenge. But their scope and freshness can often suggest new insights. Grand theories almost inevitably have elements that seem partly wrong and partly right. You will be encouraged to weigh some of the many elements in these theories. After reading the first essay, you will view visual sources and then read essays that offer support and criticism of the grand theories raised here. Then you can evaluate the theories, decide where you agree and disagree, and, perhaps, begin to develop your own grand theory as well.

1

LYNN WHITE JR.
The Historical Roots of Our Ecological Crisis, 1967

This classic essay first appeared in the magazine *Science* in 1967 and has since been reprinted and commented on many times. What do you think of White's linkage of ecological crisis and Christianity? Which of White's arguments and evidence do you find most persuasive? Which do you find least convincing? Imagine a continuum that includes all of the world's people, from the most ecologically minded "tree-huggers" on one end to the most damaging polluters and destroyers of the environment on the other end. Where on that continuum would you place the historical majority of Christians? Buddhists? Why?

THINKING HISTORICALLY

A grand theory like this — that Christianity is responsible for our environmental problems — argues far more than can be proven in such a brief essay. White concentrates on making certain kinds of connections and marshaling certain kinds of evidence. In addition to weighing the arguments he makes, consider the gaps in his argument. What sorts of evidence would you seek to make White's theory more convincing?

A conversation with Aldous Huxley[1] not infrequently put one at the receiving end of an unforgettable monologue. About a year before his lamented death he was discoursing on a favorite topic: man's unnatural treatment of nature and its sad results. To illustrate his point he told how, during the previous summer, he had returned to a little valley in England where he had spent many happy months as a child. Once it had been composed of delightful grassy glades; now it was becoming overgrown with unsightly brush because the rabbits that formerly kept such growth under control had largely succumbed to a disease, myxomatosis, that was deliberately introduced by the local farmers to reduce the rabbits' destruction of crops. Being something of a Philistine,[2] I could be silent no longer,

---

[1] Aldous Huxley (1894–1963), British author of novels, short stories, travel books, biography, and essays. Best known for *Brave New World* (1932). [Ed.]

[2] An anti-intellectual (though obviously White is not; he was only impatient with Huxley's pedantry). [Ed.]

Source: Lynn White Jr., "The Historical Roots of Our Ecological Crisis," *Science* 155 (March 1967): 1203–7.

even in the interests of great rhetoric. I interrupted to point out that the rabbit itself had been brought as a domestic animal to England in 1176, presumably to improve the protein diet of the peasantry.

All forms of life modify their contexts. The most spectacular and benign instance is doubtless the coral polyp. By serving its own ends, it has created a vast undersea world favorable to thousands of other kinds of animals and plants. Ever since man became a numerous species he has affected his environment notably. The hypothesis that his firedrive[3] method of hunting created the world's great grasslands and helped to exterminate the monster mammals of the Pleistocene from much of the globe is plausible, if not proved. For six millennia at least, the banks of the lower Nile have been a human artifact rather than the swampy African jungle which nature, apart from man, would have made it. The Aswan Dam, flooding five thousand square miles, is only the latest stage in a long process. In many regions terracing or irrigation, overgrazing, and the cutting of forests by Romans to build ships to fight Carthaginians or by Crusaders to solve the logistics problems of their expeditions have profoundly changed some ecologies. Observation that the French landscape falls into two basic types, the open fields of the north and the *bocage*[4] of the south and west, inspired Marc Bloch to undertake his classic study of medieval agricultural methods. Quite unintentionally, changes in human ways often affect nonhuman nature. It has been noted, for example, that the advent of the automobile eliminated huge flocks of sparrows that once fed on the horse manure littering every street.

The history of ecologic change is still so rudimentary that we know little about what really happened, or what the results were. The extinction of the European aurochs[5] as late as 1627 would seem to have been a simple case of overenthusiastic hunting. On more intricate matters it often is impossible to find solid information. For a thousand years or more the Frisians and Hollanders have been pushing back the North Sea, and the process is culminating in our own time in the reclamation of the Zuider Zee.[6] What, if any, species of animals, birds, fish, shore life, or plants have died out in the process? In their epic combat with Neptune have the Netherlanders overlooked ecological values in such a way that the quality of human life in the Netherlands has suffered? I cannot discover that the questions have ever been asked, much less answered.

---

[3]Paleolithic hunters used fires to drive animals to their deaths. [Ed.]

[4]Full of groves or woodlands. Marc Bloch reasoned that the open fields north of the Loire River in France must have been plowed by teams of oxen and heavy plows because of the hard soil. In the south farmers could use scratch plows on the softer soil and therefore did not clear large fields, preserving more woodlands. [Ed.]

[5]A now extinct European wild ox believed to be the ancestor of European domestic cattle. [Ed.]

[6]Once a Dutch lake, it was joined to the North Sea by a flood in the thirteenth century but has since been reclaimed by the building of a dam. [Ed.]

People, then, have often been a dynamic element in their own environment, but in the present state of historical scholarship we usually do not know exactly when, where, or with what effects man-induced changes came. . . . But it was not until about four generations ago that Western Europe and North America arranged a marriage between science and technology, a union of the theoretical and the empirical approaches to our natural environment. The emergence in widespread practice of the Baconian creed that scientific knowledge means technological power over nature can scarcely be dated before about 1850, save in the chemical industries, where it is anticipated in the eighteenth century. Its acceptance as a normal pattern of action may mark the greatest event in human history since the invention of agriculture, and perhaps in non-human terrestrial history as well.

Almost at once the new situation forced the crystallization of the novel concept of ecology; indeed, the word *ecology* first appeared in the English language in 1873. Today, less than a century later, the impact of our race upon the environment has so increased in force that it has changed in essence. When the first cannons were fired, in the early fourteenth century, they affected ecology by sending workers scrambling to the forests and mountains for more potash, sulfur, iron ore, and charcoal, with some resulting erosion and deforestation. Hydrogen bombs are of a different order: A war fought with them might alter the genetics of all life on this planet. By 1285 London had a smog problem arising from the burning of soft coal, but our present combustion of fossil fuels threatens to change the chemistry of the globe's atmosphere as a whole, with consequences which we are only beginning to guess. With the population explosion, the carcinoma of planless urbanism, the now geological deposits of sewage and garbage, surely no creature other than man has ever managed to foul its nest in such short order. . . .

What shall we do? No one yet knows. Unless we think about fundamentals, our specific measures may produce new backlashes more serious than those they are designed to remedy.

As a beginning we should try to clarify our thinking by looking, in some historical depth, at the presuppositions that underlie modern technology and science. Science was traditionally aristocratic, speculative, intellectual in intent; technology was lower-class, empirical, action-oriented. The quite sudden fusion of these two, toward the middle of the nineteenth century, is surely related to the slightly prior and contemporary democratic revolutions which, by reducing social barriers, tended to assert a functional unity of brain and hand. Our ecologic crisis is the product of an emerging, entirely novel, democratic culture. The issue is whether a democratized world can survive its own implications. Presumably we cannot unless we rethink our axioms.

The Western Traditions of Technology and Science

One thing is so certain that it seems stupid to verbalize it: Both modern technology and modern science are distinctively *Occidental*. Our technology has absorbed elements from all over the world, notably from China; yet everywhere today, whether in Japan or in Nigeria, successful technology is Western. Our science is the heir to all the sciences of the past, especially perhaps to the work of the great Islamic scientists of the Middle Ages, who so often outdid the ancient Greeks in skill and perspicacity: al-Rāzī in medicine, for example; or ibn-al-Haytham in optics; or Omar Khayyám in mathematics. . . .

The leadership of the West, both in technology and in science, is far older than the so-called Scientific Revolution of the seventeenth century or the so-called Industrial Revolution of the eighteenth century. These terms are in fact outmoded and obscure the true nature of what they try to describe — significant stages in two long and separate developments. By A.D. 1000 at the latest — and perhaps, feebly, as much as two hundred years earlier — the West began to apply water power to industrial processes other than milling grain. This was followed in the late twelfth century by the harnessing of wind power. From simple beginnings, but with remarkable consistency of style, the West rapidly expanded its skills in the development of power machinery, labor-saving devices, and automation. Those who doubt should contemplate that most monumental achievement in the history of automation: the weight-driven mechanical clock, which appeared in two forms in the early fourteenth century. Not in craftsmanship but in basic technological capacity, the Latin West of the later Middle Ages far outstripped its elaborate, sophisticated, and esthetically magnificent sister cultures, Byzantium and Islam. In 1444 a great Greek ecclesiastic, Bessarion, who had gone to Italy, wrote a letter to a prince in Greece. He is amazed by the superiority of Western ships, arms, textiles, glass. But above all he is astonished by the spectacle of waterwheels sawing timbers and pumping the bellows of blast furnaces. Clearly, he had seen nothing of the sort in the Near East.

By the end of the fifteenth century the technological superiority of Europe was such that its small, mutually hostile nations could spill out over all the rest of the world, conquering, looting, and colonizing. The symbol of this technological superiority is the fact that Portugal, one of the weakest states of the Occident, was able to become, and to remain for a century, mistress of the East Indies. . . .

In the present-day vernacular understanding, modern science is supposed to have begun in 1543, when both Copernicus and Vesalius published their great works. It is no derogation of their accomplishments, however, to point out that such structures as the *Fabrica*[7] and the *De revolutionibus*[8] do not appear overnight. The distinctive Western tradition of science, in fact, began in the late eleventh century with a massive movement of translation of Arabic and Greek scientific works into Latin. . . . [W]ithin less than two hundred years effectively the entire corpus of Greek and Muslim science was available in Latin, and was being eagerly read and criticized in the new European universities. Out of criticism arose new observation, speculation, and increasing distrust of ancient authorities. By the late thirteenth century Europe had seized global scientific leadership from the faltering hands of Islam. . . .

Since both our technological and our scientific movements got their start, acquired their character, and achieved world dominance in the Middle Ages, it would seem that we cannot understand their nature or their present impact upon ecology without examining fundamental medieval assumptions and developments.

Medieval View of Man and Nature

Until recently, agriculture has been the chief occupation even in "advanced" societies; hence, any change in methods of tillage has much importance. Early plows, drawn by two oxen, did not normally turn the sod but merely scratched it. Thus, cross-plowing was needed and fields tended to be squarish. In the fairly light soils and semiarid climates of the Near East and Mediterranean, this worked well. But such a plow was inappropriate to the wet climate and often sticky soils of northern Europe. By the latter part of the seventh century after Christ, however, following obscure beginnings, certain northern peasants were using an entirely new kind of plow, equipped with a vertical knife to cut the line of the furrow, a horizontal share to slice under the sod, and a moldboard to turn it over. The friction of this plow with the soil was so great that it normally required not two but eight oxen. It attacked the land with such violence that cross-plowing was not needed, and fields tended to be shaped in long strips.

In the days of the scratch-plow, fields were distributed generally in units capable of supporting a single family. Subsistence farming was the presupposition. But no peasant owned eight oxen: to use the new and more efficient plow, peasants pooled their oxen to form large plowteams,

---

[7] *De Humani Corporis Fabrica* (1543), an illustrated work on human anatomy based on dissections, was produced by Andreas Vesalius (1514–1564), a Flemish anatomist, at the University of Padua in Italy. [Ed.]

[8] *De revolutionibus orbium coelestium* (1543; On the Revolution of Heavenly Bodies) was published by Nicolas Copernicus (1473–1543); it showed the Sun as the center of a system around which the Earth revolved. [Ed.]

originally receiving (it would appear) plowed strips in proportion to their contribution. Thus, distribution of land was based no longer on the needs of a family but, rather, on the capacity of a power machine to till the earth. Man's relation to the soil was profoundly changed. Formerly man had been part of nature; now he was the exploiter of nature. Nowhere else in the world did farmers develop any analogous agricultural implement. Is it coincidence that modern technology, with its ruthlessness toward nature, has so largely been produced by descendants of these peasants of northern Europe?

This same exploitive attitude appears slightly before A.D. 830 in Western illustrated calendars. In older calendars the months were shown as passive personifications. The new Frankish calendars, which set the style for the Middle Ages, are very different: They show men coercing the world around them—plowing, harvesting, chopping trees, butchering pigs. Man and nature are two things, and man is master.

These novelties seem to be in harmony with larger intellectual patterns. What people do about their ecology depends on what they think about themselves in relation to things around them. Human ecology is deeply conditioned by beliefs about our nature and destiny—that is, by religion. . . .

The victory of Christianity over paganism was the greatest psychic revolution in the history of our culture. It has become fashionable today to say that, for better or worse, we live in "the post-Christian age." Certainly the forms of our thinking and language have largely ceased to be Christian, but to my eye the substance often remains amazingly akin to that of the past. Our daily habits of action, for example, are dominated by an implicit faith in perpetual progress which was unknown either to Greco-Roman antiquity or to the Orient. It is rooted in, and is indefensible apart from, Judeo-Christian teleology.[9] The fact that Communists share it merely helps to show what can be demonstrated on many other grounds: that Marxism, like Islam, is a Judeo-Christian heresy. We continue today to live, as we have lived for about seventeen hundred years, very largely in a context of Christian axioms.

What did Christianity tell people about their relations with the environment?

. . . Christianity inherited from Judaism not only a concept of time as nonrepetitive and linear but also a striking story of creation. By gradual stages a loving and all-powerful God had created light and darkness, the heavenly bodies, the earth and all its plants, animals, birds, and fishes. Finally, God had created Adam and, as an afterthought,

---

[9]The biblical idea that God's purpose is revealed in his creation, that human history can be seen as the result of God's intentions. [Ed.]

Eve to keep man from being lonely. Man named all the animals, thus establishing his dominance over them. God planned all of this explicitly for man's benefit and rule: No item in the physical creation had any purpose save to serve man's purposes. And, although man's body is made of clay, he is not simply part of nature: He is made in God's image.

Especially in its Western form, Christianity is the most anthropocentric religion the world has seen. As early as the second century both Tertullian and Saint Irenaeus of Lyons were insisting that when God shaped Adam he was foreshadowing the image of the incarnate Christ, the Second Adam. Man shares, in great measure, God's transcendence of nature. Christianity, in absolute contrast to ancient paganism and Asia's religions (except, perhaps, Zoroastrianism), not only established a dualism of man and nature but also insisted that it is God's will that man exploit nature for his proper ends.

At the level of the common people this worked out in an interesting way. In Antiquity every tree, every spring, every stream, every hill had its own *genius loci*, its guardian spirit. These spirits were accessible to men, but were very unlike men; centaurs, fauns, and mermaids show their ambivalence. Before one cut a tree, mined a mountain, or dammed a brook, it was important to placate the spirit in charge of that particular situation, and to keep it placated. By destroying pagan animism, Christianity made it possible to exploit nature in a mood of indifference to the feelings of natural objects. . . .

When one speaks in such sweeping terms, a note of caution is in order. Christianity is a complex faith, and its consequences differ in differing contexts. What I have said may well apply to the medieval West, where in fact technology made spectacular advances. But the Greek East, a highly civilized realm of equal Christian devotion, seems to have produced no marked technological innovation after the late seventh century, when Greek fire[10] was invented. The key to the contrast may perhaps be found in a difference in the tonality of piety and thought which students of comparative theology find between the Greek and the Latin Churches. The Greeks believed that sin was intellectual blindness, and that salvation was found in illumination, orthodoxy—that is, clear thinking. The Latins, on the other hand, felt that sin was moral evil, and that salvation was to be found in right conduct. Eastern theology has been intellectualist. Western theology has been voluntarist. The Greek saint contemplates; the Western saint acts. The implications of Christianity for the conquest of nature would emerge more easily in the Western atmosphere.

---

[10] Byzantine incendiary weapon developed about seventh century. Siphon tube spewed fire on enemy. Used especially against Arab ships (material continued to burn on water). [Ed.]

The Christian dogma of creation, which is found in the first clause of all the Creeds, has another meaning for our comprehension of today's ecologic crisis. By revelation, God had given man the Bible, the Book of Scripture. But since God had made nature, nature also must reveal the divine mentality. The religious study of nature for the better understanding of God was known as natural theology. In the early Church, and always in the Greek East, nature was conceived primarily as a symbolic system through which God speaks to men: The ant is a sermon to sluggards; rising flames are the symbol of the soul's aspiration. This view of nature was essentially artistic rather than scientific. . . .

However, in the Latin West by the early thirteenth century natural theology was following a very different bent. It was ceasing to be the decoding of the physical symbols of God's communication with man and was becoming the effort to understand God's mind by discovering how his creation operates. The rainbow was no longer simply a symbol of hope first sent to Noah after the Deluge: Robert Grosseteste, Friar Roger Bacon, and Theodoric of Freiberg produced startlingly sophisticated work on the optics of the rainbow, but they did it as a venture in religious understanding. From the thirteenth century onward, up to and including Leibnitz and Newton, every major scientist, in effect, explained his motivations in religious terms. Indeed, if Galileo had not been so expert an amateur theologian he would have got into far less trouble: The professionals resented his intrusion. And Newton seems to have regarded himself more as a theologian than as a scientist. It was not until the late eighteenth century that the hypothesis of God became unnecessary to many scientists.

It is often hard for the historian to judge, when men explain why they are doing what they want to do, whether they are offering real reasons or merely culturally acceptable reasons. The consistency with which scientists during the long formative centuries of Western science said that the task and the reward of the scientist was "to think God's thoughts after him" leads one to believe that this was their real motivation. If so, then modern Western science was cast in a matrix of Christian theology. The dynamism of religious devotion, shaped by the Judeo-Christian dogma of creation, gave it impetus.

An Alternative Christian View

We would seem to be headed toward conclusions unpalatable to many Christians. Since both *science* and *technology* are blessed words in our contemporary vocabulary, some may be happy at the notions, first, that, viewed historically, modern science is an extrapolation of natural theology and, second, that modern technology is at least partly to be explained as an Occidental, voluntarist realization of the Christian dogma of man's transcendence of, and rightful mastery over, nature. But, as we now recognize, somewhat over a century ago science and technology—hitherto quite separate activities—joined to give mankind powers which, to judge by many of the ecologic effects, are out of control. If so, Christianity bears a huge burden of guilt.

I personally doubt that disastrous ecologic backlash can be avoided simply by applying to our problems more science and more technology. Our science and technology have grown out of Christian attitudes toward man's relation to nature which are almost universally held not only by Christians and neo-Christians but also by those who fondly regard themselves as post-Christians. Despite Copernicus, all the cosmos rotates around our little globe. Despite Darwin, we are *not*, in our hearts, part of the natural process. We are superior to nature, contemptuous of it, willing to use it for our slightest whim. . . .

What we do about ecology depends on our ideas of the man-nature relationship. More science and more technology are not going to get us out of the present ecologic crisis until we find a new religion, or rethink our old one. . . .

Possibly we should ponder the greatest radical in Christian history since Christ: Saint Francis of Assisi. The prime miracle of Saint Francis is the fact that he did not end at the stake, as many of his left-wing followers did. He was so clearly heretical that a General of the Franciscan Order, Saint Bonaventura, a great and perceptive Christian, tried to suppress the early accounts of Franciscanism. The key to an understanding of Francis is his belief in the virtue of humility—not merely for the individual but for man as a species. Francis tried to depose man from his monarchy over creation and set up a democracy of all God's creatures. With him the ant is no longer simply a homily for the lazy, flames a sign of the thrust of the soul toward union with God; now they are Brother Ant and Sister Fire, praising the Creator in their own ways as Brother Man does in his.

Later commentators have said that Francis preached to the birds as a rebuke to men who would not listen. The records do not read so: He urged the little birds to praise God, and in spiritual ecstasy they flapped their wings and chirped rejoicing. Legends of saints, especially the Irish saints, had long told of their dealings with animals but always, I believe, to show their human dominance over creatures. With Francis it is different. The land around Gubbio in the Apennines was being ravaged by a fierce wolf. Saint Francis, says the legend, talked to the wolf and persuaded him of the error of his ways. The wolf repented, died in the odor of sanctity, and was buried in consecrated ground.

What Sir Steven Ruciman calls "the Franciscan doctrine of the animal soul" was quickly stamped out. . . . [St. Francis's] view of nature and of man rested on a unique sort of pan-psychism of all things animate and inanimate, designed for the glorification of their transcendent Creator, who, in the ultimate gesture of cosmic humility, assumed flesh, lay helpless in a manger, and hung dying on a scaffold.

I am not suggesting that many contemporary Americans who are concerned about our ecologic crisis will be either able or willing to counsel with wolves or exhort birds. However, the present increasing disruption of the global environment is the product of a dynamic technology and science which were originating in the Western medieval world against which Saint Francis was rebelling in so original a way. Their growth cannot be understood historically apart from distinctive attitudes toward nature which are deeply grounded in Christian dogma. The fact that most people do not think of these attitudes as Christian is irrelevant. No new set of basic values has been accepted in our society to displace those of Christianity. Hence we shall continue to have a worsening ecologic crisis until we reject the Christian axiom that nature has no reason for existence save to serve man.

The greatest spiritual revolutionary in Western history, Saint Francis, proposed what he thought was an alternative Christian view of nature and man's relation to it: He tried to substitute the idea of the equality of all creatures, including man, for the idea of man's limitless rule of creation. He failed. Both our present science and our present technology are so tinctured with orthodox Christian arrogance toward nature that no solution for our ecologic crisis can be expected from them alone. Since the roots of our trouble are so largely religious, the remedy must also be essentially religious, whether we call it that or not. We must rethink and refeel our nature and destiny. The profoundly religious, but heretical, sense of the primitive Franciscans for the spiritual autonomy of all parts of nature may point a direction. I propose Francis as a patron saint for ecologists.

2

Image from a Cistercian Manuscript,
Twelfth Century

This image of a Christian monk chopping down a tree while his lay servant prunes the branches is from a manuscript of the Cistercian order of monks, from the twelfth century. The Cistercians, more than other orders, spoke out in favor of conserving forest resources, but they also celebrated manual labor. Does this image indicate that the monks were in favor of forest clearance?

Source: Image from a Cistercian manuscript, twelfth century, monk chopping tree (Dijon, Bibliothèque municipale, MS 173), duplicated in *Cambridge Illustrated History of the Middle Ages*, ed. Robert Fossier (Cambridge: Cambridge University Press, 1997), 72.

Figure 14.1 Twelfth-century manuscript.

Source: De Agostini / M. Seemuller / Getty Images.

THINKING HISTORICALLY

Does this image lend support to White's argument? Why or why not? If there were many such images, would visual evidence like this convince you of White's argument? Would it be more convincing if almost all European images of trees showed someone chopping them down and virtually no Chinese tree images showed that? In other words, how much visual evidence would convince you of White's interpretation?

3

Image from a French Calendar, Fifteenth Century

This French calendar scene for March is from the early fifteenth century. What sorts of activities does it show? How does it relate specifically to White's argument about the changing images of European calendars? (See p. 484.) The top half of the calendar shows an astrological zodiac. In what ways are these images of nature different from those in the bottom half?

THINKING HISTORICALLY

What technologies are shown here? Were any of these technologies particularly recent or European? Does this image merely illustrate White's argument, or does it support it to some extent? What other visual evidence would you want to see to be persuaded by White's argument?

Source: From *Les trés riches heures du duc de Berry*, Giraudon, Musée de Condé.

Figure 14.2 French calendar scene for March.

Source: © RMN-Grand Palais / Art Resource, NY.

Image of a Chinese *Feng-Shui* Master,
Nineteenth Century

Although the Chinese celebrated the natural landscape in their paintings, they also created drawings that showcased their advanced technologies. The Chinese made and used the compass (as well as paper, printing, and gunpowder) long before Europeans. Instead of using it to subdue the natural world, however, they used it to find harmony with nature, specifically through the practice of *feng-shui*.* *Feng-shui*, which literally means wind over water, is the Chinese art of determining the best position and placement of structures such as houses within the natural environment. In the following image we see a type of compass used in the work of a Chinese *feng-shui* master. Before building, the *feng-shui* master would use instruments like this to ascertain the flow of energy (*chi*) on the site, resulting in new buildings that would be in harmony with, rather than obstruct, this flow. How might a compass detect energy? How was the Chinese use of a compass-like device different from the modern scientific use of the compass?

THINKING HISTORICALLY

An image has many elements to read. What information is revealed about Chinese society in this image, in addition to the scientific devices? What significance do you attach to the artist's depiction of humans and the natural setting? In what ways does this image support Lynn White Jr.'s argument? In what ways does it challenge his interpretation? On balance, do you find it more supportive or critical of White's position?

* fung SHWEE

Source: Joseph Needham, *Science and Civilization in China* (Cambridge: Cambridge University Press, 1956), 2:362.

Figure 14.3 Chinese *feng-shui* master.

5

Image of European Surveying Instruments, c. 1600

Europeans used a wide range of instruments for surveying and gunnery by 1600. Here we see various instruments for figuring the height or depth of an object by making it the third side of a triangle. What does this image show us about European ideas of the Earth and the heavens? How would this knowledge be useful in war as well as surveying? What does it suggest about European ideas of nature?

THINKING HISTORICALLY

Compare this European image with the previous Chinese image. If these images are at all representative of their cultures, what does the comparison suggest about European and Chinese attitudes toward nature? How do these images support or challenge Lynn White Jr.'s thesis?

Figure 14.4 European surveying, c. 1600.
Source: Granger, NYC.

Source: Kevin Reilly, *The West and the World: A History of Civilization*, 2nd ed. (New York: Harper & Row, 1989), 344.

6

JARED DIAMOND

Easter Island's End, 1995

In comparison with the grand theory of White, an essay on a small island in the Pacific might seem to be an exercise in the recent vogue of small-bore "micro-history." It is not. Jared Diamond, author of *Guns, Germs, and Steel*, uses small examples to big effect. In this selection and in his larger book-length treatment, *Collapse: How Societies Choose to Fail or Succeed*, Diamond teases a global lesson from the history of tiny Easter Island. What is that lesson? What does Diamond's essay suggest about the causes of environmental decline? Are we in danger of duplicating the fate of Easter Island? How can we avoid the fate of Easter Island?

THINKING HISTORICALLY

How does Diamond's essay challenge the thesis of Lynn White Jr.? Do you see in this essay an alternative grand theory for understanding our environmental problems? If so, what is that theory? Do you agree or disagree with it? Why or why not?

In just a few centuries, the people of Easter Island wiped out their forest, drove their plants and animals to extinction, and saw their complex society spiral into chaos and cannibalism. Are we about to follow their lead?

Among the most riveting mysteries of human history are those posed by vanished civilizations. Everyone who has seen the abandoned buildings of the Khmer, the Maya, or the Anasazi is immediately moved to ask the same question: Why did the societies that erected those structures disappear? . . .

Among all such vanished civilizations, that of the former Polynesian society on Easter Island remains unsurpassed in mystery and isolation. The mystery stems especially from the island's gigantic stone statues and its impoverished landscape, but it is enhanced by our associations with the specific people involved: Polynesians represent for us the ultimate in exotic romance. . . .

But my interest has been revived recently by . . . painstaking research and analysis. My friend David Steadman, a paleontologist, has been working with a number of other researchers who are carrying out the first systematic excavations on Easter intended to identify the animals

Source: Jared Diamond, "Easter Island's End," *Discover* 16, no. 8 (August 1995).

and plants that once lived there. Their work is contributing to a new interpretation of the island's history that makes it a tale not only of wonder but of warning as well.

Easter Island, with an area of only 64 square miles, is the world's most isolated scrap of habitable land. It lies in the Pacific Ocean more than 2,000 miles west of the nearest continent (South America), 1,400 miles from even the nearest habitable island (Pitcairn). Its subtropical location and latitude—at 27 degrees south, it is approximately as far below the equator as Houston is north of it—help give it a rather mild climate, while its volcanic origins make its soil fertile. In theory, this combination of blessings should have made Easter a miniature paradise, remote from problems that beset the rest of the world.

The island derives its name from its "discovery" by the Dutch explorer Jacob Roggeveen, on Easter (April 5) in 1722. Roggeveen's first impression was not of a paradise but of a wasteland: "We originally, from a further distance, have considered the said Easter Island as sandy; the reason for that is this, that we counted as sand the withered grass, hay, or other scorched and burnt vegetation, because its wasted appearance could give no other impression than of a singular poverty and barrenness."

The island Roggeveen saw was a grassland without a single tree or bush over ten feet high. Modern botanists have identified only 47 species of higher plants native to Easter, most of them grasses, sedges, and ferns. The list includes just two species of small trees and two of woody shrubs. With such flora, the islanders Roggeveen encountered had no source of real firewood to warm themselves during Easter's cool, wet, windy winters. Their native animals included nothing larger than insects, not even a single species of native bat, land bird, land snail, or lizard. For domestic animals, they had only chickens. European visitors throughout the eighteenth and early nineteenth centuries estimated Easter's human population at about 2,000, a modest number considering the island's fertility. As Captain James Cook recognized during his brief visit in 1774, the islanders were Polynesians (a Tahitian man accompanying Cook was able to converse with them). Yet despite the Polynesians' well-deserved fame as a great seafaring people, the Easter Islanders who came out to Roggeveen's and Cook's ships did so by swimming or paddling canoes that Roggeveen described as "bad and frail." Their craft, he wrote, were "put together with manifold small planks and light inner timbers, which they cleverly stitched together with very fine twisted threads.... But as they lack the knowledge and particularly the materials for caulking and making tight the great number of seams of the canoes, these are accordingly very leaky, for which reason they are compelled to spend half the time in bailing." The canoes, only ten feet long, held at most two people, and only three or four canoes were observed on the entire island.

Figure 14.5   Easter Island statues.
Source: © Westend 61 GmbH / Alamy Stock Photo.

With such flimsy craft, Polynesians could never have colonized Easter from even the nearest island, nor could they have traveled far offshore to fish. The islanders Roggeveen met were totally isolated, unaware that other people existed. Investigators in all the years since his visit have discovered no trace of the islanders' having any outside contacts: not a single Easter Island rock or product has turned up elsewhere, nor has anything been found on the island that could have been brought by anyone other than the original settlers or the Europeans. Yet the people living on Easter claimed memories of visiting the uninhabited Sala y Gomez reef 260 miles away, far beyond the range of the leaky canoes seen by Roggeveen. How did the islanders' ancestors reach that reef from Easter, or reach Easter from anywhere else?

Easter Island's most famous feature is its huge stone statues, more than 200 of which once stood on massive stone platforms lining the coast. [See Figure 14.5.] At least 700 more, in all stages of completion, were abandoned in quarries or on ancient roads between the quarries and the coast, as if the carvers and moving crews had thrown down their tools and walked off the job. Most of the erected statues were carved in a single quarry and then somehow transported as far as six miles — despite heights as great as 33 feet and weights up to 82 tons. The abandoned statues, meanwhile, were as much as 65 feet tall and weighed up to 270 tons. The stone platforms were equally gigantic: up to 500 feet long and 10 feet high, with facing slabs weighing up to 10 tons.

Roggeveen himself quickly recognized the problem the statues posed: "The stone images at first caused us to be struck with astonishment," he wrote, "because we could not comprehend how it was possible that these people, who are devoid of heavy thick timber for making any machines, as well as strong ropes, nevertheless had been able to erect such images." Roggeveen might have added that the islanders had no wheels, no draft animals, and no source of power except their own muscles. How did they transport the giant statues for miles, even before erecting them? To deepen the mystery, the statues were still standing in 1770, but by 1864 all of them had been pulled down, by the islanders themselves. Why then did they carve them in the first place? And why did they stop?

The statues imply a society very different from the one Roggeveen saw in 1722. Their sheer number and size suggest a population much larger than 2,000 people. What became of everyone? Furthermore, that society must have been highly organized. Easter's resources were scattered across the island: the best stone for the statues was quarried at Rano Raraku near Easter's northeast end; red stone, used for large crowns adorning some of the statues, was quarried at Puna Pau, inland in the southwest; stone carving tools came mostly from Aroi in the northwest. Meanwhile, the best farmland lay in the south and east, and the best fishing grounds on the north and west coasts. Extracting and redistributing all those goods required complex political organization. What happened to that organization, and how could it ever have arisen in such a barren landscape? . . .

[There is] overwhelming evidence that the Easter Islanders were typical Polynesians derived from Asia rather than from the Americas and that their culture (including their statues) grew out of Polynesian culture. Their language was Polynesian, as Cook had already concluded. Specifically, they spoke an eastern Polynesian dialect related to Hawaiian and Marquesan, a dialect isolated since about A.D. 400, as estimated from slight differences in vocabulary. Their fishhooks and stone adzes resembled early Marquesan models. Last year DNA extracted from 12 Easter Island skeletons was also shown to be Polynesian. The islanders grew bananas, taro, sweet potatoes, sugarcane, and paper mulberry—typical Polynesian crops, mostly of Southeast Asian origin. Their sole domestic animal, the chicken, was also typically Polynesian and ultimately Asian, as were the rats that arrived as stowaways in the canoes of the first settlers.

What happened to those settlers? The fanciful theories of the past must give way to evidence gathered by hardworking practitioners in three fields: archeology, pollen analysis, and paleontology. Modern archeological excavations on Easter have continued since Heyerdahl's 1955 expedition. The earliest radiocarbon dates associated with human activities are around A.D. 400 to 700, in reasonable agreement with the approximate settlement date of 400 estimated by linguists. The period of statue construction peaked around 1200 to 1500, with few if any statues erected thereafter. Densities of archeological sites suggest a large population; an estimate of 7,000 people is widely quoted by archeologists, but other estimates range up to 20,000, which does not seem implausible for an island of Easter's area and fertility.

Archeologists have also enlisted surviving islanders in experiments aimed at figuring out how the statues might have been carved and erected. Twenty people, using only stone chisels, could have carved even the largest completed statue within a year. Given enough timber and fiber for making ropes, teams of at most a few hundred people could have loaded the statues onto wooden sleds, dragged them over lubricated wooden tracks or rollers, and used logs as levers to maneuver them into a standing position. Rope could have been made from the fiber of a small native tree, related to the linden, called the hauhau. However, that tree is now extremely scarce on Easter, and hauling one statue would have required hundreds of yards of rope. Did Easter's now barren landscape once support the necessary trees? . . .

. . . [Pollen analysis reveals that for] at least 30,000 years before human arrival and during the early years of Polynesian settlement, Easter was not a wasteland at all. Instead, a subtropical forest of trees and woody bushes towered over a ground layer of shrubs, herbs, ferns, and grasses. . . . The tall, unbranched trunks of the Easter Island palm would have been ideal for transporting and erecting statues and constructing large canoes. The palm would also have been a valuable food source, since its [still-surviving] Chilean relative yields edible nuts as well as sap from which Chileans make sugar, syrup, honey, and wine.

What did the first settlers of Easter Island eat when they were not glutting themselves on the local equivalent of maple syrup? Recent excavations by David Steadman, of the New York State Museum at Albany, have yielded a picture of Easter's original animal world as surprising as Flenley and King's picture of its plant world. . . . Less than a quarter of the bones in its early garbage heaps (from the period 900 to 1300) belonged to fish; instead, nearly one-third of all bones came from porpoises.

Nowhere else in Polynesia do porpoises account for even 1 percent of discarded food bones. But most other Polynesian islands offered animal food in the form of birds and mammals. . . . The porpoise species identified at Easter, the common dolphin, weighs up to 165 pounds. It generally lives out at sea, so it could not have been hunted by line fishing or spearfishing from shore. Instead, it must have been harpooned far offshore, in big seaworthy canoes built from the extinct palm tree.

In addition to porpoise meat, Steadman found, the early Polynesian settlers were feasting on seabirds. For those birds, Easter's remoteness and lack of predators made it an ideal haven as a breeding site, at least until humans arrived. Among the prodigious numbers of seabirds that bred on Easter were albatross, boobies, frigate birds, fulmars, petrels, prions, shearwaters, storm petrels, terns, and tropic birds. With at least 25 nesting species, Easter was the richest seabird breeding site in Polynesia and probably in the whole Pacific. Land birds as well went into early Easter Island cooking pots. . . .

Porpoises, seabirds, land birds, and rats did not complete the list of meat sources formerly available on Easter. A few bones hint at the possibility of breeding seal colonies as well. All these delicacies were cooked in ovens fired by wood from the island's forests.

Such evidence lets us imagine the island onto which Easter's first Polynesian colonists stepped ashore some 1,600 years ago, after a long canoe voyage from eastern Polynesia. They found themselves in a pristine paradise. What then happened to it? The pollen grains and the bones yield a grim answer.

Pollen records show that destruction of Easter's forests was well under way by the year 800, just a few centuries after the start of human settlement. Then charcoal from wood fires came to fill the sediment cores, while pollen of palms and other trees and woody shrubs decreased or disappeared, and pollen of the grasses that replaced the forest became more abundant. Not long after 1400 the palm finally became extinct, not only as a result of being chopped down but also because the now ubiquitous rats prevented its regeneration: of the dozens of preserved palm nuts discovered in caves on Easter, all had been chewed by rats and could no longer germinate. While the hauhau tree did not become extinct in Polynesian times, its numbers declined drastically until there weren't enough left to make ropes from. By the time Heyerdahl visited Easter, only a single, nearly dead toromiro tree remained on the island, and even that lone survivor has now disappeared. (Fortunately, the toromiro still grows in botanical gardens elsewhere.)

The fifteenth century marked the end not only for Easter's palm but for the forest itself. Its doom had been approaching as people cleared land to plant gardens; as they felled trees to build canoes, to transport and erect statues, and to burn; as rats devoured seeds; and probably as the native birds died out that had pollinated the trees' flowers and dispersed their fruit. The overall picture is among the most extreme examples of forest destruction anywhere in the world: the whole forest gone, and most of its tree species extinct.

The destruction of the island's animals was as extreme as that of the forest: without exception, every species of native land bird became extinct. Even shellfish were overexploited, until people had to settle for small sea snails instead of larger cowries. Porpoise bones disappeared abruptly from garbage heaps around 1500; no one could harpoon porpoises anymore, since the trees used for constructing the big seagoing canoes no longer existed. The colonies of more than half of the seabird species breeding on Easter or on its offshore islets were wiped out.

In place of these meat supplies, the Easter Islanders intensified their production of chickens, which had been only an occasional food item. They also turned to the largest remaining meat source available: humans, whose bones became common in late Easter Island garbage heaps. Oral traditions of the islanders are rife with cannibalism; the most inflammatory taunt that could be snarled at an enemy was "The flesh of your mother sticks between my teeth." With no wood available to cook these new goodies, the islanders resorted to sugarcane scraps, grass, and sedges to fuel their fires.

All these strands of evidence can be wound into a coherent narrative of a society's decline and fall. The first Polynesian colonists found themselves on an island with fertile soil, abundant food, bountiful building materials, ample lebensraum,[1] and all the prerequisites for comfortable living. They prospered and multiplied.

After a few centuries, they began erecting stone statues on platforms, like the ones their Polynesian forebears had carved. With passing years, the statues and platforms became larger and larger, and the statues began sporting ten-ton red crowns—probably in an escalating spiral of one-upmanship, as rival clans tried to surpass each other with shows of wealth and power. . . .

Eventually Easter's growing population was cutting the forest more rapidly than the forest was regenerating. The people used the land for gardens and the wood for fuel, canoes, and houses—and, of course, for lugging statues. As forest disappeared, the islanders ran out of timber and rope to transport and erect their statues. Life became more uncomfortable—springs and streams dried up, and wood was no longer available for fires.

People also found it harder to fill their stomachs, as land birds, large sea snails, and many seabirds disappeared. Because timber for building seagoing canoes vanished, fish catches declined and porpoises disappeared from the table. Crop yields also declined, since deforestation allowed the soil to be eroded by rain and wind, dried by the sun, and its nutrients to be leeched from it. Intensified chicken production and cannibalism replaced only part of all those lost foods. Preserved statuettes with sunken cheeks and visible ribs suggest that people were starving.

With the disappearance of food surpluses, Easter Island could no longer feed the chiefs, bureaucrats, and priests who had kept a complex society running. Surviving islanders described to early European visitors how local chaos replaced centralized government and a warrior class took over from the hereditary chiefs. The stone points of spears and daggers, made by the warriors during their heyday in the 1600s and 1700s, still litter the ground of Easter today. By around 1700, the population began to crash toward between one-quarter and one-tenth of its former number. People took to living in caves for protection against their enemies. Around 1770 rival clans started to topple each other's statues, breaking the heads off. By 1864 the last statue had been thrown down and desecrated.

[1] Room to live. [Ed.]

As we try to imagine the decline of Easter's civilization, we ask ourselves, "Why didn't they look around, realize what they were doing, and stop before it was too late? What were they thinking when they cut down the last palm tree?"

I suspect, though, that the disaster happened not with a bang but with a whimper. After all, there are those hundreds of abandoned statues to consider. The forest the islanders depended on for rollers and rope didn't simply disappear one day—it vanished slowly, over decades. Perhaps war interrupted the moving teams; perhaps by the time the carvers had finished their work, the last rope snapped. In the meantime, any islander who tried to warn about the dangers of progressive deforestation would have been overridden by vested interests of carvers, bureaucrats, and chiefs, whose jobs depended on continued deforestation. Our Pacific Northwest loggers are only the latest in a long line of loggers to cry, "Jobs over trees!" The changes in forest cover from year to year would have been hard to detect: yes, this year we cleared those woods over there, but trees are starting to grow back again on this abandoned garden site here. . . .

Gradually trees became fewer, smaller, and less important. By the time the last fruit-bearing adult palm tree was cut, palms had long since ceased to be of economic significance. That left only smaller and smaller palm saplings to clear each year, along with other bushes and treelets. No one would have noticed the felling of the last small palm.

By now the meaning of Easter Island for us should be chillingly obvious. Easter Island is Earth writ small. Today, again, a rising population confronts shrinking resources. We too have no emigration valve, because all human societies are linked by international transport, and we can no more escape into space than the Easter Islanders could flee into the ocean. If we continue to follow our present course, we shall have exhausted the world's major fisheries, tropical rain forests, fossil fuels, and much of our soil by the time my sons reach my current age.

. . . Our risk now is of winding down, slowly, in a whimper. Corrective action is blocked by vested interests, by well-intentioned political and business leaders, and by their electorates, all of whom are perfectly correct in not noticing big changes from year to year. Instead, each year there are just somewhat more people, and somewhat fewer resources, on Earth. It would be easy to close our eyes or to give up in despair. If mere thousands of Easter Islanders with only stone tools and their own muscle power sufficed to destroy their society, how can billions of people with metal tools and machine power fail to do worse? But there is one crucial difference. The Easter Islanders had no books and no histories of other doomed societies. Unlike the Easter Islanders, we have histories of the past—information that can save us. My main hope for my sons' generation is that we may now choose to learn from the fates of societies like Easter's.

7

TERRY HUNT
Rethinking the Fall of Easter Island, 2006

The author, an anthropologist specializing in Polynesia, thinks
research on Easter Island shows different causes for the collapse of
the Rapanui culture than those put forth by Jared Diamond in the
previous selection. What are these different causes? How persuasive
is Hunt's argument and evidence?

THINKING HISTORICALLY

This is an article that challenges a grand theory; it does not propose
one. What is the grand theory that Hunt challenges? What is his challenge? How persuasive do you find his challenge? What, if anything,
remains of Diamond's grand theory that is still convincing to you?
What parts of Hunt's essay could be used to construct an alternative
grand theory about ecological change? What would that theory be?

Every year, thousands of tourists from around the world take a long
flight across the South Pacific to see the famous stone statues of Easter
Island. Since 1722, when the first Europeans arrived, these megalithic
figures, or *moai*, have intrigued visitors. Interest in how these artifacts
were built and moved led to another puzzling question: What happened
to the people who created them?

In the prevailing account of the island's past, the native inhabitants — who refer to themselves as the Rapanui and to the island as Rapa
Nui — once had a large and thriving society, but they doomed themselves
by degrading their environment. According to this version of events, a
small group of Polynesian settlers arrived around 800 to 900 A.D., and
the island's population grew slowly at first. Around 1200 A.D., their
growing numbers and an obsession with building moai led to increased
pressure on the environment. By the end of the 17th century, the Rapanui
had deforested the island, triggering war, famine and cultural collapse.

Jared Diamond, a geographer and physiologist at the University of
California, Los Angeles, has used Rapa Nui as a parable of the dangers
of environmental destruction. "In just a few centuries," he wrote in a
1995 article for *Discover* magazine, "the people of Easter Island wiped
out their forest, drove their plants and animals to extinction, and saw

---

Source: Terry Hunt, "Rethinking the Fall of Easter Island," *American Scientist* 94 (May
2006): 412–19.

their complex society spiral into chaos and cannibalism. Are we about to follow their lead?" In his 2005 book *Collapse*, Diamond described Rapa Nui as "the clearest example of a society that destroyed itself by overexploiting its own resources."

Two key elements of Diamond's account are the large number of Polynesians living on the island and their propensity for felling trees. He reviews estimates of the island's native population and says that he would not be surprised if it exceeded 15,000 at its peak. Once the large stands of palm trees were all cut down, the result was "starvation, a population crash, and a descent into cannibalism." When Europeans arrived in the 18th century, they found only a small remnant of this civilization.

Diamond is certainly not alone in seeing Rapa Nui as an environmental morality tale. In their book *Easter Island, Earth Island*, authors John R. Flenley of Massey University in New Zealand and Paul G. Bahn worried about what the fate of Rapa Nui means for the rest of human civilization: "Humankind's covetousness is boundless. Its selfishness appears to be genetically inborn. . . . But in a limited ecosystem, selfishness leads to increasing population imbalance, population crash, and ultimately extinction."

When I first went to Rapa Nui to conduct archaeological research, I expected to help confirm this story. Instead, I found evidence that just didn't fit the underlying timeline. As I looked more closely at data from earlier archaeological excavations and at some similar work on other Pacific islands, I realized that much of what was claimed about Rapa Nui's prehistory was speculation. I am now convinced that self-induced environmental collapse simply does not explain the fall of the Rapanui.

Radiocarbon dates from work I conducted with a colleague and a number of students over the past several years and related paleoenvironmental data point to a different explanation for what happened on this small isle. The story is more complex than usually depicted.

The first colonists may not have arrived until centuries later than has been thought, and they did not travel alone. They brought along chickens and rats, both of which served as sources of food. More important, however, was what the rats ate. These prolific rodents may have been the primary cause of the island's environmental degradation. Using Rapa Nui as an example of "ecocide," as Diamond has called it, makes for a compelling narrative, but the reality of the island's tragic history is no less meaningful.

Early Investigations

More than 3,000 kilometers of ocean separate Rapa Nui from South America, the nearest continent. The closest habitable island is Pitcairn (settled by the infamous *Bounty* mutineers in the 18th century), which lies more than 2,000 kilometers to the west. Rapa Nui is small, only about 171 square kilometers, and it lies just south of the tropics, so its climate is somewhat less inviting than many tropical Pacific islands. Strong winds bearing salt spray and wide fluctuations in rainfall can make agriculture difficult.

The flora and fauna of Rapa Nui are limited. Other than chickens and rats, there are few land vertebrates. Many of the species of birds that once inhabited the island are now locally extinct. Large palm trees from the genus *Jubaea* long covered much of the island, but they, too, eventually disappeared. A recent survey of the island found only 48 different kinds of native plants, including 14 introduced by the Rapanui.

Accounts by European visitors to Rapa Nui have been used to argue that by the time of European discovery in 1722 the Rapanui were in a state of decline, but the reports are sometimes contradictory. In his log, Dutch explorer Jacob Roggeveen, who led the first Europeans to set foot on Rapa Nui, portrayed the island as impoverished and treeless. After they left, however, Roggeveen and the commanders of his three ships described it as "exceedingly fruitful, producing bananas, potatoes, sugar-cane of remarkable thickness, and many other kinds of the fruits of the earth. . . . This land, as far as its rich soil and good climate are concerned is such that it might be made into an earthly Paradise, if it were properly worked and cultivated." In his own account of the voyage, one of Roggeveen's commanders later wrote that he had spotted "whole tracts of woodland" in the distance.

A 19th-century European visitor, J. L. Palmer, stated in the *Journal of the Royal Geographic Society* that he had seen "boles of large trees, Edwardsia, coco palm, and hibiscus." Coconut trees are a recent introduction to the island, so Palmer might have seen the now-extinct *Jubaea* palm. . . .

Rats in Paradise

For thousands of years, most of Rapa Nui was covered with palm trees. Pollen records show that the *Jubaea* palm became established at least 35,000 years ago and survived a number of climatic and environmental changes. But by the time Roggeveen arrived in 1722, most of these large stands of forest had disappeared.

It is not a new observation that virtually all of the shells housing palm seeds found in caves or archaeological excavations of Rapa Nui show evidence of having been gnawed on by rats, but the impact of rats on the island's fate may have been underestimated. Evidence from elsewhere in the Pacific shows that rats have often contributed to deforestation, and they may have played a major role in Rapa Nui's environmental degradation as well. . . .

Whether rats were stowaways or a source of protein for the Polynesian voyagers, they would have found a welcoming environment on Rapa Nui—an almost unlimited supply of high-quality food and, other than people, no predators. In such an ideal setting, rats can reproduce so quickly that their population doubles about every six or seven weeks. A single mating pair could thus reach a population of almost 17 million in just over three years. On Kure Atoll in the Hawaiian Islands, at a latitude similar to Rapa Nui but with a smaller supply of food, the population density of the Polynesian rat was reported in the 1970s to have reached 45 per acre. On Rapa Nui, that would equate to a rat population of more than 1.9 million. At a density of 75 per acre, which would not be unreasonable given the past abundance of food, the rat population could have exceeded 3.1 million.

The evidence from elsewhere in the Pacific makes it hard to believe that rats would not have caused rapid and widespread environmental degradation. But there is still the question of how much of an effect rats had relative to the changes caused by humans, who cut down trees for a number of uses and practiced slash-and-burn agriculture. I believe that there is substantial evidence that it was rats, more so than humans, that led to deforestation. . . .

A Misplaced Metaphor?

. . . The first settlers arrived from other Polynesian islands around 1200 A.D. Their numbers grew quickly, perhaps at about three percent annually, which would be similar to the rapid growth shown to have taken place elsewhere in the Pacific. On Pitcairn Island, for example, the population increased by about 3.4 percent per year following the appearance of the *Bounty* mutineers in 1790. For Rapa Nui, three percent annual growth would mean that a colonizing population of 50 would have grown to more than a thousand in about a century. The rat population would have exploded even more quickly, and the combination of humans cutting down trees and rats eating the seeds would have led to rapid deforestation. Thus, in my view, there was no extended period during which the human population lived in some sort of idyllic balance with the fragile environment.

It also appears that the islanders began building moai and ahu soon after reaching the island. The human population probably reached a maximum of about 3,000, perhaps a bit higher, around 1350 A.D. and remained fairly stable until the arrival of Europeans. The environmental limitations of Rapa Nui would have kept the population from growing much larger. By the time Roggeveen arrived in 1722, most of the island's trees were gone, but deforestation did not trigger societal collapse, as Diamond and others have argued.

There is no reliable evidence that the island's population ever grew as large as 15,000 or more, and the actual downfall of the Rapanui resulted not from internal strife but from contact with Europeans. When Roggeveen landed on Rapa Nui's shores in 1722, a few days after Easter (hence the island's name), he took more than 100 of his men with him, and all were armed with muskets, pistols and cutlasses. Before he had advanced very far, Roggeveen heard shots from the rear of the party. He turned to find 10 or 12 islanders dead and a number of others wounded. His sailors claimed that some of the Rapanui had made threatening gestures. Whatever the provocation, the result did not bode well for the island's inhabitants.

Newly introduced diseases, conflict with European invaders and enslavement followed over the next century and a half, and these were the chief causes of the collapse. In the early 1860s, more than a thousand Rapanui were taken from the island as slaves, and by the late 1870s the number of native islanders numbered only around 100. In 1888, the island was annexed by Chile. It remains part of that country today.

In the 1930s, French ethnographer Alfred Metraux visited the island. He later described the demise of Rapa Nui as "one of the most hideous atrocities committed by white men in the South Seas." It was genocide, not ecocide, that caused the demise of the Rapanui. An ecological catastrophe did occur on Rapa Nui, but it was the result of a number of factors, not just human short-sightedness. . . .

8

J. R. McNEILL

Sustainable Survival, 2010

Like the previous selection, this article begins with an evaluation of Jared Diamond's *Collapse: How Societies Choose to Fail or Succeed*. But as an environmental historian, McNeill turns to his own broad view of environmental history in order to frame his own theory about ecologically sustainable societies. What is that view? How is it different from Diamond's?

Source: J. R. McNeill, "Sustainable Survival," in Patricia A. McAnany and Norman Yoffee, eds., *Questioning Collapse: Human Resilience, Ecological Vulnerability, and the Aftermath of Empire* (Cambridge: Cambridge University Press, 2010), 360–65.

McNeill writes that our environmental problems today are too different from those of Easter Island (or the other historical cases Diamond discusses) for them to be of use to us today. If he is right, what sort of history would be useful to us today? Does McNeill's own grand survey of environmental history offer useful lessons to solve our problems? If so, what are those lessons?

Judgments of success or failure, survival or collapse, are often more difficult to make than we might wish. Perspective and context matter. Can a society that survived a century be counted a success whereas one that lasted 450 years count as a failure? Can one that responds to environmental stresses by migration be judged a failure whereas one that responds by conquering neighboring lands, or enlisting resources from other continents, be judged a success?

Simplicity has its virtues, especially when trying to stir an audience to action. In *Collapse*, Diamond appears motivated by a deep concern for the environmental state of the earth. I find this prudent, appropriate, and laudable. Many environmentalists face choices between what is most intellectually rigorous (which usually involves admitting to legions of uncertainties) and what is most likely to rally people to action (which usually involves skating over uncertainties). Different authors will make different choices when confronted with this dilemma, and careful readers will be interested in them. Diamond many times acknowledges uncertainties, especially with archeological evidence. But he nevertheless has chosen to rally readers as best he can even when it leads him into intellectual difficulties.

Sustained Survival

Diamond's laudable concern for the avoidance of collapse, for sustained survival, raises the question of what that might mean. To Diamond it apparently means the maintenance of levels of population and social complexity in a given place. But there are other ways to see it. One, which is of particular interest to many anthropologists, is the maintenance of a culture. In this view survival consists of the maintenance of whatever the preferred markers of a culture may be, such as language or religion. Whether a million people share this culture or only a few thousand is less important, so long as the culture survives. Whether those sharing this culture live in cities, with complex social hierarchies, or in villages, is less important. Whether those sharing this culture live where their ancestors did, or have migrated elsewhere, is less important. What is important is that the culture survives. This is also often important to bearers of a given culture, especially if they are migrants, not just to anthropologists. The indefinite survival of Chinese culture means a lot to many Chinese, whether they live in China or in California. As chapters in this book emphasize, the same is true for some cultural (and biological) descendants of the ancient Maya and Anasazi today.

Another way to look at sustained survival is through a political lens. For some people what matters most is the survival of a specific polity, rather than a culture, or certain levels of population and complexity. This is especially true in times and places where people identify, via nationalism or some other mechanism, with their state. One thousand or 3,000 years ago almost no one aside from royalty cared about the survival of a given state. But royalty and their allies went to great lengths to try to perpetuate their own states, not least by doing all within their power to encourage ethnic, tribal, nationalist, or religious identification of the population with the state. More recently broader segments of societies have identified with their states and often have made great efforts, through voluntary military service, for example, to advance the interests of their states.

The boundary between cultural survival and political survival is, of course, often permeable. Sometimes it seems that the best way to perpetuate one's preferred culture is through the perpetuation of the state that most embodies it. Many Jews presumably feel this way about Israel, Finns about Finland, and Vietnamese about Vietnam.

In the end, of course, no culture or polity lasts forever. Survival is provisional. None of the states in existence 1,500 years ago exist today. Only with the most flexible of definitions could one say that any of the cultures in existence 1,500 years ago exist today. But for most people, this does not matter. Political or cultural survival in the short term is often worth, for most people, considerable sacrifice, even if, when seen in the long run, it is all in vain.

A third way to look at sustained survival is through an ecological lens. Diamond does this himself, emphasizing environmental factors in his analyses of various collapses. But are there any enduring ecological success stories, any cases of sustainable survival that lasted longer than the Tokugawa regime or the Dominican Republic? The answer, I think, is that there are, but they are not many, and none of them are of much use as a direct example to help us resolve the problems of today.

The most enduring ecologically sustainable societies in human history have been those that did not practice agriculture. For the great majority of the human time on earth, our ancestors foraged for food and other materials they needed. They had local environmental impacts, often unhelpful from the point of view of ensuring their own survival. But because they were few in number and the earth large, they could always walk somewhere else and find more of what they needed. The key was mobility and sparse population. It was probably a demanding life in several respects, but it was ecologically sustainable.

With the emergence of agriculture, which happened several times in several places but for the first time probably around 11,000 years ago, sustainability became a potential problem. All farming is a struggle against the depletion of soil nutrients. Crops absorb nutrients; these are eaten by people or animals; then they spend shorter or longer periods of time in human or animal bodies, before returning to the soil. If these nutrients in one manner or another return to farmers' fields, then a nutrient cycle can last indefinitely. If they do not, then those fields gradually lose nutrients and over time produce less and less food—unless some intervention such as fertilizer counteracts nutrient loss. In most farming systems, some nutrients were returned to farmers' fields as manure, "night soil," or ashes, but some was lost. In systems of shifting agriculture, where farmers raise a crop for a few years and then abandon plots for a decade or more, nutrient loss is checked. But in farming systems that supplied cities, many more nutrients were lost, because they were exported, as food, to distant places and never returned as night soil or manure. In places where soils were deep and rich, the nutrient problem might safely be ignored for centuries. But not forever.

In a few important situations, farming societies overcame this fundamental nutrient problem. Perhaps the most durable, the gold-medal winner for ecological sustainability, was Egypt. For 7,500 years people have been farming in Egypt. Until 1971 they did so in an ecologically sustainable manner. The source of Egypt's success and ecological continuity is not that elites chose to succeed in recognition of their broader interests. Rather, it is, or was, the silt carried by the Nile flood. Every year, except in the worst droughts, the Nile flooded and deposited on its banks and throughout its delta a nutrient-rich silt from the volcanic highlands of Ethiopia. In effect, Ethiopia's erosion subsidized Egyptian farmers, allowing them to sidestep problems of nutrient loss and sustainability. The annual flood also carried plenty of organic matter from the wetlands of southern Sudan (the Sudd), further enriching the silt that settled on Egyptian fields. This happy situation came to an end only when the Aswan High Dam was completed in 1971, and the Nile's silt began to accumulate in the dam's reservoir instead of spreading over farmers' fields. Nowadays Egypt is one of the world's greatest importers of artificial fertilizers—and of food—and is as far from ecological sustainability as a society can be.

Between the introduction of farming in Egypt and 1971 tremendous changes took place. One political regime followed another. The culture of the earliest Egyptians disappeared under layers of Pharaonic Egyptian, Greek, Roman, Byzantine, and Arab cultures, marbled with numerous other influences. Through it all, farmers won their daily bread from the banks of the Nile by combining seed and silt with the sweat of their brows.

Southern China and Medieval Europe also developed more or less sustainable agricultural systems as long as 1,000 to 1,500 years ago. In China it involved an interlocking system of paddy rice, fish ponds, and mulberry trees (for silkworm cultivation), which kept nutrients cycling within an almost closed system. Medieval European agriculture, if not supporting cities, was also very nearly sustainable, as livestock browsed in woodlands and in "outfields" and brought their manure to "infields," thereby constantly topping up the nutrient supply. As one sixteenth-century Polish nobleman put it, "manure is worth more than a man with a doctorate."

Like Egypt, these systems were ecologically successful over long periods of time, far longer than any of the successes offered by Diamond. States, rulers, and—in Europe if not in China—cultures came and went, but these farming systems endured. As in Egypt, their success did not result from wise leadership, but instead from centuries of trial and error and some favorable circumstances. This means that they cannot serve Diamond's hortatory purposes. He could scarcely offer them as hopeful examples for humankind today, even if they proved far more durable than, say, the ecological systems of the twentieth-century Dominican Republic or Tokugawa Japan.

Sustained survival can come in different forms, depending on what one most values. If it is ecological sustainability one prizes above other forms of continuity, then Egypt before 1971 deserves the highest marks. But it is well to remember Egypt was a unique case, the gift of the Nile.

The environmental problems that bedevil the world today are, for better or for worse, vastly different from those that beset Tokugawa Japan or Easter Island. They are different in scale, as Diamond recognizes. They do not, for the most part, readily lend themselves to solution via wise decisions by enlightened leaders, because they are all complicated, and many of them derive in large measure from the energy system that has gradually come to prevail over the past 200 years: a fossil fuel energy system.

Fossil fuels function as an Ethiopian highlands for the modern world: they represent an enormous subsidy, not from a distant place, but from a distant time, the carboniferous era. They make it possible for 6.5 billion people to eat. Fossil fuels are the fertilizer of modern agriculture. They pump up groundwater and power tractors. They serve as the feedstocks for pesticides and herbicides. They make nitrogenous fertilizers practical. And they power the vehicles that move crops to kitchens. They sustain us.

But they also make us unsustainable. First and most obviously, they exist in limited supply. Predictions of the imminent exhaustion of coal and oil go back at least to the 1860s and have always proved wrong so far. But they are not fundamentally wrong. A time will come when all that is left is too difficult to extract at reasonable cost. For oil this might be ten years off or 100. For coal it will be longer. But it will come—unless we abandon fossil fuels first. Second, fossil fuels make our global society unsustainable because of climate change. Roughly three-quarters of the carbon dioxide emitted into the atmosphere derives from the combustion of fossil fuels (most of the rest comes from the burning of biomass and destruction of forests). This has been warming the earth's atmosphere for at least the last few decades, and probably the last 150 years. If we were to use fossil fuels for the next 200 years as we have used them for the last 200, we are likely to raise temperature and sea level (through thermal expansion) to levels not experienced on earth at any time in the human career, indeed, not in many millions of years.

Our ways are radically unsustainable. Diamond is right to be concerned by that. He is right to prefer hope to despair, and admirable in that he has used his fame to draw attention to issues of sustainability. But he is, as often as not, wrong in his judgments about successes and failures among societies of the past.

■ REFLECTIONS

Grand theories are difficult to evaluate, as are these. In part the difficulty is that they cover so much. How many images or primary sources could ever establish that a particular set of Christian ideas affected the way Christians actually behaved? And yet we know, or believe, that ideas matter. How many histories of societal collapse do we need to understand the threats to our own? And yet, we know that the more knowledge we possess of how others have struggled and failed or succeeded, the better our own chances for survival.

At least two issues lie beneath the surface of the debate in this chapter. One is the issue of culture, specifically the importance of cultural or religious ideas in shaping human behavior. White argues that religious ideas have a profound impact on how societies behave. Diamond, however, sees culture as adaptive rather than formative. For the others, not only are Christian or monotheistic ideas irrelevant, but historical processes leave precious little room for thoughtful intervention. The micro view of Hunt gives center stage to rats and a walk-on role to European settlers. The macro view of McNeill is a useful reminder of basic technological constraints that cry out for cultural and political intervention.

Historians are always working between ideas and things. Historians of ideas may have a tendency to see ideas shaping history, and historians of things (economic historians, for instance) may see ideas as mere rationalizations. But good historians are not predictable. Lynn White Jr. is perhaps best known for his book *Medieval Technology and Social Change* in which he argued, among other things, that the introduction of the stirrup into medieval Europe was the cause of the society and culture we call feudalism. While this idea is much debated today, one would have a hard time finding an example of a stronger argument of how a thing created a culture. Nor does Diamond, a professor of geography and physiology, ignore the role of ideas. In addition to the case of Easter Island, he surveys the example of Viking collapse in Greenland in his recent book, *Collapse: How Societies Choose to Fail or Succeed* (a title that suggests the power of will and ideas). The Vikings, he suggests, failed in Greenland because they were unable to change their culture in ways necessary to adapt to the new environment. For Diamond, ideas and political will offer the only hope against the blind destructiveness of entrenched interests and seemingly unstoppable historical processes.

Another issue below the surface of this debate is the relationship between ecology and economic development. We tend to think that one comes at the expense of the other. White criticizes Western (Christian) environmental behavior with the same lens that has allowed others to celebrate Western (Christian) economic development. This is a reason, by the way, why many contemporary world historians find both views too centered on the West or Europe. But if Europe was not the source of modern technology, it was also not a source of our modern ecological predicament. Diamond is also critical of approaches that start and end in Europe. (His area of specialty is New Guinea.) Since he eliminated religious or cultural motives, his story of Easter Island can be read as an indictment of economic growth as the cause of ecological collapse. But the villain in Diamond's essay is not any kind of economic growth; it is the competitive economic exploitation of different tribes without any common plan or restraint. His message for our own predicament is to correct the anarchy of competing greedy corporations and interest groups with a common agenda and control.

Are not genuine economic growth and ecological balance mutually supportive? It is difficult to imagine long-term, healthy economic growth continuing while wrecking the environment. Similarly with environmental movements: White has us imagine that the true environmentalists are Buddhist mendicants and Hindu tree-huggers. But Buddhist monks might be content to cultivate their own gardens and ignore the rest of the world. After all, modern ecological political movements are largely products of rich societies with threatened environments. Might the most precarious ecologies display—by necessity—the greatest ecological concern? If that is the case, is the renewed popularity of environmental movements in our own age at least a sign of hope?

We can do nothing effective, however, without the guidance of historical knowledge. We cannot assume that any part of the world is what it always was. Nothing remains the same. The better we understand how the world is changing, the better world we can make it.

Acknowledgments, Volume One

Chapter 1

1 Virginia Hughes / National Geographic Creative.

2 "The 'Venus' Figurines: Textiles, Basketry, Gender, and Status in the Upper Paleolithic, 2000," *Current Anthropology*, August/October 2000, Vol. 41, Issue 4, pp. 511–537. Copyright © 2000 by The University of Chicago Press. Used with permission.

4 Margaret Ehrenbergm. Excerpts from "The First Farmers" from *Women in Prehistory*, University of Oklahoma. Reproduced with permission of the publisher in the format Republish in a book via Copyright Clearance Center.

5 Catherine Clay, Chandrika Paul, and Christine Senecal. "Women in the First Urban Communities" from *Envisioning Women in World History: Prehistory to 1500*, 1/e. Copyright © 2009. Reprinted by permission of McGraw-Hill, Inc.

Chapter 2

1 Kevin Reilly. "Cities and Civilization" from *West and the World: A History of Civilization*, V2. Copyright © 1988 by Kevin Reilly. Reprinted by permission of Pearson Education, Inc., Upper Saddle River, NJ.

2 Anonymous. Excerpt from *The Epic of Gilgamesh*, trans. N. K. Sanders (Penguin Classics 1930, Third Edition, 1972). Used by permission of Penguin Group (UK).

3 Source: Jeremy Allen Black, Graham Cunningham, J. Ebeling, Esther Fluckiger-Hawker, Eleanor Robson, Jonathan Taylor, and Gabor Zolyomi. *The Electronic Text Corpus of Sumerian Literature*, Oxford 1998–2006. Copyright © J. A. Black, G. Cunningham, E. Robson, and G. Zólyomi 1998, 1999, 2000; J. A. Black, G. Cunningham, E. Flückiger-Hawker, E. Robson, J. Taylor, and G. Zólyomi 2001; J. A. Black, G. Cunningham, J. Ebeling, E. Robson, J. Taylor, and G. Zólyomi 2002, 2003, 2004, 2005; G. Cunningham, J. Ebeling, E. Robson, and G. Zólyomi 2006. Used with permission.

4 Martha T. Roth. Excerpt from *Law Collections from Mesopotamia and Asia Minor*, Second Edition. Copyright © 1997. Reprinted with the permission of the Society of Biblical Literature.

5 TALE OF SINUHE AND OTHER ANCIENT EGYPTIAN POEMS, 1940–1640 BCE, translated with an introduction by Parkinson (1997), 320 lines of poetry from "The Tale of the Eloquent Peasant," pp. 54–88. By permission of Oxford University Press.

7 Martha T. Roth. Excerpt from *Law Collections from Mesopotamia and Asia Minor*, Second Edition. Copyright © 1997. Reprinted with the permission of the Society of Biblical Literature.

8 "First City in the New World," *Smithsonian.com*, August 2002. Copyright © 2002 Smithsonian Magazine. Used with permission.

Chapter 3

1 William H. McNeill. "Greek and Indian Civilization" from *A World History*, Second Edition: 2,904 words (pp. 78–83, 88, 90, 95, 99–100). Copyright © 1967, 1971, 1979 by William H. McNeill. By permission of Oxford University Press USA.

2 Ainslee T. Embree, excerpt from "The Rig Veda: Sacrifice as Creation" from *Sources of Indian Tradition*, Second Edition. Copyright © 1988 by Columbia University Press. Reprinted with permission of the publisher.

3 THE THIRTEEN PRINCIPAL UPANISHADS ed. and trans. Hume (1954) "Brihad Aranyaka, IV: 4: 5–6," pp. 140–141. By permission of Oxford University Press, USA.

4 Anonymous. Excerpt from "The Upanishads: Brahman and Atman" from "Chandogya Upanishad" in *The Upanishads*, trans. Juan Mascaro. Copyright © 1965 by Juan Mascaro. Used by permission of Penguin Group (UK).

5 Barbara Stoler Miller. From *Bhagavad Gita*, trans. Barbara Stoler Miller. Translation copyright © 1986 by Barbara Stoler Miller. Used by permission of Bantam Books, a division of Random House, Inc.

6 Aristotle. "The Athenian Constitution: Territorial Sovereignty," trans. John Warrington, from *Aristotle, Politics, and the Athenian Constitution* (J. M. Dent & Sons, 1959) is reproduced by permission of Everyman's Library, an imprint of Alfred A. Knopf.

Chapter 4

2 "The Tao-te Ching," *Sacred Books of the East*, trans. James Legge, ed. Müller, Vol. 39 (Oxford University Press, 1891). Also from: http://classics.mit.edu/Lao/taote.html.

3 Hai Fei. From *Sources of Chinese Tradition*, Volume 1, ed. William Theodore de Bary. Copyright © 1963 by Columbia University Press. Reprinted with the permission of the publisher.

4 From *Sources of Chinese Tradition*, Second Edition, ed. Wm. Theodore de Bary and Irene Bloom. Copyright © Columbia University Press. Reprinted with permission of the publisher.

5 THE OXFORD HISTORY OF THE CLASSICAL WORLD: THE ROMAN WORLD, ed. John Boardman, Jasper Griffin, and Oswyn Murray (1988), 734 words from "Rome: The Arts of Government" pp. 154–156, 170–174, 175–177. By permission of Oxford University Press.

Chapter 5

1 Sarah Shaver Hughes and Brady Hughes. "Women in Ancient Civilizations" from *Women's History in Global Perspective*, Volume II, ed. Bonnie G. Smith. Copyright © 2005 American Historical Association. Used with permission.

2 Ban Zhao. "Lessons for Women" excerpt from *Pan Chao: Foremost Woman Scholar of China, First Century A.D.: Background, Ancestry, Life and Writings of the Most Celebrated Chinese Woman of Letters*, trans. Nancy Lee Swann. Copyright © East Asian Library and the Gest Collection, Princeton University.

5 Ovid. "The Art of Love," trans. A. S. Kline. Reprinted with permission.

Chapter 6

Chapter 7

Chapter 8

1 From *Migration in World History*, Patrick Manning, Copyright © 2005, published by Routledge. Reproduced by permission of Taylor & Francis Books UK.

2 JOURNAL OF WORLD HISTORY—HONOLULU—by University of Hawaii at Manoa Dept. of History. Reproduced with permission of UNIVERSITY OF HAWAII PRESS in the format Republish in a book via Copyright Clearance Center.

4 Ibn Battuta. Excerpt from *The Travels of Ibn Battutah*, abridged and annotated by Tim Mackintosh-Smith, copyright © 1958, 1962, 1971, 1994, 2000 The Hakluyt Society, originally published by The Hakluyt Society in four volumes, 1958–1994. Reprinted by permission of David Higham Associates and from HAR Gibb.

Chapter 9

1a Kevin Reilly. "Love in Medieval Europe, India and Japan" from *The West and the World*, Third Edition. Copyright © 1997 by Kevin Reilly. Reprinted with the permission of Markus Wiener Publishers.

1b PILLOW BOOK OF SEI SHONAGON edited and translated by Ivan Morris (1967): 225 words from pp. 49–50 © Ivan Morris 1967. By permission of Oxford University Press.

2 From ULRICH VON LIECHTENSTEIN'S "SERVICE OF LADIES" by J. W. Thomas. Copyright © 1969 by the University of North Carolina Press. Used by permission of the publisher. www.uncpress.unc.edu.

3 Andreas Capellanus. Excerpt from *The Art of Courtly Love*, trans. John J. Parry. Copyright © Columbia University Press. Reprinted with permission of the publisher.

5 Omar Khayyam, *Rubaiyat of Omar Khayyam*, trans. Edward Fitzgerald (New York: St Martin's Press, 1983), 53, 54, 56–60, 66–67, 70, 74, 76, 84, 87, 90–95, 104.

6 Murasaki Shikibu. From *The Tale of Genji*, trans. Royall Tyler, translation copyright © 2001 by Royall Tyler. Used by permission of Viking Penguin, a division of Penguin Group (USA) Inc.

7 Zhou Daguan. Excerpt from *A Record of Cambodia: The Land and Its People*, trans. Peter Harris. Copyright © 2007 by Peter Harris. Reprinted with permission of Silkworm Books.

Chapter 10

1 S. D. Goitein, *Mediterranean Society*, Vol II. Copyright © 1969 by University of California Press. Used with permission.

2 Altmann and Bernheim, eds., *Ausgeuvahlte Urkunden zur Erlauterung der Verfassungsge schichte Deutschlands im Mitzelalter* (Berlin: Weidmannsche Buchhandlung, 1904), p. 156, reprinted in Roy C. Cave and Herbert H. Coulson, *A Source Book for Medieval Economic History* (Milwaukee: The Bruce Publishing Co., 1936; reprint ed., New York: Biblo & Tannen, 1965), pp. 101–102.

3   Fulcher of Chartres, "Pope Urban at Clermont" from *The First Crusade: The Chronicle of Fulcher of Chartres and Other Source Materials*, ed. Edward Peters. pp. 72–73. Copyright © 1998. Reprinted with permission of the University of Pennsylvania Press.

4   Solomon bar Simson. "Chronicle of Solomon bar Simson" from *The Jews and the Crusaders: The Hebrew Chronicles of the First and Second Crusades*, ed. and trans. Shlomo Eidelberg. Copyright © 1977. Reprinted with the permission of KTAV Publishing House.

5   Ibn al-Athir. From *Arab Historians of the Crusades*, ed. and trans. Francesco Gabrieli. Copyright © 1969 by Routledge & Kegan Paul Ltd. Published by the University of California Press. Reprinted by permission of the publisher.

6   Ibn al-Athir. From *Arab Historians of the Crusades*, ed. and trans. Francesco Gabrieli. Copyright © 1969 by Routledge & Kegan Paul Ltd. Published by the University of California Press. Reprinted by permission of the publisher.

7   "Letter from a Jewish Pilgrim in Egypt, 1100" from "Contemporary Letters on the Capture of Jerusalem by the Crusaders" in *Journal of Jewish Studies* 3, No. 4, 1952, trans. S. D. Goitein. Copyright © 1952 by S. D. Goitein. Reprinted with the permission of the Journal of Jewish Studies.

Chapter 11

1   *The Historian: A Journal of History* by PHI ALPHA THETA. Reproduced with permission of BLACKWELL PUBLISHING, INC. in the format Republish in a book via Copyright Clearance Center.

2   Ibn Fadlan. "Ibn Fadlan's Account of Scandinavian Merchants on the Volga in 1922" from *Journal of English and Germanic Philology* 22:1, 1923, pp. 56–63. Copyright © 1923 by the Board of Trustees of the University of Illinois. Used with permission of the authors and the University of Illinois Press.

3   "Eirik's Saga" from *The Vinland Sagas: The Norse Discovery of America*, trans. Magnus Magnusson and Hermann Palsson. Copyright © 1965 by Magnus Magnusson and Hermann Palsson. Reprinted by permission of Penguin UK.

5   K. Reilly. "The Secret History of the Mongols," adapted from R. P. Lister, *Genghis Khan*. Reprinted with the permission of Cooper Square Press.

7   © Christopher Dawson, 1955, *Mission to Asia: Narratives and Letters of the Franciscan Missionaries in Mongolia and China in the Thirteenth and Fourteenth Centuries*, Sheed & Ward, an imprint of Bloomsbury Publishing PLC.

Chapter 12

2   Gabriel de' Mussis. "Origins of the Black Death" from *The Black Death*, by Rosemary Horrox (Trans & Ed.). Copyright © 1996 Manchester University Press. Used with permission.

3   Giovanni Boccacio, "The Plague in Florence" from *The Decameron*, trans. G. H. McWilliam. Copyright © 1972 by G. H. McWilliam. Reprinted by permission of Penguin UK.

Chapter 13

1 Fisher, H. J. "The Eastern Maghrib and the Central Sudan." In *The Cambridge History of Africa: From c. 1050 to c. 1600*, Vol. 3 (London: Cambridge University Press, 1977), 3320–3324. Reprinted with the permission of Cambridge University Press.

2 From *China's Examination Hell*, by Ichisada Miyazaki, translated by Conrad Schirokauer, First Edition, 1976. Protected by copyright under terms of the International Copyright Union. Reprinted by arrangement with The Permissions Company, Inc., on behalf of Shambhala Publications Inc., www.shambhala.com.

3 *Sources of Japanese Traditions: From Earliest Times to 1600*, Second Edition, vol. I, compiled by Wm. Theodore de Bary et. al. Copyright © 2001 Columbia University Press. Reprinted with permission of the publisher.

4 *Sources of Korean Tradition, Volume One: From Early Times to the Sixteenth Century*, eds. Peter H. Lee and Wm. Theodore de Bary. Copyright © 1997 Columbia University Press. Reprinted with permission of the publisher.

5 Murasaki Shikibu. From *The Tale of Genji*, trans. Royall Tyler, translation copyright © 2001 by Royall Tyler. Used by permission of Viking Penguin, a division of Penguin Group (USA) Inc.

Chapter 14

1 Lynn White, Jr. "The Historical Roots of Our Ecologic Crisis" from *Science* by American Association for the Advancement of Science. Reproduced with permission of American Association for the Advancement of Science in the format reuse in a book/textbook via Copyright Clearance Center.

6 Jared Diamond. Excerpt from "Easter Island's End" from *Discover* 16, no. 8, August 1995. Copyright © 1995 by Jared Diamond. Reprinted with the permission of the author.

7 Terry Hunt. "Rethinking the Fall of Easter Island" from *American Scientist*, Volume 94, Number 5, September-October 2006. Copyright © 2006 Sigma Xi, The Scientific Research Society. Used with permission.

8 J. R. McNeill. "Sustainable Survival" in *Questioning Collapse: Human Resilience, Ecological Vulnerability, and the Aftermath of Empire*, Cambridge University Press, 2010. Copyright © 2010 Cambridge University Press. Reprinted with the permission of Cambridge University Press.